History and Development of Airline Cabin Safety

History and Development of Airline Cabin Safety offers an understanding of how cabin safety evolved over time. It covers six key areas: impact protection, fire protection, egress potential, life support equipment, information and instructions, and cabin professionals.

Exploring the organic choreography of accidents, research, technological progress, rulemaking, and industry response, the book clarifies that cabin safety enhancements were not well planned but came incidentally and step by step. Each step was triggered by accidents with survivability issues, except in one area where a proactive approach proved to be first time right: oxygen for passengers. The step improvements, which mainly occurred in the U.S., concentrated in three waves centered around 1950, 1970, and 1985, respectively.

The book will interest aviation regulators, aircraft manufacturers and operators, cabin safety professionals (including cabin crew), and accident investigation professionals.

History and Development of Airline Cabin Safety

Fons Schaefers

CRC Press
Taylor & Francis Group
Boca Raton London New York

CRC Press is an imprint of the
Taylor & Francis Group, an **informa** business

Designed cover image: Courtesy of Embry-Riddle Aeronautical University
Lockheed Constellation evacuation test, August 1946

First edition published 2025
by CRC Press
2385 NW Executive Center Drive, Suite 320, Boca Raton FL 33431

and by CRC Press
4 Park Square, Milton Park, Abingdon, Oxon, OX14 4RN

CRC Press is an imprint of Taylor & Francis Group, LLC

© 2025 Fons Schaefers

Reasonable efforts have been made to publish reliable data and information, but the author and publisher cannot assume responsibility for the validity of all materials or the consequences of their use. The authors and publishers have attempted to trace the copyright holders of all material reproduced in this publication and apologize to copyright holders if permission to publish in this form has not been obtained. If any copyright material has not been acknowledged please write and let us know so we may rectify in any future reprint.

Except as permitted under U.S. Copyright Law, no part of this book may be reprinted, reproduced, transmitted, or utilized in any form by any electronic, mechanical, or other means, now known or hereafter invented, including photocopying, microfilming, and recording, or in any information storage or retrieval system, without written permission from the publishers.

For permission to photocopy or use material electronically from this work, access www.copyright.com or contact the Copyright Clearance Center, Inc. (CCC), 222 Rosewood Drive, Danvers, MA 01923, 978–750–8400. For works that are not available on CCC please contact mpkbookspermissions@tandf.co.uk

Trademark notice: Product or corporate names may be trademarks or registered trademarks and are used only for identification and explanation without intent to infringe.

Library of Congress Cataloging-in-Publication Data
Names: Schaefers, Fons (Writer on aviation), author.
Title: History and development of airline cabin safety / Fons Schaefers.
Description: First edition. | Boca Raton, FL : CRC Press, 2025. | Includes
  bibliographical references and index.
Identifiers: LCCN 2024043789 (print) | LCCN 2024043790 (ebook) |
  ISBN 9781032711003 (hardback) | ISBN 9781032711041 (paperback) |
  ISBN 9781032711027 (ebook)
Subjects: LCSH: Aircraft cabins—Safety measures. | Aircraft cabins—
  Safety measures—History. | Airlines—Safety measures—History.
Classification: LCC TL681.C3 S34 2025 (print) | LCC TL681.C3 (ebook) |
  DDC 629.134/45—dc23/eng/20241216
LC record available at https://lccn.loc.gov/2024043789
LC ebook record available at https://lccn.loc.gov/2024043790

ISBN: 978-1-032-71100-3 (hbk)
ISBN: 978-1-032-71104-1 (pbk)
ISBN: 978-1-032-71102-7 (ebk)

DOI: 10.1201/9781032711027

Typeset in Times
by Apex CoVantage, LLC

Contents

About the Author xiii
Preface xv
    0.1   Introduction xv
    0.2   Scope xv
    0.3   Conventions xvi
              0.3.1   Units xvi
              0.3.2   Dates xvi
              0.3.3   References xvi
    0.4   General notes on aircraft certification xvii
              0.4.1   Long lead times xvii
              0.4.2   The derivative concept xvii
    0.5   Abbreviations and acronyms xviii
    0.6   Acknowledgements xix

Chapter 1   Prologue 1

Chapter 2   Introduction 5
    2.1   An Accident-Driven Métier 5
    2.2   Waves and Troughs 6
    2.3   Reader Guidance 6
              2.3.1   Impact Protection 6
              2.3.2   Fire Protection 7
              2.3.3   Escape Potential 7
              2.3.4   Life Support 7
              2.3.5   Information and Instructions 7
              2.3.6   Cabin Professionals 7
    2.4   U.S. Standards Dominate 7

Chapter 3   Pioneering Years (1919–1944) 9
    3.1   Early Developments 9
              3.1.1   Europe Was First 9
              3.1.2   The Six Domains 10
              3.1.3   U.S. Follows 11
              3.1.4   Aircraft Development 11
    3.2   Accidents with Cabin Safety Elements 12
              3.2.1   Bermuda Bound 13
              3.2.2   Oklahoma City 13
              3.2.3   Trammel, Kentucky 13
    3.3   Cabin Safety Regulations up to 1945 15
              3.3.1   Beginning 15
              3.3.2   Impact Protection 16
              3.3.3   Fire Protection 18
              3.3.4   Escape Potential 18
              3.3.5   Life Support 21
              3.3.6   Information and Instructions 22

Chapter 4	Regulatory Framework Developments	25
	4.1 Introduction	25
	4.2 U.S. 1926–1938	25
	4.3 U.S. 1939–1958	26
	4.4 U.S. 1959 and Up	28
	4.5 U.S. Rule Gestation and Publication	29
	4.6 U.S. Accident Investigations	29
	4.7 Developments in Europe	29
	4.7.1 Pre-war	29
	4.7.2 European Civil Aviation Conference	30
	4.7.3 Joint Aviation Authorities	30
	4.7.4 European Union Aviation Safety Agency	31
	4.8 International Civil Aviation Organization	31

Chapter 5	First Wave (1945–1953)	33
	5.1 Introduction	33
	5.2 Prelude	33
	5.3 Aircraft and Cabin Developments	34
	5.3.1 Aircraft	34
	5.3.2 Passenger Seats	35
	5.3.3 Safety Belts	35
	5.3.4 Doors and Emergency Exits	35
	5.3.5 Emergency Equipment	37
	5.3.6 Means of Communication	37
	5.4 Research	37
	5.4.1 Impact Protection	37
	5.4.2 Evacuation Research	38
	5.4.3 The Quest for a Safe Evacuation Time	42
	5.5 Regulatory Developments 1945–1953	43
	5.5.1 Impact Protection	43
	5.5.2 Fire Protection	48
	5.5.3 Escape Potential	50
	5.5.4 Life Support	59
	5.5.5 Information and Instructions	60
	5.6 Summary of the First Wave	62

Chapter 6	Oxygen	65
	6.1 Oxygen Basics	65
	6.2 Experimenting	66
	6.3 Pressurizing the Cabin	69
	6.4 Firming the Oxygen Regulations	70
	6.4.1 Toward Three Altitude Bands	70
	6.4.2 Pressurized Airplanes	70
	6.4.3 Turbine-Powered Airplanes	71
	6.5 Types of Oxygen Supply for Passengers	72
	6.6 Survivability of Decompressions	73

Contents

6.7		Later Regulatory Updates	75
	6.7.1	Medical Oxygen	75
	6.7.2	Masks Connected to Portable Oxygen Equipment	76
	6.7.3	High-Elevation Airports	76
	6.7.4	Higher-Altitude Operations	76
	6.7.5	Tampering-Resistant Lavatory Oxygen Generators	77

Chapter 7 First Trough (1954–1964) 79

7.1	Introduction	79
7.2	The Operational Leftovers from the First Wave	80
	7.2.1 Crash Axe	80
	7.2.2 Chop Marks and Exterior Exit Markings	81
	7.2.3 Exit and Operating Handle Marking and Illumination	81
	7.2.4 Evacuation Means	82
7.3	The Ditching Years	82
	7.3.1 Ditching Troubles	82
	7.3.2 Assignment of Functions	84
	7.3.3 Life Raft Boarding Tests	85
	7.3.4 Ditching Success Stories	86
7.4	Impact Protection	87
7.5	Escape Potential: Preparing for the Jets	89
	7.5.1 Exit Dimensions and Table Update	89
	7.5.2 Inflatable Slide Credit	91
	7.5.3 Aisle Width for Smaller Airplanes	91
7.6	Life Support	92
	7.6.1 Extended Overwater Operations	92
	7.6.2 First-Aid Kit and Survival Equipment	92
7.7	Information and Instructions	93

Chapter 8 The Cabin Professional 95

8.1	A Brief History	95
	8.1.1 Pioneers	95
	8.1.2 Enter the Air Hostess	96
	8.1.3 Female Attraction	97
	8.1.4 Equal Opportunity	99
	8.1.5 Shift of Work	99
	8.1.6 Shift of Title	101
	8.1.7 Statistics	102
8.2	Recognition of the Safety Role	102
8.3	Regulations	105
	8.3.1 1930–1953	105
	8.3.2 1954–Present	107
	8.3.3 Expansion of Scope	108
	8.3.4 Lower Cut-Off: 10 or 20?	108
	8.3.5 Duties and Responsibilities	109
	8.3.6 Where Located?	110
	8.3.7 Protection	113

		8.3.8	How Many?.. 114
		8.3.9	Training 117
		8.3.10	Licensing 120
		8.3.11	Flight and Rest Times... 121
	8.4	Challenges and Hazards.. 121

Chapter 9 Second Wave (1965–1972) 126

	9.1	Introduction... 126
	9.2	First Set (1965).. 128
		9.2.1	Escape Potential 128
		9.2.2	Life Support: Any Overwater Operation.. 130
	9.3	Second Set (1967) 130
		9.3.1	Introduction 130
		9.3.2	Impact Protection 131
		9.3.3	Fire Protection.. 132
		9.3.4	Escape Potential 133
		9.3.5	United Airlines 136
	9.4	Third Set (1972).. 137
		9.4.1	Introduction 137
		9.4.2	Impact Protection 137
		9.4.3	Fire Protection.. 138
		9.4.4	Escape Potential 138
	9.5	Summary of the Second Wave.. 139

Chapter 10 Regulation Proposals That Were Rejected 142

	10.1	Introduction... 142
	10.2	Parachutes 142
	10.3	Aft-Facing Seats.. 143
	10.4	Passenger Smoke Hoods 144
	10.5	Flight Attendant Clothing 147
	10.6	Strobe Lights... 147
	10.7	Lavatory-Occupied Sign 148
	10.8	Evacuation Alarm System... 148
	10.9	Water Mist System 148
	10.10	Passageway between Bulkheads 150

Chapter 11 Second Trough (1973–1981) 153

	11.1	Introduction... 153
	11.2	Accidents... 153
	11.3	Hearings... 154
	11.4	FAA Getting to Grips with Cabin Safety 155
	11.5	FAA Rulemaking 156
		11.5.1	Impact Protection 156
		11.5.2	Fire Protection.. 156
		11.5.3	Escape Potential 159
		11.5.4	Life Support—Segregated Smoking Sections.................................. 159
		11.5.5	Information and Instructions.. 160

Contents ix

Chapter 12 Evacuation Demonstrations 162
    12.1   Introduction 162
    12.2   Optional Demonstrations 162
            12.2.1   30 Seconds or 1 Second per Person 162
            12.2.2   60 or 90 Seconds? 164
    12.3   United Airlines 164
            12.3.1   1952—Safety or Promotion? 164
            12.3.2   1963–1964: United versus Pan Am 168
    12.4   First Evacuation Demonstrations 169
    12.5   Research 169
    12.6   Mandatory Demonstrations 170
            12.6.1   1965–1967: Airlines Only 170
            12.6.2   1967: Extension to Manufacturers 171
            12.6.3   1968–1981: Demonstrations by Both Manufacturers
                        and Airlines 173
            12.6.4   1982: Introduction of the Mini Demo 174
            12.6.5   1982–1996: Manufacturer-Only Full-Scale
                        Demonstrations 174
            12.6.6   Regulatory Guidance and Changes 175
            12.6.7   Post-1996: Analyses Take Over Full-Scales 175
            12.6.8   A380 Evacuation Demonstration 175
    12.7   How Realistic Should the Demonstration Be? 176
    12.8   Evacuation Demonstrations in Practice 177

Chapter 13 Third Wave (1982–1996) 181
    13.1   Introduction 181
    13.2   Accidents 181
    13.3   Hearings 183
    13.4   Research 184
            13.4.1   Fire Safety 184
            13.4.2   Crash-in-the-Desert 186
    13.5   Regulatory Developments 186
            13.5.1   Impact Protection 186
            13.5.2   Fire Protection 191
            13.5.3   Escape Potential 195
            13.5.4   Life Support—Medical Kit 202
            13.5.5   Information and Instructions 202

Chapter 14 Different Opinions among Authorities 206
    14.1   Introduction 206
    14.2   Impact Protection 206
            14.2.1   Infant Supplemental Loop Belt 206
            14.2.2   Crash Loads 207
    14.3   Escape Potential 207
            14.3.1   Dispatch Relief 207
            14.3.2   Type III Exits 209
            14.3.3   Green Man Running 220

14.4	Life Support		222
	14.4.1	Flotation Cushion versus Life Vest	222
	14.4.2	Polar Flights	222
	14.4.3	Oxygen	224
14.5	Instructions and Information		225
	14.5.1	Addressing Passengers	225
	14.5.2	Country of Assembly	225
14.6	Security		226
	14.6.1	Monitoring Cockpit Entry Area	226
	14.6.2	Second Axe	228
	14.6.3	Second Barrier	228
14.7	Cabin Professionals		230
	14.7.1	Introduction	230
	14.7.2	Required Minimum Number of Cabin Crew	230
	14.7.3	Qualification and Training	234
	14.7.4	Licensing	234
	14.7.5	Flight Time Limitations	234

Chapter 15 Developments since 1997 ... 238

15.1	Introduction		238
15.2	Reports and Guidance Material		239
	15.2.1	Reviews	239
	15.2.2	Regulatory Development Support	239
	15.2.3	Guidance	240
	15.2.4	Conferences	240
15.3	Regulatory Committees		241
	15.3.1	U.S.	241
	15.3.2	Europe	243
15.4	Turbulence		243
15.5	Brace-for-Impact		244
15.6	Air Contamination		247
15.7	Pandemics		248
15.8	Regulatory Developments		248
	15.8.1	Europe	248
	15.8.2	Impact Protection	248
	15.8.3	Fire Protection	250
	15.8.4	Escape Potential	250
	15.8.5	Life Support	251

Chapter 16 Exit Credit Creativity ... 254

16.1	Introduction		254
16.2	Seeking Higher Maximum Capacities		255
	16.2.1	Non-standard Exits	255
	16.2.2	Over-Sized Exit	256
	16.2.3	Alternate Exit Configurations	257
	16.2.4	Grandfather Rights	257
	16.2.5	Overperforming Exits	258

Contents xi

      16.3   Optimizing Exit Configurations for Lesser Capacities 258
            16.3.1   De-rating 258
            16.3.2   Deactivation 258
            16.3.3   Single Pair of Exits 259

Chapter 17 Reaping the Benefits of Cabin Safety Measures 261

      17.1   Introduction 261
      17.2   Accident Trends since 1935 261
            17.2.1   Criteria 261
            17.2.2   Trend 1: Number of Survivable, Yet Life-Threatening,
                        Accidents 261
            17.2.3   Trend 2: Number of Fatalities in Survivable Accidents 262
            17.2.4   Trend 3: Number of Survivors in Life-Threatening
                        Accidents 263
            17.2.5   Trend 4: Percentage of Survivors 263
      17.3   Reaping from Cabin Safety Measures 264
            17.3.1   Introduction 264
            17.3.2   Impact Protection (Restraint) 264
            17.3.3   Fire Protection (Flammability) 265
            17.3.4   Escape Potential (Descent Assist Means, Floor Lighting) 266
            17.3.5   Life Support (Flotation Devices) 266
            17.3.6   Cabin Professionals 266

Chapter 18 Exit Usage 269

      18.1   Introduction 269
      18.2   King, Piston (1948–1951) 269
      18.3   CAMI, Jets (1961–1990) 270
      18.4   University of Greenwich 270
      18.5   Author, Jets (1960–2024) 271
            18.5.1   Introduction 271
            18.5.2   Results—Longitudinal 276
            18.5.3   Results—Lateral 278
            18.5.4   Results—Distribution Patterns 278
            18.5.5   Results—Proportion of Exits Used 278
            18.5.6   Results—Average Usage Rates per Exit 279
      18.6   Conclusions 279

Chapter 19 Possible Future Cabin Safety Developments 281

      19.1   Introduction 281
      19.2   In the Pipeline 281
      19.3   New Concepts 282
            19.3.1   Airplane Level 282
            19.3.2   Cabin Level 282
      19.4   Selected Cabin Safety Challenges 283
            19.4.1   Carry-On Baggage 283
            19.4.2   Evacuation Initiation 284

		19.4.3	PED Fire Containment	284
		19.4.4	Tail Exits	285
		19.4.5	Safety Instructions	285
		19.4.6	Cabin Safety Accident Investigations	285

Chapter 20 Acquainting Passengers 287

	20.1	Introduction	287
	20.2	1924: The First Safety Pamphlet	287
	20.3	1920s—1944	287
	20.4	Post World War Two: The Ditching Years	289
	20.5	1965 Onward: Mandated, Guided	292
	20.6	Designing and Testing Safety Cards	294
	20.7	Video	295
	20.8	Studies and Research	295
	20.9	Effectivity in Accidents	296

Chapter 21 Epilogue 300

	21.1	History Summarized	300
	21.2	Reactive, Not Proactive	301
	21.3	Stamina	301
	21.4	Rejection Rule	302
	21.5	U.S. Dominance Challenged	302

Appendices 304

Appendix 1—Accidents Referred to 304
Appendix 2a—U.S. Regulations 1926–1936 (Pre-Federal Register) 309
Appendix 2b—U.S. Regulations 1937–1964 310
Appendix 2c—U.S. Final Rules and Preceding Proposals since 1941 312
Appendix 2d—Withdrawn U.S. Proposals 317
Appendix 3—Exit Types and Dimensions 318

Index 319

About the Author

Fons Schaefers has over 40 years of aviation regulatory experience, gained in various aviation sectors. Between 1981 and 1996, he held several aircraft certification, research, and development positions in the field of cabin safety within Fokker Aircraft. He participated in five aircraft accident investigation teams on three different continents. In 1996, he joined a Dutch airline to manage the application for an Air Operator Certificate and developed its Safety Management System. He participated in international bodies engaged in aviation safety advice and rulemaking, including the U.S. FAA's Aviation Rulemaking Advisory Committee (ARAC) and the European EASA Safety Standards Consultative Committee. In 2010, he joined SGI Aviation Services for whom he performed consultancy and training activities in the general subject of aviation safety regulations. In 2012, following SGI's selection by the Government of Guernsey as the service provider for the Guernsey Aircraft Registry, he developed its policies, protocols, and procedures. He managed the registry on a day-to-day basis between 2013 and 2018. He retired in early 2019 but is still engaged as an independent consultant.

Preface

0.1 INTRODUCTION

Cabin safety is one of the more visible aspects of aviation safety. All who board an airliner will meet some of its features. When passengers stow their belongings, take a seat, and fasten their seat belts, they engage, perhaps unknowingly, in cabin safety. And when they decide to watch the safety briefing or study the safety card, this goes a step further. Obviously, they expect their flight to be safe so that they arrive in the same state of health as they departed and need not rely on more cabin safety. The crew working in the cabin will exercise cabin safety in many of their activities, all of which should be of a preparatory nature only. But they are prepared for any contingency. While extremely rare, a serious incident can develop which requires them to practice what they learned in their training. During cruise flight, this may be a medical situation or worse, the effects of heavy turbulence, a decompression, or a fire. On or closer to the ground, there may be mishaps where the aircraft becomes damaged and an evacuation is required.

All of the cabin safety features, be they of a design nature, a procedure, or training, have developed over time into what they are now, in 2024. While there are publications that give a good overview of the current state of cabin safety, few, if any, have attempted to trace its history and development over time. It is with that purpose in mind that the author embarked on this project. In doing so, he used many sources which stretched over a century, from a 1924 safety leaflet to multiple accident investigation reports and rules and acts as recent as 2024. As to rules, the majority of these are of U.S. origin, which corresponds to the dominance that the country had in cabin safety development.

0.2 SCOPE

While cabin safety prima facie may seem to be a well-contained concept, readers may have different expectations from it. A definition of cabin safety is therefore justified. But before defining cabin safety, cabin should be defined. The cabin is that part of a civil air transport aircraft that is designed for occupancy by passengers and cabin professionals. It includes those areas where they sit or work and can move about in flight. This includes the main cabin or cabins, all galleys, lavatories, and, where available, lounges. It excludes the cockpit and cargo compartments, which are normally inaccessible during flight. Cargo compartments that are accessible during flight, such as those on combi aircraft, are excluded as well.

For the purpose of this book, cabin safety includes all those cabin-related design features and operational procedures that are intended to ensure that aircraft occupants survive an accident or incident uninjured. An accident or incident, in this respect, can occur in any phase of flight. This spans the entire cycle from the aircraft being boarded for flight, in motion on the ground, taking-off, being in-flight, and back to being on the stand again for deboarding.

While cabin safety applies to all kinds of aircraft and operations, including helicopters and air taxi services, more commonly, it concerns large transport airplanes, operated by an airline.[1] In this book, the focus is on those kinds of airplanes and airlines.

Excluded from the concept of cabin safety are some subjects that balance on the edges of the definition. They are primarily operational and often rely on procedures controlled outside the aircraft but with an on-board element. They typically rely on cabin crew and their training, so some will be considered to be part of cabin safety. The excluded subjects are:

- Security measures (i.e. measures to prevent unlawful interference)
- Dangerous goods, either declared or undeclared

- Measures for special categories of passengers, such as physically impaired, obese, and, unique for the U.S., the use of emotional support animals
- Procedures for unruly passengers
- Food and water safety
- Hygiene and sanitation procedures, both in normal times and during a pandemic

0.3 CONVENTIONS

0.3.1 Units

Aviation is not yet aligned with the SI system for units. Altitude is measured in feet, cabin dimensions in inches and distances between exits in feet. These units prevail in this book. It has been attempted to add SI units, but there may be cases where this is omitted. There is a psychological element here, as well. The 60-foot rule is not the same as the 18.3-meter rule. If that rule had been conceived in the metric system, it probably would have been the 18-meter rule or maybe even the 20-meter rule. In the chapter about oxygen, a table is provided that converts feet to meters, to avoid converting altitudes in the rest of that chapter.

0.3.2 Dates

When Americans write 12/02/1955 they mean a day that the rest of the world knows as 02/12/1955. They do not mean 12 February 1955 but 2 December 1955. To avoid any confusion all dates are written with the month in letters, not numbers. But as many of the dates come from U.S. sources, in such cases, their style of the month preceding the day is kept.

0.3.3 References

Naturally, the author had to make selections in the depth of discussing subjects. Readers may find that their specific area of interest could have benefited from more detail. To help those readers, many references are included to source documents, which appear at the end of each chapter. References to website links have been kept to a minimum because of their volatile nature.

As the history of cabin safety is heavily intertwined with regulations, many of the references are to regulatory publications. An overview of the successive U.S. regulatory frameworks is given in Chapter 4. Appendix 2a and 2b list the sets of requirements as they came into force in the U.S. in the periods 1926–1936 and 1937–1967, respectively. Of more interest from a historical perspective are changes to these regulations, particularly when accompanied by their rationales. Appendix 2c gives publication details for rule change proposals and final rules. Both follow a numerical designation. Proposals, in the form of a Draft Release (DR) or Notice of Proposed Rulemaking (NPRM), start with the year of publication, followed by a sequence number. Examples are *DR 52–26; NPRM 90–4*. Final rules were published as Amendments to the relevant Civil Air Regulation or, from 1965 onward, Federal Aviation Requirements. *Amdt. 4b-4* and *Amdt. 121–381* are examples of, respectively, an amendment to CAR 4b and FAR 121. Since 1936, with few exceptions, the requirements, rule proposals, and final rules were published in the Federal Register. References to this register use the following format: a number indicating the year of publication (starting in 1936 as year 1), followed by FR (for Federal Register), and a page number. Example: *55 FR 29756*.

In the preparation of this book, a number of website links have frequently been used. They are:

- For U.S. aviation regulations:
  - Federal Register 1936 to 1993: www.loc.gov/collections/federal-register/index/partofs/?sp=1

Preface   xvii

- Federal Register from 1994 onward: www.federalregister.gov/documents/search
- FAA reference data: drs.faa.gov
- For accident information: www.aviationsafety.net and www.baaa-acro.com.

The referenced websites are considered stable and expected to last.

0.4 GENERAL NOTES ON AIRCRAFT CERTIFICATION

0.4.1 LONG LEAD TIMES

In aviation safety, and cabin safety is no exception, it can take many years before a new requirement takes effect. Why is that? For changes involving the design ('hardware') of airplanes, this can best be answered by explaining the concepts of Type Certification, forward fit, retrofit, and the Airworthiness Directive. Requirements not affecting hardware, but addressing such aspects as training or operational procedures typically have shorter lead times.

It takes many years for a new airplane type to be designed. And when the design is frozen, it can take another five years of tests and reviews to show that it meets all of the airworthiness requirements. This certification process starts with an application for a type certificate and the manufacturer and the certificating authority agreeing on the applicable set of requirements. This is called the type certification basis. Later changes to the requirements fall outside that certification basis so that the manufacturer is not confronted with a moving target. In practice, this means that new design requirements are typically followed up with a time lag of up to five years. And, as they apply to new types only, it will take a long time before the new safety feature becomes widespread. There have been cases, particularly in cabin safety, where it was felt that this was too long, and a quicker means of implementation was needed. Three such methods have been employed: the forward fit, the retrofit, and, rarely, the Airworthiness Directive. The forward fit refers to new samples of an airplane type already certificated coming off the production line to meet the new requirement. The retrofit goes much further and also applies to existing fleets. Typically, for both forward fit and retrofit, a lead time is applied of one or two years between the publication of a new rule and its effectivity date so that manufacturers and airlines have time for implementation. In a few cases, where urgency so stipulates, the instrument of an Airworthiness Directive is used to implement a new safety feature at short notice.

0.4.2 THE DERIVATIVE CONCEPT

Another certification aspect that needs explanation is that of the derivatives. The design of a new airplane type is an extensive, costly process and not easily undertaken. Rather, manufacturers have found a way to capitalize on an existing design by modifying it over the years. Such changes may exist of stretching it, shrinking it, using new engines, updating instrumentation, and so on. All these changes involve a modification to the type certificate of the base model. The advantage in terms of aircraft certification is that, for those design elements which are not changed, the original certification basis remains valid. This can lead to aircraft variants which rely on regulations that are decades-old. This practice is known as 'grandfathering'.

The ultimate example is the Boeing 737. This emerged as a new type in 1965. It was first flown in April 1967 and type certificated on December 15 of the same year as the 737–100. The first amendment of the type certificate was one week later when the next variant, the 737–200, was added. Major changes came in 1984–1990 (737–300, 737–400, 737–500, later referred to as the 'Boeing 737 Classic', the 737–100 and 737–200 being referred to as the 'Original' series), the 737 Next Generation in 1997–2001 (737–600, 737–700, 737–800, 737–900) and, finally, the 737 Max in 2017–2018 (Max 8, Max 9, with Max 7 and Max 10 not yet certificated by end-2024). Even the latest model, or derivative, still uses certification elements dating back to 1965. A cabin safety example is the credit of ten passenger seats for inflatable slides. This requirement was dropped in 1972, but as the Max 8 and 9 use the same exit design as the original Boeing 737, the FAA allowed its use five decades after the original type certification.

0.5 ABBREVIATIONS AND ACRONYMS

AECMA	European Association of Aerospace Industries
AFA	Association of Flight Attendants
ALPA	Airline Pilots Association
ALSSA	Airline Stewards and Stewardesses Association
amdt.	Amendment (to a set of regulatory requirements)
ANPRM	Advance Notice of Proposed Rulemaking
AOG	Aircraft on Ground
APFA	Association of Professional Flight Attendants
ARAC	Aviation Rulemaking Advisory Committee
ARC	Aviation Rulemaking Committee
ATA	Air Transport Association
AvCIR	Aviation Crash Injury Research
AvSER	Aviation Safety Engineering and Research
CAA	Civil Aeronautics Authority (U.S., 1938–1940)
	Civil Aeronautics Administration (U.S., 1940–1957)
CAA	Civil Aviation Authority (United Kingdom, 1972–)
CAB	Civil Aeronautics Board
CAM	Civil Aeronautics Manual
CAR	Civil Air Regulations
CASA	Civil Aviation Safety Authority (Australia)
CS	Certification Specifications
CSSG	Cabin Safety Study Group
DR	Draft Release
EASA	European Safety Aviation Agency (2002–2018)
	European Union Safety Aviation Agency (2018–)
ECAC	European Civil Aviation Conference
FAA	Federal Aviation Agency (1959–1967)
	Federal Aviation Administration (1967–)
FAA CAMI	Federal Aviation Administration, Civil Aeromedical Institute
FAA CARI	Federal Aviation Agency, Civil Aeromedical Research Institute
FAA OAM	Federal Aviation Administration, Office of Aviation Medicine
FAA TC	Federal Aviation Administration, Technical Center
FAR	Federal Aviation Requirements
FPEEPM	Floor proximity emergency escape path marking
FSF	Flight Safety Foundation
HIC	Head Injury Criterion
IATA	International Air Transport Association
ICAO	International Civil Aviation Organization
ICPTF	International Certification Procedures Task Force
JAA	Joint Airworthiness Authorities
	Joint Aviation Authorities

JAR	Joint Airworthiness Requirements
	Joint Aviation Requirements
MEL	Minimum Equipment List
MMEL	Master Minimum Equipment List
NACA	National Advisory Committee for Aeronautics
	National Air Carrier Association
NAFEC	National Aviation Facilities Experimental Center
NASA	National Aeronautics and Space Administration
NM	Nautical Mile
NPA	Notice of Proposed Amendment
NPRM	Notice of Proposed Rulemaking
NTSB	National Transportation Safety Board
PA	Public Address System
PBE	Protective Breathing Equipment
PED	Portable Electronic Device
SAE	Society of Automotive Engineers
SAFER	Special Aviation Fire and Explosion Reduction
SNPRM	Supplemental Notice of Proposed Rulemaking
TSO	Technical Standard Order
U.S.	United States of America
USAF	U.S. Air Force

0.6 ACKNOWLEDGEMENTS

The author is grateful for all the authors and organizations of the referenced documents, as they helped paint the historical picture. Equally, he is indebted to all the professionals that he met and conversed with during his 15 years of engagement in the world of cabin safety while working for the Dutch airplane manufacturer Fokker. (That period, incidentally, coincided with the third cabin safety wave.) Their number is too vast to even attempt to make a list. Some, however, are mentioned herein.

The author wishes to express warm gratitude to those who helped during the preparation of this book: Rudi den Hertog (Fokker) for his encouragement to this book, Yves Morier (JAA, EASA) for his professional and detailed comments, David Rice for proofreading the manuscript, and Melissa Gottwald (Embry Riddle University, Prescott, AZ) for giving access to the archives of Jerome Lederer and Richard Chandler.

The websites of Ronan Hubert (baaa-aro.com) and Harro Ranter (aviation-safety.net) proved to be invaluable sources of information for accidents and formal accident reports.

Finally, the following persons have been very helpful in various other ways: Gunnar Berntsen, Peter Chittenden, Wayne Hammer, Ron Huisman, and Fern Koning.

No work can be complete and free of errors, and this book is no exception. Readers who wish to communicate errors or provide other comments are kindly invited to do so by messaging f.schaefers@planet.nl.

Surhuizum, the Netherlands, 24 December 2024.

NOTE

1 A large transport airplane is defined by its take-off mass: more than 5,700 kg or 12,500 pounds.

1 Prologue

Imagine a parallel world where the following cabin safety rules and practices apply. And read on to find out where and when this parallel world exists or perhaps used to exist.

Cabin arrangement

The cabin aisle must be as narrow as possible, especially in a long cabin, to prevent passengers from rushing to the back in a panic or go promenading and disturb other passengers. An aisle width of 9 to 10 inch (23 to 25 cm) is sufficient, even though it means that passengers must walk sideways. Besides, there is no need for promenading on journeys of less than 10 hours. Yet, to aid passengers when they need to walk the aisle to visit the lavatory (perhaps to use the special vomiting basin), provide ceiling-mounted handholds for stability.

Each passenger must have a separate window, openable in flight for ventilation and, if needed, to throw out the airsickness bag. With respect to ventilation, a system must be designed that ensures proper ventilation so that there is no need for opening windows while not producing a noticeable draught. As to promenading, for very large planes, an open-air platform might be an interesting feature, which passengers then enter at their own risk. In that case, some official needs to be on board, with whose instructions passengers would have to comply.

Preferably, break the cabin up into small compartments, seating two or four, as this facilitates conversation. They can also be used to separate seasick persons from the rest. Use lockable doors between the compartments. Also, in larger planes, use a door to separate the passenger cabin from the flight deck. Yet, when there is no mechanic or steward carried, passengers must still be allowed to enter the flight deck as they sometimes are able to give a pilot useful information on damage to some part of the machine and to help out find the route. Also, passengers should be allowed to use the radiophone. If the aircraft design does not permit the installation of a door, either a speaking tube or a means for passing a message or a note should be provided.

Special baggage compartments are essential, yet if there are empty seats, they may be used for baggage. The practice of stowing baggage in the cockpit is not advised as it is very dangerous in case of bad weather or a crash.

Seats and belts

Attach seats to the floor by means of a ball joint. Consider a headrest to allow sleeping in the seat and thus counter airsickness. However, mind that a headrest may be resented by lady passengers, as it crushes their hats or disturbs their hair. Pad the seats so that in a crash legbones do not break when flailing against it. For maximum seating convenience, use wicker chairs with cushions. Footrests are not necessary as they are in the way and add weight.

Safety belts are optional, as passengers never use them, anyway. Yet, they may be useful as in rough weather passengers are sometimes thrown to the ceiling. But then it is somebody's business to tell the passengers when they should be fastened. So, in all, it may be better to just provide substantial chairs well secured to the floor than to provide belts.

Fire protection

A hand-type fire extinguisher is sufficient for cabin use. The chemical employed must be such as to injure neither cabin nor passengers. If no steward is carried, the extinguisher must be accessible to the passengers, with a clear notice of instructions and a warning against improper use.

Cabin interior furnishing materials may be like those of an automobile or Pullman car. The floor should be covered with thin, light linoleum. Cabin walls may be of airplane fabric or have leather coverings.

Crashworthiness

As aircraft crashes have the outcome of being either fatal or negligible importance, it is better to concentrate design efforts on making the aircraft itself safer rather than trying to decrease the effects of a crash. Shock-absorbing devices are unlikely to be useful in case of a crash and only add weight. Besides, wicker chairs already have good absorbing properties. The use of safety belts for crashes is not recommended, as they are not reassuring to the passengers. In a crash, passengers must grasp their chairs, which should be well fastened to the floor. Also, sponge rubber as padding on wooden or metal parts on the upper parts of seats will help. A recommended brace for impact position is as follows: knees to the chin, neck bowed, and forehead protected by one of the forearms.

Evacuation

For aircraft seating less than 14, one entrance door is sufficient. It does not matter whether this door is on the right or the left side, but the best location is at the rear as the height of the step will be less. Avoid placing doors in the plane of the propellers. Doors must have a positive lock to prevent passengers from opening them in flight and mistaking them for the toilet door. The door need not be rectangular. In fact, a triangular shape may be better with the lower part being only 7 inch (18 cm) wide. The height should be at least 5 ft 2 inch (157 cm).

The size of the cabin windows should be at least 14 by 20 inch (36 by 50 cm) so they can serve as an emergency exit on the ground. In-flight escape is not an option as the provisioning of individual parachutes for passengers present insuperable difficulties. Aircraft are controllable at the stalling angle, and pilots should make the best of a crash by pancaking on trees, sideslipping, or allowing the low wing to absorb most of the crash. Emergency exits in the roof are desirable and should be large enough to enable corpulent passengers to get out without difficulty. There should be at least one such exit for every six passengers. Where the windows are too small, there should be at least an emergency exit opposite the entrance door and in the lavatory.

Communication and steward

Passengers are interested in knowing the flight altitude, so there should be an altimeter in the cabin, preferably on the front wall. Add an airspeed indicator as well. Give passengers a map with the route and distances so they can follow the course and recognize cities and other points of interest.

The mechanic or navigator, when on board, will be the intermediary between the pilot and the passengers. He may assist passengers, for example, in the case of a medical emergency. When more than eight passengers are carried, a steward is desirable, who should then be well versed in the use of the first aid box and administration of first aid. Also, he has control over the hand fire extinguisher.

Indeed, this is a totally different world of cabin safety than what the reader is used to. The author may be accused of having too rich an imagination. The reality, however, is that this parallel world sketch did not spring from that but is simply a report of what was real, in Europe, in 1928.

It is paraphrased from a study made by the (U.S.) Daniel Guggenheim Fund for the Promotion of Aeronautics in 1928.[1] Passenger air transport in the U.S. was then still embryonic, while in Europe it was already in its tenth year. The report was based on a questionnaire prepared by the fund and sent to its representatives in the United Kingdom, France, Germany, and the Netherlands.[2] Each of these countries had its own aircraft manufacturers bearing famous names such as Dornier and Junkers (Germany), de Havilland and Handley Page (UK), Farman (France), and Fokker (Netherlands). Aircraft of the time were made of wood and fabric, seating up to 15 passengers. The cabin arrangement was typically two abreast, with a narrow aisle in between. A lavatory was in the back.

The routes these aircraft flew were mainly between the capitals and other major cities of these four countries plus neighboring countries. Single-sector flight durations ranged from a mere 25 minutes to 3 hours.

It was hoped that the study was of help American designers, constructors, and operators. As such, it gives an excellent, contemporary sketch of the state-of-the-art cabin design and operation in Europe in 1928. While in many areas there was consensus on the practices between the

Prologue

FIGURE 1.1 Dornier Komet interior (Safety and Accommodation in European Passenger Planes—Pamphlet Number Three—the Daniel Guggenheim Fund for the Promotion of Aeronautics, Inc., December 17, 1928).

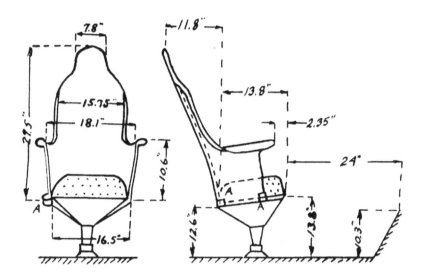

FIGURE 1.2 German sketch for a comfortable seat fastened to the cabin floor by a ball joint and with eyes, marked A, to fasten it to the cabin wall (Safety and Accommodation in European Passenger Planes—Pamphlet Number Three—The Daniel Guggenheim Fund for the Promotion of Aeronautics, Inc., December 17, 1928).

four countries, there were some differences. Stewards were initially only employed in the UK and Germany. Germany did not allow passengers to enter the cockpit. In the Netherlands, two fire extinguishers were prescribed for commercial airplanes; in other countries, one sufficed. Germany insisted on seat belts, whereas the British were against them and the French were indifferent 'as passengers never use them'. An item not mentioned in the report is the life vest. This is possible because the questionnaire was compiled by the Americans with continental U.S. air transport in mind, so flights over water were not anticipated. Yet, other sources tell us that in the epoch life vests, then known as life belts, were common in Europe, particularly for cross-Channel flights. In fact, on the very early flights, in 1919, they not only were carried on board but actually needed to be worn as contemporary trip reports witness.

Did the Americans indeed learn from Europe in designing and operating passenger transport aircraft? And did they copy the cabin safety features? The answers are in the chapters that follow.

NOTES

1 Safety and Accommodation in European Passenger Planes—Pamphlet Number Three—The Daniel Guggenheim Fund for the Promotion of Aeronautics, Inc., December 17, 1928.
2 United Kingdom and the Netherlands were then referred to as England and Holland, respectively.

2 Introduction

ABSTRACT

The history of cabin safety saw waves and troughs. Three waves with two intermediate troughs, spanning the period from 1945 to 1996, are discussed in the chronological chapters (the odd-numbered chapters). To give the reader some grip on the broad concept of cabin safety, the chronological chapters are structured per five domains: impact protection, fire protection, escape potential, life support, information, and instructions. (A sixth domain, cabin professionals, has a chapter of its own.) The even-numbered chapters cover subjects by theme, such as the regulatory framework, or are dedicated to subdomains, such as oxygen, which is an element of the life support domain.

2.1 AN ACCIDENT-DRIVEN MÉTIER

In all, all action that it seems sensible to take has already been taken.

This is what the investigators of a DC-4 crash at New York La Guardia on May 29, 1947, concluded in their September 16, 1947, report.[1] Their statement was about the corrective actions. It may have been true for those actions aimed at preventing a future accident from the same causes. But it certainly was not true for the dramatic cabin safety consequences. The aircraft was departing from a short runway when the pilot felt compelled to abort the take-off. It overran the runway, crossed the airport fence, and 'half-bounced, half-flew across the Grand Central Parkway', coming to rest next to, ironically, a school of aeronautics.

The report, rated by the aviation press as 'one of the most voluminous and detailed accident reports ever', ignored survivability aspects.[2] It very factually said that all the seats 'with the exception of the hostesses' seats' came loose.[3] Other than that, the investigators did not pay any attention to what must have been a horrific situation inside. A fire broke out immediately. In the cabin, it must have been total chaos, with passengers trapped by the loose seats which obstructed passage to the exits and the exits themselves. King's May 1952 report has more details about the evacuation:[4]

> The LaGuardia accident (May 1947) presented unusual difficulties. The airplane came to rest with the cockpit windows about one foot above water; other exits were as much as ten feet above usable footing.
>
> [The Captain] went out through the cockpit side window and entered the plane by the rear service door. He opened the main cabin door with an axe and chopped holes in the fuselage through which passengers were evacuated. Eight passengers and two stewardesses, all seriously injured, were rescued. Five passengers and one stewardess subsequently died of burns or injuries.
>
> It was estimated that three minutes elapsed before evacuation of the passengers was begun.

This cruel accident shocked many, including the president of the airline involved, United Air Lines: William Patterson. He became an advocate for cabin safety.

While this accident did not result in cabin safety improvements (at least, not instantly), many other accidents, with associated losses of lives, followed that did. The following chapters are full of references to such accidents. For the benefit of the reader, a complete list of referred accidents appears in Appendix 1.

After about 50 years, aircraft cabin safety matured to a level which is generally considered acceptable: seats that stay attached to the aircraft in all but the severest crashes, cabin materials that delay fire propagation sufficient to allow timely egress of all on board, adequate means of escape, life support features such oxygen supply and water survival devices, and, last but not least, well-trained cabin crew in adequate numbers.

In 2003, in a lecture for the International Society for Air Safety Investigators (ISASI), Thomas Farrier of the Air Transport Association of America concluded that 'as far as survivability and aircraft design criteria are concerned, much of what needs to be done, has been done'.[5] This time, the author concurs. Yet, stagnation means decline. Cabin safety development never finishes. New developments need new measures.

2.2 WAVES AND TROUGHS

Cabin safety measures came in fits and starts, in response to a single accident or a group of successive, similar accidents, or when there were major aircraft developments, such as the introduction of jets or wide bodies. Three periods can be discerned as being pivotal, called waves. With each wave, new concepts were introduced and existing concepts were enhanced. The first wave was from 1945 to 1953. Bad luck no longer was an excuse for ignoring the consequences of crashes to aircraft occupants. Up till then crash fatalities and serious injuries were simply considered an inevitable by-product of flying. Crashworthiness and survivability issues became recognized as worth studying and remedying. Pioneers such as A. Howard Hasbrook, Barry G. King, and Ross A. McFarland plowed the fields of impact protection, evacuation provisions, and oxygen needs. The second wave started about 1965 and ended in 1972, responding to the first lessons of jet accidents and anticipating the new widebodies. The third and final waves closed the remaining open items such as cabin material flammability characteristics and dynamically tested seats. It can be pinned to the period 1982 to 1996. In between the three waves, there were two periods of lesser activity, called troughs.

Since then, there have been minor, incremental improvements, in reaction to societal and technological developments. None of those however were as decisive for the current state of cabin safety as those of the three waves.

2.3 READER GUIDANCE

Cabin safety encompasses many different elements. For the benefit of the reader, they are divided into six domains: (1) impact protection; (2) fire protection; (3) escape potential; (4) life support; (5) instructions and information; and (6) the cabin professional.

While in all domains there is a mix of design and operational measures, for the first four the emphasis is on design, whereas for the latter two it is operational.

The developments in all the domains are chronologically spread over the odd-numbered chapters. Thus, readers interested in the full history of a particular cabin safety subject (such as exits) will find a chronology of events by referring to the successive odd chapters. For some subjects, however, it was decided to concentrate them in dedicated chapters (the even chapters): oxygen, cabin professionals, evacuation demonstrations, exit credits, exit usage, and safety education. The remaining even-numbered chapters contain an explanation of the leading regulatory framework systems, an overview of cabin safety developments that became moot, and a number of subjects where other countries went a different way than the U.S. The two last odd chapters contain some comments as to possible future developments and general conclusions.

2.3.1 IMPACT PROTECTION

Impact protection measures serve to mitigate the effects of an aircraft impact with the ground (a 'crash') by absorbing the energy in the load path between the cabin floor and each occupant, preventing injury to each occupant when hitting objects, and keeping cabin structures from blocking escape routes. Impact protection measures are a subset of the broader set of crash dynamics measures, which include design features outside the scope of cabin safety such as energy-absorbing fuselage structures. Conversely, and slightly beyond the semantic meaning of 'impact', this area includes protection against the effects of turbulence in flight.

2.3.2 Fire Protection

Fire protection has two different faces: (1) primarily for the in-flight phase (although also of use when on the ground): preventing the onset of any fire or smoke in the aircraft cabin or, when it occurs, containing it or, when that fails, mitigate its effects; (2) in the case of a crash, delay the onset and propagation of fire and smoke inside the cabin. Like crash dynamics, fire protection is an area larger than cabin safety and extends to measures aimed at preventing the occurrence, or mitigating the effects, of any fire starting in the aircraft at large. This includes not only the containment of powerplant combustion but also the proper positioning of engines relative to fuel tanks, securing of fuel tanks and fuel lines, and provisions for safe shearing off of landing gears and engines. These measures are not considered herein.

Crash response measures by external parties (such as fire rescue services) fall outside the concept of cabin safety, except for such design elements as marking exits on the outside.

2.3.3 Escape Potential

Escape potential includes all those design measures that afford occupants a quick means of evacuation from the aircraft when on the ground, either post-crash or not. This includes internal passageways; signage, lighting, and marking; exits; as well as external means of escape to the ground.

2.3.4 Life Support

Life support consists of a variety of equipment that is on board to preserve life in the case of an accident. Like the fire protection measures, they are either meant for in-flight use or following a forced landing or mild crash. For the in-flight incidents, this consists of oxygen provisions and medical equipment. For landings, when remote from an airfield, it includes survival equipment, appropriate to the area overflown, be it water, desert, arctic, or, otherwise, plus equipment to contact rescue facilities. Life support systems that are part of the aircraft design and which keep the cabin normally habitable, such as ventilation, temperature, and humidity control, are not considered to fall under cabin safety.

2.3.5 Information and Instructions

Cabin safety information and instructions include such elements as cabin-mounted placards and signs, safety briefings (either given by cabin crew or videotaped), and literature, such as passenger information cards.

2.3.6 Cabin Professionals

Finally, with cabin professionals are meant cabin crew, known as flight attendants in the U.S. They are trained to act and assist in such cases as an in-flight fire, decompression, medical incident, or when an evacuation is needed.

2.4 U.S. STANDARDS DOMINATE

Aviation is prohibited . . . unless. Aviation, anywhere in the world, is tightly controlled and subject to laws, rules, and regulations, collectively called requirements. These requirements, set by governments, regulate permissions to those who wish to fly. Such permissions take the form of a license, a certificate, an approval, or another form of authorization. Over the years, the standards have gained in volume. While in 1926 all the aviation standards in the U.S. fitted a 51-page small format document, today, when printed, they would occupy all the shelfs of a sizeable university library.[6]

Equally, the degree of specialization has grown exponentially. While some cabin safety measures were introduced by industry ahead of being regulated, in general, many were in response to regulations imposed by aviation authorities. Sometimes this came with some help from unions or political superiors.

The U.S. has been leading in cabin safety standards since World War Two. This is consistent with the dominant role that it took in commercial air transport. Similarly, virtually all cabin safety research was done there. There were only a few cases where other countries were ahead of, or differed from, the U.S. and then only in some particular subjects. Most simply adopted the U.S. regulations, although not all at the same pace.

This concentration of developments in one country makes it easy to trace its history. Particularly so because the U.S. has a very transparent system of rulemaking. Aviation safety regulation in the U.S. is a federal task, subject to federal procedures for publication. This applies both to rulemaking proposals and final rules. Proposals often give an explanation of why a rule change is needed. Final rules are accompanied by an appreciation of the views of industry and the wider public. Since 1936, the U.S. government has published these in the Federal Register which is issued every weekday. Copies of the Federal Register are available on the internet and can thus readily be consulted. A list of cabin safety-related proposals and final rules referred to herein is given in Appendix 2, which also includes an overview of the successive sets of airworthiness and operational requirements.

NOTES

1 Civil Aeronautics Board, Safety Bureau, Accident Investigation Report, United Air Lines, Inc., La Guardia Field, New York, May 29, 1947, SA-144, Released September 16, 1947, Supplemental Data, p. iv.
2 Aviation Week, September 29, 1949, p. 11.
3 Civil Aeronautics Board, SA-144, p. 5.
4 Aircraft Emergency Evacuation, Operating Experience and Industrial Trials, Report No. 2, U.S. Department of Commerce, Civil Aeronautics Administration, Office of Aviation Safety, May 1952.
5 Investigating Survival Factors in Aircraft Accidents: Revisiting the Past to Look to the Future, by Thomas A. Farrier, Air Transport Association of America, Inc. in Proceedings of the 34th Annual International Seminar, ISASI, August 2003.
6 Air Commerce Regulations, Effective December 31, 1926, Midnight, United States of America, Department of Commerce, Aeronautics Branch.

3 Pioneering Years (1919–1944)

ABSTRACT

This is the second of the chronological chapters. It starts with a description of the nascent air transport in Europe and one of the first of many accidents with cabin safety elements. The Guggenheim findings are briefly reviewed for the six domains. It then shifts focus to the U.S. airliner developments and discusses three early accidents which had an impact on cabin safety regulations. The history of U.S. regulations from 1926 to 1944 is reviewed for five of the six domains.

3.1 EARLY DEVELOPMENTS

3.1.1 Europe Was First

Ignoring the brief stint of passenger flights by airships within Germany before the outbreak of the Great War (World War One) and the short-lived flying boat service across Tampa Bay in Florida, civil air transport properly started in 1919 in Europe. The war had ended in November 1918, and the ensuing peace conference arranged for international passenger air transport. This started in summer 1919 between London and Paris, only shortly after the first domestic service within Great Britain. The first decade saw airplanes being developed from surplus military airplanes where the open position for the gunner was now offered to a passenger, to dedicated passenger airplanes with seating for up to 24 guests and a steward in a closed cabin. The early development of passenger accommodations is well illustrated by John Stroud.[1] Photographs of these cabins show seats, often of the wicker type, facing forward and lined up next to the windows along the length of the cabin, with an aisle in between. In some cases, the cabin was split up into several compartments with seats facing each other, thus both in the forward and in the rearward flight direction. Some airplane types had ball-shaped handholds attached to the ceiling, and in another life jackets were seen stowed above the windows.

The Guggenheim study, as reported in Chapter 1, gives a good impression of what the first ten years of commercial air transport brought in cabin safety: seats for all occupants, a fire extinguisher, a first-aid kit, a narrow aisle and safety belts, and a steward as an option. A British accident investigation report from July 1929 gives additional insights.[2] An accident happened on 17 June 1929, to a Handley Page W.10 operated by Imperial Airways on a flight from London Croydon to Paris Le Bourget. On board were a pilot, an engineer, and 11 passengers, of whom seven did not survive. Following engine trouble over the Channel, the pilot returned to the coast and attempted a water landing 3 miles (5 km) off Dungeness, Kent, next to a trawler. This was only partially successful. The pilot himself was thrown out on impact but survived. In the cabin, 'when the machine struck the water, the passengers on their seats were hurled forward in a heap against the front of the cabin'. This likely caused the death of the seven passengers. The seat's fixing to the floor was questionable, and there were no belts that strapped passengers to their seats, as 'found in some continental aircraft'. (continental, in this respect, referred to aircraft built in the Netherlands, Germany, or France.) There were lifebelts (i.e. life vests), but these did not inflate properly. There were leaflets explaining their operation, but these were found unclear. As the emergency situation unfolded, the engineer, so instructed by the pilot, had gone to the cabin to demonstrate the use of the lifebelt and answer questions. But, during the inquiry, when asked in the witness box to demonstrate how to put the lifebelt on, and how to inflate it, it was apparent 'that he was not adept in the use of the appliance'.

FIGURE 3.1 Imperial Airways life belt, extract from safety pamphlet. Items A and B were not explained in the text (Safety Leaflet, c. 1930).

For a 21st-century investigator, this array of events would prompt many recommendations. Yet, the 1929 investigators decided to make none. Possibly this was all so new to them that they were unsure as to what could be expected from the operator. It is unlikely that any regulatory standard for cabin safety items existed at the time. The Guggenheim study mentions them neither. It appears that, rather than being forced upon by governments, manufacturers, and operators used their own standards, which developed naturally from technological evolution, commercial insights, and entrepreneurial actions. There may have been little appetite for regulatory cabin safety standards owing to the belief, so well expressed by the British contribution in the Guggenheim report, that a crash was either well survivable or fatal. The Dungeness accident happened only six months after its publication and proved this assumption wrong, as there were both survivors and fatalities. It was one of the first survivable accidents with fatalities.

3.1.2 The Six Domains

So, when digesting the Guggenheim report, and looking at the Dungeness accident, it appears that all the six cabin safety domains, as introduced in Section 2.3, were covered in those early years, even though in a very basic way and not always adequately.

There were **impact protection** measures, but with significant differences between countries, with Britain lagging. On the continent, seats were attached to the floor, and there were safety belts and padding. The use of safety belts was not always encouraged.

Fire protection in the cabin was generally limited to the prohibition of smoking and the provision of a hand fire extinguisher or two.

Escape potential provisions consisted of the entrance door, openable windows, and in some cases a hatch in the roof of the cabin. Yet, there was more concern that in flight the entrance door could likely be mistakenly opened by passengers than it could readily be opened when needed for rapid evacuation.

Life support equipment was limited. Life vests (called life belts) for overwater operations and the 'medical box' were the main examples.

The door, or an aperture in it, between the cockpit and the cabin was meant for **communication**, if not audible then by means of written notes. In some cases, a mechanic or **steward** was carried on board.

Pioneering Years (1919–1944)

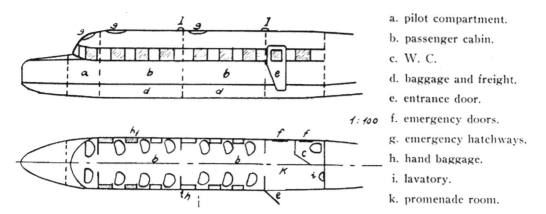

FIGURE 3.2 German design proposal, c. 1928. Note the roof exits (Safety and Accommodation in European Passenger Planes—Pamphlet Number Three—The Daniel Guggenheim Fund for the Promotion of Aeronautics, Inc., December 17, 1928).

3.1.3 U.S. Follows

While in Europe commercial air transport in the 1920s was developing at a significant pace, the U.S. lagged. Airlines there began to start carrying passengers, next to the more lucrative mail, around 1926. From then on, however, things moved quickly, and soon the U.S. took the lead for the number of passengers carried by air. The roots of four domestic air carriers (American, Eastern, TWA, United) and one international air carrier (Pan Am) stem from this period. For an indication of the fledgling cabin safety developments, we can glean some information from a report on a flight with Pan American Airways. The Director of Research of the Department of Commerce's Aviation Business Bureau flew in 1929 on a Sikorsky S-38 twin-engined amphibian craft between Miami and Nassau. He enthusiastically mentioned some of the company's passenger safety policies:[3]

> In anticipation of possible crashes, all passenger chairs are securely attached to the floor and wherever possible to the actual structure of the airplane. In addition, the company supplies several emergency exists [sic] through the top of the cabin, individual life preservers, and an inflatable life raft for overwater flights. Smoking on planes is absolutely prohibited. The pilot is equipped with a Very pistol in order to summon aid when required, and at each terminal a rescue party is fully organized ready to depart on a minute's notice, and arrangements are made to secure the immediate services of a doctor and ambulances.

This matches with what was learned from Europe. The means of water survival were probably unique to Pan Am, being the only American operator that flew over water.

3.1.4 Aircraft Development

As in Europe, in the U.S., it was initially tubular steel, wood, and fabric that were used in the construction of aircraft such as the American-built Fokker F-10. Fokker, the famous Dutch aircraft designer who helped Germany in the Great War and then formed the Fokker factory in Amsterdam, spread his wings in the U.S. as he rightly saw that the future of air transport was there. But the accident in May 1931 of an F-10, which killed eight passengers including then-famous American football coach Knute Rockne, changed this. His competitors replaced wood with metal for both the fuselage and wings. Examples included the Ford Trimotor and Boeing 247 that went into service in 1926 and 1933, respectively. In 1934, the Douglas DC-2 entered the scene and, two years later,

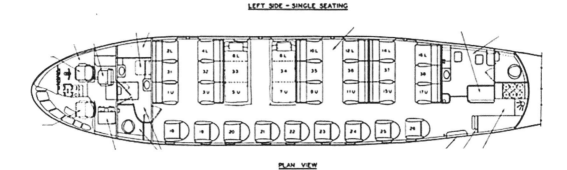

FIGURE 3.3 TWA Boeing 307 cabin layout (TWA, 1940).

the ubiquitous DC-3. The DC-3 was originally designed as a sleeper (the Douglas DST—Douglas Sleeper Transport) with 14 sleeper berths, 6 ft 5 in long (196 cm), in two tiers.

In Europe, the 1930s saw a more eclectic assortment of aircraft types, too many to list here. Photos of the interiors show seats predominantly facing forward, with single or double seats on either side of an aisle. Occasionally, there were club arrangements with seats facing each other with a table in between. Seat belts can be discerned, as well as provisions near the ceilings for light luggage, the hat racks, and curtains for the windows. Larger cabins were typically divided into separate compartments.

A separate class of aircraft were the flying boats. Germany pioneered them in the late 1920s, but their heydays were in the second half of the 1930s, the manufacturing countries then being Britain, France, and the U.S. The largest of them all was the Boeing 314, with seven sequential compartments along the length of the fuselage. Each compartment seated from 8 to 14, with a total capacity of up to 74 passengers. Other flying boats were double-decked, with the main compartments on the boarding deck and more on the upper deck, aft of the high wing. The era of flying boats came to an end around 1950, with the last of the Short, Latécoère, and Boeing examples being retired.

An interesting category of aircraft, albeit not in terms of cabin safety, was the airships. They pioneered the use of cabin staff but not for safety reasons. Their demise came with the crash of the LZ 129 Hindenburg in 1937, before the true development of cabin safety.

The Boeing 307, which came into service in 1939, was a novelty in more than one aspect. Not only did it have four engines, but it was also the first-pressurized airliner ever, capable of flying up to 26,200 ft (8,000 m) and the first with a position for a flight engineer, who was added for managing the pressurization. Conservative, however, was the landing gear layout: it was a tail dragger. The seating arrangement deviated from what was common: it had four compartments on the right side, each seating six in opposite-facing triple seats, and a line of nine single seats on the left side (see Figure 3.3). The aisle was thus off-center. For night flights, each of the four compartments was converted into four berths, closed off with a curtain. The windows on either side matched the different seating arrangement: on the right side there were pairs of windows, with small windows for the upper berths, and on the left side a traditional line-up of windows.

The few Boeing 307s which were built were used by two U.S. airlines (TWA and Pan Am) and confiscated by the U.S. military in early 1942. Post-war they returned to civil service but now with a classic, four-abreast, center aisle, configuration.

3.2 ACCIDENTS WITH CABIN SAFETY ELEMENTS

Accidents were common in the pioneering years, in spite of the low traffic numbers. Passenger capacities were low, so consequently the number of fatalities per accident was low. Seldom did fatalities in one accident exceed 20. Accident investigations, if conducted at all, or made public, focused on the cause of the accident and not on survivability issues. There were quite a few cases with both fatalities and survivors, but how the survivors escaped was seldom reported. In one case, regarding an Eastern DC-3 crash in February 1941, it was reported that the aircraft ended up inverted and all survivors were rescued from outside.[4] One of them was the airline's president, Eddie Rickenbacker, who was severely injured. Among the fatalities was Congressman William D. Byron (Maryland—D). In a few cases, toward the end of the period, the first cabin safety recommendations were made.

3.2.1 Bermuda Bound

On its way from New York to Bermuda on January 21, 1939, an Imperial Airways Short Empire flying boat named Cavalier had to make a forced landing halfway along its oceanic journey.[5] It broke up upon impact and sank shortly afterward. It did not have seat belts, but all 13 occupants survived the impact, although one passenger suffered a head injury. The flying boat had no life rafts on board. The only life-saving equipment were 22 'seat-type' and six 'crew-type' 'rubber life belts' (life vests). Of these 28 vests only eight were used, four of each. All occupants were able to abandon the boat. They clung to the vests for ten hours in the water, which was moderately warm, before rescue came. One passenger, Edna Watson, was later praised for her morale boosting with song, gossip, and jokes. Steward Spence exhausted himself by continually attending to his passengers and drowned, as did two of the passengers, including the barely conscious person who had been injured.[6] The British Air Ministry Inspector of Accidents made a list of recommendations for safety improvements on flying boats, including the requirement for seat belts and life rafts as standard equipment and instructing passengers on the fastening of seat belts on take-off and landings, the pointing out of emergency exits and instruction on how to fasten life belts.

3.2.2 Oklahoma City

On March 26, 1939, a Braniff Airways Douglas DC-2 crashed shortly after departure from Oklahoma City. Of the 12 occupants, 8 died and 4, including the 2 pilots, were seriously injured. The two passengers who survived both had difficulty in releasing their seat belts, as a result of which they sustained serious burns while extricating themselves from the wreckage.[7] The board:

> recommended that the Civil Aeronautics Authority require that all aircraft of United States registry be equipped with safety belts having uniform type quick-release devices, which device, when a safety belt is in use, shall be in such position and of such type that it can be quickly and easily released with either hand. It is further recommended that this requirement be made effective on the earliest practicable date.

There is no record of any follow-up. However, the standard in force at the time already called for a quick-release mechanism, albeit it did not specify a uniform type.

3.2.3 Trammel, Kentucky

Late in the evening of July 28, 1943, an American Airlines DC-3 bound for Memphis, Tennessee, crashed one mile west of Trammel, Kentucky, on the Louisville–Nashville sector.[8] At about 10.43 p.m. it had entered a violent, local thunderstorm with vigorous downdrafts. The investigators later concluded that the DC-3 was caught in such a downdraft, as a result of which it lost altitude and speed and crashed. It struck trees and then ground in a level attitude. The cockpit broke off, and the flight crew were killed. A fire broke out and destroyed the cabin. Of the 19 persons in the cabin, only 2 managed to escape from the cabin and survived, albeit with serious injuries. Inside the cabin, the coroner found 13 victims, one of whom was the stewardess, 'piled up against and adjacent to the door in the rear of the cabin'. The report says that

> from the slight descending angle of the aircraft at the time of the impact with the trees, which undoubtedly broke the fall to the ground, it is reasonable to assume that the passengers were not seriously injured by the crash but had probably crowded the cabin door in an effort to escape the flames.

One of the survivors managed with great difficulty to open an emergency exit, initially unsuccessful, and, having tried in vain, tried the one on the opposite side as well. Once outside, he then attempted to open the access door, which had not been opened from inside. The other survivor, who had been seated at the front of the cabin, found a hole and escaped from the aircraft. They had both been lucky. This luck was extended to the investigators as they could glean from the survivors' first-hand information on what had happened. In his testimony, the first survivor said that his attempt to open the main door from the outside failed. In trying to understand why the other passengers could not escape and why the door could not be opened, the investigators focused on the operating mechanism of the door. It had a separate safety latch which needed to be operated first before the door handle itself could be used to open the door. The stewardess would have known this but had perhaps been incapacitated. The passengers were unlikely aware of the safety latch. Yet, on checking the wreck, they found it disengaged, so why could the door not be opened? They considered that 'the emergency exits as well as the door had been jammed by severe distortion of the fuselage, caused by impact, and that heat from the subsequent fire later released the jam and allowed the door to swing open'. The latter was testified by the first survivor as happening approximately one-half hour after the crash.

As a result of this crash, two proposals were made to change the Civil Air Regulations. The first called for all emergency exits, and their handles, to be clearly marked with luminous paint. This change became effective on February 1, 1944.[9] Until then, this was not a common practice. Two years later, McFarland explained why 'in the early stages of air transportation the operators hesitated to provide clearly marked emergency escape hatches because of a belief that there would be an unfavorably reaction on the passengers'. He continued saying that 'Subsequent experience has shown a definite need for them, and there is little evidence that the provision of emergency exits has had a disturbing influence on air travelers'.[10]

The second proposed change was threefold and asked that:[11]

- 'It shall be possible to open [the external door] from either inside or outside by the operation of one conveniently located handle';
- 'Hinged doors shall open outward';
- 'The latched and unlatched positions of the handle [. . .] shall be plainly marked'.

The first of these three change proposals may have caused quite some debate. The likely reason for the safety latch was to prevent the in-flight opening of the door by passengers who mistook it for the lavatory door. That event type was so common that preventing this featured on all of the cabin attendant's task lists at the time. Removing the latch would cause other issues, and a further study regarding the redesign of doors was started instead. However, the accident report does say that the operators would alter the door-latching mechanisms in the meantime.[12]

One operator, Chicago and Southern Air Lines, based in Memphis, Tennessee, followed up on a suggestion from a local newspaper. In an editorial it was pointed out that passengers needed to be educated on exits and their operation. The airline announced that they would add to its DC-3s 'electric signs [that] flash over the doors [and exits] at each takeoff and landing, and during rough weather'.[13] In addition, it would expand the flight kit, which was given to each passenger with a pamphlet describing the operation of the exits. At least two other airlines did the same: TWA and United Air Lines.

Pioneering Years (1919–1944) 15

FIGURE 3.4 United Air Lines DC-3 auxiliary exit description in flight kit folder (c. 1943).

With today's knowledge of cabin safety measures such as interior emergency lighting, floor proximity lighting, lighted exit markings, fireproof interiors, and more, the CAB's corrective action proposals may seem quite futile. It must be appreciated, however, that in those days lessons learned from accidents focused on the causes, not the consequences. The thought was that accidents could be eliminated completely by adhering to the lessons learned about causes. Giving attention to the consequences of accidents and improving survivability was not in the contemporary minds. In that respect, this action prompted by a single accident may be seen as an early baby step in a lifetime of cabin safety growing up.

3.3 CABIN SAFETY REGULATIONS UP TO 1945

3.3.1 Beginning

Before governments in the U.S., at the state or federal level, issued safety regulations, the National Advisory Committee of Aeronautics (NACA, the predecessor of NASA), already in 1922, issued recommendations for the safety of passenger-carrying airplanes:[14]

> (T)he suffering and loss of life attending forced landings of aircraft on land and water could be lessened by making use of existing knowledge and facilities. To that end, [NACA] urged that large seaplanes should be provided with radio and other signaling equipment, be seaworthy as well as airworthy, and carry at all times fire extinguishers, life preservers, a first-aid kit, and a supply of food and fresh water; and that airplane [sic] operating over the land should carry radio or other signaling equipment, fire extinguishers, and a first-aid kit.

The first federal regulations for aviation were published in 1926 and became effective January 1, 1927.[15] Cabin safety relevant changes became effective in June 1928, May 1930, January and October 1931, March 1933, October 1934, and January 1936.[16] Significant further changes followed in November 1937, when the Aeronautics Bulletins were replaced by Civil Air Regulations.[17] These remained largely unchanged until 1945, except for some changes in 1941 related to oxygen and in 1943 related to exit operation. It was the time when the world was enveloped in a war of global dimensions. The U.S. was heavily engaged in it, but its home territory remained unscathed. Civil aviation there could not only continue but actually grow by volume. The number of passenger miles flown between 1941 and 1945 grew by a factor of 2.3. This was in spite of the number of airplanes remaining fairly stable (from 358 to 411 with a low of 179 in 1942). The growth was because of higher load factors and, of even more significance, increased frequencies.[18] Almost all the airplanes were of the same type: the Douglas DC-3.

The following subsection summarizes the regulatory developments in the U.S. between 1927 and 1943, per domain

3.3.2 IMPACT PROTECTION

In the domain of impact protection, initially the regulations addressed only four aspects: aircraft nosing over (a phenomenon typical to tail draggers in which the aircraft rotates when the wheels are suddenly kept from moving forward during landing); the aircraft completely rolling over and ending inverted (called turnover); seat belts; and seats.

3.3.2.1 Nose-Over and Turnover

The earliest crashworthiness regulation, per the 1927 regulations, required that the front parts of the fuselage needed to be designed to resist the forces of a nose-over and to protect against propeller breakage:

> Nosing over: the front parts of the fuselage shall be designed to resist the forces to which they would be subjected in nosing over, unless the landing gear is of such construction that the probability of such an accident is remote[19]
>
> the cockpit must be constructed to afford (. . .) reasonable protection to pilot and passengers against possible propeller breakage.[20]

In 1931 the nose-over protection requirement was expanded with a complete turnover protection requirement, clearly stating the objective: preventing the heads of the pilot or passengers from striking the ground and providing room for egress.[21]

In 1937, the load factor of 3 for the scenario of a complete turnover, introduced in 1934, was raised to an ultimate load factor of 4.5. The fuselage and cabin needed to be designed to protect the occupants, assuming safety belts were fastened and adequate provisions were made to permit the egress of passengers and crew.[22] The nose-over condition was deleted.

3.3.2.2 Safety Belts

The 1927 regulations introduced safety belts as follows:

> Safety belts or equivalent apparatus for pilots and passengers in open-cockpit airplanes carrying passengers for hire or reward.[23]

So, safety belts were initially only required for open-cockpit aircraft. In those days passengers either sat in open cockpits or closed cabins. The belts were not meant for crash protection but for preventing persons from being tossed around during turbulence or even falling out of the cockpit when flying inverted. This standard only applied to passengers carried for hire or reward. Non-paying passengers were apparently not worth government protection.

Around 1931, the reason for the safety belt changed from preventing people from being tossed around or falling out of the aircraft to a restraining device in the case of a crash. This item was one of many for which detailed technical requirements were codified in Aeronautics Bulletin 7-F (airworthiness requirements for aircraft components and accessories). This became effective on March 1, 1933. A load of 1,000 pounds (4,448 N) was prescribed. The safety belt had to be adjustable and equipped with a quick-release mechanism capable of being operated by hand under a load of 400 pounds (1,779 N).[24]

In 1934 a change to the design standards required that safety belts be individual, so no longer could the same belt be used for more than one person, except for children under five years of age. The 1,000-pound load had to be applied in the upward direction and forward under a 45° angle. In the same year, the following cryptic regulation appeared in the operational standards:[25]

> (H) Individual seat bolts, easily adjustable, shall be provided for each passenger.

Pioneering Years (1919–1944)

But what is a 'seat bolt'? One assumes it must be a typo for seat belt. Where the airworthiness regulations consistently spoke of safety belts, the operational regulations then used the term 'seat belt'.

From 1937, the attachment of the safety belt itself now had to be such that no part of it failed below the load introduced in 1934. Also, the quick-release mechanism had to be not prone to inadvertent release.[26]

3.3.2.3 Seats

In 1927, there was no legal requirement for seats. Perhaps because it was obvious that a passenger always needed one? Yet, in June 1928 the following was added to the safety belt requirement:

Seats or chairs shall be firmly secured in place.[27]

No further guidance was given as to how this should be accomplished. Also added on that date was the requirement that seats were to be positioned more than 12 inch (30.5 cm) forward or aft of the propeller disks. Neither was there a regulation that stated that the number of passengers on board was restricted by the passenger seating capacity of an aircraft. This was, however, regulated in a roundabout way: a pilot's license could be suspended or revoked when carrying passengers 'in excess of the original designed seating arrangements of the aircraft', except for infants under two years.[28]

In 1931 a minor change was proposed: 'Seats or chairs in open or closed cabins shall be securely fastened in place even though the safety-belt load is not transmitted through the seat'.

In 1934 the pilot's clause was relaxed: individual children under 12 years were no longer required to have their own seat. In practice, this meant that two such children could share the same seat.[29]

In 1937, the requirement, now transposed into the new Civil Air Regulations, remained virtually unchanged but appeared twice in the same set of design requirements.[30,31]

> **04.464—PASSENGER CHAIRS.**—Seats or chairs for passengers shall be securely fastened in place in both open and closed airplanes, whether or not the safety belt load is transmitted through the seat. (See CAR 15 and CAR 04.2640 for safety belt requirements.)

FIGURE 3.5 Fokker F-VII seats (photograph by the author).

> **04.5890**—*Seats.*—Seats or chairs, even though adjustable, in open or closed airplanes, shall be securely fastened in place whether or not the safety belt load is transmitted through the seat.

3.3.3 FIRE PROTECTION

3.3.3.1 Fire Extinguisher

The first regulation in the U.S. relating to fire protection was straightforward: one portable fire extinguisher was sufficient. It was needed only for aircraft carrying passengers for hire or reward, and it had to be accessible to those passengers.[32]

In 1931 a minimum capacity for portable extinguishers was introduced: 1-quart (1.14 l), except that 1-pint (0.57 l) extinguishers may be used in light airplanes. The term 'light' was defined in 1934: 'airplanes employing 40 horsepower (29.8 kW) or less'.[33]

From 1934 onward a second portable fire extinguisher was required for all passenger-carrying airplanes. In the 1937 CAR version, the requirement was stated as follows.[34]

> (j) A portable fire extinguisher in cabin airplanes, which extinguisher shall be of an approved type which shall have a minimum capacity, if carbon tetrachloride, of one quart or, if carbon dioxide, of two pounds or, if other, of equivalent effectiveness; except that any extinguisher of not less than half the above capacity may be used in an airplane equipped with an engine whose maximum rating is 40 horsepower or less. (See CAR 04.5811 for installation requirements.)
>
> (b) One additional portable fire extinguisher of the type specified in CAR 04.510 (j). (See CAR 04.5811 for installation requirements.)

3.3.3.2 Ash Containers

In 1930 an operational regulation was added requiring suitable containers on aircraft in which passengers were permitted to smoke.[35] In the 1934 version, the word 'ash' was added in front of 'container'.[36] In 1937, smoking by passengers was made not only contingent on ash containers but also on 'a second pilot or cabin attendant who shall notify passengers when and where smoking is prohibited'.[37]

3.3.4 ESCAPE POTENTIAL

The foremost measure in this domain was related to exits, with a minority role for lighting.

3.3.4.1 Exits

The first regulations, effective on January 1, 1927, had a requirement as follows:[38]

> (B) Closed cabins on airplanes carrying passengers for hire or reward must have not less than two exits affording maximum ease of operation.

Thus, where safety belts were required only for open cockpits to prevent involuntary egress, exits were needed only for closed cabins as open cockpits would offer an immediate egress opportunity. Also, the requirement was limited to those aircraft carrying passengers for hire or reward. In 1928, the requirement for at least two exits was augmented with a clause that the size, location, and method of operation were subject to approval:

> Closed cabins of airplanes carrying passengers for hire shall have not less than two exits, affording maximum ease of operation. One of such exits may be an emergency exit, in which case the size, location and method of operation shall be subject to the approval of the Secretary of Commerce.[39]

In 1931 an exit-to-occupants ratio was introduced: at least one exit per every six persons carried, and not less than two, on different sides of the cabin. Additionally, a minimum size for window

Pioneering Years (1919–1944)

exits was introduced: 14 by 20 inch (35.5 by 51 cm) if elliptical or 20 inch if circular. The location and method of operation for window exits remained subject to approval. No door was to be located in the plane of rotation of a propeller. These requirements still applied to closed cabins only, but now to any airplane carrying passengers, irrespective of whether or not it was operated commercially.[40]

On July 31, 1931, a conference was held between the Department of Commerce and aircraft manufacturers who recommended that 'closed cabins carrying more than one occupant should in all cases have at least two exits on different sides or top of the cabin'.[41] The manufacturers additionally suggested at least one additional emergency exit if the cabin provided for more than 15 occupants. The department proposed an increase in the size of window exits to 18 by 24 inch (46 by 61 cm) for a rectangular or elliptical opening or 24 inch in diameter for a circular opening. During the conference this was slightly amended: the figure 18 was replaced by 17 (43 cm). It was further proposed that where cockpits were separate from the cabin, the cockpit would not serve as an emergency exit route for passengers.

In the 1934 change of Aeronautics Bulletin 7-A, these recommendations were adopted. The minimum size was indeed specified as 17 by 24 inch if rectangular or elliptical and 24 inch in diameter if circular. The number of exits was increased to three for 16 to 22 persons and four for 23 persons or more, so one additional exit for each additional 7 persons or fraction thereof.[42] A maximum of four was considered sufficient as airplanes with capacities beyond 30 were unforeseen. When three or more exits were specified, a location at the top of the aircraft was now permitted. On an amphibian such as the Sikorsky S-38, this was the preferred location as side exits were below the waterline.

FIGURE 3.6 Boeing 247 escape hatch, interior view (photograph by the author).

FIGURE 3.7 Boeing 247 escape hatch, exterior view (photograph by the author).

The 1937 edition of the regulations, now in the form of the Civil Air Regulations (CAR), brought the following new or changed design elements in CAR 04:[43]

- A requirement that the entrance door on landplanes certificated for airline service be on the left side
- Increase in size of the window exits to 19 by 26 inch (48 by 66 cm) for rectangular or elliptical or 26 inch in diameter for circular

The operational requirements of CAR 40 added a requirement for 'one or more suitable emergency exists [sic] located in the upper half of the fuselage'.[44]

Except for a 1940 editorial change with respect to the 19-by-26-inch dimension, no further changes were made to the exit requirements until 1943 when the lessons from the Trammel accident were followed up. On November 8, 1943, a draft release was issued proposing changes to the operation, location, and marking of door-latching mechanism on cabin exits.[45]

On the design of doors, it was proposed that:

> It shall be possible to open such door from either inside or outside by the operation of one conveniently located handle. Hinged doors shall open outward.

This proposal did not make it, probably because it would create the hazard of doors being too easily opened in flight. An operational proposal however became a rule effective February 1, 1944. The proposal called for the latched and unlatched positions of the door handle to be plainly marked. The rule text was more precise:[46]

> Emergency exits of aircraft carrying passengers shall be clearly marked as such in letters not less than ¾ Inch high with luminous paint, such markings to be located either on or immediately adjacent to the pertinent exit and readily, visible to passengers. Location and method of operation of the handles shall be marked with luminous paint.

Thus, in the domain of escape potential, the following regulatory concepts and measures were in place in the U.S. by early 1945:

- All door and exit requirements only apply to closed cabins.
- There must be at least one external door on the left side.
- Each external door must be adequate and easily accessible.
- Each external door must neither be located in the plane of rotation of an inboard propeller, nor within 5° thereof, as measured from the propeller hub.
- Additional emergency exits, consisting of movable windows or panels, or additional doors, must provide a clear and unobstructed opening and be dimensioned such that an ellipse of at least 19 by 26 inch can be inscribed.
- The location of the additional emergency exits is subject to approval.
- The method of operation of the additional emergency exits is subject to approval.
- The location and method of operation of the door and exit handles must be marked with luminous paint.
- The regulation for the number of exits was simple: a minimum of two, one on each side, and, for a capacity of 15 persons or more, one additional exit per 7 persons, either in the side of the cabin or in the top, with a cap of 4 exits, including doors, in total.
- For overwater operations: one or more suitable exits in the upper half of the cabin.

For the all-present DC-3 this worked. It could typically carry 24 persons (21 passengers, two pilots, and a cabin attendant); thus, it required four exits: one door and two emergency exits in the cabin

Pioneering Years (1919–1944)

and a top escape or side escape in or near the cockpit. The largest pre-war airliner, the Boeing 307, was equipped with one entrance door, five side emergency exits (one left, four right, one per compartment), and a top hatch in the cockpit.

3.3.4.2 Lighting
The first mention of cabin lighting in the U.S. regulations was in 1930, when for scheduled intrastate airline services cabin lighting and two flashlights were prescribed when flying at night.[47]

3.3.5 LIFE SUPPORT

Life support measures came in four different kinds of equipment: food and water, medical equipment, such as first-aid kits, water survival and rescue equipment (life vests, life rafts, flare guns), and oxygen equipment. For the latter, see Chapter 8.

3.3.5.1 Food and Water
As NACA had already pleaded in 1922, when the first regulation was enacted in 1926, it indeed required airplanes 'flying over large bodies of water' to have 'an adequate supply of food and potable water'.[48] There was no definition of 'large bodies of water'. The range of aircraft at the time meant that certainly trans-oceanic flights were not considered and even flights across the Great Lakes were perhaps beyond the capabilities of the aircraft at the time. So, what large body of water was left when looking at the map of the continental U.S.? Miami to Key West? Los Angeles to Catalina Island? The food and water requirements did not last long. It disappeared from the regulations in 1930.

3.3.5.2 First-Aid Kit
Starting with the first regulation of 1926, first-aid kits were prescribed but only when carrying passengers for hire or reward.[49] Note that the plural was used, although in practice only one first-aid kit was carried. With the split of the regulations in 1930 in design and operations, the first-aid kit stayed in the design rules. In 1941, it was added to operational rules and further explained as being 'adequate for proper first aid treatment of passengers and crew which shall contain certain medical equipment and supplies approved by the Administrator as suitable and sufficient for the type of operation involved'.[50]

3.3.5.3 Flare Gun
Initially, in 1927, a Very's pistol was prescribed when carrying passengers at night and for flights over water. Very's pistol was the common name for a flare gun. In 1930, with the regulatory split between design and operations, this landed in the operational requirements.

3.3.5.4 Water Survival Equipment
For flights over water, from the start in 1927, life preservers or other flotation devices 'approved by the Secretary of Commerce' were required.[51] Neither 'flotation device' nor 'over water' was defined, but in 1934 the latter was interpreted as flying 'during daylight only on an authorized route beyond gliding distance from the shore but not beyond 50 mile (80 km) from the shore'.[52] It was restricted to flying boats, amphibians or seaplanes, or multi-engine landplanes 'capable of landing on the water and remaining afloat for at least 10 hours'. This effectively restricted operations overseas beyond the coasts of the U.S. except for the routes to the Bahamas (80 miles, 129 km) and Cuba (90 miles, 145 km). The only U.S. airline that flew these routes was Pan Am, which found ways to circumvent this regulation. Island hopping all the way from Florida across the Caribbean bead string of islands to South America, it maintained operations within 50 miles of a shore. Pan Am also flew direct from Kingston, Jamaica, to Cristobal, Panama Canal Zone, which was 600 miles (966 km) over water.[53]

In 1937 this regulation was relaxed and incorporated into a performance standard, specifying that the 'aircraft on the proposed route or part thereof are capable, with any one engine completely out of commission, of maintaining level flight with authorized load at an altitude of at least 1,000 ft (305 m) above the water'.[54] The requirement for the Very's pistol and flotation devices was now changed to not applicable 'where the operation over water is merely that of landings and take-offs, provided there is marine rescue equipment deemed suitable by the Secretary'.[55] Here, a regulation was introduced that for many years allowed airlines to fly over—and occasionally end in—water without any means for occupants to keep themselves floating. The companion design requirement, meanwhile specified:

> **04.501**—An approved life preserver or flotation device is one approved by the Secretary for such usage on sea-going vessels.

Flotation device was still not defined.

3.3.6 Information and Instructions

The first requirement calling for some form of communication between pilots and passengers came in the 1931 set of interpretations for the operational requirements. It required: 'a suitable method of communication when the pilot is separated from the passenger cabin'.[56] What such a suitable method was, was left to the airline.

In 1933, United Air Lines introduced a signal light system.

> A small red light, which can be operated from the pilot's cockpit, has been installed on the forward cabin wall of all airplanes. When the signal appears the stewardess immediately requests the fastening of safety belts or imparts any desired information to passengers.

This replaced the co-pilot coming back to the cabin and informing the stewardess that areas of bumpy air were approaching or that a landing was contemplated. Such visits occasionally had a disturbing effect upon certain slightly nervous passengers, Aviation reported in May 1933.[57]

Conspicuous signs indicating when smoking was, or was not permitted, became a requirement in 1934.[58] From 1937 a safety belt sign or signal, as already applied by United Air Lines, became required per airworthiness standards to inform passengers when the safety belt should be fastened.[59] In 1941 this requirement was extended to the operational requirements, thus covering the existing fleets of Douglas DC-3s which had been type certificated before 1937.[60] So, by 1941, both the no smoking sign and the fasten seat belt sign were required.

NOTES

1. Passenger Aircraft and Their Interiors 1910–2006, John Stroud, 2012.
2. The Channel Disaster, Air Ministry Report, as Published in Flight, 1 August 1929. The report was dated July 12, 1929, so only 25 days after the accident.
3. Air Commerce Bulletin, Department of Commerce, Aeronautics Branch, Vol. 1, July 1, 1929, p. 7.
4. Report of the Civil Aeronautics Board on the Investigation of an Accident Involving Civil Aircraft of the United States NC 28394 Which Occurred Near Atlanta, Georgia, on February 26, 1941, Released June 13, 1941.
5. Press Summary of Report of the Investigation of the Accident to the Imperial Airways Aircraft G-ADUU (Cavalier) on January 21, 1939, Office of the Air Attaché British Embassy, Washington D.C., March 25, 1939.
6. Adventurous Empires: The Story of the Short Empire Flying Boats, Phillip E. Sims, 2013.
7. Air Safety Board Report to the Civil Aeronautics Authority as a Result of an Investigation of an Accident Involving Aircraft NC 13727 of Braniff Airways, Inc., Near Oklahoma City, Oklahoma, March 26, 1939.

8 Report of the Civil Aeronautics Board on the Investigation of an Accident Involving Aircraft in Scheduled Air Carrier Operation, File No. 3525-43, April 22, 1944.
9 CAR 61.797, 1944.
10 Human Factors in Air Transport Design, Ross A. McFarland, 1946, p. 581.
11 DR 43.
12 CAB 3525-43.
13 Aviation News, October 4, 1943, p. 29.
14 Eighth Annual Report of the National Advisory Committee for Aeronautics, 1922, Washington, D.C., 1923, p. 8.
15 Air Commerce Regulations, Effective December 31, 1926, Midnight, United States of America, Department of Commerce, Aeronautics Branch.
16 1928: Air Commerce Regulations, Information Bulletin No. 7, Department of Commerce, Aeronautics Branch, Effective as Amended June 1, 1928;

1930: Air Commerce Regulations Governing Scheduled Operation of Interstate Passenger Air Transport, Aeronautic Bulletin No. 7-E, Department of Commerce, Aeronautics Branch, Effective Midnight May 31, 1930;
Letter by Clarence M. Young, Assistant Secretary of Commerce for Aeronautics dated June 12, 1930 with proposed interpretations of the new regulations governing scheduled operation of interstate passenger air transport services;
1931: Airworthiness Requirements of Air Commerce Regulations for Aircraft, Aeronautics Bulletin No. 7-A, U.S. Department of Commerce, Aeronautics Branch, Effective January 1, 1931;
Air Commerce Regulations Governing Scheduled Operation of Interstate Passenger air Transport Services Effective as Amended October 1, 1931 (Aeronautics Bulletin No. 7-E);
Interpretations of Regulations Governing Scheduled Operation of Interstate Passenger Air Transport Services Effective as Amended October 1, 1931;
1933: Aeronautics Bulletin No. 7-F, Airworthiness Requirements for Aircraft Components and Accessories, U.S. Department of Commerce, Aeronautics Branch, eff. March 1, 1933;
1934: Air Commerce Regulations, Aeronautics Bulletin No. 7, U.S. Department of Commerce, Aeronautics Branch, Effective as Amended January 1, 1934, (included inter alia Aeronautics Bulletins 7-A Airworthiness Requirements for Aircraft; 7-E Air Commerce Regulations Governing Scheduled Operation of Interstate Air Line Services; 7-F—Airworthiness Requirements for Aircraft Components and Accessories);
1935: Amendment No. 2 to Aeronautics Bulletin No. 7-E, in Air Commerce Bulletin, Vol. 7, p. 167. (Effective January 1936).

17 Civil Air Regulations, U.S. Department of Commerce, Bureau of Air Commerce, Effective November 1, 1937 (included inter alia 04.—Airplane Airworthiness; 15.—Aircraft Equipment Airworthiness; 40.—Scheduled Airline Certification (Interstate); 61—Scheduled Airline Rules (Interstate).
18 Aircraft Yearbook 1946, Aeronautical Chamber of Commerce of America, Inc., p. 518.
19 Air Commerce Regulations 1926, sec. 12(E)5.
20 Air Commerce Regulations 1926, sec. 13(A)3.
21 Aeronautics Bulletin No. 7-A, 1931, sec. 58.
22 CAR 04.247; 04.460, 1937.
23 Air Commerce Regulations 1926, sec. 15(A)3.
24 Aeronautics Bulletin No. 7-F, 1933, sec. 27.
25 Aeronautics Bulletin No. 7-E, 1934, chapter 4, sec. 1(H).
26 CAR 15.30, 1937.
27 Information Bulletin No. 7, 1928, sec. 10(I)(1)(c).
28 Information Bulletin No. 7, 1928, sec. 62(I).
29 Aeronautics Bulletin No. 7, 1934, sec. 59(I).
30 CAR 04.464, 1937.
31 CAR 04.5890, 1937.
32 Air Commerce Regulations 1926, sec. 15(A)1.
33 Aeronautics Bulletin No. 7-A, 1931, sec. 75.
34 CAR 04.510(j); 04.530(b), 1937.
35 Letter Young, 1930 with Proposed Interpretations, sec. A.
36 Aeronautics Bulletin No. 7-E, 1934, chapter 4, sec. 6(B).
37 CAR. 61.792, 1937.

38 Air Commerce Regulations 1926, sec. 13(B).
39 Information Bulletin No. 7, 1928, sec. 10(D).
40 Information Bulletin No. 7-A, 1931, sec. 71.
41 Conference with manufacturers on airworthiness requirements, July 31, 1931, Air Commerce Bulletin, U.S. Department of Commerce, Aeronautics Branch, Vol. 3, No. 4, August 15, 1934, p. 92. The largest delegation of conference attendees was from Fokker Aircraft Corporation of America. There were no representatives from either Boeing or Douglas.
42 Aeronautics Bulletin No. 7-A, 1934, sec. 64.
43 CAR 04.462, 1937.
44 CAR 40.233, 1937.
45 DR 43.
46 Amdt 61-13.
47 Letter Young, 1930 with Proposed Interpretations, sec. A.
48 Air Commerce Regulations 1926, sec. 53.
49 Air Commerce Regulations 1926, sec. 15(A)(2).
50 Amdt No. 122.
51 Air Commerce Regulations 1926, sec. 51; sec. 53.
52 Aeronautics Bulletin No. 7-E, 1934, chapter 4, sec. 4.
53 Airlines of the United States since 1914, REG Davies, p. 220.
54 CAR 40.233, 1937.
55 CAR 40.233, 1937.
56 Interpretations 1931, sec. 4.
57 Aviation, May 1933, p. 171.
58 Aeronautics Bulletin No. 7-E, 1934, chapter 4, sec. 6.
59 CAR 04.5812, 1937.
60 Amdt No. 129 (corrected by Amdt No. 130).

4 Regulatory Framework Developments

ABSTRACT

Until 1967, the aviation safety regulatory framework in the U.S. was subject to many changes, in terms of who made them, who was responsible for oversight as well as the regulatory structure itself. To help readers understand the regulatory context for those years, this chapter gives an overview. A key diagram displays it graphically. In 1967 the situation stabilized. Since, the Federal Aviation Administration is in charge of both rulemaking and oversight and the National Transportation Safety Board of accident investigations.

Similarly, regulatory developments in Europe are sketched, but here with an emphasis on the years since 1970 and the roles of the Joint Aviation Authorities (JAA) and its successor, the European Aviation Safety Agency (EASA). Finally, the involvement of the International Civil Aviation Organisation (ICAO) is briefly explained.

4.1 INTRODUCTION

The many references in this book to the U.S. regulations deserve some information about the U.S. air safety regulatory context, both in terms of its architecture and the many changes over time. Figure 4.2 on page 27 gives a graphic representation. Additionally, this chapter reviews the international and pan-European regulatory developments.

4.2 U.S. 1926–1938

The U.S. was late with an aviation act. Although several of its constituent states, and even individual cities, introduced aviation laws and regulations from 1911 onward, these primarily addressed pilot licensing, overflying, and liability issues, rather than safety.[1,2] The first federal aviation law came into force in 1926. It was called the Air Commerce Act. The name exposed its primary intent: the fostering of aviation. Safety was only a secondary consideration. The Department of Commerce was the government body that oversaw the implementation of the act. It created for that purpose the Aeronautics Branch, which was headquartered in Washington, D.C.[3] It was renamed into Bureau of Air Commerce on July 1, 1934. Under the Air Commerce Act, the first set of technical regulations became effective on 1 January 1927: the Air Commerce Regulations.[4]

This had been compiled in close cooperation with members of the aviation community.[5] It covered five areas of aviation: aircraft registration, airworthiness, pilot and mechanic licensing, flight operations, and rules of the air.

Being a federal document, it applied to interstate (i.e. between states) flying as well as to or from foreign countries. To explain the interstate concept it gave multiple examples of when a flight was interstate or not. For intrastate (i.e. within one state) use, each state still made its own regulations or adopted the federal regulations. This was corrected in the years to come, and eventually the federal regulations became applicable to any U.S. air operation, not only in the 48 states that the U.S. then counted but also its territories (including, at the time, Alaska and Hawaii, which only later became states) and possessions, such as Puerto Rico and, then, the Philippine Islands.

The Air Commerce Regulations were soon expanded, and on June 1, 1928, a revised edition was issued, now called 'Information Bulletin No. 7'. In 1930, the first split took place and

FIGURE 4.1 Front page of the first set of Air Commerce Regulations.

separate sets of standards were issued for airworthiness and for operations. They were renamed into Aeronautics Bulletins.[6] Design regulations for aircraft came in Aeronautics Bulletin No. 7-A, called Airworthiness Regulations, while operational rules came in no. 7-E.

They were limited to scheduled interstate and foreign passenger air transport. Non-scheduled operations remained unregulated until 1946. While the Air Commerce Act in 1926 gave powers to the Department of Commerce to regulate airworthiness, until 1934 it did not have full authority to regulate the airlines. The operational rules had the status of interpretations only.[7] An amendment to the act provided for this, with the express condition that this was limited to safety aspects of airline operation, so excluding route and other licenses.

While safety had become a prime consideration for these bulletins, it needed an accident to appreciate that there was still room for enhancement. In May 1935 a TWA DC-2 crashed near Atlanta, Georgia, killing all occupants including a senator, Bronson M. Cutting. What followed was a major shake-up of the governmental responsibilities for aviation safety. A new Civil Aeronautics Authority (CAA) was created in 1938, which took over from the Bureau of Air Commerce. But, before that, in 1937, the Bureau had replaced the Aeronautics Bulletins with a new system of regulations called the Civil Air Regulations (CAR). A completely new set of numbering was introduced. Airworthiness regulations came in Chapters CAR 04 and CAR 15 for airplanes and equipment, respectively, and operational regulations came in Chapters CAR 40 and CAR 61. The difference between 40 and 61 was that 40 contained the regulations for certification, whereas 61 detailed the safety regulations for those airlines. The term 'Chapter' was replaced in 1938 by 'Part'.

4.3 U.S. 1939–1958

After two years, in 1940, the task of maintaining the CAR Parts was transferred from the CAA to the newly created Civil Aeronautics Board (CAB) and, more in particular, its Office of Safety Regulation. The CAA, now with the last A standing for Administration (thus Civil Aeronautics Administration in full), remained the authority that applied the CARs, issued authorizations, and oversaw compliance. Although the CAA was no longer tasked with making formal regulations, it added policies and interpretations to CAB regulations, using the same numbering system. The material added by the CAA was published in the Federal Register. Together with the regulations they were published as Civil Aeronautics Manuals (CAM).

Regulatory Framework Developments

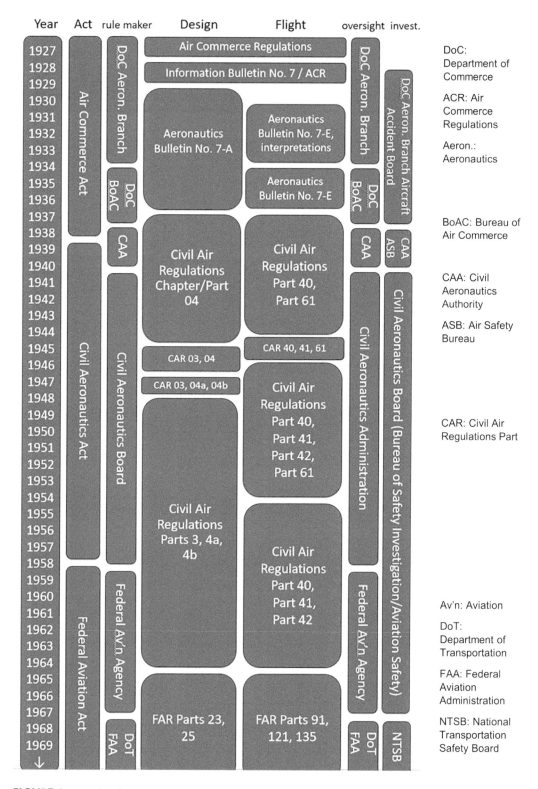

FIGURE 4.2   U.S. aviation regulatory framework 1927–1967 and up.

The end of World War Two in August 1945 gave an impetus to commercial air transport, both by U.S. and other airlines. In the U.S., Pan Am was joined by other scheduled airlines (TWA, American Export Airlines, United, Northwest) on overseas routes. In anticipation, on July 10 a new Part was published to cover such operations:

Part 41—Certification and operation rules for scheduled air carrier operations outside the continental limits of the United States.

The end of the war also led to an increase in non-scheduled air carriers, typically operating surplus military aircraft such as the C-46 (Curtiss Commando) and Douglas C-47 (DC-3). Standards for such U.S. operators, operating either within the U.S. or outside, followed in 1946:

Part 42—Nonscheduled air carrier certification and operation rules.

Compared to Parts 40/61 and 41, Part 42 standards were significantly more lenient. Unlike 40/61, the new Parts 41 and 42 each combined the certification and the operating rules in a single Part. This difference was repaired in 1954 when Parts 40 and 61 were merged into a single Part as well: new Part 40. Part 42 initially had 'nonscheduled' in its title. This changed twice. In 1949 it was replaced by 'irregular' and in 1963 by 'supplemental'.

For design standards, a new set of airworthiness regulations for transport category airplanes, Part 04, became effective November 9, 1945. It applied to aircraft type certificated after January 1, 1948, and co-existed next to the previous edition of Part 04.[8] The existence of two sets of Part 04 regulations, only distinguished by promulgation date, was confusing. In December 1946 they were renamed as Part 04b and Part 04a, respectively, two years later spelled as Part 4b and Part 4a,[9,10] In 1945, a companion set of airworthiness regulations for other-than-transport-airplanes was created as Part 03, later Part 3.

4.4 U.S. 1959 AND UP

Just as the 1935 accident led to a new aviation act and a reorganization of the aviation department, the same occurred in the second half of the 1950s. On June 30, 1956, two airliners crashed over the Grand

FIGURE 4.3 Memorial plaquette at Navajo Point, Grand Canyon (photograph by the author).

Canyon while flying in Visual Flight Rules in uncongested, uncontrolled airspace. Both had departed from Los Angeles, with a three-minute interval, on their way to Kansas City and Chicago, respectively.

The accident, with 128 fatalities and no survivors, triggered a new aviation act, the Federal Aviation Act, and, in its wake, a new agency: the Federal Aviation Agency (FAA). Next to its air traffic control tasks, it assumed statutory responsibility for aviation safety rulemaking on December 31, 1958. Initially, the new agency had to use temporary offices dispersed over Washington, D.C. The day in 1963 that its staff moved to its permanent location, at 800 Independence Ave, SW, was that of President Kennedy's assassination. Between 1961 and 1964 a major recodification process took place in which the Civil Air Regulations were replaced by Federal Aviation Requirements (FAR). This was completed on December 31, 1964, when new FAR Part 121 was published. This part replaced CARs 40, 41, and 42. One week earlier, CAR 4b had been replaced by FAR 25. For interpretation and guidance material, Advisory Circulars were created.

The Federal Aviation Agency lost its independence in 1967 when it became part of the new Department of Transportation. It was renamed the Federal Aviation Administration (FAA). It has been responsible for aviation safety rulemaking in the U.S. since.

4.5 U.S. RULE GESTATION AND PUBLICATION

The U.S. has a very transparent system of rulemaking. Each rule is typically first proposed to the public and interested parties, by circulation of a draft, with an explanation of its rationale and an ultimate date for sending in comments. The next step normally is the publication of a Final Rule together with an assessment of the comments. In some cases, however, a proposal may be withdrawn or a supplemental proposal is issued. Until 1963, Notices of Proposed Rulemaking (NPRM) were called Draft Releases (DR). The majority of the DRs and all NPRMs and Final Rules were published in the Federal Register. Appendix 2c gives an overview of the DRs, NPRMs, and Final Rules as referred to herein. Appendix 2d lists the proposals that were withdrawn.

4.6 U.S. ACCIDENT INVESTIGATIONS

In 1928, the Aircraft Accident Board of the Aeronautics Branch became the first agency to conduct accident investigations. This was later transferred to the Bureau of Air Commerce and in 1938 to the Air Safety Board of the Civil Aeronautics Authority. In 1940 it was transferred again, now to the Bureau of Aviation Safety of the Civil Aeronautics Board. In turn, in 1967 the new National Transportation Safety Board became responsible for aviation accident investigations. Until its independence in 1974, it resorted under the Department of Transportation.

4.7 DEVELOPMENTS IN EUROPE

4.7.1 Pre-war

Before World War Two, coordination on aviation between states was under the umbrella of the International Commission for Aerial Navigation (ICAN). It resulted from the International Air Conference held in Paris in 1919 where *The Convention Relating to the Regulation of Aerial Navigation* was signed on October 13, 1919, by 27 countries from around the globe. As the convention had been prepared on the occasion of the peace conference following World War One, these were allied and associated countries only. Many neutral countries had not been invited. This included Scandinavian countries, the Netherlands, Spain, and Switzerland. They joined much later, as did Germany, Austria, and Hungary, the central powers in the 1914–1918 conflict.

Airworthiness was addressed in Annex B, which was very succinct. For operations there was no annex, except for rules of the air. The only cabin safety aspect that appears to have been addressed by ICAN was the 'organization of emergency medical boxes on board aircraft', in other words, first-aid kits.[11]

4.7.2 European Civil Aviation Conference

Post World War Two, the first aviation association of European countries was the European Civil Aviation Conference (ECAC), established in 1955 and affiliated to ICAO. It issued a number of agreements and documents, of which one pertained to cabin safety. That was Doc No. 18 first issued in 1979.[12] As ECAC Documents had advisory status only, its historical importance was limited. This was also because many European countries preferred to continue basing their regulations on U.S. and ICAO regulations.

4.7.3 Joint Aviation Authorities

In the 1970s, the aviation authorities of European countries with a manufacturing industry formed the Airworthiness Authorities Steering Committee (AASC). Its objective was to formulate common standards for airworthiness of aircraft products. Previously, the United Kingdom had its own British Civil Airworthiness Regulations, and France had its AIR 2051. Other European countries typically adopted the American CAR 4b and FAR-25 requirements.

The AASC standards became known as Joint Airworthiness Requirements (JAR). The first was JAR-25, initially published in August 1974. This document was modeled after the U.S. FAR-25 and dealt with Large Aeroplanes. (FAR-25 was titled Airworthiness Standards: Transport Category Airplanes.) Later, the AASC was renamed into Joint Airworthiness Authorities. Its secretariat was domiciled with the UK CAA near London Gatwick, but in 1991 moved to Hoofddorp, the Netherlands. It changed its name to Joint Aviation Authorities (JAA). This reflected the expansion of its scope beyond airworthiness to licensing and operations. The second A (Authorities, plural) has often been misrepresented as Authority (singular). However, the JAA was not an authority with legal powers but rather a forum where the member authorities cooperated. Informally it was often referred to as a club or even a charity, as its legal status under Dutch law was that of a foundation.

JAR-25, as its U.S. ancestor, addressed many cabin safety design subjects. Starting in 1983, it became the principal set of certification standards for new European products such as the BAe 146, Saab 340, Fokker 50 and 100, and Airbus A320. Initially, the certification work was done against JAR-25 by the national authority of the country where the product was made. Later, JAA organized joint certifications, but the legal responsibility remained with the member states. The JAA teams did the technical work and the Certification Director together with the Certification Committee issued a recommendation to member states.

FIGURE 4.4 Joint Aviation Authorities sign on its headquarters in Hoofddorp, the Netherlands, 2001 (photograph by the author).

Development of a set of operational standards started in 1989. In 1995 it was completed as JAR-OPS 1 Commercial Air Transportation (Aeroplanes) and an implementation date of 1 April 1998, was agreed. However, each member country had to adopt it by means of a national regulation and not all countries did that in time.

Despite the limitations inherent in its legal status, the JAA played a key role in promoting harmonized aviation safety regulations in Europe and paved the way for EASA.

4.7.4 EUROPEAN UNION AVIATION SAFETY AGENCY

Since its creation as an agency of the European Commission (EC) in 2002, the European Aviation Safety Agency (EASA, since 2018 European Union Aviation Safety Agency) has grown quickly. It became, next to the FAA, the most important aviation safety agency in the world. Initially, from 2003 onward, its remit was limited to initial and continuing airworthiness, both in terms of proposing regulations for adoption by the EC and applying them by issuing certificates related to the design of products such as aircraft and engines, foreign production, and foreign maintenance organizations. In 2008 it inherited the responsibility for proposing operational and personnel licensing regulations for adoption by the EC and to approve foreign operators and training organizations. The certification of individual European airlines remained with the national aviation authorities of the EASA member states, which comprise all European Union countries plus four other countries.[13] EASA's remit was later extended to aerodromes and airspace regulations, thus covering the whole spectrum of aviation safety except accident investigations, which remained a national obligation.

For cabin safety, the relevant sets of requirements are in:

- airworthiness requirements (specifically CS-23 for small aeroplanes, CS-25 for large aeroplanes, CS-27 and CS-29 for small and large helicopters);[14]
- additional airworthiness requirements, including CS-26;[15]
- aircrew regulations, specifically Part Cabin Crew;[16]
- air operations regulations.[17]

4.8 INTERNATIONAL CIVIL AVIATION ORGANIZATION

The Paris Convention of 1919, which established the ICAN, was superseded in 1944 by the Convention on International Civil Aviation, better known as the Chicago Convention. It established the International Civil Aviation Organization, domiciled in Montreal, Canada, and formed a framework for international regulations. These were in the form of Standards and Recommended Practices (SARPs). Standards are binding for all member countries (eventually effectively all countries of the world), which should also endeavor to comply with the Recommended Practices. The SARPs are published in the form of Annexes to the Chicago Convention. For cabin safety, two Annexes are of relevance:

- Annex 6—Operation of aircraft
- Annex 8—Airworthiness

ICAO also publishes lower-level guidance in the form of ICAO Documents.

NOTES

1. Bonfires to Beacons: Federal Civil Aviation Policy under the Air Commerce Act, 1926–1938, by Nick A. Komons, p. 27.
2. Civil Aviation in the Department of Commerce, Hearing Before a Subcommittee of the Committee on Commerce, Unites States Senate, 67th Congress, Second Session, December 19, 1921.

3. Air Commerce Bulletin, U.S. Department of Commerce, Aeronautics Branch, Vol. 6, No. 1, July 15, 1934, p. 3.
4. Air Commerce Regulations, Effective December 31, 1926, Unites States of America, Department of Commerce, Aeronautics Branch, sec. 89: 'These regulations shall take effect midnight, December 31, 1926'.
5. Bonfires to Beacons, p. 96.
6. Not to be confused with the Aeronautical Bulletins, which were published between 1923 and 1925 by the Office of the Chief of Air Service, the forerunner of the Air Force.
7. Air Commerce Bulletin, U.S. Department of Commerce, Aeronautics Branch, Vol. 6, No. 1, July 15, 1934, p. 2.
8. Amdt 04-0.
9. 11 FR 14134.
10. 13 FR 5488.
11. The Organization and Program of the International Commission for Air Navigation (C.I.N.A.), Albert Roper, in Journal of Air Law and Commerce, Vol. 3, No. 2, 1932.
12. European Aviation Civil Aviation Conference, ECAC.CEAC Doc No. 18, Joint Requirements for Emergency and Safety Airborne Equipment, Training and Procedures.
13. Iceland, Liechtenstein, Norway, Switzerland.
14. Certification Specifications for Normal, Utility, Aerobatic, and Commuter Category Aeroplanes, CS-23, 14 November 2003; Certification Specifications for Large Aeroplanes, CS-25, 14 October 2003; Certification Specifications for Small Rotorcraft, CS-27, 14 November 2003; Certification Specifications for Large Rotorcraft, CS-29, 14 November 2003, all Initial Issues by European Aviation Safety Agency.
15. Certification Specifications and Guidance Material for Additional Airworthiness Specifications for Operators, European Aviation Safety Agency, Initial Issue 8 May 2015.
16. www.easa.europa.eu/en/regulations/aircrew.
17. www.easa.europa.eu/en/regulations/air-operations.

5 First Wave (1945–1953)

ABSTRACT

This chapter is about a key period in cabin safety history. Many cabin safety concepts were conceived in this period. Even the term 'cabin safety' stemmed from it. Yet, developments of this period do not form part of the collective memory of later generations. This chapter, therefore, helps the reader in understanding the origin of many of the cabin safety concepts that became commonplace.

It starts with the Chicago Convention of 1944, an event with massive consequences for civil aviation, followed by a description of aircraft and cabin developments of the period immediately following World War Two. Two important lines of research are narrated: evacuation research led by Barry G. King of the CAA medical division and post-crash-fire behavior by NACA. Additionally, Howard Hasbrook is introduced, a pioneer in field investigations of impact protection.

For four and a half of the six domains, the chapter contains a very detailed description of the regulatory developments, each starting with a summary of what was already in place. A key cabin safety attribute that was introduced in this period was the escape chute.

A summary is added for the benefit of those readers who wish to have a quick overview of what happened in this crucial, yet forgotten, period of cabin safety development.

5.1 INTRODUCTION

In the century-old history of cabin safety, there has not been a period as decisive as the years 1945–1953. As discussed in Chapter 3, the first 25 years of air transport saw basic cabin safety elements that were borrowed from the maritime world such as flotation means, fire extinguishers, first-aid kits, and exits. To that were added items dictated by two aspects unique to aviation, high speed and altitude: the securing of occupants in seats with seat belts, and embryonic oxygen rules. But, from 1945 through 1953, concepts were introduced that laid the foundation for crashworthiness, fire protection, survivability, and cabin safety at large for decades to come.

What were the triggers for that? Was it the Zeitgeist that was ripe? Was it a societal demand for more safety? Were it visionary pioneers who saw opportunities for improvement? Did the larger aircraft that became available immediately after the war highlight the need for increased attention to cabin safety? Was it the spur in research, for which funds became available? Were it accidents that proved that, while they could be survivable, survival rates would benefit from dedicated measures? Probably, it was a combination of all that.

5.2 PRELUDE

A global event that occurred while the world was at the peak of war was a significant prelude. It was the international aviation experts gathering in Chicago that started on Wednesday, November 1, 1944, and, although planned for three weeks, ended five weeks later. The venue was The Stevens hotel, in its time the world's largest. Close to 1,000 delegates from 54 countries convened for what would become a historic meeting that was concluded with the ceremonial signing of the Chicago Convention on Thursday, December 7, 1944. Most of the allied countries were represented, including a few that were occupied, plus a number of neutral countries. Naturally, none of the Axis countries (Germany, Japan, Italy) had been invited.

The conference dealt with a multitude of subjects, both of a commercial nature and more technical. While the former, which included matters of traffic rights, proved less successful, the latter went well. It was agreed to form an International Civil Aviation Organization (ICAO). Technical standards for a variety of subjects were tabled and agreed upon. One of those pertained to the airworthiness of aircraft. To facilitate the work, the U.S. had proposed at the start a set of airworthiness regulations. Unsurprisingly, this was a copy of their own CAR Part 04 as then in force, albeit with some revisions that had not been fully processed yet but were considered necessary to include in a draft which was to have international consideration.[1]

They were reviewed and debated in detail by a subcommittee composed of 55 delegates from 30 countries. Although there had been international conventions on aviation standards before, none had focused on such technical details. It may have been the first time that the U.S. airworthiness regulations, which had been developed in isolation over the previous 15 years, were reviewed extensively by other countries. Changes and additions were made and precisely recorded in the minutes of the meetings.[2] In the area of cabin safety, there were several proposals for new standards:

- By the U.S.:
  - Evacuation demonstration—land
  - Evacuation demonstration—ditching
  - Exit distribution longitudinally and laterally so as to facilitate egress without crowding
  - Exit operation simple and obvious, considering the possibility of darkness
  - Provision to prevent jamming of exits due to deformation of the fuselage structure
- By the UK: provisions for restraining occupants, expressed in acceleration g values
- By the Netherlands: fireproofing of cabin materials

The ditching demonstration proposal was not adopted, but all others found their way into the first edition of ICAO's airworthiness standards, published in 1949 as Annex 8.[3] Meanwhile the U.S. CAB continued with its own update of the airworthiness regulations. They were issued in 1945 and became effective on November 9 of that year and included most of the suggestions raised in Chicago.[4]

5.3 AIRCRAFT AND CABIN DEVELOPMENTS

5.3.1 Aircraft

When the war ended in August 1945 the enormous energy that it had unleashed was now turned to civil use. Many new air transport types were added to the airline fleets. Initially, the unpressurized DC-4 took over the main routes in the U.S., with its lower number, smaller stalemate (the DC-3) seconded to the feeder routes. The fleets of both types predominantly consisted of surplus military aircraft. But soon new, dedicated, civil aircraft types augmented the fleets. The Lockheed Constellation series and the DC-6 were pressurized and flew higher and faster. In 1949, Boeing's first airliner that was produced in significant numbers (by period standards), the model 377, was introduced. Passenger capacities increased from a mere 21 in the DC-3 up to 99 in the Constellation and Boeing 377. Even much larger aircraft were built, such as the Lockheed Constitution (168 passengers) and Convair 37 (204 passengers). Both were double-decked. Yet, they proved too large for their time and did not mature beyond the prototype stage. A similar fate occurred to two British projects: the Bristol 167 Brabazon and the Saunders-Roe Princess flying boat.

For the shorter hauls, the 'feeders' of the time, Martin offered the 2–0–2 and Convair the 240. Until the late 1950s, all U.S. air transport aircraft had piston engines.

Elsewhere, in Britain and France, many new types were developed, but only a few of them were successful and built in sizeable numbers. Among those were in Britain the Airspeed Ambassador (1952, 47 passengers), the Avro Tudor (32 seats), the Vickers Viking (1946, 36 seats), the first turboprop, the Vickers Viscount (1953, 32 seats initially), and the first jet, the ill-fated De Havilland Comet (1952, 36 seats initially). In France, types given names after French regions emerged from 1945 onward: the 43-seat Sud-Ouest Bretagne, the 44-seat Sud-Est Languedoc, and the largest of all: the Sud-Est Armagnac. The latter was designed for up to 160 passengers, but it is doubtful that it was ever so equipped, with normal capacities of 87 and 107 being cited instead. It was built in limited numbers and proved unsuccessful.

In the Soviet Union, a parallel development took place. Ilyushin became the main design house, with the Il-12 and Il-14 as early mainstay transport aircraft, seating each up to 32 passengers, but with many variations.

A class of aircraft that was dwindling was that of the flying boats. The heydays of these were the years just before World War Two, when flying boats pioneered crossing two oceans: the Pacific, from the U.S. west coast multi-stop to China, and the Atlantic from the U.S. east coast to Europe with stops either in Canada and Ireland or in the Azores. Flying boats were also used on routes from Europe to Africa and to Australia. Most routes stopped during the war, but, after that, some were resumed. By the mid-1950s, most flying boats had disappeared; some continued flying around in some pockets of the world. They were replaced by long-range, four piston-engine landplanes, which flew higher and faster.

5.3.2 Passenger Seats

Passenger seats in this period typically faced forward and were quite massive. Double seats were often configured as two adjacent, and linked, single seats. Alternatively, benches for two were used, some even without a center armrest. Backrests normally included headrests; however, they were lacking on some short-haul airplanes, leaving the passenger's head unsupported.

Seats were individually bolted to the floor at fixed positions. With single-class configurations this went well. But in the late 1940s airlines started to offer passengers a second class, called coach or tourist class. Pan Am introduced a 63-passenger coach class layout (previously 44) on their DC-4s for flights between New York and Puerto Rico.[5] The service offered was less and so was the fare. Fitting more seats in the same space meant legroom was sacrificed. With the fixed floor positions, reconfiguration was not easy. The solution came with the invention of the seat track in 1952. Four parallel seat tracks were mounted to the floor, with slots at one-inch intervals for securing the seat's front and back legs. Now seats could be mounted in a modular fashion. And it could be done quickly. This invention brought the term seat pitch, which was always expressed in whole inches, thanks to the slot's spacing of 1 inch (2.54 cm). Who invented the seat track, that has stayed ever since? At least two airlines claimed they did: Pan Am and SAS.[6] In both cases they introduced it in their new Douglas DC-6B. So, perhaps it was actually someone at Douglas?

5.3.3 Safety Belts

Safety belts came in many varieties and designs but commonly consisted of a two-piece lap belt, anchored at the sides of the seat. The method of attaching the two ends differed from manufacturer to manufacturer and so did the adjusting. An early 1950s safety leaflet of the British airline Airwork shows three different designs, see Figure 5.1. Each was unique to an aircraft type, which suggests that they came from the aircraft manufacturer, together with the seats. In later days, seats and safety belts were typically acquired from dedicated suppliers.

5.3.4 Doors and Emergency Exits

The typical configuration of doors and exits was one boarding door at the rear of the cabin on the left side. Some larger aircraft also had a service or crew door at the front on the right side. Spread around the cabin were openable windows that served as emergency exits. Some aircraft, including flying boats, had a top hatch in the ceiling, with ditching in mind. Doors typically opened outward

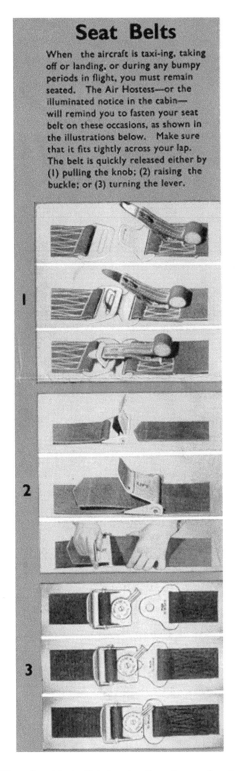

FIGURE 5.1 Extract from Airwork safety leaflet showing three types of seat belts (c. 1950).

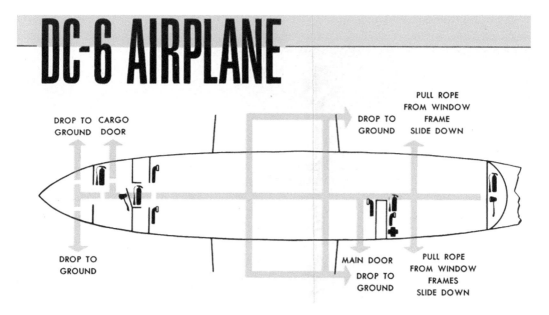

FIGURE 5.2 United Air Lines safety leaflet extract showing DC-6 exit locations and emergency equipment (c. 1954).

and had a safety catch to prevent immediate opening in flight. There were several reports that opening on the ground in an emergency was hampered by this.

5.3.5 Emergency Equipment

Emergency equipment in the cabin included fire extinguishers, a first-aid kit, and, for routes that carried well over water, life vests, life rafts, and emergency flares.

5.3.6 Means of Communication

In the cabin there were signs notifying when safety belts needed to be fastened and when smoking was allowed. Airlines flying long routes over water typically handed out to their passengers a leaflet with ditching-oriented safety instructions. Such a leaflet more often than not was one of many that came in what was called the 'flight kit'. Other leaflets included timetables, menus, postcards, and other promotional material, making the safety leaflet not always readily apparent.

5.4 RESEARCH

5.4.1 Impact Protection

Research in the field of impact protection was done by the U.S. military between 1947 and 1954.[7] Colonel John Paul Stapp had at his disposal a rocket-powered sled, which he used for deceleration tests to test various types of body restraints.

In the private sector, there was a development which may be described as being of a truly amazing pioneering spirit. Hugh De Haven in 1942 started the Crash Injury Research (CIR) project at Cornell University Medical College, New York, initially sponsored by Dr. Eugene F. DuBois of that college. De Haven had been involved himself in 1917 in a midair collision from which he survived with serious injuries. This prompted him to start 'observing injury patterns and theorizing that wounds can be prevented by redesigning and reconfiguring the elements in the plane's interior'.[8] He quickly became known as the expert in the field and received encouragement from domestic and foreign airlines, as well as the CAB Safety Bureau. At one stage De Haven started to focus on automotive injury research. Howard Hasbrook, who had joined him in 1949, then came in charge of the aviation division, now named AvCIR.[9] He became the world expert in the field of civil airplane crashworthiness and participated in the investigation of many U.S. airliner crashes. He soon began to lecture on the subject.

5.4.2 Evacuation Research

On May 29, 1947, a United Airlines Douglas DC-4 crashed after taking off from New York La Guardia. Out of 48 occupants, only 5 survived; see Section 2.1. The investigators found that most if not all of the occupants would have survived the impact yet perished in the ensuing fire. In the 1950 House hearings on a bill to create an independent safety board, the president of the Air Line Pilots Association said that:

> passengers were seen by witnesses drumming on the inside of the cabin windows, burning to death.

He added that had this airplane been equipped with

> trapped-passenger escape tools, similar to the escape tools that are regular equipment in railroad passenger coaches, [. . .], the results would have been different.[10]

Eight months later, on January 21, 1948, a Lockheed Constellation of Eastern Airlines crashed in Boston. This time, the investigators concluded that:

> this accident forcibly points toward the necessity for the development of more suitable passenger evacuation facilities.[11]

The aircraft had been diverted to Boston due to fog at its original destination, New York. During its landing roll in the dark, control was lost, the right landing gear failed and the aircraft ended partially in a snowbank. A fire ensued, but all occupants (5 crewmembers and 20 passengers) managed to escape. The main exit, on the left, was higher than normal because of the gear collapse on the opposite side. The distance from the exit sill to the ground was estimated to be 12 to 16 ft (3.6 to 4.9 m). Five passengers who jumped from this exit were injured as a result. The aircraft was equipped with a rope and a ladder as descent assist means, but neither had been deployed. The report mentions that:

> although the crew made no attempt to use any emergency equipment with which the aircraft was equipped, there is considerable question as to whether the use of the rope would have minimized injuries during the evacuation, and there is no doubt that use of the ladder would have materially increased the time required for evacuation;

and

> in the darkness the placards describing the location and operation of evacuation equipment and emergency doors were not legible. None of the passengers, therefore was able to open the cabin entrance door or any of the emergency doors, nor was any of the passengers aware that emergency evacuation equipment was carried aboard the aircraft.

The report does not mention who opened the door and exits, but it is believed that the crew did. At the presentation of the report, the CAB added that:[12]

First Wave (1945–1953)

the accident indicates the necessity of independent auxiliary lighting facilities to illuminate such areas as emergency exits, emergency evacuation equipment, first aid equipment, and survival craft equipment in the event of electrical system failure.

On November 29, 1949, an American Airlines DC-6 attempted to land at Dallas Love Field with only two out of four engines working. It struck the ground hard, tail first, broke in pieces, and came on fire. Of the 46 occupants, 15 passengers and the flight crew managed to evacuate, using three emergency exits and gaps in the fuselage, but 25 passengers and 2 cabin attendants were trapped and died because of the fire.[13,14]

Likely, these three accidents prompted research on the subject of emergency evacuation. In early 1950, a Working Group was formed for that purpose under the chairmanship of Dr. Barry G. King of the Medical Division of the CAA Office of Aviation Safety. On March 13, 1950, the research program was announced by the CAA in House of Representatives hearings.[15] The study plan was adopted the next month.[16] The Working Group was a joint effort of the CAA Medical Division, the CAB Bureau of Safety Investigation, the Air Transport Association (representing U.S. airlines), the USAF Military Air Transport Service, and the George Washington University (GWU). All these organizations were based in or near Washington, D.C. It operated under the name of the 'CAA-CAB Working Group, Subcommittee Emergency Evacuation'.

One study element was a review by King of exit usage in survivable accidents.[17] Availability and use of exits in 43 landplane accidents in the period 1948 to 1951 that involved U.S. operators were analyzed (see Section 18.2). In addition, an appraisal was made of known evacuation tests carried out so far (see Section 12.2.1).

The research program called for a series of tests on actual aircraft. The first took place later in 1950 or perhaps early in 1951 on a military Douglas C-54 (DC-4) at Andrews AFB near Washington, D.C.[18] These tests aimed at developing a satisfactory test method. They did not involve speed evacuations but rather were meant to understand how individuals negotiated exits. Exits used were the main door, 8 ft (2.4 m) above the ground, and a left overwing exit which led to a descent route over the—lowered—wing flaps. Four different kinds of assist means at the main door were compared: an evacuation chute, a rigid ladder, a rope ladder (Jacob's ladder), and a rope.

Thirty-one civilians and 14 military subjects were employed, most of whom tried all four different assist means. The civilians ranged in age from 6 to 82 years; the military from 19 to 39 years. Five of the military served as patients. They had—simulated—injuries such as a thigh that was splinted, a broken leg in splints, or a splinted arm supported by a sling. One person acted as a 'psychotic patient' under restraint. These patients were all removed from the aircraft by means of the evacuation slide but not tested on the other assist means. This marked the first case where handicapped persons (albeit simulated) were used in evacuation tests.

These tests indeed gave insight into the method of testing and also which kind of assist means was best. The evacuation chute came as the 'winner'. At the time, slides were known as chutes and were made of various materials, such as nylon. Inflatable slides had yet to be developed. This chute was of the type that had loops at the lower end which were meant to be pulled by men on either side so that it indeed formed a good 'chute'. The tests scientifically confirmed that, next to stairs, this was the best descent means, what was already believed at the time.

The next tests were completely civil operations. American Airlines made available a Convair 240 at Washington National Airport ('WNA'), Pan American a Boeing 377, and TWA a Lockheed Constellation. The Convair was used in five different tests, all in daylight, on April 9, 1951. Alternatively, a built-in stair, an external stair, and a hand-held evacuation chute were used, in addition to exits over the wing and an exit with a significant jump-down distance. This time, the evacuees used the exit and assist means successively but without any sense of urgency. Film footage of these tests is kept and made available by the San Diego Air & Space Museum.[19] This museum specializes in Convair memorabilia as their factory was at the local airport. The Pan Am Boeing 377 and TWA Constellation tests, both assumed to also have taken place in Q2 1951, were meant to establish evacuation rates so done with speed.

FIGURE 5.3 USAF MATS Douglas C-54 evacuation trial, rope ladder (Embry Riddle Aeronautical University, Aviation Safety & Security Archives, Richard F. Chandler Papers—Binder: Emergency Evacuation from Airplanes).

FIGURES 5.4 AND 5.5 Pan Am Boeing 377 evacuation test (Embry Riddle Aeronautical University, Aviation Safety & Security Archives, Richard F. Chandler Papers—Binder: Emergency Evacuation from Airplanes).

More photos of the 377 and Constellation tests appeared in a commemorative issue of a 2005 FAA CAMI publication.[20] Reports of the tests are difficult to find. However, they are well summarized in an excellent study by Douglas in September 1961 as well as in lectures delivered by Barry King, such as at the 1954 Flight Safety Foundation seminar.[21,22]

Separately, but as part of the program, the George Washington University conducted trials using a mock-up of the interior of an aircraft with exits and doors of variable sizes and, for the exits, variable step-up and step-down distances.[23] Approximately 600 trials were carried out with 137 subjects, 3 of whom were infants and 6 were children below the age of 15. The infants were carried throughout, while the children were typically picked up by male adults when passing the exit. Four exit sizes and three door sizes were tested and, per exit size, four combinations of step-up and step-down distance. In these tests the step-down was onto a wing surface. In actual aircraft of the time, not all exits were located over the wing, thus resulting in real step-down distances as large as 6 to 10 ft (1.8 to 3 m).

The exit sizes consisted of:

- The existing size (as employed on the Convair and Constellation), as regulated: 19 by 26 inch (48 by 66 cm)
- A smaller size: 17 by 26 inch (43 by 66 cm)
- Two larger sizes: 24 by 31 inch (61 by 79 cm) and 24 by 36 inch (61 by 91 cm)

The step-up-step-down distances, tested for all four exit sizes, were:

- 23 inch (48.5 cm) up, 25 inch (63.5 cm) down (as employed on the DC-6)
- 26 inch (66 cm) up, 30 inch (76 cm) down (as employed on the Constellation)
- 29 inch (73.5 cm) up, 30 inch (76 cm) down (as employed on the Convair 240)
- 29 inch (73.5 cm) up, 36 inch (91 cm) down (as employed on the Constellation)

The door sizes were:

- 24 by 44 inch (61 by 112 cm)
- 24 by 48 inch (61 by 112 cm) (the later 'Type I')
- 24 by 72 inch (61 by 183 cm)

In all three door cases the step-up was 0 inch and the step-down was 7 inch (18 cm).

Most of the conclusions were as would be expected; however, those less intuitive were the following.

For exits:

- Exit size itself was not a factor in the speed of egress.
- Neither was the step-up–step-down condition in itself a factor in the speed of egress.
- However, the combination of smallest-sized exit (19 by 26 inch) with the largest step-up–step-down condition (29/36 inch) yielded a significantly lower egress rate than the combination of the largest-sized exit (24 by 36 inch) with the smallest step-up–step-down condition (23/25 inch).

For doors:

- The middle-sized door (24 by 48 inch) yielded a slightly greater egress rate than the largest (24 by 72 inch).

A preliminary report was issued on September 4, just in time for the decisive meeting of the CAA-CAB Working Group on September 5 and 6.

5.4.3 The Quest for a Safe Evacuation Time

5.4.3.1 NACA Crash-Fire Tests

At the same time, the notion landed that a fire often accompanied an air carrier crash. Until then, in their designs, manufacturers focused on in-flight fires rather than post-crash fires. The latter, however, started to cause more fatalities. This had been picked up by the public, as well as by Congress, resulting in negative publicity for the airlines. The larger aircraft being introduced at the time such as the DC-4 and Constellation could fly further than the DC-3 but also carried more fuel in the wing tanks, close to the engine and associated sources of ignition. In 1947, William Littlewood, chairman of the NACA Committee on Operating Problems (and associated with American Airlines), suggested that NACA study the crash-fire problem.[24] Their Cleveland, Ohio, based Flight Propulsion Research Laboratory had a team of fire experts, led by Irving Pinkel.[25] They started in 1949 a study of previous airplane fire accidents to determine initial ignition sources and combustibles. A total of 282 fires that had occurred in the ten-year period ending July 1, 1948, were investigated. Sixty-one of these were associated with a crash. For those, data about the combustibles and ignition source was scarce. This was explained by the fact that in most cases evidence was destroyed by the very fire and that accidents were primarily investigated to determine their cause and not why or how a fire ensued.[26] Yet, the study said that it appeared that 'gasoline' was 'the most hazardous of the combustibles' in a crash. Cabin items, including baggage, interior lining and insulation, and seat upholstery were not seen as potentially significant combustible materials. As to ignition sources, sufficient data for conclusions was available neither, so it could only be speculated upon. Yet, of the many candidates, the report said most such as backfires, torching at exhaust-duct outlet, arcs, sliding friction, and exhaust gases would only exist for a short period of time. The exhaust system however would be hot for a longer time and thus create a lasting source of ignition. Fuel spillage, in general, was seen as a significant cause of a crash fire, but it was decided that only tests could provide 'additional information concerning the causes and physical mechanism of crash fires'.[27] Rather than using models out of uncertainty about scale effects, NACA decided to perform full-scale tests using actual aircraft. Luckily, an abundance of aircraft was available. 'Service-weary' military transports were found, having last served in the Berlin airlift of 1948–1949. With their doors open so that the pilot could jump, if necessary, they were flown to the Army Ravenna Arsenal, east of Ravenna, Ohio.[28] This site, located about 75 km southeast of Cleveland (where NACA's Flight Propulsion Laboratory sat, later called NASA Glenn Research Center) had been selected for the tests. A 1,700 ft (518 m) 'runway' constructed of two concrete strips was prepared. A guiding monorail in the center steered the aircraft toward a crash barrier, which they hit at typical take-off speed. Together with poles simulating trees behind it, these sheared off the landing gear and propellers and ruptured fuel tanks. Two transport aircraft types of different general configurations were used: the Curtiss C-46 (a low-wing tail dragger) and the Fairchild C-82 Packet (high-wing, tricycle gear) from which the Fairchild C-119 was later developed. The C-46 is best known for its role in the 'hump' route, ferrying cargo from Assam, India to Kunming, China during World War Two, at a high human and material cost. The C-82 became famous for its star role in the 1965 movie 'The Flight of the Phoenix'. Four C-46s and 13 C-82s were so crashed. Most of the tests were done in 1952, possibly preceded by some earlier testing in the two preceding years. The unmanned aircraft were remotely operated and started their run at take-off power after release of a cable that held them from going forward. The aircraft were equipped to measure deceleration, temperatures, cabin air concentrations (carbon monoxide, carbon dioxide, oxygen and hydrocarbons) and other parameters. Several 200 pound (91 kg) dummies were strapped in and forces applied on them were recorded. The crash area was monitored by a series of motion and still cameras.[29] The results were revealing and for the first time gave insight into the mechanics of a crash fire. Recommendations were given with respect to spanwise distribution of fuel, cut-off of fuel flow to engine just prior to crash, wetting the runway before a crash landing. The data were insufficient to predict the effect of low volatility fuels on reducing the crash-fire hazard.

First Wave (1945–1953)

5.4.3.2 NACA Escape Time Tests

In four of the dynamic tests, measurements were made to appraise the hazards to human survival.[30] These were augmented by two static burn tests of aircraft hulks that had survived the crashes. Time intervals for safe escape were determined by measuring cabin temperatures and toxic gas concentrations at both cockpit and cabin locations. These were set against data known at the time for what humans could tolerate to the level that this would impair their ability to self-escape. These tolerances addressed skin burning and inhalation of hot or toxic gases. For skin burning temperatures at head level were taken, as that is usually unprotected by clothing and therefore deemed more rapidly affected than clothed parts of the body. Skin temperature levels up to where escape was still considered possible were those where pain would become unbearable (42–45°C) or where a second-degree burn would be inflicted. The gases sampled were oxygen, carbon dioxide, carbon monoxide, and aldehyde concentrations. 'Skin injury was imminent in as little as 53 seconds' in the worst location in one of the dynamic tests and the respiratory threshold there was reached six seconds later. Critical measurements for the other location in that test, as well as in the other three dynamic tests ranged from 90 to 220 seconds for severe pain, 95 to 306 seconds for second-degree burn, and 60 to 296 seconds for the respiratory limit. In the two static tests, carbon dioxide, carbon monoxide, and oxygen depletion concentrations were measured as well as time to second-degree burns. The latter times were most critical, ranging from 55 to 319 seconds. These measurements were taken from military aircraft without any sound or thermal insulation. Tests with insulation showed a positive effect on survival time until the insulation itself burned through. Although not measured scientifically, smoke was also observed as a factor that may impede escape by significantly reducing visibility. The report on these tests by Gerard Pesman has been frequently cited. This proves its importance as a pioneering study into available evacuation time in air transport ground fire cases. It is occasionally referred to as the scientific basis for the 90-second evacuation time, even though the most critical times were well below that figure. The crash-fire test program was completed in 1953 and the site was dismantled in the following years.

5.4.3.3 Escape Avenues

Escape avenues were analyzed for four cases. These were determined with hindsight, using camera footage and outside observations, which acting evacuees would have lacked. For one of the four cases, it is reproduced here in Figure 5.6. It shows per quadrant location where and when escape is possible. In none of the four cases was there a clear split between left and right, in two cases (including that shown here) there was, between forward and aft. Key variables of influence, according to Pesman were: (1) the circumstances of the fuel spillage; (2) the location of the bulk of fuel with respect to the occupants; (3) the wind direction.

The report concluded that 'generally, the most likely location of escape avenues will be toward the upwind portions of the airplane unless fire exists on only one side of the fuselage'.

5.5 REGULATORY DEVELOPMENTS 1945–1953

The Chicago Convention was but one of the triggers that led to an increase in cabin safety standards. The larger size of airliners, the strive for an increase in safety in general, research activities, and accident experience were others. This section reviews the cabin safety regulatory developments in the first wave in the U.S. for five domains (Chapter 8 narrates the sixth). For ease of reference purposes, a summary is given of the measures already in place before 1945.

5.5.1 IMPACT PROTECTION

5.5.1.1 In Place before 1945

In the domain of crash impact, the following regulatory measures were in place in the U.S. by 1945:

- Occupant protection and room for egress for the scenario of a complete turnover, at an ultimate load factor of 4.5

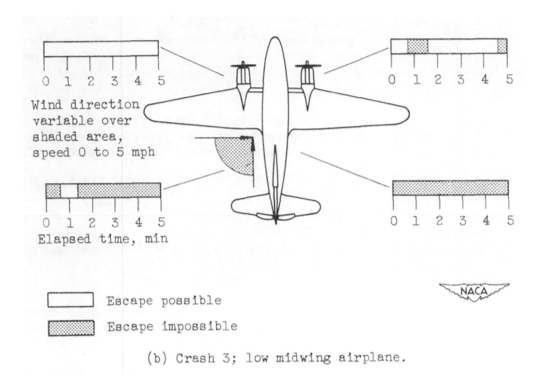

FIGURE 5.6 C-46 escape avenues, crash 3, out of 4 (Appraisal of Hazards to Human Survival in Airplane Crash Fires, by Gerard J. Pesman).

- Seats securely fastened 'in place' (but no explicit requirement for seats for each occupant in the first place)
- Certificated safety belts for all occupants
- Safety belts and structures to which they are attached to withstand an ultimate load of 1,000 pounds

5.5.1.2 State-of-the-Art and Regulatory Measures

Crash impact measures introduced or improved in the first wave by the CAB were about four subjects: the requirement for a seat for each occupant, safety belts, crash inertia loads, and the padding of projecting objects.

5.5.1.2.1 A Seat for Each Occupant

The November 1945 edition of CAR 04 introduced a firm requirement for 'a seat for each occupant', albeit that it was listed as 'miscellaneous equipment'.[31] As this would affect new airplane types only, a companion operational rule would have helped, but this was not consistently arranged. The new operational requirements for the non-scheduled airlines (CAR 42) in 1946 listed a 'suitable seat' for each passenger carried, albeit as guidance only.[32] In CAR 40 (domestic operations) seats were not formally required, but only inferred, until 1954. CAR 41 ignored seats completely until 1962. By then, however, the fleets of the overseas air carriers would have consisted entirely of airplanes subject to the 1945 type certification change for a seat for each occupant anyway.

5.5.1.2.2 Safety Belts

5.5.1.2.2.1 Objectives In 1945, the new design requirements specified two objectives for the belt:

- Prevent serious injuries in the event of an emergency landing as a result of contact of a vulnerable part of the body with any penetrating or relatively solid object
- Protection from head injuries[33]

For the latter, it offered three combinations to reach this objective:

- A safety belt plus a shoulder harness
- A safety belt and the elimination of all injurious objects
- A safety belt and a cushioned rest

These requirements still exist in 2024, with minor textual adjustments made over time.

5.5.1.2.2.2 Strength As to strength, the 1,000 pound (4,448 N) tensile strength requirement of 1931 remained. In 1946, a proposal was made to increase this to 1,500 pound (6,672 N) because 'in numerous instances safety belts have not withstood the loads imposed on them, allowing the user to be thrown against the airplane's structure, instrument panel, controls or other protruding objects with resulting severe or even fatal injuries'. Many such injuries probably could have been avoided had the strength of the safety belt been greater.[34] This was further elaborated in 1947, when it was explained that the webbing degrades over time, so an end time of 30 months after manufacture was proposed. Also, a minimum width of 2 inch was proposed.[35]

From 1947 onward, airworthiness standards for equipment, including safety belts, were regulated under the new Technical Standard Order system in which reliance was made on industry standards, such as National Aerospace Standards.[36] A change to CAR 4b effective February 6, 1950, specified that the rated strength, as well as the attachment of the belts, be the same as that of the inertia loads.[37] Thus, with a nominal mass of 170 pound (77 kg) of an occupant, at 6 g this yielded a tensile strength of 1,020 pound (4,537 N), and at 9 g, 1,530 pound (6,806 N).

5.5.1.2.2.3 Quick Release The 1946 and 1947 proposals called for 'an easily-operable quick release mechanism which will enable the wearer to release himself easily under a load simulating the wearer hanging in the belt after an application of a load'.[38] This proposal may be traced back to the accident at Oklahoma City mentioned in Section 3.3.2.

5.5.1.2.2.4 Wearing Passengers were not always keen to wear the belt. One accident in particular may have caused that. On 31 October 1950, a BEA Viking crashed in thick fog at London Airport (later Heathrow). Twenty-eight out of 30 occupants did not survive. Dr. Donald Teare, a well-known British forensic pathologist, published an article in the British Medical Journal in which he stated that '[t]he immediate cause of death in more than half of the victims was acute flexion of the body over the seat-belt'.[39] While this unlikely was his intent, the popular *Scientific American* magazine took this over and coined it as '[t]he dangerous safety-belt'. Airline passengers became apprehensive and fastened their belts loosely, if at all.[40] The public sentiment that Hugh De Haven had carefully tried to overcome by his crash research work was back. A later study of the Viking accident sequence published in the same journal by Eugene DuBois of Cornell University titled 'Safety-belts are not dangerous' proved Teare's conclusions were wrong.[41] The seats had broken loose and there was much tumbling of the victims. The cause of death was that passengers had hit hard objects. This included six passengers in aft-facing seats. But his article was not picked up by the media. It took years before the public had gained confidence in seat belts again. A similar, if not even more severe, struggle to convince the public to wear safety belts took place over automobiles.

Passengers in the U.S. were not formally required to wear seat belts until 1963 (Part 41) or 1964 (Part 40).[42]

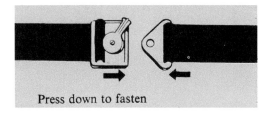

FIGURE 5.7 Safety belt fastening instruction, BOAC safety leaflet (1960).

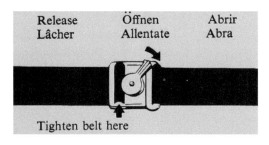

FIGURE 5.9 Safety belt release instruction, BOAC safety leaflet (1960).

FIGURE 5.8 Safety belt of Comet 1 as displayed in the De Havilland Museum, London Colney (photograph by the author).

5.5.1.2.2.5 Infants The retention of infants, or rather the lack thereof, was first mentioned in November 1949, in guidance material for the non-scheduleds (CAR 42): 'When a child under 2 years of age is held by an adult person, the safety belt shall be used only for the adult'.[43]

5.5.1.3 Crash Loads

5.5.1.3.1 From Pounds to g's

In the first wave, a new concept for crash loads was introduced. Rather than the fixed, static, load expressed in pounds that had been in use since 1933, they were now expressed as inertia loads in g's (g being the inertia force of gravity). In Chicago, this was proposed by the British delegation, which suggests that they already used this concept. Initially, the loads were only applied to seats and safety belts. For safety belts, a maximum tensile load of 1,000 pounds (4,448 N), applied to a person having the standard mass of 170 pounds (77 kg), equated to 5.9 g. In the CAR 04 revision of 1945, this was now extended to the entire aircraft structure and set at 6 g in the forward direction and lesser values in the other directions. The new airworthiness requirements that became effective November 9, 1945, read[44]:

> The structure shall be designed to give every reasonable probability that all the occupants, if they make proper use of the seats, belts and other provisions made in the design [. . .] will escape serious injury in

the event of a minor crash landing (with wheels up if the airplane is equipped with retractable landing gear) in which the occupants experience all combinations[45] of the following ultimate inertia forces relative to the surrounding structure.

Forward	0 to 6.0 g
Sideward	0 to 1.5 g
Vertical	0 to 4.5 g (down)
	0 to 2.0 g (up)

At the same time, a separate set of airworthiness requirements was first created for non-transport airplanes. This had the same g values, except in the forward direction, where it was 0 to 9.0 g.

The rationale for the inertia forces chosen is not well documented. Snyder, in 1981, investigated this and found 'no source [. . .] to document the CAB's Civil Air Regulations on this point'.[46] Referring to human body impact tolerance data available at the time (i.e. 1940s), he concluded that 'the occupant crash protection standards published by the CAB in 1945 [. . .] were outdated from the start'.[47]

McFarland in 1953 reported that research on human tolerance to deceleration 'indicated that forces up to 20 g are very common' and many passengers survived this and higher values. 'This suggests that 20 g protection represents the minimum acceptable level of airworthiness and that levels up to 40 g are desirable'. 'The critical element in restraining a person was not considered limited to the seat and belt, but included the entire aircraft structure and that 'solutions will be found only when all aspects of the problem are considered as an integrated whole'.[48]

The U.S. Air Force and Navy used crash load factors of 17 and 40 g, respectively, and the British Royal Air Force 25 g.

Snyder suggested that the values chosen in 1945 aligned with the capabilities of contemporary aircraft designs rather than having been inspired by research on human tolerances. To prove his point, he remarked that in at least one direction (sidewards) the load was the same as the structural load for the landing gear that had already been introduced in 1927 by the Department of Air Commerce.

5.5.1.3.2 From 6 g to 9 g

In 1952, the design emergency landing load in the forward direction was increased to 9 g for all new transport aircraft types.[49] At the same time, the fitting factor of 1.15 for attachments of seat to structure, and safety belt to seat or structure, was elevated to 1.33 and renamed 'safety factor'. The fitting factor was only needed when seats or belts were not actually tested. The safety factor however applied always to such attachments. As seats were normally tested, some therefore argued that the inertia force was in fact doubled, from 6 to 12 (being 1.33 × 9).

Why was the inertia force load raised? A rationale is found in the 1977 FAA Staff Study that is reproduced in Petition Notice PR 80–9:[50]

> After a number of transport accidents having extensive numbers of seat failures under the 6.0 g requirement, the transport criteria was changed [. . .] to require 9.0 g seats, the same as for small airplanes. As far as can be determined, these strength levels were selected as an envelope condition to provide 50% greater strength.[51]

In a November 1980 letter by the then administrator to the chairman of the U.S. House of Representatives Subcommittee, the following explanation was given:[52]

> In 1948, the CAA recommended that the forward crash load factor be increased from 6g's to 12g's. [. . .] This particular crash load factor increase was considered at the 1950 and 1951 [annual airworthiness] reviews, and the CAA position at both was to recommend moderate increase in crash load factors, such as 9g's forward. It was considered that the crash acceleration values in CAR 4b should be increased to at least the values in CAR 3 for small airplanes and, hence, the 9g forward load factor recommendation. The CAB later offered, in a draft release stemming from the 1951 review, that they consider the

proposed increase in crash load factor essential for the protection of occupants in crash landings. The CAB went on to add that the experience had indicated rather conclusively that the presently effective rules were not wholly adequate in that respect.

5.5.1.4 Padding of Projecting Objects

The design standards of 1945 introduced a requirement for the padding of projecting objects 'likely to cause injury to persons seated or moving about the airplane in normal flight' not for the crash scenario but rather for 'rough air flights'.[53] In 1950, it was proposed to copy this in the operational requirements, but that was not pursued.[54]

5.5.2 Fire Protection

5.5.2.1 In Place before 1945

In the domain of fire precautions, the only regulatory measures in place in the U.S. before 1945 consisted of portable fire extinguishers and ash containers. For airliners, two portable fire extinguishers were required by both the design requirements and the operational requirements.[55] Ash containers were required by operational regulation 'when smoking is permitted and the aircraft carries a second pilot or cabin attendant, who shall notify passengers when and where smoking is prohibited'.[56]

In Chicago, the Dutch delegation had proposed to add a requirement for the fireproofing of cabin materials. This may well have been inspired by two accidents where KLM had learned that aircraft cabins were susceptible to fire. In December 1934, the Douglas DC-2 named *Uiver* crashed in the western Iraqi desert, near Rutbah Wells. Although all occupants likely perished as a result of the impact, the fuselage and cabin were destroyed by fire. Only two months earlier, the *Uiver* had become famous as the winner of the handicap prize in the MacRobertson race from London to Melbourne. In July 1937, another KLM Douglas DC-2 while flying over Belgium suffered from an enigmatic accident. The co-pilot's cap, an emergency exit hatch, and passenger's baggage were strewn out before the aircraft itself crashed.[57] The cause was a riddle for the investigators and was never found. What was clear though was that a severe fire had developed in-flight inside the cabin.

The proposal led to the following agreed text in Chicago:

> 2.317 Cabin Fireproofing. All materials used in cockpit and cabins for soundproofing, upholstering, and further furnishing shall be of non-inflammable material. Smoking shall be prohibited in sleepers, when the interior is converted into the sleeper arrangement.[58]

5.5.2.2 Fire Protection of Materials

In November 1945, the U.S. airworthiness regulations adopted this in a slightly different format:[59]

> 04.38240 Cabin interiors. In compartments where smoking is to be permitted, the materials of the cabin lining, floors, upholstery, and furnishings shall be sufficiently flame resistant to preclude ignition by cigarettes or matches, and suitable ash containers shall be provided. All other compartments shall be placarded against smoking.

Compared to the Chicago text, the term 'non-inflammable material' was replaced by 'sufficiently flame-resistant', and the condition was added that this was only needed when smoking would be allowed. The thought at the time was apparently that only smoking could lead to a cabin fire.

Around 1946, the manufacturers, together with the CAA, the CAB Safety Bureau, and the airlines, met frequently to develop 'more stringent fire prevention regulations which will provide the basis for installation of extensive fire protection equipment and design features so that all probable sources of fire hazard are being eliminated'.[60] The need for more rigorous requirements was confirmed by a DC-3 accident that occurred on January 18, 1946, near Cheshire, Connecticut. All occupants died in this crash where the investigators determined that a fire had developed in the left engine which eventually led to the left wing breaking off. The report does not mention any fire in the cabin, but does say that:

> As the result of the investigation of this and other accidents, both prior to and subsequent to this one, the Board has, after months of study and coordination with the parties concerned on the part of the Safety Bureau, promulgated additional fire prevention regulations.

The new regulation, effectuated in both airworthiness and operational regulations, asked, as could be expected, for improved engine fire safety but also added fire safety in the cabin. The condition that cabin material met only certain flammability standards when smoking was to be permitted was removed:

> All coverings, linings, upholstery, carpets, etc., in the passenger and crew compartments are to be for the most part of flame-resistant materials but in all other cases of flash-resistant materials. All receptacles for waste material are to be of fire-resistant materials and provided with covers to smother any fire which may originate within.[61]

Definitions for the terms 'fire proof', 'fire resistant', 'flame resistant', and 'flash resistant' were introduced and so were test methods.[62] The terms 'fire proof' and 'fire resistant' meant that a material 'will withstand heat equally well or better than steel [fire proof] or aluminum alloy [fire resistant] in dimensions appropriate for the purpose for which it is to be used'. The term 'flame resistant' meant that 'material will not support combustion to the point of propagation, beyond safe limits, a flame after removal of the ignition source'. The term 'flash-resistant' was defined as materials 'which will not burn violently when ignited'. The ignition source was a Bunsen burner with the test specimen held horizontally. The test method was specified by the CAB in Safety Regulation Release No. 259 in 1947. Materials in the cabin needed to be at least flash-resistant and walls, ceilings, and the coverings of all upholstering, floors, and furnishing at least flame-resistant. The new requirements became effective for aircraft manufactured from October 1, 1947. For operators of existing aircraft an ultimate date of January 1, 1948, applied for implementing the changes in their fleets.[63]

5.5.2.3 Ash Containers and Receptacles

Since 1930, ash containers had been required by operational standards but not by design standards. This changed in November 1945, when the operational requirement was copied into the design standards, now prescribing 'suitable ash containers' in compartments where smoking is to be permitted. Effective October 1, 1947, this was changed into: 'compartments where smoking is to be permitted shall be equipped with ash trays of the self-contained type which are completely removable'.[64] And it was extended: 'all receptacles for used towels, papers, and waste shall be of fire-resistant material, and shall incorporate covers or other provisions for containing possible fires started in the receptacles'.[65]

5.5.2.4 Fire Extinguishers

Since before the war, portable fire extinguishers were required in airworthiness standards: one for 'non-airline carrier' (NAC) airplanes and two for 'Airline Carriers—Passengers' (ACP). They had to be of an approved type and contain either carbon tetrachloride or carbon monoxide.

From 1945 onward, the design requirements specified one extinguisher for use by the pilot and co-pilot, plus extinguishers in the cabin as specified in the operational standards. In 1952, the number of fire extinguishers was specified in CAR 4b as a function of the passenger capacity.[66] In addition to one hand fire extinguisher for use by the flight crew, the minimum numbers in the cabin were as follows.

TABLE 5.1
Number of Cabin Fire Extinguishers, 1952

Passenger Capacity	Minimum Number of Fire Extinguishers
6 or less	0
7 through 30	1
31 through 60	2
61 or more	3

5.5.3 Escape Potential

5.5.3.1 Introduction

Until 1945, the requirements for doors and exits were essentially those of 1934. The only addition that had been made was in 1944 in response to the Trammel DC-3 accident which called for identifying the exits and the operating handle using luminous paint. Virtually all of the airlines in the U.S., both domestic and overseas, used the Douglas DC-3.[67] That was before the massive influx of military DC-3s after the war had ended that were converted for civil use. But during 1945, also new types became available: the four-engined Douglas DC-4 and Lockheed Constellation. Other aircraft types were in development. McFarland in 1946 listed 11 landplanes (excluding the DC-4 and Constellation) and 2 seaplane types being in development, by five different manufacturers. As it turned out, only four of these actually came into service.[68] These were the Convair 240, the Martin 2–0-2, the Douglas DC-6, and the Boeing 377, all landplanes, see Table 5.2 on page 53.

In anticipation of the new equipment, toward the end of the war, the CAB developed a major revision of the exit standards. This revision was introduced at short notice in late 1945. Later, following the first accidents with evacuation issues, a research program was conducted in 1950 and 1951 (see Section 5.4.2). That led to a new scheme for specifying the size and number of exits that came into force in November 1951 for new airplane types. That scheme in essence still exists in 2024 and will do so for many more years.

The following reviews the developments in 1945, continues with the 1951 scheme for new types, and finishes with the retroactive actions for existing types. The concept of a safe evacuation time, first mentioned in Chicago, was introduced in the first wave but did not become a firm standard. That would take another decade or two.

5.5.3.2 Exit Standards 1945

The measures in existence at the start of 1945 matched the aircraft of the day, mainly the Douglas DC-3. But the new transport aircraft that became available from that year onward were different. They were significantly larger. Where the DC-3 sat 21 passengers, the new Douglas DC-4 and Lockheed Constellation could accommodate 56 and 62 passengers, respectively. Another novelty was the tricycle landing gear: no longer a tailwheel but a nose gear. This brought the main door, which was kept in the rear of the airplane, significantly higher from the ground. With gear down, the distance from the sill to the ground went from 1.3 m (4.2 ft) on a DC-3 to 2.5 m (8.3 ft) on a DC-4 and even 3 m (10 ft) on a Lockheed Constellation.[69] Even with gear-up, distances were considerable. It was recognized that these distances were too high to jump and descent assist means were provided in the form of ladders, escape ropes, or stairs in the door.

The CAB reacted. In November 1945 it issued new standards for the evacuation potential of airliners.[70] These were embedded in the complete revision of Part 04, airworthiness regulations, which was published without any explanation. They introduced a number of new concepts. While there

First Wave (1945–1953) 51

is no indication that these were preceded by research, or even public consultation, they must have resulted from quite some in-office brainstorming on the possible effects on escape potential of the new generation of airplanes.

5.5.3.2.1   Doors versus Exits

As was previously the case, there were separate requirements for doors and exits. This may seem to be a futile difference as it would be obvious that standards for emergency exits would automatically apply to doors. But that was not the case. The U.S. regulations offered an option not to count an external door as an emergency exit, in which case it did not need to meet those standards. The effect was that doors through which passengers had entered and, where they had a tendency to rely on escape in an emergency, could in fact be inadequate. An example was the Martin 2–0–2, which had a ventral door that was used for normal embarkation and disembarkation but was not an emergency exit.

5.5.3.2.2   Number of Exits

- Instead of the entire cabin, evacuation regulations now focused on cabin compartments. The definition of a compartment was 'a closed space to which normal access is by a door, passageway, or stair that is likely to become a bottleneck in evacuating the airplane'. For each compartment, the number of exits was a function of the number of persons for which seats were provided:

> § 04.38120 *Number of exits.* The minimum number of exits per compartment is as follows:
>
> | Number of persons for which seats are provided: | Minimum number of exits required |
> |---|---|
> | 5 or less | 1 |
> | Exceeding 5, not exceeding 15 | 2 |
> | Exceeding 15, not exceeding 22 | 3 |
> | Exceeding 22, not exceeding 29 | 4 |
> | Exceeding 29, not exceeding 36 | 5 |
> | Exceeding 36, not exceeding 50 | 6 |

  There was a proviso that, if there was only a passageway, so not a door, between two adjacent compartments, the number of exits could be combined, so long as there was at least one exit per eight passengers. Of the period airplanes, the Boeing 314 flying boat had many compartments (seven for passengers, plus one for crew, all on the main deck. On the upper deck was the cockpit with an extended facility for crew resting). Barry King was against this concept and pleaded for 'clean' cabin interiors: 'The less the compartmentation of the interior the better is the opportunity for instructing and controlling passengers in an emergency situation'.[71]
- A ratio was added for the number of exits on either side to the total number of exits of not less than one-third. So, as an example, if the number of required exits is six, there had to be at least two exits on one side.
- For airplanes certificated for ditching, it was added that 'at least one emergency exit per 16 passengers is located above the waterline'. This was supplementary to the operational requirement in CAR 40 that multi-engine aircraft operating over water must have 'one or more suitable emergency exits located in the upper half of the fuselage'.[72]
- A slightly different set of exit rules, albeit only having the status of guidance, was presented in CAM 42, issue September 1, 1949:[73] For up to 50 persons it was identical to that of CAR 04, but, beyond that and up to 78 persons, it required an extra exit for each additional 14 persons.

5.5.3.2.3 Location
- The location of exits, previously subject to approval, was now specified to be 'so as to give the maximum likelihood of their being usable in the emergency landing with wheels up' and to 'be distributed so as to facilitate egress without crowding'. The requirement that the external door be on the left side, was removed.
- The requirement that doors not be located in the plane of rotation of an inboard propeller nor within 5° thereof as measured from the propeller hub, was reworded as a more general performance standard: they must be located such that persons using it would not be endangered by the propellers. This requirement was not meant to cover emergencies but intended to safeguard against persons being struck by rotating propellers during regular use. In 1950, when some editorial changes were made to Part 04, the condition 'when appropriate procedures are employed' was added.

5.5.3.2.4 Size
The size of emergency exits remained the same: 'such that a 19 by 26 inch [48 by 66 cm] ellipse may be inscribed therein'. There was no requirement for the size of doors, other than the minimum for qualification as an exit. They were assumed to be adequate as they would be large enough for normal use.

5.5.3.2.5 Accessibility
- A new requirement was that 'exits shall be readily accessible' and doors 'easily accessible'. No further specification in terms of passageway widths was given.
- Similarly, the requirement that each exit provided a clear and unobstructed opening to the outside remained unchanged.

5.5.3.2.6 Ease of Operation
- As to ease of operation of emergency exits, the lessons of Trammel echoed in Chicago. In 1943, the only requirement for the method of operation of emergency exits was that it be approved. The 1944 U.S. proposal to ICAO included several elements learned from the July 1943 Trammel accident. The operation of emergency exits must be 'simple and obvious', also 'in darkness'. To this, the Chicago conference added: 'The exits shall not require exceptional agility of a person using them'. All these proposals were adopted in the November 1945 CAR Part 04 edition, except that for darkness reliance was put on the luminous paint requirement that had been introduced in 1944.
- Also following the Trammel accident, the CAB had issued a proposal that cabin doors be opened by the operation of a single handle.[74] This was not adopted as quickly as the other post-Trammel proposal for marking the exit and the handle but did appear in the November 1945 edition of Part 04:
  It shall be possible to open such door from either inside or outside by the operation of only one handle inside or one handle outside even though the persons using the exit may be crowded near it.[75]

In 1951, this requirement was removed again, citing the following reason:

It has been brought to the attention of the Board that interpretations of the present rule do not allow any separate safetying devices and that an incipient hazardous condition may be created in certain situations. Although this change is needed to permit operators in their discretion to provide additional safety devices against inadvertent opening of doors in flight, it is of a minor nature and imposes no additional burden on any person.[76]

First Wave (1945–1953)

5.5.3.2.7 Jamming

Both doors and exits now had to have reasonable provisions against jamming as a result of fuselage deformation in a minor crash. This requirement, proposed by the U.S. in Chicago, may also have been inspired by Trammel.

5.5.3.2.8 Marking of Exits and Handles

The requirements for marking the door as exit and the operation handle with luminous paint were now copied from the operational standards to the airworthiness standards and reworded as a performance standard: 'marked that [the door] can be readily located and operated, even in darkness'[77]. This requirement was confined to external doors and not extended to exits, as it was in the operational standards.

5.5.3.2.9 Operation from Outside

For doors it was now required that they also be openable from the outside. In addition, 'at least one exit on the opposite side from the main door shall be operatable [sic] from the outside and shall be marked accordingly for the guidance of rescue personnel'.[78]

5.5.3.3 Descent Assist Means

The increased distance from the cabin floor to the ground posed a challenge for manufacturers. The CAB introduced in 1945 a requirement that:

> landplane exits which are more than 10 feet from the ground with the airplane on the ground and wheels retracted, suitable means shall be provided by which the occupants can safely descent to the ground.[79]

TABLE 5.2
Escape Facilities on Airplane Types, Existing and Projected, 1946

Model	Maximum Number of Passengers	Doors	Emergency Hatches	Decks	Cockpit, ft.	Main deck, ft.	Lower deck, ft.	Means of Escape
B-307	41	1	6	1	12	5	—	None
B-377	100	3	7	2	10	10	5.6	Escape ropes
C-97	132	3	5	2	10	10	5.6	None
CV-104	53	2	5	1	6	3	—	None
CV-240	30	3	6	1	8.2	7.5	—	Stairs; escape ropes
CV-37	204	4	6+	2	20	20	11	
DC-3	24	2	3	1	9	4.2	—	None
DC-4	56	2	4	1	8.3	8.3	—	Ladder
DC-6	56	2	6	1	8.9	8.9	—	Escape ropes
DC-7	118	3	9	1	13	12	—	Escape ropes
DC-8	48	2	3	1	7	5	—	Steps in door
L-49	62	2	4	1	10.7	10	—	Ropes and ladder
L-89	160	5	11	2	15	13	7.8	Telescoping ladders
M-202	40	2	6	1	8	7	—	Escape ropes
RC-2	46	2	6	1	7	5	—	Escape ropes
CW-20	37	2	3	1	10	6	—	None

In 1946, McFarland gave an extensive overview of the various types of descent assist means that the manufacturers applied or contemplated for all the new aircraft types.[80] The table, which he named 'General Escape Facilities on Representative Civilian Air Transports in Normal Ground Position with Landing Gear Down' and reproduced in Table 5.2, included several airplane types that did not come to fruition such as the Convairs 104 and 37, the Douglas DC-7 and DC-8 (these identifications were later used for different aircraft types), the Lockheed L-89 Constitution, and the Republic RC-2.

The means included escape ropes, stairs, ladders, and telescoping ladders. Devices tested but rejected included rope ladders, automatically extended metal ladders, telescope firemen's poles, and inertial escape reels. The latter, known as 'Davy emergency escape units', were tried but considered to require too much agility on the part of the passenger.

The 10-feet (3-m) criterion applied to the wheels retracted scenario. This translated to distances of more than 15 ft (5 m) for the normal, landing gear down, configuration. A distance that people could not jump without the risk of injury so would cause hesitation or refusal. And that is what accident experience would soon confirm. In the January 1948 crash of a Constellation in Boston the nose gear failed and the distance from the rear exit was as high as about 15 or 16 ft. This must have been an eye opener. For the first time, people actually had to jump such a distance from an airliner. It would have stimulated the invention of the chute, but records vary as to when it indeed was invented. This is how Jerome Lederer remembers it. When orally recapitulating his memories in 1994, he said:

> At the meeting, [TWA] Capt. [Robert] 'Bob' Buck had just come from a tour of the South by car with his family, and he had noticed that the schools in the South had metal chutes from the third story down to the ground, so that, in the event of a fire, the students could slide down the chutes to safety. He wondered why it would not be a good idea to use escape chutes for the quick evacuation of airplanes when they had a crash. Otto Krishner, who was working with the [Flight Safety] Foundation on loan from American Airlines, thought this was a very good idea. The next day, Otto went back to La Guardia Airport [in New York, New York], where American Airlines had a hangar and repair shops, put a sewing machine in the hangar, got a bunch of nylon and made the first chute.[81,82]

The meeting that he referred to was probably the aviation meeting of the Society of Automotive Engineers in New York in April 1948, just after the Flight Safety Foundation had been founded, and only three months after the Boston crash.

Lederer's memory at age 92 may have suffered, or it was his modesty, but earlier, in October 1946, he had already suggested chutes as a descent assist means:[83]

> The use of fireproof cloth chutes from the main and emergency doors, the chutes to be held rigid by expelling compressed air of CO_2 into tubular cloth girders has been suggested.

Not only is this a description of a slide, but even an inflatable slide, complete with a fireproof element such as would only be introduced following the 1978 DC-10 Los Angeles accident.

McFarland also mentioned the escape chute in 1946. When listing in his book means 'to facilitate the rapidity of exit' he proposed that 'some method of emergency descent such as ropes, slides, or chutes must be devised so that the passengers will not need to jump in free space'.[84]

So, while the concept of a chute arose to those that pondered in a theoretical fashion as how to jump from the new airliners, it still took some years, and possibly a vacation trip, before theory was put into practice. But from then it caught on and the chute, and later the inflatable slide, became the principal assist means for emergency escape from airliners.

The CAB followed up. In 1950 it published a draft release to change the operational rules and specified chutes for the first time, albeit as one option out of several.[85] It did not set a distance when such equipment was required, but did heed the lesson of January 1948 by specifically mentioning the scenario of aircraft tipping:

First Wave (1945–1953)

> Where the aircraft design is such that, when the aircraft is tipped to an attitude likely to result from a landing accident, the regular exits would not be sufficiently close to the ground to enable passengers and crew to be safely and expeditiously evacuated without danger of injury, adequate evacuation equipment such as chutes, rigid ladders, etc., shall be provided.

This proposal was one of a quartet that raised opposition from the Air Transport Association, the strong trade organization of the airlines (see Chapter 7.2 for the other three). In an October 1951 sequel to the draft release, the proposal was slightly reworded. No longer were chutes explicitly mentioned, but rather 'adequate evacuation equipment'. Now also the normal landing configuration was mentioned next to that of tipping. This was a correction to the 1950 proposal where the January 1948 accident apparently had narrowed down the focus to just the tipping scenario:

> where the aircraft design is such that, when the aircraft is in normal landing configuration or is tipped to an attitude likely to result from a landing accident, the regular exits would not be sufficiently close to the ground to enable passengers and crew to be safely and expeditiously evacuated, adequate evacuation equipment shall be provided.[86]

The proposal did not materialize into a rule. The matter was postponed for resolution in the period of the first trough (see Section 7.2).

5.5.3.4 The 1951 Exit Scheme

The following summarizes the insights gained from the research program conducted by Dr. Barry King and his team:[87]

- There is a limit on the time available for successful evacuation in the event of a fire following a landing.
- The aft portion of the fuselage is less vulnerable to structural damage in crash landings.
- Doors are the preferred way of evacuation over emergency window exits.
- Principal exits must be at (cabin) floor level and of such size as to allow the occupants to step or jump in a partially upright position, rather than climb out through a small opening and drop.
- Currently prescribed window exits are almost never used and the time required for evacuation through such exits is too great.
- Wheels-down crash landings are much more frequent than wheels-up landings and present significantly higher jump-down distances, thereby slowing down evacuation and increasing the risk of injuries.

Neither an insight from the research program, nor necessarily supported by the findings of Barry King's exit usage survey, but a notion already held for quite some time, was that there should be exits on both sides of the fuselage. The U.S. had proposed in Chicago that:[88]

> The exits shall be distributed longitudinally and laterally so as to facilitate egress without crowding.

In 1945, this consideration had been codified as a requirement that on either side there be not less than one-third of the exits.

At a meeting of the CAA-CAB Working Group on September 5 and 6, the findings were discussed and translated into the following notions and concepts that formed the basis for a new set of requirements for size, location, and number of exits:

- 'Experience indicates that the currently effective requirements for emergency exits are not sufficiently realistic, especially with respect to larger airplanes. Consideration of the rapid

increase in recent years in the size of transport aircraft, the number of passengers carried, and the increased seriousness of fire in the event of crash landings because of the greater volume of fuel carried, all point to the need for a re-examination of the emergency evacuation problem'.[89]
- Classify exits into exit types (to be called Type I, II, III, and IV), defined by their dimensions, and draft a scheme in which seating capacity ranges are linked to frequencies of these exit types.
- Consider exits as pairs, one on either side of the fuselage.
- Discontinue the exits per compartments concept.
- Recognize that certain locations are safer than others.
- Prescribe escape assist means from a sill to ground distance of 6 ft (1.8 m) with gear extended.

The new scheme consisted of two elements: the definition of exit types by size and location and a table prescribing their number as a function of passenger seating capacity ranges. It was circulated for comments on October 4, 1951, with a tight response period: until October 26.[90] The final rule was then quickly adopted and published, on November 15.[91]

The new rule applied from December 20, 1951. So, in only 16 weeks from the meeting, a new set of regulations had been drafted, circulated for comments, comments-reviewed, published, and made applicable. This would be a record, never to be repeated again for cabin safety regulations that would have such a lasting impact.

Its effectivity was limited to future aircraft types, that is, those for which type certification had yet to be applied. Aircraft already in production or new aircraft types well advanced on the drawing boards were not affected. While previous designs typically had one main door in the left aft fuselage plus a service or crew door at the right front and a number of small emergency exits spread along the two fuselage sides, the new designs were to have at least one floor-level door on the right side in addition to the boarding door on the left. This door did not need to be directly opposite the entrance door. One of the first designs to which the new requirements applied, albeit partially, was the Douglas DC-7, which came into service in November 1953. It had the right side door at the extreme aft end of the cabin. Actually, rather than a door it was a hatch that could be removed completely from the frame but had door dimensions.

5.5.3.4.1 The New Exit Types

Each exit type was defined by minimum size and location and in one case maximum step-up and step-down distances. The latter, clearly a result of the GWU findings, were added in the final rule without having appeared in the draft release, so they were left outside of the consultation. Four types were introduced. Type I exits would be the largest, Type IV the smallest:

TABLE 5.3
Exit Types Definition, 1951

	Width (inch)	Height (inch)	Location	Step-Up (inch)	Step-Down (inch)
Type I	24	48	aft	0	n/d
Type II	20	44	aft	0	n/d
Type IIII	20	36	aft	n/d	n/d
Type IV	19	26	Over the wing	29	36

n/d: not defined.

First Wave (1945–1953)

Except for Type IV exits, which must be located over the wing, all exits should be located as far aft as possible, at least for those airplanes 'where the major portion of the passenger area is aft of the powerplant and the fuel tanks'. For other configurations, variations would be acceptable.

Appendix 3 presents a graphical size comparison of the exit types, including those added later. The widths and heights have remained the same per type.

The Type IV exit size was the same as that prescribed for emergency exits since 1937. It was the only exit type for which step-up and step-down dimensions were specified, for both inside and outside (onto the wing), respectively. These dimensions were the same as the highest in the GWU tests and resembled those of the Constellation. Both the Type I and Type II exits were prescribed as floor level (so 0-inch step-up), for Type III it was left open.

The step-down outside was not defined, except that beyond a distance to the ground of 6 ft (1.8 m) (measured with gear extended), a descent assist means was prescribed for Type I, II, and III exits. This requirement was previously 10 ft (3 m) and with the gear retracted, quite an improvement. Other than for the Type IV exits, no correlation of exit dimensions as chosen could be traced to the tests of 1951.

5.5.3.4.2 Number Prescribed

The required number of exits was now prescribed by means of a table specifying the number of exit types as a function of passenger seating capacity ranges. Above a certain capacity, a flat ratio was used. The proposal was as follows:[92]

(c) **Passenger emergency exits – number required.** Emergency exits of type and location prescribed in paragraph (b) of this section shall be accessible to the passengers and shall be provided on each side of the fuselage in accordance with the following:

Passenger seating capacity	Emergency exits required on each side of fuselage			
	Type I	Type II	Type III	Type IV
1 to 19 inclusive	–	–	1	–
20 to 39 inclusive	–	1	–	1
40 to 69 inclusive	1	–	–	1
70 to 99 inclusive	1	–	–	2
100 to 149 inclusive	2	–	–	2

For airplanes with a passenger capacity of over 149 there shall be, in addition to the emergency exits prescribed for a passenger seating capacity of 100 to 149, inclusive, on each side of the fuselage, one Type I emergency exit for additional passengers up to 50, these exits to be located at such strategic points as would contribute most to the safe evacuation of passengers.

NOTE: Although similar exits and their locations are prescribed for each side of the fuselage, it is not the intent of this regulation to require that the exits necessarily be at locations diametrically opposite each other.

The Type I and Type IV exits dominated. This is not surprising as they were already well used, even though the doors often were larger than what was prescribed for a Type I exit. The Type II and Type III exits were only prescribed for smaller airplanes (of up to a capacity of 39), so they were possibly chosen as a trade-off for the smaller size of those aircraft, where larger exits would pose structural issues. For capacities from 100 and up, extra pairs of Type I exits were prescribed, giving a credit of 50 passenger seats for each additional pair. The first such increment was embedded in the table, which ended at a seating capacity of 149. This was indeed linked to seating capacity, but the next increments were in plain text and linked to passengers carried, not capacity. In the final rule, dated November 15, 1951, the cut-off of 149 was changed to 139, which meant a credit of 40 instead of 50 for a pair of Type I exits. No reason for this change was given in the preamble to the final rule. Beyond 139, the plain text was kept, including that each extra Type I pair was good for 50 more passengers. Thus, an inconsistency was introduced: was a Type I exit worth 40 or 50 seats (or passengers)? This inconsistency not only remained uncorrected but, as discussed in Section 7.5.1, was actually amplified in 1957.

Adding a Type IV exit was good for 30 seats (69 to 99). Adding 4 inch (10 cm) of width and 4 inch of height to a Type II to make it a Type I was also good for 30 seats extra (39 to 69). These increments were not consistent with the performance of the exits. This new system also significantly changed the ratio of exits per passenger. For higher capacities up to one exit per 17 passengers was considered sufficient.

The number of exits for the ditching scenario, which was one emergency exit above the waterline for every 16 passengers, was now elevated to one *on each side* for every 35 passengers, except that an overhead hatch of Type III dimensions would be considered to be an acceptable alternative.

5.5.3.5 Other Changes 1951

5.5.3.5.1 Aisles, Passageways, Access, Assist Space

The 1951 draft release proposed a requirement for aisle width. A minimum of 14 inch (35.5 cm) was set. However, the final rule came with quite a more restrictive dimension, or actually two: 15 inch (37 cm) up to 25 inch (63.5 cm) from the floor and 20 inch (51 cm) above. The preamble to the final rule gave no explanation.

As per the new insights gained, no longer needed exits be installed per compartment. The only compartment-related requirement that remained was that there must be an unobstructed passageway between individual compartments of 20 inch (51 cm) wide. The same criteria—unobstructed and at least 20 inch wide—were now proposed for passageways giving access to Type I and Type II exits. In addition, space was required adjacent to exits with assisting means, except Type IV exits, to allow a crewmember to assist in the evacuation of passengers.

5.5.3.5.2 Marking and Lighting

On the subject of exit marking, it was added that the 'identity and location of emergency exits shall be recognizable from a distance equal to the width of the cabin'. 'The location of the emergency exit operating handle and the instructions for opening shall be marked on or adjacent to the exit and be readable from a distance of 30 inch' (76 cm). Where exits previously could be illuminated by means of luminous paint, the 1951 standards now required a source, or sources of light, with an energy supply independent of the main lighting system, to illuminate all emergency exit markings. 'Such lights shall be designed to function automatically in a crash landing and shall also be operable manually'.[93]

5.5.3.5.3 Locking Against Inadvertent Opening in Flight

A new element was that each exit was to have a means to lock it in flight so that it would not inadvertently open, with a means for the crew to ascertain whether the exits were indeed fully locked.

5.5.3.5.4 Crowding

A new requirement for opening external doors was that this be possible, from either inside or outside, even though persons may be crowding against the door from the inside. This requirement was not extended to emergency exits, as it was considered unlikely that crowding would occur at exits other than the main door.

First Wave (1945–1953)

5.5.3.5.5 Descent Assist Means

The criterion for when assist means, such as chutes, was now required for landplanes was significantly reduced from 10 ft (3 m) (with wheels retracted) to 6 ft (1.8 m) from the ground with the airplane on the ground and the landing gear extended. This applied to all types of exits, except Type IV, which was prescribed for over-the-wing applications, where it was assumed that evacuees could jump from the wing to the ground.

5.5.3.6 Not Changed

Not changed significantly compared to the 1945 requirements were those for the method of operation (the words 'not requiring exceptional effort' were added to 'simple and obvious') and for doors or exits becoming jammed. Also, the difference in approach between doors and exits remained. Doors were not necessarily seen as emergency exits.

5.5.3.7 Existing Aircraft Types

Concurrent with the development of the new rules and the insights gained with the research program, the CAB appreciated that action was needed to redefine maximum passenger capacities for existing large transport aircraft types. This coincided with a trend that higher-density seating arrangements were applied, the coach class.

In December 1951, with updates in May and July 1952, the CAB proposed a special CAR that essentially did the following:

- Recognize the maxima for the numbers of occupants earlier authorized.
- Set new capacities in a table listing, for each of the existing types, the maximum number of occupants (so crew and passengers).
- Allow eight additional occupants per additional exit above the number in the list.
- Require, when allowing additional occupants for aircraft where the ratio of occupants to exits in the list is greater than 14 to 1, an additional floor-level exit in the rearward portion of the cabin.
- Set a maximum of 115 occupants, unless there are at least two full-size door-type exits in the rearward portion of the cabin, one on each side of the fuselage.
- Alternatively, allow exits as per the new requirements for new aircraft types.

In the drafting stage, the proposal included an evacuation test that would allow higher capacities. However, based on comments received, this was deleted from the final rule when it appeared in September 1952.[94] The special CAR, initially numbered SR-387 (soon after re-numbered into SR-389), saw several iterations of the table and some of the conditions.

In 1957, a condition was added to reduce by 8 the number of occupants per exit when reducing the number of exits below that of the list. The table listed 16 airplane types. All but one of these stopped being operated many decades ago. The only type that is still in operation, even though sparsely and mainly for nostalgic flights, is the oldest from the list: the DC-3. In 1964, the contents of SR-389 were shifted to FAR 91.607, where it still sits.

5.5.4 Life Support

5.5.4.1 In Place by 1945

In the domain of life support, regulatory measures were in place in the U.S. by 1945 for:

- First-aid kit (in both design and operational requirements)
- For domestic and overseas operations when operating over water beyond gliding distance from land, except for landings and take-offs: life preservers or other adequate flotation devices, with a Very pistol or equivalent signal equipment (no distinction was made between landplanes and seaplanes)

- For domestic operations when operation above 10,000 ft. (3.048 m) for more than 30 minutes or above 12,000 ft. (3,658 m) for any length of time: oxygen apparatus and adequate supply of oxygen (see Chapter 6)

5.5.4.2 First-Aid Kit

Since the first requirement for a first-aid kit in 1927, it was left to each airline to decide on the contents of its first-aid kit. The broadly worded post-war requirement was for 'a conveniently accessible first-aid kit adequate for proper first-aid treatment of passengers and crew which shall contain medical equipment and supplies approved by the Administrator as suitable and sufficient for the category of operation involved'. To give guidance as to what would be approved, a detailed specification for the first-aid kit was published as policy material by the CAA in 1952 for all three operational CARs. Three different kit sets were prescribed, subject to passenger capacity (1 to 5, 5 to 25, or more than 25).[95]

5.5.4.3 Overwater and Survival Equipment

The simple pre-war measures for overwater equipment initially stayed so during the first wave. When sets of regulations for overseas (Part 41) and non-scheduled operations (Part 42) were added in 1945 and 1946, respectively, the pre-war requirements were copied and expanded with equipment not applicable to domestic operations but very much so for these: sufficient life rafts when flying long distances over water and 'as the Administrator designates' for long distances over uninhabited terrain.

In 1946, the first guidance material for life raft ancillaries such as a police whistle, sea marker dye, mirrors, fishing kit, and water stills appeared but only for Part 42.[96] This was expanded in 1949 when four different sets of survival equipment were specified: tropical land, frigid land, tropical water, and frigid water. Each prescribed equipment specific for the area such as rifles, mosquito headnets, blankets, snowshoes, seawater desalting kits, and survival guide books (general, jungle, arctic). For all areas but tropical land, a five-day supply of emergency food ration per person was prescribed.[97] Later, this was reduced to two-day portions.[98]

Pan Am, the pioneer U.S. airline for overseas operations, and subject to Part 41, not 42, published the contents of its survival kit on its safety pamphlet. It included all the items of the CAA guidance material, and more, such as a bible (see Figure 20.3 on page 290).

5.5.5 INFORMATION AND INSTRUCTIONS

5.5.5.1 In Place by 1945

In the domain of communication, the following regulatory measures were in place in the U.S. before 1945:

- A conspicuously located safety belt sign or signal
- No smoking placards in compartments where smoking is prohibited (CAR 04.38240).

5.5.5.2 Signs

Upon introduction of Part 41 in 1945, 'use oxygen equipment' signs were required, located in the cabin of non-pressurized aircraft when operating at altitudes above 12,000 ft. (3,658 m). However, this sign was not needed when 'a competent cabin attendant is provided to care for passengers'. For neither domestic operations (Part 61) nor non-scheduled operations (Part 42), such a sign was considered needed. It is not known whether they were actually installed. They were, however, decades later in all-freighter airplanes to inform cargo attendants (see Figure 5.10).

From 1949, next to the fasten seat belt sign, a lighted no smoking sign was now required for overseas operations, replacing the no smoking placards. For domestic operations, the sign was required

First Wave (1945–1953)   61

FIGURE 5.10 Don oxygen mask sign, Airbus A300–600F (photograph by the author).

only in berths, the rationale being that smoking was permitted only under the supervision of a crewmember who would tell when it was allowed.

In 1950, a consolidation was proposed of regulations for all scheduled operations, be it domestic or overseas, and merging them into a single part. As part of that, a more uniform requirement was proposed for the signs, as follows:[99]

> § 40.78 Passenger information for all operations. All aircraft shall be equipped with signs located in the passenger compartment in such a manner as to be visible to passengers and cabin attendants to notify such persons when smoking is prohibited, when safety belts should be fastened, and. where applicable, when oxygen should be used. These signs shall be capable of on-off operation by the crew. Additional means of informing passengers and cabin attendants of matters pertaining to safety, such as a public address system, may be used.

While the consolidation effort itself failed, this text appeared, in a more concise form, in the 1953 change of Part 40 that became effective in April 1954:[100]

> § 40.177 Passenger information for all operations. All airplanes shall be equipped with signs visible to passengers and cabin attendants to notify such persons when smoking is prohibited and when safety belts should be fastened. These signs shall be capable of on-off operation by the crew.

Part 41 kept its existing requirements; Part 42 remained without.

5.5.5.3 Pamphlets

Since its introduction in 1945, Part 41 requirements for airlines operating overseas (also known as the flag airlines) demanded that:

> Passengers shall be acquainted with the location of emergency exits, with emergency equipment provided for individual use, and with the procedure to be followed in the case of an emergency landing on the water.[101]

This requirement was generally met by the flag operators giving the passengers a safety pamphlet. Such pamphlets were typically one of the many leaflets in a flight kit that was either handed out before the flight or on board. The emphasis of the requirement was on the 'emergency landing on water', a scenario that at the time was considered to be survivable. For the non-scheduleds, a slightly differently phrased requirement was introduced in 1949, stating:

> The air carrier shall establish procedures for familiarizing passengers with the location and use of emergency equipment.[102]

No equivalent requirement existed for domestic operators until 1956. More on safety briefings and pamphlets appears in Chapter 20.

5.6 SUMMARY OF THE FIRST WAVE

In the period 1945 to 1953, cabin safety started to become recognized.

There were two major improvements in the area of impact protection. One was a new design performance requirement for safety belts, introduced in 1945. The belts were now aimed to protect the occupant from serious injuries to the head and other parts of the body. The other was the rise in 1952 of structural crash design loads from 6 to 9 g.

Flammability requirements for cabin interior materials, as well as test methods, were defined. These applied to both new and existing airplanes.

Research by NACA involving the deliberate crashing of airplanes yielded data as to how post-crash fires develop and affect survivability and escape. Estimates for the time that a crashed airplane could be evacuated were obtained, ranging from about one to five minutes.

With airplanes becoming of size, and having tricycle gears, distances from exits to the ground increased significantly. They could no longer be negotiated by a simple jump. Descent assist means of diverse kinds such as ropes and ladders were applied, but when the escape chute was invented in 1948, this quickly became the principal means of escape. Requirements for the exits themselves were defined in 1945. Following three accidents which were impact survivable but in which many occupants died of fire, evacuation research started. This was managed by Barry G. King of the CAA medical section and involved many parties, including airlines, a university, and the air force. It led to a major update of the exit regulations. These addressed such aspects as their location, number, size, ease of operation, marking, lighting, and accessibility. For location, number, and size, in 1951 a system of exit types was developed. Four types were defined (Types I, II, III, and IV), and a table was created specifying which type of exits to apply as a function of passenger seating capacity.

With airplanes becoming capable of flying longer distances, they increasingly crossed oceans and uninhabited land areas. This occasionally led to ditchings and landings remote from civilization. Airlines started to equip the airplanes accordingly. Survival gear was added, appropriate for the area overflown, be it water or land, tropical, or frigid. Passengers were given safety pamphlets with instructions on the location of exits and emergency equipment.

Separately, oxygen standards were set, both for non-pressurized and for pressurized airplanes.

NOTES

1. International Airworthiness Standards by Edward Warren in SAE Aerospace Journal, October 1945, p. 563.
2. Proceedings of the International Civil Aviation Conference, Chicago, Illinois, November 1—December 7, 1944, Department of State Publication 2820, 1948.
3. Uniquely Published in the Federal Register: 14 FR 3922.
4. Amdt 04-0.
5. Aviation Week, December 6, 1948.
6. Aviation Week, April 7, 1952, p. 54; Scandinavian Airline System, Aircraft Fleet Development 1946–2016, Birger Holmer, Ulf Abrahamsson, Bengt Olav Nas, Swedish Aviation Historical Society, 23 February 2016.
7. General Aircraft Crashworthiness, An Evaluation of FAA Safety Standards for Protection of Occupants in Crashes, by Richard G. Snyder, The Highway Safety Research Institute, Final Report UM-HSRI-81-10, p. 57, May 15, 1982.
8. www.icorsi.org/hugh-dehaven-1895-1980.
9. Special issue, Jerry Lederer: Mr. Aviation Safety, Flight Safety Digest August-September 2002, Flight Safety Foundation, p. 33.
10. Air Safety Board, Hearings Before a Subcommittee of the Committee on Interstate and Foreign Commerce, House of Representatives, 81st Congress, Second Session, February 14, 1950, p. 52.
11. CAB Accident Investigation Report, Eastern Air Lines, Inc., East Boston, Massachusetts, January 21, 1948, SA-162, Released April 26, 1948.
12. Aviation Week, May 10, 1948, p. 15.

First Wave (1945–1953)

13 CAB Accident Investigation Report American Airlines Inc., Dallas Tex, November 29, 1949, Released August 30, 1950.
14 Aircraft Emergency Evacuation, Operating Experience and Industrial Trials, Report No. 2, U.S. Department of Commerce, Civil Aeronautics Administration, Office of Aviation Safety, May 1952.
15 Air Safety Board, Hearings before a Subcommittee of the Committee on Interstate and Foreign Commerce, House of Representatives, 81st Congress, Second Session, March 13, 1950, p. 194.
16 An Experimental Plan for the Study of Emergency Evacuation of Aircraft, Barry G. King, Adopted April 18, 1950.
17 Report No. 2.
18 Aircraft Emergency Evacuation—A Method for Evaluating Devices, Procedures and Exit Provisions, CAA, Office of Aviation Safety, April 1951.
19 Search for F 3553 American Airlines Convair 240 Evacuation Test.
20 A Milestone of Aeromedical Research Contributions to Civil Aviation Safety: The 1000th Report in the CARI/OAM Series, William E. Collins, Katherine Wade, FAA CAMI, DOT/FAA/AM-05/3, March 2005.
21 Aircraft Ground Emergency Exit Design Considerations, John A. Roebuck, Jr., B.H. Levedahl, Human Factors Group, Interior Design Section, Transport Aircraft Engineering, Douglas Aircraft Co., Inc., in The Journal of the Human Factors and Ergonomics Society, September 1961.
22 Some Survival Lessons Learned from Recent Accidents, by Barry G. King, Presented at the Flight Safety Foundation Air Safety Seminar, Santa Fe, New Mexico, November 10–12, 1954.
23 A Report of Results and Conclusions from Tests on the Effect of Size of Doors and Windows on Emergency Escape Time, Preliminary Report, J.G. Slavin, George Washington University, September 4, 1951.
24 Engines and Innovation, Lewis Laboratory and American Propulsion Technology, Virginia P. Dawson, NASA SP-4306, 1991, p. 117.
25 Renamed Lewis Laboratory in 1948 after the death of George W. Lewis.
26 Analysis of Multiengine Transport Airplane Fire Records, Gerard J. Pesman, NACA RM E9J19, 1950, p. 16.
27 Pesman, 1950, p. 16.
28 Dawson, 1991, p. 119.
29 Facilities and Methods Used in Full-Scale Airplane Crash-Fire Investigation, Dugald O. Black. NACA RM E51L06, 1952.
30 Appraisal of Hazards to Human Survival in Airplane Crash Fires, by Gerard J. Pesman, Lewis Flight Propulsion Laboratory, NASA Technical Note 2996, September 1953.
31 CAR 04.51(c)(1), 1945.
32 CAM 42.21-1, 1946.
33 CAR 04.38220, 1945.
34 DR 46-8.
35 DR 47-9.
36 Aircraft Safety Belts, National Aerospace Standard (NAS) 802, January 1, 1950.
37 Amdt 4b-2 (1950).
38 DR 47-9.
39 Post-Mortem Examinations on Air-Crash Victims, British Medical Journal, September 22, 1951.
40 The Dangerous Safety-Belt, Scientific American, December 1951.
41 Safety-Belts Are Not Dangerous by Eugene F. DuBois, British Medical Journal, September 27, 1952.
42 Amdt 41-0 (1945), Amdt 40-43.
43 Supp. 3 to CAM 42 (1949).
44 CAR 04.260, 1945.
45 The phrase 'all combinations' was deleted two years later (Amdt 04b-5).
46 General Aircraft Crashworthiness, An Evaluation of FAA Safety Standards for Protection of Occupants in Crashes, by Richard G. Snyder, The Highway Safety Research Institute, Final Report UM-HSRI-81-10, May 15, 1981, p. 55.
47 Snyder, 1981, p. 57.
48 Human Factors in Air Transportation—Occupational Health and Safety, Ross A. McFarland, 1953, p. 556.
49 Amdt 4b-6 (1952).
50 45 FR 41439.
51 When separate airworthiness requirements for small airplanes were introduced in 1945, a forward load of 9.0 g was required.

52 Cabin Safety: "SAFER Committee" Update (Aircraft Passenger Seat Structural Design), Hearings Before the Subcommittee on Oversight and Review of the Committee on Public Works and Transportation, House of Representatives, 96th Congress, Second Session, p. 687.
53 CAR 04.38220, 1945.
54 DR 50-8.
55 CAR 04.510(j); 04.530(b), 1937.
56 CAR 61.792, 1937.
57 www.hdekker.info/Nieuwe%20map/1937.html#28.07.1937, Visited 3 June 2024.
58 International Civil Aviation Conference, Final Act and Related Documents, 1945, p. 213.
59 CAR 04-0.
60 The Aircraft Year Book for 1947, Aircraft Industries Association of America, Inc., p. 30.
61 CAB Accident Investigation report Eastern Airlines, Cheshire, Connecticut, 144-46, January 18, 1946.
62 Amdt 04-1 (of Part 04 as Promulgated on November 9, 1945).
63 Amdt 41-3, 42-2, 61-2.
64 Amdt 04-1 (of Part 04 as Promulgated on November 9, 1945), CAR 04.3824(c).
65 Amdt 04-1 (of Part 04 as Promulgated on November 9, 1945), CAR 04.3824(d).
66 Amdt 4b-6 (1952).
67 Aircraft Yearbook 1946, Aeronautical Chamber of Commerce of America, Inc., p. 206.
68 Human Factors in Air Transport Design, Ross A. McFarland, 1946, p. 646.
69 McFarland, 1946, p. 582.
70 CAR 04-0.
71 Some Survival Lessons Learned from Recent Accidents, by Barry G. King, Presented at the Flight Safety Foundation Air Safety Seminar, Santa Fe, New Mexico, November 10–12, 1954.
72 CAR 40.233, 1937.
73 Supp. 3 to CAM 42 (1949).
74 DR 43.
75 CAR 04.3821, 1945.
76 Amdt 4b-4 (1951).
77 CAR 04.3821, 1945.
78 CAR 04.38121, 1945.
79 CAR 04.38121, 1945.
80 Human Factors in Air Transport Design, Ross A. McFarland, 1946, p. 582.
81 Special Issue, Jerry Lederer: Mr. Aviation Safety, Flight Safety Digest August-September 2002, Flight Safety Foundation, p. 33.
82 'Krishner' was a typo for 'Kirchner'. The interview was audio taped and later transcribed.
83 Safety in Air Navigation, Hearings Before the Committee on Interstate and Foreign Commerce, House of Representatives, 80th Congress, First Session, Part 1, February 13, 1947.
84 McFarland, 1946, p. 583.
85 DR 50-8.
86 DR 51-6.
87 DR 51-8.
88 Chicago Convention Conference Proceedings, Vol. I, p. 299: U.S. Proposed Requirement 2.3164.
89 DR 51-8.
90 DR 51-8.
91 Amdt 4b-4 (1951).
92 DR 51-8.
93 Amdt 4b-4 (1951).
94 SR-387; SR-389.
95 Supp. 14 to CAM 41; Supp. 11 to CAM 42; Supp. 20 to CAM 61 (1952).
96 CAM 42, November 1, 1946.
97 Supp. 3 to CAM 42, 14 FR 7034.
98 Supp. 43 to CAM 42.
99 DR 50-8.
100 Amdt. 40-0, 1953.
101 CAR 41.507, 1945, later 41.127.
102 Revised Part 42, 42.59 (1949).

6 Oxygen

ABSTRACT

This chapter is entirely dedicated to oxygen provisions, the other half of the life support domain. Oxygen became topical in the mid-1930s when the improved performance of airplanes brought them to altitudes where oxygen was an issue. The requirements initially developed haphazardly. Ross A. McFarland, who joined an international altitude expedition in Chile in 1935, conducted pioneering research work on the subject. The first-pressurized air transport airplane, the Boeing 307, entered service in 1940. Immediately after World War Two, more pressurized airplanes became available. By 1950, oxygen requirements for both unpressurized and pressurized airplanes became stable. Operating ceilings were then about 25,000 ft. When turbine-engined airplanes (turboprops and jets) entered the market in the late 1950s, stricter oxygen provisions were required, including automatic drop-out oxygen masks. The 1950 requirements were updated in 1958 for that category of airplanes and have remained essentially unaltered. Since, only minor changes specific to some aspects were required. The chapter lists five types of oxygen supplies and reviews the excellent accident experience of in-flight decompressions. It concludes that the oxygen requirements as set out in the 1950s have worked well. Unlike the other cabin safety domains, where accidents drove developments, the requirements for oxygen provisions were proactive and 'first time right'.

6.1 OXYGEN BASICS

Before unveiling the history of oxygen regulations, a mini-lecture is presented to understand the basics. The air in the earth's atmosphere has a constant composition. It consists of various gases but primarily two: nitrogen, for circa 78%, and oxygen, for 20.95%. The remaining 1% is made up of argon (0.93%) and various other gases including much-discussed carbon dioxide (CO_2) as well as water vapor. This composition is perfect for sustaining life. Should the percentage of oxygen drop below this value, the lungs of humans, and other living creatures, start taking less oxygen from the air, especially when performing physical activity. At concentrations below 16%, this becomes noticeable. Concentrations below about 6% are not survivable. Higher than standard oxygen concentrations are less harmful but increase the risk of fire.

The air composition remains fairly constant, both horizontally across the earth's surface at sea level and vertically. At sea level, the pressure of the air is ideal for humans and other living creatures. With altitude increasing, the pressure drops. This is because there is less air above it, so there is less mass pushing on the air below it. This means that, even though the composition of the air remains constant with 20.95% oxygen in it, the amount of oxygen reduces with altitude.

The internationally accepted unit for pressure is Pascal (Pa). At sea level, the average air pressure is 101325 or 1013.25 hPa. However, for atmospheric pressure, other units are in use such as the millimeter mercury, or mmHg (1 mmHg = 133.1224 hPa). This unit is still used in medicine and is used here to illustrate the effects of altitude. At sea level, pressure is 760 mmHg. At that level, the partial pressure of oxygen is $0.209 \times 760 = 159$ mmHg.

Table 6.1 for various key altitudes gives the corresponding values for pressure, partial O_2 pressure in mmHg, and corresponding sea level oxygen concentrations ('equivalent O_2 percentage'). The latter is a good indicator. Remember from 16% down, there is noticeable deterioration; below 6%, it becomes non-survivable. It also gives geographical examples.

The phenomenon of less oxygen the higher one gets became known in the 19th century when manned balloons ascended to dangerous altitudes and caused fatalities. Humans have no primary senses for reduced oxygen levels. Oxygen itself, or air for that matter, is invisible, so a reduction

TABLE 6.1
Oxygen versus Altitude Data

Altitude		Pressure	Partial O$_2$ Pressure	Equivalent O$_2$ Percentage	Example
Feet	Meters	hPa	mmHg		(meters)
0	0	1,013	159	20.9	Sea level
8,000	2,438	753	118	15.4	Mexico City (2,230), Quito (2,400)
10,000	3,048	697	109	14.3	
13,000	3,962	620	97	12.7	El Alto, Bolivia (4,150)
14,000	4,267	595	93	12.3	Daocheng Yading, China (4,411)
16,404	5,000	540	84	11.3	Mont Blanc (4,810)
18,000	5,486	506	79	10.5	
19,685	6,000	472	74	9.8	Aucunquilcha mine, Chile (5,950)
22,966	7,000	411	64	8.5	
25,000	7,620	376	59	8.1	
30,000	9,144	301	47	6.3	Mount Everest (8,848)
35,000	10,668	238	38	4.9	
40,000	12,192	187	29		
50,000	15,240	120			
60,000	18,288	72			

cannot be seen. Neither can the other senses discern it. And neither are there clear secondary symptoms such as pain. However, there are some more subtle indicators, such as loss of visual acuity, paralysis of arms and legs, and fingers and nails becoming pink that can alert a trained person in time that oxygen deprivation is imminent.

How long can humans function at altitudes when not provided with supplementary oxygen? Until the 1930s, this was not known.

6.2 EXPERIMENTING

The airliners that were introduced in the mid-1930s such as the Boeing 247 (1933) and Douglas DC-2 (1934) had ceilings much higher than their predecessors. They could fly well higher than 20,000 ft. (6,096 m). This enabled them to cross mountainous areas such as the Alps in Europe, the Rocky Mountains in the western U.S., and the Andes in South America, were it not that the lack of oxygen at those altitudes formed an obstacle. But to what extent was still unknown. Table 6.1 could only be made following experiments that were still due.

In appreciation of airliners capable of flying higher, the U.S. Bureau of Air Commerce introduced in October 1934 a section on maximum altitudes of flight,[1] initially only for 'scheduled operation of inter-state air-line services'. This section primarily dealt with oxygen provision:

> Oxygen and/or supercharged cabins shall be provided for crew and passengers above 18,000 feet or when operations are for more than 15 minutes above 14,000 feet, and such requirements shall be made part of the Operations Manual and approved by the Bureau of Air Commerce.
>
> If passengers' consent is obtained as a safety measure, flights for more than 15 minutes above 14,000 feet may be made without providing oxygen.

Both the 18,000 ft. and the 14,000 ft. limits, by later standards, were very high. They did not match human needs at those altitudes, but at the time there was a lot of ignorance on the subject, on the part of both the Bureau and pilots. Pilots believed they were not seriously affected. And in the absence of cabin crew, nobody observed how passengers reacted to these altitudes.[2] Little more than amazing is the notion that passengers could opt and consent to flying at a higher altitude and/or for a longer duration than prescribed. As if passengers would know the safety consequences when even science did not.

In 1933, Panagra, for the 20- to 30-minute crossing of the Andes at altitudes of 14,500 ft. (4,420 m) or above, started to offer oxygen to pilots by means of a pipestem and to passengers by means of a tube, both connected to oxygen cylinders.[3] Somewhat later, the use of oxygen on board Pan Am DC-3s crossing the Andes at 18,000 ft. en route from Santiago to Buenos Aires was described at the time as such:

> New planes purchased for the service in 1937 are Douglas DC-3 transports, especially fitted out for this high altitude operation with the latest thing in supercharged engines and also with improved oxygen equipment for passengers. Flying at such altitudes it is not unusual for the passengers to require an occasional whiff of oxygen to keep him feeling fit.[4]

Note the use of the word 'whiff', which matched the period attitude toward the use of oxygen.

In 1935, before starting a route across the Alps to Milan, where the flight altitude would be 6,000 m, KLM's medical department experimented with two options. One was that supplemental oxygen was supplied in the cabin at large when above a certain altitude. The other was to individually provide oxygen to passengers by means of tubes connected to an oxygen cylinder. Both were tested and it was decided to apply the latter. The first option was rejected as it would prevent proper ventilation of the cabin. Passengers were briefed by a mechanic or cabin attendant before the flight on how to use the tubes. Once at an altitude of 3,500 m (11,482 ft.), a pamphlet was then issued to passengers to use it.[5] It had the following text, in five languages:

> The aeroplane has by now reached the altitude at which, according to medical regulations, extra oxygen may be obtained. Passengers are requested to follow the instructions of the stewardess.

KLM's early stewardess Bongertman, in her 1936 book, complained that passengers often were stubborn. They told her that they did not need oxygen. Also in the U.S. and South America, there were reports that both crew and passengers did not always take the warnings seriously. In the absence of clear indicators of upcoming oxygen deprivation, they did not always don their masks when they should have.[6]

In 1935, Ross McFarland joined the International High Altitude Expedition in Chile to study the effects of altitude and oxygen deprivation on humans. Together with scientists from Denmark, the UK, and the U.S., he went to Aucunquilcha in the Antafogasta region, a volcano close to the border with Bolivia.[7] Here, a sulfur mine with an aerial tramway was in operation at an altitude of just below 6,000 m (19,685 ft.). The scientific expedition lasted several months. Experiments were carried out at various altitudes, ranging from 9,200 ft. (2,804 m) to 20,150 ft. (6,142 m). The main laboratory was at 17,500 ft. (5,334 m) where McFarland said that 'contrary to expectations based on the experience of previous scientific expeditions, the majority of the party were able to live very comfortable'.[8] This was also the altitude where the local miners lived, who commuted daily to the mines.

McFarland became the key expert on the subject and, more generally, on human factors and aerospace medicine. His 1953 book *Human Factors in Air Transportation* became the textbook that no airline medical department could afford not to have.

In the U.S., in the 1930s, airlines crossing the Rocky Mountains typically flew at altitudes of 12,500 ft. (3,810 m) and on rare occasions up to 14,000 ft. (4,267 m). Oxygen was not used on these flights. There are unconfirmed reports that this may have caused some fatal accidents.

Experiments in the U.S. with oxygen on board were done by TWA in 1936. A non-passenger, laboratory Northrop Gamma was flown to 35,000 ft. altitude and used 'to chart the problems which must be solved before passengers can be carried at those levels'.[9]

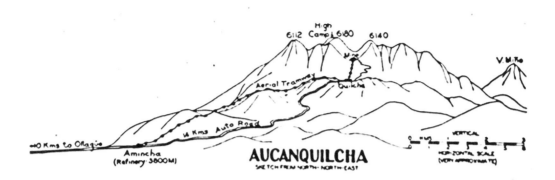

FIGURE 6.1 Sketch of Aucanquilcha showing the aerial tramway and the locations of the mine and the high camp (Wright State University, Dayton, Ohio, University Libraries' Special Collections and Archives, Ross McFarland Collection).

In a 1936 revision of the requirements for interstate airlines, the 18,000 ft. limit became more firm.[10] It could only be exceeded by permission and when oxygen was provided. There was no requirement though stipulating its use. The time between 15,000 and 18,000 ft. should be kept to a minimum and only 'as may be necessary to clear obstructions to flight and to avoid hazardous weather conditions'. This requirement actually relaxed that of 1934 in that no longer was oxygen equipment required when flying above 14,000 ft. for more than 15 minutes. New was a requirement for a 'competent cabin attendant' for flights between 15,000 and 18,000 ft. His or her function was loosely described as 'to observe and care for passengers'. There was no mention of any oxygen equipment for, or use by, that cabin attendant. Both the 1934 and 1936 regulations offered, as an alternative to the operational restrictions, a 'supercharged' cabin. In that case, no oxygen was required at all. However, at the time there were no aircraft with 'supercharged', or pressurized, cabins. This is probably the first example where a cabin safety requirement pre-dated the actual application of new technology.

The new CAR of 1937 changed the requirement for oxygen above 18,000 ft. into a prohibition to fly above that altitude, except with prior permission in the form of a 'weather competency letter'. Oxygen was no longer prescribed. Similarly, the more than 15 minutes at 14,000 ft provision was changed into a prohibition to fly above 15,000 ft. 'except for the periods of time which are necessary to clear obstructions to flight and to avoid hazardous weather conditions'.[11] Again, no oxygen was prescribed, but instead 'a competent cabin attendant to observe and care for the passengers'.

Northwest Airlines announced that, as the first airline, it 'began installation of oxygen equipment on its planes in February 1939 after a test flight in which one of the company's planes climbed to 20,200 ft with no discomfort to passengers or crew'.[12]

> Taken through a special mask developed by Dr. Lovelace and his associates oxygen was easily administered to those needing or desiring it. The mask may be worn during eating, smoking or talking. To a metal pipe, running from the oxygen bottle placed in the lavatory compartment of the Northwest airliners, was attached a small rubber tube from the mask.

'Dr. Lovelace pointed out after the test flight that the installation of the equipment would not necessarily mean that all persons flying at high altitudes would be given oxygen'. He said:

> Oxygen is necessary to the physical requirements of the individual. Some persons require it at lower altitudes than other; still others can stand atmospheric pressure at high altitudes without any oxygen. Its installation is for the comfort of the passenger. It is easier to stand the high sub-stratosphere flying by using oxygen. And when descending, a mixture of oxygen and helium helps to equalize air pressure

on one's ears. We believe this installation is very noteworthy. Northwest Airlines is the first air line to use it.

In 1937, the Bureau of Air Commerce sponsored an extensive investigation, conducted by Ross McFarland, of the effects of altitude on the average airline passenger. This involved more than 200 subjects between the ages of 18 and 72 years. A pressure chamber at Columbia University was used for simulating altitudes up to 18,000 ft. Both slow and rapid ascents were made, but rapid descents were not. Key altitudes at which measurements were made were 10,000, 12,000, 14,000, and 16,000 ft.

Possibly influenced by the work of McFarland, in May 1941 the CAB issued a firm requirement for the use of 'oxygen apparatus'.[13] It applied to pilots of domestic scheduled air transportation when flying above 12,000 ft. or after 30 minutes above 10,000 ft. This requirement did not extend to passengers, but later in the same year the CAB issued a maximum ceiling for scheduled air carriers of 17,000 ft. and addressed passengers. But rather than prescribing oxygen for them, the CAB continued to require 'a competent cabin attendant to care for passengers'. This time from a much lower altitude onward: 12.000 ft. instead of 15,000 ft. as previously. The nature of the care was not specified further.

6.3 PRESSURIZING THE CABIN

The practice of crew, and, where applicable, passengers using oxygen was far from ideal. The performance of airplanes developed further and allowed higher flight altitudes to take advantage of less weather. This led to the invention of pressurization of the cabin. This had the advantage that passengers were no longer tied to their seats to use oxygen from masks that they might not find hygienic or even understand how to use. The Boeing 307 was the first airliner with a pressurized cabin. It started airline operations with Pan Am and TWA in 1940 but due to the outbreak of World War Two did not enter widespread civil operation. Although built in limited numbers, it formed a major milestone in the development of civil aviation. Until the altitude of 8,000 ft. the pressure in the cabin was the same as outside. Above that, the cabin pressure decreased less than outside. At 16,000 ft. outside pressure, the cabin pressure was at 10,000 ft. and at 20,000 ft. outside the cabin was at 12,400 ft. Above that, oxygen would need to be used. During one flight with McFarland as an observer on board, a window was purposely broken to see what would happen. Sudden fogging of all of the windows and cabin occurred from the rapid change of temperature.[14]

During the war, cabin pressurization was further developed. The Boeing B-29 bomber had two compartments that were pressurized, thus relieving the crew to constantly be on oxygen when on bombing missions to Japan flying at high altitudes to avoid enemy contact. The pressure differential was significantly higher than on the 307: 6.55 psi (45 kPa) as opposed to 2.5 psi (17 kPa), allowing a cabin altitude of 8,000 ft. up to a flight altitude of 30,000 ft.

The Lockheed Constellation, also developed during the war, became the first-pressurized airliner that could be put to use on long-distance, international flights. This happened in late 1945, initially between the U.S. and Europe. It had a higher pressure differential ratio than the Boeing 307, allowing a flight at a true altitude of 20,000 ft. with the cabin at 8,000 ft.

At the same time, the CAB issued new sets of Civil Air Regulations specific for overseas operations (Part 41) and for non-scheduled operations (Part 42).[15] With respect to oxygen supply, Part 41 had requirements for both non-pressurized and pressurized airplanes, but Part 42 was only for non-pressurized airplanes.

For non-pressurized airplanes, both Part 41 and 42 copied the 1941 requirements of Part 61 for domestic operations as far as flight crew was concerned. For passengers, both parts prescribed oxygen when flying above 12,000 ft., but for domestic operations (Part 61) no oxygen for passengers was prescribed. Instead, a competent cabin attendant remained required for operations above that altitude.[16] This cabin attendant was also prescribed for overseas operations (Part 41) but could be traded in for a 'use oxygen equipment' sign in the cabin. This gives some insight into what the CAB at the time considered 'care': apparently it was only the signal function: informing passengers when to use oxygen. In practice, all U.S. overseas carriers employed such personnel.

For pressurized airplanes (only Part 41, overseas), the oxygen supply for crew and passengers needed to be the same for non-pressurized airplanes when operating above 10,000 ft. When the flight would exceed an altitude of 18,000 ft., an additional, adequate emergency oxygen supply was required, but only for the flight crew and apparently to cover the scenario of depressurization and emergency descent.

6.4 FIRMING THE OXYGEN REGULATIONS

6.4.1 Toward Three Altitude Bands

In the early post-war years, the CAB saw a need for re-arranging the regulations for oxygen. However, it struggled. In a 1947 proposal, circulated to 'those interested in the subject matter' (and not published in the Federal Register), it proposed a mix of rules for both unpressurized and pressurized ('supercharged') cabins.[17] One comment to an earlier, lighter, version of May 1946, neither published in the Federal Register, was that no oxygen be provided for passengers at altitudes below 14,000 ft. The CAB, however, based on a 'careful review of medical evidence', argued that there was 'an increase in workload of the heart of about 200% at 14,000 feet'. 'Since among passengers are included individuals with heart and lung ailments', 'a small amount of oxygen appears necessary'. It proposed 12,000 ft as 'a reasonable limiting altitude above which oxygen should be available for all passengers'. This would apply to unpressurized airplanes, of which there were still many flying around. This proposal was not followed up. It was succeeded in 1949 by another proposal, in which two altitude bands, with escalating oxygen requirements, were proposed.[18] A lower band and an upper band. The lower band ranged from 8,000 to 14,000 ft. Oxygen was specified for 10% of the number of passenger seats but only after 30 minutes of flying in that band. The upper band was above 14,000 ft., for which oxygen for all passengers was specified. When this proposal was transformed into a rule, made applicable, and consistent to all three kinds of operation (domestic, international, irregular), and effective on March 1, 1950, there were two changes.[19] The 10% of the lower band was now linked to the actual number of passengers carried, not the number of seats. The upper band (14,000 ft. and above) was split in two. A small band between 14,000 and 15,000 ft. was created to

> permit an air carrier to operate older-type aircraft at such altitudes for the short periods of time necessary to clear terrain or to fly over localized weather or traffic conditions without imposing the economic penalty that strict compliance with these regulations would require and which flight experience in the past several years would not indicate to be necessary.[20]

In this middle band, oxygen was not required for all passengers but only for 30%. Above that, oxygen was required for all passengers. Cabin attendants were not addressed, as they were not required at the time.

The introduction of these standards ended a period of 16 years (1934–1950) of inconsistent, constantly changing standards for unpressurized airplanes. The new requirements brought stability and coherence. Table 6.2 summarizes the developments.

6.4.2 Pressurized Airplanes

Shortly after the introduction of pressurized airplanes, depressurization events started to occur. These were not expected and suddenly exposed a need for regulations for this failure condition. In 1947 the CAB proposed that no oxygen needed to be available for passengers when 'the altitude at the time of failure is less than 18,000 feet and an altitude of 12,000 feet or less can be attained within 6 minutes from the time of such failure'.[21] The 12,000 ft. altitude coincided with the limiting

TABLE 6.2
U.S. Regulatory Developments for Non-pressurized Airplanes

Altitudes in Feet	1934	1936	1937	1941	1945/46	1950
Aeronautics Bulletin/CAR	7-E	7-E	61	61	41,42	41,42,61
Oxygen required when flying above	18,000	18,000	—	—	—	—
Oxygen required after 15 minutes except with passenger consent when flying above	14,000	—	—	—	—	—
Except per prior permission, flying prohibited above	—	—	18,000	17,000	—	—
Except for obstructions or weather, flying prohibited above	—	—	15,000	—	—	—
Competent cabin attendant required when flying above	—	15,000	15,000	12,000	12,000	—
Use oxygen sign as an alternative when flying above (Part 41 only)	—	—	—	—	12,000	—
Supply of oxygen required when flying above	—	—	—	—	12,000	—
Oxygen supply after 30 minutes for 10% of occupants, when flying	—	—	—	—	—	>8,000, ≤14,000
Oxygen supply for 30% of occupants, when flying	—	—	—	—	—	>14,000, ≤15,000
Oxygen supply for all occupants, when flying above	—	—	—	—	—	15,000

altitude as proposed for non-pressurized airplanes. In a successive proposal, the emergency descent profile was revised to be from 25,000 to 14,000 ft. within four minutes.[22] If such descent was not possible, the proposal asked for oxygen after those four minutes for all passengers, except 'on those particular routes where the Administrator finds that flight above 14,000 feet would be of [. . .] short duration'. In other cases, when the post-depressurization flight continued at altitudes above 8,000 ft. for some time, the new three-altitude-bands rules for unpressurized airplanes applied.

The first pressurized airplane, the Boeing 307, only had a limited capability. At higher altitudes, it could not maintain the cabin pressure altitude below 8,000 ft. All subsequent airplanes performed better and were designed to keep that cabin altitude up to their flight ceiling or were even better than that and could maintain a lower cabin altitude. In 1957, this was reflected in the regulations when a standard was introduced for pressurized airplanes that set a cabin pressure altitude of 8,000 ft. as a design maximum.[23]

6.4.3 Turbine-Powered Airplanes

In the late 1950s, turbine-powered airliners were introduced. These had operating ceilings significantly higher than the piston-engined machines. This resulted in a major revision of both the design and operational oxygen standards that were adopted in 1958.[24] These changes centered on the issue of depressurization at altitude. It was recognized that at high altitudes oxygen would need to be urgently furnished to all occupants during the descent to a habitable environment. The changes thus focused on operations above 25,000 ft. and left untouched the requirements for reciprocating engine airplanes, even when above 25,000 ft., and airplanes not flying above 25,000 ft.

For flight crew, it was required that the pilot at the controls wore an oxygen mask at all times, or had one immediately available, when flying above 25,000 ft. For other flight crewmembers, it needed to be available timely. Later, and based on positive experience, the 25,000 ft. criterion was lifted several times. In 2020, ordered by Congress via the FAA Reauthorization Act of 2018, the FAA raised the limit for a pilot actively wearing an oxygen mask to 41,000 ft. or above and only when the other pilot is temporarily not in the cockpit.[25]

For cabin attendants (as they were referred to then), portable oxygen equipment became required, except when extra outlets of the passenger system would be immediately available regardless of the location of the cabin attendant at the time of depressurization.

For passengers, oxygen dispensing units were devised for airplanes certificated to fly above 25,000 ft., located within reach of each passenger, and immediately available in case of depressurization. In airplanes certificated to fly above 30,000 ft. they needed to be automatically presented. A supply of at least ten minutes was prescribed. More was required when the airplane was not able to descend to below 14,000 ft. within those ten minutes. This might be the case due to terrain or other operational reasons. This new regulation prompted the invention of oxygen boxes in the vicinity of all passenger seats plus in the lavatories. The drop-out system was invented.

Also introduced was first-aid oxygen, to cater to passengers suffering from disabilities that require undiluted oxygen following the rapid descent. A supply for 2% of the passengers was prescribed. In exchange, the base altitude of 8,000 ft. was raised to 10,000 ft.

When an airplane operated above 25,000 ft., the same three bands and percentages as outlined in Section 6.4.1 applied for flights after depressurization and emergency descent, except that the four-minute lapse did not apply.

These standards applied to operators of large turbine aircraft, initially under the three CARs (40, 41, 42) and later Part 121. For operations with commuter aircraft, under Part 135, introduced in 1964, different oxygen regulations applied. These were simpler. For Part 121, they distinguished between pressurized and non-pressurized airplanes, but the kind of engine mode was not a discriminant. Most Part 135 operations were done using airplanes with two turboprop engines and passenger seating capacities of up to 19 and no cabin crew. The 25,000 ft. cut-off applied as well, but the quick descent option was slightly more lenient. Rather than being capable of descending to 14,000 ft. in four minutes, for Part 135 operations it was only to 15,000 ft. in four minutes. The rationale for this difference was not documented in the regulations drafting history.

These 1950 and 1958 requirements in essence still stand in the U.S. in 2024. Other countries had slightly different standards (see Section 14.4.2).

6.5 TYPES OF OXYGEN SUPPLY FOR PASSENGERS

How have airplane oxygen systems for passenger use developed over the years?

Five types could be discerned:

- Portable oxygen bottles. Airplanes with an operational ceiling of up to 25,000 ft., and capable of a quick descent, typically had a few portable bottles with oxygen under pressure. This satisfied the rule of a 30-minute supply for 10% of the passengers. Portable oxygen bottles are also employed for use by cabin crew walking around, or for therapeutic oxygen for passengers still in need of oxygen after an emergency descent following a decompression.
- Central bottles with gaseous oxygen under pressure with a piping system delivering oxygen to outlets, with a plug-in system. This is the next level, typically employed on commuter

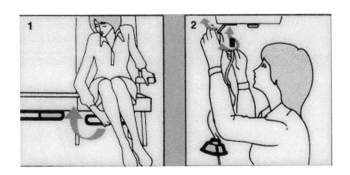

FIGURE 6.2 Oxygen equipment DLT Fokker 50 safety card (1988).

and regional airplanes which do not operate higher than 30,000 ft., so they do not require automatic deployment. It is also used on regional aircraft with a ceiling of 25,000 ft. when no descent to four minutes would be possible, or when specifically required by the local aviation authority. It has the advantage that no bottles need to be carried for passengers. The location of the mask varies from under the seat to centrally stored and distributed by the cabin crew. Similarly, the plugging of the mask into the socket is tasked to either the cabin crew or the passenger.

- Central bottles with gaseous oxygen under pressure with a piping system delivering oxygen to automatically deployable masks. This method was widely used on first- and second-generation jets such as the Boeing 707, 727, and early models of the 737 and 747, the Douglas DC-8 and DC-9. The location of the masks typically was in units located overhead of the passengers, although in some cases the masks were seat back mounted.
- Chemical oxygen generator. This method relies on a chemical reaction of two substances interacting and thereby producing oxygen. This means no oxygen needs to be stored. The generators are stowed locally, typically in the passenger service units above the seat rows. It was first employed in civil aviation in 1971 on the Douglas DC-10 and Lockheed L-1011, where it was stowed in the seats.

  This concept, which was earlier developed for submarine applications, became the most widely used for jet airplanes. The generator system is light and has the advantage that it does not require any piping nor does it store oxygen. Once the system is activated, for example, by pulling the mask and the attached lanyard, oxygen is generated in a chemical process and then flows continuously until depletion. This is typically for 12 to 15 minutes, so sufficient for a descent from maximum operating altitude to a safe altitude. Some airlines that have routes over high terrain, where no such descent can immediately take place, specify a higher duration of up to 22 minutes. A disadvantage is that the chemical reaction is exothermic, in other words produces heat.
- Small bottles with pulse supply. This is the latest version, first introduced on the Boeing 787 when it entered service in 2010. It uses small bottles, locally stowed overhead seat rows. It has an electronics-controlled system that monitors when the user inhales and thus needs oxygen. This makes it more efficient than a continuous flow system such as the chemical generators or the gaseous oxygen bottle systems.

6.6 SURVIVABILITY OF DECOMPRESSIONS

How did the pressurized airplanes perform in the case of a decompression? And were the oxygen provisions adequate?

With both the concept of cabin pressurization and oxygen provisions still fresh, McFarland in 1953 posed these questions and tried to answer them. Up to September 1952, he found there had been 16 rapid decompressions. They were caused by door problems—in some cases resulting in the door opening in flight—the loss of an astrodome, failure of a window, or a propeller blade entering the fuselage. The altitude where this happened typically was 20,000 ft. with one at 23,500 ft. Four persons were killed in these accidents, but not because of lack of oxygen. They were either blown out of the aircraft through the open door or astrodome or struck by a propeller blade. McFarland noted that 'none of the passengers experienced any discomfort due to changes in pressure alone, although the outrush of air and the sudden descent of the airplane gave rise to considerable apprehension'.[26] McFarland predicted that a decompression at higher altitudes could, however, be more dramatic and suggested that a built-in oxygen system with individual outlets at each seat be provided. Tests in 1948 with chemical oxygen generators containing pressed and crystallized potassium superoxide were promising.

In 1971, in the Harry G. Armstrong lecture, and with the benefit of data accumulated for 15 more years, including for the higher flying jets, McFarland repeated his survey of rapid decompressions.

He counted approximately ten decompressions with oxygen mask deployments per year in the U.S., all without serious medical problems.[27] This number and result were confirmed by FAA and NTSB data.[28]

In 1976, the NTSB investigated four rapid decompressions on the Douglas DC-10 and Lockheed L-1011, with chemically generated oxygen systems that had occurred in the U.S. in 1973 (April 1 and November 3), 1974 (October 3), and 1975 (May 1). In one case, where the cabin pressure altitude had reached 25,000 ft., only 2 out of 53 passengers used the masks correctly. One flight attendant, who was in the lower lobe galley, temporarily lost consciousness. In another case, in which the cabin pressure altitude reached 18,000 ft., only 2 out of 180 passengers properly actuated and donned masks without assistance from flight attendants. In the third case, passenger reaction was generally good except that some donned the mask wrongly and that other masks did not deploy. The most serious of the four cases was a decompression due to an uncontained engine failure with fragments penetrating the fuselage while at 39,000 ft. altitude. The cabin pressure peaked at 34,000 ft. and stayed above 30,000 ft. for one minute and above 25,000 ft. for more than two minutes. One passenger was ejected through a broken window. Some oxygen masks only deployed after three minutes, causing flight attendants and passengers to force open the seat-mounted oxygen compartments. This resulted in some cases in the generators causing burns to upholstery. Again, not all passengers knew how to use the masks. Two flight attendants in the lower galley lost consciousness as did three passengers who were standing in the main cabin. They all recovered.

It is striking that the poor performance of passengers in serving themselves oxygen did not harm. Apparently, there is more resilience in humans than was thought. This was dramatically demonstrated in the much-publicized accident of a high-cycle Boeing 737 of Aloha Airlines in April 1988. At 24,000 ft. (7,315 m) altitude, the aircraft lost its roof along the length of the forward cabin, about 18 ft. (5.5 m) long. This instantly exposed all cabin occupants to ambient pressure. The roof rupture disabled the oxygen system, so no masks were presented. Yet, there were no reports of hypoxia.[29] One flight attendant was ejected, but an otherwise safe landing could be made and there were no further fatalities.

A review by Fokker in 1990 of data from three different sources identified five fatalities and one serious injury due to decompressions or, in one case, failure to pressurize.[30] Three of the five fatalities were passengers, in one case with a confirmed medical condition.

1975 May 7: Boeing 707, passenger flight, over Canada. Flight altitude 10,650 m (35,000 ft.), cabin altitude 1,700 m (5,500 ft.): cabin altitude climbed sharply due to outflow valve failure. Emergency descent to 20,000 ft., with cabin altitude peak at 4,200 m (13,800 ft.). When reaching 20,000 ft., a 71-year-old man with a cardiac problem was found slumped over in his seat and dead.

1976 June 8: Boeing 737, ferry flight, USA. The pressure controller is shorted by water ingestion, giving a signal to the outflow valve to open. Cabin altitude went from about 2,450 m (8,000 ft.) to 4,270–4,880 m (14–16,000 ft.) at a rate of 20–25 m/s (4,000–5,000 ft./min). One of the six airline employees on board was hospitalized due to a collapsed lung condition, for which he had a medical history.

1977 November 3: Boeing 747, passenger flight, over Yugoslavia. Depressurization at 33,000 ft. Emergency descent to 14,000 ft. One passenger was taken ill and subsequently died.

1982 November 11: Boeing 707, cargo flight, USA: Cabin pressure drop during climb out. All crewmembers donned oxygen and the cabin altitude stabilized at 20,000 ft. About 40 minutes from the destination trainee flight engineer slumped down. Emergency descent was made and the trainee was taken to the hospital where he died later in the day. Death was due to aeroembolism. The trainee had a history of seizures and loss of consciousness following decompression.

1989 February 9: Douglas DC-9. Cargo flight, USA. Unknown to pilots, the hatch in the aft pressure bulkhead had been removed for maintenance and was not re-installed. During the initial climb cabin would not pressurize but the pilot ordered the co-pilot to continue to the assigned flight level 330 (33,000 ft.). Co-pilot reluctantly complied. The pilot left the cockpit with a portable oxygen bottle with a 15-minute supply but did not return. Some 30 minutes later, the co-pilot then descended 13,000 ft. and left the cockpit. He found the pilot with his foot entangled in a cargo net covering a pallet. The pilot had died from hypoxia.

1989 March 9: Boeing 737: Passenger flight, USA. The crew lost control of cabin pressure at FL 130. It climbed from 13,000 ft. to 31,000 ft. in a very short time. Masks were deployed, but one passenger became ill and later died in hospital.

Around 2001, FAA's ARAC did a comprehensive assessment of the frequency and nature of the need for supplemental oxygen systems in service. It identified 2,800 instances over a 40-year period and categorized them by cause, severity, and consequence. The majority of these instances were caused by malfunctions in the cabin pressurization system. However, in none of those 2,800 instances was there a loss of life reported due to lack of oxygen.[31]

The Aviation Herald has a very comprehensive online list of aviation occurrences since 1994.[32] It has no records of fatalities due to lack of oxygen.

These data indicate that the passenger fatality rate owing to hypoxia is extremely low. Apparently, the standards as set in 1950, and even more those in 1958 for the jets, were 'first time right'.

Although not by lack of oxygen following a decompression, airplane oxygen systems have caused fatalities. While these fall outside the definition of cabin safety, they are worth mentioning. In several cases of depressurization, or failure to pressurize, pilots became incapacitated and thus were no longer able to fly the airplane, eventually resulting in a crash. This occurred in 2005 to a Helios Airways Boeing 737 flying from Cyprus that, after two hours, when its fuel had depleted, crashed in Greece. Several corporate jets suffered the same fate. A different scenario evolved in 1996 when a Valujet Douglas DC-9 crashed in the Everglades in Florida as a result of a fire that had quickly developed in the forward cargo compartment. Chemical oxygen generators had been loosely stowed there, in spite of dangerous goods regulations, and got activated. The exothermic reaction started a fire that within minutes developed and made the airplane unflyable.

There have been crashes where oxygen cylinders were ruptured and contributed to a fire. An example was the collision at Los Angeles on February 1, 1991. In addition, there have been quite a number of cases of aircraft destroyed on the ground by fire during oxygen replenishing servicing.

6.7 LATER REGULATORY UPDATES

The 1950 and 1958 regulations still stand and, as demonstrated in Section 6.6, for good reasons as they were first time right. Since then, the FAA has issued a number of regulatory updates. These were in most cases not necessarily to further improve survivability but rather in response to societal and technical developments.

6.7.1 MEDICAL OXYGEN

In the 1970s, passengers who needed oxygen for medical reasons increasingly asked airlines for permission to bring their own oxygen equipment on board. As this posed safety risks and there were no rules allowing it, such requests had to be denied. The Air Transport Association petitioned for rulemaking with the FAA. This resulted in a 1974 regulation allowing such oxygen on board, provided it was controlled by the airline.[33] Some 20 years later, a new method became available for providing medical oxygen: portable oxygen concentrators (POC). Rather than containing oxygen, these devices work by filtering nitrogen from the air and providing the POC user with oxygen at a concentration of approximately 90%. Thus, POCs do not require the same level of special handling as compressed oxygen. Yet, they still needed regulatory acceptance. Initially, in the U.S. this was done by the FAA permitting such devices by make and model. Later, acceptance criteria were set, which eased the administrative process.[34]

6.7.2 Masks Connected to Portable Oxygen Equipment

A rare amendment to the traditional oxygen standards resulted from another accident near Hawaii that involved a sudden hole in the fuselage. Ten months after the Aloha accident, a cargo door of a 747 flying at about 23,000 ft. (7,010 m) blew open, taking with it fuselage skin of about 10 by 15 ft (3 by 5 m). Nine passengers were ejected, but again the pilots were able to land the crippled aircraft. Even though oxygen bottles were required to 'be immediately available to flight attendants', they were not as the masks were not attached to the regulators. The NTSB issued a recommendation and the pertinent FAR was corrected, albeit that it only became effective 16¾ years after the accident.[35]

6.7.3 High-Elevation Airports

The pressure inside the cabin of airplanes must not exceed that equivalent to 8,000 ft. A warning must be given to the pilots when it exceeds 10,000 ft. But what when an airplane goes to an airport with a higher elevation? There are numerous such airports in the world, with some even at an elevation where the oxygen system would automatically deploy. Examples are several airports in Tibet, China which are above 4,000 meters, the highest lying at 4,411 meters (14,472 ft.): Daocheng. Outside China, Bolivia's El Alto is the highest at just above 4,000 meters. In the U.S. the highest airport is at 2,767 meters (9,078 ft.). For many years, the FAA for airplanes that operated at such airports issued exemptions. In 2023, this was formally codified by the FAA, obviating the need for issuing exemptions.[36]

6.7.4 Higher-Altitude Operations

The regulations introduced in 1958 for the jets assumed maximum operating altitudes in the region of 41,000/42,000 ft. Since, there have been airplanes that fly much higher, up to 51,000 ft. The hypoxia risks to occupants in case of decompression at such altitudes are much more severe. Initially on a case-by-case basis, but later by means of a standard issued in 1996, the FAA required additional safeguards for such operations.[37] They required that the airplane design be such that it is extremely improbable that in the case of decompression, the cabin altitude reaches 40,000 ft. or higher. Additionally, during the descent, the cabin altitude may not be above 25,000 ft. for more than two minutes. In setting these altitudes and times, the FAA used the concept of 'Time of Safe Unconsciousness', as developed by James Gaume of Douglas Aircraft in 1970.[38] In this concept, it is accepted that airplane occupants (other than the pilots) may lose consciousness, provided that within a matter of minutes, they are brought to a safe altitude, where they will then recover again without suffering permanent damage. This phenomenon was confirmed in a number of accidents in the 1970s as discussed in Section 6.6. A similar approach had been followed for Concorde, which operated up to 60,000 ft. (18,300 m) and was designed not to reach unsafe cabin altitudes following a decompression. One of the means to guarantee that was the very small cabin windows.

FIGURE 6.3 Concorde Mach and altitude meter (photograph by the author).

6.7.5 TAMPERING-RESISTANT LAVATORY OXYGEN GENERATORS

In early 2011, the FAA became aware of a security vulnerability issue with respect to chemical oxygen generators installed in lavatories. Other than that the generators were vulnerable to tampering, the nature was not disclosed publicly for security reasons. An Airworthiness Directive was issued ordering U.S. airlines to expend or remove the generators.[39] But before the FAA publicly issued this AD, all U.S. airlines were informed and completed the required action. The FAA had assessed that the risk of a passenger being in the lavatory at the time of decompression and not having access to oxygen was acceptable: the probability was only about 5×10^{-9} per flighthour. EASA did not adopt the AD, but at least one EASA member state did.

To come up with a more permanent solution, an ARC subcommittee was installed, the Lavatory Oxygen ARC, which issued its final report in August 2011.[40] It recommended changes to the design standards and a retrofit with a four-year compliance period. Design standards were indeed issued in March 2014 but only for new airplane type certificates.[41] For the existing U.S. fleet, a second AD replaced the first AD.[42] That AD required bringing back oxygen provisions in lavatories, but now of a secure type, within 37 months.

NOTES

1. Aeronautics Bulletin No. 7-E, 1934, chapter 4, sec. 1(M); 1(N)
2. Human Factors in Air Transport Design, Ross A. McFarland, 1946, p. 56.
3. McFarland, 1946, p. 57.
4. Aircraft Yearbook 1938, Aeronautical Chamber of Commerce of America, Inc., p. 168.
5. Schiphol uitstappen!—Ervaringen van een K.L.M. Stewardess, Hilda Bongertman (1936).
6. Human Factors in Relation to the Development of Pressurized Cabins, the Harry G. Armstrong Lecture, Ross Armstrong McFarland, in Aerospace Medicine, December 1971, p. 1308.
7. The Physiology of Life at High Altitudes, the International High Altitude Expedition to Chile, Ancel Keys, in Scientific Monthly, Vol. 43, No. 4, October 1936.
8. McFarland, 1946, p. 51.
9. Aircraft Yearbook 1937, Aeronautical Chamber of Commerce of America, Inc., p. 178.
10. Amendment No. 2 to Aeronautics Bulletin No. 7-E, Air Commerce Bulletin, Vol. 7, No. 7, January 15, 1936.
11. CAR 61, Effective November 1, 1937.
12. Aircraft Yearbook 1939, Aeronautical Chamber of Commerce of America, Inc., p. 202.
13. Amdt No. 94.
14. McFarland, 1971.
15. Amdt 41-0 (1945); 42-0 (1946).
16. Amdt No. 120.
17. DR 47-8.
18. DR (unnumbered, 14 FR 1333).
19. Amdt 4b-13, 41-5, 42-2, 61-63.
20. Amdt 4b-13.
21. DR 47-8.
22. DR (unnumbered, 14 FR 1333).
23. Amdt 4b-6 (1957).
24. Amdt 4b-9,40-12,41-18,42-15.
25. Amdt 121-383.
26. Human Factors in Air Transportation—Occupational Health and Safety, Ross A. McFarland, 1953, p. 688.
27. McFarland, 1971.
28. Special Study, Chemically Generated Supplement Oxygen Systems in DC-10 and L-1011 Aircraft, NTSB-AAS-76-1, March 3, 1976.
29. Aircraft Accident Report, Aloha Airlines, Flight 243, Boeing 737-200, N73711, Near Maui, Hawaii, April 28, 1988, NTSB-AAR-89/03, June 14, 1989.

30 World Aircraft Accident Summary, CAP 479, UK CAA (1960–1989, global), Service Difficulty Reports, UK CAA (1976–1989, UK), FAA CAMI (1974–1981, US).
31 NPRM 13-01.
32 https://avherald.com.
33 Amdt 121-113/135-40.
34 Amdt 121-374.
35 Amdt 25-116/121-306.
36 Amdt 25-148.
37 Amdt 25-87.
38 Factors Influencing the Time of Safe Unconsciousness (TSU) for Commercial Jet Passengers Following Cabin Decompression" by James G. Gaume, Aerospace Medicine, April 1970.
39 AD 2011-04-09.
40 Lavatory Oxygen Aviation Rulemaking Committee Final Report, August 3, 2011.
41 Amdt 25-138.
42 AD 2012-11-09.

7 First Trough (1954–1964)

ABSTRACT

This chapter discusses the period following that of the first wave. While in terms of cabin safety developments and requirements it was leaner, that was not the case in airplane technology. A new means of propulsion was introduced: the turbine engine. Air transport airplanes became larger and flew higher.

In this period, some subjects left over from the previous period were dealt with, such as crash axes and chop marks (both essentially quashed) and better exit and escape means.

The main cabin safety focus of this period was the ditching: the planned, and more often unplanned, landing of an airplane on water. Serious ditchings occurred at a frequency of about one per year and gradually became more survivable, as lessons were learned.

Meanwhile, Howard Hasbrook perfected his work of investigating impact protection and toured the world to advocate his recommendations.

A revision of the exit types and table was made in anticipation of the new jet airplanes.

The invention in 1955 of the inflatable slide was soon followed by its promotion by means of a policy offering a bonus of up to 10 passenger seats for its use. This policy was later elevated to regulation status and would have a significant positive commercial impact in the decades to come.

7.1 INTRODUCTION

The first wave subsided in 1953. An 11-year period followed with few cabin safety enhancements. This period however was marked with what may have been the most exciting in terms of transport aircraft development. In May 1952 the first commercial jet service was inaugurated. The United Kingdom's British Overseas Airways Corporation (BOAC) flew the new De Havilland Comet, with its wing-root mounted jet engines, from London to Johannesburg at a speed twice of what the piston-engined airliners achieved. The next year, the first turboprop airliner, the Vickers Viscount, also of UK origin, started to fly passengers. The epic rise of the Comet was followed in 1954 by an Icarian fall when soon after each other, two airplanes of the type literally fell into the sea. The type was grounded. The circumstances have been well documented and need not be repeated here. Cabin safety was not a factor. In 1956, the Soviet Union took over the baton from the UK and restarted, this time sustained, jet air transport with the Tupolev 104, which also had wing-root jet engines. And two more years later, in October 1958, the jet age had come to the western world for good. Both a revamped Comet (the Comet 4) and the Boeing 707 with its four jet engines in pods under the wing confirmed that by flying transatlantic between New York and Europe. Other jet types soon followed, such as the American Douglas DC-8 and the French Sud-Est Caravelle. Meanwhile, the development of the piston-engined airliners came to an end with the Douglas DC-7C 'Seven Seas' and the Lockheed L-1649 Starliner, the ultimate iterations of the Douglas pistons and the Constellation breed, respectively.

These developments contrasted in volume with the few that occurred in cabin safety. And what happened there were either leftovers from the first wave, responses to a phenomenon that was unique to the decade—the ditching—or were triggered by the characteristics of the new jets (higher capacity, so more exits, and higher altitude, so oxygen).

Where the first wave's cabin safety measures had landed well with the manufacturers, the airlines appeared less pleased with proposals of the operational kind. Already in 1950, the CAB had started to propose new cabin safety rules addressed to airlines. They were about such measures as improved exit marking and lighting, assignment of emergency functions, briefing of passengers,

DOI: 10.1201/9781032711027-7

evacuation equipment such as slides, and crash axes. But these met with opposition from the Air Transport Association (ATA), the powerful trade organization of the airlines. It took a long time—in some cases until 1957—before they became mandated, or were either withdrawn. Similarly, CAB's regulatory proposals in response to the lessons of the ditchings suffered the same fate of being delayed by the airlines. Less opposition came for measures inevitable for the new jets.

Meanwhile Howard Hasbrook continued his important work in the field of impact protection.

7.2   THE OPERATIONAL LEFTOVERS FROM THE FIRST WAVE

As described in Chapter 5, in the first wave many new requirements were proposed and introduced. However, a number of proposed standards in the evacuation and communications domains, all of an operational nature, met with resistance from the ATA. Hearings were held with interested parties and numerous iterations of the proposals followed. The proposals were adjusted and augmented as new insights were gained.

This had all started in 1950 when the CAB issued a draft release in which it explained that:

> requirements for emergency equipment have been considerably strengthened in light of the increasing fund of knowledge as to the necessity for survival in an accident. For example, provision is made for carrying axes to permit persons in the cabins to provide additional means of egress, for marking exterior areas of the fuselage to indicate areas suitable for cutting to facilitate rescue from the outside.

This rather cryptical description calls to mind the United Airlines accident in 1947 at New York La Guardia, where the pilot used an axe to force the main extra door open and chopped holes in the fuselage. The 1950 draft release proposed several new requirements, all in the evacuation domain, for:[1]

- a crash axe for each 30 occupants, or portion thereof, readily available for use and clearly marked;
- exterior marking of areas suitable for cutting, also known as chop marks;
- for aircraft already type certificated:
  - the marking of opening handles;
  - the marking and illumination of exits, either with luminous paint or with a source independent from the main lighting system;
  - concise instructions for opening exits;
  - emergency evacuation means.

To that, a proposal was added in 1951 for procedures for briefing and familiarizing passengers with the use of emergency equipment during flight.[2]

The following discusses how the 1950 and 1951 proposals morphed into rules, and how they were further modified.

7.2.1   CRASH AXE

With the May 1947 horrific crash still fresh in the minds, and in response to the recommendations made by the President's Special Board of Inquiry on Air Safety following that crash, the CAB proposed in 1950 that each airliner should have one crash axe per 30 persons so that people could force their way out.[3] This would mean for a typical large airplane of the time, such as the Lockheed Constellation, three to four axes. Under pressure from the airlines, the next year this was reduced to a maximum of two, 'to be stowed in conspicuous places'.[4] CAA policy issued in 1955 suggested at least one axe should be located in the passenger compartment.[5] But the ATA still questioned the effectiveness of the axe for cutting through the fuselage of an airplane and as to the advisability from a safety standpoint of stowing a crash axe in the passenger compartment. The CAB thereupon obtained data from both the U.S. Air Force and NACA. These put doubt as to whether the average passenger could chop an adequate opening through the fuselage by means of an axe. And when succeeding, such an opening would create sharp jagged edges. To cope with that, the military required that an axe be supplemented by such equipment as a saw or a six pound sledge hammer. This new information prompted the CAB to withdraw the requirement for the second axe. It kept the requirement for the first, as 'one axe adequately served to meet certain emergency situations, as a cutting instrument, wrecking bar, and lever'. It became effective September 1, 1956.[6]

The issue of a crash axe seems to be a minor, almost futile, item. Yet, the CAB discussed it in five draft releases and as many final rules, albeit that some of these rules were only issued to postpone the effectivity date of the rule.

7.2.2 Chop Marks and Exterior Exit Markings

The chop marks were proposed at the same time as the crash axes and will also have been inspired by the 1947 La Guardia crash. But, like the crash axe, it raised opposition from the airlines who said that the fuselages of modern pressurized airplanes are so strong that chopping or cutting with hand tools would not be possible. Meanwhile, for new aircraft types, the airworthiness requirements were enhanced in 1951 by adding that the exits and their means of opening be marked on the outside for the guidance of rescue personnel. This gave the CAB a good excuse to delete the proposal for chop marks, which would have been located randomly across the fuselage. Rather, attention should be directed to those areas already designed for opening. Or, in their words: 'the existence of chop marks may induce rescue personnel to engage in fruitless chopping or cutting when expeditious means of access are readily available'.[7] Per January 1, 1956, they required all exits operable from the outside to be clearly identifiable as such with the method of opening be marked on the outside.

For those exits that are only openable from the inside, an interim proposal that instructions should be added for the most suitable procedure for forcible entry was withdrawn, following comments by the ATA, the Flight Safety Foundation (FSF), and the National Fire Protection Association. They argued that 'the limitations of language are such that it would be difficult to avoid instructions, the length and complexity of which would defeat the objective sought, unless a system of universal symbols, not currently in existence, is developed'. Rather, they did see merit in an educational program for rescue personnel.[8]

So, while the U.S. dropped the requirement for chop marks, other countries did not. ICAO retained them in the airworthiness standards, albeit as an option. Many countries copied this, and some made it mandatory. Their practical application however has been nil.

7.2.3 Exit and Operating Handle Marking and Illumination

Prior to 1950, the only operational requirements for exit marking, lighting, and identifying exit opening handles were those resulting from the 1943 Trammel crash. They were applicable to both domestic (Part 61) and overseas (Part 41) operators but not to the non-scheduled operators (Part 42), for which only a sparse airworthiness standard applied. In 1950 a proposal was issued that would require Part 61 and Part 41 operators to:[9]

- mark and illuminate all exits to permit ready identification and to attract the attention of occupants either in the light or in the dark;
- mark the exit operating handles and add clear, concise instructions for opening exits;
- illuminate the operating handle either with luminous paint or a source of light independent of the main electrical system, functioning automatically or by manual activation.

Effective December 1951, the airworthiness requirements had been improved, mirroring these requirements, but minus the luminous paint option. These requirements only applied to new aircraft types and not to existing fleets or new aircraft of types already certificated or in the certification process. This effectively meant that it would only affect new aircraft types being produced from

c. 1954 onward. Covering these features in operational requirements was therefore important to close this gap. In a 1952 update of the proposal, it was extended to irregular operators (as the non-scheduleds were now called), now covering all U.S. air carrier passenger aircraft.[10] Also, and in line with the design standard, it was considered that the luminous paint option was not stringent enough. This left as the only illumination option lights powered by an electric energy supply. That supply would need to be independent of the main electrical system and have both a manual and an automatic, crash-initiated, activation means. The latter was considered controversial, and, when issuing the final rule in December 1955, the CAB softened the requirement.[11] No crash-initiated activation was required provided that the lights be turned on before each night take-off and landing and would continue to function after a crash landing. In this form, the exit and operating handle marking and illumination rules became effective on August 31, 1957. This was limited to passenger-carrying aircraft and so excluded all-cargo operations.

The requirement only applied to night operations. Soon, it would prove that this had been a bit short-sighted. On September 14, 1960, an American Airlines Lockheed Electra crashed at New York La Guardia in daylight conditions. All on board survived, in spite of (1) a fire, (2) the fact that the aircraft came to rest inverted, which made the evacuation more difficult, and (3) the lack of light inside. To quote from the investigation report: 'The inside of the cabin was darkened by mud and soot on the outside window panes. The emergency lights in the cabin were not lighted'.[12] The investigators recommended 'that the present procedures for providing illumination of passenger exit markings be reexamined'. This led to a draft release issued by the FAA in September 1961 proposing that the lighting system of exit markings functions regardless of the time of the day. This time, no adverse comments were received and the rule became effective March 20, 1962.[13]

7.2.4 Evacuation Means

Now that a maximum safe distance that evacuees can jump—6 ft (1.8 m)—had been established for new aircraft types and regulated in CAR 4b (see Section 5.5.3.5.5), the CAB proposed the same for existing fleets. They did that in an August 1951 draft release.[14] The proposal did not state a distance to the ground when such equipment would be required but did include the scenario of the aircraft tipped. It proposed the equipment 'to be stowed in a location readily accessible for use at the appropriate exit'. In 1952 the proposal, together with others (for emergency lighting and passenger briefing), was withdrawn 'because of the considerable controversy they engendered'.[15] A meeting with industry representatives was held. The next year, 1953, the proposal was repeated in a new draft release in a slightly different form.[16] Now at main-door exits more than 6 ft (1.8 m) from the ground with the landing gear extended, a chute or equivalent device was proposed, to be 'in a position for ready use'. What that meant was the subject of further discussion with industry. The CAB conceded that chutes installed immediately above exit doors, or on brackets attached to the fuselage immediately adjacent to the doors, were within the meaning of 'ready for use'. This actually was how airlines had already installed them. This thus became the final rule text, with one more condition added: the location of the chute may not create a hazard by obstructing the exit. The tilting of the fuselage was no longer a condition to be reckoned with. The operational rule was published in late 1955 and after some postponements became effective for all U.S. air carriers on August 31, 1957.[17] By that time, quite a number of aircraft subject to the 1951 CAR 4b change for a mandatory chute had been delivered and many existing aircraft had already been equipped with chutes on a voluntary basis. The rule ensured that the remaining fleets followed suit.

7.3 THE DITCHING YEARS

7.3.1 Ditching Troubles

In the first wave period, ditchings became a frequent accident scenario. From 1949 onward, there was a ditching to an American airliner on average about once each year, in addition to those of other countries. Reviewing the investigation reports, a pattern arises where airlines initially were poorly prepared, but this gradually improved.

In August 1949, due to poor flight planning and navigation, a Transocean Airlines DC-4 successfully ditched off the coast of Ireland. The aircraft remained afloat for 15 minutes, and all but one of the life rafts were launched. Pending the rescue operations, seven passengers and one crewmember died as a result of exposure or drowning.[18]

In June 1950, Air France suffered two crashes within two days at the same location, Bahrain. Both involved a Douglas DC-4 hitting the water on approach to the runway. In the second, 13 of the 53 occupants survived. The report mentions that there had been no safety briefing for the passengers. The life vests were not accessible as they were hidden under luggage.[19]

In 1952, there were three ditchings, all with procedural imperfections and many fatalities. On January 19, 1952, just after midnight a Douglas DC-4 crashed into very cold water one mile (1.6 km) beyond the runway of Sandspit, British Colombia. Three crew and 33 passengers succumbed due to exposure and drowning. Most if not all occupants evacuated the aircraft with no known serious injuries. Many had clambered on top of the fuselage but could not hold on. They slid off one by one. Only seven passengers were rescued in near-freezing conditions after about 1 hour 15 minutes. They had clustered on the right-wing tip which stayed above the water line when the aircraft had settled to the bottom of the sea. The landing at Sandspit was not planned but precautionary as one of the four engines had been shut down earlier in the flight. Considering this as a potential and not an actual emergency and as no ditching was planned, the passengers had not been instructed to don life vests or otherwise prepared for an abnormal landing. Only one passenger is known to have donned a life vest; several others lost it during their efforts to get on top of the settling aircraft. The report notes that while there were safety pamphlets on board, which the stewardess had instructed passengers to read before departure from Tokyo, they showed life vests of a collar-type instead of the vest-type that was on board. There were three life rafts on board, two 20-man and one 15-man. The first officer and others made strenuous but futile attempts to get the 15-man life raft out through the astrodome opening. This was the only opening in the top of the aircraft, all the other exits were in the side, which were below the water line.[20,21]

Three months later, on April 11, a Pan Am Douglas DC-4 made an intentional ditching off Puerto Rico.[22] The aircraft sank after approximately three minutes. Of the 64 passengers, 52 died. All of the 5 crew survived. There were issues with the location of the rafts (all stowed aft of the flight deck and not well accessible); no notification of the pending ditching by the flight crew to the cabin crew; and once the cabin crew was aware, they did not warn the passengers nor instructed them in the location and use of the life vests until after the aircraft was in the water. Immediately following the ditching the captain went into the cabin and ordered the passengers to abandon ship; however, there was very little response. He then aided a passenger to open the main cabin door and began forcibly evacuating passengers through that door. While so engaged, the door slammed closed and the captain gripped the handle in an effort to open it again, but as he did so a wave caught the door violently pushing it outside, throwing him into the water. Due to the heavy seas, he was unable to return to the aircraft. The CAB, in its accident investigation report, recommended that airlines establish procedures for orally briefing the location and method of operation of life vests, emergency exits, and life rafts. This was for extended overwater operations only.

Another four months later, on 25 August, a Handley Page Hermes 4-A operated by the British airline Airwork carried out a ditching in the dark in the Mediterranean Sea off Trapani, Sicily. The ditching maneuver was perfect. The preparation was not. The hostesses, rather than instructing passengers to retrieve life vests and don them, merely suggested that. One hostess was not aware of how the life vest be put on. Nevertheless, passengers managed to don them, a few reading the instructions as posted in the cabin. Some life vests did not inflate, either because of defects or inadequate instructions. There were not enough life vests on board as the number was based on the number of seats rather than souls on board. Some young children shared seats so did not count. But even if there had been enough, they would not do as the vests were for adults and did not fit young children. Of the six passenger fatalities, four were young children, aged from three to six.[23]

The CAB reacted quickly to the two U.S. accidents and proposed in August 1952 new regulations addressing life rafts' ready accessibility, crew assignments in cases of emergency and ditching, and the briefing of passengers.[24] However, due to resistance by the airlines, similar to the leftovers discussed earlier, it took five years before the proposals took effect as a final rule.[25]

One way of meeting the raft accessibility requirement was to place them flush in the wings so that they would be available for wing evacuees. This was a solution that was applied to the Lockheed Constellation. In later ditchings, it proved to have its own drawbacks.

Northwest Airlines and Pan Am did not wait for the CAB proposals to become mandatory and improved their procedures and relocated emergency equipment. Also, they supplemented their safety pamphlets with oral briefings of passengers on the location of exits and how to open them, and the location of rafts and their use. Northwest introduced personal demonstrations to groups of four passengers in the use of life vests.

The 1952 cascade of ditching trouble alarmed airlines outside the U.S. as well. Many countries in the world followed closely the regulatory developments in the U.S. and adopted those, either formally or informally. Although France is not believed to have been such a country, as it rather developed its own operational regulations, based on those of ICAO, it had learned its lessons in Bahrain. When Air France had to ditch a Lockheed Constellation in the dark along the coast of Turkey on 3 August 1953, near Fethiye, the evacuation went much better.[26] The hostess' control over the passengers was such that at no time was there any panic inside the cabin. There were no life rafts, as the flight did not go beyond the coast more than what ICAO then described as the limit for rafts. Passengers, all with life vests, either swam the distance of 2 nautical miles (3.6 km) to the coast, were rescued by a small boat from the local lighthouse, or stayed on the aircraft wings until the airplane sank after about two hours, and then swam to the coast. Out of eight crewmembers and 34 passengers, four passengers did not survive. They were later found wearing inflated vests.

Also less fortunate were three passengers of a Swissair Convair 240 that had insufficient fuel to reach London from Geneva and ditched in the Channel, off Folkestone, late on 19 June 1954. They could not swim. No life vests were carried as, like in the U.S., this was only required for extended overwater flights. The cross-Channel section was not so rated. The three crewmembers and three other passengers were rescued.

Later in the same year, in the early morning of 5 September, a KLM Constellation failed to climb when departing from Shannon on its way to New York. About two miles from runway 14 it landed on the tidal muds of the river Shannon after about 39 seconds of flying. The landing had been so mild that one passenger later stated that he thought they were still at the airport. The fuselage cracked open forward of the wing. The aircraft lighting was shut off. It was pitch dark. The light impact on the mudbank and the reputation of the captain (who had months earlier been promoted to the elite rank of 'commodore') may have caused the cabin crew to underestimate the seriousness of the conditions until it became too late. A ruptured fuel tank quickly caused heavy petrol fumes to enter the cabin. Water entered the airplane. No ditching briefing had been given prior to departure. No life vests were handed out and the main passenger entry door remained closed. Rescue was only initiated after the co-pilot had waded for two and a half hours back toward the airport. Despite the absence of any radio report from the airplane, nobody there had suspected a crash. One of the circular life rafts, packed with crew and passengers, was used to try and reach the airport, but all it did was go around in circles until a sail was made out of the weather protector. Of the 56 occupants, half, including all flight crew, survived. The three cabin crewmembers and 25 passengers had died.[27]

7.3.2 ASSIGNMENT OF FUNCTIONS

Triggered by the 1952 ditchings, the CAB proposed that air carriers improve the preparation for evacuations by prescribing the assignment of functions to each crewmember. These were not limited to ditchings but also meant to cover land evacuations. The air carriers had to demonstrate that

First Trough (1954–1964)

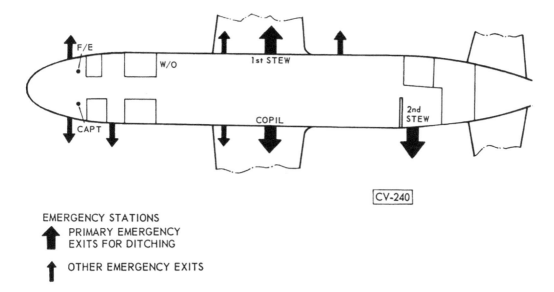

FIGURE 7.1 KLM Convair 240 ditching stations (1954).

the assigned duties were practicable and could be accomplished in practice. Additionally, the crew should be trained, both initially and recurrent.

Thus, airlines started to issue detailed assignments and instructions for their flight and cabin crew for all aircraft types for both land and water emergencies. This was not limited to U.S. airlines. As early as February 1953 KLM Royal Dutch Airlines followed this rule, even though it was still only a proposal. It defined in minute detail per crewmember the tasks before the emergency landing or ditching, which emergency stations to occupy, and the tasks during and after the emergency landing or ditching (see also Figure 8.2).

The proposal became effective in the U.S. on May 31, 1956.[28] Some airlines set up a mock evacuation of an aircraft to demonstrate the practicality of the assignments and instructions. Evacuation speed was not an objective; it was mainly a demonstration of whether the assigned tasks could indeed be accomplished. In Europe, both KLM and SAS are known to have done that around 1955, but there will have been more.

7.3.3 Life Raft Boarding Tests

In June 1955, Barry King, assisted by the U.S. Navy, an airline, and a life raft manufacturer (Air Cruisers) staged a series of life raft boarding tests from an airplane hull in the ocean, called 'Operation Ditch'.[29] In November 1957 he presented the results.[30] No formal report of the trials is known. It may well never have been written; Dr. King had left the CAA that same year. He had managed to get a hull of a Martin 4–0–4 floating in the Atlantic Ocean off Norfolk, Virginia, together with a number of 20-man life rafts. Two rafts were stowed outside, one in the left wing, another near the main door. In the cabin, rafts were stowed one near the main door, one near the overwing exits, and one in the baggage compartment forward of the main cabin. In all, 40 successive launchings took place, involving more than 500 life raft boardings by individuals. In many cases, a raft took an excessive time to inflate or, in four cases, failed to inflate completely. The weather was nice and swells were low (sea state one, wind between 2 and 12 knots). Boarding of the rafts took place from the wing, the door, or the water, the latter, as expected, taking the longest time. Two different passenger groups were employed: civilian and military, the latter showing a more orderly boarding. Due to the slow inflation of the life rafts, early evacuees tended to board the raft while it still unfolded, in some cases trapping them, or spewing them into the water. But even when the life rafts were inflated, boarding did not always go smooth. Quite a few evacuees failed to properly step into it and landed in the water.

7.3.4 DITCHING SUCCESS STORIES

From 1955 onward, the upcoming regulations, even though they were still proposals and not yet mandatory, started to pay off. In 1955 and 1956, there were three successive ditchings involving Boeing 377s. In two cases there was ample time for preparation. The first involved Pan Am and took place 35 miles off the coast of Oregon.[31] All occupants had donned their life vests. Before departure, a life jacket demonstration had been given by the steward, and each passenger was handed a folder 'Just in Case' (of a ditching). The ditching itself went smoothly. The evacuation was orderly, and all life rafts could be launched. However, they drifted away. Yet, some passengers could still reach them by swimming to them. Out of the 23 occupants, 4 succumbed as a result of shock, exposure, and/or drowning. The purser, a woman, although suffering from shock swam and towed the only seriously injured passenger to the nearest raft, some 200 ft. (60 m) away.

The second was a Northwest Boeing 377 that on April 2, 1956 ditched in Puget Sound, close to Seattle Tacoma airport. This was a last moment decision by the captain. The evacuation was orderly. As this involved a domestic flight, there were neither life rafts nor life jackets on board. Instead, a stewardess remembered that the seat cushions were buoyant and could be used for flotation. This was not listed in the manual. It contributed to survival. Of the 38 occupants, five drowned.[32,33]

The third involved Pan Am again. That ditching became a classic of a well-prepared ditching. On the stretch from Hawaii to San Francisco on October 16, 1956, the aircraft suffered an engine problem that prevented reaching land. It circled for hours over the ocean, waiting for daylight, and then ditched close to a U.S. weather station, from which rescue could be staged. Like in 1955, prior to departure, a life jacket demonstration had been given and each passenger had been provided with the 'just in case' ditching folder. In preparation for the ditching, the cabin attendants gave instructions to all passengers to remove eye-glasses, shoes, and sharp objects and to put on the life jackets. For the children, adult-sized life jackets were improvised. Passengers were relocated in the safest seats, forward of the tail section, which the captain believed would break off, as it indeed did. Some children were placed on the floor and held tightly between their parents' feet. Other children were held by their mothers in their arms, but this did not work during the impact. Following the successful ditching, all life rafts were launched and boarded in 20 minutes. Three minutes later, the aircraft sank.[34] All 31 occupants survived.

The three last major ditchings of the ditching period came in 1960 and 1962. The first and third had a good outcome, but the second fared worse, particularly due to wing-mounted rafts not being available.

On the night of July 14, 1960, a Northwest DC-7 was ditched in the Pacific Ocean, 67 nautical miles (124 km) from Manila, the Philippines, following a failure of the no. 2 engine.[35] All 58 occupants evacuated the aircraft, but one woman passenger died. The whole episode of the ditching and post-ditching survival went by the book. Prior to the ditching, the cabin attendants instructed passengers to don life vests and activate the light on the life vest. Both the captain and the purser, using the loudspeaker system, directed the passengers to remove their shoes, ties, glasses, and other pertinent objects. The cabin's emergency lights were turned on. Seat rows that aligned the no. 2 propeller were vacated and these passengers sat on the cabin floor with their backs to the compartment walls. The life rafts were placed near exits with lanyards attached. Passengers were allocated to life rafts by cabin seating area, in accordance with the company's procedures. During the ditching, the emergency lights stayed on, whereas the normal cabin lights went out. The cabin started to fill with smoke from the fire in the left wing that had prompted the ditching. All occupants evacuated successfully. Some boarded rafts; others used a section of the left wing that had broken off and was floating, yet others floated in the water. These passengers could be easily located by the lights on their life vests and were taken on board the life rafts. Passengers were transferred from one life raft to another to even the loads. Life raft leaks caused by the jagged wing were patched and the bailing bucket was used, as was the survival pack. There was no panic or hysteria. Smoke flares were used when rescue airplanes were heard and seen. In particular, the investigators commended that Northwest had equipped its airplanes with life vests with lights. This was not required for overseas flights of U.S. air carriers at the time. It had 'materially aided the occupants in the liferafts in locating survivors in the sea during hours of darkness'.

The importance of light was demonstrated again in the ditching of a Flying Tiger Super Constellation on September 23, 1962, in the Atlantic Ocean some 500 miles (800 km) from Ireland. The flight was civil, but the passengers were military, mostly paratroops with seven service wives and two children.[36] This was another ditching with sufficient time for preparing the passengers. It occurred in hours of darkness. Again, the company instructions as contained in the manuals helped and were followed, although the investigators criticized some of the preparation actions. There was confusion with respect to the brace-for-impact position, with the stewardess giving instructions different from those in the ditching folder. After the ditching, the flight crew left the cockpit into the cabin to evacuate from there. On second thoughts, the captain returned to collect a flashlight. This later turned out to be vital, as it was the only source of light for successfully making contact with the rescuers using SOS signals. This Super Constellation had four life rafts stowed in the wing, but as the left wing had separated on impact, these two were not available. Neither were the two right-wing rafts ever seen by the survivors. All these four life rafts were later found inflated by rescue personnel, either empty or laden with fatalities. The only raft that was available had been carried prior to the ditching from the crew compartment to the main exit at the rear. This 25-man raft was launched and eventually boarded by 51 persons. Rescue arrived after about six hours. Three of those in the raft died, as did the remaining 25 aircraft occupants.[37,38] The investigators recommended that both life rafts and life vests be equipped with lights and suggested to no longer carry life rafts in wings.

A month later, on October 22, a Douglas DC-7 with 102 occupants ditched off Biorka Island, Alaska. There had been ample time for preparation with passengers donning life vests, removing all sharp objects, and rehearsing the brace position. The cabin crew (one steward and two stewardesses)

> had 28 passengers move out of the first five rows of seats on the right and the first six rows on the left. These persons were seated in unoccupied seats or on the floor between seats, off the aisle and facing sideways.

Thus, they were kept away from the plane of the propeller that had oversped and was the reason for the ditching. 'Passengers seated near emergency exits were instructed in the method of opening the exits and launching liferafts'. Deceleration forces were mild. All occupants managed to evacuate and board the six rafts.[39]

7.4 IMPACT PROTECTION

Howard Hasbrook continued his research on crash survival for Cornell University. He investigated accidents with survivability issues wherever he could. An early investigation that he did was of a Douglas DC-6 that crashed shortly after take-off from Newark airport on February 11, 1952. That report has some very good crash dynamics drawings.[40] It is often cited.

Another investigation with many recommendations was that of a De Havilland Dove that crashed on Staten Island on December 9, 1952, which cartwheeled 180° along the vertical axis.[41] Thus, the forward-facing seats became aft-facing in the process. One of his last investigations, now working for FAA CAMI, was that of the evacuation pattern of the United Airlines DC-8 at Denver in July 1961.[42] One of the co-authors was Clyde Snow, who in 1970 studied this accident again, together with John Carroll of the NTSB.

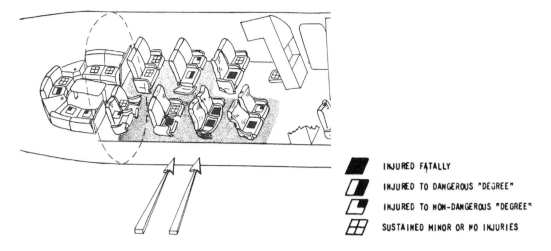

FIGURE 7.2 Extract from Hasbrook's Newark DC-6 crash injury investigation (Crash Survival Study National Airlines DC-6 Accident at Elizabeth, NJ, February 11, 1952).

Hasbrook also spent quite some time on lectures and visiting airlines and manufacturers, both in the U.S. and abroad. Pan Am, when introducing the 'Super 6' (the DC-6B) in spring 1952, had two seat features as recommended by Hasbrook: (1) 'no tubing is used where the head is likely to strike. Top of seat backs is formed of sheet metal designed to "give" on impact and absorb head blows'; (2) 'seat backs are built to collapse forward at a specified crash load'.[43] In April 1957, he delivered his lecture on 'Design of Passenger "Tie-down"' in Essen, Germany. The main points of that lecture also appeared in Aviation Week. He described victims as being a far-flung missile or a near-flung missile.[44] A far-flung missile is somebody whose tie-down to the airplane structure fails and is hurled to the ground or against distant parts of the airplane. The tie-down of a near-flung missile holds, but his head, torso, or legs are smashed against nearby lethal objects.

The month before, he was at the airport of Amsterdam, visiting Fokker on March 25 and KLM the next day. At Fokker, he inspected the prototype of the F-27 and made numerous suggestions for delethalization of the cockpit and interior. He repeated his two missile analogies. At KLM, hosted by George van Messel, the head of the new safety department, he inspected DC-6 and Constellation aircraft and again identified areas for delethalization.

In 1959, the Aviation Crash Injury Research (AvCIR) division moved from Cornell University to the Flight Safety Foundation (FSF). Hasbrook moved to FAA CAMI in 1960. In 1963 AvCIR was renamed into Aviation Safety Engineering and Research (AvSER, a similarly pronounced acronym), still with FSF. In this period, AvSER conducted many crash tests, mainly on smaller aircraft and helicopters, but toward the end of this period, it had the opportunity to stage two crashes of large transport aircraft, sponsored by the Federal Aviation Agency. The objectives of the tests were many, ranging from measuring the dynamic crash forces to evaluating various seat designs and understanding fuel tank rupture mechanisms. In 1964, both a DC-7 and a Lockheed Starliner were put to the test, which consisted of a horizontal acceleration under their own power into a hill.[45]

As testified in 1980 by James King of the NTSB to the House of Representatives, around 1960,

> there was considerable interest among industry to improve on the obvious problems with passenger seat retention. The major seat manufacturers experimented with dynamic seat-testing methods and energy-absorption mechanisms. Some air carriers required that load-limiting devices be installed on seats which they purchased for their aircraft. Others specified that the seats be tested in a dynamic impact facility.[46]

First Trough (1954–1964)

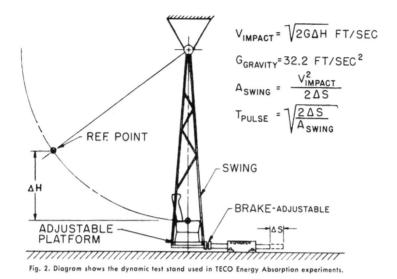

Fig. 2. Diagram shows the dynamic test stand used in TECO Energy Absorption experiments.

FIGURE 7.3 Swing for the dynamic testing of seats as displayed in a sales brochure of Teco (c. 1960).

Some seat manufacturers used a swing.

British seat manufacturers had their seats tested on a horizontal sled at the British Standards Institution in Hemel Hempstead. In an early attempt to discuss uniform dynamic seat testing, the 'usual suspects' in cabin safety of the latter 1950s met in a hotel in Palo Alto, California.[47] Absent was Howard Hasbrook, but the group included William Littlewood (VP of American Airlines), Irving Pinkel (NASA Lewis Research Center), Otto Kirchner (Boeing and chairman of the SAE S9 Committee), and Jerome Lederer (manager Flight Safety Foundation). The practice of dynamic testing was not followed up by rulemaking and was gradually discontinued.

7.5 ESCAPE POTENTIAL: PREPARING FOR THE JETS

7.5.1 Exit Dimensions and Table Update

In the second half of the 1950s, a new category of airliners was under development in the U.S.: turbine-powered airplanes. Three U.S. manufacturers were projecting jets (Boeing 707, Convair 880, Douglas DC-8) and two projected turboprops (Lockheed Electra and Fairchild F-27, under license to Fokker of the Netherlands). These aircraft were low-wing airplanes, except for the F-27, which would be the first high-wing airliner to be produced after World War Two. Additionally, the British-made Vickers Viscount turboprop was imported into the U.S., and in both Britain (the De Havilland Comet 4) and France (the Sud-Est Caravelle) jets were being developed. In Amsterdam, Fokker made the F-27, from which the Fairchild F-27 was copied. The CAB recognized these new designs and proposed in October 1956 an expansion of the exit requirements that they had introduced in 1951.[48] They explained that these new airplanes would be 'considerably larger than the transport category airplanes now in service and, accordingly, will have provisions for a larger number of passengers'. The proposed changes were 'to permit greater flexibility'.

The proposal included several changes. Type II exits were now allowed either as a floor-level exit or as an overwing exit with minimum step-up and step-down dimensions added.

Where previously Type III exits were required to be located as far aft as practicable, they were now proposed to be over the wing. Thus, a maximum step-up and step-down distance was added, which were less than for Type IV exits. One Type III exit was considered equal to two Type IV exits. For high-wing airplanes, where there is no wing to step onto, Type II exits were proposed. The dimensions as given in Appendix 3 for these types applied. Two major changes to the table were proposed:

- A revision to the existing ranges by splitting them up into smaller ranges. These had the effect that for some capacity ranges larger exits (Type IIIs in lieu of Type IVs) were prescribed, while for one range (100 to 119) a reduction (Type II in lieu of Type I) was allowed.
- An expansion with new capacity ranges covering the 140 to 239 passenger capacities, with progressive prescription of larger exits. In the final range (220 to 239) only Type I exits (4 pairs) were prescribed.

With the table now extended to 239, the plain text credit of 50 passengers per Type I pair beyond 139 disappeared.

The new rule, adopted within five months after the publication of the proposal, partially adopted it, but had some significant changes:[49]

- Double pairs of Type IVs were replaced by Type III pairs.
- For the 110 to 179 ranges, combinations of Type IV and Type II exit pairs with one or two Type I exit pairs were replaced by the combination of two Type I exit pairs with either one or two Type III exit pairs.
- Rather than having a closed end (at 239), the open-ended nature of the previous table remained. The cut-off was raised from 139 to 219. Beyond that, the new requirement prescribed that:
  Additional exits shall be provided on airplanes having 220 or more passengers. The additional exits shall provide an effective means of passenger evacuation consistent with the minima provided in the table in subparagraph (1) of this paragraph.

The word 'consistent' is noteworthy. Previously, there was already an inconsistency in that a pair of Type I exits was either worth 40 or 50 seats or passengers (see Section 5.5.3.4.2). With the new table this was only amplified. Adding a pair of Type I exits to an airplane with 19 seats (1 pair of Type III) would qualify it for 79 seats, an increase of 60. Similarly, adding such a pair to an airplane with 79 seats (1 pair of Type Is, one pair of Type IIIs) would qualify it for 139 seats, again an increase of 60. Adding a pair of Type III exits to an airplane with 59 seats would mean an increase of 50, so bringing it on a par with a Type I.

1956 proposal:

Passenger seating capacity	Emergency exits required on each side of the fuselage			
	Type I	Type II	Type III	Type IV
1 to 19 inclusive			1	
20 to 39 inclusive		1		1
40 to 59 inclusive	1			1
60 to 79 inclusive	1			2
80 to 99 inclusive	1		1	1
100 to 119 inclusive	1	1		2
120 to 139 inclusive	2			2
140 to 159 inclusive	2		1	2
160 to 179 inclusive	2	1		2
180 to 199 inclusive	2	2		
200 to 219 inclusive	3	1		
220 to 239 inclusive	4			

1957 rule:

Passenger seating capacity	Emergency exits required on each side of the fuselage			
	Type I	Type II	Type III	Type IV
1 to 19 inclusive			1	
20 to 39 inclusive		1		1
40 to 59 inclusive	1			1
60 to 79 inclusive	1		1	
80 to 109 inclusive	1		1	1
110 to 139 inclusive	2		1	
140 to 179 inclusive	2		2	
180 to 219 inclusive	2	2		

Another significant change was to the capacity range of 110 to 179. That was adjusted to match the exit configurations of the imminent first generation of jet airplanes (707, DC-8, 880) which had projected capacities in this band. They would also spell out the exit configurations of later airliner families that would become highly prolific: the Boeing 737 and Airbus A320 families. Thus, these changes, which went unexplained by the CAB at the time of their publication, determined airplane exit configurations and associated passenger capacities for the next 65 years, and beyond.

7.5.2 Inflatable Slide Credit

The chute as an escape means from aircraft had been introduced around 1948. This consisted of a single sliding surface that needed support from persons on the ground. Life vests at the time were of the inflatable type and it did not take long that it was considered that chutes could be made inflatable as well so that they would be self-supporting. James Boyle filed a patent application in May 1954, for an 'inflatable escape chute assembly'.[50] His company, Air Cruisers Company, based in New Jersey, developed such a slide. It was first tested by the USAF on a Douglas C-54 on May 13, 1955, at Andrews AFB near Washington, DC. Three tests were held. Forty-seven airmen were employed as passenger subjects in all the tests. There was a steady drizzle throughout the test period.[51] The inflated slide was compared to an uninflated slide. Not surprisingly, the inflatable slide proved superior, both in slide preparation time and in the rate of evacuees per second.

This started the production of inflatable slides. They were embodied in all the new aircraft types then under development. This was stimulated by the Civil Aeronautics Administration in May 1958. They issued a policy (not a requirement, as that could only be done by the CAB) to promote the use of such slides by offering a capacity increase bonus of five passengers per pair of floor-level exits so equipped.[52] This effectively raised the maximum capacity of the Boeing 707 and Douglas DC-8 from 170 to 189. The policy would be transposed into a proper standard when CAR 4b became FAR Part 25 in 1964.

7.5.3 Aisle Width for Smaller Airplanes

In 1962 the aisle width requirements were modified, allowing a smaller aisle of 18 inch (46 cm) for smaller airplanes.[53] A further reduction to 16 inch (41 cm) was rejected, citing research into biometric data that a significant percentage of passengers had a standing hip-breadth exceeding 16 inch, whereas the percentage exceeding 18 inch was negligible. This would

> introduce [] the probability that a single passenger may jam the aisle between seats in the excitement and near-panic of an emergency evacuation; and, in any event, movement along the aisle would be retarded by the awkward sideward gait which large-hipped passengers must assume for passage.

7.6 LIFE SUPPORT

7.6.1 EXTENDED OVERWATER OPERATIONS

Toward the end of the first wave, the 'long distances' for which flotation devices were required received more detail: it was now required for operations beyond 50 miles (80.5 km) from the nearest shore line; the flotation devices were further specified into life preservers for each occupant (or other flotation devices) and life-saving rafts. For rescue purposes, the Very pistol requirement was replaced by a more generically termed requirement (pyrotechnic signaling equipment) to which was added portable, self-buoyant, and water-resistant emergency radio signaling equipment.[54] After several postponements, this equipment became mandatory from April 1, 1954, but for domestic operators only.

For overseas and irregular operators, for which these specifications were more important as they indeed flew over water, it took much longer. When Parts 41 and 42 were finally aligned with Part 40 in 1957, the life vests and rafts were required to be located such that they 'be readily available and easily accessible to the crew and passengers in the event of ditching'.[55] As discussed in Section 7.3.1, there had been cases where this equipment was on board, but hidden in a cargo compartment, unavailable to the occupants.

Meanwhile, in 1953, CAR Part 4b had been amended accordingly so that new aircraft (type certificated from about 1957 onward) were subject to the same requirement for ditching equipment. There were some subtle differences, however, between the operational and the design requirements. Per Part 4b life vests needed to be 'reversible and contain obvious markings of instruction on their use'.[56] This was not repeated in the operational regulations, so it would technically only apply to the newest portions of fleets. The reversible life vest requirement was withdrawn in 1959 from Part 4b, in favor of the technical standards for equipment covered in Technical Standard Orders.[57] An operational proposal that life rafts be sufficient for all occupants even when one raft of the largest capacity is lost was not adopted in 1955 as the CAB claimed there was insufficient data specific to life raft capacities.[58] However, the airworthiness requirements already required this since 1953.[59]

A proposal to equip life vests and life rafts with a means of illumination was adopted neither, for the lack of adequate equipment. Adequate in this respect refers to such properties as serviceable, reliable, lightweight, inexpensive, and of indefinite shelf life.

But, inspired by the experience gained in the various ditchings, other elements were added in the first trough period:

- In 1957: a lifeline for use on the wing[60]
- As a result of the 1956 Puget Sound ditching, where seat cushions were used as impromptu flotation means, it was proposed that flotation means be required on all flights flying over water. These means may consist of cushions which normally serve as seat cushions but must have an arm strap or other simple means of holding onto it. The CAB had found that there had been 12 other cases involving crash landings on water by aircraft which were being flown on other than extended overwater flights. These 12 accidents resulted in 25 deaths from drowning and a potential loss of life from drowning of an additional 262 persons.[61] In 1958, the flotation cushion requirement was introduced in the airworthiness regulations (CAR 4b), but the operational proposal was still lingering.[62] It was withdrawn in 1962 and then reproposed again in 1965.[63,64] It finally became effective in 1967.[65]
- Spurred by the 1962 Flying Tiger Line ditching, in 1964 the FAA finally mandated a light on each life vest and life raft.[66]

7.6.2 FIRST-AID KIT AND SURVIVAL EQUIPMENT

In 1963, the detailed first-aid kit contents list that existed as guidance was elevated into a firm requirement in Parts 41 and 42.[67] The first-aid kit requirement reached Part 40 in May 1964.[68]

First Trough (1954–1964)

When the life rafts finally became mandatory in 1957, a requirement for a survival kit, 'appropriately equipped for the route to be flown', came along.[69] For Part 42 (irregulars), there had already been guidance material for the survival kit since 1946 (see Section 5.5.4.3). This was however not the case for Part 41 (overseas), and neither was it done now. Obviously, no survival kit proposals had been made for Part 40 (domestic), as the 48 contiguous states were not considered to be challenging enough.

7.7 INFORMATION AND INSTRUCTIONS

The main changes in the area of information and instructions took place with respect to cabin professionals (see Chapter 8). Other than that, the only change in this domain was that from the early 1960s passengers were legally required to observe the no smoking and fasten seat belt signs.[70]

NOTES

1. DR 50-8.
2. DR 51-6.
3. DR 50-8.
4. DR 51-6.
5. Amdt 40-0 (1953).
6. Amdt 40-18.
7. Amdt 40-18.
8. Amdt 40-18.
9. DR 50-8.
10. DR 52-26.
11. Amdt 40-20, 41-6, 42-6.
12. CAB Aircraft Accident Report, American Airlines, Inc., Lockheed Electra, L-188A, N 6217A, Laguardia Airport, New York, N.Y., September 14, 1960, I-0032, Released August 28, 1961.
13. CAR 40-36, 41-44, 42-3, 1962.
14. DR 51-6.
15. DR 52-6.
16. DR 53-15.
17. Amdt 40-20.
18. CAB Accident Investigation Report Transocean Air Lines Inc., Shannon, Ireland, August 15, 1949, SA-198, Released September 15, 1950.
19. Rapport d'accident Civil No. CA.135 (avion Douglas DC.4 F.BBDM), à Bahrein le 14 Juin 1950, Journal Officiel de la Republique Française, 28 Mars 1952, p. 301.
20. CAB Accident Investigation Report, Northwest Airlines, Inc., Sandspit, British Columbia, January 19, 1952, SA-255, Released September 15, 1952.
21. Aviation Week, May 12, 1952, p. 84.
22. CAB Accident Investigation Report, Pan American World Airways, Inc., San Juan, Puerto Rico, April 11, 1952, SA-258, Released September 26, 1952.
23. Air Work Limited, Hermes 4-A, Ditched between Port of Trapani and the Island of Formica on 21 August 1952, in ICAO Circular 38-AN/33.
24. DR 52-26.
25. Amdt 40-20, 41-6, 42-6; Postponed by Amdt 40-4, 41-10, 42-9.
26. Rapport d'enquête sur l'accident survenu à Fethiye (Turquie), le 3 août 1953, à l'avion Lockheed 749 A-F. BAZS, Journal Officiel de la Republique Française, 16 Mars 1954.
27. Interview notes by anonymous, in Embry Riddle Jerome Lederer papers.
28. Amdt 40-20, 41-6, 42-6.
29. Aviation Week, June 27, 1955, p. 97.
30. An Experimental Study of Escape and Survival in Aircraft Ditchings, Barry G. King, Mary C. Richardson, Presented at Flight Safety Foundation International Air Safety Seminar, Palo Alto, California, November 11–15, 1957.
31. CAB Accident Investigation Report, Pan American World Airways, Inc., off the Coast of Oregon in the Pacific Ocean, March 26, 1955, SA-304, Released November 15, 1955.

32. CAB Accident Investigation Report, Northwest Airlines, Inc., Boeing 377, N 74608, in Puget Sound, Near Seattle, Washington, April 2, 1956, SA-319, Released November 14, 1956.
33. Review of the Federal Aviation Act (Pilot Qualification and Certification and Military Participation in the Federal Aviation Agency), Hearings Before the Aviation Subcommittee of the Committee on Interstate and Foreign Commerce, United States Senate, 86th Congress, Part 3, June 7, 1960, p. 963.
34. CAB Accident Investigation Report, Pan American World Airways, Inc., Boeing 377, N 90943 in the Pacific Ocean, between Honolulu and San Francisco, October 16, 1956, 1-0121, Released July 11, 1957.
35. CAB Aircraft Accident Report, Northwest Airlines, Inc., Douglas DC-7C, N 292, near Manila, Philippine Islands, July 14, 1960, 1-0026, November 23, 1962.
36. Lessons of the Flying Tiger Ditching, B.W. Townshend, in The Aeroplane and Commercial Aviation News, February 28, 1963.
37. CAB Aircraft Accident Report, The Flying Tiger Line, Inc., Lockheed 1049H, N 6923C, Ditching in the North Atlantic, September 23, 1962, SA-367, Released September 13, 1963.
38. Tiger in the Sea: The Ditching of Flying Tiger 923 and the Desperate Struggle for Survival, Eric Lindner, 2021.
39. Civil Aeronautics Board Aircraft Accident Report, Northeast Airlines, Inc., DC-7C, N 285, Ditching in the Sitka Sound, Alaska, October 22, 1962, 1-0030, Released September 19, 1963.
40. Crash Survival Study National Airlines DC-6 Accident at Elizabeth, NJ, February 11, 1952, Hasbrook AH, Crash Injury Research, Cornell University Medical College, October 1953.
41. Aviation Week, January 17, 1955, p. 21.
42. Evacuation Pattern Analysis of a Survivable Commercial Aircraft Crash, 62-9, by A. Howard Hasbrook, J.D. Garner, Clyde C. Snow, FAA CARI, May 1962.
43. Aviation Week, April 7, 1952, p. 55.
44. Aviation Week, November 5, 1956, p. 61.
45. Crash Safety Tests of Two Transport Aircraft, Herbert C. Spicer, Jr., Donald W. Voyls, Federal Aviation Agency, and Donald F. Carroll, Flight Safety Foundation, SAE Paper 920C, October 1964.
46. Cabin Safety: "SAFER Committee" Update (Aircraft Passenger Seat Structural Design), Hearings Before the Subcommittee on Oversight and Review of the Committee on Public Works and Transportation, House of Representatives, 96th Congress, Second Session, June 3, 1980, p. 11.
47. Research in Occupant Safety, Dynamic Testing of Seats, Meeting—Thursday, November 19, 1959, Rickey's Inn, Palo Alto, California, in Jerry Lederer Papers.
48. DR 56-25.
49. Amdt 4b-5 (1957).
50. Unites States Patent Office No. 2,765,131.
51. Passenger Escape from Aircraft Employing the Inflatable Slide, Ralph Ostrich, CAA and William Starr, USAF MATS, February 1956.
52. Supp. 37 to CAR 4b.
53. Amdt 4b-12.
54. Amdt 40-20, postponed twice.
55. DR 52-26.
56. Amdt 4b-8 (1953).
57. Amdt 4b-11.
58. DR 55-8.
59. Amdt 4b-8 (1953).
60. Amdt 4b-6 (1957).
61. DR 56-26.
62. Amdt 4b-11.
63. 27 FR 12412.
64. NPRM 65-12.
65. Amdt 121-17.
66. Amdt 40-44, 41-9, 42-8.
67. Amdt 41-0 (1962), 42-0 (1963), 40-43.
68. Amdt 40-43.
69. Amdt 40-20.
70. Amdt 41-0 (1962), 42-0 (1963), 40-43.

8 The Cabin Professional

ABSTRACT

The sixth domain differs from the other five in that it is about persons, not technology. It deserves its own chapter, one but the largest.

The history of cabin professionals started in 1912 in Germany and initially involved males only. The female element was introduced in 1930 in the U.S. and has dominated the profession ever since. Until the 1950s, safety was not an essential element of the job, even though there were some heroic examples of stewardesses evacuating passengers from airplanes on fire. This changed when in 1954 a firm requirement was introduced in the U.S. for a flight attendant but only on domestic scheduled flights. No rationale was given, and much was left in the open. Matters such as duties and responsibilities, their number in larger airplanes, whether they were needed on international and non-scheduled flights, where they were supposed to sit and how they were protected in a crash, their qualifications, the amount and nature of training, flight duty and rest times, and so on, would all gradually be filled in over the next decades.

8.1 A BRIEF HISTORY

8.1.1 Pioneers

As civil air transport started earlier in Europe than in other parts of the world, it is only logical that the first flight attendants were employed in that continent. And that was indeed the case, however, not on an airplane but on an airship. Heinrich Kubis was a waiter with DELAG, a German airship airline that made sightseeing flights across Germany. He started his aerial career in 1912 on airship LZ 10 *Schwaben*. It was interrupted by the Great War. After the war, he kept serving on airships for two more decades. Eventually, 25 years later, he oversaw a staff of about 15 persons. On the LZ 129 *Hindenburg*'s May 1937 last, ill-fated flight from Germany to the U.S. there were seven stewards (including Kubis), one stewardess, a doctor, five cooks, and a mess boy, in addition to 46 other crewmembers and 36 passengers. On arrival at Lakehurst, New Jersey, Kubis survived the fiery crash by jumping to the ground from the infernal sinking airship at exactly the right time. When doing so, and in the right spirit of a safety-minded cabin attendant, he gave a jump command to passengers. All but four of his staff survived.

Although Ellen Church is generally considered to have been the first female flight attendant in 1930, eight years earlier, Ms. Jeanne Fontaine (1897–1994) served as an air hostess to reassure passengers on sightseeing flights from Le Bourget, operated by *Compagnie Aérienne Française*. She was the secretary to the founder, Henri Balleyguier, and reportedly also served on the Paris–Brussels route.[1]

In England, Daimler Airway started to employ in 1922 a trio of what they called 'cabin boys' on their De Havilland D.H. 34 passenger aircraft. These boys were only 14 years of age, so they weighed less than an adult.[2] Any mass brought on board an aircraft impacts the performance of an aircraft. This impact is proportionally bigger the smaller the aircraft, as those early aircraft were. The boys were dressed like bellboys. Their tasks were minimal, providing reassurance and general assistance to passengers. The first of these boys was Jack Sanderson. His initial flight was on 2 April 1922. Unfortunately, he died on 14 September 1923, at the age of 15 in an air crash near Ivinghoe, Buckinghamshire, thereby becoming the first flight attendant who 'died in harness' and the youngest, a record that he will likely posthumously keep forever.

In the following years, other airline companies started to hire stewards, all male. This included Air Union in France, Imperial Airways in Britain, Lufthansa in Germany, and Mexico's Mexicana.

KLM Royal Dutch Airlines, on the other hand, had the on-board mechanic double as cabin attendant, but from 1934 employed dedicated stewards, mainly on the long route to Netherlands East Indies.

In the U.S., Stout Air Services was the first to employ the services of an aerial courier.[3] That was in 1926. Transcontinental Air Transport (TAT), a predecessor of TWA, employed some male couriers from 1928 to 1930, who were the sons of the financiers.[4] They were replaced by co-pilots, also known as first mates, in an early effort to economize on resources. Western Air Express (also a predecessor of TWA) experimented with stewards from 1928 to 1931. Pan Am's first steward was a 19-year-old native of Puerto Rico. He was based in 1928 in Miami and regularly flew from there to Havana. By 1930, Pan Am employed ten stewards, the youngest of whom was 17. They initially flew on Fokker F-7 and F-10 landplanes, followed later by seaplanes such as the Sikorsky S-40.[5]

8.1.2 Enter the Air Hostess

In 1930, Boeing Air Transport (BAT), a predecessor of United Airlines, made the bold step to introduce females to the role of what then became known as the 'air hostess'. Many in aviation know by heart the name of the first of the 'initial eight'—Ellen Church—and the fact that she and her colleagues were registered nurses. They started flying on the Boeing 80 between Oakland and Chicago, with 13 intermediate stops. Cheyenne, about halfway, was where they transferred. The female element appealed to the flying public, and other U.S. airlines copied the concept. Eastern Air Transport (later Eastern Airlines) hired seven air hostesses in 1931 for operation on the 18-seat Curtiss Condor.[6] American Airways (later American Airlines) hired four in 1933, who also flew on the Condor as well as the Ford Trimotor. TWA's first air hostesses were hired in December 1935, to work on the Douglas DC-2.

In Europe, Swissair in 1934 was the first to introduce an air hostess, by the name of Nelly Diener. She served on the company's Curtiss Condor. A year later KLM followed with a group of four, all nurses, and called them 'stewardesses'. They flew the Douglas DC-2, but only on the European routes. The long route to the East Indies was considered too exhaustive for female but not for male stewards. The first and only pre-war British air hostess began in May 1936 on a 16-seat Avro 642 operated by Air Despatch between London Croydon and Paris.[7]

The first air hostess in Australia worked in 1936 with Tasmanian Aerial Services, the forerunner of Ansett Airlines of Australia, on the De Havilland D.H. 86.[8] In the Soviet Union, Elsa A. Gorodetskaya became the first stewardess. On 5 May 1939, she flew from Moscow to Ashkhabad on a Lisunov Li-2, which was a Soviet-built, modified version of the American DC-3. It was a 13-hour flight with two landings.[9]

The new job for women was all but risk-free. Nelly died in an air crash within three months of starting. Of the first four KLM stewardesses, one died in her first month during a familiarization flight that was part of her initial training. Another, Hilda Bongertman, was the sole survivor of an air crash at London Croydon in her second year of employment. When TWA Flight 1 crashed in Pennsylvania's Chestnut Ridge mountains in April 1936, there were some survivors, including Nellie Granger, the air hostess. She walked four miles (6.4 km) over rough mountain terrain to the nearest telephone and called her airline, breaking the news. She then insisted on returning to the crash site with the rescue party. They found two persons alive, one of whom later died. Nellie was declared a national heroin.

One of Deutsche Lufthansa's first *Flugbegleiterinnen*, Brigitte Abel, died in an air crash of a Junkers Ju 90 near Brauna, Sachsen, on November 8, 1940.[10] Although Germany was at war, the airline maintained many air routes within its extended territory and beyond to such destinations as Madrid and Lisbon. The accident was not caused by war action but by icing. With 29 fatalities, it was one of the worst air disasters at the time.

The introduction of females in the crew was an immediate success. It appeared to attract more passengers. One idea behind it was to convey a sense of reassurance: if a woman could work and fly

The Cabin Professional

unnerved, then certainly men could. Eastern Air Transport added that 'hostesses answer the average woman's desire for the company of another woman on a flight'.[11] But the allurement of the opposite sex was certainly also a factor. Passengers in those days were predominantly men. By the 1940s most U.S. airlines hired exclusively female hostesses and saw passenger numbers increase accordingly. Pan Am was the exception. It continued to only use male stewards until 1944.[12] This had to do with the extra clerical work and the physical challenges of the long overseas routes which were considered too strenuous for women.[13] Possibly, the lack of competition played a role as well. Pan Am had a monopoly on its routes. During World War Two, U.S. airlines continued to fly and employ female hostesses, but the requirement that they be a nurse was dropped, as the war demanded their services elsewhere. Probably, the need for their skills had diminished, if they were indeed ever needed.

Hiring criteria for hostesses were very stringent: registered nurse, white, not married, and within strict size and age limits, as specified below for some airlines (see Tables 8.1, 8.2 and 8.3). Added with prescriptions for make-up, haircut, and all having been subjected to a beauty make-over, a new class of graduates looked like 'a regiment of Barbie dolls'.[14]

Continental Airlines in 1941 exceptionally allowed married women but only when their husbands were with the armed forces overseas. Pan Am went further and allowed their newly-hired female cabin attendants to be married and keep their jobs.[15] Air France's first air hostesses, in 1946, met the following criteria: not married, speaking French, English, and preferably a third language, and, importantly, attractive, elegant, being present, and having a natural ease plus moral and social qualities.

8.1.3 Female Attraction

In the 1950s and 1960s, while international carriers such as Northwest and TWA kept male stewards, primarily in senior positions, most U.S. domestic airlines exploited the female attraction element and introduced a women-only policy for cabin staff. By 21st-century standards, they were indeed themselves exploited and there was gender discrimination. Air hostesses had to leave the airline when getting married, as opposed to their male colleagues. Many considered the job as a temporary sojourn between college and wifedom. But not all. Some stayed and reached their thirties. Airlines

FIGURE 8.1 Line-up of 34 TWA stewardesses in front of a Boeing 307 (courtesy of TWA Museum, Kansas City, MO).

TABLE 8.1
Height Limits for Cabin Attendants

Female Minimum	Maximum	Airline, Year	Male Minimum	Maximum
5' (1.52 m)		Delta 1940, Continental 1941		
1.55 m		Air France 1946		
5' 2" (1.57 m)		TWA 1945		
5' 3" (1.60 m)		American Airlines 1940		
5' 3" (1.60 m)		Pan Am 1944 (ideal)		
	1.60 m	Air France 1946		
	5' 4" (1.63 m)	BAT 1930		
	5' 5" (1.65 m)	Delta 1940, Continental 1941		
		Pan Am 1929	5' 5" (1.65 m)	
	5' 6" (1.68 m)	American Airlines 1940		
	5' 7" (1.70 m)	TWA 1945		
	5' 8" (1.73 m)	United		
		Pan Am 1929		5' 9" (1.75 m)

TABLE 8.2
Weight Limits of Cabin Attendants

Female Minimum	Maximum	Airline, year	Male Maximum
45 kg		Air France 1946	
100 lbs (45 kg)		Continental 1941, TWA 1945	
105 lbs (48 kg)		American Airlines 1940	
	115 lbs (52 kg)	BAT 1930	
115 lbs (52 kg)		Pan Am 1944 (ideal)	
	120 lbs (54 kg)	American Airlines 1940, Continental 1941	
	125 lbs (57 kg)	Delta 1940	
	130 lbs (59 kg)	United	
	60 kg	Air France 1946	
	135 lbs (61 kg)	TWA 1945	
		Pan Am 1929	150 lbs (68 kg)

TABLE 8.3
Age Limits (at Hiring) of Cabin Attendants

Minimum	Female	Male	Maximum
21	Air France 1946, Delta 1940, TWA, American 1940		
22	KLM 1950		
23	Pan Am 1944 (ideal)	Pan Am 1929	
	BAT 1930, American Airlines 1940		26
	Delta 1940		28
	United, KLM 1950, Air France 1946		30
		Pan Am 1929	32

reacted by imposing maximum ages of 32 or 35. American Airlines was the first to do that, in 1953. Now unionized, those already employed managed to have this new rule not imposed on them, but it was on all new hires. The exempted were referred to as having been 'grandmothered', even though they were only in their mid-thirties! This trend was not constrained to the U.S. KLM from 1954 onward contracted stewardesses for five years only, while stewards could remain until the age of 50. BOAC retired stewardesses after ten years or at age 35, whichever came first.[16] Males at BOAC kept their retirement age of 60. In 1958, an attempt by KLM to fire stewardesses aged 35 or above failed, but a second attempt in 1964, now for those aged 40 or above succeeded, except that they kept their wages, plus a pension from age 50.[17]

In the 1960s, and mainly in the U.S., one female aspect started to be even more explicitly exploited: her sex appeal. While this was already subtly present since the 1930s, it became more profound. In 1967, Mary Wells of Braniff explained to Business Week that 'when a tired businessman gets on an airplane, we think he ought to be allowed to look at a pretty girl'.[18] In the late 1960s and 1970s, U.S. airlines openly advertised sexual teases such as 'Fly Me' and 'We really move our tails for you'.[19]

As to race, 'airlines were forced to cede ground on racial discrimination when African American breached the color barrier in airline passenger service in the late 1950s'.[20]

8.1.4 Equal Opportunity

Societal changes in the 1960s, both in the U.S. and Europe led stewardesses, supported by unions, to fight for less exploiting and more rights. In the U.S., on July 2, 1964, the Civil Rights Act was signed into action by president Lyndon B. Johnson. Title VII of that act prohibited employers from discriminating on the basis of race, color, sex, religion, or national origin. Yet, it took another five to ten years and many court cases before the profession could reap the benefits of that new law. Gradually, airlines dropped the no-marriage rule and raised the age limits. The weight limit was the toughest to get lifted, lasting until the early 1990s. The women turnover rate declined sharply. Where an employment stay of 1.5 to 2 years was normal in the 1960s, in the latter 1970s it had risen to 6 to 8 years.

But not only women profited. There were also men who now won court cases for getting a job in a female-dominated profession.[21] This notably occurred at Pan Am in 1972, which earlier had traded in its male-only status to join the vast stewardess-only league of airlines.

Outside the U.S., similar trends developed. Sabena allowed married stewardesses from 1963 onward. Air France resisted such but lost its case in 1967 at the highest court in France, *la cour de cassation*. KLM dropped the no-marriage rule only in 1970 and the five-year contracts in 1977. It allowed women to be promoted to cabin chiefs (called pursers) as late as 1985.[22]

In the UK, the Equal Opportunity Act of 1975 relaxed the age restrictions for British female cabin attendants. The recruitment age went up to 49, and the retirement age became 55.[23]

Fast forward 50 years, the profession of flight attendants has become much more inclusive. Hiring standards in 2024 for airlines worldwide typically only include a minimum age (ranging from 18 to 21). Occasionally, a maximum age at application applies (Cebu Pacific 25 years, JAL 28 years, Scoot, 30 years). There are height minima (females 1.52 to 1.60 m, males 1.70 m) and occasionally maxima (females 1.80 m, males 1.90 to 1.95 m). Some airlines specify a minimum arm reach on tiptoes (2.08 to 2.12 m). There are no specific weight limitations, other than in general terms ('weight in proportion to height' or simply 'healthy'). Education skills and language skills remain specified, and some airlines require swimming skills (at least 25 or 50 m). While there are no criteria specific to race, as that would be discriminatory, quite a few airlines specify that only nationals from the home country are admitted for the job.[24]

8.1.5 Shift of Work

The early boys of Daimler Airway handed out leather steamer rugs, hot water bottles, and cotton ear plugs, next to offering reassurance to the passengers and general assistance.

The 1928 TAT couriers had a wide range of tasks. From Helen McLaughlin's Footsteps in the Sky:[25]

> They collected passengers at a downtown location and drove them to the airport. Along the way they stopped by the caterers to pick-up the meals. They weighed and loaded baggage and mail after helping their passengers to board. In flight, they were responsible for attending to the passengers' needs by adjusting seats, safety belts, ventilators and heaters, as well as serving meals.

In the same year, Pan Am used stewards. Their tasks included the checking in of luggage, mail, and express (the period term for cargo) next to greeting passengers and making them comfortable.[26] It also included rowing the passengers from shore to the flying boat when they were not moored alongside a pier.

Eastern Air Transport, in their early 1930s service manual, listed the following tasks:[27]

- *Offer to passengers newspapers, gums, cotton for the ears, ammonia capsules.*
- *Serve coffee from thermos bottles and bags of donuts.*
- *Adjust the altimeter at each stop.*
- *Assist in fuelling, using buckets.*
- *Clean the cabin, sweep the floor, dust off seats.*
- *Make sure all seats are fastened to the floor.*
- *Warn passengers against throwing cigars and cigarettes out the windows.*
- *Carry a railroad timetable.*
- *Prevent passengers from mistaking the entry door for the lavatory door.*
- *As prohibition is in force, be alert on passengers bringing their own flask on board.*

The hostess of UK airline Air Despatch in 1936 served salmon and caviar, typed business passengers' dictation, and mixed cocktails.[28]

In 1939, the Civil Aeronautics Authority (CAA) published in its periodical the results of a questionnaire by the U.S. Office of Education among airlines on air hostesses.[29] It listed the following duties:

> 1 *Is in charge of the cabin.*
> 2 *Acts as hostess to the passengers on board.*
> 3 *Assists passengers with connections and reservations.*
> 4 *Provides reading (magazine and papers) and writing materials (stationary and post cards).*
> 5 *Answers questions about the plane and airways, and points of interest along the route.*
> 6 *Serves complimentary meals at the breakfast and dinner hours.*
> 7 *Serves light refreshments on all trips flown between the regular meal hours.*
> 8 *Makes night passengers comfortable for sleeping.*
> 9 *Assists elderly persons in making trips by air.*
> 10 *Helps mothers who are traveling with children.*
> 11 *Helps out occasionally with a game of checkers, backgammon, or chess, and is often called upon to make a fourth at bridge.*
> 12 *At the completion of the trip, ascertains that all personal belongings are delivered to the passengers.*
> 13 *Takes care of certain company routine work in connection with tickets, etc.*
> 14 *Sees that all passengers routed for each flight are on board with baggage and effects.*
> 15 *Sees that the ship is supplied with sufficient items for passenger use, and does anything which may help to keep the passengers comfortable during air travel.*

It is noteworthy that the three safety-related duties (with respect to oxygen, refueling, and smoking) as mentioned in the period safety regulations were not listed by the CAA.

Gradually, the tasks shifted from providing general duties and being a guide to serving food and drinks and making up beds. In the 1950s this was quite a personal service, involving bringing food on a plate to each passenger from the galley. As Kathleen Barry put it, stewardesses walked miles and worked hard yet were expected to be glamorous and seemed not to be working at all.[30]

With the jets came more passengers but less time to do the same work. The trolley was invented allowing 'mass production of passenger care', transforming the gracious servants into mindless robots.[31] Passengers, more in number, changed from well-behaved, smartly dressed upper class to a wider cross-section of the public. Barry cited veteran stewardesses in the *Chicago Tribune* in October 1978: '[Passengers included] the barroom brawlers, the drunks, the types who get violent, the kind with no class at all'.[32] She added however that 'some elitism was surely at play in these stewardesses' complaint' and that 'the "class" desired in passengers had less to do with wealth or breeding than with courtesy and sobriety'.[33] On the latter subject, in the late 1950s, the House of Representatives proposed a bill to prohibit any alcohol serving or consumption on airliners, but this was not supported by the Senate. Drunkenness on board aircraft remained one of those challenges that flight attendants needed to cope with.

Before the jet age air hostesses spent much time serving and conversing with passengers, this changed with increasing passenger numbers. A time-motion study in 1968 found that a stewardess had exactly 23 seconds on average to interact with each passenger.[34]

A key element of the flight attendant's job is interaction with passengers. In a confined tube full of people, isolated from the world for many hours, he or she represents not only the airline but the rest of society. That notion, and her decade-long experience as a stewardess, inspired KLM stewardess Geeri Bakker to sum up the qualifications of a stewardess as follows: she is a waitress, police officer, baby caregiver, manager, riot policewoman, toilet attendant, firefighter, nurse, midwife, cook, safety consultant, photographer, film critic, salesperson, bouncer, barkeeper, technician, telecom expert, kindergarten teacher, supernanny, detective, actor, psychologist, or physician.[35]

Except for the firefighter role, perhaps missing from her list are the many other safety duties that a flight attendant is trained for. The workload of a typical cabin crewmember was well expressed by 'Singapore girl' Connie Ming in Flight International: 'We work like horses, think like men and act like ladies'.[36]

8.1.6 SHIFT OF TITLE

Over the years, flight attendants have been titled differently. The first titles used in Europe were waiter (on the German airship, in 1912) and cabin boy, in the UK, 1922. In the U.S. it was (aerial) courier in 1926. In the 1930s in Europe came stewards and stewardesses, while in the U.S. the terms 'steward' and 'air hostess' were preferred. At Pan Am, stewards were also called pursers. Later, that term was used by other airlines for the person in charge of the cabin crew, being either male or female. Air France called its first stewards barmen.

In the U.S., informally, variations to the condescending word 'girl' were used such as sky girl and cabin service girl. As an alternative to steward and stewardess, the gender-neutral term 'cabin attendant' was generally used in the 1930s, notably formally. Following World War Two, British South American Airways, which named its airplanes Stars (e.g. Star Tiger and Star Ariel, both Avro Tudors that happened to disappear forever near Bermuda), called its all-female cabin staff Stargirls.

From 1954, the U.S. started to use the term 'flight attendant' in regulations. But, on board, they remained stewardesses until the 1970s, next to the incidental steward and purser. Since the late 1970s flight attendant has been the common title in the U.S. The Federal Aviation Regulations consistently use this term, although in some cases there are still inherited references to 'cabin attendant'.[37] Outside the U.S., many countries call them cabin crew, or cabin crewmembers, either in English or in a local translation. ICAO, in 1967, used 'cabin attendant' in its standards but in 1999 changed that to 'cabin crew' and 'cabin crewmember'.

The European Union Aviation Safety Agency (EASA) refers to them as cabin crew and has a Part Cabin Crew (Part-CC) in its repository of regulations. The term 'stewardess' remains in use outside the U.S. on a more informal basis.

In France, the formal term is PNC—*Personnel Navigant Commercial*—or commercial air crew, as opposed to *Personnel Navigant Technique*—PNT—technical air crew or flight crew. The term was introduced formally in 1953 and one year later subdivided into (1) *Commissaires de bord*, (2) *Hôtesses de l'air*, and (3) *Stewards*.[38,39]

8.1.7 STATISTICS

8.1.7.1 Numbers

The number of cabin crew has grown exponentially over the years. In the U.S., in 1953 there were about 6,000 flight attendants active. This climbed to 23,000 in 1967 and 78,000 in 2005.[40,41]

In 2024, the total number of persons employed as a flight attendant, worldwide, is estimated to be roughly 400,000. There are no exact figures, but data for the U.S. airlines from various sources hover around 110,000 flight attendants. In terms of seating capacity, the U.S. airliner fleet represents just over 25% of that of the world. Hence the rough estimate of about 400,000 active flight attendants worldwide. An estimate of the total number of persons that have ever been a flight attendant since the start of aviation is even more difficult. It will amount to several million people worldwide.

8.1.7.2 Diminishing Flight Crew, Increasing Cabin Crew

The year 1958 is often cited as the year when the number of transatlantic passengers by sea was overtaken by the number of such passengers by air. Eventually, sealiners stopped altogether from sailing between the two continents.

When looking at the distribution of crew in the airliners flying transatlantic, and later elsewhere, a similar transgression took place inside. The same year, 1958, may well have been the year that more crew worked aft of the cockpit door than in front of it. Shortly after World War Two, the number of crew on the flight deck was far greater than that in the cabin. A flight crew consisted of a pilot, a second pilot, a flight engineer, a navigator, and a radio operator. And often even more as back-ups needed to be on board for relief on long flights. The cabin was then manned by two or three stewards and possibly a stewardess. Continuous sophistication of cockpit instruments and equipment led to the retirement in the 1950s of the radio operator, in the 1960s of the navigator, and in the 1990s of the flight engineer. Some prophesize that the second pilot is the next to become redundant. And, with the advent of Advanced Air Mobility, even the first pilot. Cabin crew numbers however have expanded with the growth in size of the airplane. The Airbus A380 has up to 24 qualified cabin crew. Emirates adds to that two cabin service assistants, also known as shower attendants, as their duties include refreshing the showers after each use.

8.2 RECOGNITION OF THE SAFETY ROLE

In the early 1950s, attention to evacuation grew and, thus, the awareness of the flight attendants' safety role. That was not yet the case in 1947 when a DC-4 crashed on take-off from New York—La Guardia with horrifying survivability issues, killing 43 out of 48 occupants. The investigators omitted the entire subject of cabin safety, including the fact that there were two stewardesses on board. Perhaps they were told that next time they should look beyond the cause and also study the consequences of an accident. If so, that next time came quickly. In January 1948, a Lockheed Constellation crashed at Boston, on diversion from La Guardia, in wintery conditions. Again, there was a fire but now all on board survived. This time, the investigators did pay attention to survivability factors, yet the role of the cabin attendants was not discussed other than in a general statement that 'the conduct of the passengers and crew was orderly during the evacuation and no panic was noted'.

In accidents where survivability was a factor, the investigators and the board not only spent time investigating and reporting these but went so far as praising individual crewmembers. In January 1951 a stewardess died in a survivable accident of a DC-4 that overshot on landing at Philadelphia and burned. The CAB reported that she had rendered her utmost assistance and was highly praised for her courageous efforts by the passengers who escaped. 'The board is of the opinion that Mary Frances Housley, the stewardess, acted in a most courageous manner and that she lost her life because of a high sense of duty in attempting to evacuate the passengers'.[42]

The CAB commended more stewardesses in the years to come:

December 7, 1952—TWA Constellation, Fallon NAS, Nevada—'The Board also desires to commend both stewardesses for the most efficient manner in which they carried out the cabin emergency procedures'.[43]

June 15, 1954—Great Lakes DC-4; Gage airport, Oklahoma—'Miss Muller, the stewardess, is also to be complemented for the prompt and efficient manner in which she supervised the evacuation of all passengers from the burning aircraft without injury to any of them'.[44]

March 26, 1955—PAWA 377, Oregon—'Purser Natalie Parker displayed courage and devotion to duty which was exemplary'. The vice chairman of the CAB, a panel member at the accident hearing, praised her publicly but referred to her as 'a fellow citizen, or just a fellow human being'.[45] (A later generation would likely have referred to her as a professional.)

The safety role of cabin attendants was slowly being appreciated. But even the visionary McFarland had not recognized their potential for other safety duties than first-aid. In his 1953 book, he described flight attendants—he used the new term already, next to stewardess—as passenger service personnel, and the stewardesses for their qualities as a nurse. Reacting to American Airlines' new age restriction of 32 for stewardesses, Aviation Week however did. In an editorial titled 'Age before Beauty' in February 1954 it said:

Stewardesses play an important role in reassuring new air passengers, in managing occasionally difficult passengers, in directing passenger rescue evacuation in emergency or accident. To put it bluntly, I'd rather have an orderly, safe exit from a ground-looped plane with an old (34-year-old) stewardess than be trapped inside with even Marilyn Monroe. In recent months, I've flown largely with the 'sweet young things'—beautiful, yes—but they hardly knew which end of the plane was the front. And what's worse, they showed their immaturity and ignorance. In the air, I'll take maturity in preference to beauty or youth any day.

Dr. King, in a presentation delivered at the FSF seminar in Santa Fe in November 1954 echoed this:[46]

The responsibility for initiating and carrying out emergency passenger handling procedures without supervision rests directly with the members of the cabin crew.
Survival of the cabin crew is of major importance, since knowledge and effective leadership are perhaps the most significant factors in successful escape of the passengers in landing emergencies.

The CAB in August 1952 first proposed regulations for crew duty assignments in case of emergency and ditching.[47] Due to opposition from the airlines, it took until 1956 before they became firm. Yet, they created attention, and major airlines, both in the U.S. and abroad, actively started to draft emergency protocols and tested them in practice. The term 'crew', at the time, referred to flight crew only. Cabin attendants were not yet recognized as crewmembers. This was reflected in the detailed schemes that airlines started to introduce. Pan Am c. 1952 introduced crew assignments and duties for fire and emergency landings. It had tasks spelled out for the captain; the first, second, and third officer; the first and second engineer; and the first and second radio officer. For the purser, no tasks remained but open exits in the cabin on short-range flights with fewer cockpit crew, secure the galley, and 'assist passengers'. For the other cabin crew, the stewards and stewardess, 'assisting passengers' was their only task.[48] KLM, starting in February 1953, made similar schemes. Here, at least, appeared some evacuation duties for the cabin crew.

	BEFORE DITCHING			EMERG. STATION	AFTER DITCHING
CAPTAIN	CO-PILOT	THIRD PILOT	WIRELESS OPERATOR	FLIGHT ENGINEER	CABIN PERSONNEL
Warns crew by command: 'Prepare for ditching'. Gives time available and instructs W.O. to transmit emergency signals. Takes necessary preparations. Transmits emerg. signals on R/T, giving if possible pertinent information. Immediately before landing gives command 'em. stations'.	Takes necessary preparations. Gives speed, magn. course, altitude estimated time and position of ditching to W.O. Goes to cabin and assumes command. Fastens door between crew comp. and cabin in the open pos. Assists in preparing crew emerg. stations. Remains in contact with Captain through 2nd W.O. On command emergency station warns pass. and crew to prepare for landing.	Takes necessary preparations. Assists in nav. duties and assembles necessary nav. equipment. Informs Captain of its location.	1st W.O. Takes necessary preparations. Transmits emerg signals. On command 'emergency stations' locks key. 2nd W.O. Distributes crew life vests and flashlights. Relays messages from Capt. to Co-Pilot. Stows loose objects in crew compartment.	1st F.E. Takes necessary preparations. Stows on his person aeroplane log papers. Is at disposal of Captain. 2nd F.E. Takes necessary preparations. Goes to cabin and prepares dinghies for launching.	Take necessary preparations. 1st. Steward. Is responsible for preparing seats beside emergency exits on port side and reseating pass. Repeats command 'emergency stations' to passengers in rear cabin. 2nd Steward. Distributes life vests and flashlights to cabin personnel. Collects and distributes child life vests. Assists with dinghies. Stew. (ess) Assists with general duties. Collects first aid kits, collects and packs suitable food and drink.
In Captain's seat.	In front cabin beside emergency exit on port side and over wing area.	In front cabin beside aft emergency exit on port side.	1st W.O In crew compartment, in rear seat. 2nd W.O. In rear cabin on floor, facing aft.	1st F.E. In Co-Pilots seat. 2nd F.E. On floor near main door facing aft.	1st Steward. In rear cabin against partition facing aft. 2nd Steward Near main door. Stew.(ess) In rear cabin on starboard side.
Collects nav. gear proceeds to cabin. Is last man to leave aircraft through main door.	Opens emerg. exit and climbs on wing. Contacts 1st Stew. in dinghy No. 2 Assists passengers to evacuate a/c and enter dinghy.	Opens emergency exit and climbs on wing. Contacts 2nd F.E. in dinghy No. 1. Assists passengers to evacuate a/c and enter dinghy.	1st W.O. Assists Captain or 1st F.E. to evacuate aircraft if necessary. Collects axe and proceeds to cabin. Ensures that emergency radio is aboard correct dinghy. 2nd W.O. Assists in launching dinghies. Ensures that emerg radio goes into dinghy assigned to Captain.	1st F.E. Proceeds to cabin with Captain and 1st W.O. and evacuates aircraft. 2nd F.E. Opens main door and launches dinghies. Hauls in 2 dinghies fastened to forward ring near door. Boards dinghy No 1 contacts 3rd Pilot on wing and assists passengers to enter dinghy.	1st Stew. Enters dinghy No. 2. Contacts Co-Pilot on wing and assists pass. 2nd Stew. Assists passengers in evacuating aircraft. Takes large first aid kit with him. Stew. (ess) Takes position near main door and assists pass. Ensures that food and drink go aboard of the dinghies. Takes small first aid kit with her in dinghy.

GENERAL INSTRUCTIONS TO CABIN PERSONNEL

After command 'prepare for ditching' instruct passengers to don life vest, but not to inflate, and to remain in seat with safety belt fastened. Don own life vest and check each passenger personnally. Place back of seat in upright position. Request passengers to remove footwear spectacles, pointed objects, etc. and to loosen collars. Instruct passengers to adopt standard KLM. position for emergency landing. Inform each passenger through which exit he has to evacuate. Remove and stow loose baggage etc. preferably in forward upper cargo compartment or under seats. Clear baggage racks and cloakroom of all articles.

FIGURE 8.2 Assignment of tasks for ditching, KLM, February 1953.

Thus, gradually, the safety role of the stewardess developed. In the first half of the 1950s, they had evacuated passengers in actual emergencies (some even with loss of their life), Barry King had completed his evacuation research in 1952. Airlines had started to issue evacuation tasks for cabin crew the same year. United Airlines was concerned about how to evacuate densely populated airplanes also that year, and, most importantly, a regulatory safety rule for cabin crew on board was pending. If asked to pin a year when cabin crewmembers became regarded as safety staff, then 1952 would be a good candidate. This was also the year when the term 'cabin safety' appeared for the first time. American Airlines' VP Engineering, William Littlewood, in the 16th Annual Wright Brothers Lecture delivered in Washington in late 1952 used the phrase in the context of evacuation and the positioning of emergency exits.[49]

In July 1956 the Flight Safety Foundation, always at the forefront of aviation safety developments under the dedicated leadership of Jerome Lederer, started a periodical for cabin safety, called 'Cabin Crew Safety Exchange'.

But things did not change instantly. Rather, it took a decade before the safety role was recognized widely. In January 1956, Rowland Quinn of the Airline Stewards and Stewardesses Association (ALSSA) sent a statement to a Congress hearing about the nation's civil air policy. His subject was the licensing of flight attendants and associated safety training. He observed resistance on the part of airlines, one executive of which he quoted as having 'expressed the view that emergency training was undesirable because it was a morbid subject and depressing for new stewardesses'.[50]

In July 1960, Mr. Quinn repeated his warning. This time he referred to the trade organization of the airlines, the Air Transport Association, as having taken the position, as recent as December 1957, 'that the use of flight attendants aboard aircraft was solely for reasons of service to passengers and not for reasons of safety'.[51] He added that 'the cabin attendant's primary job is taking command of the situation in an emergency and directing the action of the passengers so that those passengers will be provided the maximum amount of protection in that particular condition'.

During the 1960s, this view, which essentially was an elaboration of the CAB's decision in 1954 to require flight attendants for safety, became less controversial and more widely accepted, not only in the U.S. but globally. In 1967, ICAO added a chapter about cabin attendants in Annex 6 to the Chicago Convention, operation of aircraft. This meant that they became mandatory in all of its member states.

8.3 REGULATIONS

The first regulations about cabin attendants appeared in the U.S. already in 1930. They were of an optional nature. This changed when in 1954 there came a firm requirement for a flight attendant. That requirement was simple but gradually raised questions. What were their duties and responsibilities, on what kind of operations, how many were required, what training should they have, should they be licensed, where should they sit, and should their duty and rest times be regulated? Answers to these, and other questions, spanned five decades of rulemaking, eventually stabilizing in the 2000s.

8.3.1   1930–1953

Soon after the introduction of the first standards for commercial air transport, regulations specific to cabin attendants appeared in the U.S. In 1930, a proposal was made for a 'steward or cabin attendant' in aircraft having a passenger capacity in excess of eight. The proposed requirement continued by saying that:[52]

> the co-pilot or radio operator may serve as such, unless unusual circumstances attendant upon a particular route or service make a different arrangement advisable.

In a conference between the Aeronautics Branch and the airline industry and pilots on July 28, 1931, this regulation was challenged. This was in spite of the fact that it already left the door open to the practice of relying on the co-pilot. A summary of that conference says that a:

> recommendation was made [by industry] that the requirement concerning the provision of a steward or cabin attendant be eliminated, as it was not believed that such a requirement is necessary in the interest of safety. The department stated that it is ready to eliminate this clause.[53]

In 1934, they indeed eliminated it, and rephrased the section addressing the co-pilot as follows:[54]

> The co-pilot or radio operator may serve as steward or cabin attendant, unless unusual circumstances attendant upon a particular route or service make a different arrangement reasonable and necessary.

Co-pilots were only required for aircraft with a passenger capacity of 15 or more or 8 or more when the first pilot flew on a schedule of more than five hours within any 24-hour period without any rest or the airplane had a gross weight of 15,000 pounds (6,800 kg) or more.[55] At the time, the only aircraft types operating in the U.S. having such a capacity were some models of the Ford Trimotor and the Boeing 80A. But there were many aircraft in the 8- to 15-passenger bracket, which were now excluded by the lighter requirement. These included the Fokker F-10, the Boeing 247, the Douglas DC-2, Lockheed Models 10 and 14, and some models of the Curtiss Condor and Boeing 80A.

So, the function stayed, but it was neither mandatory nor did it require a dedicated person to serve it. Nor were its tasks defined. Many operators however still carried a cabin attendant.

By the early 1930s, the continuous improvement of aircraft designs brought them into a new space: higher altitudes. Service ceilings reached 18,000 ft (5,486 m) and higher. Aircraft at the time were all unpressurized, so cabin altitude generally equaled flight altitude. At these altitudes, oxygen is an issue and, thus, in 1934, regulations addressing oxygen were introduced in Aeronautics Bulletin No. 7-E (see Chapter 6). In 1936 these were adapted to require 'a competent cabin attendant to observe and care for passengers' when flying between 15,000 and 18,000 ft. How to interpret the terms 'competent' and 'care' was not further explained, thus left to the operator.

In 1937, the Civil Air Regulations (CAR) replaced the Aeronautics Bulletins. The contents of Bulletin No. 7-E landed in new CAR 61, which contained the regulations for scheduled interstate airlines.[56] In addition to the requirement for a competent cabin attendant when flying above 15,000 ft., it now required a 'responsible cabin attendant' who 'shall remain in the cabin at or near the main door' 'when passengers are permitted to remain in the cabin while refueling is being accomplished'.[57] However, elsewhere in the same set of regulations, it appeared that person not necessarily needed to be a cabin attendant, as it read:[58]

> Passengers aboard during refueling—Passengers may be permitted in the cabin during refueling, provided [. . .] an employee of the operator is stationed in the entrance to the passenger cabin and remains there alert for any emergency until refueling is completed.

The first of these two duplicating and possibly conflicting requirements appeared in the chapter on maintenance (of aircraft) and the second in the flight operations section: two domains that traditionally struggle. Both requirements stayed in CAR 61 until it was merged with CAR 40 in 1954. Finally, CAR 61 had a section saying that when smoking was permitted on board, a cabin attendant needed to be carried 'who shall notify passengers where and when smoking is prohibited'.[59] Yet, this regulation, too, allowed this function to be assigned to the co-pilot as an alternate.

CAR 61 contained specific qualification and duty requirements for airmen, ranging from first pilots to dispatchers. That section however remained silent on cabin attendants, so left it to the operators to decide on the qualifications and duties of cabin attendants. CAR 61 also provided for the operator to compile and distribute an operations manual and list all recipients. Cabin attendants were not on that list. These are all indications that the cabin attendant function was not taken too seriously by the regulators of the day or, at least, not recognized as important for safety.

In 1945 and 1946 two new CARs were added, CAR 41 and 42. CAR 41 was for scheduled air carriers outside the continental U.S., that is, foreign operations by U.S. air carriers such as Pan Am, American Overseas Airlines (formerly American Export Airlines), and TWA. CAR 42 set regulations for non-scheduled air carriers. In the latter, there was no mention of cabin attendants at all. In CAR 41, there was only one instance of it, where it mentioned a competent cabin attendant as an alternative to the 'use of oxygen equipment sign'.[60] The CAR 61 requirements with respect to cabin attendants caring for passengers at high cabin altitudes and for refueling and smoking were not copied. Thus, while requirements for a cabin attendant were in force in the U.S. from as early as 1930, they could either be avoided (by not flying high or not flying scheduled) or replaced by other personnel or even a sign.

8.3.2 1954–Present

The year 1954 saw for the first time a U.S. unconditional requirement for a cabin attendant. In a protracted rulemaking process that had started in 1950 and only finished on the effectivity date, April 1, 1954, CAR 61 was merged into existing CAR 40. The outcome was a new CAR that combined the operational rules of scheduled interstate air carriers in CAR 61 with the (air operator) certification rules of CAR 40.

Among many other changes, it introduced a firm requirement for a cabin attendant. Yet, the process of specifying when and how saw numerous iterations. The end result was that a *flight attendant* was now required for all scheduled interstate operations with aircraft having a passenger capacity of 10 or more.

The proposal did not raise significant opposition from industry. Typically, proposals that met with industry resistance are well documented, but in this case there is no trace of such a debate. An example of a contemporary rule proposal that was challenged was one that called for a formal briefing before flight of the passengers of emergency procedures. Industry commented heavily, so it was set aside and dealt with in a separate rulemaking process. The fact that neither there was an explanation for the new cabin attendant requirement nor any documented form of opposition confirms that this new regulation simply codified a practice common at the time, for which the airlines saw no reason to protest. By analyzing the successive text versions—see Table 8.4—it can be concluded that one element may have been slightly controversial. We have no access to the comments that were raised to the proposals, if any, but can draw some assumptions from these successive versions. In the initial proposal, the phrase 'commensurate with number of passengers' suggests that it was the intent to have more than one cabin attendant for larger numbers of passengers. In later drafts, and the final version, this phrase was removed, possibly in response to feedback so that only one flight attendant was required, irrespective of the number of passengers. The ratio matter would only be dealt with a decade later. The other changes were more of a semantical or technical nature. The identifier 'cabin attendant' was replaced by 'flight attendant'. The discriminant when to carry a flight attendant was set to airplanes having a passenger capacity of at least ten and carrying passengers. Airplane weight was initially proposed as a discriminant but then dropped.

So, the situation in spring 1954 was as follows:

A rule mandating at least one flight attendant on airplanes when carrying passengers, but:

1. only for those engaged in scheduled interstate (i.e. domestic) U.S. air services;
2. specifying as lower cut-off a passenger seating capacity of 10;
3. without any clue as to duties and responsibilities;
4. without specifying their seating location;
5. without clarity as to when additional flight attendants would be required and at what increments;

TABLE 8.4
Gestation of CAR 40 Flight Attendant Rule

Version	Number	Identifier	Ratio to Passengers	When On flights Carrying...	In...
Draft Release 50–8	One or more	Competent cabin attendants	Commensurate with the number of passengers carried	Passengers	Aircraft of more than 12,500 pounds max. certificated take-off weight
Draft Release 51–6	At least one	Cabin attendant	n/d	Ten or more passengers, or	Aircraft of more than 12,500 pounds max. certificated take-off weight
Draft Release 52–6	At least one	Flight attendant	n/d	Passengers	Aircraft of ten-passenger capacity or more
Final rule effective on April 1, 1954	At least one	Flight attendant	n/d	Passengers	Airplane of ten-passenger capacity or more

n/d: not defined.

6. without training requirements;
7. without a license requirement;
8. without associated regulations for flight and rest times;
9. without specifications for crash protection offered by seats.

Most of these open areas would be filled in or changed in successive years, some sooner than others. The next subsections describe developments for each of these areas since 1954 and, in some cases, even before that.

8.3.3 Expansion of Scope

The 1954 regulation for one flight attendant applied to Part 40 operations only, that is, domestic services. It would take until 1963, almost 10 years later, before flight attendants were formally required for overseas (Part 41) and supplemental operations (CAR 42). But then, those requirements surpassed those of Part 40 in that they regulated numbers beyond the first and only flight attendant. They required second and third flight attendants as a function of the number of passenger seats. Part 40, however, kept a requirement for one flight attendant only, irrespective of the number of passengers, or seats, until it was superseded by FAR 121 in 1965.

8.3.4 Lower Cut-Off: 10 or 20?

When the flight attendant rule was first introduced in CAR 40 in 1954, it applied to airplanes with a seating capacity of ten or more. When CAR 40 was replaced by FAR 121 in 1965, this remained the case and still is so in 2024. Yet, the common threshold for the first flight attendant for decades has been 20 passenger seats, not 10. What is the explanation for this contradiction? A 1995 change in FAR 121 gives a clue.[61] The threshold number of 10 became 20 for airplanes with a payload capacity of 7,500 lbs (3,400 kg) or less. That figure amounts to about 40 passengers. This means that for FAR 121 operators with airplanes with less than 40 passenger seats, the cut-off of 10 does not apply. Rather, it is 20.

But this still does not provide the full answer. For that we have to go back to FAR 135 of 1970 and CAR 46 of 1958. FAR 135 was introduced in 1964 and initially covered air taxi operations only. Later it was extended to the so-called commuter operators. These operators emerged in the U.S. in the mid-1960s. Initially, FAR 135 did not specify a flight attendant at all as its scope was limited to small aircraft not capable of carrying more than nine passengers. Cabin safety duties such as the briefing of passengers before flight were tasked to the pilot. But in the mid-1960s there was a technological breakthrough in power plants for smaller aircraft with the development of a lightweight turboprop engine: the Pratt and Whitney (Canada) PT-6.[62] This promoted such airplane types as the De Havilland Twin Otter and Beechcraft 99, with seating capacities in the 15 to 19 range. The new commuter operators put these airplanes to work under Part 135. This raised the question of whether a flight attendant would be needed as well. After all, for large airplanes, ten passenger seats were the discriminant. In a 1969 NPRM it was proposed that a trained flight attendant would be required in commuter aircraft:[63]

- when the passenger capacity is more than nine and the pilot compartment is separate from the passenger compartment; or
- regardless of the interior configuration, when the passenger capacity is more than 15.

This proposal raised significant opposition and the FAA relented. When it published the final rule in 1970, it said:[64]

> The proposed requirement for a flight attendant is changed in this amendment to apply to aircraft having a passenger seating capacity of 20 or more. This change is made in view of the requirement in Part 127 for a flight attendant in helicopters with a passenger capacity of more than 19 and in view of the second-in-command requirement.

The reference to helicopters gave a clue: it was Part 127 (the helicopter regulation) that swung the cut-off threshold from 10 to 20. Part 127 had started its life in 1958 when the CAB introduced it as CAR Part 46. That included a requirement for a flight attendant for helicopters with a passenger seating capacity of 20 or more. In the drafting stage of CAR 46, this discriminant had been proposed as being 10, but it was changed to 20 in the final rule.[65,66] The preamble gave no rationale for that change. At the time, it was probably not seen as significant as there were very few helicopter airlines. But that changed in 1970 when it formed a precedent for the nascent group of commuter airplanes. The cut-off discriminant of 20 has never been challenged in the U.S.

8.3.5 Duties and Responsibilities

When, in the 1930s, the CAB specified cabin attendants as an option they clarified why: to care for passengers when oxygen was needed or to guard the entrance door during refueling. But when they made them mandatory, in 1954, no reason was given. In fact, they left that to the airlines. In a separate rulemaking process, the CAB prescribed that operators in their operations manual assign functions to each crewmember in cases of an evacuation following a crash landing or ditching. This became effective in 1956.[67] This regulation prompted airlines to draft detailed schemes of tasks for individual crewmembers, including stewards and stewardesses. These were not limited to the two emergency evacuation scenarios (on land and ditching) but also to other scenarios such as a fire on board. The drafting of these schemes was taken seriously and some airlines went as far as organizing evacuation tests to validate the schemes.

Only in 1958, when the CAB proposed more than one flight attendant for overseas operators, did it give a hint of their duties for the first time:[68]

It is believed that in present-day airplanes with large passenger capacities, including jets, more than one cabin attendant may be required in case of emergency evacuation, explosive or rapid decompression or other emergency situation.

Two years later, in a further proposal to Part 41, the CAB referred to these areas as 'problems':[69]

Considering the problems associated with evacuation, decompression, and other possible emergency situations, it is provided in this section that when more than 100 passengers are carried, the air carrier shall assign at least 3 flight attendants to serve on the aircraft.

In 1960 (and also in 1962), in Congress hearings, the Airline Steward and Stewardesses Association (ALSSA) testified that flight attendants had two roles: service and safety:

The second, in our opinion, the most important function of the cabin attendant is the responsibility for the in-flight safety of the airline passenger. This can be broken down into three important duties:

1. Surveillance of passengers and cabin to prevent dangerous acts on the part of passengers.
2. To take action to protect passengers in the event of decompression, turbulence, mechanical malfunction, illness, injury of unconsciousness.
3. To handle passenger evacuation in the event of emergency crash landings and ditchings.

In essence, the cabin attendant's primary job is taking command of the situation in an emergency and directing the action of the passengers so that those passengers will be provided with the maximum amount of protection in that particular condition.[70]

In 1962, when freezing the flight attendant standards in CAR 41, the FAA echoed the views of the ALSSA and explained that flight attendants' tasks consisted of both routine duties and emergency duties. In 1965, when the FAA established the 1 to 50 ratio, they explained the rationale for flight attendants as follows:

'the need for expeditious performance of emergency functions'; and
'the handling of passengers in survivable accidents'.[71]

Much later, when the FAA first introduced flight time and rest limitations for flight attendants, they gave a more comprehensive description of their duties and responsibilities:

Flight attendants are crewmembers who perform essential routine and emergency safety duties. Routine duties include ensuring that carry-on baggage is correctly stowed; verifying that exit seating requirements are met, that passenger seat belts are fastened, and that galley service items are properly stowed; and conducting passenger briefings before takeoff. Emergency duties include conducting land and water evacuations, controlling inflight fires, handling passengers who threaten the safety of other passengers or the flight, managing medical emergencies such as passenger illness or injury, managing in flight emergencies such as smoke or fire in the cabin, and managing turbulent air penetrations, airplane decompressions, and hijackings.[72]

8.3.6 WHERE LOCATED?

The early airplane types like the DC-2 and DC-3 did not have a dedicated seat for the steward or hostess. They typically used a passenger seat. The Boeing 307 may have been the first aircraft type with a dedicated seat for the hostess. It was a folding seat, situated next to the entrance door. This would become the standard practice in many aircraft types that followed: one or more folding seats near the entry door and other doors. Until 1967, the rule was singular: the seat needed to be near a floor-level exit. In that year, a second location criterion was added: uniform distribution, and, in 1981, a third, direct view of the cabin. This created some regulatory friction.

8.3.6.1 Near Floor-Level Exit

Until 1958, the location of flight attendant seats was not regulated. This changed when the following design rule was introduced:[73]

> § 4b.358 Seats, berths, and safety belts. * * *
> (b) Arrangement. * * *
> (6) Seats for cabin attendants shall be disposed within the passenger compartment near approved floor level emergency exits. (See § 4b.362 (g).)

Note the use of the term 'cabin attendant', where since 1954 the operational rules referred to 'flight attendant'. The design rules persisted in using this term until 1981. While the requirement specified that all cabin attendants needed to be seated next to floor-level exits, it was not reciprocal. In other words, it did not specify that all floor-level exits needed cabin attendants near it. In the 1965 Salt Lake City 727 accident, the galley door on the right side just forward of the wing was allocated to a cabin attendant who sat next to the boarding door on the left, eight rows away. The accident report said that 'the speed with which the passengers progressed toward the exits' (referring to this exit) 'prevented the stewardess from reaching [it]'.[74] The short 727 was unique in having the forward exits not diametrically opposed. Such a configuration was not repeated on either the longer 727 or other airplane types. Typically, with exits opposite each other, cabin attendants were better able to control two exits, but this did not always work out.

8.3.6.2 Uniform Distribution

The location requirement was made dualistic when in 1967 the FAA additionally specified that flight attendants 'be uniformly distributed throughout the airplane in order to provide the most effective egress of passengers in event of an emergency evacuation'. This was done in both the airworthiness and the operational requirements.[75]

FIGURE 8.3 Boeing 727 tail exit door with double flight attendant seat (photograph by the author).

This eased a configuration such as on the Fokker F-28 and derivatives (Fokker 100 and 70), which only had one pair of floor-level exits, at the front. Fokker had argued that it would be better to spread the flight attendants over the cabin rather than have them all at the front, as the initial requirement ('near approved floor level exits') mandated. In most cases, the second flight attendant was located at the very end of the cabin, but some airlines preferred a location near the overwing exits, at the cost of a passenger seat. Period airplane types with a similar configuration were the Boeing 727, Douglas DC-9 (all variants), the BAC One-Eleven and the Sud-Est Caravelle. There was one difference: those types had a ventral or tail cone exit at the very rear which justified a flight attendant seat there.

In 1980, the uniform distribution requirement was dropped from the airworthiness requirements of FAR 25.[76] This was possibly unintentional. The intent of that regulatory rewording was improved protection. The reference to uniform distribution perished in the process. It remained however in the operational requirements, thus indicating that this was not an intended change of policy. The FAR 25 change created a formal non-compliance situation for the Fokker 100 when it was type certificated in 1987. It had inherited the flight attendants' distribution pattern of the F-28. The non-compliance was not recognized by the many airworthiness authorities that certificated it, including the Dutch CAA and the FAA. Only Canada spotted this, but they offered to issue an exemption as they saw merit in Fokker's approach. In 1990, the FAA repaired FAR 25.785(h) by putting back the uniform distribution rule; this time worded as 'must be [n]ear a required floor level emergency exit, except that another location if the emergency egress of passengers would be enhanced with that location'.[77] With that change, the exemption for Fokker became moot.

Also in 1990, it was required that a flight attendant seat be placed at each Type A exit. These exits were only used on wide-body airplanes, for which it was considered that the width of the cabin was too large for flight attendants to manage two opposite exits. That same year, the preference for locating flight attendant seats near floor-level exits, as opposed to such exits as the overwing hatches, was further confirmed by a new requirement that remaining flight attendant seats be evenly distributed among the required floor-level emergency exits to the extent feasible.

8.3.6.3 Direct View

Since the 1980 change to FAR 25, the flight attendants had to have a direct view over the cabin area for which they were responsible.[78] This requirement was not copied in the operational requirements, so it applied only to new aircraft types, certificated from about 1985 onward.

But what did direct view mean and why was it important? Did flight attendants need to be able to see the entire cabin, from side wall to side wall, or would it be sufficient that they at least saw the aisle so that passengers standing up were seen? Should the flight attendants be able to sense any unrest developing in the cabin when passengers perceive a dangerous situation? The latter may have occurred in the 1985 Manchester accident. Passengers on the left side saw the fierce engine fire but could not signal the cabin crew, whose view of that part of the cabin was blocked by a bulkhead. But even if they could have seen those signals, would they have understood the magnitude of the

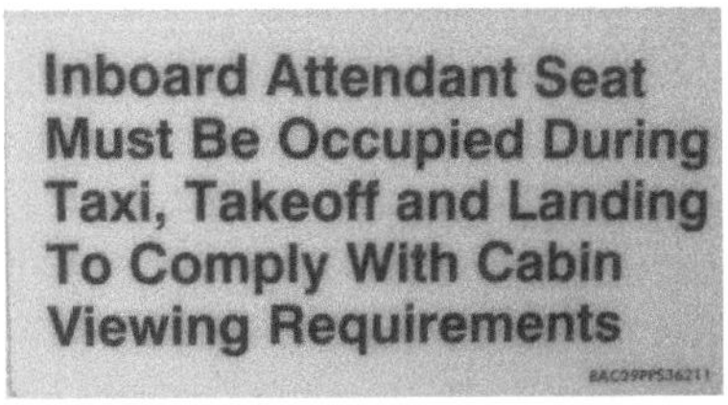

FIGURE 8.4 *Placard adjacent to a double, forward cabin attendant station of a Boeing 737-800* identifying mandatory flight attendant seat for direct view reasons (photograph by the author).

The Cabin Professional

FIGURES 8.5 AND 8.6   BAe 146 mirror coverage from cabin crew seat, forward (left), and aft (right) (photographs by the author).

fire, and, if they had, would they have been able to convince the pilot to stop the airplane earlier for an evacuation?

In some airplane types placing the flight attendant seats next to the exits, and at the same time providing a direct view created a problem. An example was the BAe 146: at the front doors, the seat unit faced forward, and in the rear it faced aft, so in both cases away from the cabin. The solution consisted of strategically placed mirrors, which enabled the cabin crew to monitor the cabin when seated during take-off and landing.

Protracted ARAC meetings in 1992–1994 with interested parties were held to advise on how to interpret the direct view rule and whether mirrors would be acceptable. A flight attendant union representative questioned this solution. John Goglia (whose career went from being an airplane mechanic to NTSB board member) wondered why thousands of U.S. truck drivers could back up using mirrors but flight attendants could not use mirrors to watch passengers. In other aircraft designs, seats were placed such that they both were near floor-level exits and faced the passengers or, such as in the rear cabin of the Airbus A320, placed in the aisle with an excellent view of the cabin. The results of the ARAC meetings are extensively reflected in an FAA Advisory Circular.[79]

8.3.7 Protection

Early cabin attendant seats were of a simple design. They provided minimal support and the user was only restrained by means of a simple safety belt. Typically, the wall to which the seat was mounted provided a hard and uncomfortable support.

Since 1945, seats for both passengers and crew were required to be designed such as to protect from head injuries. This could be achieved by either (1) a safety belt with a shoulder harness, (2) the elimination of objects in the striking radius, or (3) a safety belt and a cushioned rest which will support the arms, shoulders, head, and spine. It can be questioned whether the simple folding seats for cabin professionals indeed provided the requisite protection.

The primitive, bulkhead-mounted, folding seat, or jump seat as it became known, lasted well into the 1960s and 1970s. Accidents investigated by the NTSB repeatedly identified injuries to flight attendants sitting on jump seats in cramped areas and restrained by only a lap belt. An example was a recommendation that stemmed from three different December 1972 accidents. It called for a shoulder harness on each flight attendant seat.[80] Another was the case of an August 1975 survivable impact crash just after take-off in which two forward flight attendants submarined under their safety belts. They lost consciousness as they struck obstacles. Passengers had to initiate the evacuation. Luckily, there was no fire.[81,82]

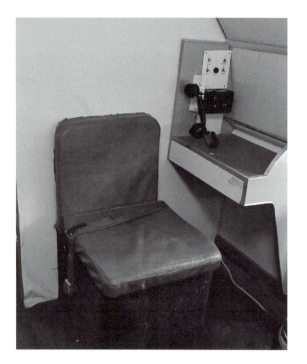

FIGURE 8.7 Cabin crew station on De Havilland Comet 1 (photograph by the author).

FIGURE 8.8 Cabin crew seat on an Antonov 24 (photograph by the author).

Side-facing flight attendant seats were found so dangerous that their use was prohibited by means of an Airworthiness Directive in 1976.[83] In 1975, the FAA proposed to significantly improve the standards for folding seats. The safety belt had to be combined with a shoulder harness, and there had to be proper support for the arms, shoulder, head, and spine. It took until 1980 before a final rule was issued.[84] It pertained not only to new airplane types but, importantly, also to the existing fleet. This required a major redesign effort by both manufacturers and airlines for which, eventually, a two-year period was granted. By March 1982, all U.S. fleets were compliant.

A further improvement occurred in 1988, when flight attendant seats, like passenger seats, were required to be dynamically tested (see Section 13.5.1). Initially, this requirement applied only to new airplane types with a type certification date from around 1993, such as Boeing 777 and Airbus A330 and A340. A companion proposal to similarly equip the existing fleet lingered on and on. It was finally issued as a rule in 2005 and was limited to aircraft manufactured from 27 October 2009 onward.[85] But, by then, a significant portion of the newer fleets complied.

8.3.8 How Many?

Four years after the requirement for one flight attendant was issued in the U.S., the CAB started to ponder about how many flight attendants should be required for the higher-capacity airplanes. In 1958, the largest airplanes in service sat about 100 passengers. With the new jets seating up to 150 or more coming up, this matter became pressing. On December 24, 1958, one week before its demise, and as part of a major change proposal for CAR 41, the CAB proposed to add a sentence for an additional flight attendant:[86]

> At least one flight attendant shall be provided by the air carrier on all flights carrying passengers in airplanes of 10-passenger capacity or more. In airplanes of 45-passenger capacity or more an additional

The Cabin Professional

flight attendant may be required by the Administrator if found necessary due to the type of operation, services rendered, or the interior configuration of the airplane.

This proposal did not reach far: only beyond 45 passenger seats. In 1960 the new FAA extended the proposal by adding a line for a third flight attendant beyond 100. However, like a decade before, there was some shuttling between two bases: passenger seating capacity or actual number of passengers. In 1958 it was the former (capacity), in 1960 the latter (passengers), but when the CAR 41 rule became effective in 1963 it was capacity-based again. CAR 42 followed in November 1963. Neither affected domestic operations (CAR 40), for which only one flight attendant remained specified until 1965, when the rules for domestic operators were harmonized with those for flag and supplemental operators, now consolidated in the new FAR 121. At the same time, a fourth band was introduced for more than 149 passengers, specifying a fourth flight attendant.[87]

By 1972 a formula was reached that has since remained virtually unchanged. From 51 passenger seats onward, additional flight attendants were required based on the ratio of 1 attendant per 50 passenger seats. But for reaching this ratio, the CAB, and its successor, the FAA, went through quite a few steps. The evolution focused on the following questions:

1. Should the number of flight attendants be based on the number of passengers actually carried, or on the capacity of the aircraft?
2. Or should it be linked to the number of emergency exits?
3. And what should the ratio be?

Later, in 1981, another discriminant was added: the number used in the evacuation demonstration.

8.3.8.1 Seats or Passengers?

As to question 1, what to use as the basis—passengers or passenger seats—the 1954 rule was a bit of both. It had the criterion of airplane capacity (10 or more passenger seats) as well as the criterion of 'carrying passengers'. Note the plural in the word 'passengers'. Could this be interpreted as meaning that the requirement only stood when there were at least two passengers? After all, it did not use the singular 'carrying at least one passenger'. Probably this subtle difference was not intended at the time and had no implication in practice.

In 1958, the CAB proposal for an additional flight attendant was based on seating capacity. In 1960, its successor, the FAA, suggested to use as the basis the actual number of passengers carried.[88] When the rule became effective in CAR 41 and 42 in 1963 (and for domestic operation in 1965, now under FAR 121), it was shuttled back to capacity again. The capacity-based ratio had won over the actual passengers-based ratio. As a solace, the FAA kept the door open for reductions on a case-by-case basis:[89]

> Upon application by the certificate holder, the Administrator may approve the use of an airplane in a particular operation with less than the number of flight attendants required by paragraph (a) of this section, if the certificate holder shows that, based on the following, safety and emergency procedures and functions established under § 121.397 for the particular type of airplane and operations can be adequately performed by fewer flight attendants:
>
> 1. Kind-of operation.
> 2. The number of passenger seats.
> 3. The number of compartments.
> 4. The number of emergency exits.
> 5. Emergency equipment.
> 6. The presence of other trained flight crewmembers, not on flight deck duty, whose services may be used in emergencies.

This option was deleted in 1967.

The capacity-based solution meant that even with only one passenger on board, a 400-seater needed at least eight flight attendants. For commuter operators, it was even more strict. Per Part 135, for airplanes with 20 seats or more, a flight attendant crewmember (*sic*) has been required since 1970, regardless of whether or not there is a passenger on board.[90]

In 1981, the FAA launched a proposal that the number of flight attendants could be reduced, under strict conditions, with seats physically blocked off. This was to accommodate, for example, scheduled flights where the passenger load was consistently low and well less than the number of seats, or in sudden cases of illness of a flight attendant.[91] Previously, the FAA had granted exemptions on a case-by-case basis. The proposal raised fierce opposition from the flight attendant unions, who went to Congress, resulting in a House of Representatives hearing in April. The FAA withdrew its proposal in December.[92] The only way for airlines to reduce the number of required flight attendants was to remove so many seats that it landed in a lower 1 to 50 band.

8.3.8.2 . . . or Exits?

When defining the number of flight attendants in 1965, the FAA responded to a comment submitted during the consultation process that there should be one flight attendant for each Type I exit. The FAA 'concluded that this is not essential, since in survivable accidents, one or more flight crewmembers likely could be available to assist in the emergency evacuation of occupants'.[93] This response is a bit puzzling, as it seems to confuse two separate aspects: floor-level exits (Type I exits at the time were the only floor-level exits) and the assistance of flight crewmembers. But it did close the door for a direct link between exits and flight attendants. This should not be confused with the requirement for locating flight attendant seats near floor-level exits, as that does not necessarily specify the number of flight attendants.

8.3.8.3 Ratio of Flight Attendants to Passenger Capacity

In the first draft for a regulation for a cabin attendant, as the term then was, issued in 1950, their number was proposed to be 'commensurate with the number of passengers carried'.[94]

In the next proposals, and the final rule of 1954, the requirement was for 'at least one' flight attendant, without a further specification. Airplane passenger capacities, at the time, stretched to close to 100. Yet, the regulator saw no reason to match these capacities by explicitly specifying more than one flight attendant. The first time that the CAB proposed a second flight attendant was in 1958 when it proposed to change Part 41 (foreign operations). The threshold was 45 passenger seats, but a second flight attendant was required only when 'found necessary due to the type of operation, services rendered, or the interior configuration of the airplane'.[95] In a follow-up, 1960 proposal this soft attempt to regulate the second flight attendant gave way to a much firmer proposal. That proposal unconditionally required a second flight attendant from a capacity of 45 onward and a third from 101 onward.[96] This became a rule in 1963, albeit only for foreign and supplemental operations, but not yet for domestic operations. And it was far from being consistent. The first flight attendant covered a maximum of 44 passenger seats; the second a maximum of 55 (45 to 100). The third was open-ended. At the time (1963–1965), maximum aircraft capacities had reached 187 (Pan Am, 1963, Boeing 707). These capacities were certificated on an individual basis. Pan Am conducted in September 1963 an evacuation demonstration to convince the FAA that it was safe to carry 187 passengers in their Boeing 707 (see Section 12.3.2). Apparently, four stewardesses were used in that demonstration, even though the regulation allowed three. Thus, they set four as the minimum number required for that capacity.

For domestic operations, the situation was even more skewed, as legally only one flight attendant was required. This would in theory allow a 1 to 187 ratio. Yet, for service reasons, most airlines at the time allocated three to four flight attendants to their new jetliners. In the 1965 FAR 121 amendment, the FAA confirmed that a fourth flight attendant was needed for seating capacities of 150 onward.[97] This shifted the open end from somewhere well beyond 101 to somewhere well beyond

151. Aircraft still grew in size, and the FAA kept lagging behind with its regulations. To stop this, it decided in 1967 to take a different approach. The rationale for this was described as being in anticipation 'of much higher passenger seating capacity airplanes presently being planned'. That was a reference to the Boeing 747 that in 1967 was on the drawing boards. The FAA introduced a blanket ratio of 1 to 50. For each increment of 50 passenger seats, an additional flight attendant was required. No longer did it need to revise the rules each time aircraft grew larger. The ratio approach worked infinitely, regardless of the size of an airplane. If there would ever be an airplane with 1,000 passenger seats, the minimum number of flight attendants for safety could already be calculated: it was 20. The new ratio applied from the third flight attendant onward (capacity 101 onward). For the second flight attendant the discriminant stayed at 45, rather than 51, as true application of the 1 to 50 ratio would dictate. That was corrected in 1972, at the instigation of the ATA.[98] Since then, the 1 to 50 ratio has been stable and copied by many other countries in the world.

But what is the 1 to 50 ratio based on? Why not 45 or 55 or any other number? In the 1962 hearing about the licensing of flight attendants, Barbara Roads of the ALSSA suggested a 'formula of at least 1 flight attendant for every 30 seats' on the jets.[99] On other occasions, a ratio of 1 to 40 was proposed. Other countries, as discussed in Section 14.7.2, chose ratios of 1 to 36 and 1 to 40.

The number was not based on any research or scientific evidence but simply picked by the FAA as a nice, rounded figure. In 1962, when choosing 101 for the third flight attendant, the FAA explained it as follows:

> There appears to be no formula of general applicability which can be established which will not under certain circumstances be considered unnecessary or arbitrary. We agree that a minimum fixed ratio of flight attendants to passengers may, as stated in some comments, be unnecessary over certain routes or on certain types of airplanes now used, or to be used in the future. However, it has been determined that the number of flight attendants in ratio to the number of passengers contained in the proposal should be prescribed as a basic minimum standard for the guidance of all operators.[100]

The key word here is 'arbitrary'. The FAA found it of greater importance that a minimum standard was set than that its rationale would stand any criticism.

8.3.8.4 Number Used in the Evacuation Demonstration

Later, an additional criterion for the number of flight attendants was added. When the evacuation demonstration requirements for air carriers were reviewed in 1981, the FAA added that the number of flight attendants employed in the demonstration became leading.[101] This referred to the demonstration by the operator, not the manufacturer. For example, if an airline used four flight attendants in its demonstration for an airplane configuration of 145 seats—for which the 1:50 ratio prescribed only three flight attendants—it was bound to always use four flight attendants. However, they could then change the seating configuration to beyond 150 without a further demonstration (provided this was within the type certification limit and the change would not alter the duties and flight attendant locations). Conversely, if they wished to reduce the number of flight attendants back to three, another demonstration would be needed.

8.3.9 Training

The training of early stewards focused on quite different subjects than those of today. Pan Am, the international operator of flying boats around 1929, had very intensive training. It lasted two months, of which five weeks were dedicated to first aid, in addition to life raft operation and other emergency skills. American Airways, on the other hand, in 1933 gave their first air hostesses a map of the cities overflown and a timetable and that was about it.[102] They started a formal training course three years later. In 1940, now named American Airlines, in stewardess school, the stewardesses studied the following subjects: (1) maps of the airlines, including all the stops by each line; (2) the parts and construction of a plane, what makes it go and what keeps it in the air, (3) flight control, radio, communication; (4) aviation meteorology, ticketing and reservations, food service; (5) duties of a stewardess.[103]

TWA, in 1936, trained their second hostess on the job, in a 12-hour familiarization flight from Kansas City to Los Angeles.[104] She later organized a two-week training course herself.

A 1939 questionnaire by the U.S. Office of Education indicated that training periods typically took two to three weeks and focused on (1) the scenic points over the routes to be flown; (2) instructions in the handling of tickets, manifests, and baggage stubs; (3) the duties relative to making passengers comfortable before and after take-off; and (4) other flight duties. After two or more familiarization trips, the hostess was assigned to regular duties.[105]

In 1941, Continental Airlines' first class of hostesses received training on (1) the airline; (2) the CAB and the CAA, including their histories; (3) technical aspects of the aircraft (the Lockheed Lodestar); (4) meteorology and causes of turbulence; (5) reservations, ticketing procedures and airline codes; (6) food service aloft as well as other in-flight services; (7) a Red Cross course to qualify each trainee to administer first aid; (8) the points of interest on the routes, as well as a review of the geography of the U.S.[106] Except for first aid, the list did not include any cabin safety element. That may either have been completely absent or touched upon so briefly that it was not worth mentioning. If so, it would have been limited to exits and the fire extinguisher. Another period report for another airline said that not more than 1.5 hours was needed for such subjects and that included the first-aid kit.

BOAC, next to Pan Am, was one of the first airlines that spent much time and effort on cabin safety training. Already in the early 1950s, its air/sea rescue training included combating a fire and finding the way out to the exit through a smoke-filled building. The first-aid syllabus had an extensive section, with a 'film in glorious Technicolour', about how to deliver a baby and care for both mother and baby. There were ditching drills, either in the Hounslow swimming pool or in a dinghy (life raft) on the Staines reservoir, both near Heathrow airport. While the crew were taught that singing in dinghies was promoted, they should not be hymns. Other elements were post-crash oriented: jungle, arctic, and desert survival with such practical suggestions as dried camel dung making a good energy fuel.[107]

KLM started a cabin safety training program in 1952. While since World War Two airplanes had been equipped with life vests, life rafts, flashlights, and Gibson girls (emergency radio equipment), the crew had not been trained in their use. This now changed, although initially some crew was quite skeptical as to whether it would work out in practice.[108]

With the introduction in 1954 in the U.S. of the requirement for a flight attendant (albeit only for domestic operations), training requirements became applicable to them. These requirements, both for initial and recurrent training applied to all crewmembers, flight attendants included. Those for initial training, although generally worded, made reference to such cabin safety events as decompression, fire, ditching, and evacuation.[109] The requirement for recurrent training did not.[110]

Rowland Quinn of the ALSSA, in a 1958 House of Representatives hearing, described the poor state of training for flight attendants. In a written statement, he explained that emergency training by the airlines 'ranges from barely adequate to none at all. Some of the procedures are impossible of implementation'. The requirements at the time (CAR 40.286), although setting forth the basic subjects to be covered, provided no minimum standards or requirements for the maintenance of qualifications.[111]

In a congressional hearing two years later, Quinn lamented again about the poor state of training by the airlines, now in person. 'In those cases where safety training is provided, the percentage of time devoted to safety—as compared to that given to "charm" and other allied service training—is perhaps 5 percent of the total'. And the training was on a group basis: only one out of perhaps 40 students would actually operate an exit. The others were supposed to learn by watching it. Some airlines confined their emergency training to explaining the location of the fire extinguisher and the operation of the main entrance door and spent not more than 15 to 20 minutes doing so.[112]

Per January 1, 1961, air carrier training programs for crewmembers were made subject to approval by the FAA.[113] The amendments to CAR 40, 41, and 42 that introduced these, however, did not specify minimum standards. The Flight Standards division of the FAA filled this gap by circulating memoranda containing training criteria. In 1962 these criteria were proposed to be elevated to the level of regulations, which occurred in 1965.[114,115] These regulations formed a template for flight attendant training that would last for decades. The standards as they apply in 2024 can be traced to this amendment, although there have of course been additions and improvements over the decades. In 1970, the list of training subjects was enlarged. Such items were added as drills on smoke control, instructions in the handling of such emergencies as illness or injury of passengers or crewmembers, and instructions in the use of first-aid equipment. For portable fire extinguishers, the instructions had to include which type of extinguisher to use on the different classes of fires.[116]

Other additions and improvements followed in 1977 (in the context of air transport for the handicapped) and 1978.[117] The 1965 standards prescribed that each trainee actually opened exits and participated in an evacuation drill. However, a clause had been added that the FAA could permit watching a demonstration as a lesser alternative. In a 1974 safety study, the NTSB, when evaluating performance during actual evacuations, found that this option was often used and condemned it.[118] Thereupon, the FAA changed the regulation so that flight attendants both during initial and recurrent training (performed every 24 months) actually operated each type of emergency exit. The same NTSB study prompted some other changes to the training standards in 1978, such as the review and discussion of previous aircraft accidents and incidents pertaining to actual emergency situations, operating exits in the emergency mode with the slide attached, and emphasis on electrical equipment and related circuit breakers found in cabin areas when combating a fire.

In 1992, the NTSB reviewed again the training standards of flight attendants and their application by the airlines. It found no major issue with the standards themselves but rather with the

FIGURE 8.9 Air France cabin training simulators (photograph by the author).

methods of oversight by the FAA. In addition, many airlines did not perform drills during recurrent training as required since 1978 and some airlines had flight attendants working on as many as seven different airplane types. Recommendations for the drills were made but not for reducing the number of aircraft types.[119]

Later changes to the training standards followed in 1995 about Protective Breathing Equipment and Crew Resource Management and in 2004 about in-flight medical events, including the use of Automatic External Defibrillators and Emergency Medical Kits.[120,121]

Major airlines started to use cabin training simulators in the 1970s, which included exit doors and slides. The more sophisticated models could be tilted and had smoke and crash sounds added for realism. This was done on a voluntary basis and, like flight simulators, for efficiency reasons: to avoid the use of actual aircraft for training. The U.S. introduced formal requirements for such equipment in 2014.[122] But already 20 years earlier it had issued guidance to its inspectors with respect to such devices.[123] This was in response to an NTSB recommendation following a December 1990 runway collision.[124] European regulators allowed the use of a 'representative training device' in the same period and provided guidance material for it.

8.3.10 LICENSING

In France, the safety role of cabin crew was recognized early and confirmed by a certificate. This was in the mid-1950s, following the recognition by law in 1953 of the PNC role on board.[125,126] It was called *Certificate de Sécurité et Sauvetage* (Safety and rescue certificate).[127] Many Latin-speaking European countries adopted the same practice.

In the U.S., even before cabin attendants were required, a suggestion for their licensing was made not by a cabin attendant but by a pilot. In a column in December 1952 in Aviation Week, Captain R.C. Robson suggested this.[128] He did it in the context of United Airlines' concerns about the evacuation of high-density DC-4s. He observed that in high-capacity aircoach operations there would be only 'one fair maiden versus 80 people'. Sometimes, even, a ticket agent would stand in to look after the passengers in flight. His plea was for a curriculum and examination of cabin attendants, including licensing.

Later that decade, the ALSSA union repeated pleas for flight attendant licensing wherever they could. One such occasion was the 1960 hearing where Rowland Quinn argued that in France such personnel is certificated.[129] He complained that '[t]he cabin attendants are the only crewmembers that the government neglected'.

The next year, and no doubt some lobbying later, a bill was proposed to include flight attendants within the definition of 'airman' so that they needed a license.[130] This bill was discussed in 1962 in a House of Representatives committee. The poor state of training of flight attendants by the airlines was brought up again, as was the importance of the flight attendant's role in an emergency. The Federal Aviation Agency, on stand, was against the bill. It argued that it was in the process of improving the training standards for flight attendants and that the administrative burden of issuing 10,000 licenses each year would be prohibitive. The training standards were indeed improved, but there would be no license.

Pleas for a license were repeated in the next decade and possibly in all successive decades until, in the next millennium, they no longer fell on deaf ears. In 2003, finally, Congress listened. As part of the Vision 100-Century of Aviation Reauthorization Act, it ordered the FAA to set up a flight attendant licensing program. The license is called a 'Certificate of demonstrated proficiency' and relies on the airlines for whom the flight attendants work. Using modern technology, the airlines inform the FAA once an attendant has qualified. The FAA then sends the certificate card directly to the flight attendant. Other than meeting the requisite training standards, there are no additional requirements, such as a medical certificate. Although the practical value of the license is quite limited, the flight attendant fraternity sees it as a token of recognition for the profession.

8.3.11 Flight and Rest Times

For pilots, legal flight time limitations, even though rudimentary, were already introduced in 1930. Flight attendants had to wait until 1994. Meanwhile, cabin crew, particularly on long, international flights, made many hours. On a KLM flight by Lockheed Constellation from Amsterdam to Montreal in the 1950s, with stops in Glasgow-Prestwick, Scotland, and Gander, Newfoundland, a 24-hour duty was normal. A compounding circumstance was that it started in the evening Amsterdam time, after being awake for a day.[131] Anecdotal reports even mention cases of 36 hours of continuous work.

Rowland Quinn in 1958 made a plea for flight time limitation rules for flight attendants, but this ended moot. Three decades later, in 1989, a flight attendant duty time act was proposed but failed to get passed in Congress.[132] A second attempt, in 1992, was more successful and caused the FAA to propose in 1993 flight duty and rest regulations for flight attendants. They became effective the next year.[133] The FAA explained that while

> no accident/incident data currently exists to provide a direct correlation between flight attendant fatigue and passenger survivability [. . .] the FAA recognizes that a flight attendant who is excessively fatigued is less likely to be capable of performing safety duties than an adequately rested flight attendant' and considered this an unacceptable risk.

Since then a flight duty time limit of 14 hours applies, but this can be extended under certain conditions to up to 20 hours. For such extended duties, a rest opportunity on board is needed. Long-range airliners are equipped with crew rest compartments, typically either below the passenger cabin or in the attic above. From a cabin safety point of view, these are small cabins of their own, with emergency equipment, emergency lighting, and a second means of egress. Minimum rest periods range from 10 to 12 hours. Until January 2023 there was a minimum of eight hours, but this was amended as ordered by Congress as part of the 2018 FAA Reauthorization Act.[134] Alternatively, an operator can choose to apply to flight attendants the flight duty and rest times for flight crew.

8.4 CHALLENGES AND HAZARDS

Next to long hours, flight attendants are exposed to a variety of societal challenges and physiological hazards. Although these are generally considered to be outside the scope of cabin safety, they may influence their ability to perform, routinely or in an emergency, hence their inclusion here.

Societal challenges include passenger behavior, excessive carry-on baggage, and portable electronic devices. They come primarily on the plate of airlines and their staff, with flight attendants at the forefront. While these challenges are frequent, very infrequent but contrary in impact are unlawful acts such as hijacking and terrorism.

The physiological hazards consist of exceedances of the physical variables which support life and to which humans are adapted. This pertains to pressure (and thus oxygen concentration), ventilation, temperature, humidity, acceleration, motion (a trigger for air sickness), noise, and vibration. Ross McFarland wrote two standard works on all these aspects, for airplane designers and airlines, respectively.[135] He distinguished psychological boundaries (e.g. for temperature below 18°C or above 24°C) and physiological boundaries (e.g. below −1°C or above 43°C). Airplane designs cover these hazards. Additionally, there are physiological hazards in domains not needed to support life, such as geophysical (ozone, cosmic radiation), cabin air contamination, sanitation, and health. Some of these are covered by regulations; others are not. Table 8.5 gives an overview for the U.S. situation, which is indicative and not necessarily complete. Other jurisdictions may have different arrangements. Cosmic radiation measuring equipment has been required since 1972 by ICAO Annex 6 for airplanes operating above 15,000 m (49,000 ft.). Concorde was so equipped.

TABLE 8.5
Physiological Hazards for Domains Not Needed for Life Support

		Regulated? U.S.
Geophysical hazards	Ozone (O_3)	Since 1980
	Cosmic radiation	Advisory only, since 1994
Cabin air quality	Carbon monoxide (CO)	Since 1937
	Carbon dioxide (CO_2)	Since 1952
	Smoking	Since 2000
	Air contaminants	No
	Airborne infectious agents	No
	Disinsection	No
Sanitation and health	Food, water, waste, vermin	By FDA or EPA
	Other health hazards	No

When it comes to the organization of regulation and oversight of these aspects, countries have different structures. Several of these elements do not necessarily resort under the civil aviation authority (such as the FAA in the U.S.), but under:

- sanitation authorities (in the U.S. the Food and Drug Administration, Department of Health and Human Services regulations for galley and lavatory construction);
- drinking water quality authorities (in the U.S. the Environmental Protection Agency);
- occupational safety and health authorities (in the U.S. this is de facto delegated by the Occupational Safety and Health Administration, Department of Labor, to the FAA per a Memorandum of Understanding).[136]

One area still in development is that of cabin air contaminants (see Section 15.6).

NOTES

1. Saint-Exupéry, le paladin du ciel, Michel Lhospice, Éditions France-Empire, 1994.
2. Human Factors in Multi-Crew Flight Operations, Harry W. Orlady, Linda M. Orlady, Ashgate 2016.
3. Feminity in Flight, A History of Flight Attendants, Kathleen M. Barry, 2007, p.17.
4. Footsteps in the Sky—An informal Review of U.S. Airlines Inflight Service—1920-Present, Helen E. McLaughlin, 1994, p. 234.
5. Fasten Your Seat Belts!—History and Heroism in the Pan Am Cabin, Valerie Lester, 1995, p. 3, 4.
6. Footsteps in the Sky, p. 33.
7. Glamour in the Skies—The Golden Age of the Air Stewardess, Libbie Escolme-Schmidt, 2009, p. 41.
8. Glamour in the Skies, p. 41.
9. Psychology of Flight Attendant's Profession Tatyana V. Filipieva, Association of Aviation, Space, Naval, Extremal and Environmental Medicine of Russia 2012, p. 336.
10. Lufthansa im Krieg—die Jahre 1939-1945, Werner Brittner, 2012, p. 47.
11. Aviation, April 1931, p. 245.
12. Footsteps in the Sky, p. 86.
13. Feminity in Flight, p. 21.
14. Feminity in Flight, p. 47.
15. Feminity in Flight, p. 246.
16. Glamour in the Skies, p. 19.
17. Cabine—koffie op hoog niveau, Peter Steinmetz, 2000, p. 81.

18 Feminity in Flight, p. 100.
19 Feminity in Flight, p. 100.
20 Feminity in Flight, p. 97.
21 Not just a Pretty Face: The Evolution of the Flight Attendant by Angelica Rose Gertel, May 2014, p. 73.
22 Cabine, p. 109.
23 Glamour in the Skies, p. 184.
24 cabincrew24.com/category/airline-requirements; cabincrewhq.com/recruitment.
25 Footsteps in the Sky, p. 5.
26 Footsteps in the Sky, p. 6.
27 Footsteps in the Sky, p. 37, p. 196.
28 Glamour in the Skies, p. 41.
29 Air Commerce Bulletin, U.S. Civil Aeronautics Authority, Vol. 11, No. 2, August 15, 1939.
30 Feminity in Flight, p. 3.
31 Feminity in Flight, p. 105.
32 Feminity in Flight, p. 107.
33 Feminity in Flight, p. 107.
34 Feminity in Flight, p. 106.
35 Stewardess@work, Geeri Bakker, 2008 (translated from Dutch by the author).
36 Flight International, 13 August 1983, p. 426.
37 e.g. 14 CFR 121.333(d) (in 2024).
38 Loi No. 53-285 du 4 avril 1953 Statut du Personnel Navigant Professionnel de l'Aeronautique Civile.
39 Arrêté du 25 août 1954 relatif à la classification du personnel navigant professionnel de l'aéronautique civile.
40 Feminity in Flight, p. 113, p. 159, p. 166.
41 Psychology of Flight Attendants, p. 337.
42 CAB Accident Investigation Report, National Airlines, Inc., Philadelphia International airport, Philadelphia, Pennsylvania, January 14, 1951, SA-226, Released October 26, 1951.
43 CAB Accident Investigation Report, Trans World Airlines, Inc., Fallon, Nevada, December 7, 1952, SA-267, Released July 13, 1953.
44 CAB Accident Investigation Report, Great Lakes Airlines, Inc., at Gage, Oklahoma, June 15, 1954, 1-0135, Released February 3, 1955.
45 CAB Accident Investigation Report, Pan American World Airways, Inc., off the Coast of Oregon in the Pacific Ocean, March 26, 1955, SA-304, Released November 15, 1955.
46 Some Survival Lessons Learned from Recent Accidents, by Barry G. King, Presented at the Flight Safety Foundation Air Safety Seminar, Santa Fe, New Mexico, November 10-12, 1954.
47 DR 52-26.
48 Human Factors in Air Transportation—Occupational Health and Safety, Ross A. McFarland, 1953, p. 550.
49 Aviation Week, February 9, 1953, p. 20.
50 Civil Air Policy, Hearings Before a Subcommittee of the Committee on Interstate and Foreign Commerce, House of Representatives, 84th Congress, January 20, 1956, p. 322.
51 Review of the Federal Aviation Act (Pilot Qualification and Certification and Military Participation in the Federal Aviation Agency), Hearings Before the Aviation Subcommittee of the Committee on Interstate and Foreign Commerce, United States Senate, 86th Congress, Part 3, June 7, 1960, p. 930.
52 Letter by Clarence M. Young, Assistant Secretary of Commerce for Aeronautics dated June 12, 1930 with proposed interpretations of the new regulations governing schedule operation of interstate passenger air transport services.
53 Scheduled Air-Line Conference, July 28, 1931, Air Commerce Bulletin, Vol. 3, p. 87. Conference attendees are listed and include illustrious names such as Paul Braniff and Jack Frye.
54 Aeronautics Bulletin No. 7-E, 1934, chapter 5, sec. 2.
55 Aeronautics Bulletin No. 7-E, 1934, chapter 5, sec. 2.
56 Together with Part 40 which contained the certification rules.
57 CAR 61.35147, 1937.
58 CAR 61.7042, 1937.
59 CAR 61.7920, 1937.
60 CAR 41.504(c), 1945: a 'use of oxygen equipment' sign is required 'in the cabin of aircraft not having pressurized cabins when operated at altitudes in excess of 12,000 ft above sea level for any period of time, unless a competent cabin attendant is provided to care for passengers'.

61 Amdt 121-251.
62 Commuter Airlines and Federal Regulation 1926–1979, U.S. Department of Transportation, Federal Aviation Administration, January 1980.
63 NPRM 69-4.
64 Amdt 135-12.
65 DR 56-2.
66 Amdt 46-0.
67 Amdt 40-20.
68 DR 58-24.
69 DR 60-19.
70 Review of the Federal Aviation Act, 1960, p. 930.
71 Amdt 121-2.
72 Amdt 121-241.
73 Amdt 4b-8 (1958).
74 CAB Aircraft Accident Report, United Air Lines, Inc. Boeing 727, N7030U, Salt Lake City, Utah, November 11, 1965, SA-388, Released June 7, 1966.
75 Amdt 25-15/121-30.
76 Amdt 25-51.
77 Amdt 25-72.
78 Amdt 25-51.
79 Flight Attendant Seat and Torso Restraint System Installations, Advisory Circular 25.785-1B, U.S. Department of Transportation, Federal Aviation Administration, May 11, 2010.
80 NTSB Recommendation A-73-40.
81 Aircraft Accident Report, Continental Air Lines, Inc., Boeing 727-224, N88777, Stapleton International Airport, Denver, Colorado, August 7, 1975, NTSB-AAR-76-14, May 5, 1976.
82 Air Carrier Cabin Safety—A Survey, Federal Aviation Administration, December 1976; p. VI-3.
83 AD 76-05-02.
84 Amdt 25-51/121-155.
85 Amdt 121-315.
86 DR 58-24.
87 Amdt 121-2.
88 DR 60-19.
89 FAR 121.391(b), 1964.
90 Amdt 135-12.
91 NPRM 81-1.
92 46 FR 61489.
93 Amdt 121-2.
94 DR 50-8.
95 DR 58-24.
96 DR 60-19.
97 Amdt 121-2.
98 Amdt 121-88.
99 To include Flight Attendants within the Definition of "Airman", Hearings Before a Subcommittee of the Committee on Interstate and Foreign Commerce, House of Representatives, 87th Congress, Second Session, May 1, 1962, p. 36.
100 Amdt. 41-0 (1962).
101 Amdt 121-176.
102 Footsteps in the Sky, p. 45.
103 Aviation, October 1940, p. 45.
104 Footsteps in the Sky, p. 53.
105 Air Commerce Bulletin, U.S. Civil Aeronautics Authority, Vol. 11, No. 2, August 15, 1939.
106 Footsteps in the Sky, p. 67.
107 Glamour in the Skies, p. 32.
108 Cabine—koffie op hoog niveau, 2000, p. 195.
109 CAR 40.286, 1954.
110 CAR 40.289, 1954.
111 Federal Aviation Agency Act, Hearings Before a Subcommittee on Aviation of the Committee on Interstate and Foreign Commerce, United States Senate, 85th Congress, Second Session, June 17, 1958, p. 278.

112 Review of the Federal Aviation Act, 1960, p. 931.
113 Amdt 40-21, 41-28, 42-23.
114 DR 62-9.
115 Amdt 121-7.
116 Amdt 121-55.
117 Amdt 121-133, 121-143.
118 Special Study, Safety Aspects of Emergency Evacuations from Air Carrier Aircraft, NTSB-AAS-74-3, November 13, 1974.
119 Special Investigation Report, Flight Attendant Training and Performance During Emergency Situations, NTSB/SIR-92/02, Adopted June 2, 1992.
120 Amdt 121-250.
121 Amdt 121-281.
122 Amdt 121-366.
123 Crewmember Emergency Training; Use of Mockups, Air Carrier Operations Bulletin (ACOB) 8-76-46, FAA, July 13, 1992.
124 NTSB Recommendation A-91-60.
125 Loi No. 53-285 du 4 avril 1953 Statut du Personnel Navigant Professional de l'Aeronautique Civile.
126 Review of the Federal Aviation Act, 1960, p. 934.
127 La vraie histoire des Hôtesses de l'air, Olivier Magnan, 2015.
128 Aviation Week, December 8, 1952.
129 Review of the Federal Aviation Act, 1960, p. 934.
130 H.R. 8160—A Bill to Amend sec. 101(7) of the Federal Aviation Act of 1958, so as to include flight attendants within the definition of "airman", 1961.
131 Een vrouw vloog mee—herinneringen van een stewardess, Trix Terwindt, 1951.
132 A Bill to Amend the Federal Aviation At of 1958 to Provide for the Establishment of Limitations on the Duty Time for Flight Attendants, in the House of Representatives, H.R.638, 101st Congress, January 24, 1989.
133 Amdt 121-241.
134 Amdt 121-386.
135 Human Factors in Air Transport Design, Ross A. McFarland, 1946; Human Factors in Air Transportation—Occupational Health and Safety, Ross A. McFarland, 1953.
136 FAA/OSHA Aviation Safety and Health Team (First Report), December 2000, including a Memorandum of Understanding between the FAA and OSHA signed August 7, 2000.

9 Second Wave (1965–1972)

ABSTRACT

The second wave of cabin safety activities in the U.S. counted three episodes of regulatory activity. The first two were each triggered by survivable, yet fatal accidents to new jets; the third resulted from recommendations made by the manufacturing industry. In all three episodes, escape potential improvements were first and foremost. These ranged from the introduction of mandatory evacuation tests and improved exit marking and lighting requirements to passenger briefing standards and the mandatory use of safety cards for passengers. In the second and third sets minor impact protection measures were introduced plus, more importantly, more demanding test protocols for interior materials flammability.

9.1 INTRODUCTION

While the 1944 prelude to the first wave of cabin safety measures can perhaps be debated, there is no doubt as to the origin, both by location and by time, of the second wave. That was at Denver-Stapleton airport, Colorado, on July 11, 1961, at 11:36 local time.

> A Douglas DC-8 of United Airlines veered off the runway on landing and slid over an 18-inch sharp edge of an unfinished concrete taxi strip. Three of the four engines tore free. Deceleration forces were very low. After the aircraft had come to rest, two major fires developed. The cabin was compartmentized, as follows, from forward to aft:
>
> - a first-class lounge with 8 seats plus a cabin attendant seat, with access to the entrance door on the left;
> - a galley area, with access to a door on the right;
> - a 4-abreast first-class cabin with 36 seats stretching until just behind the two pairs of over-wing exits;
> - a partition with a door;
> - a 6-abreast second-class cabin of 12 rows with 72 passenger seats;
> - a second-class lounge with 5 seats with a galley and access to the right aft door;
> - immediately behind the aft lounge, the left aft door.
>
> Thus, there were 6 exits in first class and two in second class.
> Passenger occupancy was high. In first class, all but one seat were occupied; in second class there were eight seats vacant. Four seats were occupied by a parent with an infant each. In the forward area, one stewardess occupied a dedicated jump seat and one sat in the lounge. In the rear, similarly one occupied a dedicated seat and one a lounge seat.
> Of the six exits in first class, three were used for evacuation: the entrance door on the left side and two adjacent overwing exits on the right. In second class, only the right aft door could be used.
> In first class, everybody evacuated safely. But not so in second class, where 16 passengers perished because of carbon monoxide poisoning. They had been lined up to escape via the single rear door, neatly waiting in turn. Yet, by the time that those furthest away from the door were advancing aft, circumstances inside had become so grave that they succumbed. Some of the second-class passengers managed to escape via the first-class cabin and thus survived. The evacuation in first class was described as being 'one of controlled haste with little evidence of irrational behavior of confusion'.[1] The second class was 'in an orderly and relatively calm manner; little shoving or shouting occurred and many persons took their time to collect their personal belongings'.[2] The evacuation was later estimated to have lasted about two minutes.

The evacuation aspects of the accident were investigated by Howard Hasbrook and two assistants and published as an FAA CAMI report in May 1962.[3] The formal CAB investigation report

Second Wave (1965–1972)

FIGURE 9.1 Denver DC-8 accident (FAA).

was published two months later but did not delve into survivability aspects. In a later study by FAA CAMI, the accident was compared with two other survivable jet accidents.[4] That study, which became a classic in airplane survivability investigation, added very detailed information.

The May 1962 report contained six recommendations, five of which pertained directly to cabin safety. They called for:

- passenger briefings prior to unusual landings;
- exit location placards;
- re-evaluation of the number and location of exits in relation to aisle width, passenger capacity, and cabin compartmentation;
- research into the effect of impaired breathing and sight on evacuation time and aisle widths;
- research into protective breathing means.

About five months after the Denver accident, on November 8, there was another major accident in the U.S. which was impact survivable but with carbon monoxide poisoning fatalities. All but two of the 79 occupants died.

> The aircraft was a piston-engined Lockheed Constellation carrying young army recruits.[5] The airplane, operated by a non-scheduled operator, Imperial Airlines, suffered crew-induced engine failures while en route from Baltimore, Maryland to Columbia, South Carolina. During the diversion landing attempt at Richmond, Virginia, it crashed one mile (1.6 km) short of the runway. The fire broke out immediately. The time available for escape was later estimated as between 30 seconds and 2 minutes. The crew in the cabin consisted of a single stewardess. Passengers were found piling up against the main cabin entrance door 'which either had been jammed by the ground impact or by trees and debris' and so remained closed. 'There was no evidence [...] that attempts had been made to use any of the emergency over-the-wing window exits'.[6] The CAB investigation concluded that this operator was operating below standards, a fact known by the FAA.

The Denver accident resulted in massive attention for cabin safety, but the Richmond accident, which was far worse in the number of lives lost, did not. Why was that?

The answer may lie in differences in equipment, operator, and social strata. In Denver, a modern jet was involved, representing the future fleet of transport aircraft, operated by one of the major, trunk air carriers, with passengers that likely represented the wealthier classes. In Richmond, on the other hand, the aircraft was a second-hand piston-engined aircraft reminiscent of days gone by, operated by a small non-scheduled airline of dubious standard and carrying young soldiers-to-be. Where United had a cabin crew complement of four, thus about 1 per 28 passengers, Imperial only had one stewardess for 72 passengers.

The fate of the jet and its passengers set in motion actions to improve crashworthiness features. Jets represented the future of commercial aviation and it was felt that their safety needed to be improved, if only to uphold their reputation. Following the release of Hasbrook's report, manufacturers, operators, and the FAA started working together on improving passenger safety in jets and, in their wake, turbo-propeller airplanes.

This marked the start of a ten-year period of cabin safety improvements which was characterized by a high degree of cooperation between the industry and the FAA. The improvements came in three distinct sets, one each in 1965, 1967, and 1972. The focus of the first set was to increase the escape potential of survivable accidents. The second set was triggered by another accident, in Salt Lake City, 1965, to a Boeing 727 which exposed the vulnerability of design aspects of rear jet-engined airplanes.

Survivability was approached from two angles: (1) reduce the likelihood, and intensity, of a fire in the cabin and (2) further improve the escape potential. In the third set, many of the improvements resulted from recommendations made by the Aerospace Industries Association (AIA), the organization of the aircraft design industry. They had initiated a crashworthiness development program in response to the second set of changes. In between the three sets, there were some minor cabin safety requirement changes that were primarily clarifications and corrections.

For three other subjects, the second wave saw major developments as well: evacuation demonstrations, flight attendants, and safety cards. They are dealt with in Chapters 8, 12, and 20, respectively. During this period, the FAA sharpened one aspect of the life support domain: equipment needed for any overwater operation.

9.2   FIRST SET (1965)

9.2.1   Escape Potential

The FAA studied the Denver and Richmond accidents, plus two more in the period 1960–1963 where there were difficulties and delays encountered in evacuating the airplane.[7] It undertook a broad study of transport cabin interiors and found that significant improvements were reasonably attainable to raise the level of evacuation safety. It discussed these with the airline industry.[8] In August 1962 there was a conference in Washington, D.C., where Hasbrook's recommendations were discussed. On a voluntary basis and for evaluation purposes, two airlines and two manufacturers modified sample aircraft by making exits more conspicuous by improving paint, placards, and lighting.[9,10]

Yet, to reach other airlines as well, it was found necessary to update the rules. For that purpose, the FAA issued in October 1963 a Notice of Proposed Rulemaking (NPRM—the new term used by the FAA, replacing the term 'Draft Release' as used by its predecessor). It proposed both design and operational requirements aimed at improving evacuation potential.

On the design side, exit marking signs were now required next to floor-level exits, above the aisle abeam overwing exits, and on bulkheads that prevented fore and aft vision. Overall emergency lighting was required for the first time. To increase passenger awareness of exits, the exit signs needed to be electrically illuminated or radioactively self-illuminated. Previously, the exits only had to be illuminated by a source of light that shone onto them.

Second Wave (1965–1972)

Opening instructions for Type I and II exits were proposed to be larger and complete, no longer missing essential steps. For the exterior came a requirement to outline each exit by means of a contrasting two-inch (5 cm) band, to ease quick recognition by rescue personnel. Also, doors between passenger compartments were prohibited. However, a door between a passenger area and an exit remained allowed, as long as it could be firmly latched in the open position.[11] Earlier, following a suggestion made during the 1958 airworthiness review, the design rules had been amended to require that internal doors have a means to latch them in the open position during take-off and landing.[12]

On the operational side, it proposed requirements of several kinds. Flight attendant numbers were specified and emergency duties and functions for crewmembers needed to be established for all types of airplanes. All airlines needed to orally brief their passengers. Previously, a briefing requirement only applied to airlines operating extended overwater or high-altitude (>25,000 ft., >7,620 m) flights. Now, in addition to ditching and oxygen provisions, the items to be briefed included smoking, the use of safety belts, and the location of emergency exits. To supplement the oral briefing, printed cards were required containing diagrams of, and methods of operating, the emergency exits and other instructions necessary for use of emergency equipment.[13]

As 'immediately after an accident has occurred, there is a considerable amount of confusion resulting from the sudden disorderliness of the cabin, flying debris, lack of adequate lighting, lack of orientation and fear', crewmembers shouting instructions would no longer be heard 'over the various noises associated with a crash landing'.[14] For airplanes with a seating capacity of 60 or more, a megaphone was therefore required and even two when the capacity was 100 or more.[15] Finally, a live evacuation demonstration was prescribed to verify the operator's cabin procedures and training (see Chapter 12).

Measures contemplated at the time, but later rejected and thus not proposed in the NPRM, were public address systems and audio systems to warn when fasten seat belts and no smoking signs were turned on, and wider aisles. Also, research into 'uncontaminated breathing air for periods long enough to evacuate a burning aircraft', later known as passenger smoke hoods, was suggested.[16]

Public hearings on the proposals were held in June 1964 and March 1965, which rendered few changes. The proposals became rules coming into force on June 7, 1965. One element that was added as a result of comments was that the oral briefing on the location of exits was supplemented

FIGURE 9.2 ATR 42 with improper outlining band (photograph by the author).

by printed cards with diagrams of the emergency exits. Such safety briefing cards were already in use by major airlines on a voluntary basis.

For most of the measures, compliance was set from July 1, 1966 onward, giving airlines time to modify their airplanes. The new requirements applied both to new airplane designs and as a retrofit to the existing air carrier fleet. Other countries adopted the measures in a matter of a few years. In the United Kingdom, the Ministry of Aviation adopted most, but not all, of the measures.[17] One measure adopted with a significant delay was that for the two-inch band outlining exits on the exterior. British airliners were still spotted without such a band as late as 1977. As such, they stood out, as airliners from all other countries had by then long been modified. Whether this measure has indeed ever helped outside assistants to locate emergency exits is not known. It has not been reported in investigation reports.

The reason for the band is not always recognized by those who apply it. There have been several cases where large cargo doors not being emergency exits have been provided with the two-inch band. Some were in passenger aircraft, but even in all-cargo aircraft, doors far away from where the occupants are have been so outlined, see Figure 9.2.

9.2.2 Life Support: Any Overwater Operation

An operational rule existed since the 1950s that required flotation means for extended overwater operations. These were defined as operations beyond 50 miles (80.5 km) from the nearest shoreline. They did not cover operations which stayed closer to shore, such as over large lakes and rivers or along the coastline, especially immediately after take-off or before landing. To close this gap, in 1967 an operational requirement was added that, for any overwater operation, at least a flotation cushion was required.[18]

9.3 SECOND SET (1967)

9.3.1 Introduction

Following the dramatic accident involving a United DC-8 in 1961, and while the measures of the first series were being implemented, another accident occurred that was impact survivable but in which many people died. It would raise a host of new cabin safety measures.

> On November 11, 1965, a United Airlines Boeing 727 touched down short of the runway at Salt Lake City airport and crash-landed. Both main landing gears sheared off and the aircraft skidded on its aft fuselage along the runway and veered off.[19] A fuel line serving the right rear engine from the wing tanks was ruptured by the failed right gear, then ignited and burned through the cabin floor. Passengers described it as a 'flame-thrower'. The interior furnishings contributed greatly to the spread of the fire and the emission of heavy black smoke, both of which contributed to the fatalities.[20] All six side exits were used for evacuation. Five, including the mid-ship galley door, were opened by passengers. By the air carrier's procedures, that exit was assigned to one of the two stewardesses seated adjacent to the forward door on the left. Yet, that was eight seat rows away and unreachable for her because of the crowd quickly occupying the aisle. Even the left forward door could not be opened by the senior stewardess who sat immediately adjacent because of passengers blocking the vestibule area. It could however be opened by the co-pilot after shoving some passengers aside. The stewardess seated against the ventral stair door in the aft end of the cabin opened that door to attempt evacuation via the tail. Together with two passengers however, she became trapped as the stairs would not deploy because the tail sat on the ground. Via a very small opening they were able to alert fire rescue services. The latter's efforts to chop and cut through the fuselage using axes and blow torches were unsuccessful. Rescue finally came after 25 minutes when the fire was sufficiently under control. The escape route, ironically, was a gap in the fuselage skin at the location of the original fire, four rows forward of the entrance to the tail. One of these two passengers died seven days later from severe, third degree burns. Many other passengers did not escape in time from the heavy internal fire, aggravated by the dense smoke that obscured any vision and in itself was lethal. The death toll in this accident was much higher than United's earlier accident: 43 fatalities out of a total of 85 occupants.

Second Wave (1965–1972)

FIGURE 9.3 Salt Lake City accident (FAA).

The Salt Lake City accident triggered an appreciation that much more could, and should, be done to protect occupants of a survivable accident and allow them to escape in time. In January 1966, only two months after the accident, the FAA established an Agency Task Force to study factors affecting crashworthiness and evacuation.[21] That Task Force included manufacturers from the U.S. In March and April, the FAA organized conferences to discuss possible improvements to cabin safety regulations. This was followed by an NPRM in July.[22]

Where the 1965 measures were limited to evacuation aspects, this time the scope was broader. It included several fire protection measures, and one impact protection measure, in addition to numerous escape potential improvements. The measures were both of a design nature and an operational nature. The former were made not only applicable to new types and amendments to existing types, but in some cases also to the existing fleets.

Just over one year later a Final Rule was issued which became effective October 24, 1967.[23] Some elements that required modification of existing aircraft had later compliance dates, ranging until October 1, 1969.

Subjects being under research, for possible future rulemaking consideration, included individual passenger portable smoke masks (the term 'smoke hood' or 'PBE' had not yet caught on), delethalized seat backs, individual passenger single strap inertial reel torso restraints, dynamic testing of 40 g (all directional) passenger seats, and emergency escape procedures in 400–1,000 passenger aircraft.[24]

9.3.2 Impact Protection

Not a result of the Salt Lake City accident but otherwise triggered, the FAA proposed a requirement to prevent head injury by side-facing passengers flailing sideways, that is, in the airplane's forward direction. Proposed was 'a cushioned rest supporting the arms, shoulder, head and spine'. Following up on comments, the final rule offered a shoulder harness as an alternative, and the word 'cushioned' was replaced by 'energy absorbing', thus allowing alternatives to cushion pads.[25] This effectively meant that lounges disappeared as these appeared incompatible with the new rule.

In the same amendment, it was regulated that passenger seat backs be in the upright position for take-offs and landings and that passengers must obey instructions to do so by the crew.[26] Additionally, articles were only allowed to be stowed under seats when they would not 'slide forward under crash impacts severe enough to induce the inertia loads' as specified.[27] One way of doing that would be by means of a restraint bar, but the requirement did not specify so. This regulation was a reaction to the increased use of carry-on baggage. In the NPRM the FAA had observed that 'recent developments such as "shuttle" flights and "space, available student fares"' 'increased the number of situations where passengers are boarding the airplane at the last minute carrying more baggage than probably would be the case if they had a confirmed reservation and checked in at the ticket counter prior to departure'.[28]

Two petitions for increased strength of seats and seat attachments were discussed in the same NPRM and rejected for lack of evidence. However, the FAA mentioned that the National Aviation Facilities Experimental Center (NAFEC) would determine the relationship between static and dynamic load.[29] Values of load factor, occupant weight, and time duration of load application, it announced, would be quantitatively determined so that fully dynamic crash load standards could be formulated.

9.3.3 Fire Protection

9.3.3.1 Cabin Interior Materials

The CAB Bureau of Aviation Safety, investigating the Salt Lake City accident, recommended within five weeks of the accident in 1965 to improve the flammability characteristics of interior compartment materials.[30] This recommendation was quite generic. The CAB only substantiated that 'we have been advised that the aforementioned fire tests have disclosed a number of deficiencies in the materials presently being installed in aircraft interiors and that materials are available which could be far superior to those being used today'.

The fire tests that the CAB referred to were those that the FAA had performed in 1963. They were the first fire laboratory tests they had done, using the test equipment and facilities of the Fire Protection Section, National Bureau of Standards, Washington, D.C. The January 1964 report said:

> The events that preceded this project and were responsible for it being conducted were foremost: (1) concern with recent fire experience involving interior materials in air transport passenger cabins, (2) increased use of plastics and synthetics in interior furnishings, and (3) development of new laboratory test methods and criteria for evaluating flame-resistant characteristics of materials.[31]

Until then, an FAA document established both a test method and a burn-rate limit of 4 inch (10 cm) per minute for showing compliance.[32] 'However, a burn rate of this magnitude is now generally considered very lenient'.[33]

Where previously cabin fire protection requirements 'were designed primarily to prevent serious fires from passenger carelessness, such as cigarette burns', it now dawned that the increased use of plastics had become a concern of its own. Burning plastics produces gases more toxic than carbon monoxide and in concentrations sufficient to become hazardous. As demonstrated in Salt Lake City, they also emitted large quantities of smoke. Yet, the mechanics were not yet understood and further tests utilizing a full-scale test article to simulate an actual fire in an aircraft were recommended.[34] In 1969, following a petition by Du Pont who suggested the adoption of National Bureau of Standards smoke generation tests for cabin materials, the FAA issued an Advance NPRM to solicit views on the availability of materials that emit less smoke yet still meet the flammability standards.[35]

The FAA decided that 'within the present state of the art, it is considered possible, and practicable to require that materials used in passenger and crew compartments meet a specified horizontal and vertical burn rate'.[36] The proposed new standard effectively called for the interior materials to be self-extinguishing. In the horizontal test, the specimen must be exposed to a flame of a Bunsen burner for 15 seconds; in the vertical test 12 seconds. This requirement was not proposed for retrofit application, but only for replacement material and, obviously, new airplane types certified per FAR 25. The final rule of September 1967 introduced a new Appendix to FAR 25: Appendix F, which specified the fire test methods.[37]

Second Wave (1965–1972)

So, for the first time since 1947, cabin interior fire resistance improvements were made. While recognized as being important as well, smoke and toxicity propagation characteristics of materials were insufficiently understood at the time. More research in that area was foreseen so no regulations in that respect were drafted.

9.33.2 Electrical Cables and Fuel Lines

A key design aspect that the investigation identified as hazardous was the vulnerability of fuel and electrical lines through the aft fuselage. In the 727, this was so constructed because its three engines were mounted at the far end of the fuselage. The fuel lines fed the engines with fuel from the wing tanks. In the opposite direction, electrical lines fed the aircraft systems with electrical power from the engines, where it was generated. The 727 was the first U.S. design so configured. But more were in the pipeline: the DC-9 and smaller corporate jets such as the Lockheed JetStar, the Lear Jet, and the Jet Commander. Outside the U.S., this concept had already been applied on the Sud-Est Caravelle and the BAC One-Eleven. In correspondence from their Brussels office to the Dutch *Rijksluchtvaartdienst* (Civil Aviation Authority), the FAA informed Dutch aircraft manufacturer Fokker of these hazards as well.[38] At the time, Fokker was developing the F-28, an aircraft using the same engine location concept. The FAA proposed 'that electrical cables be isolated from fuel lines and that both be designed to allow a reasonable degree of deformation and stretching without failure or leakage'.[39] In 1967 these requirements became effective for new types and derivatives of existing types when increased in capacity.[40]

9.3.4 Escape Potential

As in 1965, the majority of the 1967 improvements were about evacuation provisions. They came in many different kinds and there were many, more than at any other rulemaking update. Most were not a direct result of the Salt Lake City accident but probably stemmed from discussions of the conferences held in March and April 1966. Significant changes to the evacuation demonstration requirements introduced in 1965 were made (see Chapter 12).

9.3.4.1 Exit Table

The exit table, last amended in 1957, was proposed to be modified again. It would now extend to seating capacities up to 339, so well beyond the previous cap of 219. For the highest increment, (300 to 339 seats) six pairs of Type I exits were proposed plus two pairs of floor-level, overwing, Type II exits. Beyond 299, no Type III exits would be allowed, only Type Is and IIs. The limit for Type IV exits would be 59.

Passenger seating capacity (cabin attendants not included)	Type I	Type II	Type III	Type IV
1 to 10 inclusive				1
11 to 19 inclusive			1 or 2	
20 to 39 inclusive		1		1
40 to 59 inclusive	1			1
60 to 79 inclusive	1		1	
80 to 109 inclusive	1		2	
110 to 139 inclusive	2	1	1	
140 to 179 inclusive	2	1	2	
180 to 219 inclusive	3	1	1	
220 to 259 inclusive	4		2	
260 to 299 inclusive	5	1 [1]	1	
300 to 339 inclusive	6	1 [2]		

[1] These Type II exits must be floor level, over-the-wing, with a stepdown outside the airplane of not more than 17 inches.

Above 339, a credit of 40 would be given for each extra pair of Type I exit and 30 for each extra pair of Type IIs.[41] This table would have added to the list of inconsistencies. Adding a pair of Type I exits to an airplane with a capacity of 109 would be good for 70 seats, and from 139 even 80 seats.

Still, the proposal did not fall well with the manufacturers. They responded 'that the combination of exit types was arbitrary and inconsistent with evacuation capabilities of the larger aircraft' and that 'the nonlinear assignment of exit credit versus the number of passengers was without sufficient justification'.[42] Boeing was in the early design phase of the huge Boeing 747 and poised for a much larger exit permitting two-abreast evacuation. This exit type had already gained the informal designation of 'Type A'.

The FAA relented and withdrew the proposed table in favor of keeping the 1957 table, but now curtailed at 179 instead of 219. Beyond 179 and up to 299, it offered credits per pair of exits as follows: Type III: 35; Type II: 40; Type I: 45; and the new Type A: 100. Beyond 299, only Type A and Type I exits were allowed, with the same credits. The leap of 80 seats for an additional pair of Type I exits had disappeared, but that of 70 seats remained.

9.3.4.2 Uniform Distribution

Until 1965, the FAA had focused on exits being as far aft as possible. This had led to situations where most, if not all, of the exits were located in the rear cabin, close to each other. A good example of that was the Fokker F-27, with a pair of floor-level exits at the end of the cabin and a pair of non-floor-level exits just a few seat rows forward, with the majority of the cabin ahead of that without any exits.

In this NPRM, the FAA introduced a requirement that exits be distributed as uniformly as practicable taking into account passenger distribution. The FAA argued that 'It does not require any detailed research or accident investigations to show that there is a direct relationship between the proximity of an exit to a passenger and that passenger's chances for escape'. The aft location preference for Type I and Type II exits was removed from their definition.

9.3.4.3 Inflatable Slides Credit

By the mid-1960s, 'substantial improvements have been made in the design and installation of inflatable slides at floor level exits', the FAA said.[43] To capitalize on that, they proposed that all exits more than 6 ft (1.8 m) from the ground be equipped with automatically deployable and inflatable slides. Earlier, such slides were promoted by means of a CAA policy that awarded a credit of five seats for each pair of exits so equipped. That option was now proposed to be eliminated. However, in the final rule, FAR 25 Amendment 15, it was retained, but with a cap of 189 seats. No further justification was given. In practice, this decision would very much help the Boeing 737, which was type certificated by the FAA on December 15, 1967, about two months after Amendment 15 became effective. Boeing would make use of this credit for many decades of 737 production.

Technology was not yet so advanced that all doors could be equipped with automatic slides. For doors used regularly, such as entry and service doors, an exception was made. There, the slides 'may be inflated in a different manner'. In practice that meant that the slides required some more action by the cabin crew, such as putting a slide in position at the door sill and pulling an inflation cord.

9.3.4.4 Entrance Door: An Emergency Exit

At the time, entrance doors were not always furnished as an emergency exit. Some missed the exit marking, lighting, and perhaps even an escape slide, because they were not a required emergency exit. They were surplus doors. An example of that was the entrance door of the Lockheed L-188 Electra. This door was located left forward, whereas the mandatory floor-level emergency exit pair was at the rear. The FAA found that in actual emergencies as well as in demonstrations, passengers showed a natural tendency to try to leave by the same route they entered the airplane.[44] Thus, passengers would risk going to an exit which they could then not locate or properly descend from. A new proposal, adopted in 1967, required therefore that all entrance doors meet the emergency exit requirements as either a Type II, Type I, or Type A exit.[45]

Second Wave (1965–1972)

9.3.4.5 Tail Exits

Several new airplane types featured entrance steps in the tail of the aircraft. These were fitted to a fuselage panel that could be lowered to the ground, thus allowing a means of entering the airplane independent of ground equipment. Access into the cabin was then through a door in the pressure bulkhead. Earlier, some of the 1950s Martin and Convair twin piston-engined airliners had the same, but now many of the new, 1960s, short-, and medium-haul jets were so equipped.

The French Sud-Est Caravelle was the first, followed by the Boeing 727, the Douglas DC-9, and the British BAC One-Eleven. The stairs doubled as an evacuation route, now called 'ventral exit', except for the DC-9 where not the stairs formed the exit route, but a deployable tail cone. The FAA had granted credits for these exits on an individual basis, ranging from 10 seats for a ventral exit to up to 20 seats for a tail cone exit in combination with a door of Type I size in the pressure bulkhead. In the 1966 NPRM the FAA proposed to add these exits to the formal set of exit types.[46] It said that it had:

> given considerable thought to these type exits and has concluded that while they have merit, they nevertheless have an inherent limitation relative to conventional exits in that they are a single exit per airplane rather than one per side. This, plus their location makes them somewhat less effective than a pair of fuselage side doors.

When this proposal was adopted in 1967, the FAA generously set higher exit credits: 12 for the ventral exit (as already granted for Boeing 727) and even 25 for a tail cone exit in combination with a door in the pressure bulkhead of 24 by 60 inch (thus higher than a Type I).[47] For a tail cone exit in combination with a Type III size bulkhead door, the credit was 15.

9.3.4.6 Access to Type III and IV Exits

Access to Type III and IV exits was regulated such that seats did not obstruct it to an extent that the effectiveness of the exit would be reduced. However, minor obstructions were allowed if there were compensating factors to maintain the effectiveness of the exit. This changed in 1967, when it was required that the projected opening of the exit had to be free from any protrusion for a distance equal to a seat. For airplanes with less than 20 passenger seats, the minor obstructions allowance remained.

9.3.4.7 Excess Exits

Until 1967, excess exits did not need to meet the standards for emergency exits. Excess exits are additional doors or exits above the minimum required per the regulations. Unlike entrance doors, they are not used for boarding passengers, but they may give access to galleys or baggage compartments. The rationale for equipping excess exits as emergency exits was that passengers would not know whether an exit was required or not. For them all exits are exits.

9.3.4.8 Exit Marking

The FAA proposed improvements to exit marking, including means to assist the occupants in locating exits in conditions of dense smoke. This was a rather broadly worded standard which according to the FAA could be met using distinctive materials on seats adjacent to an exit or a strobe light under seats at exits.[48] In practice, however, airlines applied a different means: three buttons on the handrail forming the bottom of overhead racks, posing a tactile indication for persons moving along the cabin steadying themselves using the handrail.

9.3.4.9 Emergency Lighting

In Salt Lake City all cabin lights went out as the aircraft stopped. A requirement for an emergency lighting system was now proposed that would work independently of the airplane's normal electrical power.[49] This battery-powered system would need to continue to operate after the break-up of the fuselage. Its duration was proposed to be at least 30 minutes, but this was reduced to 10 minutes in the final rule.[50] Not only would it need to feed exit signs and illuminate aisles and routes from aisles to exits, but also the overwing escape route on the outside. The lighting system would be activated automatically on interruption of normal power. In addition, switches were needed both in the cockpit and at least one point in the cabin.

9.3.4.10 Maximum Number of Seats Abreast

The number of seats on either side of the aisle typically was two or three. Only two cases are known where more than three seats were used: in Britain, a charter airline used a Trident 1E with seven rows seating four on the left side of the aisle, dedicated for families, see Figure 9.4.

In the Soviet Union in the 1960s, the large long-haul Tupolev 114 turboprop briefly flew short-haul routes in a high-density version with four seats on either side of the single aisle.[51]

Although no such application in the U.S. is known, in 1966 it was proposed to restrict by a rule the maximum number of seats abreast.[52] It was initially ill-worded, risking confusion, but this was corrected in the final rule. Here is the proposed text followed by that of the final rule:

Proposal:

'On airplanes having only one passenger aisle, the number of seats abreast must not be more than six'.

Final rule:

'On airplanes having only one passenger aisle, no more than 3 seats abreast may be placed on each side of the aisle in any one row'.

The intent is clear: any passenger was not to be separated from an aisle by more than two other seat places. The text of the requirement has not been changed since. Interestingly, it only addressed airplane types with one aisle. Yet, the consequence of this rule is that any airplane wider than fitting six seats across will need to have more than one aisle. The maximum number of seats between two aisles would be six. So, in theory, a twin-aisled airplane can have 12 seats abreast: 3–6–3. The maximum in practice has been ten, although eleven has been pondered at several instances.

9.3.5 UNITED AIRLINES

The 1965 Salt Lake City accident, like the 1961 Denver crash and the 1947 La Guardia accident were all triggers for cabin safety, and notably evacuation improvements. They also involved one and the same airline: United Airlines. This was coincidental. The accidents were not a result of specific actions or procedures unique to that airline. Yet, they had a major effect on it. A Salt Lale

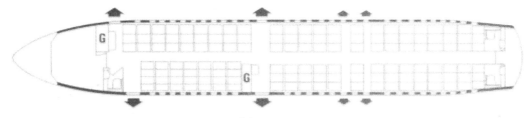

Interior arrangement of the HS. Trident 1E-140 (G=galley)

FIGURE 9.4 Channel Airways Trident 1E layout with 139 seats, of which 28 are four-seat assemblies (The Trident Preservation Society).

City passenger, who lost a close business associate in the accident and had a safety background at Du Pont, one week after the accident wrote to United.[53] He criticized the exit layout of the 727, pointing out that 'five of the six exits were concentrated within six rows'. (He omitted the tail exit.) He said there should be more exits along the entire length of the cabin. Whether or not influenced by this letter, United decided that new airplane acquisitions needed more exits. When ordering in the second half of the 1960s the stretched Douglas DC-8 and the Boeing 727-200, it specified extra pairs of exits. United's 727-200s were the only samples with a pair of Type I exits just forward of the wings. Their Douglas DC-8–61s had an extra pair of Type I exits just aft of the wings, bringing the number of cabin exits to 14.[54] No other airline had these exits. One of their so-equipped DC-8–61s was involved in December 1978 in Portland in a survivable crash, without fire, followed by an evacuation. Although 8 of the 14 cabin exits were used, the unique extra pair of exits was not. In the next year, United decided to de-activate these extra exits.

9.4 THIRD SET (1972)

9.4.1 Introduction

The NPRM of the second series raised many comments. Among those, there was one that went further than the rest. The Aerospace Industries Association (AIA) not only commented on the rule proposals but announced a research and development program to further increase passenger survivability. It was called the AIA Crashworthiness Development Program (CDP). The AIA is the trade organization of U.S. aircraft manufacturers. In the CDP, nine of its members participated. That included the five suppliers of transport aircraft (Boeing, Convair, Douglas, Fairchild-Hiller, and Lockheed) plus four manufacturers of corporate aircraft (Aero Commander, Grumman, Lear Jet, and North American Aviation). Of these Boeing and Douglas contributed the most. During the course of the program, in April 1967, Douglas merged with McDonnell Aircraft to form McDonnell Douglas.

The CDP was welcomed by the FAA, which sent a letter of encouragement on February 7, 1967. Yet, they did not pause to wait for its outcome but issued the second series Final Rule in September 1967 as discussed above.

The CDP focused on five subjects. Two in the domain of fire control and three in the domain of evacuation. Additionally, it briefly looked at passenger communication. The two fire subjects dealt with improvements in interior materials and fire suppression/smoke/fume protection systems, respectively. In the evacuation domain, the subjects were emergency lighting, exit awareness, and evacuation systems. The research constituted analyses of past accidents, a review of 134 evacuation demonstrations, and many human performance and interaction tests done by Boeing and Douglas. The FAA also hoped that industry would look at 'gelled fuels', but AIA decided that was beyond the scope of the CDP. The results were published in July 1968 and contained detailed text proposals for rule changes.[55] Also, areas for further research and development were identified which, the AIA said, should then be funded by government rather than industry. While interior material fire improvements were supported, in the area of fire suppression/smoke/fume protection, no solutions were found feasible for implementation.

Backed up by the CDP results, the AIA filed a petition for rulemaking in April 1969. NPRM 69–33, published by the FAA in August 1969, contained quite a few of the subjects recommended by the AIA CDP. It contained other proposals as well, in the areas of both impact protection and escape potential. They were followed up with regulations becoming effective May 1, 1972, offering a two-year grace period for some subjects.

9.4.2 Impact Protection

In the field of impact protection, the FAA proposed a number of measures. These fell outside the AIA CDP recommendations. A proposal was made to add a crash load in the aft direction (of 1.5 g) and to increase the upward and sideward load factors. The FAA considered that seats and seat attachments were compatible, but industry explained that these new factors would increase airplane weights and lead to significant costs. The FAA put it on hold.[56]

Period overhead stowage compartments, the 'hat racks', were typically open. It was now proposed that they be completely enclosed, to better retain its contents. A counterproposal to keep the compartment open but use tie-down straps or webbing was rejected by the FAA. Since then, closed stowage compartments in the cabin became the norm. At the same time, weight placards for these compartments were required.[57]

Similarly, underseat stowage areas, while remaining open, would need to have means to prevent the sliding forward of items stowed there. This was already required in 1967, but it was now clarified that this needed 'a means'.[58] That means would be a restraint bar. Initially, such bars would only restrain in the forward direction, but gradually they were extended to the sideward direction. Also intended to restrain equipment and prevent items from becoming missiles, as Howard Hasbrook already advocated in the 1950s, were means to keep galley equipment and carts in place under inertia loads. For the same reason, food and beverage service were prohibited during take-off and landing, and a FAR section was added that passengers comply with instructions given by a crewmember in this respect.[59]

9.4.3 Fire Protection

AIA had proposed more severe burn test requirements, which were adopted by the FAA. This included exposing materials such as ceiling panels, interior wall panels, and other large structures, to a vertical Bunsen burner test for 60 seconds instead of 12 seconds. Other materials, used for floor coverings, seat cushions, and others needed to pass a lesser test. The AIA based its recommendation on tests and the availability of better materials. Yet, it acknowledged that

> it is not expected that improved self-extinguishing interior materials can contribute heavily to survivability when they are exposed to relatively hostile small fires [. . .] let alone when they are exposed to the overpowering effects of fires from large fuel spills. These materials, however, do prevent flame propagation from small ignition or fire sources because of their self-extinguishing characteristics.[60]

The recommendation was adopted by the FAA in 1972 for airplanes type certificated from May 1972 onward.

The AIA did not venture into proposing smoke or noxious gases criteria. The FAA followed this, saying there was no standardized testing method nor were there materials available that would emit significantly less smoke. Hence, it issued in 1969 an Advanced NPRM to solicit input from industry.[61]

9.4.4 Escape Potential

Again, evacuation was a subject well addressed, making the second wave the most prolific when it comes to escape potential measures. The subjects varied.

9.4.4.1 Exit Table

This time, a minor change to the exit table was proposed: deleting entirely the Type IV exit. The FAA reasoned that Type III exits offered a significant improvement in egress rate over Type IV exits, so 'there is very little justification for continuing to provide for the Type IV exit'.[62] On reflection, it was maintained but only for airplanes with a capacity of up to 9.

9.4.4.2 Exit Location

In the previous iteration, Type I and Type II exits were no longer bound to the aft location, but Type III exits were still restricted to the overwing location. This was now let loose, the FAA saying that this particularly would promote its use as a ditching exit. However, when a non-overwing Type III exit had a sill more than 6 ft from the ground, an escape slide would be required. In practice, no Type III exits not over the wing were employed.

9.4.4.3 Opening and Ready-for-Use Times

The AIA had recommended that each required emergency exit be openable within ten seconds, in each landing gear collapse condition. Especially for larger aircraft, such as the 747, this would require power boost or power-operated systems. In the final rule, following a pertinent comment, it was added that this requirement only applied 'when there is no fuselage deformation'.[63] Additionally, it recommended that escape slides at all locations (so including passenger and service doors) be automatically erected within ten seconds of the start of its deployment, eliminating the actions needed by the flight attendant.

9.4.4.4 Inflatable Slides Bonus Deletion

The FAA again proposed to eliminate the bonus of 5 for a pair of inflatable slides, with a maximum of 10. This time it used the argument that inflatable escape slides had now become the norm, so 'there appears to be no rational basis for the current rule'. It pursued and deleted the bonus, but only for new aircraft types. Previously type certificated types, such as the 737, kept using it on its derivatives for many decades to come.

9.4.4.5 Exit Marking and Lighting

The AIA proposed more and brighter exit markings. Since 1967, only required floor-level exits needed to have an exit sign. This was now extended to all emergency exits. Exit operating handles on Type III exits were required to be self-illuminated. The size of the letters forming the word EXIT, in red, was increased from 1 inch (2.5 cm) to 1.5 inch (4 cm).

9.4.4.6 Wing Escape Route

In the second set, a requirement had been added for marking and covering with a slip-resistant surface the escape route from each overwing escape route.[64] The AIA proposed a reflectance standard for the marking of 80% and a contrast ratio of at least 5:1. The FAA agreed and added a minimum width: 4 ft (1.22 m) for Type A exits and 2 ft (61 cm) for all other exits. In practice, manufacturers applied routes wider than 2 ft for double overwing exits.[65]

9.5 SUMMARY OF THE SECOND WAVE

The cabin safety measures of the second wave largely were corrections to, and enhancements of, those introduced in the first wave. They were primarily triggered by two accidents with jets that occurred in 1961 (Denver) and 1965 (Salt Lake City). The first led to a host of escape potential improvements that became effective in 1965. The second led two years later to further escape potential measures and tighter flammability test standards and fire prevention measures unique to airplanes with tail-mounted engines. In 1972, further enhancements were introduced in response to input from the American manufacturing industry.

Minor changes were introduced in the impact protection domain, such as improved protection of side-facing seats (which led to the deletion of lounges) and overhead and underseat baggage restraints. Overhead, closed baggage compartments became the norm; underseat, restraint bars were added.

The Salt Lake City accident was one of the first survivable accidents to an airplane with engines mounted aft. It exposed a construction element that had not been flagged before: the vulnerability of the cabin to fire resulting from the rupture of the fuel lines and the generator lines between the wings and the engines. These lines transport fuel from the wings to the engines and, in the reverse direction, electrical power from the engines. Measures were introduced to isolate electrical cables from fuel lines and that both be designed to allow a reasonable degree of deformation and stretching without failure or leakage.

As to the flammability of interior materials, vertical Bunsen burner tests were introduced in addition to horizontal tests.

The escape potential improvements were a mix of design and operational measures. The exit table for the number, location, and size of exits was updated; the requirements for exit marking, lighting, and accessibility were extended to all exits, including those above the minimum required. This meant that boarding doors and so-called excess exits were no longer treated differently. A new kind of exit, unique to airplanes with tail-mounted engines was addressed: tail exits. In anticipation of the Boeing 747, a new exit type allowing two evacuee lines was introduced: the Type A exit.

Inflatable slides had become the norm and the FAA in 1967 was about to cancel the bonus of 10 seats for such slides that had been introduced in 1957. But in a move that would have a huge commercial benefit for Boeing, this decision was delayed until 1972. Thus, the Boeing 737, with a type certificate date of December 1967, would make use of this bonus for all of its derivatives in the next six decades.

Exit marking and lighting requirements were improved in two steps, in 1967 and again in 1972 following up on suggestions made by industry.

NOTES

1. Survival in Emergency Escape from Passenger Aircraft by Clyde C. Snow, John J. Carroll, Mackie A. Allgood, Department of Transportation, AM 70-16, FAA CAMI, October 1970, p. 12.
2. Survival in Emergency Escape from Passenger Aircraft, p. 13.
3. Evacuation Pattern Analysis of a Survivable Commercial Aircraft Crash, 62-9, by A. Howard Hasbrook, J.D. Garner, Clyde C. Snow, FAA CARI, May 1962.
4. Survival in Emergency Escape from Passenger Aircraft.
5. CAB Aircraft Accident Report, Imperial Airlines, Inc., Lockheed Constellation L-049, N 2737A, Byrd Field, Richmond, Virginia, November 8, 1961, SA-365, Released February 6, 1962.
6. To include Flight Attendants within the Definition of "Airman", Hearings Before a Subcommittee of the Committee on Interstate and Foreign Commerce, House of Representatives, 87th Congress, Second Session, May 1, 1962, p. 28.
7. Amdt 25-1/121-2.
8. NPRM 63-42.
9. Aviation Week & Space Technology, September 17, 1962.
10. Delta Airlines on a Convair 880, American Airlines on a Lockheed Electra and a Convair 990, Douglas on a DC-8 and Boeing on a 707 and a 720.
11. NPRM 63-42; Amdt 25-1/121-2.
12. Amdt 4b-11.
13. Amdt 25-1/121-2.
14. NPRM 63-42.
15. Amdt 121-20.
16. Aviation Week & Space Technology, September 17, 1962, p. 43.
17. Flight International, 18 June 1964.
18. Amdt 121-17.
19. Survival in Emergency Escape from Passenger Aircraft, p. 18.
20. [No Subject], Letter CAB Bureau of Safety to FAA, December 16, 1965, in CAB Aircraft Accident Report, United Air Lines, Inc., Boeing 727, N7030U, Salt Lake City, Utah, November 11, 1965, SA-388, Released June 7, 1967.
21. NPRM 66-26.
22. NPRM 66-26.
23. Amdt 25-15/121-30.
24. Federal Aviation Agency Air Traffic Control Operations, Hearings Before a Subcommittee of the Committee on Government Operations, House of Representatives, 89th Congress, Second Session, April 26, 1966, p. 71.

25. Amdt 25-15, 25.785(c).
26. Amdt 121-30, 121.311(d).
27. Amdt 121-30, 121.589(b).
28. NPRM 66-26.
29. NPRM 66-26.
30. Letter CAB Bureau of Safety to FAA, December 16, 1965.
31. Flammability and Smoke Characteristics of Aircraft Interior Materials, Technical Report ADS-3 by John F. Marcy E.B. Nicholas, J.E. Demaree, Federal Aviation Agency, January 1964.
32. FAA Flight Standards Service (FSS) Release No. 453, issued in 1961 as a Replacement of Safety Regulation Release 259 of August 1947.
33. Flammability and Smoke Characteristics of Aircraft Interior Materials.
34. Flammability and Smoke Characteristics of Aircraft Interior Materials.
35. ANPRM 69-30.
36. NPRM 66-26.
37. Amdt 25-15/121-30.
38. Crashworthiness Aspects of Transport Aircraft with Engines Mounted in the Rear, Letter Raymond B. Maloy, Assistant Administrator, Europe, Africa, Middle East to Rijksluchtvaartdienst, January 14, 1966.
39. NPRM 66-26.
40. Amdt 25-15.
41. NPRM 66-26.
42. Amdt 25-15/121-30.
43. NPRM 66-26.
44. NPRM 66-26.
45. Amdt 25-15.
46. NPRM 66-26.
47. Amdt 25-15.
48. NPRM 66-26.
49. NPRM 66-26.
50. Amdt 25-15.
51. Aeroflot: An Airline and Its Aircraft, R.E.G. Davies, 1992, p. 52.
52. NPRM 66-26, Amdt 25-15.
53. [No Subject], Letter R.H. Dawson to George E. Keck, United Air Lines, Inc., November 18, 1965, in Jerry Lederer Papers, Embry Riddle University, Prescott.
54. This was not the highest number of exits ever. Early Vickers Viscounts had up to 18 exits, including all the oval windows being an emergency exit.
55. Recommended Regulation Changes, Crashworthiness Development Program, AIA CDP-RC, Aerospace Industries Association of America, Inc., July 1968.
56. Amdt 25-32/121-84.
57. Amdt 25-32/121-84.
58. Amdt 25-32/121-84.
59. Amdt 25-32/121-84.
60. AIA CDP-RC, p. 10.
61. ANPRM 69-30.
62. NPRM 69-33.
63. Amdt 25-32.
64. Amdt 25-15.
65. Amdt 25-32.

10 Regulation Proposals That Were Rejected

ABSTRACT

While success stories are remembered, failures are forgotten. Yet, they form an equally important part of history and are a lesson of their own. In this chapter, nine cabin safety initiatives for novel features are reviewed that failed. The more salient are aft-facing seats, smoke hoods for passengers, which were tried to be introduced twice, and the cabin water spray system.

10.1 INTRODUCTION

Since the first cabin safety measures were introduced in the early 1920s, many have followed, as the other chapters narrate. Some came instantly as their benefit was obvious; others were discussed at length or extensively researched before being adopted. Yet other proposed measures looked promising but were rejected. Such measures share the fate that they are quickly forgotten, or pop up again, only to find their rejection repeated. This chapter discusses the more salient of such measures and why they were rejected.

10.2 PARACHUTES

An early proposal for saving passengers in a crash, or better, from an impending crash was the parachute. Several pre-World War Two sources mention individual parachutes as an option for passengers to escape in-flight from an airplane in trouble. When Knute Rockne, American football's most-renowned coach, Norwegian by birth, died in the 1931 Fokker F-10 accident at Bazaar, Kansas, people said that it was a tragedy that he did not even have a chance to save himself using a parachute.[1]

Particularly noteworthy was a proposal for equipping an entire cabin with a parachute. This was already a question in the 1928 Guggenheim survey and mentioned again in the hearing following the DC-2 crash in 1935 in which Senator Cutting was killed.[2,3] It was argued that in time such parachutes would be seen as normal as the retractable landing gear, against which airlines and manufacturers initially were opposed as well as it was too heavy and had too many extra parts that would give trouble.

The last time that there was a serious discussion about parachutes for passengers was in a report to President Harry S. Truman in December 1947. The president had installed a Special Board of Inquiry on Air Safety following three air accidents, two of which occurred on two consecutive days: the DC-4 accident on May 29, 1947, at La Guardia, another DC-4 accident, non-survivable, the day after and a third all-fatal DC-4 accident on June 13. The verdict was clear: while 'their use might seem to be highly desirable', the board disagreed and found them 'undesirable as well as impracticable'.[4] Most airline accidents come without advance warning, so there is no time for an organized abandonment in flight. But even if there were, could passengers be quickly taught the 'jump discipline'? And what about infants-in-arms, elderly passengers, or women, the report remarks. And in the case they do land safely, there are more challenges when this is in a remote or inaccessible area. On top of all these questions comes the fact that modern transport aircraft fly at altitudes and speeds that make in-flight jumping extremely dangerous, the report said.

The only reported case where an aircraft load of passengers used parachutes to evacuate a stricken aircraft in-flight was on August 2, 1943. The airplane was a military C-46, brand new, flying over the 'hump', the link between India and China over Japanese-occupied Burma. The 17 passengers, all male, were a mix of U.S. civil servants, U.S. and Chinese military staff, and a well-known CBS news correspondent. Their jumps resulted in some broken bones and landed them in an area that was hostile—not because of the Japanese but because of the indigenous population that had a reputation for headhunting. One of the four crewmembers' parachutes became entangled in the airplane's tail, with which he crashed, fatally. All the others reached safety after about three weeks including a brutal six-day trek.[5]

And then there is the infamous case of hijacker 'D B Cooper' who jumped out of the tail of a Boeing 727 in November 1971. This event led to rulemaking to prevent such cases by 'requiring that a means be provided to prevent the opening of central [sic] exits and tail cone exits during flight'.[6] The rule, effective August 1973, consisted of a design solution that became known as the 'Cooper vane' and a placard located next to the door in the pressure bulkhead stating that it cannot be opened in flight.[7] The vane is a simple device: an aerodynamic paddle that moves by airflow and blocks the door from opening in-flight but is spring loaded so that on the ground it is free from the door.

10.3 AFT-FACING SEATS

Of the cabin safety measures that over the years were proposed for regulation but rejected, the orientation of seats in the aft-facing direction probably came closest to having been adopted. There were attempts to introduce such a requirement, but they met with insufficient reasons for a convincing case. Yet, airplanes have been so equipped. During World War Two, there were many crashes with military transport aircraft. It was realized that those seated in aft-facing positions with adequate head support could tolerate higher crash forces than their forward-facing colleagues.

> This can be attributed to the distribution of the decelerating force over a much larger and more suitable surface than that covered by the conventional harness.[8]

The first organization that applied rearward-facing seats in their transport aircraft was the British Royal Air Force (RAF). They did this from 1946 onward on all their new transport aircraft and continued this practice for many decades. The U.S. Air Force followed in 1951 and continued to do so when their Military Air Transport Service (MATS) arm, later renamed Military Airlift Command, introduced the Boeing C-135, Lockheed C-141 and C-5 large transports. The U.S. Navy specified it for those transport aircraft types that landed on aircraft carriers such as the Grumman C-2 Greyhound.

On the civil side, aft-facing seats became a topic from 1947 onward. The committee that reported to President Truman in December 1947 recommended that 'an intensive study should be undertaken as to the advantages and disadvantages of rear-facing seats'.[9] In March 1952, *Flying*, the magazine, reported that the Airworthiness Division of ICAO had discussed it but 'it was pointed out that this would rule out other and perhaps better ways of accomplishing the same thing'.[10] In the same year, the CAB recommended aft-facing seats but did not go as far as starting rulemaking.[11] The debate continued. Those in favor of aft-facing often used data from crashes which appeared to prove their point. Evidence from the RAF, which had both forward-facing DC-3s and Yorks and aft-facing Hastings and Varsity aircraft, seemed to confirm the wisdom of their choice. Opponents said that a crash is never perfectly in the forward direction but has sideward components. This may cause a person's back and head to miss the support of the seat and cause injuries unique to that orientation. Another argument raised against rearward-facing is the risk of being injured by loose objects in the cabin flying forward.

Fokker originally decided on backward-facing seats for its F-27 'Friendship', but as 'practically all customers require forward facing', that became the standard.[12]

Howard Hasbrook, at the time a world expert on 'passenger tie-down' as he phrased it, had no preference. Either was good, he said, as long as the seat and belt restrain the occupant in crash conditions, and there are no objects around that can cause incapacitating or dangerous injuries.[13]

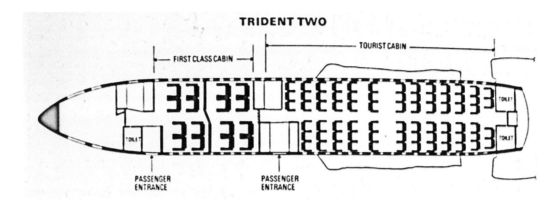

FIGURE 10.1 Cabin layout of BEA Trident Two (BEA timetable 1971).

In 1963, Australia was on the verge of requiring rearward-facing seats for the new Boeing 727. In a May 26, 1963, press release, Shane Paltridge, the Australian Minister for Civil Aviation, said that 'the Department of Civil Aviation was convinced that the chance of survival of passengers involved in some types of aircraft accident would be substantially increased if they were accommodated in a properly designed system of rearward facing seats'. However, Boeing had informed them that the floor structure of the 727 was not strong enough for this. Australia would try through ICAO 'to increase the design strength of the floors of regular public transport aircraft manufactured overseas'.[14] Even if tried, it failed, just as it had a decade earlier.

Boeing was correct in stating that the tensile load of a rearward-facing seat's aft leg is higher than that of a forward-facing seat. This is explained by the fact that the occupant's center of gravity when flailing forward is lower than that of a person who essentially remains upright in an aft-facing seat.

The main reason that airlines have always been against it is that they think passengers will not accept flying backward. While there is anecdotal evidence supporting this, there seems to be no scientific evidence and opinions vary considerably. Hawker Siddeley Trident Twos, operated by British European Airways in the 1960s and 1970s, had about half of the tourist class seats facing rearward.

Dan-Air, in testimony to the parliamentary inquiry in the United Kingdom following the Manchester 1985 and Kegworth 1989 accidents, said: 'It was very obviously noticeable that passengers preferred to face forward'.[15] McFarland cited a 1947 survey among passengers flying reverse in a USAF Douglas C-54 (DC-4) on a transcontinental run. The majority preferred it, and only one out of each five passengers found it objecting. Ninety-nine percent thought the view from the window was better and one passenger in three felt less airsick.[16] The RAF required airlines that they contracted for troop transport to place seats rearward-facing. In one case, such an airplane returned to normal airline service unmodified so that civil passengers sat aft-facing, with no appreciable negative feedback.[17]

In the 1960s the subject subsided but never got away completely. Often a survivable accident with fatalities kindled a debate between proponents and opponents of rear-facing seats.

10.4 PASSENGER SMOKE HOODS

In the 1965 Salt Lake City accident, when the aircraft hit the ground short of the runway, a fuel line running below the cabin from the wing to the tail engine ruptured. Within seconds it started a fire inside the cabin. The aircraft skidded for less than half a minute before it came to a stop, and the evacuation started. That half a minute of helplessness was perceived by some occupants as having lasted much longer, up to one and a half minutes. Ernest McFadden of FAA CAMI pictured himself

Regulation Proposals That Were Rejected

in that situation and thought of a piece of equipment that would have helped the people inside to bear that ordeal: a smoke hood. Instantly, he started fabricating a prototype: a simple, lightweight, protective, bag-shaped hood with a neck seal. He found a commercial company, named Schjeldahl, to further develop the concept.[18] The hoods were tested with flames aimed directly at it when worn and proved to work, even though its purpose was to only keep smoke out. In a hearing to Congress in April 1966, FAA CAMI demonstrated the hood. The concept was further developed and in 1967 the FAA installed the smoke hoods on its own transport aircraft N1 (a Lockheed Jetstar) and N3 (a Grumman Gulfstream 1). Before flight, passengers were briefed on the smoke hood. On these aircraft, they were never needed to be used in practice. The smoke hood, when properly donned, would protect the entire head against the effects of heat, smoke, and toxic gases and provide breathing air for about eight minutes.

In July 1967 evacuation tests were conducted in the FAA CAMI facility to determine the reactions of a naive group of subjects to the use of the hoods in the presence of smoke.[19] Evacuations with smoke were much slower than those without smoke. The use of the hoods alone did not seem to affect the evacuation rate. In February 1968 evacuation tests were done in the FAA Boeing 720 with four Braniff stewardesses. There were six runs, both with and without smoke hoods. The primary conclusion was that the use of smoke hoods would cause a small increase (approximately 8%) in the overall evacuation time.[20] The ATA, in their comments to the NPRM, criticized that these tests were not sufficiently realistic and not as per FAA's own evacuation demonstration criteria. CAMI thereupon did further tests in a Lockheed L-749 forward cabin, using dense smoke and applying FAA evacuation demonstration criteria.[21] Two groups of 64 subjects were employed in a Latin Square test set-up, with the test variables being no-smoke/no smoke hood and dense smoke/smoke hood. The latter condition again proved significantly slower, thus not supporting the hood's benefit. An additional test with smoke hood on but without smoke showed no significant loss of egress rate.

FAA CAMI continued its research in 1968 and 1969. In February 1969, the FAA issued an NPRM for protective smoke hoods for emergency use by passengers and crewmembers, soliciting comments. The FAA substantiated its proposal by referring to past accidents and the belief that smoke hoods would significantly increase occupant survival and 'that the economic burden of fitting airplanes with such hoods is reasonable in relation to expected benefits'.[22]

In support of the proposal was the pilot union, but for passengers only, asking for more sophisticated protection for crewmembers. The flight attendant union was opposed due to the increase in evacuation time and the limited useful time without air supply.[23]

Around 1968, AIA had done its own research. Comparative tests of ten different smoke mask samples (not in all cases a hood) were done by Boeing and McDonnell Douglas in a closed environment in which irritant smoke was introduced. The series of tests included evacuation tests in a Boeing 727 mock-up, with 316 subjects. They found that the hoods would delay evacuation by 30% in emergency lighting conditions and by 50% in dense smoke.[24] Additionally, a significant proportion of the naive subjects appeared to actually not don the hood at all and some removed it again before completing evacuation. Unsurprisingly, AIA concluded that the hoods might actually be more dangerous. ATA agreed with AIA. They strongly opposed the mandatory introduction of the hoods and went as far as saying that they would be a potential death trap. They found the technical specification that came with the proposal to be written specifically to one model (that of Schjeldahl) without allowing other designs. They further added that the smoke hood would be a pilferable item, driving the airlines' costs for replacements well beyond those estimated by the FAA. ATA's very extensive, 39-page-long comments were made public during the 1976 hearings.[25] It provides useful lessons for rule makers and those being regulated alike.

In addition to the ATA, two other commenters mentioned the risk of suffocation: the Flight Safety Foundation and an individual who was concerned that the briefing demonstration would cause children to put plastic bags over their heads. In August 1970 the FAA announced it withdrew the proposal. Reasons were the (1) increase in evacuation time; (2) the smoke hood, in itself, being a potential hazard caused by the consumption of oxygen in the trapped air; (3) and practical considerations such as deployment, pilferage, and liability.[26,27] FAA CAMI stopped its research the same year.

Renewed interest in smoke hoods, now dubbed protective breathing equipment (PBE), followed the Cincinnati 1983 accident, but only as a means to protect cabin crew when dealing with a fire.

Two years later, the Manchester 1985 accident brought back interest in a passenger smoke hood, now called Passenger Protective Breathing Equipment. This interest was restricted to the United Kingdom, where the accident received massive public attention. The UK AAIB, the investigator of this accident, was very positive about the hoods. It cited a comprehensive study made for the FAA in 1982 that said it was the most cost effective option for improving survivability in aircraft fires. The AAIB thought that smoke hoods would reduce the level of 'panic' during a critical evacuation 'which is triggered frequently by the sudden envelopment of passengers in dense black smoke and toxic/irritant gasses'.[28] (The use of the word 'frequently' by the AAIB suggested that they, like others, saw the Manchester accident as a 'typical' accident.)

Within five months after the accident, so well in advance of the publication of the final report in December 1988, the AAIB urged the CAA to 'give consideration to the formulation of a requirement for the provisions of smoke hoods/masks to afford passengers an effective level of protection during fires which produce a toxic environment within the aircraft cabin'.

The CAA responded in May 1988 by publishing a technical specification asking for breathing air-equipped hoods of at least 20-minute duration. The AAIB was disappointed as this was quite demanding and reduced the chances that a matching smoke hood would become available. The CAA had chosen 20 minutes to also cover the scenario of a fire starting in-flight, such as in the Cincinnati case in which there were 17 minutes from the first observation of smoke to the start of evacuation on the ground. The AAIB suggested as an alternative a filter-type device (so without its own breathing air supply) with protection for 10 minutes. The AAIB also thought that when no passenger would be offered a PBE, the existing cabin crew PBEs would introduce competitive behavior, with passengers creating critical disorder when they see that cabin crew have survival equipment that they do not have. The AAIB itself organized trials with smoke hoods protecting for five minutes. The survivor lobby organization SCI-SAFE reckoned that seven to ten minutes would be enough for ground evacuation. They discounted the in-flight fire scenario.

Like 20 years before in the U.S., post-Manchester in the UK little attention was paid to the psychological aversion of an untrained person to deliberately put a bag over the head and thus risk suffocation. Nor, when put on and it reached the end of supplying oxygen, whether the stimuli of taking it off again were sufficiently strong, knowing that hypoxia could cause a sense of euphoria.

The CAA studied the possible number of lives saved by a 'perfect' smoke hood, worldwide, and concluded that would be an average of nine per year. But it warned that this figure was optimistic and smoke hoods might actually delay an evacuation and thus increase the number of fatalities. After coordination with authorities in the U.S., Canada, and France, in December 1987 it concluded that a mandatory requirement for smoke hoods was not justified, also considering other cabin safety improvements introduced at the time.[29]

The UK parliament select committee inquiry that was set up in 1989 in the wake of the Manchester and Kegworth crashes still recommended in December 1990 'the mandatory carriage by UK-registered aircraft of the best smokehoods currently available'.[30] This was not followed up either.

In the 20 years between Salt Lake City and Manchester, there have been quite a few accidents mirroring their scenarios of an intact cabin full of smoke with passengers waiting for an escape opportunity but failing to evacuate. The more salient of these were three cases where the fire started in the cabin in-flight (Paris Orly 1973, Riyadh 1980, and Cincinnati 1983) and three post-crash-fire and smoke-entering-cabin cases (Monrovia 1967, Pago Pago 1974, and Malaga 1982). Yet, none of these led to a recommendation for smoke hoods by the investigators, or even mention of them. Why is that? Perhaps the answer is that it needs an individual to step forward as a strong proponent, such as CAMI's McFadden.

In the 40 years since Manchester, there have been about ten cases where the accident investigation report confirmed smoke in the cabin before, or entering during, the evacuation. Of these, in three cases there were fatalities that can be positively or likely attributed to failure to evacuate.[31] In the remaining seven cases where smoke was reported all occupants evacuated safely, except that in one case three passengers had been incapacitated by the impact, not by the smoke.[32] In another half a dozen or so cases conditions were similar, and there may have been smoke; however, this is not confirmed in the investigation reports.[33] In those cases, fatalities ranged from one to 70% of the occupants. Out of these 16 cases, PBE was mentioned in four reports, two of which involved Airbus A310 accidents, in Khartoum (2008) and Irkutsk (2006).[34] In the former, it was reported that the cabin crew did not use 'Personnel Protective Equipments'. What was meant here, was the cabin crew PBE that had been introduced earlier. The Russian accident report about the Irkutsk accident mentioned the lack of PBEs and included a recommendation aimed at EASA and manufacturers of large transport aircraft:

> to evaluate the usefulness of cabin crew smoke hood devices in assisting the evacuation of airplanes; to evaluate the possibility of equipping large transport airplanes with devices for passengers and/or flight attendants to be used in case of an emergency evacuation without suffering from the effects of smoke and toxic fumes.

In its annual review of safety recommendations for 2007, EASA confirmed receipt but did not include its response. Likely, EASA rejected the recommendation, thereby confirming the school of thought on passenger PBEs that the FAA started in 1970 and the UK CAA affirmed in 1987. That school said not to mandate Passenger Protective Breathing Equipment. Accident history has proven it right.

10.5 FLIGHT ATTENDANT CLOTHING

In March 1975 the FAA issued an Advance NPRM (ANPRM) for soliciting comments about research and current technology with respect to the flammability of flight attendant clothing.[35] It said it had:

> become aware of the urgent requirements for such standards as a result of recent flammability tests in which flight attendant uniforms readily caught fire and, in some instances, did not afford sufficient coverage to provide protection from exposure to heat and flame. These tests indicated that uniforms made of polyester cotton blends, vinyl and other synthetics, can be ignited by small fires, and will continue to burn independently after ignition.

It formulated eight specific questions, most of them about the effects of treating uniforms with fire retardants on durability, styling, tailoring, laundering, and so on.

What it did not disclose was the nature of the 'tests' that had triggered this ANPRM. The tests were protests. In the wake of a societal trend, in 1972, the Stewardesses for Women's Rights was formed. It was a movement that protested against the image that the profession, which predominantly consisted of women, had gained: that of an over-sexualized waitress instead of a safety professional. At a protest in 1974 where they burned uniforms, they found 'the synthetic fabrics melted and burned with shocking rapidity'.[36] The Association of Flight Attendants informed the FAA about the safety risk.

The ANPRM generated answers that were not specific but of a nature too general for the FAA to proceed. In 1980 it followed up with a second NPRM which was gender-neutral as it expanded the scope to all crewmember uniforms, not only those of (female) flight attendants, and with more questions.[37] It also announced a public hearing. But the response was meager, even after extending the comment period to eight months. The notice was withdrawn in May 1981.[38]

10.6 STROBE LIGHTS

In 1966, the FAA published two proposals for strobe lights, for both inside and outside. Inside, strobe lights were suggested under seats at exits to assist passengers in locating exits. This was aimed particularly at the condition of the cabin filled with smoke. On the outside, instead of the two-inch contrasting band outlining each emergency exit, the American Association of Airport Executives suggested a crash inertia-activated strobe light mounted in the exit windows to inform crash rescue services.

The FAA did make mandatory neither of the two suggestions and these ideas both died. Later, and unrelated, Airbus performed tests with strobe lights to see whether they would be effective in attracting passengers to exits. They proved not, so the FAA decision in 1967 not to require such lights appeared just.

10.7 LAVATORY-OCCUPIED SIGN

As part of the Airworthiness Review Program, the FAA proposed in 1975 a mandatory sign indicating when lavatories are occupied. It reasoned that this would minimize aisle congestion and possible injuries during flight in turbulent air.[39] Commenters pointed out that such signs already existed but did not reduce aisle congestion and that there may be other reasons for such congestion. The proposal was withdrawn in 1980.[40]

FIGURE 10.2 Lavatory-occupied sign in a Boeing 717 (photograph by the author).

10.8 EVACUATION ALARM SYSTEM

From the 1960s onward, some major airlines equipped their jet fleets with an evacuation alarm system. Like in office buildings, these systems give a specific aural sound, accompanied by red flashing lights, prompting an evacuation. In its 1974 cabin safety review, the NTSB called for such a system, independently powered and supplementing passenger address systems, which did not always function as intended. In 1975, as part of the Airworthiness Review program, the FAA indeed proposed a mandatory evacuation alarm system: 'The FAA believes that during an emergency, an alarm system which can be perceived by all passengers and crewmembers located anywhere on the airplane is vital'.[41] But there was much opposition, and the FAA withdrew its proposal.[42] The NTSB repeated its recommendations in 1981 and 1998 but to no avail.[43] Yet, some airlines kept them. It was activated in the Boeing 777 accident at London Heathrow, in January 2008. The investigators did not report whether it materially contributed to the evacuation, which itself was successful.[44] In the Toronto Airbus A340 August 2005 accident its activation failed.[45]

10.9 WATER MIST SYSTEM

The history of the water spray system paralleled that of the passenger smoke hoods. The investigators of the Manchester 1985 accident launched the idea of a sprinkler system in airliners which they called the water mist system. The idea was not new. A passenger of the 1965 Salt Lake City accident, in a letter to United Airlines written one week later, suggested 'that a dry (empty) sprinkler system is incorporated into every fuselage', for quick attachment of foam hoses from the fire trucks.[46] The concept was further described by Roebuck in 1968 and more extensively in 1982 by the IIT Research Institute for the FAA.[47,48] Resembling a sprinkler system, there is a water reservoir on-board and a piping system for distributing water to be released in mist form from multiple nozzles in the ceiling and along the luggage bins. Alternatively, the system does not have an on-board supply, but a connection in the fuselage hull for fire tenders to connect their supplies or a combination of both. In either case, the system, when activated, douses the cabin with a mist of tiny water droplets. This will inhibit flame spread, cool the cabin and delay flashover, and so extend the evacuation time for its occupants.

In 1987 and 1988 the system was tested on a surplus VC-10 at RAF Catterick, Yorkshire, and Tridents in Teesside, Durham, both in Northeastern England. In February 1988 the system was demonstrated to aircraft cabin safety experts from both authorities and manufacturers.

In 1989, the FAA Technical Centre repeated the tests, initially in a DC-7 fuselage and later a DC-10-based wide-body fuselage dubbed 'TC-10'.[49] Also in 1989, the CAA continued testing on a Boeing 707 fuselage parked in one of the two huge airship hangars in Cardington, near Bedford, UK. In the summer of 1992, the Applied Psychology Unit of the College of Aeronautics, Cranfield Institute of Technology, jointly with the Institute of Sound and Vibration Research, University of Southampton, performed a series of eight tests, with 45 participants each time. Both dry and wet runs were done. No difference in evacuation rate was found.[50]

While the system was impressive at first sight, it raised many practical questions. What is the effect of inadvertent activation in-flight on aircraft systems that are vital for continuing flight? What about a precautionary evacuation in subfreezing temperatures, with the passengers, now wet and shivering outside in the cold, waiting hours for transport to somewhere warm? Boeing, in 1992 contracted by the FAA, did a disbenefit study. In addition to giving negative answers to both questions, it found that, like smoke hoods, the system might increase evacuation time. Also, it concluded that passenger reaction to the system is unknown.[51] Another negative aspect of the system was that it did not remove carbon monoxide from the cabin air as that is a non-water-soluble gas. Particularly in an in-flight fire, this could be disastrous.[52]

Research continued until late 1993, when the CAA together with the FAA decided not to pursue the system. The costs 'per potential life saved' would be too high but they also cited the benefits of the other cabin safety measures. In the words of the CAA's project manager for the system, Nick Povey: 'We are running out of lives to save'.[53] This decision saved them from having to address the in-flight and wet-and-cold-outside questions.

After that, occasionally the water mist system popped up again. In 2002, Ray Cherry conducted a benefit analysis which estimated that it would save 27 to 34 lives worldwide, for 'western-built' aircraft.[54] He based those figures on accidents over the 30-year period 1967 to 1996 and inferred

FIGURE 10.3 Cabin water spray system demonstration on a Trident (photograph by the author).

that accident rates would remain the same in the future. Two decades later, this prophecy can be proven as falsified.

10.10 PASSAGEWAY BETWEEN BULKHEADS

One of the tragedies that happened in Manchester in 1985 was the surge of people at the forward cabin end. The passageway there, between two galley units, was only 22.5 inch (57 cm) wide and became a bottleneck. Because of the smoke, people en masse came forward, not only through the aisle but also climbing over seats. This led to a blockage and hampered speedy evacuation. The report says:[55]

> At the start of evacuation from the L1 door, the stewardess stated that passengers seemed to be jammed in the cabin aisle and entrance to the galley (ie between the twin forward bulkheads).
>
> The aisle aperture between the twin forward bulkheads in this configuration was 22½ inches wide, effectively restricting passengers approaching along the aisle and over the seat backs to a single-line exit flow in spite of both forward doors being open from approximately 1 minute 10 seconds after the aircraft stopped. Many passengers [. . .] collapsed in this area but survived.

Within four weeks after the accident, the AAIB sent a letter to the CAA recommending a review of the approval of the cabin configuration with respect to the forward aisle restriction. Unlike with the Type III overwing exits, for which it issued an Airworthiness Notice in January 1986 (see Section 14.3.2.2), the CAA did not take quick action. Rather, it asked Helen Muir of the Cranfield Institute of Technology to extend her program of competitive testing to such apertures. Cranfield tested the effect of various widths on the speed of evacuation. The widths were 20, 24, 27, 30, and 36 inch (51, 61, 68.5, 76, and 91.5 cm). The first (20 inch) met the requirements in force at the time. Evacuation times for the smaller three configurations were significantly slower than for the two wider configurations and Cranfield suggested a minimum of 30 inch for a passageway through a bulkhead.[56]

The CAA indeed promoted such a proposed regulation but, as it was a member of the JAA, needed to do that via that organization. The JAA Cabin Safety Study Group prepared a Notice of Proposed Amendment in the period 1991–1993. After some debate, it was decided that it would affect aircraft with 110 passenger seats and up. The affected passageways would not only be those at the front of the cabin (where it happened in Manchester) but also elsewhere in the cabin, as well as in cross aisles. It was proposed to not only make the requirement applicable to future aircraft types (via JAR-25) but also on a retrofit basis to the existing fleet (via JAR-26). The proposal initially met with reservations within the JAA community but was eventually published in 1996 as an Advance NPA for soliciting comments.[57] It was not transposed as a final rule by the JAA but landed on the to-do list of EASA when it inherited the JAA's tasks in 2003. EASA decided in 2008 not to pursue the matter further as the safety benefit would be insignificant but costs incurred would be significant.[58] Since 1985, the accident scenario that led to this NPA has not been repeated.

NOTES

1 Bonfires to Beacons: Federal Civil Aviation Policy under the Air Commerce Act, 1926-1938, by Nick A. Komons, p. 116.
2 Safety and Accommodation in European Passenger Planes—Pamphlet Number Three—The Daniel Guggenheim Fund for the Promotion of Aeronautics, Inc., December 17, 1928, p. 68.
3 Safety in Air, Hearings Before a Subcommittee of the Committee on Commerce, United States Senate, 74th Congress, Second Session, June 5, 1936, p. 1253.
4 Report to the President of the United States by the President's Special Board of Inquiry on Air Safety, December 29, 1947.
5 The August 2, 1943 Crash of C-46 # 41-12420 and Significance of the Rescue of Its Crew and Passengers, John F. Cassidy, July 17, 2013.

Regulation Proposals That Were Rejected 151

6. NPRM 72-15.
7. Amdt 25-34/121-99.
8. Advanced Techniques in Crash Impact Protection and Emergency Egress from Air Transport Aircraft by R.G. Snyder, AGARDograph No. 221, NATO, June 1976, p. 67.
9. Report to the President of the United States.
10. Flying, March 1952.
11. Aviation Week, August 11, 1952.
12. Safety Aspects of the F-27 "Friendship', by H.C. van Meerten, presented at the Fifth Annual Air Safety Forum, March 5, 6, 7, 1957.
13. Design of Passenger "Tie-Down"—Some Factors for Consideration in the Crash-Survival Design of Passenger Seats in Transport Aircraft, A. Howard Hasbrook, Aviation Crash Injury Research, Av-CIR-44-0-66, September 1956.
14. Rear Facing Seats not Mandatory for Boeing 727, Statement by the Minister for Civil Aviation, Senator Shane Paltridge, Melbourne, May 26, 1963, press release.
15. Aircraft Cabin Safety, Vol. 1, Appendix 7, United Kingdom, House of Commons, Transport Committee, First Report, Printed 5 December 1990.
16. Human Factors in Air Transportation—Occupational Health and Safety, Ross A. McFarland, 1953, p. 561.
17. Fatal Civil Aircraft Accidents, Their Medical and Pathological Investigation, Peter J. Stevens, 1970, p. 60.
18. Summary Report of the History and Events Pertinent to the Civil Aeromedical Institute's Evaluation of Providing Smoke/Fume Protective Breathing Equipment for Airline Passenger Use, Arnold Higgins, FAA CAMI, DOT/FAA/AM-87/5, June 1987.
19. DOT/FAA/AM-87/5.
20. DOT/FAA/AM-87/5.
21. Protective Smoke Hood Studies, Ernest B. McFadden, Roger C. Smith, AM 70-20, FAA OAM, December 1970.
22. NPRM 69-2.
23. DOT/FAA/AM-87/5.
24. Aviation Safety Volume II (Aircraft Cabin Environment). Hearings Before the Subcommittee on Investigations and Review of the Committee on Public Works and Transportation, U.S. House of Representatives, 94th Congress, Second Session, February 5, 1976, p. 260.
25. Aviation Safety Volume II, 1976, p. 253.
26. 35 FR 13138.
27. Engineering·and Development Program Plan Aircraft Systems Fire Safety, DOT/FAA/CT-84/1, FAA TC, November 1983.
28. Report on the Accident to Boeing 737-236 Series 1, G-BGJL at Manchester International Airport on 22 August 1985, 8/88, Department of Transport, Air Accidents Investigation Branch, 15 December 1988, p. 148.
29. Aircraft Cabin Safety, Minutes of Evidence, Wednesday 24 January 1989, United Kingdom, House of Commons, Transport Committee, p. 99.
30. Aircraft Cabin Safety, Volume 1, United Kingdom, House of Commons, Transport Committee, First Report, p. xx, Printed 5 December 1990.
31. Busan 2002, Irkutsk 2006, Khartoum 2008.
32. Warsaw 1993, Jeju 1994 (smoke unconfirmed, but likely), Fukuoka 1996, Hualien 1999, Toronto 2005, Dubai 2016, Durango 2018.
33. Bangalore 1990, Aurangabad 1993, Buenos Aires 1999, Phuket 2007, Yichun 2010, Heho 2012.
34. The other two were the A340 accident in Toronto, August 2, 2005 and the 777 accident in Dubai, August 3, 2016.
35. ANPRM 75-13.
36. Feminity in Flight, A History of Flight Attendants, Kathleen M. Barry, 2007, p. 193.
37. NPRM 75-13A.
38. 46 FR 32409.
39. NPRM 75-31, Proposal 8-38.
40. Amdt 25-54, Proposal 8-38.
41. NPRM 75-26, Proposal 7-39.
42. Amdt 25-46.
43. NTSB Recommendations A-81-129; A-98-22.

44 Report on the Accident to Boeing 777-236ER, G-YMMM, at London Heathrow Airport on 17 January 2008, 1/2010, Department for Transport, Air Accidents Investigation Branch, published 9 February 2010.
45 Aviation Investigation Report Runway Overrun and Fire Air France Airbus A340-313 F-GLZQ Toronto/Lester B. Pearson International Airport, Ontario 02 August 2005, Transportation Safety Board of Canada, A05H0002, Released 16 October 2007.
46 [No Subject], Letter R.H. Dawson to George E. Keck, United Air Lines, Inc., November 18, 1965, in Jerry Lederer Papers, Embry Riddle University, Prescott.
47 New Concepts for Emergency Evacuation of Transport Aircraft Following Survivable Accidents, J.A. Roebuck, Jr. North American Rockwell Corporation, ADS-68-2, January 1968.
48 Fire Management/Suppression Systems/Concepts Relating to Aircraft Cabin Fire Safety, K.R. Miniszewski, T.E. Waterman, IIT Research Institute and J.A. Campbell, F. Salzberg, Gage-Babcock and Associates, Inc., DOT/FAA/CT-82/134, October 1983.
49 Flight International, 13 May 1989, p. 18.
50 Aircraft Evacuations: the Effect of a Cabin Water Spray System Upon Evacuation Rates and Behaviour, D.M. Bottomley, H.C. Muir, M.C. Lower, CAA Paper 93008, March 1993.
51 Aircraft Cabin Water Spray Disbenefits Study, Thomas L. Reynolds, Kent W. Porter, Boeing, DOT/FAA-CT92/6, October 1993.
52 Aircraft Cabin Safety, Minutes of Evidence, Wednesday 17 January 1990, United Kingdom, House of Commons, Transport Committee, p. 71.
53 Flight International, 24–30 November 1993, p. 8.
54 A Benefit Analysis for Cabin Water Spray Systems and Enhanced Fuselage Burnthrough Protection, by R.G.W. Cherry & Associates Limited, CAA Paper 2002/04, 7 April 2003.
55 AAIB 8/88, p. 172.
56 Aircraft Evacuations: The Effect of Passenger Motivation and Cabin Configuration Adjacent to the Exit, Helen Muir, Claire Marrison, Alyson Evans, CAA Paper 89019, 1989.
57 ANPA 25D-224 Emergency Exit Access, Joint Aviation Authorities, Issue 1, 1 November 1996.
58 Access through Bulkheads, European Aviation Safety Agency Notice of Proposed Amendment (NPA) No. 2008-18, 13 June 2008; EASA NPA 2008-18, 13 June 2008; Comment Response Document (CRD) to NPA 2008-18, 14 October 2008.

11 Second Trough (1973–1981)

ABSTRACT

The trough period between the second and third waves indeed was a lean period in terms of cabin safety developments. However, quite to the contrary in terms of accidents with survivability factors. In a period of about seven months, there were two such accidents with Boeing 707s. In the short run, they led to some improvements in lavatory fire protection. Proposals to regulate smoke emission and the reduction of toxicity from burning cabin materials, however, were stifled. Hearings started to be held in U.S. Congress about the state of airline cabin safety in the nation. They would be held about annually for ten years. The FAA took cabin safety more seriously but still lacked a visionary plan addressing the underlying causes for the increase in fatalities since 1970: fire and impact. Its activities were limited to educating airlines. Toward the end of the period, and under congressional pressure, the FAA formed a committee together with industry to find solutions for aircraft occupants to survive a post-crash-fire environment: the SAFER committee. It started a fire research program at its Technical Center location in Atlantic City and a crash dynamics program.

11.1 INTRODUCTION

Following the second wave, there was no noticeable decline in cabin safety accidents. Quite to the contrary. The number of airline accidents increased, and so did the number of accidents with survivability issues.

The increase in airline accidents was alarming and led to U.S. Congress coming into action. In 1975 a House Committee arranged hearings, which focused on the prevention of accidents. In February 1976 they convened follow-up hearings specific on the subject of the 'aircraft cabin environment'. This became a series on its own. There would be annual follow-up hearings dedicated to cabin safety subjects each year until the mid-1980s.

Responding, the FAA started to recognize that cabin safety was more than just facilitating speedy evacuation. It was a subject well worthy of attention. This started slowly and needed some external pressure from unions and, more effectively, Congress. Regulatory action was limited until after the turn of the decade, when research initiatives started to yield results that could be transposed into rules. This pertained mainly to two domains: impact protection and fire protection. With the benefit of hindsight, the period of the second trough can be characterized as one of consolidation, with little regulatory output.

11.2 ACCIDENTS

The decade of the 1970s saw more survivable but fatal accidents than any other decade in history. On U.S. soil, one of the first occurred to a Douglas DC-8 in November 1970, at Anchorage, Alaska. Impact forces were mild and not debilitating. Yet, 47 persons, out of 229 on board, died because of a fire. Like in Richmond nine years earlier, all passengers were active military personnel (213) or their dependents (6). The eight weeks from November 28, 1972, to January 22, 1973, saw six accidents, worldwide, with both fatalities and survivors, 434 and 178, respectively. This included the first accident to a wide-body: a Lockheed L-1011 that came down in the Everglades, Florida.

Frank Taylor of the Cranfield Institute of Technology, who kept records of survivable accidents and causes of death (impact or fire) for turbine-engined aircraft, counted a peak for this decade compared to the previous and next, particularly for fire-caused fatalities.[1]

TABLE 11.1
Accident Statistics for Survivable Accidents by Frank Taylor

	Number of Accidents	Death by Fire	Death by Impact	Total
1960–1969	41	584	1048	1632
1970–1979	56	1312	1287	2599
1980–1989	18	554	919	1473

It should be noted that not all these accidents are classified as cabin safety accidents. Some were so severe that few survivors resulted from chance circumstances that could not be mitigated by improving cabin safety. One striking example was the August 1985 Japan Airlines in-flight loss of control accident with 520 fatalities but also 4 'lucky survivors', thereby qualifying for the records of Taylor. The same applied to the March 1977 Tenerife collision accident, where a 747 taking off struck another 747 that was taxiing. On the latter airplane, there were 335 fatalities but also 77 survivors. (None of the occupants of the 747 taking off survived.) The crash dynamics of that accident were so random that no cabin safety improvements could be envisaged that would save fatalities in a future similar occurrence.

Two significant accidents which triggered cabin safety improvements occurred to Boeing 707s, at Paris Orly, in July 1973 and in Pago Pago, American Samoa, in January 1974. The former suffered an in-flight fire that led to drastic changes in lavatory fire safety. The latter was impact survivable yet almost all occupants were unable to escape and perished due to smoke and fire.

But there were also good news stories. Early in the decade, a DC-8 crashed in Rome in a fierce fuel fire scenario, yet all occupants could escape. Later in the decade, there were about 15 more accidents where a fire had developed, yet all occupants managed to escape.

11.3 HEARINGS

The rise in accidents with cabin safety elements caused concerns at all levels. This included the heart of the U.S. government: Capitol hill in Washington, D.C. Starting in 1976, cabin safety would be the subject of House of Representatives Subcommittee hearings on an annual basis for the next 10 years.

In February 1976 hearings were held on the subject of 'Aircraft cabin environment', another term for cabin safety. In the three-day hearings one day was spent listening to flight attendants who had been involved in accidents. They aired their disappointment with the FAA and its inaction on the poor standards of 'jump seats'. These seats, used by flight attendants during take-off and landing, in many cases were simple fold-out seat pans in galley areas. Inadequate training standards were another target. One of the speakers summarized these as 'spotty training procedures that seem to be flirting with danger'.[2] Other subjects on which there were testimonies included the flammability of cabin interiors, flight attendant uniforms, toxicity and smoke generation during post-crash fires, and adequacy and availability of safety equipment provided for occupant protection, including smoke hoods.

In the next year, July 1977, the subject was 'Aircraft Passenger Education: the missing link'. There was again testimony by a flight attendant who had experienced a crash. The main subject was the human behavior of passengers in accidents and how this could be influenced by safety briefings and safety cards. In September 1977 hearings took place on the overarching subject of airline deregulation and what it meant for safety. Cabin safety was addressed in passing and in particular the policies of the FAA with respect to granting exemptions.

No cabin safety subjects were addressed in 1978, but in 1979 they returned on two occasions. In April 1979, the House Subcommittee, this time chaired by Congressman Norman Mineta, spent two days on interior compartment materials. Looking back on the second wave of regulatory improvements with respect to flammability and evacuation and citing the Pago Pago accident, the NTSB representative accused the FAA of a band-aid approach.[3] Later in the year, with the broader subject of 'FAA safety issues' on the agenda, the subject of evacuation demonstrations was raised by the Association of Flight Attendants.[4]

In 1980 Norman Mineta chaired four days of hearings (three in June, one in September) on two major cabin safety subjects where the FAA was seen as footdragging. Interior compartment materials were addressed again, now by testimony on the perceived slow progress of the SAFER committee. The other subject was the aircraft passenger seat structural design. Here, the FAA took the stance that its standards, and notably the 9 g static test, were adequate and needed no update.

The next year, in April 1981, accident-experienced flight attendants were again invited to deliver testimonies. This time the main subject was the FAA's January proposal to allow airlines to reduce the number of flight attendants when passenger seats were blocked.[5] The flight attendant's engagement of Congress was successful: the proposal was withdrawn by the FAA in December.[6]

11.4 FAA GETTING TO GRIPS WITH CABIN SAFETY

The second wave of cabin safety measures had not brought the reduction of passenger fatalities in survivable accidents that was hoped for. While those measures had been proudly supported by industry (airplane manufacturers and airlines), this time it were the NTSB and the flight attendant unions that signaled the disappointing accident trend. The two regulation review programs commenced in 1974 and 1975 for airworthiness and operations, respectively, generated many proposals in the cabin safety domain. And, as discussed earlier, in February 1976 a Congress hearing was held on the subject. This all prompted the FAA to take the subject more seriously. In 1975 it hired the first cabin safety specialist, a former stewardess from Hughes Air West.

In December 1976 it published a report on Air Carrier Cabin Safety, detailing the results of a survey conducted in the summer months.[7] The study identified many contemporary, valid cabin safety issues and recognized ongoing research by its two research facilities: the National Aviation Facilities Experimental Center (NAFEC) in Atlantic City, New Jersey, and the Civil Aeromedical Institute (CAMI) in Oklahoma City. Yet it lacked an action plan for mitigating the issues. The deputy director of the FAA flight standards service however looked back with satisfaction and concluded that 'considerable progress had been made in the past 15 years'. The recommendations of the study were correspondingly quite soft. They were addressed internally (to either the Flight Standards Service or the Office of Aviation Medicine) and were about educating airlines in cabin safety operational and training elements and further research. What was lacking was a visionary plan, addressing the underlying causes for the increase in fatalities since 1970: impact and fire. Of these two, fire was the first that was acknowledged by the FAA as requiring action. In the course of 1977, the FAA started research on post-crash fires at NAFEC using a surplus Douglas C-133 airframe. In the same year, it signed an agreement with the United Kingdom on cooperation in developing anti-misting kerosene (AMK) fuel. These were the first steps in a fire safety research program that would lead to drastic regulatory changes some ten years later.

During the 1960s and 1970s, several petitions were filed by aviation users and professional organizations asking the FAA to improve the standards for seat and seat tie-down strength and specify dynamic testing.[8] They said that jet airplanes were larger than the propeller airplanes for which the standards were made and had higher landing speeds. In addition, human tolerance limits had been shown to be much higher than the 9 g's of the FAA standards. They are as high as 20 g. In 1969, NAFEC had already studied criteria for dynamic seat testing for type certification purposes.[9] At CAMI, Richard Chandler and others were a proponent of dynamic seat testing. In 1981, the NTSB issued recommendations to the same effect.[10]

The FAA, until 1980, consistently denied such petitions and recommendations arguing that jet transport airplanes have extensive crushable structures. It further negated the evidence that the petitioners cited in 11 documented accidents in which passenger seats failed as a result of inadequate standards. The FAA countered by saying that they were the result of loss of airframe integrity. In other words, because the crash caused the fuselage or the floors to break or flex, it could not be expected that a passenger seat performed in protecting its occupant. The FAA, however, accepted that making seats more energy absorbent would help and said this would need more research. Such research was indeed being done by its CAMI research facility, as well as at NASA's Langley Research Center. The ultimate research goal was to define one, or more, dynamic pulse standards, which could then be used for testing the seats. This required a sequential approach. First, based on actual past accidents, crash scenarios needed to be chosen. These then defined candidate scenarios for further modeling and testing. The schedule for this program would progress well into the first half of the 1980s. It indeed started in 1980 with the three U.S. airframe manufacturers (Boeing, Lockheed, McDonnell Douglas) being contracted by NASA to assess the failure mechanisms and impact resistance performance in past accidents. One conclusion was that the primary cause of seat failure was floor deformation. In the next step, a joint team of NASA Langley and FAA Technical Center (the new name for NAFEC) defined three crash scenarios: ground-to-ground (overrun), air-to-ground (hard landing), and air-to-ground (impact).[11] These scenarios were then worked out in mathematical computer models, such as KRASH, drop tests of fuselage sections, and full-scale tests and cross validated.

Mineta, as chairman of two hearings in which the FAA was grilled, had been quite instrumental in the progress that the FAA eventually geared into. Looking back in December 1984 on the process, he said that he had a number of bills ready that would have required the FAA to issue certain regulations by specified dates, no matter what. But, rather, he gave them some leeway on the schedules for research and rulemaking that they promised.[12] And it worked. The FAA was indeed getting to grips with cabin safety. Proof came with the third wave.

11.5 FAA RULEMAKING

The period 1973–1981 was a lean period when it comes to new cabin safety regulations. Of the few regulations that did appear, the majority resulted from an FAA initiative to invite the aviation industry and aviation public to propose subjects for rulemaking. These were the first biennial Airworthiness Review (1974–1975) and the first biennial Operations Review (1975–1976).

11.5.1 Impact Protection

There was only one subject in the impact protection domain that was conclusively regulated in this period. Metal-to-fabric safety belts were prohibited as they were found susceptible to wear and deterioration, thus losing friction and failure of the belt to lock effectively.[13] The change, which stemmed from the airworthiness review, became effective in the U.S. in December 1980 for all fleets.[14]

Also stemming from the airworthiness review, and supported by recommendations from the NTSB as well as congressional pressure, were the rigorous changes to improve flight attendant seats and the securing of galleys against inadvertent spillage of contents. They were prepared toward the end of the period. Their becoming mandatory, in early 1982, heralded the start of the third wave of cabin safety enhancements (see Chapter 13).

11.5.2 Fire Protection

As to fire protection, the period of the second trough was more productive, albeit in the form of planting seeds, the reaping of which would come in the next period, the third wave. This was mainly because of two dramatic accidents involving smoke and toxic gases.

11.5.2.1 Paris Orly 11 July 1973

On 11 July 1973, 12 years to the date after the Denver accident, the pilot of a Brazilian Boeing 707 landed in a field 5 km short of the runway at Paris Orly. He did so with his side window open to be able to look outside. His view inside was compromised by intense smoke. That smoke came from a cabin fire that had developed five to ten minutes earlier in the aft cabin. At the time of the landing, the fire was confined to the aft lavatories area, but smoke had filled the entire cabin and poisoned all of its occupants. Although the forced landing was successful, the accident was fatal to all but 11 occupants. Eight crewmembers, out of nine who had congregated in the cockpit, escaped via the cockpit windows.[15] One flight engineer, who had been standing, was fatally injured by the impact, but three cabin crewmembers, also standing in the cockpit, survived. One steward, seated at a forward cabin door, said that, since he was sick from smoke, he was too weak to open the emergency door. He leaned against it and it opened, but it closed partially after he fell out.[16] Another cabin crewmember, seated next to the opposite door, managed to use it and escaped. Two more cabin crewmembers were later found deceased close to these exits. Fire rescue services, who arrived after six to seven minutes, extricated one crewmember and three passengers, one of whom survived. The other cabin exits remained closed. In the cabin, 122 persons were found deceased, all asphyxiated. The accident investigators were able to trace the origin of the fire to the right aft lavatory but were unable to determine the cause. Was it a cigarette that had been carelessly disposed of, or was it an electrical failure?

The accident had occurred outside the U.S. and did not involve a U.S. operator, but the aircraft type was of U.S. design. The NTSB thus became involved and issued recommendations to the FAA for:

- early detection of lavatory fires;
- full-face masks on each emergency oxygen bottle for each cabin attendant;
- re-evaluating the cabin interior flame resistance requirements of Boeing 707;
- organizing a government/industry task force on aircraft fire prevention and improvements with respect to the fire potential of enclosed areas such as lavatories.[17]

The FAA used its quickest regulatory means to introduce mitigating measures addressing the first and, allegedly, the third recommendation: the Airworthiness Directive (AD). On April 30, 1974, it issued AD 74–08–09. This applied not only to the Boeing 707 but also to all other contemporary aircraft types in service. It called for no smoking placards on the lavatory door, no cigarette disposal placards on waste containers, ashtrays on or near the lavatory door, no smoking in lavatory announcements to passengers, and regular inspection of the lavatories in flight. In 1991, this AD was complemented, but not replaced, by a change to the FARs.[18] Another AD (AD 74–21–03), issued in October 1974, called for an inspection for wear, abrasion, and corrosion of electrical items within lavatory waste container areas. Both ADs are still active in 2024 and often appear as the oldest ADs on the lists that airworthiness inspectors consult.

The second recommendation was not followed up. However, much later, a requirement for protective breathing equipment for cabin crew was introduced (see Section 13.5.2.4). The fourth recommendation was initially responded to by the FAA by reference to the fire safety development program that it had initiated, also following the Pago Pago accident. Later, the SAFER program followed this up.

11.5.2.2 Pago Pago, January 30, 1974

Shortly after the 1973 disaster at Paris Orly, there was another dramatic accident in which smoke and toxicity played a fatal role: in Pago Pago, American Samoa, on January 30, 1974. The aircraft crashed into jungle vegetation about 1 km short of the runway. Of the 101 occupants, nine passengers and one crewmember survived the crash and fire, but the crewmember and three of the nine passengers died within the next days. An overwing exit on the right side was opened but closed again as flames came in through it. All survivors used a left overwing exit. The investigation report says:

> It could not be determined why the primary emergency exits were not opened on the left side of the aircraft. The fire outside the aircraft on the right side or the press of passengers may explain why the doors on the right side were not opened.
> It is also possible that the passengers crowded against the doors, and for that reason, the flight attendants were unable to open the exits.

Except for the co-pilot, who received impact injuries, all fatalities were due to smoke inhalation and massive first-, second-, and third-degree burns and complications from those massive burns.[19] As American Samoa was a U.S. territory, the investigation was done by the NTSB. The report did not include cabin safety-related recommendations.

11.5.2.3 FAA Follow-Up

Triggered by the two accidents, the FAA proposed the development of smoke emission criteria for interior materials, to be applied to new airplane types and, after five years, the existing fleet. A companion standard for toxicity levels was the subject of a separate Advance NPRM (ANPRM), issued in 1974.[20] But in August 1978 it was decided against pursuing it as it was felt that smoke was the overriding incapacitating element so a separate toxicity standard would add nothing.[21]

As part of the 1975 airworthiness review program, it was proposed to make applicable to the existing fleet the 1972 FAR 25 upgrade of the Bunsen burner test. This was withdrawn again in August 1978 because of developments described hereunder.[22]

A further step to advance on these proposals was to involve industry, as the NTSB had already recommended in 1973. Thereto, in 1977 two public hearings were held: in June on fuel tank safety (fire and explosion hazard reduction) and in November on cabin compartment interior materials. There, it was appreciated that these four proposals (fuel tank safety, flammability retrofit, smoke, and toxicity of interior materials) should not be treated in isolation but would benefit from a unified look. The risk of such an isolationist approach had already manifested itself: materials developed to meet the new flammability requirements actually created more smoke and toxic gases, thus negating the net safety gain. Industry was also negative about the lack of an adequate test methodology and the high cost with a questionable safety benefit.[23] They proposed that the FAA would employ that unified look together with them. On June 8, 1978, the FAA indeed invited industry for such an advisory committee. Soon after, it dropped the four rulemaking proposals.[24] The FAA named the committee SAFER—Special Aviation Fire and Explosion Reduction. Its mandate was for two years. Its mission was 'to examine the factors affecting the ability of the aircraft cabin occupant to survive in the post-crash environment and the range of solutions available'.[25] Unfortunately, the first 11 months were taken by its formation, leaving only 13 months for the actual work. Eventually, it comprised about '150 top experts in fire research, accident investigation, materials development and related fields' under the chairmanship of John Enders, head of the FSF. A report was issued in June 1980.[26]

The SAFER committee looked at both fuel system fire hazards and interior materials. It concluded that the existing FARs were adequate. Yet, going forward, it considered as the most promising development for reducing post-crash-fire risk that of the AMK: 'The Committee is of the view that, if successful, the AMK technology could provide the single most significant safety improvement to reduce the post-crash fire hazard'.[27]

With respect to interior materials, one recommendation was that the fire-blocking layer concept be developed for aircraft seat cushions as a means of retarding flame spread. Seat cushions formed, by volume, a significant portion of the flammable material in a typical cabin. A further recommendation was to expedite further development of test methods for flammability, smoke, and toxicity. In that respect, the Ohio State University test chamber was specifically mentioned.

From then on, an extensive full-scale testing program was undertaken using the Douglas C-133 fuselage sited at the FAA Technical Center in Atlantic City. The C-133 was a military transport airplane but its size represented that of the civil widebodies, thus forming a well-sized test bed. The test set-up was that of a fuel fire external to the fuselage so that the interior was exposed to radiant heat rather than flames. This mimicked the scenario that was found typical for airplane fire accidents. It had a CO_2 total flooding fire protection system to stop each test cycle. Initially, the C-133 was in open air, but later it was housed in a special facility. An extensive description of the tests by the two principal scientists, Constantine (Gus) Sarkos and Richard (Dick) Hill, is given in ICAO Bulletin, October 1982 edition. 'Sarkos and Hill' became a siamese expression in the cabin fire safety world.

Their tests confirmed a known phenomenon that earlier small-scale tests had not uncovered: the 'flashover'. Flashover is the sudden and rapid uncontrolled growth of fire from a relatively small area surrounding the ignition source to the remainder of the cabin.[28] The hot smoke layer in the upper part of the cabin ignites adjacent materials, which leads to increased thermal radiation upon materials in the lower cabin, which then also ignites. Additionally, burning ceiling panels fall upon and ignite seats.[29] Typically, before flashover smoke and toxic gas levels are minimal and survival is clearly possible, but this changes rapidly after the onset of flashover. The tests also demonstrated that the use of a fire-blocking layer on seat cushions would improve the survival time in the cabin by 60 seconds.

The full-scale test program started in 1980. The C-133 survived about 150 test cycles although occasionally needed extensive repairs.

11.5.3 ESCAPE POTENTIAL

The second wave had brought many escape potential improvements. In the period of the second trough, there were two escape potential initiatives of relaxation plus some minor rulemaking adjustments. One relaxation involved dispatch relief for exits (see Section 14.3.1).

Another involved a credit raise for Type A exits. In 1974, the FAA issued an ANPRM to gauge opinions as to increasing the rated capacity of the Type A exit.[30] That exit type had been introduced in 1967, on request of Boeing, in anticipation of the introduction of its 747. The Type A exit rating was initially set at 100 for a pair, but Boeing felt that this was overly conservative. Tests and evacuation demonstrations had shown that more than 100 persons could be evacuated via a Type A exit within 90 seconds. In NPRM 75–40, the FAA proposed an increase to 110. In response to it, a rating of 117 was proposed, being 85% of what was actually achieved in tests. The FAA disagreed with that higher number but in the subsequent FAR 25 rule change adopted 110 as the new exit rating for Type A exits.[31] Contrary to what is normal for FAR Part 25 changes, this change also applied to existing airplanes. The reason for that was its relaxative nature.

11.5.4 LIFE SUPPORT—SEGREGATED SMOKING SECTIONS

Smoking in society was very common and until 1973 there was no legal segregation between smoking and non-smoking passengers. In 1969 Ralph Nader petitioned the FAA to ban smoking on board airliners, citing that smoking presents (1) a fire hazard, (2) a health hazard, and (3) an annoyance to non-smoking passengers. The FAA denied the petition. It said that there was no fire hazard as interior materials were self-extinguishing, and a fire would anyway easily be spotted and extinguished (this was before the July 1973 Paris Orly accident proved otherwise). The FAA had no answer to the second question and therefore issued an Advance NPRM seeking input.[32] The third question was beyond the remit of the FAA and the CAB became involved. The answer to the second question (health hazard) appeared to be no, as a study done jointly by the FAA and the National Institute for Occupational Safety and Health found no air contamination from smoking. To answer the third question, military passengers on civil flights were questioned. This yielded an emphatic yes: 'many comments filed by nonsmokers in this proceeding [. . .] forcefully illustrate that antipathy against unsegregated smoking runs deep'.[33] United Airlines was the first airline to introduce smoking segregation in 1971.[34] In 1972, the CAB proposed a rule to formally segregate the two groups. Most other U.S. airlines, with the exception of Overseas National Airways, were against it, but the CAB pursued it nonetheless. A total ban, as asked for by Ralph Nader, would take another 17 years, but here was a first step. Effective July 1973, the CAB published a new Part 252, requiring formal segregation of smokers from non-smokers on U.S. airlines.[35] Since then, and until the later banning of smoking altogether, the last rows of an aircraft, or class, were typically reserved for smokers.

11.5.5 Information and Instructions

11.5.5.1 PA and Interphone

In 1972, the FAA identified the need for a public address system which served to keep passengers and crewmembers apprised of necessary information prior to and during an emergency.[36] Similarly, it saw a need for a system enabling communication between crewmembers, called the interphone system. The latter was inspired by the 'increase in recent years of aircraft hijacking'. The interphone system would offer a means of communication between crewmembers without passengers overhearing. Many aircraft were already so equipped, so the proposed rule served to formalize an existing application. The rule was published in August 1973 and became effective in September 1975.[37]

11.5.5.2 Fasten Seat Belt Placard

In 1978, the FAA proposed to require that passengers keep their safety belts fastened at all times, except when leaving their seat 'for physiological reasons' or when so authorized by a crewmember.[38] This proposal was meant to reduce injuries due to turbulence. It raised quite some opposition, including that passengers should have the right to decide themselves when to fasten the belt. Also, there was a perceived mismatch with the lighted fasten seat belt sign, which would not be on the whole flight. A compromise was reached by only requiring a placard on each seat back reading 'Fasten Seat Belt While Seated'.[39]

NOTES

1. Data based on: Aircraft Fires—A Study of Transport Accidents from 1975 to the Present, A.F. Taylor, Cranfield Institute of Technology, in Aircraft Fire Safety, AGARD Conference Proceedings No. 467, NATO, October 1989.
2. Aviation Safety Volume II (Aircraft Cabin Environment). Hearings Before the Subcommittee on Investigations and Review of the Committee on Public Works and Transportation, U.S. House of Representatives, 94th Congress, Second Session, February 3, 1976, p. 22.
3. Aviation Safety (Interior Compartment Materials), Hearings Before the Subcommittee on Oversight and Review of the Committee on Public Works and Transportation, House of Representatives, 96th Congress, First Session, April 25, 1979, p. 7.
4. FAA Aviation Safety Issues, Hearings Before a Subcommittee of the Committee on Government Operations, House of Representatives, 96th Congress, First Session, August 13, 1979, p. 3.
5. NPRM 81-1.
6. 46 FR 61489.
7. Air Carrier Cabin Safety—A Survey, Federal Aviation Administration, December 1976.
8. 45 FR 41439.
9. Dynamic Test Criteria for Aircraft Seats, Donald W. Foyls, FAA NAFEC, October 1, 1969.
10. NTSB Safety Recommendation A-81-142.
11. Structural Response of Transport Airplanes in Crash Situations, R.G. Thomson, C. Caiafa, NASA Technical Memorandum 85654, June 1983, p. 13.

12. Statement by Congressman Norman Y. Mineta, in Proceedings of Cabin Safety Conference and Workshop, December 11-14, 1984, Flight Safety Foundation, DOT/FAA/ASF100-85/01, August 1985, p. 9.
13. NPRM 77-20.
14. Amdt 25-44, 91-33.
15. Rapport Final de la Commission d'Enquête sur l'accident survenu au Boeing 707 PP-VJZ de la Compagnie Varig à Saulx-les-Chartreux, le 11 juillet 1973, Journal Officiel de la République Française, 6 April 1976.
16. An Analysis of Aircraft Accidents Involving Fires by G.V. Lucha. M.A. Robertson, F.A. Schooley, NASA CR 137690, May 1975.
17. NTSB Recommendations A-73-67 through A-73-70.
18. Amdt 25-74.
19. Aircraft Accident Report, Pan American World Airways, Inc., Boeing 707-321B, N454A, Pago Pago, American Samoa, January 30, 1974, NTSB-AAR-77-7, report date: October 6, 197.
20. ANPRM 74-38.
21. 43 FR 37703.
22. NPRM 75-31, 43 FR 37703.
23. NPRM 85-10.
24. 43 FR 37703.
25. NPRM 85-10.
26. Final Report of the Special Aviation Fire and Explosion Reduction (SAFER) Advisory Committee, Vol. I, FAA-ASF-80-4, June 26, 1980.
27. FAA-ASF-80-4, Vol. I, p. 16.
28. Development of Improved Fire Safety Standards Adopted by the Federal Aviation Administration by C.P. Sarkos, in Aircraft Fire Safety, AGARD Conference Proceedings No. 467, NATO, October 1989.
29. Effectiveness of Seat Cushion Bocking Layer Materials Against Cabin Fires, Constantine P. Sarkos, Richard G. Hill, in Proceedings of Cabin Safety Conference and Workshop, December 11-14, 1984, Flight Safety Foundation, DOT/FAA/ASF100-85/01, August 1985, p. 107.
30. ANPRM 74-19.
31. Amdt 25-39.
32. ANPRM 70-14.
33. 38 FR 12207.
34. Inflight Smoking, Wikipedia, Visited April 28, 2024.
35. 38 FR 12207.
36. NPRM 72-6.
37. Amdt 121-205.
38. NPRM 78-7.
39. Amdt 25-53/121-159.

12 Evacuation Demonstrations

ABSTRACT

Evacuation demonstrations are a very visible element of airplane cabin safety certification. It has a checkered history, deserving a separate chapter. While 90 seconds for the complete evacuation of an airplane has been the target for many decades, this has not always been the case. It varied from 30 to 120 seconds, or was it even seven minutes? The conditions also developed over time. Initially, all exits were allowed to be used, in daylight conditions, but gradually tighter conditions were set. As the number of injuries grew, alternatives to the demonstrations were allowed, ranging from ramps as alternatives to slides to analyses or combinations of analyses and partial tests.

12.1 INTRODUCTION

Until 1944, the concept of a safe evacuation time was not considered or at least not codified. The U.S. brought the idea to Chicago in its draft airworthiness regulations. It was in the form of a 30-second evacuation test, so a performance standard. (The rules for the number of exits were prescriptive.) This 30-second rule had not yet been adopted in the U.S. regulations, but apparently the CAB was considering it and tested the idea in Chicago first. As this is believed to be the first time that an evacuation demonstration is mentioned, it is worth repeating the proposed text here:[1]

> In case of question concerning the adequacy and suitability of emergency exits, it shall be demonstrated that the airplane can be completely evacuated in 30 seconds under conditions simulating a forced landing. The maximum number of persons for which seats are provided shall be used in this demonstration, and they shall not have been previously trained in the evacuation procedures.

No documents were found that explained the rationale of this proposal. Quite certainly, it was not backed up by research. That would only start six years later. So, it may have been merely visionary, stimulated by the imminent introduction of significantly larger transport aircraft.

The idea of an evacuation test caught on and the convention adopted it with one minor change. Rather than not allowing any previous training, as proposed, it was accepted that 'persons may be instructed in the evacuation procedures before making the test'. The 30-second criterion itself was not challenged.

12.2 OPTIONAL DEMONSTRATIONS

12.2.1 30 Seconds or 1 Second per Person

It was however later. When the U.S. issued its November 1945 revision of the airworthiness code, including major changes with respect to emergency exits, the evacuation test now appeared in it, for the first time in U.S. regulations.[2] Like in Chicago, the test was required only 'in case of question concerning the adequacy and suitability of emergency exits', so it supplemented the exit regulations and was optional. The maximum time, however, was relaxed by adding after '30 seconds' the words: 'or in a time equal to one second per occupant, whichever is greater'. This was probably done in view of larger aircraft coming for which a 30-second evacuation time was felt unrealistic. Yet, the open-ended wording effectively would have allowed much higher evacuation times. If the 204-passenger Convair 37 had been put in passenger service an evacuation time of more than 3.6 minutes would have been acceptable.[3]

Evacuation Demonstrations 163

Other than that a forced landing needed to be simulated and that participants 'may be briefed once', there were no further conditions. Thus, all exits would have been allowed to be used, in daylight conditions. A demonstration of the same passenger and crew load under later standards (half of the exits, dark of the night, demographical restrictions, etc.) would have taken about twice that time, so about 7 minutes or 420 seconds. Twice because only half of the exits could be used. But, actually, it would be somewhat less when recognizing that feeding two exits opposite each other from the same line will not optimally feed the exits, as opposed to one line feeding one exit. In line with the notion that there should be an equal number of exits on both sides (see Section 5.5.3.4), later evacuation demonstrations employed only half of the installed exits, but never both of an opposite pair, thus providing single lines to exits at cabin ends. The advantage so offered, however, is assumed to be compensated by the effects of the absence of daylight and tighter demographics, which will prolong the egress time. It can therefore be argued that the 1945 demonstration time was almost five times more lenient than the later standards (420 seconds in lieu of 90 seconds). This is theoretical, as the Convair Model 37 was never put in passenger service.

But was there ever a one-second-per-passenger test done? Dr. King listed manufacturer demonstrations conducted in the period 1946 to 1951 on six different airplane types.[4] These included both tests for the complete aircraft and individual exits. Table 12.1 summarizes the results of the all-aircraft tests, in which all doors and exits were employed for evacuation. For non-overwing exits, stands and ramps were placed simulating a wheels-up landing so that jump-down distances were limited or almost zero.

All tests were done in daylight conditions. In all cases except for the Lockheed 49, the tests started with the door and exits closed and occupants belted in. In some cases all subjects were men; in other cases there was a mix of males and females of various age groups. The results varied from 12 seconds for the small Beechcraft, with 4 occupants only, to 43 seconds for the Douglas C-54 (DC-4) test with 102 occupants and one of the two Lockheed 49 tests with 66 occupants. Clearly, the one-person-per-second limit was easily met.

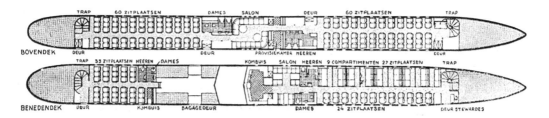

FIGURE 12.1 Convair 37 proposed cabin layout for 204 passengers, seated in two decks (Vliegwereld, 1945).

TABLE 12.1
Full-Scale Evacuation Tests by Manufacturers, 1946–1951

Month	Airplane Type	Number of Occupants	Result in Seconds	Remarks
April 1946	Beechcraft D-18	4, 8, 10	12; 19.5; 25	Same participants
August 1946	Lockheed 49	63, 53, 63	27; 21; 26	
August 1946	Lockheed 49	66, 66	38; 43	Including two attendants
June 1947	Martin 202	42	29	
August 1949	Curtiss C-46	60, 60	37; 38	Same participants
November 1949	Boeing 307	58	32	
March 1951	Douglas C-54	102	43	Including two attendants

Apart from the small Beechcraft, the Lockheed 49 Constellation (L-049) was the first airliner subjected to evacuation tests. These took place on two different dates in August 1946, on two different ships.[5] The illustration on the cover shows one of the tests. The type had been grounded by the CAA following a fatal accident during a training flight on July 11, 1946. This was lifted late in August, but airplanes standing idle as a result might well have played a role in the decision to conduct these tests. The first set of tests, on August 15, was observed by a delegation from the Dutch CAA. At the time, KLM Royal Dutch Airlines had received a number of L-049s, which had been kept in California for training purposes before being ferried to the Netherlands in September after the ban was lifted. The second set of tests, on August 27, involving a different ship, was observed by the CAA. In both cases, the wheels-up scenario was represented, with platforms simulating the ground. Lockheed concluded that the airplane met both the July 1944 CAR-04.462 and the November 1945 CAR 04.3812 requirements.

The C-54 (military version of the DC-4) test, with a very high-density occupancy, was done amazingly quickly: in only 43 seconds 102 occupants (100 passengers and 2 cabin attendants) escaped.[6] The subjects were airline personnel; 10% of whom were women. They had been briefed and were told to get out as quickly as possible, but the location of exits and their method of operation were not disclosed. They were belted in and exits were closed before the start. Just over half (53 occupants) used the main door; usage of the 21 by 24 inch (53 by 61 cm) exits varied from 5 to 19. One pair of these exits was over the wing and had a fairly low step-down of 25 inch (63.5 cm). The other pair had a higher step-down to the ramp and consequentially a low egress rate and was used by fewer occupants.

12.2.2   60 or 90 Seconds?

In 1950 George Haldeman, chief of the aircraft division at the CAA Office of Aviation Safety, suggested that a cap should be put on the demonstration time, possibly one minute, 'since a fire will develop just as rapidly whether there are 30 or 60 persons aboard the plane'.[7] The notion that there was a limit on the time available for successful evacuation was further worked out in 1951. In that year's summer, it was suggested to be set at 90 seconds.[8]

In November 1951, a new set of exit regulations was introduced for new airplane types (see Section 5.5.3.4). For existing types, a catch-up exercise was done. For each aircraft type, a maximum number of occupants (passengers plus crew) was set (see Section 5.5.3.7). It was proposed to offer the option of an evacuation demonstration to those operators wishing to have a higher number. The time limit would still be 30 seconds or one occupant per second, as in the previous regulation but now with a cap of 90 seconds. For the first time, detailed conditions for an evacuation demonstration were formulated.[9] While the conditions were light compared to later criteria, they would still be quite demanding. Table 12.2 compares the 1951 proposed criteria with those of 1965 (introduction of mandatory evacuation demonstrations for operators) and 1978 (manufacturer demonstration requirements, which may be used by operators).

These conditions were formally proposed in December 1951 and again in May 1952.[10,11] However, due to comments and further study, the evacuation demonstration option was deleted 'because of difficulty making such demonstrations sufficiently realistic'.[12] Instead, maximum capacity numbers for certain aircraft types were raised compared to the initial 1951 proposal. This apparently appeased the operators. The time was not yet ripe for mandating evacuation tests.

12.3   UNITED AIRLINES

12.3.1   1952—Safety or Promotion?

United Airlines, in 1952, performed full-scale evacuation tests on a voluntary basis and was probably the first. The reason, however, was not solely driven by safety. In that year, the CAB allowed

TABLE 12.2
Comparison of 1951, 1965, and 1978 Evacuation Demonstration Conditions

	1951 Proposal	1965	1978
Objective	Substantiate capacity increases beyond that listed	Show that the operator's procedures allow evacuation as specified below	Show that maximum seating capacity can be evacuated as specified below
Conducted by	Any operator requesting a higher capacity than the listed	Air certificate holder (air operator)	Design approval holder (manufacturer)
Applicable to			Aircraft with > 44 pax seats
Time limit	30 s or 1/s, with a cap of 90 s	Two minutes (from 1967: 90 seconds)	90 seconds
Completion condition	All participants on the ground	Not regulated	The last occupant on the ground or on a stand or ramp
Number of seats	Not regulated	Seating density and arrangement representative of the highest passenger version used by the operator	Maximum seating capacity for which certification is requested
Aircraft attitude	Wheels down or wheels up, whichever is most critical	Both gear down and gear up (two demos)	Gear down
Exits to be used	All	Not more than 50%, at least one floor-level exit	Not more than 50% of required exits on the side of the fuselage, representative of all exits, approved by FAA, at least one-floor level
Stands and ramps	Not regulated	At wings trailing edge for wheels-down; at all exits for wheels-up	At wings. Mats and inverted rafts may be placed on the ground
Day/night	Not regulated	Night for wheels-down demo; day for wheels up	Night
Aisle cluttering	Not regulated	Carry-on baggage, blankets, pillows and similar articles	Approximately one half of the total average amount of carry-on baggage, blankets, pillows, and similar articles in aisle and access ways
Exits at the start of the test	Closed and latched	As in normal flight	In take-off configuration
Descent assist means	Installed as required	All emergency equipment installed	
Adjustable seat backs near exits	In position giving maximum interference, may be moved during the test	Not regulated	
Seats and belts	Seated and belts fastened	Seat belts and shoulder harness (as required) fastened	
Seat assignments	Not regulated; standees allowed in case not all seats are installed	Crew in normally assigned seats; no passenger may be assigned a specified seat	Crew in normally assigned seats; no passenger may be assigned a specified seat except as required by the FAA

(Continued)

TABLE 12.2 (*Continued*)
Comparison of 1951, 1965, and 1978 Evacuation Demonstration Conditions

	1951 Proposal	1965	1978
Crew	May assist as per operator procedures	Regular crew (for gear-up flight attendants only)	Regular line crew
Passenger age mix (as nearly as possible)	Age 15–26: 20% Age 27–45: 60% Age 46–65: 20% Female: 20% per age group	Age < 12: 5 to 10%, prorated Age > 60: 5% Female: ≥ 30% Three life-size dolls	
Prohibited passengers	Not regulated		Crewmembers, mechanics, training personnel
Participant's previous demo experience	Not regulated	Not in the previous six months (however, in practice same occupants were allowed for both demos)	Not in the previous six months
Practice or rehearsal	Not regulated	Prohibited	
Prior knowledge	Not regulated	Participants may not have knowledge of usable exits	
Briefing	Once, no disclosure of the location and method of operation of exits	Normal pre-take-off briefing as required by operating rules	
Clothing and shoes	As normally worn in traveling	Not regulated	

airlines to offer their customers a second class, the coach or airtourist class. One of the conditions was a high-density seating configuration so that comfort levels were lower than those for first class. For the Douglas DC-4, then the mainstay of the airlines, the *minimum* number of passengers in coach was set by the CAB as 66. William (Pat) Patterson, the head of United Airlines, considered that too much. He still remembered the carnage to the DC-4 that crashed in New York La Guardia in 1947 and thought 66 passengers would be unable to evacuate a burning airplane in time, but offering comfort to his passengers might also have been a drive. Patterson went for 54 seats, at four abreast instead of five, and thus with a wider aisle.[13] To demonstrate the safety point he staged a series of evacuation tests. These tests were not done the way they were done later—static in a darkened hanger. Rather, he invited passengers for a short sightseeing flight over Niagara Falls that would be followed by an evacuation on the runway. The flights took off and landed in Buffalo, New York, on the weekend of September 13 and 14. Cornell University, based there, helped.[14] They took care of the entire set-up, from recruiting and selecting passengers, including a medical check, to recording (6 outside and 17 inside cameras) and analyzing the results. The purpose of the test was advertised as 'to study time, ease and efficiency' (of airplane evacuations). About 250 volunteers were drafted, who were divided into three groups. Members of each group took part in four successive tests, three of which started with a flight. To minimize education effects, for each test at least 25% of the passengers on board were new. The four tests per group involved three different combinations of exits. This was the main door, combined with either the left forward overwing exit, both forward overwing exits or all four overwing exits. The airplane was configured with 66 passenger seats. However, the numbers of participants per test were 44, 60, or 66, respectively, for the three groups. That is, for the first three tests per group. Each fourth test was an 'overload test', not preceded by a flight, with 60, 75, and 83 passengers, respectively. In the latter case there were 17 'standees'. The number 44 was chosen as that was the airplane's limit at original certification in 1946. The number 83 was based on the new maximum that the CAB pondered at the time (see Section 5.5.3.7). The number 66 was the aircoach limit set by the CAB.

The same crew, consisting of two pilots and only one stewardess, Edith Lauterbach, did all 12 tests. Unlike duty assignment procedures as developed later in which flight crew had an active evacuation role, here the pilots abandoned ship through the crew door just behind the cockpit without entering the cabin. The report does not mention whether they assisted from the outside. This left Edith to handle the cabin entirely on her own. During each short flight, she instructed men next to the overwing exits when to open them ('until the propellers have stopped completely') and to assist outside. Similarly, she selected men to climb down at the main door and hold the chute taut. She herself took position at the main door from where she guided passengers on to the chute. She exited herself last.

Time-motion recording methods gleaned from Barry King's test were used. Results varied from 44 passengers out through all five exits in just over 62 seconds to 60 passengers through two exits in 115 seconds and 83 passengers through three exits in 95 seconds. Cornell analyzed the results scientifically, applying a correction factor for the experience gained along the way by the crew and even the passengers. They concluded that to meet an evacuation time target of 60 seconds and assuming that three exits (out of five) would be usable, the passenger limit would be 48. Aisle width was not a factor, they found. The report concluded that 'evacuation time appeared to be limited only by the speed at which the passengers could get thru the hatches or down the slide'.

As with later tests, these tests had their hitches. One person got injured, another refused to exit, and in the dress rehearsal test on Friday a chute was ripped 'when the heel of one of the girl's shoes punctured' it. Would this have been the source for the perennial order for females to remove their shoes?

Patterson used the results of these tests in an appeal to the CAB to allow his 54-seat coach operation, but they denied it.[15] Their response to Patterson's claim that seat configuration is a key survival factor is interesting: they contended, based on King's research, that crew training is more important. In 1952, cabin attendants were not yet required, so did this statement refer to flight crew?

FIGURE 12.2 UAL DC-4 evacuation test 1952, Buffalo, New York (Collection of SFO Museum, gift of Edith Lauterbach).

12.3.2 1963–1964: United versus Pan Am

About 12 years later, in another marketing struggle, Pat Patterson played the evacuation safety card again. This time the platforms were the new jets, and the route was the U.S. West Coast to Hawaii. This market had a high appeal for senior citizens paying their own fares, as opposed to businessmen who typically had their company pay the fare. At stake was the maximum number of passengers allowed and the associated seat pitch. Pan Am had applied with the CAB to carry as much as 189 passengers in a high-density, 'thrift class' Boeing 707 with a seat pitch of 36 inch. Before that, Pan Am used its 707s in much lower-density configurations. The Federal Aviation Agency required Pan Am to do an evacuation test. Actually, two were held, on September 17, 1963, with only exits on one side of the plane used to simulate the realism of an accident. The first test took 2 minutes and 20 seconds to evacuate 189 people, ranging in age from 17 to 56 years, plus seven crewmembers. The FAA found this too long and felt that two seats adjacent to the overwing emergency exits should be removed. A second test, with the two seats removed, was indeed significantly quicker: 96 seconds. It is not clear whether the same participants were used in that second test.[16]

United protested, saying that Pan Am's passengers were 'too closely packed for safety'. It initially asked the FAA to set more stringent demonstration criteria, including a typical passenger load and representative clothing. At the time, passengers dressed fashionably and certainly not in running apparel. For Hawaii flights, this meant a higher percentage of persons over 65 years of age. United suggested no prior knowledge by participants, the use of smoke, and a maximum time of 90 seconds.

United's plea was not honored. So, in the same manner as 12 years before, Patterson, who did not want to reduce the seat pitch from 38 inch to 36 inch, thought he could prove his point by showing that a high load airplane could not be evacuated safely in time. In the spring of 1964 he staged a series of DC-8 evacuation demonstrations with added elements of reality. This time the airplane stayed on the ground. United led participants, including the crew, believe that they were to participate in a publicity stunt rather than a simulated emergency.[17] Engine sounds were played with 'a crescendo in the pitch' and 'as metal grinding into a concrete runway'.[18] Rather than a representative mixture of the general public, the participants were present and retired United employees and their families, including young children and elderly persons. 'Heavy mineral oil smoke was pumped into the cabin' from both ends which in less than 20 seconds made it almost impossible to see where the emergency exits were. United thereby tried to replicate the conditions of the crash of one of its DC-8s at Denver on July 11, 1961.[19] The test showed signs of panic among the passengers. One escape slide failed to inflate. The result was accordingly poor: the DC-8 was evacuated via all exits on the left by 174 passengers plus crew in as much as 4 minutes 50 seconds (290 seconds). Following the test, the same participants went back three times for repeat evacuations, albeit no longer with the smoke. In the second test, there were only 160 passengers, which led to a quicker evacuation, variably reported as 3 minutes 10 seconds and 2 minutes 20 seconds. The third and fourth tests were done with yet fewer persons (147 and 126 respectively), but still from the same group as in the first and second tests. Each time the egress rate improved, which undoubtedly resulted from an experience gain, as was the case in Buffalo 12 years earlier for the crew. United had set itself a goal of 90 seconds, which they almost reached in the fourth and final test that took 100 seconds. United decided to fly the DC-8 on the Hawaii route with only 95 'thrift fare' passengers plus 24 first class seats as opposed to Pan Am's 187 seats in a comparable size Boeing 707.

12.4 FIRST EVACUATION DEMONSTRATIONS

The Pan Am evacuation demonstration of September 1963 had not been the first. That honor went to Delta Airlines. After having operated its DC-8s for about two years in a low-density arrangement of 147, it wanted to increase it to 177, a 20% increase. The FAA would only authorize that when Delta would demonstrate the adequacy of the emergency equipment (i.e. slides), procedures, and crewmember training. They did two tests on December 11, 1961, using half the available exits. One test was conducted at night, the other during daylight. One result was 3 minutes 30 seconds; the other is unknown.[20]

By early 1964 some 20 evacuation tests had been done on the new jets (707, 720, 880, DC-8). The average passenger load was 125, so well below that of the examples mentioned earlier. The average evacuation time was 2.14 minutes and the average individual evacuation time was 1 second.[21]

12.5 RESEARCH

In 1964, two full-scale crash tests had been conducted by AvSER on a DC-7 and an L-1649 Starliner, respectively (see Section 7.4). The Lockheed Starliner had broken in three sections. The center and aft sections, stretching from the wing aft remained fairly intact, albeit that there was a circumferential break and that the sections were laying tilted on a hill, so posing unnatural floor angles. All the exits were still usable. Seeing this, it was suggested to use it for evacuation research. Four tests were done in April 1965 by FAA CAMI, two by daylight and two in the dark. 'The general purpose of the tests was to observe the reactions of unindoctrinated passenger populations under different test conditions rather than to compare one test with another'.[22] In each test, 2 stewardesses and about 45 passengers participated, some being 'injured', others with poor visibility conditions and some carrying dolls simulating infants and children. To make it all more realistic, the passengers stayed one hour in the cabin and were even served lunch in a box.[23] Then, crash sound effects and smoke announced that it was time to abandon ship. Of the report's 15 conclusions, the more remarkable were that (1)

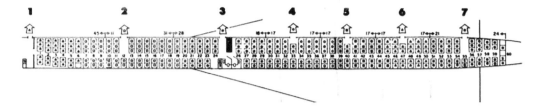

FIGURE 12.3 SST mock-up right side, with 4 Type I and 3 Type III exits (FAA AM 70–19).

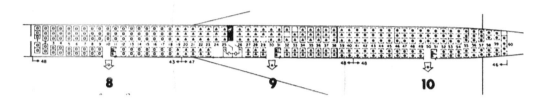

FIGURE 12.4 SST mock-up left side, with three Type A exits (FAA AM 70–19).

the night tests took significantly longer than the daylight tests (c. 190 vs. c. 110 seconds); (2) elderly passengers may require aid in release of seat belts; (3) the tilted floor did not impede egress, except for those handling the injured; (4) seating elderly and incapacitated passengers adjacent to an exit could delay use of the exits; (5) not seat pitch in the row leading to an exit but exit size is the determining factor for speed of egress.

In the 1960s, both in Europe and in the U.S., supersonic transport airplanes were in development. In Europe, Concorde started to fly with paying passengers in 1976, but government funding for the U.S. program was canceled in 1971, killing the Boeing 2707, prototypes of which were being manufactured. The competing Lockheed L-2000 had already earlier lost the race. Both Boeing and Lockheed had made full-size wooden mock-ups furnished with seats. In March 1967, Lockheed shipped its mock-up, with 280 seats in 59 rows, mostly five abreast, to CAMI in Oklahoma for evacuation tests. Around 1969, a series of evacuation tests were done, involving a total of 560 subjects.[24] United Airlines provided six flight attendants. The mock-up had an asymmetric exit configuration, with 4 Type I and 3 Type III exits on the right side and 3 Type As on the left side.

The step-down varied per location and ranged between 7 inch (18 cm) and 27 inch (68.5 cm), so no slides were needed. The first test used the right side exits, and the second, with a new group of 280 subjects, the left side. The difference in egress time was significant: right side: 70.7 seconds, left side: 45.4 seconds. Each group was then subjected to a follow-up test involving only two exits to gauge, respectively, the effect of a different Type I exit height (right side) and the mechanisms of redistribution of evacuees when one exit is unavailable (left side). The single-aisle cabin was very long, and it appeared that the unamplified instructions of the flight attendants were not heard by many, so people started to copy what they saw others did. The combination of a single aisle and Type A exits was unique. The tests identified the importance of an assist space near Type A exits and ample cross aisles or routes to maintain two continuous lines from two different sources. It also showed that there was no difference in flow rate for Type I exits of 48 inch (122 cm) high versus 60 inch (152 cm) high.

12.6 MANDATORY DEMONSTRATIONS

12.6.1 1965–1967: Airlines Only

In October 1963 the FAA published a Notice of Proposed Rulemaking for mandatory demonstrations by airlines. It referred to the evacuation tests done so far, such as by Pan Am the month before.

Evacuation Demonstrations

The FAA explained that 'it was evident that a more realistic assignment of functions within the cabin would have resulted in a lesser time to evacuate the airplane satisfactorily'.[25] To stimulate airlines to develop such a better assignment, it decided to make mandatory evacuation demonstrations. The rationale behind it was to ensure that airlines developed proper procedures, not only for crew functions but also as a check of the training adequacy. In addition, faults in design, such as of escape slides, would be revealed. The final rule ordered that an airline would need to run two tests per airplane type: one for the wheels-down situation simulating an aborted take-off and one with wheels-up representing a crash landing. Those carriers that flew extended overwater would additionally need to do a simulated ditching. The time limit for the first two demonstrations was set at two minutes 'in order to assist the air carriers in having a means by which they can establish and subsequently measure their ability to execute the evacuation procedures'.[26] In other words, the two minutes was more of a goal and a yardstick than a realistic, scientifically supported time limit. No time limit was considered necessary for the ditching demonstration.

The aborted take-off demonstration needed to be conducted in night conditions, unlike the gear-up crash landing and the ditching demonstrations. For the two land demonstrations, there were demographical limitations of the participants, such as at least 30% female, at least 5% over 60 years of age, and between 5% and 10% children under the age of 12. Also, three life-size dolls needed to participate, carried by passengers. This number was not expressed as a percentage, which meant in practice that it could vary from 1.5% of the participants on a large airplane to almost 7% on a smaller one. The rationale for the number of three was not explained, but it is noted that in the 1951 test by GWU, three live infants participated (see Section 5.4.2). Possibly, the rule maker remembered this and wanted to replicate it but decided that it was unethical to call for the participation of infants. No dress code was set. The same set of participants was allowed for both land demonstrations. For the ditching test, no passengers needed to participate, unless the airline's 'manual requires the use of passengers to assist in the launching of liferafts'. The exits to be used in the two land scenarios were those on one side only. This reflected the contemporary thinking that a fire would typically develop on one side only. For the gear-up scenario, it was allowed to use stands at each exit or the wing at a height representing ground level after a gear-up landing. Similarly, for the ditching scenario, stands were allowed to represent the water line following a ditching. Here, all exits through which life rafts would be launched, needed to be used. Alternatively, a mock-up of the airplane or a floating device simulating a passenger compartment was allowed for the latter demonstration but not for the first two. In March 1965, the proposal was adopted as a final rule, becoming effective for airplanes with more than 44 passenger seats by October 1965.[27] United Airlines had proposed to add smoke in one of the demonstrations, as they had done in their own test. The FAA rejected this proposal on the ground that 'this would tend to excite the passengers used, and create a hazardous condition'. A suggestion, likely also raised by United Airlines, to reduce the time limit to 90 seconds was not adopted—yet.

Up to spring 1966, the percentages of the three tests (wheels-down, wheels-up, ditching) as performed by airlines were 45, 35, and 20, respectively.[28] Of the three categories, the first was the most representative of the later evacuation demonstrations: an airplane on all its gears where passengers had to negotiate the distance from the airplane to the ground by jumping, using an escape slide, or sliding down a wing flap in the dark. By the end of 1966, about 300 tests of that category had been done, 134 of which involved jets. These included both tests before the two-minute rule became effective and after. The AIA, as part of their petition to enhance the 1967 rule changes, analyzed them.[29] They found a progression of performance over the three years 1964 to 1966. The average evacuation time reduced from 105 seconds in 1964 to 84 seconds in 1966. The number of malfunctions, mainly of slides not deploying, also reduced significantly, from 25% to 11%.

12.6.2 1967: Extension to Manufacturers

These better results were partly due to the increased use of inflatable, door-mounted slides, as opposed to ceiling-mounted non-inflatable chutes. They gave sufficient confidence for the FAA to reduce the evacuation target from 120 to 90 seconds. And that is what they proposed in 1966.[30] Some commentators said this was too short; others said it was too long.

Other proposed changes included the prohibition of using passengers who were experienced (within six months), knowledgeable (e.g. mechanics), or trained. As to the crew, normal training was allowed, but they could not participate in another demonstration for at least six months. So, where previously the same crew could do the gear-down and gear-up demonstration, this was no longer permitted. The requirement for cluttering the aisle was now more precisely specified as 'approximately one-half of the total of such items (i.e. baggage, blankets, pillows) as normally aboard a fully loaded flight'. In the gear-up demonstration airlines had placed stands a few inches away from the exit sill, claiming that the fuselage had crushed. This was now prohibited. Stands needed to be level with the bottom of the fuselage.

A major new element of the proposal was that manufacturers needed to perform an evacuation demonstration. Not to test the training of crew but rather because compliance with the prescriptive exit rules did not necessarily guarantee quick evacuation. 'Differences in the relationships between elements of the emergency evacuation system introduce a considerable variation in evacuation time, and this variation is expected to be even more marked on larger transport aircraft now under development', the FAA said in its 1966 proposal.[31] In other words, some of the prescriptive exit rules worked out too generously in practice. Thus, the FAA considered that the evacuation demonstration should now be part of type certification and with haste. Where normally such changes would affect only new applicants for a type certificate, this change affected existing airplane types when stretched.

The subsequent final rule was published in September 1967, becoming effective October 23, 1967, to both airlines (FAR 121.291) and manufacturers (FAR 25.803(c)).[32] There were minor differences in the test conditions between the two sets. For FAR 25, persons 'who have knowledge of the operation of exits and emergency equipment may be used to represent an air carrier crew' instead of a member of a regularly scheduled line crew as FAR 121 stipulated.

In either case, exits to be used would not need to be 'a one of a kind exit such as a ventral stair or tail cone exit'. Thus, only exits in the side of the fuselage needed to be used, leaving little opportunity for an evaluation of the procedures and technical qualities of the tail exits.

Shortly before the compliance date, two manufacturers did evacuation tests as part of type certification, not necessarily in accordance with the new standards in all respects. On December 11, 1966, Douglas ran a demonstration using one of the first DC-9-30 airplanes. That model had six side exits, three on each side, plus a tail exit. The side exits were a Type I at the front, equipped with a non-inflatable chute, and over the wing a Type III exit and an exit that was of Type III size but formally a Type IV because the step-down was too high but found equivalent to a Type III (see Section 16.2.1). The tail exit consisted of a door in the aft pressure bulkhead, which gave access to the tail cone area. For normal use there was a built-in stair in the tail, but for emergency use the tail cone itself could be jettisoned. In the demonstration, 130 persons were used. However, in the particular airplane used for the test, there were only 110 seats. So some people were standing in the aisle and others were even waiting on the wing on the inactive side. At some stage during the test, the overwing exit on that side was opened and persons went inside the cabin. They were interjected in the evacuation flow that was going on. This practice later got quite some criticism in a congressional hearing with a congressman ridiculing that he did not know persons could fly on the wing.[33] A second demonstration consisted of testing the tail cone exit, which yielded a high egress rate (65 persons in 90 seconds).

One day before the FAR 25 rule came into force, Boeing conducted a demonstration on a stretched 727 with 162 passengers and 7 crewmembers and set a time of 81.7 seconds. Two years later, under FAR 25 conditions, they repeated it but now with the maximum that the exit configuration (not counting the ventral exit in the tail) allowed: 189 passengers. The resulting time was well in excess of 90 seconds.

12.6.3   1968–1981: Demonstrations by Both Manufacturers and Airlines

The first demonstration by a manufacturer under the new FAR 25.803(c) rule did not take place in the U.S. but in the Netherlands. In November 1968, Fokker's first jet, the F-28, was the subject, together with 65 passengers and 5 crewmembers, of whom two were in the cabin. The result was well within the target: 78 seconds.

From 1968 to 1981, demonstrations were done by both airlines and manufacturers. As an example, the Boeing 747 was first tested by Boeing, in November 1969 in Seattle and then in January 1970 by its first customer, Pan Am, in Roswell, New Mexico, where Pan Am had a training base.

Boeing split its tests according to the deck: the large main deck and the smaller upper deck. The main deck test involved five (out of ten) Type A exits, 550 passengers, and 16 crewmembers. It was evacuated in 108.8 seconds.[34] This was 19 seconds over the limit of 90 seconds and thus a failure. Yet, no repeat test was found necessary, and the FAA granted the 747 its certificate. How was this possible? Each Type A exit was good for 100 passengers per the regulation, so the whole main deck was good for 500 passengers. Yet Boeing, being confident, decided to engage 550 passengers, presumably to convince the FAA that the 747 could do better than 500. But the slide on door 5 failed to deploy and only four other doors could be used. Doors 4 and 3 had to absorb the load of door 5, and this took well more than 90 seconds. The FAA, in the end, decided to grant Boeing its certificate as the number of passengers that had evacuated at the 90-second mark, which was 509, was more than the requisite 500. This practice of using the evacuation demonstration to empirically determine the evacuation capacity of a new airplane type was later no longer accepted. The next day, the upper deck was tried, with only 30 passengers and 4 crew, who needed 80.4 seconds, so first time right. Pan Am in their test also suffered several slide failures plus a fault in an emergency lighting system. They had to repeat the test twice more before eventually successfully evacuating 423 persons. Pan Am used only the main deck as occupancy of the upper deck during take-off and landing was initially not permitted.

The number of U.S. airline demonstrations against the 90-second target (as opposed to the 120-second target of 1965 to 1967) is estimated to have been about 100. In Europe, evacuation demonstrations were done mainly in Scandinavia, against either the 120 or 90-second limit. SAS tested a DC-8 in Copenhagen in April 1967 and a DC-9–41 in Oslo in September 1968. Sterling did a test on a Fokker F-27-500 in May 1968 with 56 passengers and one cabin crewmember, completed in 70 seconds. Braathens tested their F-28, with only one cabin crewmember and 67 passengers, in March 1969, within 95 seconds.

The period 1968 to 1981 would see manufacturers' demonstrations at an average rate of about 1.6 per year. Notable demonstrations in this period included those of the other three widebodies (the Douglas DC-10, the Lockheed L-1011, and the Airbus A300) and Concorde.

Concorde was initially subjected to three tests in February 1975, of which one failed.[35] Later, when it would fly with Braniff, another demonstration was done for the FAA.[36] McDonnell Douglas did two FAR 25.803 demonstrations on DC-9 models: on the DC-9–50 in 1975, with 139 passengers, and on the MD-80 in 1980 with 172 passengers. Initially, for the DC-9–50, they had filed a petition to perform an analysis, using the 1966 DC-9–30 test data and arguing that the increase was only nine passengers. However, the Association of Flight Attendants successfully objected to the petition.[37] McDonnell Douglas had the habit of inviting different airlines to compose a cabin crew complement. For the DC-9–50 that were Allegheny and Hawaiian, with North Central as backup; for the MD-80 one each from PSA, Hawaiian, Republic, and Air California. In both cases they just stayed under 90 seconds, although the DC-9–50 was very close: 89.6 seconds.[38]

For small aircraft, an evacuation demonstration requirement was introduced in 1970.[39] The wheels-up demonstration FAR 121 was deleted in 1969. The FAA had found that 'a successful aborted take-off demonstration was generally followed by a successful gear-up landing demonstration', and therefore would not add anything.[40]

12.6.4 1982: Introduction of the Mini Demo

The evacuation demonstrations required for air carriers since 1965 involved many injuries ranging from bruises to broken bones. To reduce those, the FAA granted over 100 exemptions, but a more solid regulatory basis was needed to address this. Therefore they issued a final rule effective January 1982 that allowed an air carrier to use the results of an evacuation demonstration conducted by either the manufacturer (under Part 25) or another air carrier (under Part 121).[41] To still demonstrate the efficacy of their procedures and training program, an air carrier would need to perform a partial demonstration, also called a mini demo. Such a mini demo was primarily required when an air carrier introduced a new airplane type. A mini demo involved no passengers. The flight attendants were required to demonstrate that they could open and deploy within 15 seconds the exit for which they were assigned, including its slide, when so equipped. The flight attendants would be selected at random by the FAA inspector and may not have been coached for the exercise. At the same time it would confirm the proper maintenance of the slide. For those carriers that operated extended overwater flights, a ditching exercise was required, involving the placement of life rafts at exits and the launching and inflating of one of the rafts. Boarding them was not required. Effectively, this rule change stopped, after about 16 years, the practice of airlines carrying out full-scale evacuation demonstrations. With the replacement of slides by slide rafts, the ditching demonstrations became redundant.

12.6.5 1982–1996: Manufacturer-Only Full-Scale Demonstrations

With the onus of conducting evacuation demonstrations now shifted from air carriers to manufacturers, and with many new airplane types entering the market, the period from 1982 became particularly busy. From 1982 until 1996, there were about 40 full-scale demonstrations by manufacturers, an average of 2.5 per year. Many new airplane types entered the market. This included airplanes with less than 44 passenger seats such as the Saab 340, the De Havilland Canada Dash 8-100 and -300, and the Dornier 328. Even though the FAA's threshold limit for a FAR 25 evacuation demonstration was 45, they were still subjected to an evacuation demonstration. Significant other demonstrations in this period were conducted on the:

- Boeing 747 with door 3 deactivated, in February 1986;
- McDonnell Douglas MD-11 in October 1991; and
- Boeing 777-200 in February 1995 which took just over 90 seconds. This led to a repeat in 1996.

The October 1991 MD-11 demonstrations turned out to be game changing, in a negative way. The stretched and updated sequel to the DC-10 was subjected to two evacuation demonstrations. Per Douglas tradition, the cabin crew was a mix from three different airlines, this time even from three different continents. Both demonstrations dramatically failed. Not only was the 90-second target not met twice (132 and 112 seconds, respectively), but also were there about 50 injuries, including one very serious. A woman aged 60 fell off a slide head first and became paralyzed from the neck down. Such an injury had never before occurred in an evacuation demonstration and shocked both the industry and the regulators. The MD-11 was thus certificated with a lower passenger capacity and additional flight attendants, until in December 1992 a repeat demonstration cleared the airplane type with the desired maximum capacity of 410 (and nine flight attendants, per the 1:50 ratio). That demonstration was done according to a new protocol, agreed upon with the FAA. The set-up was designed to prevent the use of dangerous slides. Instead, platforms at floor level were allowed. As this would accelerate the speed of egress, a time malus was set to compensate for this: rather than 90 seconds, a limit of 62 seconds was applied. This was calculated specifically for the MD-11 configuration and was not meant to be the 'new 90 seconds'. The demonstration, this time with flight attendants from one airline, from the U.S., succeeded without any injury and in 56.4 seconds.[42] The platform demonstration would remain unique in history. However, to avoid injuries by people

Evacuation Demonstrations

already jumping before an escape slide is fully deployed and inflated, in 2004 the FAR 25 demonstration requirements were changed to allow pre-deployment before the start of the demonstration.[43]

12.6.6 REGULATORY GUIDANCE AND CHANGES

In 1989, the FAA issued an Advisory Circular giving guidance on the conduct of a demonstration and when an analysis might be used in place of a full-scale demonstration.[44] It also gave an age-gender distribution, which was an alternative to that in the rules.

As already hinted at in 1989 when the 60-foot rule (18.3 m; see Section 13.5.3.3) was issued, in May 1991, under the umbrella of the newly formed Aviation Rulemaking Advisory Committee, a subcommittee was formed to discuss evacuation performance standards with a view of adding to or even replacing design standards. That, the group never did. Rather, influenced by the October 1991 MD-11 tragedy, it discussed the evacuation demonstration procedures and standards. Specifically, it focused on how to reduce the risk of injuries. One way was to make more use of analyses. Another was to amend the rules for the demonstration. A proposal for that was issued in 1995 and adopted as a final rule in 2004.[45,46]

Before that, in 1993, the demonstration conditions had also been changed.[47] No longer would there be active participation of the flight crew. To reduce the risk of injury a change of mixture of gender and age of passengers was prescribed. Instead of persons over 60 years of age, or under 12, a higher percentage of passengers above the age of 50 was required. That new percentage was chosen such that it would yield the same evacuation rates in the 90-second demonstration so that they could be compared. The new rules applied to actual demonstrations conducted after September 1993.

12.6.7 POST-1996: ANALYSES TAKE OVER FULL-SCALES

After 1996, the number of full-scale evacuation demonstrations diminished significantly. With few exceptions, the years of new airplanes coming on the market had gone. Derivatives of existing models were the norm. Boeing introduced its third generation of the Boeing 737 in the period 1997–2001. The -700, the -800, and, the largest, the -900 were all certificated by means of analyses, building on data obtained in demonstrations of the second generation (the -300 in 1984 and the -400 in 1988). Twenty years later, Boeing repeated this with the fourth generation of the Boeing 737 (the Max 8 and Max 9). The stretch version of the Boeing 777, the -300, with an additional pair of Type A exits and slated for 550 passengers, was done in 1998 by a combination of analysis and a limited test, involving 80 passengers. In 2014, a 'maxpax' version of the Airbus A320, allowing up to 190/195 passengers, was also cleared by means of an analysis.

With analyses becoming the new standard, even completely new airplane types relied on them, benefiting from similarities with previous types. The two main new widebodies of the 2010s, the Boeing 787 and the Airbus A350 used exit systems similar to, respectively, the Boeing 767/777 and the Airbus A330/A340. On the A350, as the slides were different, partial tests were done on doors 1 and 3.

12.6.8 A380 EVACUATION DEMONSTRATION

In early 2006, cabin safety experts around the world expectantly looked at Hamburg, where the largest full-scale evacuation demonstration ever would take place.

The date: Sunday, 26 March 2006.
The location: Airbus' plant in Hamburg Finkenwerder, along the river Elbe.
The airplane: Airbus A380 MSN 007.
The crew: Lufthansa's.
The passengers: predominantly German, and so was the language.

On the lower or main deck, equipped with 10 Type A exits, there were 538 passengers plus 11 cabin crewmembers (and 2 pilots). On the upper deck, with six Type A exits, the load was 315 passengers and 7 cabin crew. All exits on the right side were used. The three upper deck slides were pre-deployed for reasons of safety. It was considered that them being ready already would not be a bonus anyway, as their deployment is not subsequent to, but synchronous with, the door operation. These slides were not door mounted but stored below the door sill and erected in less than six seconds. All slides were double-laned. The evacuation was completed well in time, in 78 seconds, 12 seconds below the deadline.[48] This very good result obviated the need for a contingency test, which had been planned for one week later. There were several injuries, the most serious of which was a broken leg. Three days later, Airbus did full-scale migration tests to evaluate the crowding of people coming from the upper deck to the main deck, involving 150 passengers on the main deck and 70 on the upper deck, without adverse interaction. Later, Airbus used an analysis to extend the capacity on the upper deck by 15 seats to 330.

Airbus had initially been hesitant to do the full-scale evacuation but quickly discovered that there was no alternative. Historically, Airbus succeeded in avoiding full-scale demonstrations, having done only six in its 50+ years of existence and building 15,000 airplanes (one each on the A300, the A300-600, the A320, the A380, and two on the A310). This is a ratio of one full-scale demo per 2,500 airplanes. Boeing, on the other hand, did a total of 18 full-scales, plus 3 upper decks since 1967, and built about 22,000 airplanes, so a ratio of about 1:1,050.[49] The ratios for McDonnell Douglas (DC-9 and up) and Fokker (F-28 and up) were much lower: about 1:400 and 1:110, respectively.

12.7 HOW REALISTIC SHOULD THE DEMONSTRATION BE?

Ever since the first evacuation demonstrations were conducted, there has been criticism that they lacked the realism of an actual post-crash evacuation. This typically came from such parties as cabin crew unions, passenger action groups, or, even, U.S. Congress. But it was an airline that said it first and put it into practice. United Airlines in 1963 tried to copy the conditions of the 1961 Denver crash as close as possible in a demonstration, but that did not go well (see Section 12.3.2).

In drafting the conditions for the certification demonstration a compromise was made between reflecting the conditions of a live crash and the requisites of repeatability and participant safety. In 1990, in evidence to the House of Commons, Ron Ashford et al. of the UK CAA submitted a memorandum which worded it like this:

> A popular misconception is that the demonstration is intended to provide a guarantee that the aircraft type would be fully evacuated in 90 second under any circumstances. This is not so. It is a standardised test which assesses the main features of the aircraft's escape facilities and is the means by which the performance of one aircraft can be compared with others. Although the demonstration represents a fairly severe condition, it could not reproduce the very worst accident situation without introducing an unacceptable risk of injury to the participants.

Thirty years later, in 2020, the Office of the Inspector General (OIG) of the U.S. Department of Transportation studied how the FAA treated the issue of evacuation demonstrations. This was in the wake of the FAA Reauthorization Act of 2018 in which evacuation was topical again. That, itself, was the result of two evacuations in the U.S. in September 2015 and October 2016. Although both were successful, there were issues with evacuees taking their carry-on baggage. The OIG was critical of the number of analyses that the FAA allowed and that they neither recorded actual evacuation results nor pro-actively monitored such data as passenger demographics, behavior, and the presence of emotional support animals. The OIG, like many others before, suggested bringing more 'real-world risks' such as smoke in the demonstrations or accounting for those in the analyses. They did not go as far as recommending this. The FAA responded by saying:[50]

> Evacuation times in the accidents cited in the report bear no relation to the certification requirement for a given airplane. The certification standard is a benchmark, under a specific set of conditions, and is not relatable to an actual accident, unless all of the same conditions exist. In an actual event, the key

parameter is whether the time required to evacuate is less than the time available to evacuate. The time required is particularly difficult to establish for evacuations in non-emergency conditions.

Other parties that criticized the realism of evacuation demonstrations suggested that they should include persons with reduced mobility such as physically handicapped persons, and blind persons, or have the airplane tilted so that floors are not level. While these suggestions have merit, to keep the benchmark idea, additional testing would be needed to determine their impact so that a new benchmark target could be established. Yet, there have been evacuation tests with litter patients. The U.S. Air Force did such tests on their Douglas C-9A (the military DC-9–30) in 1968. Tyrolean Airways, the Austrian airline that often repatriated skiing victims, did them on their Dash 8. Limited tests with persons with reduced mobility have been carried out by FAA CAMI in 1977 and TÜV Rheinland in 2008.[51]

12.8 EVACUATION DEMONSTRATIONS IN PRACTICE

The key to a successful demonstration is preparation. This starts long before the actual test. It requires months of planning, with military precision. For a novel design, such as its 747 was in the late 1960s, Boeing performed many in-house tests. In a presentation delivered in October 1992, Boeing's George Veryioglou said:[52]

> Because the 747 was a 'first' for which we had no evacuation data, we ran tests. Thousands of them. We tested how people moved inside that airplane when they had two main aisles and several cross aisles to choose from. We tested escape devices. We ran jump tests. We ran development tests, verification tests and demonstration tests on the main deck system and on the upper deck systems. All in all, when we first built the 747, we ran more than 10,000 tests of its evacuation systems. Twenty-four hundred of these tests involved more than 40,000 voluntary subjects—a number equal to about one-third of the entire Boeing workforce in 1969. And it was only after we had proven the 747's evacuation systems and procedures to ourselves that we went to the FAA and said, we want to demonstrate the evacuation capability of the 747 airplane.

But even when the demonstration is due, preparation is everything. Dry rehearsal tests should be run, both under daylight and night conditions to be prepared for all contingencies. Spare participant groups should be standing by in case of failure of a test. Not all manufacturers did that.

The February 1972 Lockheed L-1011 Tristar demonstration was not well prepared. In testimony to the House of Representatives in 1983, one of the participating flight attendants, who worked for TWA, a launch customer, explained that the demonstration failed because it took four hours to get the hangar dark enough for the filming. 'By then, the "passengers" were almost comatose from sitting in a closed, unairconditioned plane for such a long time'. But, she added, 'the most interesting surprise, and the one which obviously gave an advantage to the crew, was the placement of the cameras and microphones'.[53] They gave away which doors should be opened so that no precious seconds be spent on trying to open doors that would not do so. In a chrono-twist of fate, the time clocked for this demonstration underscored the airplane type's identification: 1011 deciseconds.[54] The second attempt, the next day, was successful, with a time of 82.7 seconds.

In another case, involving a Boeing 747, a delay was caused by one evacuee who sat on the wing and refused to descend the slide, requiring physical assistance from a flight attendant. In yet another case, a captain, being the last one out, or nearly, remained sitting at the toe end of the slide and consumed precious seconds.

A British manufacturer had not tested the method of mechanically blocking the exits not to be used. When the demonstration started, all doors and exits opened, so it failed. The story goes that, as there was no contingency set of passengers, and not to wait for another day, it went to a local pub to round up some volunteers. A group of farmers, with their 'wellies' (boots) still on, was happy to participate and saved the day. But, even with a perfect preparation, there remains one unpredictable element: the human factor. In a demonstration of the Fokker 100, equipped with four overwing exits in addition to floor-level exits, the two Type III overwing exits on the right side were blocked, and the two on the left side were not. As is common on all airplane types, such exits have passengers sitting beside them, who are relied upon for opening these hatch-type exits. When the test started, only the aft left exit was opened. It took about 45 seconds, and the direction of a flight attendant, for the person sitting next to the forward left exit to open it. He later explained that, seeing that the aft exit opened he assumed that his was a blocked one, so there was no reason to try it. During the briefing that the passengers had been given earlier, it was mentioned that only half of the exits would function. Even with this hiccup, the test succeeded, in 80 seconds.

But not only naive participants can be unpredictable. On the same night, in which three demonstrations took place in succession, to test two exit variants, the first test took 93 seconds, so was a failure. At least in the perception of Fokker. A launch customer was a U.S. airline, which had provided a flight attendant contingent so that the demonstration could double as a FAR 121 evacuation demonstration. Their FAA inspector had clocked 89 seconds on his stopwatch and considered it a success. How could this mismatch happen? It appeared the FAA inspector used different cues for both the start and finish of the test. Where the Fokker timing started with the 'Evacuate' command over the PA system by the pilot, the FAA inspector waited for the emergency lights to come on, which was seconds later. Also, he was used to seeing ramps placed near the wings, as was allowed by the FARs but not done by Fokker. In their absence, he stopped his stopwatch when the last person

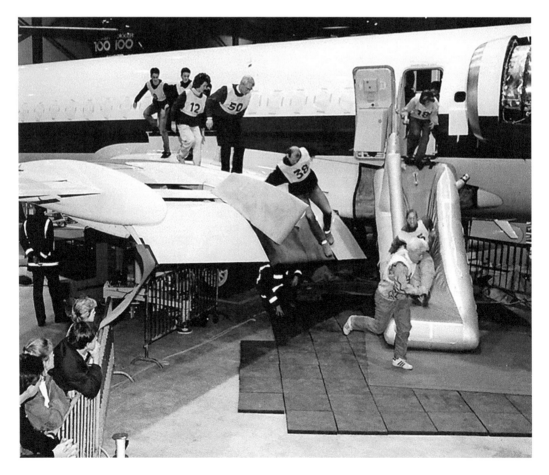

FIGURE 12.5 Evacuation demonstration Fokker 100—training run (photograph by the author).

was on the wing. Fokker used the last person off the wing for the end time. The video recordings were consulted, and it was agreed that the official time was 93 seconds, not 89 seconds. The demonstration had to be repeated.

That was done about two hours later. It brought an unexpected element that turned out favorably. The crew of the repeat test was the backup crew provided by the same U.S. airline. The first crew was now watching outside and started to cheer for their colleagues. That cheering was taken over by the rest of the watching crowd (most of whom were Dutch, whose culture is apparently less for cheering). As later confirmed by some of the passenger participants, this motivated them to speed up. The result was accordingly good: the same amount of passengers were now evacuated in 13 seconds less than the first time, in spite of the late opening of the overwing exit. Another difference between the two tests was the better distribution of participants over available exits, as directed by the flight attendants.

NOTES

1. Chicago Convention Conference Proceedings, Vol. II, p. 1086.
2. Amdt 04-0, CAR 04.3812.
3. The number of crew envisaged for the Convair 37 is not known, but assuming it was 12, this would mean a total occupancy of 216.
4. Aircraft Emergency Evacuation, Operating Experience and Industrial Trials, Report No. 2, U.S. Department of Commerce, Civil Aeronautics Administration, Office of Aviation Safety, May 1952.
5. Constellation Evacuation Test, Lockheed Aircraft Corporation Report No. 5869, August 27, 1946.
6. Report No. 2.
7. Aviation Week, September 18, 1950, p. 45.
8. Aviation Week, June 11, 1951, p. 57.
9. DR 51-16.
10. DR 51-16.
11. DR 52-13.
12. DR 52-21.
13. Aviation Week, December 8, 1952; February 2, 1953.
14. DC-4 – 66-Passenger Aircoach Evacuation Tests, Report No. JA-829D-1, Milton D. Smith, Cornell Aeronautics Laboratory, November 5, 1952.
15. Aviation Week, December 8, 1952, February 9, 1953.
16. Aviation Week and Space Technology, November 25, 1963.
17. Aviation Week and Space Technology, April 20, 1964.
18. Flight International, 30 April 1964.
19. Aviation Week and Space Technology, April 20, 1964.
20. Human Factors of Emergency Evacuation, Stanley R. Mohler, John J. Swearingen, Ernest B. McFadden, J.D. Garner, AM-65-7, FAA CARI, September 1964.
21. Human Factors of Emergency Evacuation, Stanley R. Mohler, John J. Swearingen, Ernest B. McFadden, J.D. Garner, SAE 851B, FAA OAM, April 1964.
22. Emergency Evacuation Tests of a Crashed L-1649, J.D. Garner, John G. Blethrow, AM 66-42, FAA OAM, August 1966.
23. A Milestone of Aeromedical Research Contributions to Civil Aviation Safety: The 1000th Report in the CARI/OAM Series, William E. Collins, Katherine Wade, FAA CAMI, DOT/FAA/AM-05/3, March 2005.
24. Evacuation Tests from an SST Mock-up, J.D. Garner, John G. Blethrow, Department of Transportation, AM 70-19, FAA OAM, December 1970.
25. NPRM 63-42.
26. NPRM 63-42.
27. Amdt 25-1/121-2.
28. Congressional Record, Proceedings and Debates of the 91st Congress, First Session, Vol. 115, Part 16, August 1, 1969, p. 21845.
29. Evacuation, Crashworthiness Development Program Technical Report, AIA CDP-4, Aerospace Industries Association of America, Inc., July 1968.
30. NPRM 66-26.

31 NPRM 66-26.
32 Amdt 25-15/121-30.
33 FAA Aviation Safety Issues, Hearings Before a Subcommittee of the Committee on Government Operations, House of Representatives, 96th Congress, First Session, August 13, 1979, p. 5.
34 Aviation Safety (FAA's Near Midair Collision Reporting System and the Proposed Boeing-747 Overwing Exit Removal), Hearings Before the Subcommittee on Investigations and Oversight of the Committee on Public Works and Transportation, U.S. House of Representatives, 99th Congress, First Session, June 1986, p. 297.
35 Advanced Techniques in Crash Impact Protection and Emergency Egress from Air Transport Aircraft by R.G. Snyder, AGARDograph No. 221, NATO, June 1976.
36 Mach 2 Concorde Magazine, Issue 20, February 2019.
37 Airline Deregulation and Aviation Safety, Hearings Before a Subcommittee of the Committee on Government Operations, House of Representatives, 95th Congress, First Session, September 9, 1977, p. 595.
38 FAA Aviation Safety Issues, p. 20.
39 Amdt 135-18.
40 NPRM 68-28; Amdt 121-46.
41 NPRM 81-1; Amdt 121-176.
42 Aircraft Evacuation Testing: Research and Technology Issues, Office of Technology Assessment, OTA-BP-SET-121, September 1993.
43 Amdt 25-117/121-307.
44 Emergency Evacuation Demonstrations, Advisory Circular 25.803-1, U.S. Department of Transportation, Federal Aviation Administration, November 13, 1989.
45 NPRM 95-9.
46 Amdt 25-117/121-307.
47 Amdt 25-79,121-233.
48 Flight International, 4–10 April 2006, p. 16; Over in a Flash, FSF Aerosafety World, January 2007, p. 46.
49 The number of 18 full-scale demonstrations is an estimate.
50 FAA's Process for Updating Its Aircraft Evacuation Standards Lacks Data Collection and Analysis on Current Evacuation Risks, U.S. Department of Transportation, Office of Inspector General, Report No. AV2020045, September 16, 2020, p. 33.
51 Emergency Escape of Handicapped Air Travellers, by J.G. Blethrow, J.D. Garner, D.L. Lowry, D.E. Busby, R.F. Chandler, FAA-AM-77-11, FAA CAMI, July 1977; Carriage by Air of Special Categories of Passenger, Contract Number: EASA.2008.C.25, Martin Sperber, Dr. Hendrik Schäbe, Daniel Masling, David Toth, Jan Küting, Michael Demary, Gero Wodli, TÜV Rheinland Kraftfahrt GmbH, 9 November 2010.
52 Emergency Evacuation Demonstrations: Time for Reform? Presentation by George Veryioglou at the ATA Engineering, Maintenance & Materiel Forum, Pittsburgh, Pennsylvania, October 1, 1992.
53 Aviation Safety (Aircraft Passenger Survivability and Cabin Safety), Hearings Before the Subcommittee on Investigations and Oversight of the Committee on Public Works and Transportation, U.S. House of Representatives, 98th Congress, First Session, July 14, 1983, p. 487.
54 GPSS Computer Simulation of Aircraft Passenger Emergency Evacuations by J.D. Garner, R.F. Chandler, FAA CAMI and E.A. Cook, FAA, FAA-AM-78-23, June 1978, p. 7.

13 Third Wave (1982–1996)

ABSTRACT

The third wave was the last of the three waves of significant cabin safety regulatory updates. It started in 1982 with the implementation of something that was already well under way: the improvement of impact protection of cabin personnel. Several years later, major improvements were made to flammability requirements and seat crash resistance.

While these measures were being progressed, two events occurred, in August and September 1985, that prolonged the third wave. The first was an accident with a Boeing 737 in Manchester, UK, with the loss of many lives. The second was a conference held in Seattle in which international experts discussed evacuation regulations. The catalyst had been a decision by the FAA to allow the deactivation of the middle exits of the Boeing 747 so that a distance of about 72 ft was created between the remaining exits. The Seattle conference led to several changes to existing evacuation regulations plus a new rule: the 60-foot rule.

13.1 INTRODUCTION

The third wave finalized an unplanned scheme of cabin safety developments that spanned five decades. In the first wave (1945–1953), the focus was on impact protection, with the 9 g crash load being established, plus evacuation provisions. The second wave (1965–1972) was primarily about further improving escape potential. The third wave, responding to the sharp increase in fatalities in the 1970s, addressed the missing elements: flammability of cabin interior materials and energy absorption properties of seats.

But the domain of escape potential popped up again, due to two events in August and September 1985. The 22 August accident in Manchester, England, prompted research into passenger behavior and led to changes to Type III exits and other cabin safety initiatives that later proved stillborn. The next month, a key conference in Seattle, Washington, itself resulting from a seemingly innocent FAA decision that blew up into a major issue, set the pace for a number of evacuation improvements. Many cabin safety measures were introduced in this period. In September 1991, the FAA proudly presented 11 different 'advances in cabin safety' in its *Aviation Safety Journal* magazine. Some more were to follow, marking the remaining years of the third wave.

13.2 ACCIDENTS

The third wave itself was in response to the spur of accidents in the 1970s, described in Section 11.2. But several new accidents steered some of the developments into a new direction. This was not the case for three accidents that occurred within four weeks early in 1982, and all involved water survival (January 13, Air Florida, Washington, D.C., January 23, Boston, February 9, Tokyo Haneda). None of these generated cabin safety-related recommendations. That was different from the in-flight fire accident that resulted in a successful emergency landing at Cincinnati in June 1983. The fire had quickly spread inside, and only half of the occupants survived. This accident prompted, or accelerated, several cabin safety measures. A DC-10 accident in Malaga, Spain, in September 1982 emphasized again that interior flammability was a major issue.

The next accident with a host of survivability lessons was the 22 August 1985, accident of a Boeing 737-200 in Manchester.[1] The aircraft suffered a left engine explosion while on its take-off run. An immediate abort was conducted, and the aircraft was turned off the runway. As a fuel access panel on the lower side of the panel had been hit, fuel poured out of the wing and caught

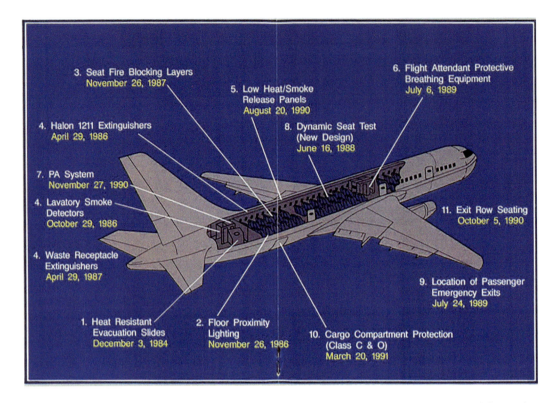

FIGURE 13.1 Overview by FAA of cabin safety improvements (*FAA Aviation Safety Journal*, September 1991).

FIGURE 13.2 Boeing 737 Manchester accident (AAIB report 8/88).

fire, causing a massive pool fire. The wind blew it toward the fuselage where it quickly melted cabin windows on the left side and entered via the right rear exit that had been opened instantly by a cabin crewmember. Out of 137 the occupants, 55 died.

This accident had three precursors involving the same, -200, variant of the Boeing 737. That variant, unlike later variants, had the engines underneath the fuel-carrying wing, making it vulnerable to fuel leakage and fire following an engine explosion. Two of them were non-fatal (22 March 1984, Calgary, and 11 May 1985, Doha), and the third was fatal to two passengers (30 August 1984, Douala). The reason that in Manchester the result was so much worse than in the three preceding cases was because there the engine fragments hit the weakest part of the wing: a fuel access panel. The Manchester accident led to passenger behavior trials in Cranfield, which, in turn, led to changes to Type III exit design and operation. Those trials also led to proposed, but never implemented, changes to bulkhead widths (see Section 10.10).

Later accidents followed with notable cabin safety lessons. Gradually, they started to confirm that the cabin safety measures of the third wave that had been imposed worked (see Section 17.3).

13.3 HEARINGS

The annual cycle of U.S. congressional hearings on cabin safety issues that had started in 1976 continued. In 1982 both the House and the Senate held hearings. The main topic of the House hearing, held in March, was the recent Air Florida accident and, thus, icing, its cause. Yet progress—or rather the lack thereof—on crashworthiness and flammability improvements was discussed again.[2] The title of the Senate hearings was 'airliner cabin safety and health standards', but the main subject was cabin air quality.[3] This was primarily about humidity but also touched upon air contamination. Smoking on board was still normal and not seen as a major source of such contamination. The air contamination issues as they would arise some decades later were not yet manifest. A bill to investigate air quality did not make it. A second subject was the provision of emergency medical kits on board airliners. This neither led to immediate regulations. Again, it would take almost two decades before that would be regulated.

The next year it was the House of Representatives again that organized two hearing series, in July and in November.[4] Subjects this time were again flammability, smoke, and toxic gases. Incidentally, when the July hearing was being planned, the Cincinnati in-flight fire occurred. In November, the FAA could announce some progress: NPRMs that had been issued on seat cushion blocking layers and, stimulated by the latter accident, low-level emergency lighting.

In 1984, the frustration of Congress with the slow progress of the FAA reached a high. Section 11.4 already mentions that Congressman Mineta had a host of bills proposed to improve cabin safety.[5] Neither of these bills passed, but the message was clear: the FAA should expedite its cabin safety program.

The 1985 edition of the House hearings dedicated to cabin safety was triggered by one element of one airplane type: the overwing exit pair of the Boeing 747.[6] In September 1983 Boeing had obtained from the FAA approval for a version of its 747 model where the two overwing exits on the main deck (out of ten exits) were removed. Removal, in this context, did not mean the physical removal of the exits but rather their deactivation and, at least on the inside, their concealment. Outside, the exits were marked as unserviceable and the exit outlining was removed. This move was found to be in compliance with the FARs as the four remaining exit pairs, each rated at 110 passengers, would allow 440 passengers in total. Many of the 747s in operation did have passenger capacities below 440, so prima facie would qualify for this modification. That this decision meant that there was now a distance of 72 ft (22 m) between exits apparently was not considered as a deterioration of safety. Yet, to many, the closing off of exits, and the creation of such a distance, felt so. That was the reason for this hearing.

In 1986, a one-day hearing was held on the specific subject of a flight attendant's strike at a particular airline (TWA) and the effect replacement staff might have had on cabin safety.[7]

In 1988, the House again heard about the 747 exit removal case.[8] The FAA by now had drafted the '60 foot rule', and Congress spent time on this subject again. As usual, the FAA administrator himself testified. He used the hearing to publicly announce his full support for the 60 feet (18.3 m) rule. Another witness, Matthew Finucane of the Association of Flight Attendants, told the audience that, in a 1964 study, research had shown that there should be not more than 44 ft (13.4 m) between exits. A flight attendant who had survived the 1977 Tenerife accident was called again (as in the 1985 hearing) and gave a moving, powerful, and compelling testimony of her horrendous experience. She reminded that the only exit that was used there and then was the overwing exit, the very exit that was the subject of the 1983 removal approval. (In fact, according to the Spanish investigation report the only exit actually used was the left number 2 exit, so an exit ahead of the wing, not over the wing. Her statement was not challenged.) Boeing testified as well. They still supported the exit removed case, also for the next 747 model (the -400) and poised a maximum distance between exits of 71 to 77 ft (21.6 to 23.5 m), claiming there was no scientific basis for the 60 feet (18.3 m), which had been suggested by a flight attendant union.

In 1989 and 1991, flight attendant duty and rest times were discussed, eventually resulting in a regulation in 1994. In 1990, the House turned its attention to child restraints. This was a direct result of the DC-10 crash at Sioux City in July of the previous year.

The U.S. was not the only country where parliamentary hearings took place. In the UK, where two major airliner accidents had taken place (1985 Manchester, 1989 East Midlands), a parliamentary inquiry was held in 1989 and 1990. All the topical cabin safety subjects were discussed such as seat designs, seat orientation (forward or aft), seat spacing, aisle widths, exit access, evacuation demonstrations, cabin material flammability, passenger smoke hoods, and water spray systems.

13.4 RESEARCH

The research programs set in motion in the U.S. in the 1970s continued, both for fire safety and crash-resistant seats, and started to yield usable results.

13.4.1 Fire Safety

Gus Sarkos, in 1989, looked back on the fire research program and explained it had led to new fire test standards in four areas: seat cushion fire-blocking layers, low heat/smoke release interior panels, radiant heat resistant evacuation slides, and, outside the aircraft cabin, burn-through resistant cargo liners.[9]

Following the SAFER recommendation, the seat cushion fire-blocking layers became the subject of intensive research by NASA Ames and FAA Technical Center. That research gave promising results: the additional time available for escape was found to be up to 60 seconds. Many tests were needed to filter the many materials offered for evaluation by the FAA. Not all met other criteria, such as weight, comfort, durability, and flotation, but eventually sufficient materials appeared adequate in all respects.[10]

Once the seat cushion blocking layers challenge was met, the next focus area of the FAA Technical Center scientists was the interior panels of an aircraft cabin, such as sidewalls, ceiling, stowage bins, and partitions. Initially, early wide-body interior panels were compared with fire-hardened panels. The safety gain, expressed in delay of onset of flashover, was from three minutes or more, to one minute, depending on the fire scenario. The most severe scenario was a ruptured fuselage; others were an external fuel fire adjacent to a door opening and an in-flight cabin fire starting from a gasoline-drenched seat. Flashover, to a large degree, is caused by the heat release rate of burning interior materials.[11] Thus, the selection criterion for interior materials became their heat release properties. The next challenge was to define a reliable and consistent method of measuring such properties. A test device designed specifically for that purpose had already been identified by the SAFER committee: the Ohio State University (OSU) rate-of-heat-release apparatus. It indeed was allocated as the equipment that would be specified in the regulation. The final step was to define a pass/fail criterion. Further testing identified this as 65 kWmin/m^2 for a two-minute duration and a peak heat release of 65 kW/m^2.

Third Wave (1982–1996)

60 SEC.   60 SEC.

These pictures, taken during actual tests of unblocked (left) and blocked seats (right) at the same times -- 60 sec. (above) and 120 sec. (below) -- and the same conditions, dramatically demonstrate the value of fireblocking. Within 60 sec., the flames had spread to unblocked seats (above left). After 120 sec., the unblocked seats were engulfed in flame (bottom left), and the fire had spread to adjoining seats and overhead panels. At this point, passenger survival would have been highly improbable. The fire-blocked seats (bottom right) remain basically intact after 120 sec.. The flames are still confined to the initial fire area; and the heat, smoke and toxic gas levels in the cabins are still well below incapacitation levels. With fire-blocked seats, passengers would still be able to evacuate the aircraft safely.

120 SEC.   120 SEC.

FIGURE 13.3 FAA Technical Center information leaflet.

Tests initiated by the Technical Center following the Los Angeles 1978 accident in which escape slides deflated because of radiant heat showed that a typical slide could fail in 25 to 30 seconds of heat exposure. Adding an aluminized coating would extend this to 70 to 75 seconds. The relevant Technical Standard Order was updated accordingly.

13.4.2 CRASH-IN-THE-DESERT

The results of the crash dynamics program of the FAA (see Section 11.4) were made public in September 1984.[12] The FAA then published an outline of its intentions to establish state-of-the-art seat and occupant restraint system design standards. The most dramatic element of the program, which gained worldwide attention, was the Controlled Impact Demonstration. This joint FAA/NASA test, which was eventually performed on December 1, 1984, involved the deliberate crashing of a remotely controlled, FAA-owned Boeing 720. The location was the Edwards Air Force Base, California, in the Muroc desert; hence, it colloquially became known as the crash-in-the-desert. A prime objective of the test was to validate the merits of anti-misting kerosene (AMK), which was developed to prevent a post-crash fire by limiting the vaporizing of the fuel into a mist that quickly ignites.

The unique event offered the opportunity to evaluate many other elements in the domains of crashworthiness and cabin fire safety. On board were 27 seat units (seating either two or three) with 73 test dummies, including infant dummies. The seat units were either of a traditional design or of a new, lightweight design with energy-absorbing features. The former met the existing design criteria (9 g forward, 1.5 g side, 4.5 g down, 2 g up), while the latter were designed and tested to meet peak dynamic loads of 18 g forward, 10 g side, 10 g down, and 6 g up in the 35/50 ft per second (10.7 to 15.2 m/s) velocity change range.[13] They were co-located so that they were subjected to the same loads as far as possible. This enabled the comparison of differences in the structural responses. Overhead stowage compartments were evaluated in a similar fashion. The crash could also be used to validate the mathematical 'KRASH' program. In the fire safety domain, half of the seat rows were furnished with fire-blocking layers, alternating with rows not so equipped, again to allow comparison. The results were convincing: all seats with the blocking layers remained superior to the standard seats. This good performance extended to the adjacent cabin wall linings.

The AMK element failed, that is, did not perform as hoped. This was largely the result of something that was not planned. On the ground, steel cutters had been constructed that were intended to cut the wing and thus release the AMK fuel. The airplane however developed a Dutch roll just before impact. The yaw caused engine number three to hit a cutter, which in turn caused the release of pressurized degraded AMK fuel and oil from hydraulic lines in the engine and strut compartments. As a result, the fuel was immediately vaporized and burned before any significant anti-misting action could develop. A portion of this burning fuel entered the interior as another cutter had made an opening in the fuselage, starting a fire which burned through the floor and entered the cabin. Thus, the impact demonstrated that there are conditions in which the jet fuel anti-misting additive is not sufficient to prevent a post-crash fire. The AMK additive initiative was quashed instantly.

In 1986, after the analysis of the data, the crash dynamics program was sufficiently ready to be converted into rulemaking.

13.5 REGULATORY DEVELOPMENTS

13.5.1 IMPACT PROTECTION

13.5.1.1 Amendment 25–51

The greatly improved protection features of flight attendant seats have already been described in Section 11.5.1. They became effective in March 1982 and were recognized not only for their primary objective—better protection of flight attendants in a crash—but also as a confirmation of their status as crewmembers with a safety mandate.[14] The features were not restricted to the seats

FIGURE 13.4 Crash-in-the-desert (photograph by NASA, Dave Howard).

but included the improved securing of galleys, on top of the measures introduced in 1972. This now meant equipping stowage compartments for galley carts and other items with double latches.

13.5.1.2 16 g Seats

The next major step was announced in July 1986 when a rule was proposed for improved seats. The crash dynamics program was nearly finished and confirmed that, with a few exceptions, the existing Part 25 design standards provided adequate impact protection for the occupants. A review of accident data showed that, for survivable accident scenarios, the airplane structure remained substantially intact and provided a livable volume for the occupants throughout the impact sequence.[15] This had been confirmed by the crash-in-the-desert. Undesirable seat performance is usually related to cabin floor displacement and excessive lateral inertial loads.

The exceptions were primarily seat related but it was also decided to upgrade the static load factors of FAR 25.561, which applied, next to seats, to other fixed items of mass in the cabin. The forward factor was kept at 9 g but a rearward factor of 1.5 g, previously not specified (although contemplated in 1975 but then withdrawn), was added. The upward and downward factors were proposed to be increased from 2 to 3.5 g and from 4.5 to 6.5 g, respectively. The sideward factor was proposed to be raised from 1.5 to 4.5 g.

The major change, however, affected the seats. It was proposed to introduce dynamic seat test standards that provided the same level of impact injury protection as that provided by the airplane structure itself. Two distinct survivable impact scenarios were developed based on the analyses of past accidents:

- The hard landing, or vertical, scenario: a combination of longitudinal and vertical loads to simulate ground impact following a high-rate vertical descent. In this scenario, spinal injury reduction is an important objective.
- The forward impact, or horizontal, scenario: this consists of a predominantly longitudinal load, simulating a horizontal impact with a ground-level obstruction such as typically occurring in an overrun or an impact survivable air-to-ground crash. In this scenario, the occupant restraint system and seat structural performance are assessed.[16]

The testing was done by subjecting seat assemblies with anthropomorphic test dummies weighing 170 pounds (77 kg) in it to sled tests. The assemblies were stopped (decelerated) to meet specific standards, as follows:

TABLE 13.1
Overview of Dynamic Test Standard Criteria

	Velocity Change (ft/s)	Axis			Floor Warping	Peak Floor Deceleration	
		Longitudinal	Lateral (wings)	Top (yaw)	Rails misalignment	Second after impact	Minimum g level
Vertical	≥ 35	30° down	Level	None	10° plus one rail	0.08	14
Longitudinal	≥ 44	Horizontal	Level	10°	rolled 10°	0.09	16

Other performance criteria were added for spinal injury, leg injuries, retention of lap belts and shoulder harnesses, seat deformation, and what is called the head injury criterion (HIC). The HIC is about secondary head impacts which can inflict debilitating injuries and result in concussion and unconsciousness. The HIC is a dimensionless variable defined by a mathematical equation and may not exceed a value of 1000. It was earlier introduced in the automotive industry. Accelerometers mounted in the head of the anthropomorphic test dummy register the impact of the head against an object and express it in the HIC value. The number 1000 is quite high. For cars to pass a crash test, a lower number, such as 700, is common. At a HIC of 1000, there is an 18% probability of a severe head injury, a 55% probability of a serious injury, and a 90% probability of a moderate head injury to the average adult.[17]

All these proposed criteria for the dynamic testing were adopted unaltered in the final rule, which was published on May 17, 1988.[18] As to the increase of the static load factors, smaller numbers were adopted as they would be 'within the existing design ultimate strength envelope for most airplanes that would be affected by this rule' (upward load 3 g, not 3.5 g, downward load 6 g, not 6.5 g). The sideward load value of 4.5 g was considered excessive in weight additions and 'without commensurate gains in safety'. It was kept at 3 g for structure but increased to 4 g for seats only.

The final rule was effective for transport airplane types for which U.S. type certification was applied after June 16, 1988. The first airplane types so affected were first delivered between April 1993 (Canadair Regional Jet to Comair) and July 1995 (Boeing 777 to United Airlines). In Europe, where the JAA had adopted the FAA standard, the Airbus A340 and BAe Jetstream 41 came earlier, both in January 1993.

The seat manufacturers redesigned their seats accordingly and had them tested, either in-house or by dedicated testing facilities. The most challenging element of the new regulation proved to be the HIC = 1000 value, particularly for front-row seats. While the sled tests showed that it could be met for occupants seated behind another seat, it was more difficult for those seated behind cabin walls such as a cabin divider, lavatory, or galley. For several of the early airplane types that had to meet the new regulation, an exemption for the HIC was given, pending further research and development. Solutions to reduce the HIC to 1000 or below included adding padding to the wall, articulating the seat pan (i.e. rotation of the seat pan upon impact, a solution used by United Airlines on their Boeing 777) and air bags. The latter were typically mounted in the seat belt.

The dynamic seat test standards were copied in the design standards for other aircraft: small airplanes (FAR 23) and helicopters (FAR 27 and 29). The variables for velocity change and deceleration were slightly different.

On the day that the rule for to-be-certificated types was published, the FAA issued an NPRM that proposed fitting 16 g seats in the existing fleets of FAR 121 air carriers, plus in airplanes yet to be assembled of types already certificated, or still in the certification process. A lead time of seven years, from publication of the NPRM, so an effectivity date of June 16, 1995, was proposed for such a retrofit.[19] That proposal raised quite some opposition from the airlines and stalled. One reason was that the introduction of 16 g seats on the new airplane types did not go as smoothly as anticipated. Attempts to comply with the new rule presented quite some teething problems. This was not so much in the seat structural integrity element, but primarily in the occupant protection portions, such as the HIC. The attention needed to solve these problems led to the appreciation that the retrofit rule was unrealistic. It was delayed indefinitely.

13.5.1.3 Child Restraints

Impact protection of children and infants had been a subject that was long a regulatory void. As early as 1941, in an accident involving a Sikorsky S-42 seaplane, two children aged one and two were thrown violently from the arms of the adults holding them.[20] The latter were almost completely submerged and unable to find the children who drowned. A larger child aged three, strapped in a safety belt, survived, as did all the other passengers and crew. Subsequently, the airline, Pan Am, devised and put into use a harness arrangement by which a child in arms is secured to the body of the person holding the child.

Since 1962, when the wearing, as opposed to the provision, of safety belts was first regulated, infants could be held loose on an adult's lap.[21] The wording of the rule was interpreted as a prohibition for infants to be belted, although the regulatory text had a 'may' in it, not a 'shall' or 'must': 'except that a person 2 years of age or less may be held by an adult person occupying a seat or berth'.[22]

The definition of infants (2 years of age or less) caused confusion: it implied that a person who has not yet reached his or her third birthday is an infant. But was that indeed intended? In 1928, infants had already been defined as those 'under 2 years of age' (see Section 3.3.2.3). In 1971 a common, unambiguous definition was introduced: 'a person who has not reached his second birthday'.

An infant on an adult's lap came at no extra charge. When child car seats became common on the roads in the U.S. in the 1970s, some parents thought they could buy an extra ticket, bring their own child seat on board, and strap it to the ticketed seat for their infant. However, the FAA prohibited that and airlines were forced to tell the passenger that the child seat was merely carry-on baggage. From 1982 onward, the FAA started to allow child seats to be used as such when they issued a TSO (C100) and the child seat brought on board indeed met that TSO. But not all airlines supported that practice and denied the use of such a seat.

In July 1989, a crippled DC-10 emergency landed in Sioux City, Iowa. Among the 285 passengers were three infants and one small child, ranging in age from 11 to 26 months, who were being held by adults. Two of the infants and the small child received minor injuries; the other infant died. Another young child, aged 32 months, sat in its own seat, restrained with the lap belt and additionally padded with cushions, and remained uninjured. In all, 111 occupants died in this crash. During the preparations for the emergency landing, the parents were instructed to place their infants on the floor and to hold them there when the parent assumed the protective brace position. One parent stated that her son 'flew up in the air' upon impact but that she was able to grab him and hold onto him. The mother of the 11-month-old girl said that she had problems placing and keeping her daughter on the floor because she was screaming and trying to stand up. She was unable to find her after the airplane impacted the ground, but the infant was rescued by a passenger who heard her cries and re-entered the fuselage to save her. The 26-month-old child sustained minor injuries and was rescued. The 23-month-old infant held on the floor died of asphyxia secondary to smoke inhalation.[23]

In the fuel exhaustion crash in New York City in January 1990, which involved a non-U.S. air carrier, there were ten infants on board. Nine survived, of which seven received serious injuries.

> They were either held by adult passengers or were belted into the same seat with the passengers. Surviving passengers who held infants reported that during the impact the infants were ejected from their grasp and that they were generally unable to locate them in the darkness after the impact.[24]

As there was no fire in this accident, there was ample time for evacuation and rescue of all occupants who had survived the impact.

The two accidents highlighted the issue and drove parties to action. Several organizations filed petitions with the FAA for mandating infant safety restraint systems that fit a passenger seat. In February 1990 Congressman Jim Ross Lightfoot of Iowa introduced a bill for the same.[25] In March, the FAA issued an NPRM intending to require air carriers to accept approved child restraint systems provided by a parent or guardian.[26] But it did not go as far as mandating child seats for infants as per the would-be bill. Two months later, together with its Sioux City accident report the NTSB issued a recommendation that the FAA require that infants and small children be restrained in an approved child restraint system. Rather than using the age discriminant of two years, the NTSB proposed a weight and length discriminant of 40 pounds (18 kg) and 40 inch (102 cm), respectively.[27]

Again two months later, in July 1990, a hearing was held in the House of Representatives to discuss Lightfoot's act and the subject at large. The FAA explained the dilemma that it had also recognized in its NPRM: mandating parents to buy an extra seat for their children would likely force them away from the air trip and decide to travel by car. But car travel had a much higher fatality rate than air travel. FAA's associate administrator for regulation and certification, Tony Broderick, estimated that 'the 100% use of child safety seats would save approximately one life aboard an aircraft over a 10-year period'.[28] Unlike other safety features on an airplane, whose cost is borne by the airline, in this case, the cost is borne directly by the passenger. He explained that

> a significant number of families who would have flown will elect to travel by automobile instead, leading to a greater risk of death not only to the children [. . .] but to their parents and brothers and sisters who will be in the automobile with them.[29]

To lift the reservations on the part of airlines in accepting child seats approved for aviation use, the FAA in September 1992 issued a final rule that ordered airlines to do so.[30] But it did not do what Congressman Lightfoot, whose bill never passed, had hoped: a firm requirement for using child safety seats.

The option of the 'belly belt', as devised by Pan Am in 1941 and in general use in Europe, was never allowed by the FAA. This belt, also called a lap belt or auxiliary child belt, 'concentrates crash forces on the child's abdomen and places the child in a position to act as a "crash pad" for the adult during a crash. Consequently, [its use] is likely to cause serious and non-reversible injury to the child'.[31] In 1996, the FAA reaffirmed this position and explicitly added its prohibition into FAR 121. At the same time, it clarified that some other types of restraints (booster seats, vests, and harness-type restraints) were also prohibited.[32] A wider acceptance of child restraint systems was only regulated years later (see Chapter 15).

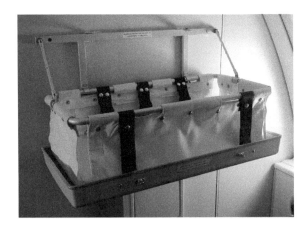

FIGURE 13.5 Baby bassinet (photograph by the author).

Third Wave (1982–1996)

Tests done at Cranfield University in the UK compared lap infants both held loose and restrained with a lap belt. Neither method was satisfactory: the former, so the U.S. preferred option (when no separate seat is purchased) 'is likely to promote fatalities and injuries to these children during impact situations'. The latter 'is not a suitable form of restraint'.[33] However, that study only looked at forward decelerations and did not appraise its possible benefit during turbulence, where the loads are vertical.

Not to be confused with a CRD is the baby bassinet. These are quite a common sight at front rows, hooked up on partitions. They have not been designed for crash loads and may only be used during the cruise portion of a flight.

13.5.2 Fire Protection

The third wave, more than the first and second, brought important fire protection measures. The most important, by any measure, were those for seat cushions and the heat release standards for interior materials. However, there were others, such as increased heat resistance for escape slides and some fire extinguishers to contain Halon as an agent.

13.5.2.1 Fire Extinguishers

In the 1980s, an update of the standards for the number and extinguishing agent of fire extinguishers was long overdue. There had been no change since 1956, in spite of the increase in the size of airplanes and the availability of better agents. The highest discriminant was 60 passenger seats, above which three extinguishers were required. But there were airplanes in service with ten times that number of seats. In 1985 the operational standards were updated, followed in 1991 by the airworthiness standards, both now listing 600 passenger seats as the highest discriminant.[34] Around the same time, Halon had become available as an extinguishing agent next to water and dry powder. However, there were concerns that Halon could release toxic gas by-products. This was investigated by the FAA Technical Center in 1980.[35] A positive result cleared the way for requiring that a proportion of the extinguishers contain Halon 1211 (bromochlorodifluoromethane). Incorporation of the requirements in FAR 25 meant that they became applicable to any user of new large airplane types, so not only airlines but also corporate and private users. Yet, this was limited to those types for which

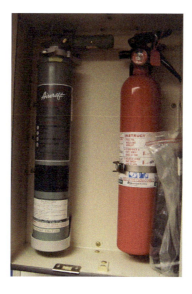

FIGURE 13.6 Fire extinguishers containing water (left) and Halon 1211 (right) as agents (photograph by the author).

certification was applied for after May 1991 and having 20 passenger seats or more. The majority of such airplanes in corporate use have lower capacities and remained excluded.

13.5.2.2 Lavatory Fire Protection

Following the in-flight fire that resulted in a forced landing short of the Paris Orly runway in 1973, the FAA issued fire standards specific to lavatories fire safety by means of Airworthiness Directives (see Section 11.5.2.1). The measures included no smoking signs, ashtrays on or near the lavatory door, periodic inspection of trash receptacles, augmented passenger briefings, and inspections for wear, abrasion, and corrosion of electrical items. The 1983 Cincinnati accident indicated that they were not enough. The FAA studied the subject again and found that in-service wear and tear to lavatory trash receptacles necessitated a stronger approach to lavatory fire safety. This resulted in a rule, published in 1985, that required air carriers to install: (1) a smoke detection system, or equivalent, in each lavatory after October 29, 1986; and (2) a built-in fire extinguisher for each lavatory disposal receptacle after April 29, 1987.[36]

13.5.2.3 Seat Cushion Fire-Blocking Layers

One of the recommendations of the SAFER Committee was that the fire-blocking layer concept be developed for aircraft seat cushions as a means of retarding flame spread. This was followed up with research by NASA Ames Research Centre (design optimization with respect to fire performance, comfort, wear, and cost) and at the FAA Atlantic City full-scale test facility.[37] The result was that a thin layer of highly fire-resistant cloth or foam material that completely encapsulates and protects the larger mass of foam core material of a cushion can significantly delay involvement in a cabin fire.

In October 1983 the FAA published an NPRM in which it explained this result.[38] It estimated that an increase of at least 40 seconds in post-crash evacuation and survival time could be gained. This would mean, according to the FAA, the evacuation of an additional 40 passengers per floor-level exit or for exits with a double-lane slide an additional 80 passengers. (This would translate into credits of 60 for a Type I exit and 120 for a Type A exit; more than the FAA regulatory credits of 45 and 110, respectively.) Even though the tests identified one material as superior, the FAA proposed a performance standard, so as not to prescribe that specific mark but allow other materials. The new standard was in the form of a two-minute oil burner fire performance test method for the seat cushion assembly. The existing Bunsen burner test would remain to cover the case that a fire directly penetrates a cushion, as opposed to being exposed to radiant heat. The final rule was published in October 1984, essentially unchanged from the proposal.[39] The entire U.S. FAR 121 fleet needed to comply by November 1987.

13.5.2.4 Flight Attendant Protective Breathing Equipment

Protective breathing equipment (PBE) was required in the cockpit since 1949 following an accident in June 1948 to a Douglas DC-6. A false fire warning caused the crew to discharge carbon dioxide (CO_2) into an area below the cockpit. That CO_2 reached the cockpit and incapacitated the pilots, which resulted in the aircraft getting uncontrolled and crashing into Mount Carmel, Pennsylvania.

The first accident which triggered a suggestion for cabin crew PBE was the accident to a Comet 4B at Ankara in December 1961. One of the cabin attendants seated at the entry door is believed to first have opened the door and then went forward to try and assist passengers. However, he died from asphyxiation. 'Had he had breathing apparatus readily available he might have saved some passengers and saved himself'.[40]

The requirement for PBEs only in the cockpit remained unchanged until 1976, when an airworthiness-only rule was adopted for installing PBE in each isolated compartment, such as upper and lower lobe galleys. The need for this rule was explained as 'recent service experience'.[41,42] This likely referred to incidents with Lockheed L-1011 and DC-10 airplanes that had such galleys. An airworthiness rule proposed at about the same time, asking for a PBE at each flight attendant seat

Third Wave (1982–1996) 193

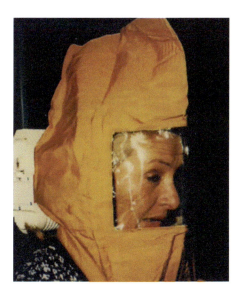

FIGURE 13.7 Smoke hood (photograph by the author).

was rejected as it was thought to overlap with the isolated compartment rule.[43] An operational rule proposal for the same was withdrawn 'in light of the need to conduct further testing of protective breathing equipment'.[44]

The Cincinnati 1983 in-flight fire stirred the need for the PBE again. The cabin crew would have benefited from adequate protection against smoke and harmful gases when fighting the lavatory fire. Responding to a recommendation by the NTSB, the FAA in October 1985 proposed to specify a portable PBE with an integral oxygen supply for at least 15 minutes.[45]

A PBE unit was proposed to be required next to each required fire extinguisher in the cabin and be accessible and conveniently located for use by flight attendants. 'Next to' was specified as 'within three feet' (1 meter). At the same time, a firefighting drill was added to the mandatory initial training curriculum for flight attendants (and other crew). The final rule essentially copied the proposal and imposed compliance by FAR 121 air carriers by July 1989, which was later postponed to January 1990.[46] The training standard compliance date was even extended to July 1992 because confusion had arisen as the FAA in an Advisory Circular (AC) had issued guidance that conflicted with the rule. The actual firefighting drill did not necessarily need to be done with a PBE. Alternatively, the PBE drill could be combined with a simulated firefighting exercise.[47] However, fighting an actual fire with a PBE on was still encouraged.

PBEs meeting the new rule came in two forms: (1) a smoke goggle, covering the mouth, nose, and eye that is connected to a portable oxygen cylinder and (2) a hood-type device that goes over the head which has a built-in chemical oxygen generator: the portable smoke hood.

There have been a few cases where the cabin crew PBE was tested in practice. One such case, the Toronto 2005 accident, demonstrated that the smoke hood prevented communication. '[T]he one cabin crew who donned a smoke hood for personal protection was unable to communicate in an intelligible manner' and removed it to make herself understood'.[48]

13.5.2.5 Flammability, Heat Release, and Smoke

All the major airplane manufacturers had internal policies for the flammability of interior materials that well exceeded those of the FARs of 1972. For example, for the Boeing 747 they included heat release and smoke emission standards. For the Boeing 757 and 767, which entered service in the early 1980s, the standards were more stringent and also included toxic gases standards. This was partly in anticipation of the FAA considering such standards since 1974. The smoke emission standards ranged from D_s>200 to D_s <50, subject to material application in the cabin (D_s = specific optical density, measured in the NBS smoke chamber). Douglas, Airbus, British Aerospace, and Fokker had similar in-house standards.[49,50]

The full-scale fire test program by the FAA Technical Center demonstrated a correlation between flammability and smoke emission characteristics in the materials tested. Those materials, unlike some then in use, were selected for their higher ignition temperatures, reduced heat release rates, and lower content of thermally unstable components.[51] The tests also showed that toxic levels before the onset of the flashover were survivable, but this changed instantly the moment flashover occurred. This led to the conclusion that no separate tests, or standards, for smoke or toxicity were necessary.

Now that the fire test program had delivered results, sufficient in volume and reliability, it was time for a rulemaking proposal additional to that for the fire-blocking of seat cushions. It was published in April 1985.[52] It proposed a radically new flammability standard for all larger interior surface materials used from the floor up. This included sidewalls, ceilings, bins, partitions, galley structures, and any coverings on these surfaces. Smaller items such as windows, window coverings, or curtains were excluded as were floor coverings. Neither were seats, as they were already the subject of the separate seat cushions rule, nor service items such as pillows, blankets, magazines, food, and alcoholic beverages. Seats with large panel assemblies, such as first and business class seats, however were included. The proposed test method involved the exposure to radiant heat of samples of material for cabin interior use in the calibrated environment of the OSU test chamber. The pass/fail criterion was expressed as the heat release rate from the material over the first two minutes of exposure, in kilowatt-minutes per square meter. Subject to the measurement method (either by thermopile or by oxygen depletion), the maximum rate would either be 40 or 70 kW min/m². In an update of the NPRM, this was changed to one test method but two pass/fail criteria: the maximum for the first two minutes would now be 65 kWmin/m² (using the thermopile method) and a new maximum would be added: a peak heat release rate of 65 kW/m².[53] The vertical Bunsen burner test requirement remained, mainly to cover extremely thin materials that might not release enough heat to exceed the proposed standards, yet be highly flammable.[54] The proposal was not confined to Part 25, so for new, to-be-certificated, airplane types only, but was aimed at newly manufactured airplanes of types already certificated. A two-year period, from the date of publication of the final rule, was proposed to allow manufacturers time to select and qualify compliant materials. Additionally, the new standard would apply when a cabin interior was replaced. A general retrofit was not proposed because of a number of practical and cost–benefit considerations.

The new standard came as quite a shock to industry. It was significantly more stringent than the in-house standards. It was seen as a means to force technology rather than adopt state-of-the-art, as it was difficult to find suitable materials that would comply. High costs would be involved in developing and testing new materials, as well as for airplane manufacturers to acquire OSU test chambers. Also, there were questions about the reliability of the test method as different laboratories using the same materials and the same test method yielded different results. But while the latter proved teething problems which were solved with a 'round robin' among the various laboratories, the new standard indeed led to an accelerated search by industry for new materials. This however needed time and investment. The FAA, for that purpose, extended the compliance period from two to four years. For the interim two-year period, less stringent maxima were set: a maximum heat release rate of 100 KWmin/m² for the first two minutes of exposure and a peak heat release rate of 100 kW/m². Thus, the rule that had already become known as the 65/65 rule temporarily became a 100/100 rule.[55] The industry was still not pleased and submitted a counterproposal.[56] This suggested keeping the 100/100 criteria but added a smoke density test to filter out materials generating significant amounts of smoke when burning. As discussed, airplane manufacturers already used smoke density as part of their own acceptance criteria for materials. The FAA, in 1988, adopted the smoke density standard, using the D_s<200 criterion, but kept the 65/65 heat release standard. The new rule now became known as the 65/65/200 rule. The addition of the smoke test may have been influenced by the Manchester 1985 accident, where many people died because of smoke inhalation. Its investigators had found that no flashover had occurred and criticized the overreliance in the FAA Technical Center tests on the importance of the flashover theory as opposed to other scenarios. In Manchester, with many doors open, there was more ventilation than in FAA's single opening test article, thus producing a different airflow pattern and circulation of smoke and toxic gases.

The FAA allowed airlines to ask for compliance extensions on a case-by-case basis, but other than that kept its stance.[57] From August 20, 1988, onward, newly manufactured airplanes had to comply with the 100/100 heat release standard. Exactly two years later, the 65/65/200 standard applied to airplanes newly manufactured from that date. The regulation also applied to complete replacements of interiors, but airlines avoided that. The General Accounting Office in February 1993 found that no U.S. airline had completely replaced interior components of even one in-service aircraft nor planned to do so.[58]

13.5.3 Escape Potential

In the escape potential domain, fewer developments took place in the third wave than in the first and second. Apart from the introduction of floor lighting, already being contemplated but accelerated by the Cincinnati accident, there were several events that led to a series of regulatory changes. Two were accidents (Manchester, UK, 1985, and Los Angeles, 1991) and one was a conference on evacuation held in September 1985 in Seattle.

13.5.3.1 Floor Lighting

Floor proximity emergency escape path marking (FPEEPM), or floor lighting, in short, is a means for guiding passengers to emergency exits under conditions of dense smoke. In 1980, the SAFER committee advised placing emergency lights at a lower level in the cabin, where in conditions of smoke, the air is relatively clear. Then current emergency lighting sources typically were located in cabin ceilings. The regulation specified a specific illumination level at armrest height. The SAFER advice was not followed up until there was an accident that made its value abundantly clear. That accident was the Cincinnati accident of June 2, 1983. By that date, the FAA was well on its way to conducting research, testing, and design studies, so it could issue a proposed rule in a short time span. About four months after the accident it issued a proposal for FPEEPM.[59]

In its research phase, the FAA evaluated different types of lighting, including three that require an electric source and one that does not: incandescent (wire filament, typically in a bulb), fluorescent (mercury-vapor gas), and electroluminescent (typically a strip). Independent of an electric source is the photoluminescent or self-illuminating light. This continuously re-emits light that it receives from another light source, even after the removal of that source. As no single system appeared superior to other systems, the FAA chose a performance standard instead of a prescriptive standard, without any illumination level prescribed, as follows:[60]

> Provide emergency evacuation guidance for passengers when all sources of illumination more than four feet above the cabin aisle floor are totally obscured. In the dark of the night, the floor proximity emergency escape path marking must enable each passenger to (1) after leaving the passenger seat, visually identify the emergency escape path along the cabin aisle floor to the first exits or pair of exits forward and aft of the seats; and (2) readily identify each exit from the emergency escape path by reference only to markings and visual features not more than four feet above the cabin floor.

The FPEEPM would be in addition to the existing requirements for emergency lighting, not instead of. The final rule was published in October 1984 without significant changes compared to the proposal and gave airlines two years to equip their fleets.[61] The performance standard did not go as far as requiring that airplane manufacturers and airlines demonstrate the effectivity of the chosen system. In the final rule's preamble, the FAA however did. This was then laid down in an Advisory

FIGURE 13.8 UV-illuminated floor-mounted escape path (photograph by the author).

Circular.[62] It prescribed an evaluation of the system in the aircraft cabin, but not necessarily by using test subjects and/or artificial smoke.

Airplane manufacturers and airlines went to select systems from the various manufacturers that offered their products. Typically, either of two systems were chosen: seat-mounted incandescent lights or floor-mounted electroluminescent lights. The former provided, by the simple fact that they were seat-mounted, intermittent illumination along the aisle. The latter system, being floor-mounted and of a strip design offered the advantage of a continuous light, with offsets at right angles where there were exits. In both cases, additional wall-mounted lights were provided in floor-level exit areas. Fokker invited five different system suppliers to demonstrate their system in a mock-up and used test subjects and artificial smoke. One supplier had a novel concept that consisted of exit markings impregnated in the floor carpet that would only become visible when shone on by a UV light source. The concept was however just that, a concept, and not yet mature. Fokker identified the ready-to-install electroluminescent system as superior and thus selected it as their preferred system. Almost all of its airline customers went along with that choice.

Later, when the photoluminescent, non-electric lights had developed so that they remained brighter for a longer time, many airlines replaced their electric FPEEPM with this non-electric version. Not only did that save maintenance costs, but it also avoided a flight being delayed or canceled when the FPEEPM, or parts of it, appeared unserviceable just before the flight.

13.5.3.2 The Seattle Conference

The events that led to the review in the period 1985 to 1996 of several evacuation-related standards began in 1983. Boeing applied in August with the Seattle Aircraft Certification Office of the FAA for a variation of the Boeing 747 in which the exit pair placed over the wing was deactivated. This was granted within four weeks.[63] No evacuation demonstration was considered necessary; the approval was based on a simple verification of compliance with the rules in place. Later, in February 1986, as a result of the uproar discussed later, a demonstration was done in which 440 passengers evacuated from the main deck plus 100 from the extended upper deck in 80.5 seconds. The cabin crew complement of 11 was from British Airways.

Although there was a requirement since 1967 that exits be distributed as uniformly as practicable taking into account passenger distribution, no further specification existed as to what that meant, so there was no ground for denying the application. The remaining four exit pairs, all of Type A size, for which the rating was 110 since 1977, supported a passenger load of up to 440 on the main deck. The airlines that were interested in this variant were Asian and European. No U.S. airline was interested. Yet, it was particularly in the U.S. that this created a row, although France followed suit. In Paris, cabin crew unions placed stickers saying 'ne vous laissez pas desactiver' (don't let yourself be deactivated).[64] Several U.S. parties, once aware of what they considered to be a downgrading of safety, objected. A hearing on the subject was held in Congress in June 1985. The FAA promised a further investigation into the matter. That confirmed that the application for the 747 door 3 deactivation was handled correctly but that at a higher level, there were questions about the efficacy of the emergency evacuation rules. This prompted the FAA to convene a technical conference on the broader subject of emergency evacuation. It was held in September 1985 in Seattle and was massively attended. All of the U.S. experts were there, representing not only the FAA, NTSB, and designers of airplanes and slides but also unions, research organizations, and an airline passenger group. But also from Europe there was a strong delegation, including representatives from several airlines and from manufacturers British Aerospace, Fokker, and, particularly, the Airbus group. Airbus in 1985 was a young company with a modest portfolio of airplane types. Its market access in the U.S. was still limited, with only two customers: Eastern and Pan Am. But it had a great potential; the fly-by-wire A320 had just been launched.

Subjects discussed at the conference covered the number, capacity, distribution, and marking of emergency exits, full-scale evacuation demonstrations, the validity of the data derived from full-scale evacuation tests versus data obtained from analyses, and the criteria to be used to decide when the analysis method would be acceptable in lieu of a full-scale demonstration.[65] Discussions also covered escape slides and the design standards and certification testing requirements for these slides, slide maintenance failure reporting and other related topics. Not on the agenda, but widely discussed informally, especially among the Europeans, was the accident that had occurred about a month earlier in Manchester, England. Fifty-five people had died while not being able to get out of a Boeing 737 on fire.

This gathering of experts led to several initiatives for reviewing the rules. One of this addressed the issue that started it all and became known as the 60-foot (18.3 m) rule. Others were about a revision of the exit table (see Section 13.5.3.4), further changes to the evacuation demonstration procedure and access to Type III exits. Less impacting changes were about mandatory reporting of slide malfunctions, exit handle illumination, and PA system improvements.

13.5.3.3 The 60-Foot Rule

In 1987, the FAA published an NPRM to limit the distance between exits to 60 ft. (18.3 m). It explained that this was based on the standard, introduced in 1967, for uniform distribution of exits. At the time, the NPRM explained, 'it was assumed that a uniform distribution of exits [. . .] would result in reasonable passenger seat-to-exit and exit-to-exit distances'.[66] Since then, maximum distances on wide-body airplanes had been employed, and not questioned during type certification, of 44 ft. (13.4 m) (Boeing 747), 47 ft. (14.3 m) (DC-10), and 50 ft. (15.2 m) (L-1011). For the Boeing 747 with door 3 deactivated it became 72 ft. (22 m). A later application (Airbus A340-600) would even have an exit-to-exit distance of 74 ft. (22.6 m), but that was now denied by the FAA.

The rationale for imposing a maximum distance was that in actual evacuations blockages in escape paths, which aisles are, had occurred that prevented passengers from reaching an exit. Such blockages could be formed by structural damage (but not to the extent that it offered a break sufficient for egress), the entry of fire and smoke, or submersion in water accidents. The longer the distance between a given seat and an exit, the higher the chances of such a blockage. Alternatively, the tilting of the fuselage without a complete blockage may reduce the flow rate through an escape path. The maximum distance between exits was arbitrarily set at 60 ft. (18.3 m), or about 20% above that which had previously been accepted (discounting the 747 deactivation). A quantitative analysis was used as well to substantiate this figure. That analysis was based on CAMI research which had measured the effect a tilted fuselage would have on the rate at which evacuees ran through an aisle. In response to criticism, in the preamble to the final rule the FAA downplayed the importance of that analysis, but without altering the 60 ft. criterion.

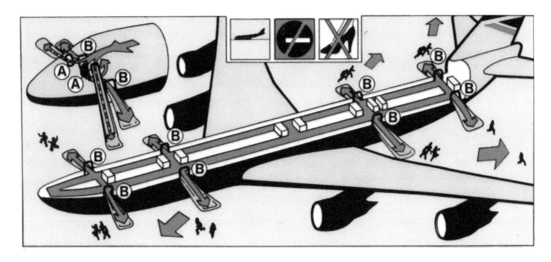

FIGURE 13.9 Boeing 747 safety card showing exit configuration with door 3 deactivated (British Airways, c. 1989).

In recognition of the economic aspects, the FAA explained that the 20% margin would still give sufficient flexibility for 'continued design development'. This phrase referred to the practice of stretching airplane types, such as exemplified by families of airplanes. The DC-9 and Boeing 737 families were good examples of such stretching, but it was also done on wide-body designs. A companion rule that would limit the distance between any given seat and the nearest exit to 30 ft. (9.1 m) was not adopted in the final rule that was issued in June 1989.[67] It was considered redundant with the existing requirement that there be at least one floor-level exit per side near each end of the cabin. But that was not entirely true. That figure would primarily have affected airplane zones that have exits only at one end. Such zones were also known as 'dead ends'. Examples formed the upper deck of the classic Boeing 747 and the section aft of the wings on the Fokker 100. On the former, the distance from the aftmost seat to the nearest main deck exit (but not the single side exit on the upper deck) was more than 30 ft. (9.1 m).

The rule prohibited U.S. air carriers from introducing the 747 with doors 3 deactivated. But as there were no such airlines in the U.S. it had no material effect. The non-U.S. airlines that operated them were allowed to keep them in use until their retirement.

However, the next generation of the 747 (the 747-400) was affected by the new rule, in all countries, and thus had all ten main deck exits activated.

In the rule preamble, the FAA announced that it would establish an emergency evacuation advisory committee to develop recommendations for an evacuation performance standard and appropriate further modifications and additions to the agency's existing evacuation regulations. That committee was indeed formed in May 1991 under the umbrella of the new Aviation Rulemaking Advisory Committee.

13.5.3.4 Revision of the Exit Table

The exit table that was devised in October 1951 had only been changed twice (disregarding a minor change in 1972). In 1957 it was expanded beyond 139 seats to 219 seats in anticipation of the jets. In 1967, expecting the wide bodies, it was curtailed back to 179 seats but augmented with a second table. That second table acted as an add-on to the first table for capacities from 180 up to 299. It prescribed exit credits of 100, 45, 40, and 35, respectively, for each Type A, Type I, II, and III exit pair. From 300 and up, it served as a stand-alone table and specified that only floor-level exits were allowed. The first table remained being prescriptive and thereby restrictive. As noted earlier, for

Third Wave (1982–1996)

Passenger seating configuration (crew member seats not included)	Emergency exits for each side of the fuselage			
	Type I	Type II	Type III	Type IV
1 to 9				1
10 to 19		O	O	1
20 to 39	60 {		1 20 1	
40 to 79		1	30 { 1	
80 to 109	60 {	1	2	
110 to 139		2 70	1 40	
140 to 179		2	2	

FIGURE 13.10 Exit table with flexible credits superimposed.

any given (maximum) passenger capacity, it prescribed in a limitative way the number and type of emergency exits. It had some quirks: it was adverse to stretching an airplane, and it contained variable credits for the same type of exit.

An airplane designed for up to 109 passenger seats required one pair of Type I exits and two pairs of Type III exits (or, until 1967, one pair of Type III and one pair of Type IV). But when such a design would be stretched beyond 109 seats, a second pair of Type I exits was required. Of the two pairs of Type III exits, one was no longer required. Typically, Type III exits are over the wing but the Type I exits need to be at the cabin ends. This made stretching a 109-seater cumbersome. One of the Type III exit pairs could not simply be enlarged into a Type I as its location was wrong (not at a cabin end). For the second pair of Type I exits, there may not be a good location due to the relative position of wings and engines. This was particularly true for airplanes with engines mounted at the rear fuselage, such as the Douglas DC-9 family, the Boeing 727 (i.e. the original model, the 727-100), and, in Europe, the BAC One-Eleven and the Fokker F-28 family. For some of these models, when being stretched, an emergency exit in the tail formed a way out to overcome the restrictive nature of the exit table.

Another peculiarity of the 1967 table (as amended in 1972) was the variable credit for exit types. When comparing the various combinations of number and type of exits, as prescribed, it appeared that an additional pair of Type I exits would allow either 60 or 70 passenger seats (and even 65 or 75 when eligible for the bonus for inflatable slides). Similarly, an additional pair of Type III exits would be good for either 30 or 40 seats.

The second table set fixed ratings for each type of exit. These were a mere 45 for Type I exits and 35 for Type III exits, which were the exit types most commonly used at the time on narrow-body airplanes. For the seldom-used Type IV and Type II exits they were 9 and 40, respectively. For the Type A exit, used in all wide bodies, it was 110, elevated from 100 in 1977. Thus, a Type I exit was worth 45, 60, or 70 seats, and a Type III exit was either 30, 35, or 40 seats. These inconsistencies, together with the prescriptive nature of the first table, made it a 'hodge podge' of a table, as a Long Beach FAA Aircraft Certification Officer informally put it.

A revision was indeed in place and the FAA published an NPRM in 1990.[68] In 1996, when this NPRM had still not been converted into a final rule, the then administrator, Thomas McSweeney, explained the reason for it in a letter to his European counterpart, Klaus Koplin, then head of the JAA:[69]

> The NPRM was not written because of safety concerns for the current regulations. The exclusive purpose of the NPRM was to provide, for new 'clean sheet of paper' designs only, a more ordered and less confusing progression of exit configurations of various seating capacities. The existing rules have produced a seemingly crazy quilt of combinations which are not orderly, and are difficult to interpret and apply.

Perhaps 'crazy quilt' is a synonym for 'hodge podge'. The letter was written in the context of the JAA not accepting the FAA's acceptance of the 737 Next Generation being based on pre-1972 exit standards.

The seeds for the revision had been planted shortly after the 1985 Seattle conference when industry experts met with the FAA in follow-up meetings. Messerschmitt–Bölkow–Blohm (MBB), acting for Airbus, made a proposal for new ratings, including a proposal for a new exit type: the Type B exit.[70] Actually, the Type B exit had already been used in a certification program. In 1972, the forward exit pair of the DC-10 was granted by exemption a credit of 80. The FAA confirmed that they would use the MBB credits in a draft proposal, albeit that for two Types (Type II and III), they made the reservation that the data was not supported by evidence. The FAA-supported credits were 110 for a Type A pair, 80 for a Type B pair, and 55 for a Type I pair. For a Type II pair, it was 45, for a Type III pair it was 40.[71]

But when five years later the proposal was indeed issued, the credits were different. For some exit types, they were much lower than promised in Seattle. Type B went back to 75, Type I to 45, Type III to 35, and for two pairs of adjacent Type IIIs, it became 65. A new Type C was introduced: 6 inch (15 cm) wider than a Type I, but with the same height and always equipped with a slide, irrespective of the height above ground. The slide would typically be single lane. It was worth 55. The table for capacities up to 179 disappeared and was replaced by requirements that still used bands, but no longer specified in a limitative way which Type to use. As an example, it now specified:[72]

> (5) For a passenger seating configuration of 41 to 110 seats, there must be at least two exits, one of which must be a Type I or larger exit, in each side of the fuselage.

However, even though the table was now removed, its basic concept remained. The proposal showed, in table format, a comparison of the existing table and the proposal.

\multicolumn{4}{c	}{Exit type}	\multicolumn{2}{c}{Maximum passenger capacity}
I	II	III	IV	Existing § 25.807(c)(1)	Proposed regulation
			1	9	9
		1		19	19
	1	1		39	40
1		1		79	80
1		2		109	110 or 115
2		1		139	125
2		2		179	155 or 160

For the exit configuration I—III–III—I, as prolifically used on the Airbus A320 and Boeing 737, already certificated for 179 and 189 passenger seats, respectively, the new proposal would yield only 155. This was made up of two times 45, plus 65 for the two pairs of closely located Type IIIs. However, as confirmed by Thomas McSweeney, the new rule would not affect types already

Third Wave (1982–1996)

certificated. The previous prohibition to use Type III exits (or Type IIs) for passenger capacities beyond 299 was deleted, as, according to the FAA's 'experience with the Airbus Model A310 and Boeing Model 767 airplanes has shown that Type III overwing exits can also be effective exits in twin-aisle airplanes'.[73] However, there was no such experience, as neither type had been involved in an accident where usage of the Type III exit was vital. The proposal raised disapproving comments, even from the JAA in Europe. The JAA argued against dropping the 299 limit for Type III exits and suggested, based on evacuation demonstration performance, higher exit credits: 65 for a Type C, 60 for a slide-equipped Type I, and 50 for a sec Type I.[74] The FAA disregarded the comments from their European counterpart and in 1996 adopted the NPRM into a rule, unaltered.[75]

13.5.3.5 Uniform Distribution

In 1967 the FAA introduced a requirement that exits 'be distributed as uniformly as practicable taking into account passenger distribution'. In the Seattle conference, it was recommended that guidance be provided for what uniform distribution entailed. The FAA published an Advisory Circular (AC) on the subject in August 1990.[76] While indeed providing useful guidance, the AC also added confusion by introducing a new concept: exit unit. This paralleled, but did not exactly match, the credits already given in the exit tables. While FAR 25.807 has been updated since, the AC has not, which suggests that its practical value is limited.

13.5.3.6 Validating the Credits

Table 13.2 presents a historical overview of the exit credit development since 1977. It serves to illustrate the various attempts of defining a uniform egress capability figure for each type of exit and assesses whether that was achieved.

Columns A and B give flow rate figures (in persons per minute), and columns C through F give exit pair credit figures. Columns G and H give conversions from flow rates into exit pair credit figures using the rates of columns A and B. Column I gives an excess percentage, as explained hereunder.

TABLE 13.2
Exit Credit Developments since 1977

	A	B	C	D	E	F	G	H	I
	Airlines	mfgrs	25.807	MBB/FAA	WG	25–88	A Based	B Based	F:H
	Evac Demos		Rule	Proposal		Rule	Conversion		Excess
	1981	1995	1977–1996	1985	1986	1996 Onward			
	Flow Rate (N/min)				Credit (per exit pair)				%
Type A	85.8	102.5	110	110	110	110	100	120	9
Type B		78		80	80	75		91	21
Type C		58.5				55		68	24
Type I	52.2	54.2	45, 60, 70	55	45–55	45	61	63	40
Type II			20, 40	45	40	40			
Type III	39.2	42	30, 35, 40	40	35	35	45	49	40
Double Type III		60.7	70	80	70	65		71	9
Type IV	36		9	20	10	9	42		

The flow rate data in column A come from the preamble to the final rule for evacuation demonstrations that was published in December 1981 and which referred to data from 89 90-second evacuation demonstrations conducted by airlines in the period.[77] The flow rate data in column B are averages from a collection of flow rate data as set in 30 full-scale evacuation demonstrations by five airplane manufacturers in the period 1967–1995. The exit pair credits in column C were those that applied from 1977 (and for some exit types even from 1951 onward) until 1996. The exit pair credits in column D were as proposed by MBB post the Seattle conference in a November 1985 working group meeting. The FAA then said that 'we will draft proposal of suggested changes to current tables by MBB'.[78] The exit pair credits in column E were as agreed in a follow-up working group meeting in February 1986.[79] There was concurrence on all figures, except for the Type I. The working group was composed of authorities, manufacturers, airlines, and unions. The exit pair credits in column F were as proposed by the FAA in 1990 and adopted, unaltered, in 1996 and since unchanged.[80] The figures in columns G and H are calculations in which the flow rates of columns A and B are converted to a 90-second performance capability. Two assumptions are made. The first is that readying an exit takes 15 seconds so 75 seconds remain available for egress. The second is a conservatism factor of 93.5%. That factor is based on explanations that the FAA gave in 1967 and 1977 when they established the Type A credit of 100 and 110, respectively. When the FAA introduced the Type A exit in 1967, it allocated a credit of 100 which it explained was 'conservatively set at 85% of the test evacuation capacity'. The test evacuation capacity was not further defined but assumed to be based on a flow rate of 108 persons/minute as confirmed by AIA in 1968 based on mock-up tests. Later the Type A credit was raised to 110, thus making the conservatism factor 93.5%. Column I, finally, compares the demonstrated performance of exits, as given in column H, with the rated credit as given in column F. The result is an excess percentage, meaning the margin that exit types have. This margin ranges from 9% for Type A and double Type III exits to 40% for Type I and single Type III exits. Thus, where the credits for Type A and double Type III exits fairly resemble their demonstrated performance, the Type I and single Type III exits perform much better than what their given credits assume.

13.5.4 Life Support—Medical Kit

Effective August 1986, the FAA introduced a requirement for a medical kit to be carried on board.[81] This was in response to a petition filed in 1981 by the Aviation Consumer Action Project (ACAP) which noted that 'any doctor on board who is called to help will find that the plane carries no lifesaving medical equipment (other than burn compound)—not even a stethoscope. As a result, a person with severe asthma or diabetic coma, for example, could die for want while a doctor stands helplessly by'.[82] ACAP observed that many foreign airlines did carry a medical kit. In response to the published petition, a number of physicians described their involvement in in-flight medical emergencies. Those emergencies included such conditions as myocardial infarction, allergic reaction to food, acute asthma, epileptic seizures, and childbirth.[83] The matter had also been discussed in a Senate hearing in 1982 on airliner cabin safety and health standards.[84] Initially, the FAA denied the petition as it felt it was not authorized to deal with this matter, which it considered was beyond its remit. It took a court case by ACAP to get the FAA back on track. This took a while. Only in 1985 did the FAA issue an NPRM, which then led to a final rule signed on the last day of the year.[85] Compared to the proposal, the contents list in the final rule was significantly reduced, notably in terms of drugs. Incidentally, the burn compound, which was prescribed in the first-aid kit, not the medical kit, was removed in 1994 as the use of ice or cold water was the preferred treatment.[86]

13.5.5 Information and Instructions

13.5.5.1 Independent Power Source for PA

Already in 1974, the NTSB recommended an independent power source for PA systems so that an audible evacuation order could be given even after normal power has been cut.[87] The FAA reacted in 1981 with a proposal for retroactive installation.[88] However, it was withdrawn because the costs would outweigh the expected benefit. In 1986 it proposed it again, but now only as a forward fit, which it found was cost effective.[89] It became effective for all airplanes with a seating capacity of 20 or more in November 1990.[90]

13.5.5.2 Passenger Briefing Enhancement

In 1992, the operational standards were amended to enhance the passenger briefing requirements. Specifically, the briefing needed to include text that passengers comply with lighted signs and posted instructions. At the same time, it became unlawful for passengers not to obey.

NOTES

1. Report on the Accident to Boeing 737-236 Series 1, G-BGJL at Manchester International Airport on 22 August 1985, 8/88, Department of Transport, Air Accidents Investigation Branch, 15 December 1988.
2. Aviation Safety Research. Hearing Before the Subcommittee on Investigations and Oversight and the Subcommittee on Transportation, Aviation and Materials of the Committee on Science and Technology, U.S. House of Representatives, 97th Congress, Second Session, March 9, 1982, p. 6.
3. Airliner Cabin Safety and Health Standards, Hearing Before the Subcommittee on Aviation of the Committee on Commerce, Science, and Transportation, United States Senate, 97th Congress, Second Session, May 20, 1982.
4. Aviation Safety (Aircraft Passenger Survivability and Cabin Safety), Hearings Before the Subcommittee on Investigations and Oversight of the Committee on Public Works and Transportation, U.S. House of Representatives, 98th Congress, First Session.
5. Statement by Congressman Norman Y. Mineta, in Proceedings of Cabin Safety Conference and Workshop, December 11–14, 1984, Flight Safety Foundation, DOT/FAA/ASF100-85/01, August 1985, p. 9.
6. Aviation Safety (FAA's Near Midair Collision Reporting System and the Proposed Boeing-747 Overwing Exit Removal), Hearings Before the Subcommittee on Investigations and Oversight of the Committee on Public Works and Transportation, U.S. House of Representatives, 99th Congress, First Session, June 1985.
7. TWA Flight Attendants' Strike—Cabin Safety, Hearing Before a Subcommittee of the Committee on Government Operations, House of Representatives, 99th Congress, Second Session, April 10, 1986.
8. Boeing's Proposal to Remove Overwing Exits from 747-Series Aircraft, Hearing Before the Subcommittee on Investigations and Oversight of the Committee on Public Works and Transportation, U.S. House of Representatives, 100th Congress, Second Session, March 2, 1988, p. 60.
9. Development of Improved Fire Safety Standards Adopted by the Federal Aviation Administration by C.P. Sarkos in Aircraft Fire Safety, AGARD Conference Proceedings No. 467, NATO, October 1989.
10. Sarkos, AGARD Conference Proceedings No. 467.
11. Sarkos, AGARD Conference Proceedings No. 467.
12. 49 FR 37111.
13. Summary Report—Full Scale Transport Controlled Impact Demonstration, FAA TC, DOT/FAA-CT87/10, September 1987.
14. Amdt 25-51/121-155.
15. NPRM 86-11.
16. Amdt 25-64.
17. The Increasing Importance of the Biomechanics of Impact Trauma, Murray MacKay, Sādhanā, Vol. 32, Part 4, August 2007, p. 397.
18. Amdt 25-64.
19. NPRM 88-8.
20. Report of the Civil Aeronautics Board of the Investigation of an Accident Involving Civil Aircraft of the United States NC 15376 Which Occurred in San Juan Harbor, Puerto Rico, On October 3, 1941, 5106-41, Released January 16, 1942.
21. In Part 41, 1963 and 1964 in Parts 42 and 40 respectively.
22. CAR 41.174, 1963.
23. Aircraft Accident Report, United Airlines, Flight 232, McDonnell Douglas DC-10-10, Sioux Gateway Airport, Sioux City, Iowa, July 19, 1989, NTSB-AAR-90/06, November 1, 1990.

24 Aircraft Accident Report, Avianca, the Airline of Colombia, Boeing 707-321B, HK 2016, Fuel Exhaustion, Cove Neck, New York, January 25, 1990, NTSB-AAR-91/04, Adopted April 30, 1992.
25 A Bill to Amend the Federal Aviation At of 1958 to Require the Use of Child Safety Restraint Systems Approved by the Secretary of Transportation on Commercial Aircraft, in the House of Representatives, H.R.4025, 101st Congress, February 20, 1990.
26 NPRM 90-6.
27 NTSB Recommendation A-90-78.
28 Child Restraint Systems on Aircraft, Hearing Before the Subcommittee on Aviation of the Committee on Public Works and Transportation, U.S. House of Representatives, 101st Congress, Second Session, July 12, 1990, p. 62.
29 Child Restraint Systems on Aircraft, p. 127.
30 Amdt 121-230.
31 Child Restraint Systems on Aircraft, p. 291.
32 Amdt 121-255.
33 Infant and Child Restraint Research, Roger N. Hardy, Cranfield Impact Centre, in Proceedings of the European Cabin Safety Conference 1990, CAP 583, April 1991, p. 131.
34 Amdt 121-185; Amdt 25-74.
35 In-Flight Aircraft Seat Fire Extinguishing Tests (Cabin Hazard Measurements), DOT/FAA/CT-82/111, Richard G. Hill, Louise C. Speitel, December 1982.
36 Amdt 121-185.
37 Optimization of Aircraft Seat Cushion Fire Blocking Layers, D.A. Kourtides, J.A. Parker, A.C. Ling, W.R. Hovatter, NASA Ames Research Center, DOT/FAA/CT-82-132, March 1983.
38 NPRM 83-14.
39 Amdt 25-59, 121-184.
40 Fatal Civil Aircraft Accidents, Their Medical and Pathological Investigation, Peter J. Stevens, 1970, p. 55.
41 NRPM 75-10 Proposal 2-91.
42 Amdt 25-38.
43 NPRM 75-31 Proposal 8-54.
44 Amdt 25-54.
45 NPRM 85-17.
46 Amdt 121-193, 121-204.
47 Amdt 121-220.
48 Aviation Investigation Report Runway Overrun and Fire Air France Airbus A340-313 F-GLZQ Toronto/Lester B. Pearson International Airport, Ontario 02 August 2005, Transportation Safety Board of Canada, Report Number A05H0002, Released 16 October 2007, p. 114.
49 Interior Materials, James M. Peterson, in International Aircraft Occupant Safety Conference and Workshop, Proceedings, Final Report, DOT/FAA/OV-89-2, August 1989, p. 189.
50 AAIB 8/88, p. 146.
51 NPRM 85-10.
52 NPRM 85-10.
53 NPRM 85-10A.
54 NPRM 85-10.
55 Amdt 25-61/121-189.
56 51 FR 26166.
57 Amdt 25-66.
58 Slow Progress in Making Aircraft Cabin Interiors Fireproof, General Accounting Office, January 1993, GAO/RCED-93-37.
59 NPRM 83-15.
60 Text of the final rule, not of the proposal, although differences are textual only.
61 Amdt 25-58, 121-183.
62 Floor Proximity Emergency Escape Path Marking, Advisory Circular 25.812-1, U.S. Department of Transportation, Federal Aviation Administration, September 30, 1985.
63 Task Force on Emergency Evacuation of Transport Airplanes, Volume II—Supporting Documentation, DOT/FAA/VS-86/1,II, July 1986, p. 252.
64 Correspondence with Yves Morier, 30 July 2024.
65 NPRM 87-5.
66 NPRM 87-10.
67 Amdt 25-67/121-205.

68 NPRM 90-4.
69 [No Subject], Letter Thomas McSweeney, Director Aircraft Certification Service, FAA, to Klaus Koplin, Secretary General, JAA, May 22, 1996.
70 DOT/FAA/VS-86/1,II, p. 365.
71 DOT/FAA/VS-86/1,II, p. 365.
72 NPRM 90-4.
73 NPRM 90-4.
74 NPRM 90-4.
75 Amdt 25-88.
76 Uniform Distribution of Exits, Advisory Circular 25.807-1, U.S. Department of Transportation, Federal Aviation Administration, August 13, 1990.
77 Amdt 121-176.
78 DOT/FAA/VS-86/1,II, p. 365.
79 DOT/FAA/VS-86/1,II, p. 378.
80 NPRM 90-4/Amdt 25-88.
81 Amdt 121-188.
82 46 FR 42278.
83 NPRM 85-9.
84 Airliner Cabin Safety and Health Standards.
85 NPRM 85-9, Amdt 121-188.
86 Amdt 121-236.
87 Special Study, Safety Aspects of Emergency Evacuations from Air Carrier Aircraft, NTSB-AAS-74-3, November 13, 1974.
88 NPRM 81-1, Proposal No. 11-7.
89 NPRM 86-5.
90 Amdt 25-70/121-209.

14 Different Opinions among Authorities

ABSTRACT

Since the first wave, when cabin safety started to properly develop, the U.S. has been leading in both research and development. Many other countries copy-pasted. However, in some countries, differences appeared. This was because they found developments in the U.S. too slow, responded to accidents in their country, or had a different opinion as to how to approach cabin safety challenges. An example of the first was regulating the number of cabin attendants. Two countries (Australia and Canada) around 1960 established ratios before the U.S. did. An example of an accident driving a country to introduce rules more specific than the U.S. was the United Kingdom following the 1985 Manchester accident. The subject was Type III exits and its 'self-help hatches'. Examples of different opinions were the method of restraining lap infants, the temporary deactivation of exits, especially on single-aisle airplanes, and the supply provisions of oxygen. But there were more.

14.1 INTRODUCTION

Primitive as they were, the first cabin safety measures were developed in Europe, as discussed in Chapter 3. The nascent U.S. airline industry in 1928 even went there to learn the trade, as narrated in Chapter 1. But as soon as air transport in the 1930s in the U.S. developed, they took the lead.

After World War Two, cabin safety research took place in several facilities across the U.S. The development of regulations domiciled in Washington, D.C. Even in cabin safety accidents the U.S. led.

Other countries copy-pasted the U.S. regulations. But not in all cases. In some areas, opinions differed. This concerned all domains except fire protection. In the domain of impact protection, there was the question about infant lap belts, and whether or not crash loads should be combined. Probably the domain where there were the most differences was escape potential: Type III exits split the U.S. and Europe, and so did the issue of dispatch relief for unserviceable exits. Europe developed the green running man as an alternative to the U.S. red exit sign. In life support, there were different opinions about flotation cushions and oxygen supply. A domain not discussed elsewhere, but with cabin safety implications and different opinions, is security. And then, last but not least, there is the group of cabin professionals for which there is no common name, a sign of a difference of opinion in itself.

14.2 IMPACT PROTECTION

14.2.1 INFANT SUPPLEMENTAL LOOP BELT

As discussed in Section 13.5.1.3, the FAA never allowed infants to be restrained by a loop belt. In other parts of the world such a belt was the preferred, and in Europe even the mandated, means of restraint, other than when the infant is in a dedicated restraint attached to a separate seat.

In the U.S., it has long been acknowledged that adults were unable to hold on to an infant when held loose in their arms. An example was a six-month-old infant in a Douglas DC-9 that crashed in Denver in November 1987. His mother could not hold him and while she survived, her infant died from blunt trauma. In the same accident, a father, seated in the last row, exceptionally was able to hold on to his six-week-old infant who was the only occupant not injured at all in that accident.[1] But, generally, the FAA accepted that 'a lap-held infant must be considered as an unrestrained flying missile'. It considered this option preferable to the injuries that a loop belt-restrained infant would suffer.[2]

14.2.2 CRASH LOADS

In Europe, unlike the U.S., it was common to combine crash loads. This meant that the loads in the X, Y, and Z directions (longitudinal, lateral, vertical) needed to be combined:[3]

> All combinations of inertia forces (which are expressed as accelerations) in the following ranges up to a maximum resultant of 9g are experienced, taking the forces in each case as relative to the aeroplane—
>
> 4.5g downward to 2.0g upward
> 9g forward to 1.5 rearward
> zero to 1.5 sideways.

When JAR-25 was copy-pasted from FAR-25, this was one of the differences. In an early move toward transatlantic harmonization, this requirement was deleted in 1989 from JAR-25.[4] Conversely, in July 1997, the FAA adopted the JAA practice to apply the 1.33 safety factor to the loads for restraining items of mass which, when coming loose, could injure occupants.[5] This was restricted to those items which were frequently removed during normal operation, such as quick-change interior items. Until then, the FAA only applied the 1.33 factor to seat and safety belt attachments.

14.3 ESCAPE POTENTIAL

14.3.1 DISPATCH RELIEF

The 1967 regulation change that required slides to deploy and inflate automatically on door opening brought a dramatic change to the speed at which exits and slides of the widebodies would be ready for use. These widebodies, such as the Boeing 747, the Douglas DC-10, and the Lockheed L-1011, all entering the market in the years 1970–1972, happened to be the first group of aircraft affected. While this meant a great safety enhancement, it had its drawbacks in normal airline operations. When a flight attendant, or perhaps catering staff, operated a door when still armed, that is with the slide engaged, there was no way back. The door would open power-assisted and the slide would inflate. On previous aircraft models, flight attendants could at an early stage sense that the slide was about to deploy and stop the process. The new wide bodies however were unforgiving. The number of times that they, perhaps distracted, lapsed in checking or registering the door armed/disarmed status was countless. When there was no spare slide available, U.S. airlines called their FAA Principal Operations Inspector (POI) begging for relief. The FAA began an unofficial policy of granting one-time, verbal/telegraphic approvals to permit airlines to 'get home' with an inoperative slide.[6] A key item was that seats in the cabin section of the unusable exit were blocked. Fewer passengers could be carried, but at least the flight could go.

This policy was formalized in October 1976 under FAA Administrator John McLucas, for the aircraft types mentioned. It was said that he did so after receiving a call from Continental's president Robert Six who had a DC-10 stuck at Miami and National Airlines refused to loan him a replacement slide. In 1978 the policy was extended to the Airbus A300. 'This relief was granted to allow these airplanes, which had new technology, automatically deploying and inflating slides to minimize the economic penalties for having service personnel inadvertently deploying slides due to unfamiliarity'.[7] One of the considerations for allowing relief was that 're-supplying AOG parts, or ferrying aircraft from distant airports, was a costly proposition', especially for large-capacity aircraft.[8]

Outside the U.S., airlines faced the same problem and local authorities acted in the same way as the FAA POIs: they granted relief on a case-by-case basis. The number of passengers to be refused boarding was thus determined quite haphazardly. More importantly, authorities other than the FAA allowed this practice not only for twin-aisle aircraft but for single-aisle aircraft as well. France, already in 1970, had issued general guidelines for dispatch relief.[9]

The U.S. airlines, aware of this, in 1992, had their trade organization, the Air Transport Association plea for an extension of the policy to other twin-aisle airplanes with less than eight exits (such as the

767) as well as single-aisle airplanes. They all had their sob stories of aircraft that got stuck because of deployed slides. And often not of their own employee doing. Customs personnel, medical personnel, and police/security personnel had all been known to open doors and inflate slides.[10] An example came from American Trans Air. In July 1993, it had a 757 that got grounded in Dhahran, Saudi Arabia, because the cleaning crew inadvertently opened the aft right door. The FAA did not grant a relief and the airline had to charter a Lear Jet to bring in a spare slide from Germany. The delay was thus kept limited to 13 hours; the costs for the airline were $ 40K. The passenger load for the 218-seat aircraft was only 106, so well safe to carry on by European standards with one exit less.

The FAA initially was open to the idea and drafted a Master Minimum Equipment List (MMEL) policy letter proposal in April 1993. Opposition was however voiced by several unions as well as a consumer advocacy group and the FAA relented half way. They did extend the policy to other twin-aisle aircraft but refused it for single-aisle aircraft. The reason they used is that the second aisle gives redundancy. This rationale was difficult to understand for rational-minded persons, like engineers. It seemed there was an element of emotion here: 'In an emergency it is vital to have every exit usable to ensure the survivability of our passengers and crew members', one flight attendant union said.[11]

The Europeans followed a different logic, which in fact was based on principles lent from the U.S. They considered that it is not the number of aisles that determined the evacuation capacity, but the number of exits as per the tables of FAR 25.807. An example was the Boeing 737 in combi configuration: the forward floor-level exits were inactive as they were in the cargo section. From the wing to the rear there were overwing and aft exits that allowed a number of passengers consistent with the 25.807 table: one pair of Type Is and one, or two, pairs of Type IIIs good for 79 or 109 passengers, respectively (and even 5 more because of the inflatable slide grandfather clause). Similarly, a Boeing 737–400 (in I-IIII-III-I configuration) with one Type III exit inoperative was like a Boeing 737–500 (with I-III-I exit configuration), for which a lower seating capacity had been certificated.

But also in Europe, it had evolved gradually. In 1988, Fokker, responding to questions from its customers, the airlines, proposed an MMEL change to allow dispatch relief for inoperative exits of the Fokker 100. It took the *Rijksluchtvaartdienst* (RLD, the Dutch CAA) one and a half years to study it, before issuing an approval. It then took one and a half days for them to withdraw it again. What had happened that changed their mind so quickly? Fokker had sent the request to the RLD's airworthiness department, as they were responsible for MMEL approvals. But on the day it sent its approval to Fokker, it informed its Flight Operations colleagues, who oversaw the airlines, the equivalent of FAA POIs. They objected to the MMEL approval, arguing that such approvals should be done on a case-by-case basis and not per MMEL. Critics said that perhaps there was an element of professional status involved as well. It took 25 more years before Fokker received its MMEL approval, now from EASA.

In the period 2001–2003, the JAA Cabin Safety Study Group, together with groups responsible for MMEL policies, drafted a policy paper on the subject. That was eventually included in EASA's CS-MMEL. It set a detailed policy for allowing dispatch relief for a door or exit on any aircraft, be it twin-aisle, or single-aisle, large or small, used by a European airline. One of the elements of the complex guidelines was that type certification data should be consulted. This led to some airlines making seemingly inexplicable decisions. One airline is known to have in its procedures for an unusable forward pair of A320 Type I exits to block not only the first 15 rows in the forward cabin, which makes sense, but also one row half way in the aft section, which is quite odd. Apparently, they based this on the evacuation demonstration, where on that day some evacuees from the rear cabin bypassed the overwing exits and egressed via the forward exit.

Thirty years on, the FAA and Europe still have different opinions. Not only on the principal matter of allowing or not dispatch relief for single-aisle aircraft but also on determining how many seats should be blocked. The U.S. policy is straightforward. It says that 'All passenger seats halfway to the next exit in each direction from the inoperative door, across the entire width of the airplane, shall be blocked' and 'seated capacity must not exceed rated capacity of remaining pairs of exits'.[12] The Europeans have a different approach which involves a multi-step, multi-variable analysis that is quite complex and needs expert cabin safety knowledge. They also differ as to the duration of the relief. The Americans prescribe one flight day; the Europeans five flights.

14.3.2 Type III Exits

14.3.2.1 Manchester 1985

Until late 1985 Type III exits were not particularly topical. That changed when information became available about what had happened in the 22 August Manchester accident. The Boeing 737–200 was equipped with two Type III exits, one on either side above the wing, in addition to four floor-level exits at the cabin ends. The left overwing exit, on the side of the fire, remained closed. Next to the right exit sat a young female. The investigator's report says:[13]

> The female in seat 10F adjacent to the right overwing hatch, upon being exhorted by passengers behind to open the door, undid her seat belt and turned in her seat to face the hatch. She saw the 'Emergency Pull' instruction at the top of the hatch, but pulled at the armrest which was fixed to the lower area of the hatch. She was not familiar with the opening procedure and unaware if the door was hinged at the top, bottom, left or right, or if it would come straight off. Her female friend in seat 10E stood up and pulled at the release handle adjacent to the instruction. The hatch, which weighed 48 lbs [22 kg], fell inboard across the chest of the passenger in 10F, trapping her in her seat. She managed to get out from under the door and a male passenger sitting behind her assisted by lifting the hatch over the back of row 10, depositing it on the vacant seat 11D. This exit was seen to be open by about 45 seconds after the aircraft stopped. The two female passenger escaped onto the right wing and both jumped down from the leading edge, the passenger from seat 10E twisting her ankle.

The subsequent use of this exit was chaotic due to the dense, black, toxic, very hot smoke inside the cabin. The path toward the exit was narrow and partly blocked as the back rest of seat 10F was pushed forward. 'Very rapidly the area around the overwing exit became a mass of bodies pushing forward to the exit'.[14] Including the two girls, two young children being carried and a 16-year-old boy pulled clear by a fireman (and the last survivor out through this exit), 27 passengers escaped from this exit. Thirty-eight were later found dead in this area. Within four weeks after the accident, the AAIB sent a letter to the CAA recommending a review of the approval of the cabin configuration with respect to access to the overwing exit and recommending that all row 10 seats be removed.[15]

14.3.2.2 Initial Response by UK CAA

The Manchester accident dramatically exposed the inherent risk posed by emergency exits consisting of hatches that were designed to be removed by uninformed, let alone trained, passengers. It also exposed the frailties of a narrow escape path to such exits. The accident caused authorities and manufacturers alike to focus on the adequacy of the Type III overwing hatches as an emergency exit. That is, in Europe. The UK Civil Aviation Authority was the first to act. In January 1986 it issued an airworthiness notice (AN No. 79) calling for increased access to the exits by either widening to at least 10 inch (25.4 cm) the path between seats from the aisle to the exits (and not having that path encroach beyond the center line of the exits; see Figure 14.1) or by removing the seat next to them (the outboard seats removed—OBR—option) (see Figure 14.2).[16]

Previously, there were no requirements for the passageway width. Access to the Type III exits is measured as the distance between the aftmost edge of the forward seat's backrest and the foremost edge of the aft seat's cushion. Thus, it measures the vertical projection of the space available. In reality, owing to the shape of seat backs, more space will be available, but of relatively little use to evacuees. In addition, the CAA required such measures as fixing seat backs to prevent climbing over and so ensure a single, uninterrupted line of evacuees from aisle to exit. Or, in the OBR case, two lines that merge at the exit. To prevent passengers from getting stuck, gaps in seat pans had to be eliminated. The seat back fixing and seat pan measures were aimed at increasing the rate of egress, but the purpose of the access width increase was to enable better opening of the hatch, not to

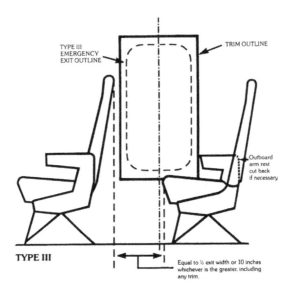

FIGURE 14.1 Minimum access dimension to Type III exit as described in AN 79 (UK CAA).

FIGURE 14.2 Outboard seat-removed configuration and displaced hatch, Boeing 737 (photograph by the author).

increase the egress rate.[17] In the 737 the hatch could best be opened from a standing position, hence the wider passageway or, alternatively, the removal of the outboard seat.

Other than by providing more space for the person to open the hatch, the notice did not aim at improving the ease of operation of Type III exits. It neither called for reducing the mass of the hatch, nor improved its handling characteristics, nor asked for restricting occupancy next to these exits to certain categories of persons only. The only other means to ease the opening was an instruction placard on the hatch and seat backs showing how to open it (see figure 14.3 on page 214).

The airworthiness notice's legal applicability range was limited to UK airlines but it was copied by several other countries that followed UK regulations. France introduced a standard in March 1987 which only copied the dimensional measures of AN 79.[18]

The airworthiness notice was an initial, temporary measure. The CAA intended to issue more elaborate regulations but appreciated that these had to be based on proper research rather than intuition. Recognizing that what had happened on board the 737 must have been a struggle for life, the CAA looked for an organization that could do tests that replicated the situation of people competing to get out. The Cranfield Institute of Technology, located north of London near Milton Keynes, had an aircraft and an expert department. The aircraft was a surplus Hawker Siddeley Trident Three, parked outside the campus. The department was the Applied Psychology Unit of the College of Aeronautics, led by Professor Helen Muir. She set up a test program of evacuations from the Trident in which an element of competition was added. That was done by promising the first half out a monetary bonus. It was quite amazing what people were willing to do to earn a £5 note. The first tests were run in 1988. In April of that year, Cranfield asked for volunteers, announcing that 'all who participate will receive £10, and the first 50 per cent of passengers off the aircraft on each evacuation will receive an additional £5'.[19] Non-competitive tests were done as well for comparison reasons. The initial set of tests was run with single-row access widths to a Type III exit of 3 inch (7.6 cm, the baseline), 13 inch (33 cm), 18 inch (46 cm), 25 inch (63.5), and 34 inch (86 cm). Separately, tests were done with two rows, and the outboard seat-removed configuration. So, where the CAA additionally thought more space would help the opening of the hatch, in the Cranfield tests the wider space was primarily for quicker egress.

The initial tests confirmed the intuitive notion that egress rates increased with wider passageways. But, surprisingly, this only worked up to 13 inch. The increase was particularly prominent in the competitive tests, with a 66% improvement over the baseline width, but less in the non-competitive tests. Beyond that, there was no further gain, and at wider widths egress rates even became longer due to two persons trying to pass at the same time.

European aircraft manufacturers Airbus and Fokker observed the tests and found a need for further tests between 3 and 13 inch. Together with Saab and Aerospatiale (for the ATR) they funded tests at widths of 6 and 10 inch (15.2 and 25.4 cm) that would fit their aircraft models. Those tests showed that 10 inch was actually even slightly better than 13 inch, while at 6 inch the results were not better than for 3 inch.[20]

Later, Helen Muir did further competitive tests with non-toxic smoke brought into the cabin and to determine the influence of hatch weight on opening performance.[21] Her competitive tests program ran for many years, and at some stage the Trident was replaced by an ex-British Airways Boeing 737–200 fuselage, parked indoors. Other evacuation elements such as the behavior and influence of cabin crewmembers, either assertive or non-assertive, were tested in 1994 in the 737. Assertive behavior, in this respect, meant cabin crewmembers 'calling volunteers to exits and actively pushing them through exits as rapidly as possible in a highly active but non-aggressive manner'. 'Non-assertive behavior involved asking volunteers to come to exits and only giving physical assistance when someone was in danger of falling'.[22] In one of the last tests, the effects of briefing passengers at Type III exits on exit opening speed and correct hatch disposal were investigated.[23]

14.3.2.3 Initial Response by European Manufacturers

Airbus in 1986 was in the advanced stages of developing its first single-aisle product. Initially simply known as 'SA' (for single aisle), it had been named in 1981 as the Airbus A320. The first sketches released by Airbus showed three floor-level exits on each side but, soon after the middle exit pair, located just behind the wing, was replaced by two Type III exits over the wing on each side.[24] Motivated by the Manchester accident and the UK Airworthiness Notice Airbus looked again at the design of those exits. It conducted a research and development program involving about 100 test sequences, typically engaging five persons each. Many variables were tested, including acoustic and flashing light options, different hatch colors, several designs of hatch opening handles, handle cover, and lower handle (grip). The program allowed Airbus to choose optimum designs and dimensions for the handle, grip, and exit trim panel. The acoustic and light features were not adopted as they proved counter-productive. The most important discriminant affecting hatch operation appeared to be its mass. The final hatch as engineered by Airbus weighed only 14.5 kg. Compared to the starting mass of 21 kg the improvement in ease of operation performance was amazing, in particular for female operators.[25] Later, Airbus also did egress rate tests.

Fokker at the time was designing a stretch of its F-28 model, the Fokker 100. Like its predecessor, the Fokker 100 had a pair of Type III exits over the wing on each side which were kept unchanged. Like Airbus, Fokker embarked on a program to improve their handling characteristics. A major difference with the 737 was that in the smaller F-28 and Fokker 100, the hatch could best be opened from a seated rather than a standing position. Creating space as intended by AN 79 would therefore not help. Fokker changed the contour of the trim panel, replaced the armrest with an assist handle, and improved the design of the lower pins that held the hatch in place. As the main hatch design stemmed from the F-28 days and could not be altered, no major mass reduction was feasible, but it could still be reduced from 16 kg to 15.5 kg.[26] When UK airlines were interested in acquiring the Fokker 100, a debate started about compliance with AN 79. The CAA stance was that as long as Fokker could demonstrate that the Fokker 100's exit was equal to or better than that of the 737, it was fine. That could either be done by comparing the two in a Latin Square test, or, alternatively, by using a 'simulated incapacitated person' seated adjacent to the exit. As Fokker had no access to a 737, it chose the latter option and hired an anthropomorphic dummy normally used for car crash tests. In a series of tests more than 200 naive persons were employed, of which 62 opened the exit across the dummy seated in the outboard position. The tests showed that the exit could still quickly be opened without first having to drag that person away. As Airbus had found, Fokker saw that the light mass of the hatch was a key aspect of good opening performance.

14.3.2.4 The U.S. Acts

On the U.S. side, the FAA and manufacturers remained silent, or so it seemed. In 1989, the FAA proposed a new requirement that prohibited certain passengers from seating in an exit row.[27] The motivation for this was not the tragedy of Manchester. Rather, it was the introduction of the Air Carrier Access Act of 1986. That act prohibited discrimination in air transportation on the basis of handicap. However, for safety reasons, an exception could be made provided that it was properly regulated. The FAA at the time gave airlines the right to refuse transportation and draft their own procedures. This however was not a proper regulation for the purpose of the Air Carrier Access Act, so the FAA had to be more forthcoming. That is what the proposed rule for exit row seating was about. It generated many comments and when the final rule was issued, in March 1990, it was accompanied by a host of pages of response, underlining what the FAA said in its introduction:[28]

> The issues addressed by the rule, are among the most difficult and controversial ever addressed by the FAA for they require, in the interest of what is essential for the safety of all passengers, that some passengers be treated differently from other passengers, depending on their physical abilities.

There was mention of accidents, but only those that had occurred in the U.S. or to a U.S. airline abroad. Manchester was far away. The rule itself was equally elaborate in that it in minute detail specified who could occupy an exit row seat and who could not. It also required flight attendants to verify that indeed passengers in exit rows were 'able-bodied'. U.S. airlines copy-pasted verbatim the text of the rule on their safety cards.

The Type III exit safety issues that the Manchester accident so dramatically exposed in 1985 started to be more widely recognized in the U.S. when a similar accident happened on U.S. soil. That was on February 1, 1991. A Boeing 737 landing at Los Angeles airport (LAX) collided with a commuter aircraft and caught fire. Inside, the scenario was as follows:[29]

> About 37 passengers escaped via the right overwing emergency exit. Their egress was hampered by the passenger seated in seat 10-F who stated that she was frightened and 'froze', and was unable to leave her seat or open the window next to her. The male passenger seated in 11-D climbed over the 10-E seatback and opened the overwing exit; he pushed the passenger seated in 10-F out the window and onto the wing

and then followed her. During the subsequent evacuation through the right overwing exit, two male passengers had an altercation at the open exit that lasted several seconds.

The outboard seatback at 10-F adjacent to the right overwing exit was found folded forward after the accident blocking approximately 25 percent of the exit opening. The retaining bolt at the seat's pivot point was sheared. The timing of this occurrence could not be determined.

Passengers seated around row 10 stated that prior to departure the flight attendant assigned to the R-1 position interviewed a young passenger who was seated in 10-D about whether he could fulfill the duties of an able-bodied person in the event of an emergency. The passenger advised the flight attendant that he was 17 years old; however, to be sure that the youth understood his responsibilities, the flight attendant conducted a special oral briefing for the persons seated in and around row 10. Passengers stated that the instructions provided by the R-1 flight attendant aided in their evacuation.

It is interesting to note the similarities between Manchester and LAX. The passenger in 10F, next to the hatch, was unable to open it, a passenger one row behind assisting, and doing this from the 10E position, the seat back of 10F folding forward and partially blocking the opening. What was different in LAX was the prior briefing of the passengers of row 10. Undoubtedly this was inspired by the 1990 rule on exit row seating and the need for verification by the crew.

And then, within months of the LAX accident, the FAA issued an NPRM for better access to Type III exits.[30] The investigation was still going on and no details had been made public. The NPRM did not mention the accident but rather said that it was work left over from the 1985 Seattle conference. It proposed wider passageways toward Type III exits, not only for future aircraft types (via FAR 25), but also for the existing fleet (via FAR 121). In a move away from tradition, the FAA acknowledged cabin safety rules coming from outside the U.S. The NPRM referred to CAA's Airworthiness Notice No. 79 (AN 79), but the proposal put forward was based on research from U.S. soil. CAMI had done some testing on Type III exit access in the period 1987–1989 (the report gave no date). The test article was a right-hand side Type III exit from a salvaged Boeing 720 section.[31] Four configurations were tested. A baseline of 6 inch (15.2 cm) met the then existing regulations, the two AN 79 options (10 inch—25.4 cm—passageway and the outboard seat-removed option) and a configuration with a 20 inch (51 cm) wide access path with an encroachment of 5 inch (12.7 cm). Encroachment in this respect meant how far the leading edge of the seat bottom cushion of the seat aft of the exit protruded forward of the aft vertical edge of the exit opening. The number of subjects in each test was 36 as there were no more seats available. No flight attendants were employed to shout instructions or urge test subjects to hurry up. An improvement of up to 14% was seen for two of the configurations (20-inch and outboard seats removed) compared to the baseline. The main focus of the NPRM (and the CAMI tests) was on access to the exits, not on ease of operation, although some hatch removal and disposal tests were done as well. These tests showed that test subjects varied in how they disposed of the exit. In some cases the hatch was left leaning against the wall partially blocking the exit. But as in those handling tests egress was not included and thus not mentally factored in by the subjects, their validity can be questioned. Leaning on the 14% improvement score, it was proposed that for all aircraft with 20 passenger seats or more only the 20-inch passageway or the outboard seat-removed option would be acceptable.

Comments poured in. As often, they could be sorted into three groups: (1) individuals whose aviation affiliation is that of frequent flyer who typically express support for stronger safety rules, (2) the aviation industry (airlines and manufacturers) who have detailed technical responses and warn that the FAA estimates the costs too low, and (3) unions who say that the proposed rules do not go far enough. A fourth group, foreign aviation authorities, is less predictable but tends to support their national interests.

In this case, almost in unison, representatives of the smaller aircraft communities reminded the FAA that not all aircraft are jets with three seats on either side of the aisle but that there are many smaller aircraft with Type III exits that already have a comfortably better exit-to-passenger ratio than the larger aircraft. Many airlines argued that they would have to remove seats from the aircraft to comply with the rule. Many also questioned the limited testing of CAMI, not only in terms of the number of variables but also its technical representativeness. Not all Type III exits are the same, have the same wall curvature, step-up and step-down height, give the same maneuvering room (as e.g. limited by overhead bins), or indeed have access paths lined by three seats. No testing was done between 10 and 20 inch, while for airlines that information would be very useful. Some even questioned whether the 20-inch passageway as tested was in fact 20 inch as the illustration in the CAMI report suggested it was much less. Many referred to the tests done in the United Kingdom which were competitive and should therefore be taken more seriously than the clinical CAMI tests. One of the commenters was the JAA who provided Cranfield data that showed that even for the baseline configuration (a passageway width of only 3 inch) a 26.5% improvement was reached by simply fixing the seat backs bordering the passageway. They argued that this element was missing in the proposed rule.

The FAA did not wait for the accident investigation report of LAX. It quickly followed up the NPRM with a final rule in May 1992.[32] The smaller aircraft community was listened to: the applicability discriminant was raised from 20 seats to 60 seats. Also, for two seaters (as opposed to three seaters), a reduced passageway width of 10 inch was allowed. The FAA had asked CAMI to run some tests with two seaters to substantiate this. Thus, the economic pain for many airlines vanished. But even for those that remained affected, the impact was much less than feared. The rule included an option for alternative compliance when the rule would otherwise have meant loss of seats and the FAA appeared quite flexible. Even when the seat pitch of all other rows was reduced by 1 inch (2.54 cm) and this would not free sufficient inches to widen the exit rows, the FAA would accept deviations. The FAA did not follow up on the JAA's suggestion to fix seat backs or copy other measures that the CAA had taken to prevent evacuees from being delayed while attempting to get out.

After the publication of the rule, and acknowledging comments that the test basis was too small, FAA commissioned CAMI to do further tests. This time the test article was their Douglas C-124 fuselage. More passageway widths were tested than previously and now included a 13 inch (33 cm) width which came out equal in performance to the 20 inch (51 cm).[33] This matched with what Cranfield had found in their competitive tests. The setting was non-competitive, although CAMI employed what they called 'competitive cooperation', in which the three top performers in a series of tests would receive an unspecified bonus.

14.3.2.5 Europe Differs in Opinion

In Europe, the NPRM did not land well. Where previously Europe tended to follow the U.S. in cabin safety rule updates, this time the JAA decided not to do that. It was felt that the 20-inch passageway

FIGURE 14.3 Boeing 757 hatch operation instruction with weight statement (photograph by the author).

width did not match the Cranfield test results and would be too onerous. And, although not explicitly stated, there was the hatch mass issue. Airbus had gone to great lengths to obtain a very low mass for its A320 hatches. Fokker also had managed to arrive at an acceptable mass. But the U.S. products kept their heavy hatches. Although the mass of the 737 hatch had been reduced from 21.5 kg on the original 737–200 to a more modest 17 kg on the Classic (-300/-400/-500), the Boeing 767 hatch was reported as weighing 27 (60 lbs) to 30 kg (67 lbs.), clearly something not manageable by the average 'naive passenger'.

The JAA asked its newly formed Cabin Safety Study Group (CSSG), in which the various national authorities worked together with the manufacturing industry and cabin crew unions, to come up with a European proposal. The CSSG formed in 1992 an ad-hoc subgroup. It started with identifying three phases for Type III exit operation:

- Awareness and responsibility—the person seated next to the exit must be aware that he or she is responsible for, and capable of, opening the exit
- Removing and disposing the hatch (ease of operation)
- Passage through seats and egress through the opening (egress rate)

With these distinct phases in mind, the group continued to work and after nine meetings, in 1995 the CSSG presented a comprehensive set of rules that addressed measures covering all three phases. It consisted of design rule change proposals for both future type designs (JAR 25) and the existing fleet (JAR-26) but also proposed operational procedures (JAR-OPS). Notably, it formulated three sets of occupancy rules: ensured occupancy (so that there always sits someone next to a Type III exit, who is deemed physically capable of handling it), preferred occupancy (by promoting that excess cabin crew or deadheading crew sit in exit rows) and denied occupancy (similar to what the FAA introduced in 1990). The design rules were published as a Notice of Proposed Amendment (NPA) with a comment period of early 1997, but the operational rules were found not suitable yet. Only a watered-down version with interpretative and explanatory material was put out for public consultation.[34]

Comments came in along the lines as sketched earlier for FAA's NPRM, except that several commenters, both from American industry and some European authorities were opposed to the entire set and pleaded for harmonization with the FAA.

14.3.2.6 Second NPRM

Meanwhile, the FAA in 1995 had issued a second NPRM on the subject, called 'Revised access to Type III exits'.[35] As mentioned, FAA CAMI had done further tests which showed that a 13-inch passageway was as good as a 20-inch one. This NPRM therefore proposed to formally reduce the 20-inch requirement for a three-seater into a 13-inch requirement. Based on the CAMI results, the FAA had issued exemptions to the rule, allowing airlines to use a 13-inch passageway width instead of 20 inch. The NTSB, in 2000, as part of a safety study on emergency evacuation, criticized the way CAMI had run the tests, citing several test design flaws—'such as the use of a flight attendant at the exit and no consideration given to exit hatch removal times', and recommended additional tests.[36]

CAMI indeed did so, reported in 2002, which not only addressed the design flaws observed by the NTSB but was much more comprehensive than previous tests done by CAMI.[37] It showed that the 20-inch passageway was marginally better than the 13-inch passageway but identified many other variables that more significantly influenced individual egress times, such as gender, age, and waist size of participants. The FAA did not progress the NPRM into a rule; it was withdrawn in 2002.[38] The formal reason was that it would be subject to harmonization, but the CAMI results and input by unions and consumer action groups may have been factors as well. Thus, the 20-inch width requirement remained the rule. In practice, however, few if any U.S. airlines with six abreast cabin layouts applied the 20-inch passageway width. For the two main airplane types affected—the Boeing 737 family and the Airbus A320 family—the manufacturers eventually obtained exemptions which allowed a 13-inch passageway width.[39]

14.3.2.7 Boeing versus JAA

In 1995, Boeing was in the process of updating the Boeing 737. The Boeing 737 Next Generation (737–700, 737–800, later also 737–600 and 737–900, collectively 737NG) was a derivative of the previous generation with improved engines and better performance. It was a direct competitor to the Airbus A320, which had a maximum passenger seating capacity, as determined by the exits, of 179.

Being a derivative, the Boeing 737NG profited from certification grandfather rights for passenger capacity, allowing ten extra seats for the inflatable escape slides at the four floor-level exits. Thus, although the exit configuration was identical to that of the A320, it was allowed 189 passengers instead of 179. At least, in the U.S. When Boeing offered it for certification with the JAA, it was told that it could no longer use that privilege, which dated back three decades. Both Boeing and the FAA were not amused. A year before, the FAA and JAA, backed by industry, had formulated and agreed on principles for how to deal with derivatives, called the ICPTF program. ICPTF stands for International Certification Procedures Task Force. It embraced a safety risk matrix model for determining whether or not later design rules should apply to derivatives. Where the FAA found that later design rules need not apply as there was no change to the 737NG's floor-level exits, the JAA disagreed, citing an ICPTF clause about 'overriding safety considerations'. The JAA had decided that the credit system of NPRM 90–4 (see Section 13.5.3.4) now be used. That NPRM however was still a proposal only; it had not yet led to a final rule. Some considered that the JAA was just protecting the A320. The JAA itself considered that the use of this decades-old grandfather right was a disincentive for the use of state-of-the-art solutions. Be that as it may, Boeing faced a problem. The first customers for the high capacity, 189-passenger seat version, were in Europe and thus subject to the dearly needed JAA approval: leisure carriers such as Germania and Hapag-Lloyd that connected their homeland (Germany) with the sun destinations in the Mediterranean area.

With its back against the wall, Boeing went creative. For the floor-level exits, it claimed that they were much larger than required for a Type I, for which the proposed credit was fixed at 45. Along the lines of NPRM 90–4, the JAA granted a credit of 55 (later, this exit size would become the Type C exit). For the 737–700 this resulted in a capacity of 145 (2 × 55 + 35), 4 short of what Boeing wanted. Similarly, for the 737–800 it meant 180 (2 × 55 + 2 × 35), 9 short of Boeing's wishes. To earn the balance, Boeing made the bold step of drastically changing the design of the hatches. It correctly sensed that no longer should their opening be at the mercy of naive passengers who have no clue how to handle them. They designed hatches that hinge at the top, are spring loaded and open by

FIGURE 14.4 Boeing 737NG canopy-style Type III exits (photograph by the author).

activating a single handle. By doing so, they significantly elevated the state-of-the-art for overwing exits. The JAA indeed awarded credit for this novel design such that Boeing reached the desired capacities of 149 and 189. Even though still a semi-plug type door, so sealed in by cabin pressure, Boeing had to add locks and in-flight logic to secure it against passengers inadvertently opening it in-flight. The new hatch design became available in 1997 and was installed on airplanes already assembled and waiting for export to Europe. Another wise decision was to equip all 737NG aircraft with the new hatches and not just those ordered by European carriers.

The whole episode taught Boeing that the world had changed and that the European authorities no longer followed the FAA suit but could have a different opinion.

14.3.2.8 Harmonization?

With the difference in passageway width now cleared and the hatch weight issue lifted (at least for the 737NG), Europe was ready for harmonization.

The 1997 NPA was parked, but it took until January 2000 before harmonization meetings started. FAA's CAMI assisted in 2001 by conducting additional and comprehensive tests, as discussed earlier. Before those tests were done, CAMI had decided to do a 'meta-analysis' of the tests done so far in Cranfield and in Oklahoma. One of the outcomes was that, overall, a 13-inch passageway width (past three seaters), was as good as passageway widths up to 20 inch and even better than still wider passageways. The reason is simple: a 13-inch passageway is perceived as giving room for only one person at a time, thus supporting a steadier flow than when persons can compete in passing.

The harmonization working group agreed on an automatically disposed hatch (ADH). This was the single most important Type III exit improvement since the start of regulatory changes in 1986. Such a hatch no longer required maneuvering by passengers, and thus much eased the education challenge. The passenger's only action would be to press a proverbial button, actually, typically a handle that must be pulled. The canopy-style hatch that Boeing had introduced in 1996 stood model.

The group did not reach consensus on all aspects. Its report had two dissenting positions, reflecting the views of unions and survivor groups on one side and those of industry (manufacturers and airlines) on the other side. The main areas of disagreement concerned:

- the minimum passageway width (10 inch or 13 inch);
- whether the outboard seat-removed option could be allowed;
- from which discriminant the ADH was needed: 20+, 41+, or 60+.

The harmonization itself failed. The JAA went on and used the group's report to prepare an NPA, but the FAA did not. Rather, it withdrew its 1995 NPRM, so formally kept the 20-inch passageway width requirement.[40]

The JAA CSSG indeed drafted a new NPA in 2003 using the harmonization group's work. It was primarily for new designs, yet mentioned its wish to also propose a revised retrofit rule. However, neither were published. EASA was being formed, and the JAA was in its last days.

14.3.2.9 EASA Takes Over from JAA

In February 2006 EASA took over the work of JAA on this subject and prepared an NPA that was published in April 2008. It essentially copied JAA's non-published NPA of 2003. With respect to the contentious items, it reached compromises: (1) a minimum passageway width past three seaters of 13 inch (in recognition particularly of the 2002 CAMI testing), (2) the outboard seat-removed option remained, and (3) the ADH was required from 41 seats or more. New was that a class divider was allowed bordering the passageway, as long as the latter was at least 20 inch wide.

The NPA was adopted in 2010, without substantial changes, in Amendment 9 of CS-25, thus applicable to new aircraft types. The retrofit rule never came, but in practice many of the airlines in Europe adopted some or most of the measures. In November 2014, the UK CAA withdrew AN 79 (by then incorporated into CAP 747 as a Generic Requirement).[41]

Since its introduction, one new aircraft type has been affected by CS-25 Amendment 9 and thus has ADHs, plus two derivatives: the Airbus A220 (née Bombardier CS). The derivatives were the second generation of the Embraer 190 family and the A321neo.

EASA's first set of pan-European operational regulations became effective in 2014. Before that they were set by JAA and, after its demise, temporarily under the custody of the European Commission. Neither were concerned with setting standards for occupancy of seats adjacent to Type III exits. In the context of 'Special Categories of Passengers' (SCP), EASA introduced standards for preventing certain categories of passengers in these rows.[42] In 2017 EASA introduced lower-order material that promoted operators to ensure that seats next to Type III exits always be occupied by passengers, deemed fit for the task, or excess cabin crewmembers and that passengers seated there receive a briefing prior to take-off.[43]

14.3.2.10 Real Briefing versus Self-help Briefing

Such a dedicated briefing had already been introduced in Britain decades earlier, not long after Manchester. Airlines in other countries in Europe and beyond had adopted the same practice, either on a voluntary or a mandatory basis, often in combination with extra placards on the seat back and the exit showing how to open and dispose of the hatch.

But not so in the U.S. The FAR 121 exit seating requirements were separate from the FAR 121 passenger briefing requirements. This is because their original objective was not safety, but meeting the non-discrimination on the basis of a handicap act. The exit seating requirements asked not for a briefing but for the flight attendant to verify that no passengers are seated in exit rows who are likely unable to open the exit. The actual briefing is delegated to the briefing card, which passengers are supposed to read and understand: a self-help briefing. However, U.S. airlines go beyond this requirement and actually instruct their flight attendants to give an oral briefing to the passengers, as in Europe. In the FAR 135.117 briefing requirements, there is a minor but remarkable difference: while mirroring their FAR 121 counterpart, it does require a briefing on location *and means for opening* of exits, whereas FAR 121.571 only requires a briefing on the location of exits.

14.3.2.11 2020 Recommendation by Aviation Rulemaking Committee

Following a congressional order in 2018, the Aviation Rulemaking Committee (ARC) again looked at emergency evacuation standards, as they had done twice before since their inception in 1991. Of the many recommendations, published in 2020, number 9 asked for harmonization of FAR 25 with the automatically disposable hatch (ADH) standard of EASA's CS-25.[44] By the end of 2024, this recommendation had not been followed up by the FAA.

On the subject of ensuring that seats next to Type III exits are always occupied, or at least the exit row, the ARC reviewed the set of evacuations documented in the period 2009–2019. Although admitting that the information source was limited, it considered that there was no need to raise a recommendation in this respect. This position, which differed from the practice in Europe, was supported in 2022 by the FAA Exit Seat Working Group.[45]

14.3.2.12 The Complex Applications on the A320 and 737

The issue of Type III exits, passageway width, and novel hatches impacted two airplane families in particular: that of the U.S. Boeing 737 and the European Airbus A320.

Being arch rivals, and in the spirit of competition, their designers continuously looked for higher capacities. In doing so, they faced the limits of the regulations, which, as we have seen, itself were changing, not necessarily in harmony across the Atlantic Ocean. At times, even the regulators were in competition.

The effects of the changing regulations and the responses by the two manufacturers led to a multitude of ways to try and meet, or underscore, them. Table 14.1 gives a summary. It is based on type certification data from the two different authorities (FAA and EASA). It lists various options:

- An ADH or not
- The number of Type III exits per side (one or two)

Different Opinions among Authorities 219

FIGURES 14.5 AND 14.6 Type III exits of Boeing 737NG (left) and Airbus A320 (right) (photographs by the author).

TABLE 14.1
Type III Exit Credits on Boeing 737 and Airbus A320 Families

		737NG, MAX		A320ceo/neo	A321neo	A321neo
	ADH Equipped?	yes		no	yes	
	Exit Configuration/Side	C-III-C	C-III-III-C	C-III-III-C	C*-III+-C-C*	C*-(III–III)+-C-C*
	# of Type III Exits/Side	1	2	2	1	2
FAA	Total credit	149	189	190		244
	ADH required?	no		no		
	Passageway width	≥ 13 inch		≥ 13 inch		
	Passageway offset	≥ 6.5 inch		≥ 6.5 inch	≥ 10.5 inch	
EASA	Total credit	149	189	195	224	244
	Total credit (OBR)		185			
	ADH required?	yes		no	yes	
	Maximum exit credit				39	73
	Inferred exit credit	35	79	65		
	Inferred exit credit (OBR)		75			
	Passageway width	≥ 13 inch		≥ 7 inch	≥ 13 inch	Fwd: ≥ 6 inch; Aft: ≥ 13 inch

- Allowed passageway width (which, for the U.S., deviates from the FAR 121 minimum of 20 inch)
- Allowed passageway offset (which, for the U.S., deviates from the FAR 121 minimum of 5 inch)
- The exit capacity credit for the entire airplane
- The maximum credit for improved Type III exits (identified as Type III+)
- Inferred credit for the Type III exits (= total credit for the airplane minus Type C credit)

The Airbus A320neo, which was launched in 2010, did not have ADH exits. Being a second-generation aircraft, it benefited from grandfather rights and continued with the light weight, removable hatches of the A320. But on the A321neo Type III exits were new, so grandfather rights did not apply. Its certification basis was past CS-25 amendment 9, so it had to meet the ADH requirement.

14.3.2.13 Epilogue

The 25 years between 1986 and 2010 saw an evolution around Type III exits that certainly resulted in improvements but also exposed different opinions between the Americans and the Europeans.

The Americans at an early stage introduced Type III exit access design requirements for all fleets of 60 seats and up and kept these since, albeit that in practice the regulatory passageway width requirement of 20 inch could in fact be met with a 13-inch passageway. On the operational side, they have a long and detailed list of persons not allowed to sit in the exit seat rows, but no requirement stipulating that somebody must sit there.

The Europeans took the step to discourage removable hatches so that airlines no longer needed to rely on passengers maneuvering a removable hatch. In 1997 they had triggered, possibly unintentionally, Boeing to design the automatically opening exit. In 2010 they introduced a requirement for such, albeit slightly less sophisticated, and now called ADH. It applied to new aircraft types with 41 seats or more. They introduced other design measures that improve the egress rate, such as fixed seat backs, as well as opening instruction placards. These measures apply to new airplane types of 20 seats or more, as opposed to the FAA's 60-seat discriminant for their package of Type III exit design rules. Since then, several new types complied. On the other hand, they seem to have forgotten to add a regulation that the existing fleets need to have these measures as well, as was the intent of UK CAA's AN79 back in 1986. But, many airlines, voluntarily and perhaps ignorant of this omission, implemented them anyway.

On the operational side, only in the second half of the 2010s, almost 25 years after they were first proposed within JAA, did EASA introduce standards for ensuring that there is always a person sitting next to a Type III exit and who is capable of opening it.[46]

The host of Type III exit measures was triggered by two accidents, in 1985 and 1991. Since then, there have been accidents where Type III exits were used for evacuation under life-threatening conditions. But, in none of these, fatalities occurred due to problems with the Type III exits.

14.3.3 GREEN MAN RUNNING

The U.S. has one official language. Canada has two. The European Union has 24 official languages. It does not come as a surprise therefore that the initiative for language-less exit signs came from Europe.

Europe had earlier copied the U.S. requirements for aircraft exit signs in red letters. Unlike its master, where only English is prescribed, the European airworthiness regulations allowed an alternative language on a sign or more than one language.

ATR, the manufacturer of regional aircraft, was one of several that often received requests for a second language on its product's exit signs. In 1994, Jean-Marc Rampin, its representative in the JAA Cabin Safety Study Group (CSSG), proposed to allow a symbolic exit sign as an alternative. That required a rule change.

He undertook the task of investigating which symbol best to use and found an ISO standard, showing a green man running. Typically, the background is green; the person is white. It was reportedly designed in Japan in 1979 by Yukio Oto and quickly found universal application in many countries but not in the U.S. In Europe, in buildings and ships, the green man running symbol is common, if not formally prescribed. Green was chosen as it is the color of safety and of sufficient contrast.

The CSSG embraced the idea and organized a test to determine the comprehensibility of the symbolic sign by multiple nationalities. In November 1995, passengers at Amsterdam Schiphol

Different Opinions among Authorities 221

FIGURES 14.7 AND 14.8 Green person running symbol, Boeing 787, exit left and exits beyond (photographs by the author).

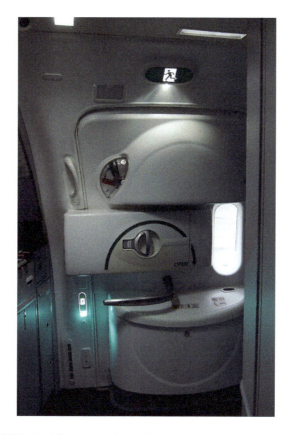

FIGURE 14.9 Boeing 787 exit with green symbol exit signs (photograph by the author).

airport were shown photographs of an aircraft interior with the new signs and were asked what it was supposed to mean. Three different signs were used: exit marking signs, which are located directly at, usually above, an exit; exit locator signs, typically placed above an aisle abeam the exits; and exit signs on a bulkhead or divider, which announce there is an exit beyond it.

Schiphol airport is connected to all corners of the world and many nationalities pass it each day. Care was taken to have all continents represented in the test. A total of 695 persons of 74 nationalities were canvassed, coming from Western Europe (50%), Eastern Europe (6%), North America (15%), Asia (11%), Africa (7%), Middle East (5%), Latin America (4%), and Australia/New Zealand (2%). The interviews were held in 12 different languages, 5 of which verbally and 7 by the use of pre-printed questionnaires. Less common languages used were Russian, Turkish, Japanese, Arabic, and Korean. The results were processed by Cranfield University's Department of Applied Psychology. Repeat tests were done at Schiphol in 1996 and in France in 1998.

The first two signs scored well above the minimum of 66% of what is considered acceptable for such tests. The comprehensibility of the bulkhead/divider mounted signs was low, but this might also have been the case had comparable tests with textual signs been done. Regions that scored best were Western Europe and North America, whereas Eastern Europe and Africa scored lowest.

The next step was to draft a rule. It was decided that the symbolic sign should be offered as an alternative to the red exit sign, not as a replacement, so that manufacturers and airlines had a choice. The JAA circulated an NPA in February 2002 which was repeated by its successor, EASA, in 2006.[47] Few comments were received, mainly from the FAA and Transport Canada. In particular the latter had a different opinion, questioning the research design and EASA's move to 'un-harmonization'.[48] But also the FAA questioned whether the Schiphol results were directly applicable as alternatives to the FAA requirements 'especially for use in the United States where text based exit signs were prevalent throughout society'.[49] Yet, EASA argued that symbolic signs were very common in Europe (and other regions of the world) and amended CS-25 accordingly in 2007.[50]

Ironically, one of the first, if not the first, manufacturer that started to apply the symbolic exit sign was from the U.S.: Boeing. For its 787 model, which came on the market in 2010, it applied for an equivalent level of safety finding with the FAA to allow its use. Many of the non-U.S. customers opted for it, and even some U.S. airlines, such as American Airlines. One condition that the FAA made was that passenger briefing cards must include the specific exit sign artwork. Some airlines took this to its extreme, by dedicating half of the front page to portraying the symbolic sign.

Airbus, with the A350, was likely the first manufacturer to offer the symbolic exit signs as standard equipment. ATR announced in April 2016 to do the same.[51] Since then, more manufacturers and airlines specified symbolic exit signs. In 2018, the ARAC Transport Aircraft Crashworthiness and Ditching Working Group recommended the harmonization of symbolic exit signs.[52]

14.4 LIFE SUPPORT

14.4.1 FLOTATION CUSHION VERSUS LIFE VEST

When in 1956 following a ditching in Puget Sound, near Seattle, a stewardess decided to use seat cushions as flotation devices, she could not imagine that she set a trend. Her initiative, which saved lives, was followed up by the FAA in 1966 to specify buoyant seat cushions as acceptable flotation equipment next to life preservers. Many countries outside the U.S. did not accept such cushions as a means of flotation. They required what is alternatively called a life vest, a life jacket, or a life preserver. A flotation cushion is inferior to a life vest. It requires the survivor to actively hold it, an action that will soon diminish in cold water. A life vest, once donned, requires no action. It will hold the head above water and will provide survival for significantly longer than a flotation cushion. Probably the only reason that cushions are still allowed in the U.S. is that they have not been put to the test.

In 2018, an ARAC group composed of representatives from manufacturers, authorities, and research institutes from multiple countries plus a U.S. flight attendant union looked into ditching standards. The scope was limited to design provisions. They recommended replacing in FAR 25.1415 the phrase 'approved flotation means' with 'approved life preserver', so as to exclude the cushions. The group did not discuss the operational requirements.[53]

14.4.2 POLAR FLIGHTS

Polar flights were pioneered by SAS. In 1954 it started regular DC-6B flights between Copenhagen and Los Angeles across the North Pole. Before doing so, it had studied the needs for occupant survival in the case of an emergency landing in the remote, vast areas of the pole, where rescue would be difficult. It equipped the airplanes with tents, shovels, four-men sleeping bags, special eiderdown clothing for the crew, emergency radio transmitters with a kite and balloon to lift the aerial, hunting and fishing tackle, and rifles for shooting polar bears.

Different Opinions among Authorities

FIGURE 14.10 Polar equipment, including a four-man sleeping bag, as displayed in the SAS museum at Oslo Gardermoen (photograph by the author).

Other European airlines followed SAS. Anchorage, Alaska became a busy international airport in the 1960s to 1980s with much traffic linking Europe and Japan. They all carried some sort of arctic survival equipment on a voluntary basis. JAA's joint European rules for operations in 1996 specified in advisory material the following equipment:[54]

- *A means for melting snow;*
- *Sleeping bags for use by 1/3 of all persons on board and space blankets for the remainder or space blankets for all passengers on board;*
- *Arctic/Polar suit for each crewmember carried.*

Later, EASA adopted similar guidance.

The U.S. had specified as early as 1957 first-aid equipment for 'frigid land areas'. It specified several pieces of equipment, including two pairs of snowshoes, blankets for each occupant, and one small bore rifle, but no other means to protect persons against the cold.[55] This only appeared in CAR 42 and was stopped when FAR 121 replaced it. Decades later, in 2001, when direct operations between East Asia and the U.S. that led over the North Pole started, the FAA issued guidance.[56] This time the only means of protection it suggested were two cold-weather anti-exposure suits so that outside coordination at a diversion airport could be accomplished safely. The policy was based on the assumption that a flight in peril could reach an airfield. The scenario of a successful emergency landing in remote areas was considered so extreme that no contingency measures were considered justified.

14.4.3 OXYGEN

As narrated in Chapter 8, the oxygen requirements are complex and confuse many. There are many variables: pressurization or not, maximum operating altitude, ability to descend, varying altitude bands, varying durations when oxygen must be supplied, the difference between supply and actual use, and so on.

The human need for oxygen is a subject for medical experts, who at times vary in opinion as to what is needed. This has led to differences in oxygen regulations between jurisdictions. The following summarizes the most prominent differences. Some are historical and disappeared, others remained.

14.4.3.1 Quick Descent Capability

For pressurized airplanes capable of a quick descent from a moderate altitude, the oxygen requirements were significantly less than for those airplanes that were unable. It may have meant the difference between just a few oxygen bottles for 10% or 15% of the passengers or a drop-out system for all occupants. The typical associated operating ceiling is 25,000 ft. (7,620 m), but that has not always been the case. Table 14.2 gives an overview of what the various authorities considered as a quick descent capability.

14.4.3.2 When Is Automatic Presentation Required?

Since 1958, automatic presentation was required in the U.S. on airplanes flying above 30,000 ft. (9,144 m). Many countries in Europe only required this above 35,000 ft. (10,668 m). Examples included France, Sweden, and the UK. Consequently, early jet airliners such as the Caravelle, Comet, Trident, and BAC One-Eleven were delivered without drop-out oxygen systems. Only when exported to the U.S. were they so equipped. The Soviet Union had an equally liberal approach to oxygen supply. Even the long-haul Soviet Union Ilyushin Il-62, used for transatlantic flights by Eastern bloc airlines in the 1970s and 1980s, was not equipped with an all-passenger oxygen system.

When JAR-OPS became effective in 1998, Europe introduced an altitude for automatic presentation of 25,000 ft. Thus it changed its earlier tune of requiring automatic presentation 5,000 ft. higher than in the U.S. to 5,000 ft. lower than in the U.S.

ICAO, in 1998, in response to a proposal by Canada, changed its standards so that automatic presentation was required for any operation with pressurized airplanes above 25,000 ft., similar to Europe. Previously, it had a general requirement that pressurized airplanes be equipped with oxygen for all crewmembers and 'a proportion of the passengers as appropriate to the circumstances of the flight being undertaken'. In addition, it required automatic presentation for airplanes built after November 1998 with a ceiling of 25,000 ft. and not capable of descending to 13,000 ft. in four minutes. This ICAO standard has been copied by Europe but not by the U.S. It would require a full drop-out oxygen system in some turboprop airplanes. An example would have been the Fokker 50 if production would have continued past November 1998. It met the (U.S.) 25,000 ft. down to 14,000

TABLE 14.2
Quick Descent Parameters

Jurisdiction	Period	Max Operating Altitude	Descend To	Within
FAA (121)	1950–current	25,000 ft. (7,620 m)	14,000 ft. (4,267 m)	4 minutes
FAA (135)	1974–current	25,000 ft. (7,620 m)	15,000 ft. (4,572 m)	4 minutes
UK option 1	1950s–1989	30,000 ft. (9,144 m)	15,000 ft. (4,572 m)	6 minutes
UK option 2	1950s–1989	35,000 ft. (10,668 m)	15,000 ft. (4,572 m)	4 minutes
ICAO	1998–current	25,000 ft. (7,620 m)	13,000 ft. (3,962 m)	4 minutes
JAA, EASA	1998–current	25,000 ft. (7,620 m)	13,000 ft. (3,962 m)	4 minutes

Different Opinions among Authorities

ft. test in four minutes for some mass ranges but not all. A level-off altitude 1,000 ft. lower, as stipulated by ICAO, would even have been more critical. On top of that, when a reaction time is added, it would have failed the descent speed test. EASA applied a reaction time of 17 seconds between the moment of decompression and the pilots starting the quick descent, a time already mentioned by Gaume in 1970.[57] This left only 3 minutes 43 seconds for the actual descent. Not many airplanes of types similar to the Fokker 50 but built after November 1998 and operated by European air carriers have been equipped with an automatic drop-out system. German air carriers formed an exception, as the German *Luftfahrt-Bundesamt* (CAA) took this new requirement seriously and demanded such a system on types as the ATR 42/72.

14.4.3.3 Cabin Crew Supply Figures

For oxygen calculation purposes the U.S. considers cabin crew as passengers, sorting them under the phrase 'passenger cabin occupants'. This goes back to when the oxygen rules for pressurized airplanes were drafted there: in 1950, before flight attendants were required. In Europe, EASA has separate rules for oxygen provision for cabin crew, which are more stringent than for passengers.

14.5 INSTRUCTIONS AND INFORMATION

14.5.1 Addressing Passengers

To whom do the aviation safety regulations apply? Obviously, such parties as aircraft manufacturers and airlines are addressed. They may also pertain to professional staff such as cabin crew, but what about passengers? Here is a difference between the U.S. and many other countries.

Some U.S. aviation regulations directly address passengers and tell them to use seats and seat belts, not to smoke on board, and observe lighted signs and posted instructions. This practice was introduced in 1963 in Part 40 and continued in Parts 121 and 135. In 1987 it was expanded to include adherence to flight attendant instructions with respect to the stowage of carry-on baggage and in 1992 for adhering to the fasten seat belt and no smoking signs.[58,59] As a consequence, each airline flight in the U.S. not only starts with a safety briefing but also with a reminder that passengers must heed lighted signs and posted placards. Since 1999, U.S. regulations also prohibit passengers from interfering with crewmembers, but obviously this is not part of the briefing.[60] Similar to the U.S., the UK Air Navigation Order has provisions that directly address passengers.

In many other countries, the airline is tasked with ensuring that passengers use seats, seat belts, and so on. More serious offenses, such as unlawful behavior, are embedded in their penal law system. ICAO has provided guidance for this by means of Document 10117.[61]

14.5.2 Country of Assembly

The FAA's policy on passenger safety briefing cards is that they should not be used for non-safety subjects, such as advertising, schedules, or promotional information. This was reaffirmed in an Advisory Circular issued in 2003.[62] Yet, in 2004, the FAA was forced to digress from their own policy. In the FAA Reauthorization Act of 2003 there appeared a section as follows:[63]

> The Secretary of Transportation shall require, beginning after the last day of the 18-month period following the date of enactment of this section, an air carrier using an aircraft to provide scheduled passenger air transportation to display a notice, on an information placard available to each passenger on the aircraft, that informs the passengers of the nation in which the aircraft was finally assembled.

The Secretary had passed this on to the FAA for action. The FAA reluctantly did and issued a Final Rule-uniquely unnumbered-requiring airlines to add to their safety card the sentence 'Final assembly of this airplane was completed in [INSERT NAME OF COUNTRY]'.[64] As congress had limited the requirement to scheduled air transportation only, the rule was not applicable to supplemental air carriers. 'The requirement was included in the bill at the direction of Rep. John Mica (R-Fla.), chairman of the House Transportation and Infrastructure Aviation Subcommittee'. Mica had said the intent was to provide the consumer with additional information, akin to that found on clothing labels, for example.[65] The FAA did not issue an NPRM, and neither did it publish a cost–benefit assessment. Its internal assessment had concluded that the rule would not be beneficial, but the FAA diplomatically stated that 'Congress, which reflects the will of the American people, has determined that providing the required information is beneficial to the public'.

Reactions were mixed. Was it indeed a consumer information measure or perhaps a protectionist measure? If it was the former, would that have the inference that foreign airplanes were less safe? After all, all aircraft, imported or not, are certificated against the same safety standards so that could not be the reason. If it indeed were the latter (protectionist), stating the country of assembly says little about the American contribution to the product. Many non-U.S. airplanes have American-made engines, avionics, and other pieces of equipment. Also, would a passenger who, once on board and reading this message, decide that he or she does not want to fly on this airplane because it is 'foreign' or allegedly less safe?

Airlines complied and added, in small print, the required sentence. For Airbus airplanes, it typically said assembly was done in France or in Germany. Some cards said 'France or Germany', because safety cards are made for an entire fleet, and some airplanes in that fleet were French-built and others German-built. That was the situation until Airbus decided to assemble airplanes in Mobile, Alabama. Airbus airplanes produced there rightly feature this sentence: 'Final assembly of this airplane was completed in the USA'. Perhaps Mica has flown on such an Airbus. Would it have made him wonder about the wisdom of his bill?

Obviously, this rule was not adopted by other countries.

14.6 SECURITY

14.6.1 MONITORING COCKPIT ENTRY AREA

Following the atrocities of 9/11, cabin security became an issue of concern. Soon after the terrorist attacks, Congress enacted in November 2001 the Aviation and Transportation Security Act which, next to creating the Transportation Security Administration, asked for Improved Flight Deck Integrity Measures. The FAA quickly came up with a rule for reinforced cockpit doors. This was soon copied by other authorities in the world, so no different opinions here.

The Act also asked that the FAA:[66]

> may develop and implement methods—(1) To use video monitors or other devices to alert pilots in the flight deck to activity in the cabin, except that use of such monitors or devices shall be subject to nondisclosure requirements applicable to cockpit video records.

ICAO confirmed in 2002 the secure door and, well ahead of the FAA, also introduced a standard for monitoring means, effective November 2003. Its broad-worded text must have been a compromise.

> In all aeroplanes which are equipped with a flight crew compartment door in accordance with 13.2.2: [. . .] means shall be provided for monitoring from either pilot's station the entire door area outside the flight crew compartment to identify persons requesting entry and to detect suspicious behaviour or potential threat.

In this text, several words or phrases have led to discussion and different opinions:

- Means shall be provided.
- Monitoring.
- Either pilot's station.

Different Opinions among Authorities

'Means' is an umbrella term. It is broader than 'system' and could include hardware, a feature, or a procedure. 'Monitoring' is a broad term as well. It refers to a person checking or watching something but does not specify which of the senses to use. The most common sense for monitoring is sight, but hearing is not excluded. A 2003 interpretation by the UK Department for Transport said that, to be properly effective, it meant a visual check. '[S]uch methods as interphone exchanges, code words, "special knocks', the passing of notes, or the temporary blocking of the area behind the flight deck door during its openings, does not offer a satisfactory degree of security'.[67] 'Either pilot's station' means either of the two pilot's stations, so not necessarily both. In Europe, the ICAO standard was initially transposed with the words 'each pilot's station', which means both. Monitoring from either pilot's station does not mean that the pilot needs to remain seated. When a CCTV is installed, this may be in their instrument panel or mounted on the back wall of the cockpit, visible to either one or both pilots by turning their heads.

All states were required to adopt ICAO standards in their national regulations, but, even though 9/11 had happened in the U.S., the FAA acted slowly. It issued an NPRM for means of monitoring only in 2005, which became a final rule in 2007.[68]

Other states were much quicker. In Europe, the JAA copied the ICAO standard, initially with some changes, but this was corrected later. The multi-interpretable character of the text made diverse the application in practice among the member states. This particularly applied to the question of whether or not a CCTV was the sole means of compliance. A study at the time showed that centrally located countries, such as France, Germany, Netherlands, and the UK, required a CCTV, but peripheral countries (Scandinavia, Iceland, Ireland, Portugal, etc.) allowed an operational solution. In some cases, this interpretation was not so much ordered by the national civil aviation authority but rather influenced by the local pilot union. When cabin crew unions were consulted on this issue, they typically responded not being in favor of a CCTV due to privacy reasons.

The FAA interpreted monitoring means broader:[69]

> In proposed § 121.313(k), the use of the phrase "a means to monitor from the flightdeck side of the door" permits at least two methods to comply with the proposed rule, covering monitoring from the flightdeck. The first method is a video system. The video system would transmit video images to a monitor or monitors appropriately situated on the flightdeck to allow viewing of the area outside the flightdeck (herein referred to the "door area") from the flightdeck side of the door. A crewmember would provide audio confirmation to the flight crew that the door area is clear, including confirmation that the lavatory is clear. A second method would involve visual identification of the door area, coupled with an audio confirmation procedure. Through a viewing device installed in the flightdeck door, one person on the flightdeck would view the door area and identify the person seeking access.

FIGURES 14.11 AND 14.12 CCTV views of the cockpit door entrance area (left) and galley with external door (right) (photographs by the author).

The Regional Airlines Association noted that nearly all their members used the peephole/audio method of confirming that the area outside the flightdeck door was secure before opening the door during flight.[70] They saw no additional security benefit of using a video camera system over using their current peephole system to monitor the area outside the flightdeck door. The Association of Professional Flight Attendants and Boeing supported a viewing device in the flightdeck door that allowed for the door and forward cabin to be monitored. In the preamble to the final rule, the FAA explained:[71]

> This rule allows U.S. air carriers options to meet requirements while remaining flexible in their methods. This flexibility provides an additional level of security to the public because air carriers will use different methods to provide flight deck security and crew communication. Different methods of compliance will make attempts to breach security more difficult because multiple systems will be more difficult to monitor and defeat.

14.6.2 Second Axe

The U.S. CAB considered requiring a second axe in the 1950s but decided against it (see Section 7.2.1). In Europe, well before the JAA was tasked with drafting operating regulations, some countries had a requirement for a second crash axe, to be placed in the cabin of aircraft with more than 200 seats. When JAR-OPS was drafted in the 1990s, this requirement was copied, in spite of an attempt by AECMA, the European Association of Aerospace Industries, to delete it. Following 9/11, several parties in Europe again asked the JAA to reconsider it, as that axe was seen as a security threat. Airbus, the Association of European Airlines, and the Dutch airline Martinair did so in 2002 and 2003, but the JAA Operations Standardization meeting rejected it, citing that it would be an important tool for firefighting. At least one European national aviation authority is known to have issued an exemption, allowing an airline to remove this axe. EASA copied the requirement in its operational rules. No reports are known of the use of the *cabin* axe for accessing hidden fire nor as a weapon. There have been reports though that the *cockpit* axe was used as a weapon, both by and against pilots. In Canada on November 13, 1971, a pilot successfully used it against a hijacker by fracturing his skull with the axe handle.[72] In the Ethiopian Airlines 767 hijack in November 1996 the hijackers grabbed the axe and used it as a threat. The investigators recommended that 'the fire axe should be stowed in such a manner as to make it inaccessible to non-flight crew members'.[73] In 2002 on a flight from Miami to Buenos Aires, a cockpit intruder who managed to break the lower panel of the cockpit door was hit on the head by a pilot using the cockpit axe.[74] In 2004 in Norway a passenger had boarded a Dornier 228 with an axe and attacked the pilots. The airport lacked a security check; the airplane lacked a cockpit door. Though hurt, the pilots, with the assistance of a passenger, managed to overpower the assailant. In the process the airplane came as close as 30 meters above houses but was landed safely.[75]

In a Brasilia crash, the cockpit axe was unsuccessfully tried to open a cockpit window. The NTSB recommended a re-evaluation of the axe specifications.[76]

14.6.3 Second Barrier

Following the events of '9/11' in 2001, quickly a design requirement came for the cockpit door to be intrusion-proof. This was in addition to the means of monitoring and operational requirements restricting access to the cockpit. As to the latter, the U.S. has been more stringent than most other countries. During flight, the cockpit door still needs to be opened frequently, for cabin crew to serve the flight crew and for the latter to go into the cabin for 'physiological reasons' (visiting the lavatory). For added security, some U.S. airlines installed a secondary barrier at a small distance from the cockpit door, called an installed physical secondary barrier (IPSB). In those airplane configurations where there is a lavatory directly behind the cockpit, it secures the path between the two.

Different Opinions among Authorities 229

FIGURE 14.13 Cockpit axe clearly displayed to passengers in a Dornier 228 (not the Norwegian case) (photograph by the author).

FIGURE 14.14 Installed physical secondary barrier (in stowed position) (photograph by the author).

While not being a second door per se, it typically hinges like a door. It can perhaps best be described as a gate constructed of metal rods and bars that are lockable and impede unauthorized access.

In 2018 Congress made the IPSB mandatory for new U.S. transport airplanes.[77] The FAA transposed it into FAR 121 in August 2023, requiring that all new airplanes delivered to U.S. air carriers from August 2025 be so equipped.[78] No other countries (with the possible exception of high-risk countries such as Israel) are known to have, or consider, a similar standard.

14.7 CABIN PROFESSIONALS

14.7.1 INTRODUCTION

The domain of cabin professionals is likely the cabin safety domain most subject to different opinions. As opposed to airworthiness subjects, where countries typically adopted the requirements of leading countries such as the U.S., and later Europe, cabin professionals are a purely operational matter for which countries tended to follow ICAO. But on this subject ICAO was late and the standards it produced were succinct.

The first ICAO standards for cabin attendants became effective in 1967. There were two: assignment of emergency duties and training.[79]

> 12.1 Assignment of emergency duties—An operator shall establish to the satisfaction of the State of the Registry the minimum number of cabin attendants required for each type of aeroplane based on seating capacity or the number of passengers carried, in order to effect a safe and expeditious evacuation of the aeroplane, and the necessary functions to be performed in an emergency evacuation. The operator shall assign these functions for each type of aeroplane.
>
> 12.2 Training—An operator shall establish and maintain a training programme, approved by the State of Registry to be completed annually by each cabin attendant who is assigned emergency functions as required by 12.1, which will ensure that each such attendant is:
>
> a) competent to execute those duties and functions which the attendant is assigned to perform in the event of an in-flight emergency or a situation requiring emergency evacuation;
> b) drilled and capable in the use of emergency and life-saving equipment required to be carried such as life jackets, life rafts, evacuation slides, emergency exits, portable fire extinguishers, oxygen equipment and first-aid kits;
> c) when serving on aeroplanes operated above 3 000 metres (10 000 ft), knowledgeable as regards the effect of lack of oxygen and, in the case of pressurized aeroplanes, as regards physiological phenomena accompanying a loss of pressurization;
> d) aware of other crewmembers' assignments and functions in the event of an emergency in so far as it is necessary to fulfil his own individual duties.

The open-ended wording of 12.1 left a lot to be decided by the individual countries, leading to a wide variety of requirements. These concerned not only the minimum required number of cabin crew but also qualification, training, and licensing issues, the allocation of senior cabin crewmembers, and flight time limitations. Since 1967, ICAO kept the standards largely unchanged. However, it published guidance for cabin crew training in 1976 and, much later, on the minimum number of cabin crew.

14.7.2 REQUIRED MINIMUM NUMBER OF CABIN CREW

ICAO in 1967 did not suggest a ratio of passengers to crew but mentioned two different bases for determining the number of cabin crew: seating capacity or the number of passengers carried. Since then, some countries added more bases: the number of floor-level exits in combination with the ratio, and the number as employed in the evacuation demonstration. Another discriminant with little international variation is the lower cut-off: from which number of passengers, or passenger seats, is a cabin crewmember required?

In practice, many airlines employ more flight attendants than the minimum required, particularly for service reasons which tend to be more on long-haul routes. In a number of cases, this has helped in actual evacuations, such as in New York, in July 1992, and Toronto, in 2005.

14.7.2.1 Ratio

In the U.S., a ratio for cabin crew to passengers was for the first time considered in December 1958 but only for overseas operators. The ratio proposed was initially 1 to 45, as a second flight attendant was required from 45 passengers onward, but became 1 to 50 when a third flight attendant was proposed for more than 100 passengers. It took a few more years, until 1963, before it became solid. For domestic operations, this was even in 1965.

In other countries, larger airplanes with capacities beyond 100 were being introduced as well from about 1960 onward. This prompted some countries which did not wish to wait for the rather slow developments in the U.S. to come up with their own ratio. At least two countries did so. Both selected the ratio concept. Unlike the U.S. they selected the actual number of passengers, not passenger seats, as the basis.

These countries were Australia and Canada. The ratios that they chose differed. Australia decided on 1 to 36, Canada for 1 to 40. In neither case is it recorded when this exactly happened, but it is likely that this was around 1960. Neither is the rationale for these figures well documented. In 2011, the issue of cabin crew ratio was discussed in a committee of the Australian parliament.[80] The reason was a proposal by CASA, the Australian civil aviation safety authority, to change the Civil Aviation Order by raising the ratio from 1:36 passengers (not seats) to the international standard of 1:50 passenger seats. Since 2006, CASA has issued exemptions to Australian operators for allowing the number of cabin crew on the 1:50 passenger seats ratio, rather than the 1:36 passengers ratio. As to the history of the 1:36 ratio, the Committee reported:

> While the origins of the 1:36 ratio in Australia are unclear, it is widely believed to be connected to the introduction of the Fokker F-27 Friendship in the late 1950s, or possibly the earlier introduction of the Douglas DC-3. Both models of aircraft contained approximately 36 passenger seats.
>
> Since this time, the 1:36 cabin crew ratio appears to have been extrapolated to cater for larger and more modern aircraft. The Committee heard that this ratio pre-dates the requirement for demonstrated and measurable safety outcomes in aviation.
>
> It is equally unclear how long the 1:50 ratio has been in place in other jurisdictions. The CASA noted that preliminary research into the issue has indicated that a 1:50 ratio was adopted in the United States no later than 1994, but perhaps as early as 1965.

Indeed, Australia was a very early customer of the F-27, which was initially configured with 36 passenger seats in Australia, so the first element appears likely. The DC-3 rarely sat 36, so that is less likely. The report also referred to an earlier discussion in Australia, in 1997–1998, about this ratio, saying:

> ... the previous review ... was extremely comprehensive. When I found out that they had been giving dispensations [exemptions to the 1:36 ratio] I was absolutely floored because everyone in the industry was involved in that. Those of us who looked at the one for 50 comparison did six months of research on it. We went everywhere. I spoke to all of my colleagues in the [United] States, Canada and everywhere else looking for some sort of justification for us to drop our standards, and we could not find anything.

Although the committee recommended against replacing the 1:36 passenger ratio with the 1:50 passenger seat ratio, the government of Australia, in 2017, decided otherwise.[81] Since then, Australia, in essence, used a ratio of 1 cabin crewmember to 50 passenger seats.

Canada issued exemptions from the 1:40 rule from 2013 onward and since 2015 offered airlines a choice between the 1:40 passenger ratio and the 1:50 passenger seat ratio. In the latter case, additional conditions applied such as a safety assessment which may involve an evacuation demonstration and clarification of the in-charge flight attendant requirements.[82]

Unlike the U.S., the Europeans specified the number of cabin crew per deck. This initially applied primarily to the Boeing 747, but later also to the Airbus A380, with its two decks stretching along the entire length of the fuselage.

14.7.2.2 Lower Cut-off

As to the lower cut-off, there was great consensus across the globe: it was 20. The rationale for that figure is explained in Section 8.3.4. Only one country is known which applied a lower cut-off: Australia. They required the first cabin crewmember from 16 passengers, but this lower cut-off only applied when the airplane was flown by a single pilot and had an aisle, thus excluding such a type as the Trislander. Australia conformed to the rest of the world in 2021.

14.7.2.3 Floor-Level Exit Based

In some countries the number of flight attendants was linked to floor-level exits. It is assumed that this was felt to be a more solid basis than selecting a ratio, as that would have an element of being arbitrary. However, it was typically only done above a certain threshold. As that threshold coincided with twin-aisle airplanes, it is believed that this method was introduced in the early 1970s. Two countries for which this is known were Australia and the UK, but there may have been more countries that used it.

In Australia, the threshold was 216 passenger seats, which equals 6 times 36. Above that

> aircraft carrying more than 216 passengers shall carry the number of cabin attendants as prescribed by CASA which shall not be less than 1 cabin attendant for each floor level exit in any cabin with 2 aisles.[83]

In 2021, Australia introduced a new set of regulations based on the 1:50 ratio. Since then, for determining the number of cabin crew, the regulations differ between single-aisle and twin-aisle airplanes. For the latter, the number of cabin crewmembers must be at least equal to the number of floor-level exits.

In the UK, the threshold for basing the number of cabin crew on floor-level exits was 200 passenger seats. Below that, the 1:50 ratio applied. Applying the per exit ratio below 200 would work against airplane types with a high proportion of floor-level exits, as that would have led to many more flight attendants than the 1:50 ratio would dictate. Examples were the BAe 146 and Fokker 50. They both had four floor-level exits and would thus require four flight attendants whereas per the 1:50 ratio two or even only one would be needed. With smaller airplane diameters, opposite exits would be proximate, so being able to be covered by one cabin crewmember. Above the threshold of 200 passenger seats, in the UK,

> the number of cabin attendants [...] shall be not less than half the number of main exits in the aircraft, and, in addition, when more than 200 passengers are carried, one additional cabin attendant for every 25, or fraction of 25, of such passengers.[84]

However, the number of cabin attendants thus calculated did not need to exceed the number of main exits. The UK changed this in 1989 to an overall 1:50 ratio.

Singapore based the number of required cabin crew on both the 1:50 ratio and floor-level exits. They specified one per exit pair for single-aisle airplanes and one per exit (so, two for a pair), for twin-aisle airplanes. This requirement was in force in 2024.

The European Civil Aviation Conference (ECAC), a European organization with only an advisory role, set a recommendation in 1988 to its member states which was based on the 1:50 ratio (passengers based, not seats) but additionally linked it to exits. The number of cabin attendants should be at least the same as that of 'Type A, I or II usable floor level exits'.[85]

Using two versions of the Boeing 767 as an example, these various regulations resulted in quite different numbers of flight attendants:

TABLE 14.3
Different Flight Attendant Numbers for Same Airplane Type and Capacity

	Number of Passengers	4 Type A, 4 Type III	6 Type A, 2 Type I
Australia (pre 2021)	290	9	9
Australia (2021–)	290	6	8
EASA (current)	290	6	6
ECAC (1988)	290	6	8
Singapore (current)	290	6	8
UK (pre-1989)	290	6	8
U.S. (current)	290	6	6

It is of interest to note that in some countries the variant with the more demanding exit configuration of heavy, passenger-dependent Type III hatches requires less cabin crew than the variant with floor-level exits only, which are easier to operate and manage by flight attendants.

14.7.2.4 Evacuation Demonstration Based

Before countries generally adopted the 1:50 ratio in some an evacuation demonstration was used to determine the minimum number of flight attendants. In Scandinavia, Sterling Airlines of Denmark ran a demonstration in May 1968 of its Fokker F-27–500 with 56 passengers and one cabin crewmember. Similarly, Norwegian carrier Braathens demonstrated its new Fokker F-28 in March 1969 with 65 passengers and only one cabin crewmember. They were subsequently allowed to fly more than 50 passengers with only one cabin crewmember until these countries adopted the 1:50 ratio.

In the mid-1990s, the JAA, when drafting pan-European operational rules, consolidated the 1:50 passenger seat ratio which by then had been in use in most of the participating countries. It however added a proviso that the relevant evacuation demonstration or analysis be taken into account. More specifically, JAR-OPS 1.990, effective in 1998, specified:[86]

> (b) [. . .] that the minimum number of cabin crew is the greater of:
> (1) One cabin crewmember for every 50, or fraction of 50, passenger seats installed on the same deck of the aeroplane; or
> (2) The number of cabin crew who actively participated in the aeroplane cabin during the relevant emergency evacuation demonstration, or who were assumed to have taken part in the relevant analysis, except that, if the maximum approved passenger seating configuration is less than the number evacuated during the demonstration by at least 50 seats, the number of cabin crew may be reduced by 1 for every whole multiple of 50 seats by which the maximum approved passenger seating configuration falls below the certificated maximum capacity.

Unlike the FAA, which referred to determining the number of flight attendants to the airline's evacuation demonstration, the JAA meant the manufacturer's evacuation demonstration or analysis. The JAA did not require airlines to conduct their own demonstration. A practical example of 1.990(b)(2) was the McDonnell Douglas MD-11 when operated with, for example, 386 passengers. According to 1.990(b)(1) the number would be 8 flight attendants. However, as the manufacturer demonstration had been done with 410 passengers, and thus 9 flight attendants, and as 386 is less than 50 lower, the provision of 1.990(b)(2) overruled that of (b)(1) and thus 9 flight attendants were required instead of 8. When EASA took over responsibility for drafting European operational requirements, a similar requirement remained.[87]

30 NPRM 91-11.
31 The Influence of Adjacent Seating Configurations on Egress Through a Type III Emergency Exit, Paul G. Rasmussen, Charles B. Chittum, FAA OAM, December 1989.
32 Amdt 25-76/121-228.
33 Aircraft Evacuations Through Type-III Exits I: Effects of Seat Placement at the Exit, G.A. McLean, M.H. George, C.B. Chittum, G.E. Funkhouser, FAA CAMI, DOT/FAA/AM-95/22, July 1995; Aircraft Evacuations Through Type-III Exits II: Effects of Individual Subject Differences, G.A. McLean, M.H. George, FAA CAMI, DOT/FAA/AM-95/25, August 1995.
34 NPA 25D-270; Type III EXITS; NPA 26-2; TYPE III EXITS; NPA-OPS-5 TYPE III EXITS, Letter by Y. Morier, Regulations Director, Joint Aviation Authorities, 15 October 1996.
35 NPRM 95-1.
36 Safety Study—Emergency Evacuation of Commercial Airplanes, NTSB, Adopted June 27, 2000.
37 Access-To-Egress I: Interactive Effects of Factors that Control the Emergency Evacuation of Naïve Passengers Through the Transport Airplane Type-III Overwing Exit, Garnet A. McLean, Cynthia L. Corbett, Kenneth G. Larcher, Jerry R. McDown, David A. Palmerton, Keith A. Porter, Robert M. Shaffstall, FAA CAMI and Rita S. Odom, Advancia Corporation, DOT/FAA/AM-02/16, August 2002.
38 67 FR 22363.
39 Equivalent Level of Safety (ELOS) Finding for the Passageway to and Opening of Overwing Exits for Boeing 737–600, -700, -700C, -800, -900 Series Aircraft, TD8301SE-T, DOT FAA, June 10, 2004; A321: AT10637IB-T-CS-3.
40 67 FR 22363.
41 Access to and Opening of Type III and Type IV Emergency Exits, in Mandatory Requirements for Airworthiness, sec. 2, Part 3 Generic Requirements, GR No. 3, CAP 747, Issue 3, 30 November 2009.
42 Commission Regulation (EU) No. 965/2012 of 5 October 2012, sec. CAT.OP.MPA.155; Annex to Decision 2014/015/R of the Executive Director of the Agency of 24 April 2014, AMC2 CAT.OP.MPA.165.
43 Annex to Executive Director Decision 2017/008/R of 28 March 2017, AMC1 CAT.OP.MPA.165; GM2 CAT.OP.MPA.165; GM1 CAT.OP.MPA.170(a).
44 Emergency Evacuation Standards Aviation Rulemaking Committee Final Report, May 20, 2020.
45 Report to Congress: Federal Aviation Administration Reauthorization Act of 2018 (Pub. L. No. 115-254)—sec. 323, submitted May 13, 2022 to the U.S. Senate Committee on Commerce, Science and Transportation and U.S. House of Representatives Committee on Transportation and Infrastructure, p. 104.
46 Executive Director Decision 2017/008/R of 28 March 2017 amending the Acceptable Means of Compliance and Guidance Material to Part-CAT of Regulation (EU) No. 965/2012 'AMC and GM to Part-CAT—Issue 2, Amendment No. 12.
47 Re: NPA 25D-327 Graphical Exit Signs as an Alternative to Red Exit Signs for Passenger Aircraft, Letter by Y. Morier, JAA Regulation Director, 1 February 2002; Notice of Proposed Amendment (NPA) No. 04/2006 Draft Decision of the Executive Director Amending Decision No. 2005/06/R of the Executive Director of 12 December 2005 on Certification Specifications for Large Aeroplanes (CS-25) Symbolic Exit Signs and Revised Standards for Cargo Compartments (D To C), 25 April 2006.
48 Comment Response Document (CRD) to Notice of Proposed Amendment (NPA) 04-2006 for Amending the Executive Director Decision No. 2006/05/R on Certification Specifications, Including Airworthiness Codes and Acceptable Means of Compliance, for Large Aeroplanes ("CS-25") Symbolic Exit Signs and Revised Standards for Cargo Compartments (D To C), 14 November 2006.
49 Equivalent Level of Safety (ELOS) Finding for Symbolic Exit Signs and Green Emergency Exit Instructions, Project Number N0698ODA0077, Memorandum, Federal Aviation Administration, August 22, 2023.
50 Certification Specifications for Large Aeroplanes, CS-25 Amendment No. 3, European Aviation Safety Agency, 19 September 2007.
51 From MSN 1211 and 1332 onward for ATR42-500 and ATR 72-212A respectively.
52 Transport Aircraft Crashworthiness and Ditching Working Group Report to FAA, Release Revision B, September 20, 2018.
53 Transport Aircraft Crashworthiness and Ditching Working Group Report to FAA.
54 Joint Aviation Requirements—Operations Part 1, AMC OPS 1.835(c) Survival Equipment, Initial Issue, Effective 1 April 1998.
55 Supp. 43 to CAM 42.
56 Guidance for Polar Operations, FAA Policy Letter, March 5, 2001.

57 Factors Influencing the Time of Safe Unconsciousness (TSU) for Commercial Jet Passengers Following Cabin Decompression" by James G. Gaume, Aerospace Medicine, April 1970.
58 Amdt 121-94.
59 Amdt 40-43, Amdt 121-230/135-44.
60 64 FR 1076.
61 Manual on the Legal Aspects of Unruly and Disruptive Passengers, ICAO Doc 10117, 2019.
62 Passenger Safety Information Briefing and Briefing Cards, Advisory Circular 121-24C, U.S. Department of Transportation, Federal Aviation Administration, July 23, 2003.
63 FAA Reauthorization Act 2003, sec. 810, December 19, 2003.
64 69 FR 39291.
65 Defense Daily, July 11, 2004.
66 NPRM 05-07.
67 [No Subject], Letter UK Department for Transport to all non-UK Airlines Serving UK Airports, 27 October 2003.
68 NPRM 05-07, Amdt 121-334.
69 NPRM 05-07.
70 Amdt 121-334.
71 Amdt 121-334.
72 Paul Joseph Cini, Wikipedia, Visited May 2, 2024.
73 Aircraft Accident Investigation Report Ethiopian Airlines B767 (ET-AIZ) Aircraft Accident in the Federal Islamic Republic of the Comores in the Indian Ocean on November 23, 1996, Ethiopian Civil Aviation Authority, Flight Safety Department, May 04, 1998.
74 Airline Crew Fends off Cockpit Crasher, Chicago Tribune, February 8, 2002, Visited May 2, 2024.
75 Aftenposten, 30 September 2004; Updated 19 October 2011.
76 NTSB Recommendation A-96-149.
77 FAA Reauthorization Act of 2018, sec. 336.
78 Amdt 25-150/121-389.
79 Operation of Aircraft, International Commercial Air Transport, ICAO Annex 6, amendment 150, effective 14 April 1967, Chapter 12.
80 House of Representatives Standing Committee on Infrastructure and Communications, Finding the Right Balance: Cabin Crew Ratios on Australian Aircraft, October 2011.
81 Australian Government Response to the House of Representatives Standing Committee on Infrastructure and Communications Inquiry Report: Finding the Right Balance: Cabin Crew Ratios on Australian Aircraft, March 2017.
82 Regulations Amending the Canadian Aviation Regulations (Parts I, VI and VII—Flight Attendants and Emergency Evacuation), Canada Gazette Vol. 149, No. 12, June 17, 2015.
83 Flight Attendants, sec. 6 of Civil Aviation Order 20.16.3—Air Service Operations—Carriage of Persons, Civil Aviation Safety Authority, Australia, eff. December 2, 2004.
84 The Air Navigation Order 1985, UK Statutory Instruments 1985 No. 1643, made 30 October 1985, section 18(7)(d).
85 European Aviation Civil Aviation Conference, ECAC.CEAC Doc No. 18, Joint Requirements for Emergency and Safety Airborne Equipment, Training and Procedures.
86 Joint Aviation Requirements—Operations Part 1, sec. 1.990 Number and Composition of Cabin Crew, Initial Issue, Effective 1 April 1998.
87 Regulation (EU) No. 965/2012, as amended, Annex III, ORO.CC.100.
88 GM 121.635 in: Acceptable Means of Compliance and Guidance Material, Australian Air Transport Operations-Larger Aeroplanes, Part 121 of CASR, Australian Government, Civil Aviation Safety Authority, December 2023.
89 Amdt 121-55.
90 Amdt 121-143.
91 Regulation (EC) No. 1899/2006 of the European Parliament and of the Council of 12 December 2006 Amending Council Regulation (EEC) No. 3922/91.

15 Developments since 1997

ABSTRACT

With most of the cabin safety challenges now addressed, from 1997 onward developments in the U.S. almost came to a standstill. The only major change involved the forward fit, from 2009 onward, of dynamically tested seats. Guidance, education, and conferences on cabin safety issues thrived, and so did committees where authorities and industry met, both in the U.S. and Europe. Also, societal and technological changes warranted minor adjustments. Society had become more safety sensitive. Where decades earlier, survivable accidents with fatalities were considered a fact of life, now even evacuations with perfect outcomes triggered questions at the highest level (Congress) and led to research. The attacks of 9/11 prompted new security provisions. This chapter also houses three perpetual subjects not specific to this period: (1) turbulence, (2) brace-for-impact positions, and (3) air contamination.

15.1 INTRODUCTION

When the third wave subsided a period commenced in which cabin safety developments came at a lower tempo. The main leftover of the third wave that needed to be finished was the retrofit application of the 16 g seats. This was concluded in the U.S. in 2009. Cabin safety interest however increased, and the period saw many reports and guidance appear on the subject. Authorities and industry formed standing regulatory committees to discuss cabin safety.

The consolidation in Europe of several aviation authorities into a unified body, the European Aviation Safety Agency (later European Union Aviation Safety Agency), created a counterpart of importance to the FAA and manufacturers alike. Having been given executive powers by the European Union, it was more powerful than its predecessor, the Joint Aviation Authorities. The regulatory world of aviation safety, and thus cabin safety, changed from monopolistic to duopolistic. To avoid the two poles to diverge, harmonization of their regulations became an important mission. The first cabin safety-related subject that was harmonized was that of crash loads in 1997.[1] In 1999, the FAA tasked ARAC with comparing a number of cabin safety design subjects between the FAA and JAA.[2] While this harmonization effort for design rules was partially successful, for operational rules there was still a world to win. Another subject of harmonization came in 2004 and polished away minor differences in protective breathing equipment and the activation time of public address systems.

Societal trends found their way into the cabin. A larger cross-section of the general population boarded aircraft. This included passengers of age, with associated ailments, who might need their own supply of oxygen and for whom medical equipment would be installed on board in the form of emergency medical kits and automatic external defibrillators (AEDs). The number of infants increased and so the wish for parents to afford them the same level of safety. Passengers not conforming to normal rules of behavior caused the phenomenon of air rage, also known as unruly or disruptive passengers. That created a new challenge for cabin crew but not the only one. They had to function as baggage stowers as passengers carried more baggage on board.

Smoking on board was banned in steps in the U.S. between 1987 (on flights up to two hours) and 2000 (completely) and in Europe in 1997, but that did not necessarily mean cleaner air in the cabin. Some airplane types more than others occasionally suffered from foul air entering the cabin, typically caused by leaks in the bleed air system. The subject of cabin air contamination is still being researched without signs of a regulatory solution.

Developments since 1997 239

In 2015, the FAA tasked the Aviation Rulemaking Advisory Committee (ARAC) to study crashworthiness at an airframe level. Two evacuations in the U.S. in 2015 and 2016, although not having caused fatalities, led to renewed attention for the subject. In 2018, U.S. Congress ordered the FAA to review it, which in turn, commissioned another ARAC group. It also led to a spur in evacuation research around 2020 by FAA's CAMI. But as if that was not enough, in 2022 other congressmen pondered yet another bill for more evacuation research, the EVAC Act, later absorbed in the FAA Reauthorization Act of 2024.

Two events in this period significantly affected cabin operations and thus cabin safety, although not originating as a cabin safety issue. One was the four-aircraft terrorist attack of September 11, 2001. That had major consequences to cabin security, and even more, cockpit security. The other was the COVID-19 pandemic of 2020–2021 (and, on a lesser scale, earlier pandemics such as SARS), which was an issue of cabin sanitation with implications for cabin safety.

15.2 REPORTS AND GUIDANCE MATERIAL

While by no means complete, the following summarizes the various 'soft' activities since 1997 on cabin safety. The period saw a significant increase in research, investigations, studies, conferences, and new guidance material. The number of 'hard' activities, in the form of new rules, however, decreased.

15.2.1 Reviews

In 2004 an excellent review of cabin safety achievements and prospects was made by the U.S. Government Accountability Office.[3] It listed 46 subjects of 'advancements', as technological (i.e. design) and operational improvements were called by them, for all the cabin safety domains, and more, such as insulation material flammability and fuel tank safety. Of these, 18 were completed at the time and 28 were prospects. The recommendations were not technical but asked for more efficient organization of research and the need for the FAA to obtain autopsy and survivor information from the NTSB.

On the subject of evacuation, the NTSB published a special study in 2000, evaluating 46 evacuations between September 1997 and June 1999.[4] All had occurred in the U.S. or territories. Only one case involved an accident with fatalities. Of the 20 recommendations, all addressed to the FAA, half was eventually rated by the NTSB as 'acceptable action'.

In 2018, and updated in 2020, the UK Royal Aeronautical Society (RAeS) issued a report on evacuations with a significant contribution by Nick Butcher, former head of UK CAA flight operations cabin safety.[5] All subjects that he had faced in his career since 1986, and more, were discussed. He stressed the importance of well-trained cabin crewmembers and addressed a number of areas of concern, including passengers taking their hand luggage with them, so delaying an evacuation. The study included 24 recommendations, mainly aimed at national aviation authorities, air operators, and ICAO. However, as the RAeS has no formal status, the addressees were not obliged to respond.

15.2.2 Regulatory Development Support

The two research centers of the FAA have been mentioned many times in the context of cabin safety research. The Technical Center in Atlantic City, New Jersey was formed in 1958 as NAFEC and changed its name in 1980 to FAA Technical Center. In 1996 it was renamed again: William J. Hughes Technical Center. Its main cabin safety expertise is fire safety. The other center is the Civil Aerospace Medical Institute (CAMI), located in Oklahoma City, Oklahoma since about 1958. This facility ran many human factor tests, including evacuation tests. It also conducted in-depth research into flight attendant fatigue, spread over many reports.

Ray Cherry of RGW Cherry & Associates has done many analyses to gauge whether new cabin safety features would be cost-beneficial. He did this for such subjects as 16 g seats, cabin water spray, fuselage burn-through, hidden cabin fires, and Type III exits. His method was to estimate how many lives would be saved by a new cabin safety feature if it had been installed in aircraft that had crashed in the past. While he took care not to count the same lives saved twice for multiple features, his use of past accidents did not always account for the fact that, over time, the number of accidents decreased, thus reducing the saving potential of the new features. Separately, he did an extensive study on cabin safety threats for EASA with a view to making recommendations for improvements to CS-25.[6] The report lists 59 recommendations. Few, if any, seem to have been followed up by EASA.

EASA's research program included several cabin safety subjects, such as special categories of passengers (SCP), child restraint systems (CRS), and air contamination.[7] The umbrella term SCP comprised such diverse passengers as children, physically disabled, mentally deficient, deaf, mute, and blind passengers, expectant mothers, tall passengers, and deportees.

Cranfield University, in 2023 took up again evacuation tests in the spirit of Helen Muir's work. When she died in 2010 her work came to a stop. In 2014, British Airways donated a Boeing 737-400 to the University. The new work is being done in cooperation with the University of Greenwich. It aims at determining the choices that people make during evacuations, in support of more reliable computer evacuation models.

15.2.3 GUIDANCE

From the 2000s onward, several organizations publish cabin safety guidance material.

Since 2007, FAA's Donald Wecklein has kept up to date a Cabin Safety Subject Index (CSSI), which provides an easy reference to FAA-related cabin safety regulations and guidance. Additionally, he publishes 'a cabin safety resource for all' on cabinsafetyinfo.com.

ICAO issues guidance in the form of non-binding manuals. Between 2013 and 2019 it issued six manuals with respect to cabin safety:

- *Cabin Crew Safety Training Manual* (Doc 10002).[8] This replaced the earlier guidance for training of cabin crew (then identified as 'cabin personnel') of 1976;[9]
- *Manual on the Approval and Use of Child Restraint Systems* (Doc 10049);
- *Manual on the Investigation of Cabin Safety Aspects in Accidents and Incidents* (Doc 10062);
- *Manual on Information and Instructions for Passenger Safety* (Doc 10086), giving guidance for safety-related instructions and information to passengers;
- *Manual on the Legal Aspects of Unruly and Disruptive Passengers* (Doc 10117), replacing and expanding on ICAO Circular 288 of 2002;
- *Manual on the Establishment of Minimum Cabin Crew Requirements* (Doc 10172), which gives guidance to countries, and other parties, in filling in the open-worded standards of Annex 6 to the Chicago Convention.

IATA, the International Air Transport Association, regularly updates its Cabin Operations Best Practices Guide. Originally published around 2015, it gives guidance of a practical nature for both airlines and staff engaged in cabin safety.

The Flight Safety Foundation publishes since 2013 cabin safety news and information online on its website. Uniquely, it had already started in 1956 by publishing cabin safety information on paper (Cabin Crew Safety Exchange, Cabin Crew Bulletin, Aerosafety World).

15.2.4 CONFERENCES

The Southern California Safety Institute since 1983 for many years organized its annual cabin safety symposium. Since 2014, IATA has held a Cabin Operations Safety Conference, which, as the organizer and name suggest, is primarily aimed at airlines and its staff.

Developments since 1997   241

In 1998, in anticipation of the Airbus A380 (then still referred to as the A3XX), the JAA organized, co-sponsored by the FAA and ICAO, the Very Large Transport Aeroplane Conference to discuss cabin safety aspects unique to this double-decker. The discussions led to several Special Conditions for the A380, such as the use of stairs between the two decks.[10]

For an update on research in fire safety and cabin safety subjects, the FAA since 1995 organizes every three years a conference that is typically venued in Atlantic City, New Jersey, the host town of the William Hughes Technical Center.

Since about the turn of the century, aviation training conferences aimed at cabin crew are held each year at several locations on the globe.

15.3 REGULATORY COMMITTEES

15.3.1 U.S.

The Aviation Rulemaking Advisory Committee, which was installed in May 1991, had three subcommittees on cabin safety subjects. The Emergency Evacuation Subcommittee, which was the first ARAC subcommittee ever, was tasked to come up with a new methodology for an evacuation performance standard. That, it did not do. Instead, it improved evacuation demonstration procedures with a view to reducing injuries. In 1998 the group changed its name to Occupants Safety Subcommittee as its focus changed to other items such as slides, exit marking, lower-deck service stations, and Type III exits. Harmonization with Europe became a key objective, but this was not always accomplished. A closing meeting of the Occupant Safety Subcommittee was held on October 17, 2002.[11]

The Transport Airplane Crashworthiness and Ditching Working Group was formed in 2015, composed mainly of manufacturers and research institutes. In the task assignment, the FAA explained:

> During the development of current airworthiness standards and regulatory guidance, the FAA assumed that airframe structure for transport airplanes would be constructed predominantly of metal, using skin-stringer-frame architecture. Therefore, certain requirements either do not address all of the issues associated with non-metallic materials, or have criteria that are based on experience with traditionally-configured large metallic airplanes. With respect to crashworthiness, there is no airframe-level standard for crashworthiness.

The assignment included a list of FAR 25 sections to be evaluated. That list extended beyond the purely crashworthiness and impact protection rules (25.561–25.563, 25.785–789). It included ditching (25.801) and ditching-related safety equipment (25.1411, 25.1415) but also emergency exits (25.807). In 2018, the Working Group submitted its report to the FAA.[12] It had interpreted its task liberally and extended it to subjects paraphernal to exits such as descent assist means, viewing devices, and exit signs. It called for some minor changes, in addition to a call for harmonization between FAA and EASA for some cabin safety subjects. By mid-2024, no rulemaking proposal had followed.

In 2015 and 2016, there were two high-profile evacuations in the U.S. Both involved wide-bodies and both ended without fatalities to the 170 occupants (in each case), but what was striking was that many passengers not only evacuated themselves but also their carry-on baggage. Such accidents had happened before and typically would not raise massive media attention. The evacuation of wide-bodies in New York JFK in November 1975 and July 1992, to just name two, were more dramatic but gained less attention at the time. The difference was that, in the 2010s, the amount of media coverage (both traditional media and the new phenomena of mobile telephone recording and social media) had changed significantly, and thus public attention. Plus that of the federal parliament, Congress. It renewed its attention to air carrier cabin safety after two decades of low profile. When the FAA's funding was again up for renewal in 2018, congressmen took the opportunity to require more research and rulemaking on evacuation issues. The Reauthorization Act of 2018 had three sections with specific tasks for the FAA with respect to evacuation. One was about seats and asked the FAA to:[13]

> issue, after notice and comment, such rules as necessary for the safety of passengers with regard to the minimum dimensions, including seat pitch, width, and length, of passenger seats.

The distance between seats, known as seat pitch, had decreased over the years in the U.S., influenced by low-cost carriers, a trend that had taken place in Europe decades earlier. In combination with the increase in the size of the traveling public (not necessarily by height but more by waist), it raised concerns about the ability to evacuate. The FAA had to act and did as congress demanded. FAA CAMI organized another series of evacuations, now focusing on the effects of seat size on evacuation. Unsurprisingly, they confirmed that seat size was not a matter that influenced the ability to evacuate. Each airliner manufacturer knew this already and so did actually the FAA. Jeffrey Gardlin, its key airworthiness cabin safety expert for close to 35 years, had stated in a formal declaration dated June 2018 that:[14]

> The FAA has seen no evidence that current seat width and pitch, on airplanes certificated to part 25 standards, create a safety issue. Neither evacuation tests nor real-world incidents requiring evacuation suggest that current seat dimensions (pitch and width) adversely affect the ability to rapidly evacuate an airplane.

The second task for the FAA was to:[15]

> conduct a review of current safety procedures regarding unoccupied exit rows on a covered aircraft in passenger air transportation during all stages of flight.

Jointly with representatives from U.S. airlines and cabin crew unions the FAA did that and concluded that evacuations would not be hindered due to unoccupied exit seats.[16] No Europeans were represented so it is unlikely that the viewpoints of EASA, which promoted assured occupancy of overwing exits, were taken into account.

The third task for the FAA was to review and report to Congress: (1) in consultation with stakeholders, the evacuation certification of aircraft and (2) recent actual evacuations.[17] Thereto, in 2019 a new ARAC (now ARC—Aviation Rulemaking Committee) subcommittee was formed: the Emergency Evacuation Standards Aviation Rulemaking Committee (EES ARC).[18] That group, composed of international cabin safety experts, looked again at emergency evacuations and went much deeper than the 1990s subcommittee. It looked at 290 evacuation events of the previous ten years, not reading formal investigation reports, but consulting the website of The Aviation Herald (www.avherald.com), which has tracked aviation incidents and accidents since March 1994. Unlike many previous U.S. studies, the scope was worldwide. Twenty-seven recommendations were made, many aimed at changing rule text. Remarkably, it also had an extensive section of 'non-recommendations': subjects looked at which did not prompt a recommendation. An example was a review of cases where evacuees had to jump distances close to 6 ft (1.8 m), such as from a wing trailing edge, where it concluded that this distance was safe to jump. None of the recommendations has yet led to rulemaking.

The FAA reported the results to Congress in March 2022 and formulated 12 recommendations.[19] It also put out a request for comments on the *Minimum Seat Dimensions Necessary for Safety of Air Passengers*. As usual, both industry representatives and the traveling public responded, along predictable lines. The industry, happy with the confirmation that the FAA CAMI tests gave, said that there is no need for further action. NACA, the association of ultralow cost carriers with such members as Allegiant Air, Avelo Air, Breeze Airways, Frontier Airlines, Spirit Airlines, and Sun Country Airlines concluded that seat size is a passenger comfort issue, not safety, and thus is an issue for the airlines but neither for the FAA nor for Congress. Opponents claimed that the FAA had incorrectly narrowed down the subject of seat safety to only one element: that of evacuation, whereas there are others. Sitting a long time in an unhealthy seat affects the safety of the passenger, they claimed. Other elements bordering between safety and health, they added, were the issues of deep vein thrombosis, blood clots, personal space, and even passenger conflicts. With respect to evacuation, they argued that families not sitting together would delay an evacuation as parents would try to get hold of their child first before moving on. Airlines charged a fee for seat allocations. The FAA did not recognize this as a safety matter, but Congress stepped in and in the next FAA reauthorization round ordered the Department of Transportation to prohibit airlines from charging for families sitting together.[20] In the same act, approved in May 2024, the FAA was tasked again to study evacuation, this time with a focus on persons with disabilities, although such subjects as carry-on baggage, seat size, service animals, and 'persons who do not speak English' slipped in as well. And, as previously, the results would then need to be reviewed by an ARC for which the composition must include, among others, representatives of the disability community, the elderly community, and 'pediatricians'.[21]

15.3.2 Europe

Since the early 1990s, Europe has increasingly become a player in cabin safety developments. There were several reasons for that. One was the single set of airworthiness requirements. When from the mid-1980s more aircraft types in Europe were certificated against JAR-25 the importance of the JAA grew. It became a single stop for the manufacturers. Previously, manufacturers had to apply for certification individually with each country in Europe. Another reason was the Manchester accident which was a sad reminder that despite the recent spur of developments in the U.S., cabin safety was all but finished.

From 1990 onward, the JAA regularly met with AECMA, the European Association of Aerospace Industries to discuss cabin safety matters. This led to the installation in 1992 of the JAA Cabin Safety Study Group (CSSG), initially chaired by Lionel Virr of the UK CAA. The Association of European Airlines and cabin crew organizations joined so that all stakeholders (bar the passengers) were engaged. This group not only discussed the adoption in Europe of new American rules but also discussed Europe-initiated subjects. The examples of the Type III exits and the green symbolic exit signs have already been discussed in the previous chapter.

15.4 TURBULENCE

The phenomenon of turbulence has been associated with aviation since its start but for a long time received little attention. Yet, already in 1965, the CAB published an overview of turbulence accidents over the years 1960–1963.[22] It concluded:

> the report clearly points out the desirability and advantages of keeping the safety belt fastened while seated and the need for prompt attention and compliance to the seat belt sign when turned on.

Except for several cases where severe turbulence led to a break-up of an airplane in the air, with the loss of all on board, turbulence has rarely caused a fatality. It has caused injuries in the cabin, occasionally serious but rarely a fatality. The worldwide rate has decreased from two to three fatalities per decade in the 1980s and 1990s to less than one in the 2010s and 2020s. A review of occurrences listed by The Aviation Herald for two randomly chosen years (2008 and 2023) indicated a frequency of about two serious cases of turbulence per month on average, with 100 to 200 passenger injuries and 30 to 60 cabin crew injuries. Among these, the number of serious injuries was much less but disproportionally higher for cabin crew than for passengers. Passengers are sedentary during flight, whereas cabin crew are active in the galleys and main cabin for the majority of the flight.

In 2021, the NTSB issued a safety study on the subject of turbulence.[23] This focused, rightly, on means to predict turbulence-inducing weather so that flying into turbulence-prone air can be avoided. With respect to injuries, like its predecessor in 1965, the NTSB found that the use of seat belts effectively eliminated these and supported the practice of airlines reminding passengers to keep their safety belts fastened. The NTSB focused on the single occupant group for which no seat belt is required in the U.S.: infants. They repeated their pleas for child restraint devices.

15.5 BRACE-FOR-IMPACT

Safety leaflets from the 1950s showed a diversity in brace-for-impact positions: (1) arms stretched with hands resting on the seat back in front; (2) arms folded against the reclined seat back, or table, in front, head braced on the arms, legs flexed forward; (3) sit with the back firmly against the seat back with hands resting on the top of that seat back; (4) upper torso and head bent forward with the face hidden in a pillow and arms either below or on top of it, feet firm on the floor. In all the positions, the person has the seat belt attached. A position where the person is unrestrained is that sitting on the floor, facing aft, with the back and head firmly against a partition, hand clasped behind the neck.

None of these postures was based on research. That came first in 1967 when CAMI started to do tests with instrumented anthropometric test dummies on a sled with two seats 35 inch (89 cm) apart.[24] The lowest head impacts 'were recorded when the dummies were seated so that their heads were resting against crossed arms which were placed against the seat back in front of the dummy'. Another position, not recommended, was: 'bend all the way forward and grab ankles', as the 'head directly against the lower seat back in front would compress the neck and the head between the torso and the seat, generating concern about cervical spinal column injury'. The results were distributed by the FAA in the form of an Air Carrier Operations Bulletin, first issued in 1969. Later tests were done and the bulletin was adjusted. However, because of the many variables in a cabin interior, no single brace-for-impact position would fit all, so only general principles were defined.

The Boeing 737-400 crash near East Midlands in 1989 triggered a new investigation by medical experts. Within one week of the accident, surgeons from four medical universities, known as the NLDB study group (Nottingham, Leicester, Derby, Belfast) started to study the injuries and looked for patterns.[25] They issued a recommended brace-for-impact position, with the head bent forward against the seat in front, with the hands on top of the head, so not crossed. They said that this posture should be drawn to the attention of passengers prior to every flight, considering that this 'is much more relevant than the routine demonstration of the life jackets'.[26]

In the 2005 Toronto Air France Airbus A340 accident, the investigators found that the airline showed two different brace-for-impact positions on its safety card: a body upright position and a bent forward position.[27] Although not mentioned in the card, the former was meant for economy class seats and the latter for business class seats, the rationale given that in economy class seats there is no space for bending forward. This was neither in line with advised brace-for-impact positions nor with what other airlines used. The airline has since changed its cards.

In 2015, FAA CAMI conducted extensive research into brace-for-impact positions.[28] This led to a correction of a previously advertised position in which occupants placed their hands on the top of the seat back and their heads against the seat back. The better position was to place the hands down by the lower legs instead of on the seat back. The latest revision of the Advisory Circular about safety briefing information was adjusted accordingly.[29]

The question of the best brace position remained being debated. In 2016, under the auspices of ICAO, a group of experts from Canada, Germany, South Korea, the U.S., and the UK was formed to produce an internationally agreed, evidence-based set of impact bracing positions for passengers and cabin crewmembers in a variety of seating configurations.[30] This is the International Board for Research into Aircraft Crash Events, a string of words engineered to form a fitting acronym:

Developments since 1997 245

FIGURE 15.1 Brace-for-impact position, Air France, 1953.

FIGURE 15.2 Brace-for-impact position, Air France, 1953, aft-facing on floor.

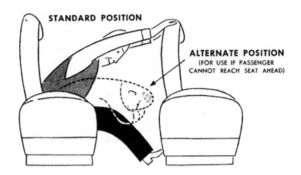

FIGURE 15.3 Brace-for-impact position, Northwest Airlines, 1953.

FIGURE 15.4 Brace-for-impact position, Lufthansa, 1957.

FIGURE 15.5 Brace-for-impact position, BOAC, 1957.

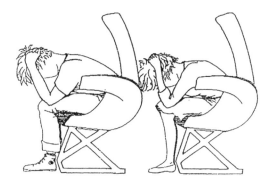

FIGURE 15.6 Recommended brace-for-impact position, NLDB group, 1990.

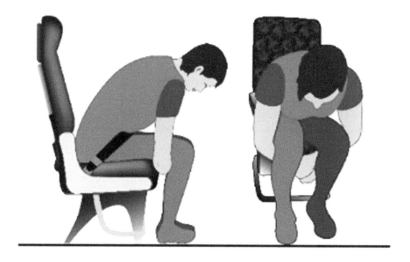

FIGURE 15.7 Brace position as reproduced in Advisory Circular 121–24D (2019).

IBRACE. They concluded that they were unable to recommend one single brace position, even for passengers seated in the most frequent seats: forward-facing economy class.

15.6 AIR CONTAMINATION

Already in the 1970s flight attendants had begun to air concerns about perceived contamination of cabin air. In 1981 a bill was proposed by Senator Inouye to commission a study into cabin air quality.[31] The FAA was against it. After more pressure from Congress, the study was eventually done in 1986 by the National Research Council but did not lead to any regulatory changes.[32]

The matter all but disappeared. It lingered on for many decades. Some airplane types appeared more susceptible than others, notably the BAe 146. In Australia, a parliamentary inquiry focused on this airplane type after multiple reports of poor quality cabin air, leading to crew health issues and crew avoiding flying this type of airplane.[33] The specific concern was that cabin air, which was supplied as bleed air from the engines, upstream of the combustion chambers, might be contaminated with lubrication oil. This led to what was referred to as 'fume events'. The bleed air concept is generally used on all airplane types but one. The Boeing 787, introduced in 2010, is bleed free. It has electrically powered compressors that take over the function of the engines in pressurizing incoming air.

In 2002, another cabin air quality study was done in the U.S., again by the National Research Council.[34] As before, it concluded that data was lacking so no recommendations for regulations were made. However, more monitoring was advised. In 2012, 2018, and again in 2024 Congress asked for the continuation of investigation of the issue.[35]

In Europe, the subject was taken seriously by EASA in the 2010s. It became the subject of a series of research projects, funded by EASA and the European Commission and led by Fraunhofer ITEM. As part of this, several workshops were held, the first of which took place in January 2020, only weeks before another phenomenon related to cabin air quality and health reared: COVID-19. Many presentations by various stakeholders were given.[36] The overall impression is that the subject is complicated, has both physiological and toxicological aspects, and is broader than the bleed air issue. In 2024, research is still in progress.[37]

15.7 PANDEMICS

Of the pandemics that struck the world, the one labeled COVID-19 by far had the largest impact on air transport. At its onset, the speed of bringing persons home sometimes overrode cabin safety. U.S. repatriation flights from Wuhan, China in January 2020 were carried out in all-cargo Boeing 747s, with about 200 passenger seats added in the huge cargo area. Apparently, dispensations had been obtained for exit and oxygen standards, but, according to media reports, they appeared not to have been met.[38] Once the pandemic struck, the airlines, together with medical and aviation authorities, introduced a host of measures that affected operations, including cabin operations. These measures were aimed at reducing the risk of transmission of the COVID-19 virus, without impinging on cabin safety standards. However, in some areas, contingencies were needed. EASA issued guidance for member states to issue exemptions for the carriage of cargo in passenger cabins.[39] ICAO issued a document prescribing alternate methods for cabin crew to remain current now that physical distancing and workplace closure made it increasingly difficult for them to attend hands-on training.[40]

15.8 REGULATORY DEVELOPMENTS

15.8.1 EUROPE

Soon after EASA took over from the JAA in 2003, the CSSG was dismantled, but EASA kept cabin safety in focus. In several cabin safety subdomains, EASA became leading, such as the formulation of regulations and guidance material for passenger amenities (showers, large display panels), the transport of special categories of passengers, and precautions with respect to lithium batteries. EASA issued a dedicated set of requirements for large airplanes used privately or by corporations (CS-25 Appendix S). EASA publishes guidance material next to regulations, as opposed to the FAA, where guidance is spread over several documents as explained in the Cabin Safety Subject Index.

15.8.2 IMPACT PROTECTION

15.8.2.1 16 g Seats

Having learned from the tedious introduction of 16 g seats for new aircraft types, in October 2002, the FAA issued a Supplemental NPRM on the subject to test the waters for its fleetwise introduction. This time it proposed a 14-year retrofit compliance period, starting not at the date of the SNPRM issue (as was done in 1988 with the seven-year compliance period), but at the date the final rule would be published. A three-pronged approach was suggested. Airplanes with pre-1993 type certificates that still were being manufactured would need to comply from four years after the publication of the Final Rule (forward fit). Earlier delivered airplanes receiving new shipsets of seats would also need 16 g seats after four years. The 14-year deadline would apply to all remaining airplanes in the fleets (retrofit). But this scheme did not make it either. When the final rule was published three years later, only the forward-fit option was mandated: airplanes newly manufactured from October 2009 onward needed to be 16 g compliant. By then many older airplane types had left the fleets, partly accelerated by the post 9/11 traffic decline. It was no longer justified to require that the remaining fleets be so equipped.

Europe was slow in copying this requirement. EASA issued an NPA in 2013, which, as in the U.S., was limited to the forward-fit option: only new airplanes of types already certificated and manufactured from a certain date onward would need to comply. That date became 26 February 2021. But by then, most of the European fleets complied. They either existed of airplanes compliant per type certificate or so equipped on a voluntary basis.

Thus came to an end a discussion of improving seat standards that had taken seven decades. Already in the early 1950s suggestions had been raised to improve seat strength standards to 20 g and more.[41] Dynamic testing of seats was first suggested by Hasbrook in 1956.[42] Seats with energy-absorbing features, and dynamically tested, were briefly in fashion on a voluntary basis in the early 1960s. Petitions for making dynamic seat testing mandatory had been filed in the 1960s and 1970s. From 1973 onward, the FAA repeatedly said it was researching the subject, but seemed not to put their actions where their mouth was. In 1981, the NTSB issued a special study on cabin safety in large transport aircraft in which it again asked for dynamic testing of seats.[43] It had even appended a detailed proposal to help the FAA formulate FAR 25 standards. In the same period, Congress put increasing pressure on the FAA. New airplane types had to comply from the mid-1990s and finally newly manufactured airplanes from 2009 (U.S.) and 2021 (Europe), respectively.

15.8.2.2 Child Restraints

On February 12, 1997, the White House Commission on Aviation Safety and Security issued a final report to President Clinton which included a recommendation on the use of CRS during flight. The following is an excerpt from the final report as it relates to CRSs:[44]

> The FAA should revise its regulations to require that all occupants be restrained during takeoff, landing, and turbulent conditions, and that all infants and small children below the weight of 40 pounds and under the height of 40 inches be restrained in an appropriate child restraint system, such as child safety seats, appropriate to their height and weight.

The FAA responded by issuing an Advance NPRM in February 1998 soliciting comments from the public on issues relating to the use of child restraint systems (CRSs) in aircraft during all phases of flight (i.e. taxi, take-off, landing, or any other time the seat belt sign is illuminated). Specifically, it sought crash performance and ease-of-use information about existing and new automotive CRSs, when used in aircraft, as well as the development of any other new or improved CRSs designed exclusively for aircraft use. In 2005 the FAA published a review.[45] There were many responses but few answered the specific questions of the FAA. Citing more recent studies, the FAA reaffirmed its earlier position that mandating the use of CRSs in aircraft would have the 'unintended consequence of causing a net increase in transportation injuries and fatalities'. To avoid the cost of an extra seat, passengers with an infant would revert to car travel, which is more dangerous.

At the same time, the FAA published a final rule allowing the use of CRS specifically designed for aircraft use and thus approved by the FAA.[46] Previously, they were permitted on an exemption basis, whereas automotive CRSs were acceptable when properly labeled for aircraft use. The use of FAA-approved CRSs however was limited to airlines. The next year, the FAA widened the options for CRSs allowed on board so that parents were no longer dependent on the airline.[47] But the subject of CRSs remained problematic. In practice, some of them, although FAA approved, did not fit airline seats. This prompted the FAA in 2015 to introduce a requirement that airlines publish on their websites seat dimensions so that caregivers, as the passengers with an infant were now called, could determine in advance whether their CRS would fit.[48]

ICAO, in 2015, published guidelines on CRS for regulators and operators. The document includes a summary of relevant research, not only of dedicated CRS but also of loop belts and even infant slings.[49] One of the research studies cited, conducted in 2008 by TÜV Rheinland, funded by EASA, comprehensively described earlier studies, accidents, available solutions, and regulatory options.[50]

15.8.3 Fire Protection

Halon, the superior agent for fire extinguishing that was introduced around 1980, had one important negative side effect: it contributes to ozone depletion and global warming and has therefore been globally banned. Civil aviation was one of the few areas where its continued use was allowed, but this has gradually been curtailed as well. Alternative agents have been identified and listed in an Advisory Circular issued in 2011.[51] EASA, together with the European Commission, published guidelines as to when Halon alternatives must be used.[52]

In 2019, after almost a decade of preparation using the ARAC system, the FAA proposed changes to the method of flammability testing by introducing performance standards.[53] Until then, the flammability standards were prescriptive and differed on the part's physical composition or function (e.g. side panel). The heat release and smoke emission standards introduced in the 1980s were proposed to be replaced by performance standards. Now, two scenarios were distinguished: in-flight cabin fires and post-crash fires. For the latter, the performance standard was simply stated as:

> During a post-crash fuel fire, the flammability characteristics of each part, component, and assembly must maintain survivable cabin conditions for enough time to allow evacuation.

For the in-flight scenario, a new subscenario was added: extensively used materials located in inaccessible areas. Such materials include electrical wiring, ducting, and composite structures. The new approach was by no means intended to reduce the level of safety but added flexibility. In the words of the FAA:

> The FAA is issuing this proposal to simplify flammability regulations and provide a higher level of safety for transport-category airplanes. The current regulations are complicated, sometimes conflicting, sometimes redundant, occasionally incomplete, and may be obsolete for dealing with present-day proposed airplanes.

A regulatory change was that the detailed test criteria were downgraded from rule material to guidance material. The changes would affect newly type certificated airplanes only. In August 2023, the proposal was reissued for a second round of comments, also giving a discussion of the comments received on the 2019 NPRM.[54]

15.8.4 Escape Potential

Augmenting the many escape-related requirements of the third wave, in 1996 the FAA proposed a series of minor improvements for the evacuation scenario.[55] They concerned both cabin fuselage doors and internal doors. An assist space next to slide-equipped exits was already required, but no dimensions were specified. The FAA went into its history books and found a 1958 policy by its ancestor, the CAA, specifying such a space: adjacent to the exit, 'adequate to permit an attendant to stand erect and to perform needed assist service in the evacuation of passengers' of 12 by 20 inch (30 cm by 51 cm).[56] This dimension was now proposed to become a legal requirement. Coming along was a proposal for an assist handle so that the person using the assist space can steady him- or herself when assisting with the evacuation and, earlier, when using the manual inflation handle of the escape slide, if needed. Although flight attendants were trained to look outside a door for fire before opening it, not all doors had the means to do so. Hence, the FAA proposed a means to view the outside. The wording deliberately avoided the word 'window' to allow other means, such as prismatic viewing devices. Finally on fuselage doors, a proposal was added for a door hold-open device to prevent opened doors from slamming back, as may particularly happen when the aircraft ends up in an unusual attitude due to partial gear collapse.

The prohibition for internal doors which had been introduced in 1967 only applied between passenger compartments, not between a passenger compartment and an emergency exit. There were many cases, especially in VIP aircraft, where there was such a door. The only requirement was that it be locked open during taxi, take-off, and landing. The new proposal prohibited such doors as well.

All these proposals were adopted in the final rule, which was published eight years after the NPRM. They became effective not only for new types (by FAR 25), but, except for the internal doors, also for aircraft newly manufactured, with a lead time of two to three years.[57] In the preamble to the final rule, the FAA concluded that:

> These amendments are deemed necessary and appropriate by the FAA considering the current state-of-the-art and existing design practice. Although nearly all existing installations already comply, these amendments will ensure that any others comply as well.

15.8.5 Life Support

In April 1998, the Aviation Medical Assistance Act was enacted. It stimulated the FAA to turn its rulemaking attention to medical situations on board. The previous time it had done so was in 1986 when a requirement for an emergency medical kit was introduced. Now, it came with two equipment improvements plus an update for associated training, mainly for flight attendants. Around that time, airlines, both U.S. and non-U.S., started to carry Automatic External Defibrillators (AEDs) on board. The FAA now proposed this to be required equipment on all aircraft on which a flight attendant is required and the payload capacity exceeds 7,500 pounds (3,402 kg).[58] It warned that the new requirements intended to provide options for treatment, not to raise expectations in the passenger or physician community regarding the level of medical care available in flight.[59] The medical kit needed to be enhanced with equipment specific to the following: to relieve symptoms associated with allergies and hay fever; to relieve muscle aches and headaches; an inhaler, used to help restore normal breathing in asthmatics. In addition, it needed equipment associated with the use of the AED. The new equipment, and the associated training, became effective to U.S. air carriers in April 2004.[60] Other countries followed suit or, based on local medical advice, made their own content lists for first-aid and medical kits.

NOTES

1. Amdt 25-91.
2. FAA Advisory and Rulemaking Committee, Occupant Safety Subcommittee (1999–2002).
3. Aviation Safety: Advancements Being Pursued to Improve Airliner Cabin Occupant Safety and Health, GAO-04-33, U.S. Government Accountability Office, October 3, 2003.
4. Emergency Evacuation of Commercial Airplanes, Special Study, NTSB SS-00/01, June 27, 2000.
5. Emergency Evacuation of Commercial Passenger Aeroplanes, Royal Aeronautical Society, Second Edition, June 2020.
6. Study on CS-25 Cabin Safety Requirements, by R.G.W. Cherry & Associates Ltd., Issue 6, December 2009.

7 Carriage by Air of Special Categories of Passenger, Contract Number: EASA.2008.C.25, Martin Sperber, Dr. Hendrik Schäbe, Daniel Masling, David Toth, Jan Küting, Michael Demary, Gero Wodli, TÜV Rheinland Kraftfahrt GmbH, November 9, 2010, Study on Child Restraint Systems, TÜV Rheinland Kraftfahrt GmbH, Contract Number: EASA.2007.C.28, 29 November 2008.
8 Cabin Crew Safety Training Manual, ICAO Doc 10002, Second Edition, 2020.
9 Training Manual—Cabin Personnel, ICAO Doc 7192-AN/857 Part E-1, First Edition, 1976.
10 Annex to TCDS EASA.A.110-A380.
11 67 FR 62281.
12 Transport Aircraft Crashworthiness and Ditching Working Group Report to FAA, Release Revision B, September 20, 2019.
13 FAA Reauthorization Act of 2018, sec. 577.
14 Declaration of Jeffrey C. Gardlin, June 21, 2018, in Docket FAA-2015-4011 on regulations.gov.
15 FAA Reauthorization Act of 2018, sec. 323.
16 Report to Congress: Federal Aviation Administration Reauthorization Act of 2018 (Pub. L. No. 115-254)—sec. 323, Issued on May 17, 2022.
17 FAA Reauthorization Act of 2018, sec. 337.
18 Emergency Evacuation Standards, Aviation Rulemaking Committee Final Report, May 20, 2020.
19 Report to Congress: Aircraft Cabin Evacuation Procedures, by FAA Aviation Safety, March 31, 2022.
20 FAA Reauthorization Act of 2024, sec. 516.
21 FAA Reauthorization Act of 2024, sec. 365.
22 Air Carrier Accidents Involving in-Flight Turbulence, Calendar Years 1960-1963, CAB Bureau of Safety, September 1965.
23 Preventing Turbulence-Related Injuries in Air Carrier Operations Conducted Under Title 14 Code if Federal Regulations Part 121, Safety Research Report, NTSB/SS-21/01, Adopted August 10, 2021.
24 Brace for Impact Positions, Richard F. Chandler, in Proceedings of the Fifth Annual International Aircraft Cabin Safety Symposium, cosponsored by USC, FAA, SCSI, February 1988.
25 Computer Simulation of Impact and Correlation with Bodily Injuries, by Professor W. Angus Wallace, John Rowles, Raf Haldar, in Proceedings of the European Cabin Safety Conference 1990, CAP 583, April 1991, p. 211.
26 CAP 583, p. 212.
27 Aviation Investigation Report Runway Overrun and Fire Air France Airbus A340-313 F-GLZQ Toronto/Lester B. Pearson International Airport, Ontario 02 August 2005, Transportation Safety Board of Canada, Report Number A05H0002, Released 16 October 2007.
28 Effect of Passenger Position on Crash Injury Risk in Transport-Category Aircraft, Amanda M. Taylor, Richard L. DeWeese, David M. Moorcroft, FAA CAMI, DOT/FAA/AM-15/17, September 2015.
29 Passenger Safety Information Briefing and Briefing Cards, Advisory Circular 121-24D, U.S. Department of Transportation, Federal Aviation Administration, March 5, 2019.
30 International Board for Research into Aircraft Crash Events, Wikipedia, Visited 25 May 2024.
31 Airliner Cabin Safety and Health Standards, Hearing Before the Subcommittee on Aviation of the Committee on Commerce, Science, and Transportation, United States Senate, 97th Congress, Second Session, May 20, 1982, p. 1.
32 The Airliner Cabin Environment: Air Quality and Safety, National Research Council, 1986.
33 Air Safety and Cabin Air Quality in the BAe 146 Aircraft, Report by the Senate Rural and Regional Affairs and Transport References Committee, Parliament of the Commonwealth of Australia, October 2000.
34 The Airliner Cabin Environment and the Health of Passengers and Crew, National Research Council (US) Committee on Air Quality in Passenger Cabins of Commercial Aircraft, 2002.
35 H.R.658—FAA Modernization and Reform Act of 2012, 112th Congress (2011–2012);
    H.R.302—FAA Reauthorization Act of 2018, 115th Congress (2017-2018); H.R. 3935—FAA Reauthorization Act of 2024, 118th Congress (2023-2024), sec. 362.
36 Workshop on Future Cabin Air Quality Research 30–31 January 2020. www.easa.europa.eu/en/newsroom-and-events/events/easa-workshop-future-cabin-air-quality-research.
37 www.easa.europa.eu/en/newsroom-and-events/events/cabin-air-quality-research-workshop.
38 www.aviation24.be/airlines/kalitta-air/boeing-747-400-freighter-repatriates-u-s-citizens-from-wuhan-china/, Visited 27 May 2024.
39 European Union Aviation Safety Agency, Guidelines Transport of Cargo in Passenger Compartment—Exemptions under Article 71(1) of Regulation (EU) 2018/1139.

40 ICAO Handbook for Cabin Crew Recurrent Training during COVID-19, Doc 10148, 2020.
41 Human Factors in Air Transportation—Occupational Health and Safety, Ross A. McFarland, 1953, p. 559.
42 Design of Passenger "Tie-Down", Av-CIR-44-0-66, A. Howard Hasbrook, Aviation Crash Injury Research of Cornell University, September 1956.
43 Special Study—Cabin Safety in Large Transport Aircraft, NTSB-AAS-81-2, September 9, 1981.
44 ANPRM 98-2.
45 70 FR 50226.
46 Amdt 121-314.
47 Amdt 121-326.
48 Amdt 121-373.
49 Manual on the Approval and Use of Child Restraint Systems, ICAO Doc 10049, 2015.
50 Study on Child Restraint Systems, 2008.
51 Hand Fire Extinguishers for Use in Aircraft, FAA, Advisory Circular 20-42D, January 14, 2011.
52 Halon Replacement in the Aviation Industry, EASA and European Commission, November 2019.
53 NPRM 19-09.
54 SNPRM 23-12.
55 NPRM 96-9.
56 Supp. 37 to CAR 4b.
57 Amdt 25-116,121-306.
58 Amdt 25-91.
59 NPRM 00-03.
60 Amdt 121-281.

16 Exit Credit Creativity

ABSTRACT

Ever since the 1951 prescription of the exit types and the exit-to-capacity table, which were soon seen as prescriptive and arbitrary, manufacturers have found ways to circumvent it. This chapter discusses the various methods employed for both increasing the seating capacity beyond that prescribed and, conversely, reducing the egress potential for reduced seating capacities. These methods resulted from dialogue between the manufacturers and the certificating authorities and saw an increasing amount of creativity.

16.1 INTRODUCTION

Exits installed in an airplane dictate how many passengers may be carried. When airlines choose a new airplane type, this is one of the criteria that can determine their decision for one type or another. Manufacturers are therefore keen to have listed in their type certification document the highest passenger capacity possible. While this, prima facie, looks like a clearcut case of simply following the regulatory exit tables, in practice, it is not.

When in the 1950s the first airplane types were designed that fell under the new 1951 exit table, its drawbacks came to light. It was restrictive and inconsistent and thus inflexible. It prescribed passenger capacities as a step function of exits installed, as opposed to a continuum. It was inconsistent in that it implied different credits for the same size of exits. Depending on the size of the airplane, a Type I exit was worth either 40 or 50 seats. Small improvements in exit height or step-up or step-down distance were not appreciated. The question arose as to how strictly the certificating authority would apply the table. The first to test this were Douglas and Fokker. They devised a method that allowed the CAA, and its successor the FAA, to exercise flexibility in applying the exit table.

Since its first appearance in 1951, the table was modified in 1957 and 1967 (with minor changes in 1972 and 1977) and replaced in 1996 by a different concept. None of these changes however removed the inconsistencies. Rather the opposite; it added more of them. The Type I range of credits was extended from 40 to 70 and other inconsistencies were added. The 1996 change, which was intended to present a 'more ordered and less confusing progression of exit configurations of various seating capacities', as McSweeny put it, did not take away the root cause of its inflexibility. That was its prescriptive and stepwise nature. The single time that the FAA, in 1991, asked ARAC to investigate whether a performance standard could replace or supplement the evacuation design requirements this resulted in a change to the evacuation demonstration requirements instead.

With the prescriptive rule remaining, over many decades two manufacturers in particular (Boeing and Airbus) developed and perfected methods that came close to converting it into a continuum. They reached, in harmony with the regulators, a degree of sophistication that resembled an art. The art of exit credit creativity. This development took many forms: non-standard exits, non-standard exit combinations (known as alternate exit configurations), over-sized exits, overperforming exits, and clever use of grandfather rights.

While the art of exit credit creativity was primarily aimed at finding and certificating the maximum capacity possible for a given exit configuration, the inflexible tables posed similar challenges for the reverse task: optimizing exit configurations for lesser capacities. This translated into such concepts as exit de-rating, exit deactivation, and defining capacities for 'truncated' cabins such as applied in combi airplanes where passengers share the same deck with cargo.

16.2 SEEKING HIGHER MAXIMUM CAPACITIES

16.2.1 Non-standard Exits

The first method to cope with the inflexible table was called 'non-standard exit'. In 1956 Douglas was in the process of designing their first jet, the DC-8. Two pairs of overwing exits were projected, but of which size? Due to the shape of the wing, its aft pair had a step-down larger than required for a Type III but still meeting that for a Type IV. Douglas had the option of reverting to the smaller Type IV exit but preferred the larger opening of the Type III. It considered this to be a safer option, but would then face non-compliance with the CAR 4b exit standard.

In January 1956, an industry-wide meeting was held with the CAB and the CAA on exit provisions for high-density jet transports. Manufacturers, airlines, and both pilot and cabin crew unions were represented. There, the authorities gave assurance that credits would be given to exit improvements when supported by sound technical data. This led Douglas to embark on a very extensive series of tests. John A. Roebuck and William G. Littlewood, working for the Human Factors Group of the Interiors Design Section, subjected participants to the overwing exit as proposed for the DC-8 and compared it with both Type III and Type IV exits.[1] Exit height and step-up and step-down heights were varied. They concluded in their report counting 382 pages that the height of the opening was the factor that most influenced the rate of egress. Next was step-down (the dimension where the DC-8 aft Type III exit was not in compliance) and third, step-up. Other results of interest, some of which counter-intuitive, were that (1) exit widths beyond 19 inch (48 cm) did not significantly alter results; (2) taller persons negotiated exits better than medium and short persons; (3) motivation and agility seemed more important discriminants than body dimensions; (4) women were generally slower than men; (5) assist handles and handholds did not help, but footholds outside did; (6) the wearing of inflated life vests did not decrease the rate of egress; and, last but not least, (7) Type III exits were significantly faster than Type IV exits.

The tests convinced the certificating authority that even though the step-down was too high, the exit as proposed by Douglas performed as good as a true Type III exit. The exit thus was credited as if it were a Type III in all respects. Later, Douglas repeated this on the DC-9.

Around the same time, Fokker managed to show equivalent safety for their non-standard exits. The turboprop Fokker F-27 (and its U.S. version built under license by Fairchild) had a Type I exit that was 5 inch (13 cm) wider but lacked 4 inch (10 cm) in height to meet the Type I dimension. Its Type IV exits were not located over the wing, as prescribed. This was not possible as the F-27 was a high-wing airplane. The 1951 regulations did not account for such a configuration. As part of certification by the Dutch CAA and the FAA in 1957, these non-standard exits were successfully subjected to tests to demonstrate that they were equivalent in performance.

The FAA issued a protocol for testing non-standard exits in May 1964, called *Test procedures for evaluating nonstandard exits for transport category airplanes*.[2] Since then, other airplane manufacturers made use of non-standard exits and airplane types were accepted using this test procedure, which became known as the Latin Square test method. It worked like this:

Two test groups of evacuees are composed and subjected to two exit configurations, one of which conforms to a regulatory exit type while the other is the exit for which equivalency is sought. Test group A is first subjected to the first exit configuration and then the second. Test group

TABLE 16.1
Latin Square Test Method for Comparing Exits

	Test Group A	Test Group B
Regulatory exit type	First test	Second test
Proposed exit	Second test	First test

TABLE 16.2
Tail Exit Credits

Exit Type	Size of Opening in Bulkhead	Descent Assist Means	Example	Credit per Exemption	NPRM	Final Rule
Ventral	Type I	Stairs	Boeing 727–100	12	10	12
Tail cone	Type III	Rope	Douglas DC-9–10	13	15	15
Tail cone	20 inch by 60 inch	Slide	Douglas DC-9–30	18	20	25

B, conversely, is first subjected to the second exit configuration and then the first. By doing this, the effects of a test group gaining experience are canceled out. If the results for the proposed exit are equal to or better than the regulatory exit, then there is a good cause for accepting the proposed exit as equivalent.

Three non-standard exits that quickly became adopted in FAR 25 in the 1960s were tail exits. The Boeing 727 was equipped with in-built stairs in the tail for boarding which gave access to the cabin via a door in the aft pressure bulkhead. These stairs could be deployed in an emergency for evacuation. Boeing gained an extra 12 passenger seats for that exit. Douglas started its DC-9 without stairs in the tail but designed the tail cone to be deployable for use as an evacuation route. This required a hole in the aft pressure bulkhead to access the tail area from the passenger cabin. That hole was of Type III exit dimensions with a step-up on the cabin side and a step-down into the tail area. Soon, however, Douglas saw the merit of built-in stairs in the tail for boarding. That required a larger opening in the pressure bulkhead, so they designed a door which offered an opening larger than Type I dimensions, with a full height for normal use. Douglas received credits of 13 and 18, respectively, for these two designs.

In 1967, these non-standard exits were codified in FAR 25.807 and so became standard exits. The associated credits were even higher than those initially awarded for the 727 and DC-9. Table 16.2 summarizes the developments.[3]

Other airplane types that employed tail exits and got a credit for it were the BAC One-Eleven (with a credit of 10 for its ventral exit) and the Sud-Est Caravelle. For the latter's last iteration, the Caravelle 12, which was approved for 131 passengers, a credit for the stairs of 17 can be inferred.[4] By 2024, all these airplane types, with the exception of a few DC-9 derivatives such as the Boeing 717 have been phased out. The last DC-9 derivative, albeit not recognized as such, is the Chinese ARJ-21. It has no tail exit but a pair of aft side exits.

16.2.2 Over-Sized Exit

When the four exit Types were introduced in 1951, the following note was added:[5]

> Larger openings than those specified in paragraph (b) of this section will be acceptable, whether or not of rectangular shape, provided the specified rectangular openings can be inscribed therein, and further provided that the base of the opening affords a flat surface not less than the width specified.

Initially, this note merely meant that exits needed not exactly be of the specified size, but could be larger. It was not an incentive for a higher credit. Only when in 1967 the second table was added and thus fixed credits were assigned per exit type, did this option theoretically allow a higher credit. The first manufacturer to realize this and take benefit from it was McDonnell Douglas (MDD). Initially, the forward exit pair of its DC-10 was certificated as a Type I pair with a credit of 45. However, it was significantly larger: 32 by 76 inch in lieu of 24 by 48 inch (81 by 193 cm in lieu of 61 by 121 cm). Within a year, MDD applied for an equivalent safety finding and got a credit of 80 for this exit.

It was dubbed a Type B exit. Much later, the Type B exit was made formal, and a credit of 75 was assigned to it.

In 1990, the FAA formalized the over-sized exit by raising the note text into a requirement.[6]

16.2.3 Alternate Exit Configurations

In some cases, the creativity went a step further than getting the maximum out of an exit size. Combinations of exits of various sizes and locations were tried. The dash 80 version of the DC-9, better known as the MD-80, is a good example. Using the DC-9–50 model as a basis, MDD stretched it and added one-floor level, Type I exit on the side, between the wing and the aft-mounted engine. This exit was on the left side only, but MDD claimed that together with the existing tail cone exit, it was now a pair. Not a pair in the sense that there were exits on either side, but rather one on the side and one at the very airplane's end. Applying the table, and arguing that both were equipped with inflatable slides so that the grandfather clause applied, it asked for a maximum capacity of 189. The FAA did not agree. After ample consideration, it granted a maximum of 172.[7] That figure was composed of 109 per the table for the forward and overwing exits (of which the aft overwing exit pair was based on an equivalent level of safety finding itself), plus 5 for the inflatable slides at the forward exits, plus 58 for the combination of the new side exit and the tail cone exit. But even that 58 stood out quite fortunate as a normal Type I exit pair was only good for 45 seats. MDD was treated well, particularly in light of the poor evacuation performance that tail exits later proved to have in real emergencies.

Another example of an alternate exit configuration was that of the British, high-wing, four-engined jet, the British Aerospace (BAe) 146 with a seating capacity of around 110. It was configured with two pairs of floor-level exits, one pair at each cabin end. That configuration did not meet the table as that prescribed a pair of Type III exits in lieu of the second-floor-level exit pair. BAe in 1982 applied for an exemption with the FAA, claiming the inability to place Type III exits in a high-wing airplane and that Type I exits would perform better. The FAA agreed, granting a capacity of 108. The British CAA granted 10 more. Later, BAe developed a stretch version for a maximum of 124 passengers, for which it did add a Type III exit pair below the wings.[8] That variant was certificated in the United Kingdom, but not put into production.

The concept of alternate exit configurations was formally adopted in 1990 when FAR 25.807(d)(5) was introduced.[9] Previously they had been approved under the more general provision for an equivalent level of safety.

16.2.4 Grandfather Rights

Another way of securing maximum passenger capacities higher than allowed by FAR 25.807 was the use of grandfather rights. In 1958, the CAA promoted the use of inflatable slides by allowing five extra seats for each pair of floor-level exits so equipped. This incentive started as a CAA policy but was elevated into a rule in 1964. As inflatable slides no longer were novelties but had become the norm, the FAA in 1966 proposed to cancel this incentive. Industry objected and the FAA paused the proposal until 1972 when it was adopted. Yet, airplane types originally certificated in that period could continue to make use of it on derivatives, so long as they did not change the door and slide system. This was called a grandfather right and applied to all 'grandchildren', that is, derivatives of the original type. Types that benefited were the Douglas DC-9, with all its derivatives including the Boeing 717, Boeing's 707 family, 727 family, and, particularly, the 737 family. On the latter type, Boeing employed this grandfather right to its extreme. It had two pairs of floor-level exits, so the gain was 10 seats more than the table allowed. The 737 has seen many derivatives and Boeing retained this option each time it updated it. It is now in its fourth generation. This explains why the Max 8 and 9 still use the same slide design as that developed in the 1960s. It still requires flight attendants to kneel down each time they must arm or disarm the slide.

16.2.5 Overperforming Exits

Airbus for many years had a competitive disadvantage with its A320 model versus the Boeing 737-800. Where Airbus was only allowed a capacity of 179, the 737 had a capacity of 189 for the same exit configuration. This difference of 10 was because of the grandfather right that the 1960s Boeing could use, but the 1980s Airbus could not. Yet, the exit systems of the Airbus were more modern, with automatic slide engagement on the floor-level exits and overwing hatches that were better to handle as they were much lighter. It had off-wing slides as opposed to the 737 with an off-wing jump distance of just below 6 ft. Airbus was unable to capitalize on that. With significant efforts, it managed to gain one extra seat in 1995. But later, it became more creative and found the certificating authorities more forthcoming. It invented the concept of overperforming exits. The difference between an over-sized exit and an overperforming exit is that the latter is about the exit system, thus including the assist means and access to the exit. The use of such exits, with double-lane slides replacing single lane slides, brought the A320 capacity up to 190 (in the U.S.) and 195 (in Europe). Airbus used the concept of overperforming exits on other types as well. The A350-1000 with so-called Type A+ exits is good for 480 seats (so a credit of 120) when there are three cabin crewmembers per exit pair.[10]

Fokker in 1994 wished to raise the capacity of its Fokker 70 beyond what the 1990 rule proposal allowed. For its two exit pairs (Type I at the front, Type III overwing) FAR 25.807 prescribed a maximum capacity of 80. Fokker conducted a Latin Square test. It compared the right forward exit, which met Type I exit dimensions and was equipped with an automatic, inflatable slide, with a Fokker 50 Type I exit without slide and a jump distance of just under 6 ft (1.8 m). (The Fokker 50's normal jump distance was lower, but the aircraft had been jacked up to increase the exit-to-ground distance.) As expected, the results were in favor of the Fokker 70 Type I exit, and a raise in the capacity of five seats was granted by the Dutch CAA and later, EASA.

For the latest Boeing 737 derivative, the Max 10, the FAA issued in March 2024 an Equivalent Level of Safety (ELOS) finding allowing 189 passenger seats in lieu of 175.[11] Such an ELOS was needed because the Max 10 grandfathering was curtailed in the wake of the two dramatic and much-publicized Max 8 crashes of 2018 and 2019. The later certification basis would limit the airplane to 175 passenger seats. Boeing had listed three compensating features to back the over-performing: the canopy-style overwing exits, the larger than Type I floor-level exits, and the fast-deploying escape slides.

16.3 OPTIMIZING EXIT CONFIGURATIONS FOR LESSER CAPACITIES

16.3.1 De-rating

Not all aircraft are filled with seats up to the certification limit. In fact, few are. In some cases there is a significant margin between the actual seating and the maximum. The seat-to-exit ratio then falls in a lower category of the exit tables. An example is the Airbus A310. (This type is almost out of service by 2024, but its value as an example remains.) It has two pairs of Type A exits (forward and aft) and a Type I pair over the wing. The maximum certificated capacity in the U.S. is 265 (2*110 + 45, in Europe it is 275), but when the Type I is considered to be a Type III, it is still 255.

Airlines operating the A310 with a capacity below 255 may decide to not use the Type I as such but indeed treat it as Type III. This is called de-rating. Assigning the exit as a Type III means that more lenient passageway width requirements apply. This then offers more flexibility in seating arrangement. Another advantage is that the exit need not be seen as a floor-level exit, and thus would not need a flight attendant adjacently.

16.3.2 Deactivation

The ultimate form of de-rating an exit is de-activating it. An exit is then not de-rated to a lower exit type (e.g. from Type I to Type III) but to no exit at all. It is simply considered not to exist. Two forms

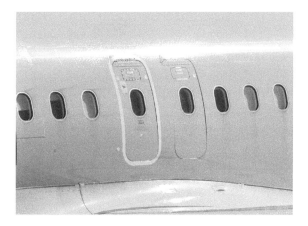

FIGURE 16.1 American Airlines A321neo aft Type III exit deactivated (photograph by the author).

of deactivation have been used: permanent and temporary. An example of a permanent deactivation was the Boeing 747 Classic with door 3 deactivated (see Section 13.5.3.3). Other examples were the United Airlines DC-8 and 727 stretch variants with the unique exit pairs (see Section 9.3.5). These were eventually deactivated, bringing the airplanes back to exit configurations identical to other airlines' DC-8–60s and 727-200s. A more recent example of deactivation is the A321neo: with one pair of Type IIIs deactivated, the maximum capacity is reduced from 244 to 204 (in Europe).

Permanent de-activations involve the removal of door controls, exit signs, and so on, and the concealing of the exit from the inside. On the outside, the outlining band and other markings are lacking.

Temporary de-activations are applied in case of a malfunction of an element of the exit system. That may be an escape slide that is inoperative, a handle, or even an exit sign. A minimum equipment list procedure is typically applied (see Section 14.3.1). The exit will not be concealed but is marked as inoperative.

16.3.3 SINGLE PAIR OF EXITS

Yet different from de-rating and deactivation is the determination of the maximum passenger capacity for combi configurations. In such airplanes, the main deck is compartmentalized in a passenger section and a cargo section. In some airplane types, such as the Douglas DC-8 and the Boeing 737, the cargo section was ahead of the passenger section. In others, it was at the rear, such as on the Boeing 747. The percentage of combi airplanes in the world's fleets has never been significant and dwindled over time, with just a few left in 2024 to serve areas where air supply of goods is essential, such as arctic Canada. In some of these configurations, only a single pair of exits remained available for evacuation. The FAA, so asked in 1987 by the UK CAA, mentioned that they had approved the following maximum passenger capacities for the various exit types:[12]

Type I—34
Oversize Type I (so-called Type B)—50
Type A—70.

These figures are in the range of 62% to 75% of the rated capacities.

NOTES

1 Overwing Emergency Exit Study, J.A. Roebuck, R.A. Littlewood, Douglas Aircraft Co. Inc., Report No. SM-22573, December 28, 1956.

2. Later adopted in the Transport Airplane Cabin Interiors Crashworthiness Handbook, FAA AC 25-17A.
3. NPRM 66-26, Amdt 25-15.
4. Caravelle – the Complete Story, John Wegg, 2005, p. 432: 'The Theoretical Limit was 139', Inferring a Credit of 25.
5. Amdt 4b-4 (1951), CAR 4b.362(b)
6. Amdt 25-72.
7. Model DC-9-80 Tail Exit Passenger Credit, Letter M.C. Beard, Federal Aviation Administration to McDonnell Douglas Corporation, November 16, 1977.
8. Type Certificate Data Sheet No. BA16, United Kingdom Civil Aviation Authority, Issue 16, March 1999.
9. Amdt 25-72.
10. Type Certificate Data Sheet No. EASA.A.151 Airbus A350, 25 October 2023.
11. Equivalent Level of Safety (ELOS) Finding for Passenger Limit on Boeing Model 737-10 Airplane, Project # PS17-0010-C11, Memorandum, Federal Aviation Administration, March 11, 2024.
12. [No Subject], Letter Leroy A. Keith to H.R.F. Duffell, Civil Aviation Authority, November 2, 1987, Filed as FAA AVS/AIR Policy Statement PS-ANM100-1987-00033.

17 Reaping the Benefits of Cabin Safety Measures

ABSTRACT

This chapter contains two different sets of trends and analyses. The first set gives, for the period 1935 through 2024, per five-year slots, trends for the number of survivable, yet life-threatening accidents, the number of fatalities, the number of survivors, and the percentage of survivors. The second set discusses, for five domains, where and how cabin safety measures have contributed to the saving of lives, in other words, where the seeds sown earlier in the form of new regulations, have reaped.

17.1 INTRODUCTION

A key question for cabin safety professionals and passengers alike is the following: have the cabin safety measures that were introduced indeed increased survivability and reduced the number of fatalities? Did the cabin safety seeds that were planted over time reap?

The short answer is yes, but not all at the same magnitude. This chapter reviews the benefits of some of the more salient cabin safety measures. But before that, it reviews four survivability accident trends over the period 1935—present.

17.2 ACCIDENT TRENDS SINCE 1935

17.2.1 Criteria

Using the criteria set out here, accidents have been selected from extensive databases available on the internet. Two internet sources in particular were used: aviation-safety.net and baaa-acro.com. Both are maintained by individuals, Harro Ranter in the Netherlands and Ronan Hubert in Switzerland, respectively. Where available, official accident investigation reports were consulted for cabin safety performance information.

- All accidents worldwide between 1935 and 2024 to transport airplanes of more than 19 passenger seats engaged in commercial passenger air transport that either:
  - occurred on the ground (land or water) and were survivable or partially survivable, or
  - started as an in-flight cabin fire forming a serious threat to cabin occupants, but where the airplane reached the ground in a controlled manner.
- Due to a lack of data, accidents that occurred to airplanes manufactured in the Soviet Union, Russian Federation, Ukraine, Iran, or China were excluded.

Thus, high-impact, non-survivable accidents, which form a large contingent of accidents but fall outside the scope of cabin safety, are excluded. Cabin safety accidents and incidents not included are decompressions, turbulence occurrences, and unlawful actions, including unruly passengers. Their occurrence rates are fairly high, but their consequences are lower.

17.2.2 Trend 1: Number of Survivable, Yet Life-Threatening, Accidents

The number of accidents that met the criteria is presented in Figure 17.1. Two kinds of survivable accidents are tabled: those in which there were fatalities and those without fatalities.

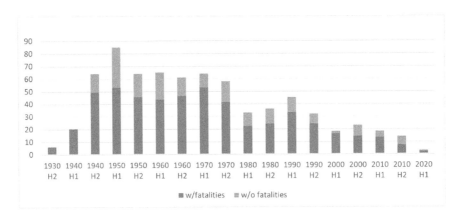

FIGURE 17.1 Number of survivable accidents.

What is immediately apparent is that from 1945 onward there is a high number of accidents per year. This stays at about the same level until 1980. Obviously, this does not indicate that there was no safety improvement. In fact, quite the opposite when appreciating that the volume of worldwide traffic grew in the 30 years 1950–1979 by a factor of about 27.5. Neither is the steady rate an indication of a cabin safety trend. It is primarily an indication that the success rate of measures aimed at preventing accidents was in balance with the traffic volume increase. Only from the 1980s onward did the safety measures win and decrease the number of accidents. These measures were of many different kinds. To name a few: turbine engines (which are more reliable than piston engines), improved navigation means (including, ultimately, satellite-based), pilot flight time limitations, ground proximity warning system (GPWS, and later Enhanced GPWS), in-flight collision prevention systems, flight simulators, Crew Resource Management and Safety Management Systems. In the period 1980–2019, traffic volume increased by a factor of 8. The multiplier over the 70-year period 1950–2019 was about 220.

The ratio between survivable accidents without fatalities and those with fatalities fluctuated between 18% and 40% with two outliers of 11% (H1 2000) and 50% (H2 2010).

17.2.3 Trend 2: Number of Fatalities in Survivable Accidents

When focusing on the number of fatalities, a slow but steady increase is apparent from 1945 until the second half of the 1960s, followed by a sharp increase in the 1970s. That increase did not correspond with the number of accidents, as that remained the same, as trend 1 shows. The increase was primarily due to the higher capacities of the aircraft involved.

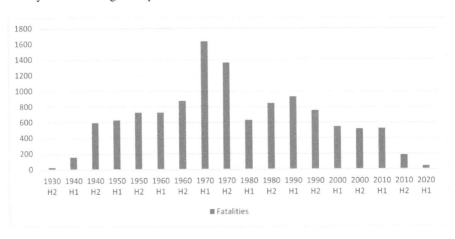

FIGURE 17.2 Number of fatalities in survivable accidents.

Reaping the Benefits of Cabin Safety Measures

The 1970s represented more than 25% of all fatalities over the nine decades. This is possibly owing to the higher capacities from that decade, while the safety measures only started to take effect in the next decade. Even though all these fatalities can obviously not solely be attributed to (the lack of) cabin safety-related issues, a significant proportion can. It explains the motivation for the drastic cabin safety measures that were introduced in the next decade, which started the third cabin safety wave. But that decade, the 1980s, itself saw a sharp reduction in the number of accidents and thus in fatalities. Both rose again in the 1990s. From the second half of the 2010s a very significant reduction is noticeable, well before the third wave measures could take effect. Again, this can primarily be attributed to a reduction in accidents, but where they did happen, the cabin safety measures did contribute to the lesser number of fatalities.

17.2.4 Trend 3: Number of Survivors in Life-Threatening Accidents

The third trend shows the fluctuations in the number of survivors in both accidents with fatalities and without, that met the criteria. After an initial increase in the 1940s, this number remained fairly stable for 25 years and then rose sharply for two decades, but for a dip in H2 1980. From H2 1990 it decreased again with a very low score in H1 2000. The three periods where the number reaches 3,000 and more (1970H2, 1980H1, and 1990H1) can be explained by a combination of the high number of accidents and higher airplane capacities.

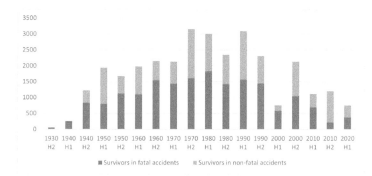

FIGURE 17.3 Number of survivors in life-threatening accidents.

17.2.5 Trend 4: Percentage of Survivors

The fourth trend shows the percentage of survivors in all accidents that met the criteria. For many decades it has been fairly constant at around 70% with lows in H1 1970 and H1 2000 and a high in H1 1980. In the final ten years it is increasing up to about 95% in H1 2020. Although some care needs to be taken because of the law of small numbers, it may well be that this positive trend can be attributed to the cabin safety measures, particularly those of the third wave, as discussed hereunder.

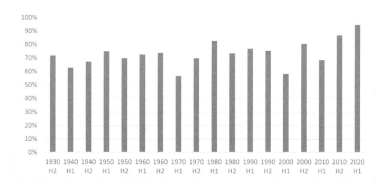

FIGURE 17.4 Percentage of survivors.

17.3 REAPING FROM CABIN SAFETY MEASURES

17.3.1 INTRODUCTION

Have the cabin safety measures as described in the previous chapters indeed contributed to an increase in cabin safety? In some of the chapters this question has already been addressed, for example, for oxygen in Section 6.6. For exits this is answered in Chapter 18 and for safety cards in Chapter 20.

A good source for determining the effects of cabin safety measures are reports from accident investigations. However, the quality of cabin safety reporting by investigators has a wide variety in quality, both over time and by investigating authority. The U.S. was early in investigating accidents, together with the British and French, but it took a while before they included cabin safety and survivability elements in their investigations. It is therefore difficult to determine how effective the early measures were. Gradually, from about the early 1960s, when the importance of cabin safety started being appreciated, it became better. This is especially true where there were fatalities due to the lack of, or poor performance of, cabin safety features. Conversely, accident investigators seldom report the contribution of cabin safety measures when positive. For example, whether the airplanes involved met the heat release standards or the dynamic seat testing standards is rarely mentioned, let alone if they had made a difference.

17.3.2 IMPACT PROTECTION (RESTRAINT)

A significant first wave measure was the raising of the 6 g seat tie-down limit to 9 g (with a 1.33 safety factor). The accident reports of the 1950s and 1960s seldom mentioned the contribution to survivability of seats and belts. Howard Hasbrook came to help here. He investigated five accidents to airplanes certificated to 6 g in the 1950s, which were, at least partially, survivable.[1] He found that, in many cases, most if not all seats had torn loose. Later accidents with 6 g aircraft, such as the Convair and Martin twins, showed the same pattern. Survivable accidents in later generations of airplanes, which met the 9 g requirements, had significantly lower rates of seats coming loose. This proved the value of the 9 g safety measure. But there were still accidents which were well survivable where seats did fail. One such accident, well investigated, was the June 23, 1976, accident to a Douglas DC-9 in Philadelphia, Pennsylvania.[2] The aft fuselage experienced a high vertical impact load of at least 10 g. In spite of the many seat failures (92% of the seats) there were no fatalities, but 80% of the 102 passengers were seriously injured. The absence of fire contributed to their survival. All seat belts stayed intact. This was one of many accidents that stimulated the 16 g/14 g dynamic testing rule decades later. The first accident where such seats were tested in practice happened in the United Kingdom in January 1989. A Boeing 737-400, trying to make an emergency landing at East Midlands airport, landed short of the runway against the embankment of the M1 motorway. Impact forces were high, with a peak value, in the center section of the airplane, of between approximately 22 and 28 g. The seat model had been tested at FAA CAMI in 1987 to the new standards.[3] The AAIB said:

> Although these [. . .] tests were for development rather than certification, the results indicated that the seat would probably meet the certification criteria, although the testing was done prior to the issue of the requirements for seat deformation.

The AAIB concluded that 'fewer injuries occurred than would probably have been the case with passenger seats of an earlier generation' and that 'seats designed to these dynamic requirements will certainly increase survivability in aircraft impacts'. Yet, the AAIB warned that for the long term, cabin floors needed to have improved strength and toughness as well.

In later accidents with 16 g/14 g seats installed, the investigation reports did not record their merit. Such accidents included three where they may have meant a difference: Toronto, 2 August 2005, Amsterdam, 25 February 2009, San Francisco, July 6, 2013. In the Toronto accident, which

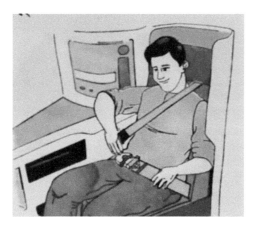

FIGURE 17.5 Shoulder harness on seat making an angle of more than 18° (photograph by the author of video briefing).

involved a runway overrun on the landing of an Airbus A340 with 297 passengers, the number of fatalities was zero. Near Amsterdam, a Boeing 737-800 impacted ground short of the runway, with a high vertical component. Except for five passengers in business class (most of whom ironically were Boeing employees), where the fuselage fractured, all other 123 passengers survived. The three cockpit occupants died. This accident was unique in that it tested real-life the 14 g element of the seats. Unfortunately, that aspect is not mentioned in the investigation report. It is even not confirmed whether the seats indeed were of the dynamically tested variant.

In San Francisco, a Boeing 777 struck a seawall on landing. Out of 291 passengers, three were ejected and died. They had not worn their safety belt. The unique motion of the airplane, spinning about 330°, led to lateral forces to occupants beyond those of the dynamic tests, and caused injuries.[4] The FAA responded to the subsequent NTSB recommendation by imposing Special Conditions for airplane seats that make an angle of more than 18° with the direction of travel.[5] On new airplane types, such seats have either a single shoulder strap or an inflatable seat belt, see Figure 17.5.

As to seat belts, there is no question as to their positive contribution to survival in all cases of impact. Yet, in a number of very severe crashes, where impact forces were hardly survivable and the fuselage ripped open, survival chances of the unbelted sometimes were better as they were ejected free of the wreckage. There have also been cases where occupants survived because they were ejected free of the airplane together with their seats.

17.3.3 Fire Protection (Flammability)

Significant interior material flammability standards were introduced in the mid-1980s: seat cushion blocking layers and the heat release standard. The first accident where the contribution of the former was noticed happened in August 1988. A Boeing 727 crashed at Dallas-Fort Worth and fire entered the cabin. The investigation report says:[6]

> The forward cabin remained survivable for about 4 minutes and 20 seconds, despite the large fuel fire at the ruptured area. Some of this survival time can be attributed to the use of fire blocking materials on the seat cushions. There was evidence of the fire blocking slowing the spread of fire into the cabin. Many seat cushions remained intact or showed signs that the blocker inhibited burning. With a large fuel fire entering the cabin, fire blocking will not stop the spread of fire, but will slow it down giving added time for escape.

It was later estimated that the blocking layers added 90 seconds to the survival time, equaling 37 evacuees.[7] The contribution of seat fire-blocking layers to survival was also mentioned in the first accident to an Airbus A320, in June 1988, where the airplane, full of passengers, flew very low as part of an airshow, hit trees, crashed, and burned.[8]

Heat release was introduced for new airplane types in 1988 with FAR amendment 25–66 and, in Europe, JAR-25 at Change 13 in October 1989. Two early types that met these requirements were the Airbus A340 and Boeing 777. Accidents of these types in which the interior was burned out, but only after all occupants had escaped, were those in Toronto in 2005, San Francisco in 2013, and Dubai in 2016. Such accidents to later airplane types so certificated happened to an Embraer 190 in 2010 in Yichun, China, an Embraer 195 in 2018 in Durango, and an Airbus A350 in 2024 in Tokyo. For the latter, no accident investigation report is available yet, but media reports suggest that the fire in the cabin was significantly delayed, allowing ample time for evacuation. Of the two Embraer accidents, the first was fatal to about half of the passengers, but no details about fire propagation were reported. In the 2018 Durango accident, the successful evacuation was reported as having taken four to five minutes. No other survivable accidents with heat-release-equipped airplanes are known, although these cannot be excluded entirely.

Thus, with the possible exception of the Yichun case, it appears that the heat release rule achieved its objective: sufficient delay of conflagration to allow evacuation of all.

17.3.4 Escape Potential (Descent Assist Means, Floor Lighting)

A key cabin safety feature since the 1950s were the chutes that morphed into inflatable slides and later automatic inflatable slides. They soon became a given. Accident investigators did not praise their existence when they were used and saved lives but rather condemned them when, for whatever reason, they failed. Yet, these inventions have possibly been the greatest inanimate life savers in cabin safety history.

In 1991 the floor path lighting was still new. This may have been a reason for the investigators of the February collision in Los Angeles to ask survivors about it. Some passengers reported using it to find the rear exit. In the 1988 Boeing 727 accident in Dallas, it was reported that no one had utilized it. The accident happened in daylight and large breaks provided visual guidance out of the aircraft.

17.3.5 Life Support (Flotation Devices)

Life rafts were the first of the cabin safety measures that accident reports covered well (see Section 7.3). But coverage and usage are not the same. Some reports mentioned that life rafts could not be used as they were inaccessible (e.g. hidden in cargo compartments) or, when launched, drifted away. Also, there were quite a few cases of water landings of airplanes not equipped with life rafts. The usage of life vests is seldom reported. When so, it is more often about problems than successes. In the 1982 Washington D.C. ice crash, the few survivors reported:[9]

> that they experienced extreme difficulty in opening the package which contained the one lifevest which was retrieved [floating]. They stated that the plastic package which contained the lifevest was finally opened by chewing and tearing at it with their teeth.

17.3.6 Cabin Professionals

Cabin crew have contributed to survival in many accidents and, of all the cabin safety resources, are most often mentioned in accident investigations. As the examples given in Section 8.2 testify this was already the case before their safety role was recognized. They concerned actions which not necessarily were implanted by training, which, at best, was primitive.

Reaping the Benefits of Cabin Safety Measures

FIGURE 17.6 ONA DC-10 accident, New York JFK (FAA, photograph by Kenneth Henry Zask).

Since the 1970s, when flight attendant training requirements matured, this paid off. Out of many, two salient examples are summarized here. The first actually consisted of two evacuations in which the first acted as a general rehearsal for the second.[10] Flight attendant Sarah Uzzell, who was on both, remembers. On November 12, 1975, a DC-10 operated by the U.S. airline Overseas National Airways (ONA) rejected its take-off from New York JFK and got on fire.

The passengers were 128 ONA staff being positioned to Jeddah as part of a contract involving hadj flights for Saudia many of whom were flight attendants. Hadj flights are an annual event in which Muslim pilgrims are flown to Jeddah (for further transport to Mecca) and back. Because of the seasonal character, companies such as ONA were chartered for that. The fire threat in the cabin was immediate but evacuation was done in less than a minute through three of the eight exits. ONA training went beyond the minimum required. All flight attendants received hands-on training not only in initial but also recurrent training. About 50 days later, a sister ship coming in to land at Istanbul from Jeddah in the dark hit short of the runway. Sarah was again on board, as a flight attendant, next to 365 Turkish passengers, one interpreter, three flight crewmembers and eight other flight attendants. The airplane bounced, landed again and veered off the runway, making a 180° turn. With the left wing broken off, fuel was released and a fire started, which was later extinguished by fire services before it could reach the cabin. Obviously an evacuation was warranted. The passengers, who she described as 'of agrarian stock, ranged in age from 50 to 80', had never been on an aircraft before they went to Mecca. They did not know what to expect and considered this just a hard landing with an abrupt stop, so saw no reason to panic. The crew and passengers did not speak a common language. The flight attendants had to unfasten their seat belts and shove them to the exits. The passengers took lots of luggage, including jugs with holy water, bags with desert sand and sacks with desert rocks, and threw these out before sliding down. Once on the ground, they stayed at the foot of the slide instead of moving away. Multiple times, the flight attendants were almost pushed out by passengers. Again, only three exits were used. Sarah recounts:

> Of the nine ONA flight attendants, eight had also been in the first accident, and I feel we were able to perform more effectively with this previous experience so fresh in our minds. This previous experience gave us the courage, the presence of mind and the patience, through understanding, to stay with this bizarre situation, where most of the passengers did not wish to evacuate and to do our job.

Almost 30 years later, an Airbus A340 overshot the runway in Toronto. The investigation report recounts the professional contribution of the well-trained cabin crew:[11]

> The evacuation was successful due to the training and actions of the whole cabin crew. With few exceptions, the performance of the cabin crew was exemplary and professional, and was a significant factor in the successful evacuation of the accident. There was effective communication between the flight crew and the cabin crew. Because the cabin crew were advised of the possibility of a missed approach, they were in a state of heightened awareness during the landing phase and were, therefore, prepared to respond immediately in the event of an emergency. The availability of three supplemental cabin crew members on AFR358 undoubtedly contributed to the success of the evacuation, as evidenced by the roles they played during the evacuation. Two were in command of passenger evacuations at emergency exits and the third played a pivotal role in opening an emergency exit and subsequently assisted passengers at the foot of the R4 slide.
>
> There was effective risk assessment and decision making. The aft purser effectively assessed the risks to passenger safety, given the presence of fire, and did not hesitate to take the decision to immediately initiate an emergency evacuation. Other cabin crew also exhibited effective risk assessment and decision making as evidenced by the actions of the R1 and the R2 cabin crews. They had initially correctly determined that their emergency exits were unusable given the creek flowing just outside the aircraft; however, as the amount of smoke in the cabin worsened, they quickly reassessed the overall risk to passenger safety and concluded that the risk presented by the creek was not as great as the immediate threat presented by the smoke in the cabin. Both crew members took actions to commence evacuation at their respective exits. When the R3 cabin crew saw that passengers were not following his emergency instructions to not use that exit, he quickly assumed a much more assertive manner, resulting in passengers responding quickly and appropriately to his commands. In spite of the fact that the L2 door opened while the aircraft was still moving and the fact that its associated slide did not deploy, the evacuation was successful, primarily due to the training and actions of the whole cabin crew.

NOTES

1. Gross Pattern of Injury of 109 Survivors of Five Transport Accidents by A. Howard Hasbrook, Aviation Crash Injury Research, July 1958.
2. Crash Injury Protection in Survivable Air Transport Accidents—U.S. Civil Aircraft Experience From 1970 to 1978 by Richard F. Chandler, Donell W. Pollard, FAA CAMI, and Lawrence M. Neri, Ceasar A. Caiafa, FAA Technical Center, Report Number DOT/FAA/CT-82-118, March 1983.
3. Report on the Accident to Boeing 737-400 G-OBME Near Kegworth, Leicestershire on 8 January 1989, Aircraft Accident Report 4/90, Department for Transport, Air Accident Investigation Branch, 25 August 1990.
4. NTSB/AAR/14-01.
5. NTSB recommendation A-14-44.
6. Delta Air Lines, Inc., Boeing 727-232, N473DA, Dallas-Fort Worth International Airport, Texas, August 31, 1988, NTSB/AAR-89/04, September 26, 1989.
7. A Review of Recent Civil Air Transport Accidents/Incidents and Their Fire Safety Implications, R.G. Hill, in Fire Safety Science 4, 1994, p. 85.
8. Commission d'enquête sur l'accident survenu le 26 juin 1988 à Mulhouse-Habsheim (68) à l'Airbus A 320, immatriculé F-GFKC, Rapport Final, Journal Officiel de la République Française, 24 avril 1990.
9. NTSB Aircraft Accident Report, Air Florida, Inc., Boeing 737-222, N62AF, Collision with 14th Street Bridge, Near Washington National Airport Washington, D.C., January 13, 1982, NTSB-AAR-82-8, August 10, 1982.
10. Successful Evacuations Following Survivable Accidents, by Sarah Uzzell, presented at 29th Annual International Air Safety Seminar, October 25–29, 1976, Anaheim, California.
11. Aviation Investigation Report Runway Overrun and Fire Air France Airbus A340-313 F-GLZQ Toronto/Lester B. Pearson International Airport, Ontario 02 August 2005, Transportation Safety Board of Canada, Report Number A05H0002, Released 16 October 2007.

18 Exit Usage

ABSTRACT

The best way to verify the adequacy of the exit regulations for location and distribution is to study their use in those accidents where they mattered: evacuations. Research into this has been done in 1951 by Barry King, in the 1970s by FAA CAMI, in 2006 by Ed Galea of the University of Greenwich, and since 1990 by the author, who specifically looked at evacuation performance under life-threatening conditions.

18.1 INTRODUCTION

One aspect relevant to cabin safety is that of exit usage. How many of the exits installed have actually been used in cases where evacuation is a matter of life or death? Are some locations or some types of exits more often used than others? Is it still true, as thought in 1951, that exits on one side are typically blocked by fire, so there is a lateral evacuation split? Or is a longitudinal split perhaps more common, with usable exits concentrated at one end of the fuselage only, be it the forward end or the aft end? Does the exit usage differ for the various threat scenarios—fire or water?

18.2 KING, PISTON (1948–1951)

The first to count the use of exits in actual accidents was Barry King.[1] He studied 43 reports of U.S. air carrier accidents that occurred between 1948 and 1951. All aircraft had piston engines. Five types had tricycle gears and two were tail draggers. In 26 cases there was a fire, in 17 there was not. In nine cases there were fatalities, in one case of which the fatality was due to runaway propellers that killed a passenger in flight, but the landing was safe.

King categorized exit types and locations as follows:

- Doors: Main door, auxiliary door forward, auxiliary door aft. The main door was always on the left, the auxiliary doors were typically on the right side.
- Emergency exits, both left and right: over the wings; forward of the wings; aft of the wings.

He allocated five use/non-use conditions to exits:

U—exit was used
O—exit open, not used
X—exit not usable
*—gaps in the fuselage were used for exits
?—undetermined

King classified the usage into three categories: (1) exits used; (2) exits available, but not used; (3) exits not available because of fire or other circumstances. Out of 73 exits used (of 264 installed), the majority (50) were doors, either the main door or a service door. Emergency exits, which typically had Type IV dimensions (as so defined from November 1951), were used significantly less: in the fire-less cases this was only 10%. In the cases with a fire, their usage was higher (between 20% and 38%), but still less than that of the doors.

Doors and exits located forward of the wings were more often used than those aft. This was in spite of the fact that the main door in those aircraft was always aft.

Descent devices were needed in 14 of the 43 cases (mainly when the wheels were down) but only used in half of those cases.

King also looked at the attitude of aircraft for 122 cases with tricycle landing gears. It showed that wheels-down cases were far more frequent than wheels-up (56% vs. 21%). Nose wheel down accounted for 17% of the cases and the remainder (5%) were partial gear failures. Wheels-down accidents posed a greater evacuation challenge because of the higher distance of exits above the ground. On a Constellation, this distance was about 10 ft (3 m).

King did not investigate whether the exit usage pattern was influenced by the presence, and location, of a fire. A re-assessment of his raw data indicates that in four accidents (out of 16) involving fire and in which more than one exit was used, this was on one side only. In two of these cases, a fire on the opposite side was mentioned, but conversely, in other cases exits on the fire side were used. Thus, King's data did not support the notion that evacuations typically took place on one side of the airplane as the other was on fire.

18.3 CAMI, JETS (1961–1990)

Two exit usage studies were published by CAMI.

The first was in response to a request in 1987 by the FAA Northwest Mountain region aircraft certification division.[2] They wanted to know how often exits at one end of the cabin were not usable. This request was in the wake of the Seattle conference and essentially asked whether the 1951 notion that exit availability was primarily laterally divided was still valid. Or was there a longitudinal element to exit availability?

The database of CAMI contained 61 cases with information on exit usage. All concerned jets and spanned the period 1961 to 1985, with only two cases outside the U.S., and not involving a U.S. operator. In 15 cases there were fatalities, of which in 11 cases due to fire or smoke and in two cases due to drowning. In 24 cases was exit usage vital to survival, the other cases involved precautionary evacuations or cases where the evacuation did not influence survivability. This reduced the value of this data. CAMI concluded that in about 7% of the cases, exit problems resulted in unusable exits at one end of the fuselage.

The second study, done in 1991, was also in response to a request by the Northwest Mountain region but this time was specific to Type III and tail exits.[3] Again, the database was limited. In general, Type III exits scored favorably compared to forward and aft exits. As to tail exits, CAMI's conclusion was contradictory: it found that 80% were not used (in half of these cases because of blockage or obstructions), yet they then concluded that their 'exit usage compared favorably with that of front, over-wing and rear exits'.

18.4 UNIVERSITY OF GREENWICH

Ed Galea of the University of Greenwich, using his AASK (Aircraft Accident Statistics and Knowledge), database, investigated three exit usage aspects:[4]

1. Whether passengers used the nearest exit
2. Whether passengers moved forward or aft
3. Percentages of exits being used

The relevant AASK database set contained accidents between 1977 and 1999, almost exclusively from the U.S. It had detailed data, including narratives taken from passengers in interviews. All accidents involved evacuations, not all of which were done under life-threatening conditions.

Re 1: Galea had found that in some reports it was surmised that passengers have a tendency to go to the exit through which they had boarded. He believed that was generally not the case and proved that postulate with AASK data. Based on 1,441 individual passenger replies he found that the number of passengers that used the nearest available exit was between 74% and 85%. The difference is a result of using two sets of data: confirmed and inferred. Reasons for not using the nearest exit (by 15% to 26% of those interviewed) were tabulated. The top four reasons (out of 11) were: (1) followed cabin crew instructions; (2) followed other passenger; (3) passenger thought this was the nearest exit (when it was not); (4) shorter queue than other exits.

Re 2: As to the direction of travel, 60% of the passengers went forward, 35% went aft and the remainder (5%) was in an exit row. Galea concluded that this suggests passengers have a propensity to move forward.

Re 3: Galea counted for 42 evacuation accidents the number of exits used versus the number installed. In one-third of the cases less than half of the exits were used, in one-sixth of cases exactly half, and in half the cases more than half. This is better than what the author found (see the following text). However, when comparing the databases it appears that Galea included many accidents which were less severe. It is noteworthy that even for the lighter cases, the rate of non-usage of exits is high.

18.5 AUTHOR, JETS (1960–2024)

18.5.1 Introduction

Since 1985, the author has maintained and kept up to date a database of exit usage on jet airliners under life-threatening conditions. It was first publicly presented in 1990 and again in 1994 and 2012.[5] The results are summarized herein, updated to the end of 2024. The selection criteria were as follows:

- Airplanes: jet air transport airplanes manufactured in countries other than the Soviet Union, Russian Federation, Ukraine, Iran, or China. The reason for excluding these countries is the lack of data.
- Operations: civil air transport operations with revenue passengers on board.
- Time range: 1960–2024.
- Regions: unlimited
- Rapid evacuation vital for life because of:
  - actual fire:
    - which started in-flight, followed by successful landing;
    - which started on the ground, either as a result of impact with the ground, a collision with another airplane, or otherwise such as an engine failure;
  - (partial) immersion in water
- At least one exit available for evacuation (thus excluding scenarios where only breaks offered escape potential).

Excluded were accidents as a result of hostile action or unlawful interference (hijackings, bomb detonation on board, etc.). The number of accidents that potentially met the criteria was 144. In one case, involving an in-flight fire, the airplane landed safely but no evacuation took place (Riyadh, August 1980). For a further 37 cases, insufficient data was available to determine exit usage. For the remaining 106 cases, usage of exits was reported. This usage is tabulated in table 18.1. In 50 of those cases, even the number of evacuees per exit was reported. The 106 cases fell in three major categories:

- A fire that started in-flight, went out of control but the aircraft could be landed: 3 cases
- Water immersion (typically following an overrun into water): 20 cases
- Fire that started on the ground: 83 cases. This category was further divided by fire entry mode:
  - Fire started inside the pressure hull (by fuel or hydraulic lines severed) or immediately below (e.g. center fuel tank explosion): 7

TABLE 18.1
Class of Airplane Occupants Exit Location

Date (yymmdd)	Type	Location	class of airplane	occupants total	occupants fatal	exits installed	exits used	1L	1R	2L	2R	3L	3R	4L	4R	5L	5R	tail	breaks used
610711	DC8	Denver	SW	121	17	6	3	32	N	x	x	N	26	x	x	N	40	x	
620820	DC8	Rio-Galeao	SW	106	14	6	2	N	N	x	x	U	U	x	x	N	N	x	
630703	CVL	Cordoba	ST	70	0	5	2	U	N	x	x	N	U	x	x	x	x	N	
640322	CMT	Singapore	SW	68	0	6	4	U	25	x	x	4	N	x	x	40	N	x	
640407	707	New York JFK	SW	145	0	6	5	U	N	x	x	U	U	x	x	U	U	x	
641123	707	Rome	SW	73	50	6	4	14	N	x	x	11	N	x	x	5	4	x	
651111	727	Salt Lake City	ST	91	43	5	4	11	x	x	x	17	5	x	x	x	x	N	
670305	DC8	Monrovia	SW	90	51	6	2	22	N	x	9	N	N	x	x	15	N	N	
670630	ST	Hong Kong	ST	80	24	5	2	53	N	x	x	N	2	x	x	x	x	N	
671105	880	Hong Kong	SW	127	1	6	4	3	U	x	x	55	55	x	x	N	N	x	✓
680408	707	London Heathrow	SW	127	5	6	4	46	45	x	x	N	18	x	x	N	10	x	
690113	DC8	Los Angeles	SW	45	15	6	2	N	N	x	x	15	15	x	x	N	N	x	
690802	CVL	Marseille	ST	45	0	5	1	N	N	x	x	41	N	x	x	x	x	N	
700419	DC8	Rome	SW	65	0	6	3	N	15	x	x	N	10	x	x	N	40	x	
700502	DC9	Nr St Croix	ST	63	23	5	3	N	6	x	x	2	30	x	x	N	x	N	
701127	DC8	Anchorage	SW	229	21	10	6	53	N	19	22	36	36	N	N	N	4	x	✓
701228	727	St Thomas	ST	55	2	7	2	N	12	x	x	N	N	N	10	x	x	N	✓
710906	111	Hamburg	ST	121	22	7	2	N	N	x	x	U	N	x	x	x	x	N	✓
720518	DC9	Ft Lauderdale	ST	10	0	5	1	10	N	x	x	N	N	x	x	x	x	N	
721208	737	Chicago Midway	SW	61	45	6	2	N	N	x	x	1	N	x	x	N	11	x	✓
721220	DC9	Chicago O'Hare	ST	45	10	5	3	30	N	x	x	5	1	x	x	x	x	N	
730122	707	Kano	SW	202	176	8	2	U	N	x	x	N	N	N	N	N	U	x	
730130	DC9	Oslo	ST	33	0	5	4	14	10	x	x	7	4	N	x	N	x	N	
730711	707	Paris Orly	SW	134	123	6	2	1	1	x	x	N	N	x	x	N	N	x	
731127	DC9	Chattanooga	ST	79	0	5	3	U	N	x	x	U	U	x	x	x	x	N	
731217	D10	Boston	T	167	0	8	4	U	N	x	x	N	U	x	N	N	N	x	✓
740116	707	Los Angeles	SW	63	0	6	6	1	15	x	U	4	4	x	x	23	15	x	

Exit Usage

740130	707	Pago Pago	SW	101	97	6	1	N	N	x	x	9	N	x	x	N	N	x	
740315	CVL	Teheran	ST	96	15	5	4	14	4	x	x	44	1	x	x	x	x	N	
741120	747	Nairobi	T	157	59	10	4	U	N	U	U	N	U	N	N	N	N	x	√
751112	D10	New York JFK	T	139	0	8	4	1	59	Z	N	N	N	x	N	43	33	x	
760102	D10	Istanbul	T	377	0	8	4	N	100	Z	N	N	N	x	x	20	N	x	
760405	727	Ketchikan	ST	50	1	5	2	12	N	100	x	28	140	x	x	x	x	x	√
760427	727	St Thomas	ST	88	37	7	1	N	N	x	x	U	N	x	N	x	x	N	√
761116	DC9	Denver	ST	86	0	5	4	U	U	x	x	N	U	x	x	x	x	U	
770327	747	Tenerife	SW	405	335	10	1	N	N	x	x	N	N	x	N	N	x	x	√
780211	737	Cranbrook	SW	49	42	6	1	N	N	U	N	N	N	x	x	N	2	x	√
780215	707	Tenerife	SW	196	0	6	6	U?	U	x	x	U?	U?	x	x	U	U	x	
780301	D10	Los Angeles	T	200	2	8	4	N	40	x	29	N	27	x	x	N	40	x	
780303	DC8	Santiago	SW	222	0	10	?	N	N	N	?	U	?	x	x	U	?	x	
780402	737	Sao Paulo	SW	44	0	6	4	U	U	x	x	N	N	U	x	U	U	x	
780508	727	Pensacola	ST	58	3	7	5	8	13	x	x	N	16	x	1	x	x	x	
781217	737	Hyderabad	SW	132	1	6	2	U	N	x	x	N	N	x	x	x	N	N	
790314	727	Doha	ST	64	45	6	2	N	N	x	x	N	?	x	N	U	x	x	
791007	DC8	Athens	SW	154	14	6	2	125	N	x	x	1	N	x	x	x	x	x	√
801119	747	Seoul	T	226	15	10	7	U	U	U	x	N	U	x	?	15	N	N	
801121	727	Yap	ST	73	0	4	1	x	x	N	U	?	N	?	?	?	U	x	
810727	DC9	Chihuahua	ST	66	32	6	2	U	U	x	N	71	N	x	x	x	x	x	
820123	D10	Boston	T	212	2	8	5	N	N	U	x	N	N	x	x	N	U	N	
820209	DC8	Tokyo Haneda	SW	174	24	10	3	N	N	N	U	U	U	x	N	N	N	x	
820317	300	Sanaa	T	124	0	8	2	N	14	N	N	x	x	U	N	110	N	x	
820826	737	Ishigaki	SW	138	0	6	4	10	N	x	x	N	30	x	N	3	95	x	
820913	D10	Malaga	T	393	50	8	6	U	U	x	4	230	N	x	x	N	N	x	
830116	727	Ankara	ST	67	47	7	2	N	N	U	N	U	?	x	x	x	x	x	√
830602	DC9	Cincinnati	ST	46	23	5	3	N	N	x	N	6	5	x	x	x	x	N	
831128	F28	Enugu	ST	72	53	4	1	9	N	x	x	N	6	x	x	x	x	N	
831218	300	Kuala Lumpur	T	247	0	8	3	90	N	140	N	x	x	N	N	10	N	x	
840322	737	Calgary	SW	119	0	6	4	20	20	x	x	N	40	x	x	N	35	x	

(*Continued*)

- Fire entered through opened doors or exits: 6
- Fire entered through breaks: 8
- Fire burned through fuselage wall: 17
- Fire burned through windows: 2
- Fire stayed outside or entered the cabin well after the evacuation was completed: 16
- Combinations of entry modes breaks, windows, fuselage wall: 3
- Fire entry not reported: 24 (but in many cases inferred as having entered through breaks).

Thirty-three of the 106 cases occurred in the U.S. or territories; 32 in Asia, 20 in Europe, 10 in Latin America, 6 in Africa, 4 in Canada, and 1 in Oceania.

The longitudinal locations of exits on the jets were defined as being in either of six locations, numbered 1 to 6 going from the front to the rear, see Figures 18.1 and 18.2 for wing-engined and tail-engined airplanes respectively. Locations 1 and 2 are forward of the wings, location 3 is above the wing;[6] locations 4 and 5 are aft of the wings. Location 6 is the tail. Not all airplane types have exits at all locations, but these six locations cover all the airplanes with one exception: upper deck exits. Although there were five cases of an aircraft with such exits (all involving a Boeing 747), only one case of usage of an upper deck exit was reported, by eight persons (Taipei, October 2000).

Location 1, left side, was the location most often used for boarding. In some airplanes, location 5, left side, or location 6 (the tail) was used for boarding.

18.5.2 Results—Longitudinal

Table 18.2 clarifies, for the 106 cases, the locations and gives the number of exits installed, and used, at each location. For the 50 cases where the number of evacuees per exit is known, it gives the number of exits used, the number of evacuees, and an average number of users per used exit.

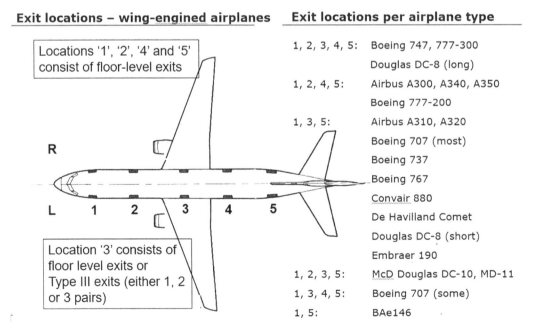

FIGURE 18.1 Exit locations—wing-engined airplanes.

Exit Usage

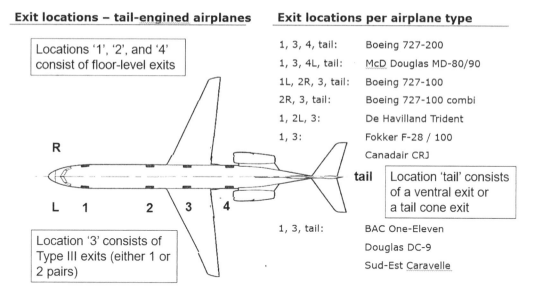

FIGURE 18.2 Exit locations—tail-engined airplanes.

TABLE 18.2
Location and Number of Exits Installed and Used (All Cases); Number of Evacuees (50 Cases)

			Overall (106 Cases)			Number of Evacuees Known (50 Cases)		
	Location	Installed on	Exits Installed	Exits Used	%	Exits Used	Number of Users	Average per Exit
1	Front of cabin	All jets except 727–100 on one side and combi 727–100 on both sides	209	114	55	52	1272	24.4
2	Forward of wings	All twin-aisle jets except A310, all long DC-8s and, on one side, 727–100 and Trident	45	24	53	10	434	43.4
3	Overwing	All jets except some twin-aisle, BAe 146	198	102	52	56	1603	28.6
4	Aft of wings	Some twin-aisle jets, some DC-8s and 707s, all 727–200 and, on one side, MD-80/-90	39	9	23	3	13	4.3
5	Aft of cabin	All jets with wing-mounted engines	142	66	46	29	1017	35.1
6	Tail exits	All single-aisle jets with tail-mounted engines, except Fokker and CRJ	29	2	7	1	12	12.0

The numbers indicate that exits above and forward of the wing have a significantly better usage rate (52% to 55%) than exits aft of the wing (7% to 46%). When looking at the number of evacuees per exit location, position 2 (forward of wings) scores best (43.4 evacuees on average). This exit position dominates on twin-aisle aircraft, which typically have wide exits with double-lane slides, thus skewing the results. The next best is the aft-of-cabin position, which, although used in less than

50% of cases, has a high average evacuee rate (35.1), again because it is a popular exit position on twin-aisle aircraft. The overwing exits come next. They are the most often used exits in water landing cases: in 76% of such cases, they are used. Position 4 and tail exits have the poorest rates, in terms of both exit usage percentages (23% and 7%, respectively) and evacuee numbers (4.3 and 12, respectively). These figures are however subject to the law of small numbers.

18.5.3   Results—Lateral

Is there a difference between the use of exits on the left and on the right side? While there were few more exits installed on the left than on the right side (320 vs. 316), the usage rate of left exits was significantly higher (54% vs. 45%). However, in terms of the average number of evacuees per exit, they were about equal: 29.2 (left) versus 28.7 (right).

18.5.4   Results—Distribution Patterns

Although not confirmed by King's actual exit usage study, in 1951, it was thought that a fire typically developed on one side, so exits on the other side should be used for an evacuation. This was later translated into the conditions for the evacuation demonstration. In the Manchester 1985 accident, hearing that there was a fire on the left side, the captain ordered his cabin crew to open the exits on the other side—'Evacuate on the starboard side please'.[7] This led to the tragic situation that the aft cabin crewmember immediately opened her exit only to let in a fierce fire that the wind blew under the fuselage and into this opening.

But how often were all, or some, exits used on one side and none on the other side in actual evacuations under life-threatening conditions? And how often was there a tendency that all exits used were either only at the front, of from the wing forward, or, conversely, at the rear or from the wing aft only? Table 18.3 presents the answers to these questions and others.

In about half of the cases (55 cases, 52%), the distribution pattern was random. In 16 cases (15%) only exits on one side were used and in 9 cases (8.5 %) the evacuation was oriented toward one end of the fuselage, of which 8 were in the forward direction.

TABLE 18.3
Exit Usage Distribution Patterns

Exit Usage Distribution Patterns		Number of Cases
Only one exit used		11
All exits used		3
Random (mix of left/right, forward/overwing/aft)		55
One side used only	All exits used on one side	9
	Some exits used on one side	7
Forward or aft orientation	Exits above wing and forward	8
	Exits above wing and aft	1
One pair used only	Forward pair	4
	Overwing pair(s)	7
	Aft pair	1

18.5.5   Results—Proportion of Exits Used

How many of the installed exits were used? Nine ratios of exits used versus exits installed are distinguished, ranging from only one used to all of the installed exits used. The distribution is reproduced in Diagram 18.1.

Exit Usage

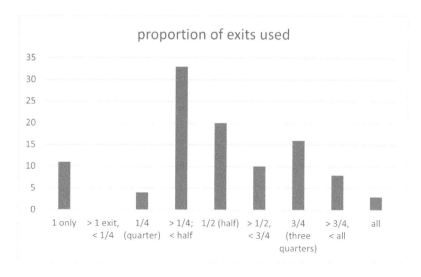

Diagram 18.1

The most frequent ratio is that where more than one quarter but less than half of the exits were used. In all, in 48 cases (46%) less than half of the exits were used, in 20 cases (19%) exactly half, and in 37 (35%) more than half.

18.5.6 RESULTS—AVERAGE USAGE RATES PER EXIT

How many persons use an exit on average? For 151 exits, spread over 55 accidents, the exact number of evacuees per exit was reported (see entries in Table 18.1 in exit location columns where a number appears).

The number per exit varies widely. The lowest is 1; the highest is 230 on a twin-aisle airplane, 125 on a single-aisle wing-engined airplane, and 53 on a single-aisle tail-engined airplane. Average numbers have been determined for two different kinds of exits (non-overwing floor level, and any overwing), two sizes of assist means (single lane and double lane), and three different categories of airplanes: single-aisle with tail-mounted engines (ST); single-aisle with wing-mounted engines (SW); twin-aisle airplanes (T). The averages and corresponding number of cases are listed in Table 18.4.

Of the 151 exits, one is not represented in this table: a tail exit, which was used once, by 12 evacuees. The averages increase with the size of the airplane but are surprisingly low. In 20 cases of a single-lane-slide-equipped floor-level exit on a tail-engine airplane, the average use was only 14. For wing-engined airplanes, this average, for 49 cases, was 26. Overwing exits on those classes of airplanes have similar averages: 17 and 24. Double-lane-slide-equipped exits, only used on twin-aisle airplanes, have an average of 54 (for 16 cases). An exceptionally high number of average usage is that for overwing exits on twin-aisle airplanes: 129. This average was for four cases only, where the numbers achieved were as follows: 27, -117, 140, 230. Not all twin-aisle airplanes have exits at this location.

18.6 CONCLUSIONS

Although the four studies differed significantly in time period, database set, and focus, still some common patterns can be discerned.[8]

All four studies found that only a proportion of the exits installed are used in actual evacuations. The numbers vary somewhat, but on average roughly one-half of the exits are used. This confirms the adequacy of the evacuation demonstration criterion to use only half of the exits.

The notion that a fire typically renders one side of the airplane unusable, which is another criterion for the demonstration, is not supported by the studies' results. Neither is it common that all exits at one end of the fuselage (either forward or aft) are used. Rather, the pattern is quite random, with

TABLE 18.4
Average Numbers of Evacuees per Exit

Exit Position:		Floor-Level Exits, Not Overwing				Overwing Exits	
Descent Assist Means:		Single Lane		Double Lane		Varies	
	Airplane Seating Capacity Range	Average	Number of Cases	Average	Number of Cases	Average	Number of Cases
ST	50 to 180	14	20	n/a	n/a	17	26
SW	100 to 250	26	49	n/a	n/a	24	26
T	200 to 550	36	9	54	16	129	4

n/a: not applicable.

a mix of exits forward and aft, left and right, being usable. This conclusion is important for crew training and decision making. Flight crew have no means to know which exits are usable and can therefore not be relied upon to make a decision in the cockpit as to which exits to use. This decision falls down on individual cabin crew at each exit. Only when there would be a crash-proof system of cameras that provide an overview of the entire fuselage in the cockpit, or another point, can a decision on which exits to use be made centrally. This would then also require a crash-resistant communication system for reaching all cabin crew and passengers. Conversely, the cabin crew should then be able to communicate exit opening to a central point.

Another pattern noticeable from the studies is that passengers have a tendency to move forward. A possible explanation that this is because passengers tend to go where they boarded (which is in most cases forward) was falsified by Ed Galea. He found a propensity among passengers to go to their nearest exit instead.

Possibly associated with the forward tendency is that exits forward of the wings have a higher usage than exits aft of the wing. Exits over the wing, however, are also used frequently, especially in cases where the airplane comes down in water.

Finally, tail exits have demonstrated poor performance in evacuations.

NOTES

1. Aircraft Emergency Evacuation, Operating Experience and Industrial Trials, Report No. 2, U.S. Department of Commerce, Civil Aeronautics Administration, Office of Aviation Safety, May 1952.
2. Usability of Transport Aircraft Emergency Exits, Richard F. Chandler, Mark H. George, Donell W. Pollard, Memorandum No. AAM-119-87-3, May 27, 1987.
3. Usage of Type III and Tail Cone Exits, Anthony L. Pennybaker, Memorandum No. AAM-610-90-1, April 12, 1991.
4. A Database to Record Human Experience of Evacuation in Aviation Accidents, The Aircraft Accident Statistics and Knowledge Database (AASK), Prepared for the CAA by Fire Safety Engineering Group, University of Greenwich, E.R. Galea, K.M. Finney, A.J.P. Dixon, A. Siddiqui, D.P. Cooney, CAA Paper 2006/01, June 2008.
5. Passenger Emergency Exit Usage in Actual Emergencies of Jet Airliners, 1960–1989, Fons Schaefers, in Proceedings of the European Cabin Safety Conference 1990, London-Gatwick, CAP 583, p. 67; Passenger Emergency Exit Usage in Actual Emergencies of Jet Airliners, Fons Schaefers, in Proceedings of the 11th Annual International Aircraft Cabin Safety Symposium and Technical Conference, SCSI and FAA CAMI, Long Beach, January 31–February 5, 1994, p. 71; Exit Usage in Survivable Accidents Under Life-Threatening Conditions, Fons Schaefers, in Proceedings of the International Cabin Safety Conference, $(L/D)_{max}$ Aviation Safety Group, Amsterdam, 23–25 October 2012.
6. Location 3 comprises all overwing exits, even when there are actually two (or even three, as on the Comet) overwing exits on each side.
7. Report on the Accident to Boeing 737-236 Series 1, G-BGJL at Manchester International Airport on 22 August 1985, 8/88, Department of Transport, Air Accidents Investigation Branch, 15 December 1988, p. 148, p. 5.
8. CAMI's two studies used the same dataset, so are counted as one study.

19 Possible Future Cabin Safety Developments

ABSTRACT

Predictions are made along three lines: an overview of cabin safety activities already in the pipeline, the cabin safety consequences of new airplane or cabin concepts, and, finally, areas that pose challenges and need a resolution of some sort. Examples of the latter include carry-on baggage and portable electronic devices and their batteries.

19.1 INTRODUCTION

Can the future be predicted by studying history? No, but it does help to know history when making predictions.

In the vast output of research into cabin safety that has been done in the U.S., and, to a lesser extent, in Europe, there were many subjects that were potential candidates for further development and even adoption as a new rule. Yet, they did not reach that stage. Going forward, what determines which research output will indeed progress into a rule? History seems to have the answer: those that were pinpointed by an accident. Once an accident identifies a specific flaw, the chances are high that a targeted 'repair' follows, typically in the form of a new rule. It might well be that the repair had already been researched and was lingering, waiting only for a matching accident to occur. Examples were the floor lighting rule, that was already 'on the shelf', but was triggered by the Cincinnati 1983 accident, and the penetration-resistant cockpit doors that came shortly after 9/11.

As the statistics in Section 17.2 show, the number of serious cabin safety accidents has diminished. And thus has the chance for new cabin safety rules. So, to predict the next cabin safety development would equal the prediction of the next accident. That, of course, is impossible. But what is possible is to predict:

- Activities that are 'in the pipeline', for example, because they have been tasked to the FAA by U.S. Congress or elsewhere
- New airplane concepts and their cabin safety implications
- Current cabin safety challenges that would benefit from a resolution

19.2 IN THE PIPELINE

The FAA Reauthorization Act of 2024, signed by President Biden on May 16, 2024, requires more research on several cabin safety aspects. It asks for the Aviation Rulemaking Committee to review and develop findings and recommendations for secondary cockpit barriers where not already required. As to first-aid and emergency medical kits, a re-evaluation per NPRM is asked to see if their contents are proper for the emergency medical needs of children and pregnant women. The longest cabin safety-related entry in the bill is about evacuation research. This seems to be a repeat of the 2018 reauthorization bill. It will lead to more testing by FAA CAMI. Computer modeling as an alternative to evacuation demonstrations is not mentioned but may well be employed as part of those studies.

Other research in the pipeline is about air contamination, as has already been conducted both in the U.S. and in Europe. Other than the conversion of heat release standards into a performance standard, no cabin safety rules are being processed as 2024 ends.

19.3 NEW CONCEPTS

19.3.1 AIRPLANE LEVEL

The airworthiness regulations address existing airplane concepts but they may not be suitable for new concepts. If so, to ensure their safety, authorities may impose Special Conditions as part of the type certification process. Special Conditions are formulated by the airworthiness authorities to address novel or unusual designs which fall outside the boundaries of existing regulations.

Such Special Conditions will certainly be needed for the following examples of emerging aviation concepts that will have significantly new cabin safety elements. They are at either end of the passenger experience spectrum: advanced air mobility (AAM) aircraft and blended wing body (BWB) transport airplanes.

AAM aircraft are short-range, small passenger capacity aircraft that may be unmanned (remotely controlled or even autonomous) and typically have vertical take-off and landing properties. They are the aviation equivalent of self-driving cars or taxis. From a cabin safety perspective, the challenges are multiple, especially for unmanned AAMs. Passengers need to be instructed on the proper use of the doors and other controls (e.g. seat and belt use, air conditioning, lighting), what to do in case of an emergency, and what not to do. Traditional safety cards will not help. Rather, new means of interaction need to be used. These are likely to employ several senses: at least visual and aural, but perhaps also tactile. Interactive video screens, together with audio, cameras, and microphones, may form a good platform for two-way communication with the machine and, where involved, the remote operator. Emergency instructions (e.g. for manual opening of exits in case of power failure) need to be intuitive and tested across diverse groups of cultures and ages.

Working at the other end of the spectrum than AAMs, airplane manufacturers are investigating new forms of long-range, large transport airplanes. One concept under investigation is that of the blended wing body (BWB). Here, the wing and fuselage are merged into a single body. The passenger cabin (and cockpit) is located inside the wing, which is thicker than for traditional airplanes. The concept of passengers sitting in the wing has been applied twice before in history in limited use: in the 1930s in Germany (Junkers G.38) and in the 1950s in the U.S. (Burnell CBY-3). In both cases, the plane form was an intermediate between the traditional fuselage plus wing rather than a full merge of the two.

Passenger cabins in the BWB will deviate from traditional layouts in the length-to-width ratio. Instead of a ratio of 10 to 1, such as a Boeing 777-300 (cabin length c. 60 m, width c. 6 m), they will have a ratio closer to 1:1. The cabin map will be drastically different. The number of lateral aisles may equal that of longitudinal aisles. New seating layouts will need to be explored and tested, both for comfort issues and for rapid egress. Current requirements specify that there may not be more than two other seats between a passenger and an aisle, but that may have to be reconsidered. The stance that the FAA took in January 1956 (see Section 16.2.1) and occasionally repeated since would help: when supported by sound technical data, alternatives are acceptable. In the case of the BWB, the challenge to get such data is a matter of volume and will involve many more tests and subjects than Boeing needed when the 747 was a new concept. Accumulating that, technical data can benefit from computer evacuation models, of which there are many available.

Ed Galea of the University of Greenwich in 2010 tested their computer model on a hypothetical BWB cabin layout of 1,020 seats with 8 longitudinal and 7 lateral aisles, 20 exits in 5 sides, and 25 cabin crew.[1] To validate elements of it, Cranfield University helped with real-life testing of a portion of the hypothetical cabin.

19.3.2 CABIN LEVEL

At the cabin level, many ideas abound, each promising a radical change in how airplane cabins will look in the future. Visitors to the Cabin Interior Expo, held annually in Hamburg, regularly see novel seating concepts. For economy class, standing-room-only options, or cinema-type seats with

Possible Future Cabin Safety Developments

FIGURE 19.1 Novel cabin seating concept involving vertical staggering of seat rows.

fold-up seat pans, have been proposed. It is thought that such a concept would increase the capacity of an airplane, but that will only work when the number of exits is increased accordingly, as current traditional high-density seating arrangements already match the maximum exit capacity. In addition, meeting impact protection requirements would pose a significant challenge. Another concept tried in Hamburg is that of using the third dimension in the cabin by vertically staggering seat rows. Its inventor, Núñez Vicente, calls it the 'chaise longue'. He is aware of the certification challenges.

At the other end of the comfort spectrum, first-class seats evolved in private suites for individuals or small companies. A next step may be suites with club or 'buddy' seating, reviving the early aviation days. The suites may even evolve into private apartments, from which it is only a small step to consider them as mini cabins, for which safety features such as a separate fire extinguisher, exit signs, and a second way out may then be specified.

19.4 SELECTED CABIN SAFETY CHALLENGES

Out of many cabin safety areas that pose challenges and need a resolution of some sort, here follows a subjective selection of items that deserve more attention in the decades to come.

19.4.1 Carry-On Baggage

Passengers tend to take more of their baggage with them on board, instead of checking it in so that it travels in the baggage compartments. There are several reasons for this: fear of checked-in baggage becoming lost and airlines charging for checked-in baggage are probably the most frequent. Airlines have increased stowage space in the cabin. In the specialist paper on evacuation by Nick Butcher of the Royal Aeronautical Society, he observed that in an evacuation people tend to take their baggage with them and delay the evacuation. He warns that one day this may cause fatalities. In this respect, two accidents are of particular interest:

- Moscow, Sukhoi Superjet, May 2019: a hard landing was made causing the wing and fuel lines to rupture. A fierce fire developed and engulfed the rear fuselage. Forty-one of the 78 occupants died. Reportedly, this aircraft was equipped with a central locking means for the luggage bins, aimed at preventing passengers from retrieving their baggage during an

evacuation. Whether that system was used, and if so, whether or not it negatively affected the evacuation, is not reported.
- Tokyo, Airbus A350, January 2024: the landing Airbus hit another aircraft on the runway and slid to a stop further down the runway. All 379 occupants survived and evacuated. According to media reports, the evacuation only started after about 5 minutes. The evacuation itself was quick and reportedly involved few, if any, passengers who took their baggage with them.

Both accidents have interesting lessons to learn as to behavioral aspects. Had the central locking of the Sukhoi indeed been a factor in the evacuation? Why did so few passengers in Tokyo take their baggage? Which groups of passengers tend to take their luggage? Do passengers make their own safety assessment when deciding to take their luggage or not? Perhaps behavioral scientists should investigate this.

Moldova in 2019 made a proposal to ICAO's 40th assembly to make mandatory the centralized lock as employed on the Sukhoi Superjet.[2] In its working paper, Moldova did not address the behavioral risks that such a means may introduce.

19.4.2 EVACUATION INITIATION

The decision to initiate an evacuation remains difficult and needs further attention. In the first moments following a mishap, the crew must assess the conditions and decide what is better: not risking passengers to potential evacuation injuries versus not exposing passengers to life-threatening conditions inside the cabin. A related question is: who may make this decision? In some airlines and cultures, this decision rests with the captain. However, there have been cases where the captain was not aware of the severity of the situation in the cabin and lingered. Examples include the Riyadh 1980 accident, in which no evacuation took place at all, at the loss of all 301 occupants on board. In 1993 when a 747 had overrun into the bay next to Hong Kong Kowloon airport, the purser ran upstairs to ask permission of the captain to start the evacuation. This may have caused a delay, but all occupants evacuated successfully.

In the January 2024 Tokyo Airbus A350 accident, the evacuation was successful as well but reportedly completed only after about eight minutes. According to media reports, the pilots were not immediately aware of a fire.[3] With communication means (public address, interphone) rendered unserviceable, the cabin crew was uncertain as to initiate the evacuation. Passengers, including a young child, reportedly pleaded for the opening of exits. After about five minutes, evacuation started which then went quickly. Megaphones were used.

In other airlines, cabin crew has a mandate to initiate an evacuation when they see a need. This still involves informing the captain, but that assumes the means of communication is serviceable. In the San Francisco accident in 2013, which involved the airplane striking a seawall and then spinning about 330°, the flight crew was hesitant to order an evacuation.[4] While one cabin crewmember coordinated with the cockpit and waited, other cabin crew started the evacuation.

In the Toronto 2005 accident, the chief purser, like the captain, was initially not aware of the fire and made a PA announcement to passengers to remain seated. But when informed by another cabin crewmember about the fire, he spoke with the captain and commanded the evacuation.

In airplanes with long cabins, and with communication means vulnerable to failure, proper initiation of an evacuation remains a challenge. Would a set of strategically located battery-powered cameras and displays using Bluetooth technology help?

19.4.3 PED FIRE CONTAINMENT

The abbreviation PED stands for Portable Electronic Devices. This encompasses an eclectic assortment of devices that crew and passengers bring on board, varying from calculators and toys to mobile phones and tablets. They all share one element: batteries. In many cases, these batteries are of the lithium-ion kind, which has an inherent risk of thermal runaway. This is a phenomenon in which cells of the battery enter an uncontrollable, self-heating state. A fire may result which can be difficult to extinguish. While the occurrence rate of a thermal runaway is extremely low, the sheer number of PEDs brought on board makes it an event that occurs from time to time. When such a PED is in checked baggage and ignites, it remains uncontrolled. EASA has therefore issued a Safety Information Bulletin advising that PEDs should not be put in checked baggage, but carried in the cabin.[5] Some airlines have added to their safety briefing and safety cards instructions that passengers contact crew at the first sign of a PED on fire, and have installed PED fire containment kits. There is no legal requirement for such a kit yet, but when the frequency of such fires increases, or when there is an accident as a result, this might change.

19.4.4 TAIL EXITS

Airplanes with tail exits have come and gone. As described in Section 16.2.1 jet airplanes so equipped appeared in the late 1950s and early 1960s. Although several thousand have been produced, there are very few remaining in service in 2024 (mainly some MD-80s and Boeing 717s). When they were certificated, the tail exits were expected to have a positive contribution to evacuations. This, however, was falsified by accident experience. In evacuations under life-threatening conditions, these exits were rarely used. In several cases, occupants who went into the tail area had to retreat and choose another exit or became fatally trapped. It would therefore be justified to reconsider the regulations for tail exits.

19.4.5 SAFETY INSTRUCTIONS

While they may be a popular source for imitation and mockery, the safety value of safety instructions (both the briefings and the safety cards), at best, is questionable. In spite of many attempts to improve the level of attention to the briefing by passengers, it is unlikely that this will succeed. The trend of cluttering many subjects on the safety cards, in small print, has further degraded their comprehensibility. For new airplane designs, a better approach would be to use a design philosophy that all controls to be operated by passengers are so designed, and placarded, that they are intuitive and need no further guidance. Again, the expertise of behavioral scientists may come of help here, possibly assisted by the same professionals who design consumer electronics. This would then reduce the need for instructions to one element: the location of emergency exits.

19.4.6 CABIN SAFETY ACCIDENT INVESTIGATIONS

An area of cabin safety where practice has not kept up with technological advances is that of accident investigations. There are few investigators that record the performance of such cabin safety measures as heat release, 16 g seats, and many more. ICAO published in 2017 a document aimed specifically at this profession.[6] Increased adherence to that document would add to knowledge about how well these features have helped in saving lives or, where there are still areas for improvement.

NOTES

1. Evacuation Analysis of 1000+ Seat Blended Wing Body Aircraft Configurations: Computer Simulations and Full-Scale Evacuation Experiment E.R. Galea, L. Filippidis, Z. Wang, P.J. Lawrence, J. Ewer, Paper presented at PED 2010, NIST, Maryland USA, March 8–10, 2010.
2. Introduction of the Centralized-Operational Locks for the Aircraft Overhead Bins, Submitted by Republic of Moldova, Working Paper A40-WP/110, 26 July 2019.

3 www.flyertalk.com/forum/japan-airlines-jal-mileage-bank/2146390-jal-a359-burst-into-flames-after-collision-coastguard-plane-haneda-2-jan-2024-a.26.html, Visited 29 May 2024.
4 Descent Below Visual Glidepath and Impact with Seawall, Asiana Airlines Flight 214, Boeing 777-200ER, HL7442, San Francisco, California, July 6, 2013, NTSB/AAR-14/01, Adopted June 24, 2014.
5 Safety Precautions Regarding the Transport by Air of Portable Electronic Devices containing Lithium Batteries carried by Passengers, EASA Safety Information Bulletin 2017-04, 5 April 2017.
6 Manual on the Investigation of Cabin Safety Aspects in Accidents and Incidents, Doc 10062, International Civil Aviation Organization, Second Edition, 2022.

20 Acquainting Passengers

ABSTRACT

One of the earliest cabin safety features were briefings to passengers, both by means of pamphlets and orally. The chapter reviews the history of the oral briefings, the safety leaflets, and the videotaped briefings. It discusses how safety leaflets were tested for comprehensibility and whether they indeed contributed to survival in accidents.

20.1 INTRODUCTION

The history of passenger safety instructions is as old as that of cabin safety. There were initially two forms: oral briefings and printed instructions. From the 1970s onward, video briefings appeared. The first safety pamphlet was issued in 1924, but it took until after World War Two before they became commonplace. In the 1950s the focus was on ditching and water survival. In the second wave, safety cards became mandatory in the U.S. and, in its wake, many other countries. Although IATA made an early attempt in 1968, it took another decade before guidance material appeared. At the same time, the subject caught the attention of the U.S. Congress, and in 1985, the investigators, the NTSB.

Little research has been done on the effectivity of printed safety instructions, either by means of tests or in accident investigations. Cranfield University was one of the few who did, and possibly the only organization that used the proper environment: an aircraft cabin. Dedicated card manufacturers, which started to emerge from 1973 onward, however, did in-house comprehensibility tests. A perpetual subject is how to improve the passenger's attention to briefings and cards.

20.2 1924: THE FIRST SAFETY PAMPHLET

The first safety pamphlet was made by KLM (Royal Dutch Air Service Co.) in 1924. The year of issue is not printed but can be inferred. It was made for the route Amsterdam (the Netherlands)—London (United Kingdom) as it described the Channel crossing and its duration (12 to 15 minutes). The English version is a translation of a Dutch original, but there are some telling differences. The Dutch version ended with the notion that KLM had never suffered an accident. The English version omits that, so, unlike the original, will have been made after 24 April 1924, when KLM suffered its first fatal accident. The English version refers to the 'Air Navigation Act', but the Dutch text does not. The United Kingdom was years ahead of the Netherlands in establishing air legislation. Text dominates. The English version has four pictures showing the life vest, then called 'lifebelt' but otherwise is text only. The only other safety feature that it explains is the emergency exit. The operation of the main door is not explained. The longest section of the pamphlet is called 'General Notes' and gives some facts about what to expect on a flight such as altitude, turbulence, and ventilation. It also explains how the pilot receives weather reports. The method described was in use before KLM equipped its aircraft with a radio, which happened in 1925. This would indeed date it to 1924. Quite possibly, there were also instructions posted in the cabin at the time.

20.3 1920s—1944

Safety pamphlets in this period were rare. In addition to KLM, which issued more versions of its pamphlet after 1924, only the UK's Imperial Airways is known to have issued safety instruction pamphlets before World War Two. The accident report of the 1929 ditching near Dungeness mentioned a leaflet explaining the use of the lifebelts, which appeared to be unclear (see Section 3.1.1).

ROYAL DUTCH AIR SERVICE CO.

GENERAL HINTS & INFORMATION FOR PASSENGERS.

1. Do not smoke or light matches in the machine.
2. Articles of any description must **not** be thrown out of the machine. In addition to it being an extremely dangerous practice, it is a breach of the Air Navigation Act.

LIFEBELTS.

3. For the channel crossing which occupies from 12 to 18 minutes, lifebelts are provided for each passenger should necessity arise.

Ordinarily the lifebelt is inflated by means of a compressed air bottle, operated by a lever, but it can also be inflated by the mouth.

TO ADJUST.

Put on the belt in waistcoat fashion, by passing the arms through the shoulderstraps, as in figure I.

FIG. I.

so that the brass operating lever comes to the bottom right hand side. Hook the brass buckles in front, as shown in Fig. II.

TO INFLATE.

Hold the air bottle (which will be felt inside the belt Fig. II. A) by the left hand and press the operating lever upwards with the right hand. If the cylinder does not work, inflate by mouth, after unscrewing the valve on the left side of the belt. (Fig II. B). When sufficiently inflated, screw down tightly the mouthpiece valve. (Fig. III).

FIG. II.

FIG. III.

EMERGENCY EXIT.

4. In the event of the door of the machine becoming blocked an emergency exit is provided. This exit is indicated in the machine and is opened as follows: — Pull with force the red ball of the linen covering, which then rips away the fabric and forms the exit, and climb out.

When making use of this emergency exit do not inflate your lifebelt until you have passed through, as the aperture would be too small.

Never tamper with the emergency exit during flight as it is extremely dangerous.

COMMUNICATION WITH PILOT.

5. In case of urgent necessity passengers can communicate with the pilot through the scuttle behind the pilot seat.

GENERAL NOTES.

Don't be concerned if the machine on starting taxies slowly towards a corner of the aerodrome. The machine always starts and lands head against the wind.

After running about 120 yards the machine almost imperceptibly rises from the ground.

The so-called „bumping" movement sometimes experienced by the irregular temperature of the air or strong winds, and it is in no way dangerous. It corresponds to the motion of a ship at sea. The machines are so stable that passengers can have every confidence and with such get quickly accustomed to the motion. It may interest passengers to know that the machines of the K. L. M. have proved their air worthiness and stability by flights across the Channel when the regular cross channel steamers have been prevented from sailing owing to stormy weather.

Good ventilation prevents air-sickness. The windows of the K. L. M. machines are so constructed that they can be opened on both sides giving perfect ventilation without causing draughts.

In case of sickness receptacles are provided and kept in the left back corner of the cabin. Do not throw these receptacles out of the machine.

A metal water bottle and tumblers are also provided and stored in the small cupboard behind the seats.

When flying in a curve machines heel slightly to one side but passengers remain sitting upright in their seats.

There is no discomfort in looking downwards when flying; dizziness is unknown in aeroplanes as there is no connection with the earth.

Machines fly at an average height of 1200 feet.

Follow your route on a map and your interest in the flight will be immeasurably increased.

Owing to the altitude of the flight the impression gained by passengers is that the machine is flying very slowly, whereas the speed is often about one hundred miles per hour.

The machines are so constructed that with the engines stopped they are able to „glide" on their wings. When gliding, for every hundred yards loss of height a distance of 800 yards horizontally is covered.

In case of engine trouble a pilot is able to circle with a diameter of 4 miles to select a field where the machine can be safely landed. These fields are situated at regular intervals on the route and are well known to pilots.

When about to land the pilot diminishes the speed of the propellor and passengers have no cause for alarm when hearing the engine slowing down, it is only an indication that the pilot is preparing to land.

When descending passengers are recommended to close the mouth and perform the operation of swallowing or „gulping" down food, so as to prevent temporary deafness.

Weather conditions are sent out every hour from wireless stations, informing the various aerodromes of such weather conditions along the route. The pilot is therefore fully aware of the weather he may expect when leaving an aerodrome. Further he will find on his route certain signals (large white figures on a dark ground) indicating weather conditions at the next station. For instance these signals displayed at Flushing inform him of the conditions at Ostend and at Ostend those for Calais. This enables him to arrange his flight accordingly and should conditions be too bad for continuing, he can finish his flight before entering the bad area. This latter condition is very exceptional as the K. L. M. machines have proved their ability to fly in practically all weather conditions. Nevertheless, pilots have received the most stringent instructions never to take any unnecessary risks and the motto of „Safety First" has been and will always remain the guiding principle of the K. L. M. flights.

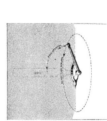

Operating lever and air tube.

FIGURE 20.1 KLM 1924 safety leaflet.

Acquainting Passengers

FIGURE 20.2   Royal Air Force Dakota ditching folder, c. 1944.

Placarded safety notices may have been more common. The January 1939 Cavalier accident report noted that 'an illustrated notice showing how lifebelts should be put on was displayed in each cabin of the flying boat'.[1]

During the war, and probably in response to the Trammel accident, U.S. airlines started to explain in their flight literature how to open emergency exits. Both TWA and United Airlines had this information, but the form differed. TWA added it in their 'for your comfort' folder, as a footnote in their cabin layout drawing. United added a small illustration showing the exit operation to the many other illustrations in their flight kit folder (see Section 3.2.3).

On the military side, the Royal Air Force around 1944 issued exquisite ditching folders to passengers of its Douglas Dakotas (the DC-3), Consolidated Liberators, and Avro Yorks.

20.4 POST WORLD WAR TWO: THE DITCHING YEARS

In 1945, the CAB issued a regulation requiring that flag carriers must acquaint passengers with (1) the location of emergency exits; (2) emergency equipment provided for individual use; and

(3) the procedure to be followed in the case of an emergency landing on water.[2] The regulation did not prescribe the form: oral, paper, or both. The U.S. airlines flying overseas selected to use safety pamphlets to meet this new standard rather than giving an oral demonstration.[3] Pan Am was possibly the first. Its leaflet had a cabin layout at the center of the folded leaflet, showing all exits and emergency equipment, plus an extremely detailed description of the life raft and its survival pack contents. Additionally, it had general instructions for preparing for an emergency landing. Two languages were used: English and French.

American Overseas Airlines, Northwest Orient Airlines, United Airlines, and TWA followed, each having its own format and style. Together with Pan Am, these airlines (bar AOA that was taken over by Pan Am in 1950) later introduced pre-flight oral briefings. This was triggered by a 1951 regulatory proposal change, which incidentally only became effective in 1956. The accident report of the March 1955 ditching off Oregon reported that 'passengers were given a life jacket demonstration by the steward at Portland, prior to departure and each handed a folder, "Just in Case" (of a ditching)'.[4]

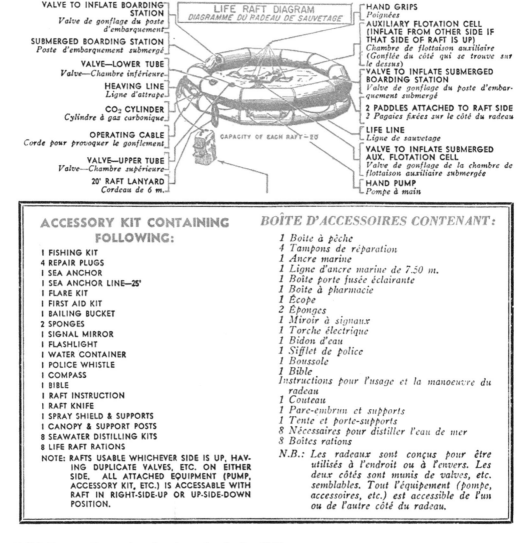

FIGURE 20.3 Extract from Pan Am safety leaflet, 1947.

Acquainting Passengers

In Britain, BOAC's 1946 pamphlet described seat belts, oxygen masks, life jackets, and the dinghy (the British term for life raft) but ignored the aircraft cabin layout or exits. On the oral side, BOAC is known to have their stewards 'lecture' passengers and describe possible emergencies before boarding.[5] This was already around 1946, likely in response to the ditching of the Cavalier. The British Air Ministry had recommended the desirability of instructing passengers in the method of fastening life belts and the location of emergency exits.[6]

In December 1946, the Search and Rescue division of the then-still provisional International Civil Aviation Organization issued recommendations for the briefing of passengers: before take-off, in the proper use of safety belts and in the location of emergency exits; after take-off, how to use the life jacket and about the principal emergency equipment.[7] In the case of an in-flight emergency, passengers should be further briefed in anticipation of an impact that, more likely than not, would be on water. It also said that the captain's authority is absolute, a line copied by at least two airlines in their safety pamphlets (Pan Am and Swissair).

FIGURE 20.4 Extract with the ICAO suggested text on the authority of the captain from safety leaflet of Swissair.

FIGURE 20.5 Extract with the ICAO suggested text on the authority of the captain from safety leaflet of Pan Am.

All the other elements suggested by ICAO were included in ditching-oriented pamphlets that all major international airlines had in the mid-1950s, a reflection of what was *en vogue*. The cover pages were remarkably similar (see Figure 20.6). With few exceptions, they all showed, with a good dose of humor, a life raft gently riding the waves with people in it singing, being played music, or still being served refreshments. The artwork was unique to each airline. The humor was an attempt to soften the impact of the message. Aviation safety was a delicate subject in those days.

Air France repeated on the back of the seats their safety pamphlet containing illustrations showing precautions to take in case of an emergency landing and instructions for the evacuation of the aircraft, in both French and English.[8]

The 1945 requirement for air carriers to acquaint passengers with the exits, emergency equipment, and ditching procedures was copied in 1949 for irregular (Part 42) operations but not for domestic operations. In 1950, the CAB proposed to correct this by requiring those operators to have in their Operations Manual:[9]

> Procedures for briefing and familiarizing passengers with the use of emergency equipment during flight.

This proposal raised 'considerable controversy'. It was followed up in 1952 by the CAB explaining that the different wording ('briefing' instead of 'acquainting') was intentional. It noted that 'many air carriers construe this requirement [of acquainting passengers] to permit passenger briefing by means of pamphlets or cards and do not actually demonstrate the use of life vests, etc.' It considered that such a form of briefing (on paper) was not adequate unless it was oral. Hence, that was now proposed for the location and method of operation of life vests and emergency exits and the location—only—of life rafts. This oral briefing was only needed for extended overwater flights and could be delayed until sometime prior to reaching the overwater portion of the flight.[10] There were still objections from the airlines but the CAB kept its stance that this change would increase safety. The only compromise it was willing to make was an extension of the compliance period. Eventually, the rule became effective on May 31, 1956, for all U.S. air carriers.[11] Although not specified, it was obvious who would give the oral briefing: the cabin attendant.

20.5 1965 ONWARD: MANDATED, GUIDED

In 1965, in the wake of the United 1961 Denver accident, there were further changes. The oral briefing was extended to smoking, the use of seat belts, and the location of exits. At the same time, printed cards were required containing diagrams of, and methods of operating, the exits, plus other instructions necessary for the use of emergency equipment.[12] This was the first time that safety cards were mandated. It led to many new cards by U.S. air carriers.

In 1966, two new requirements were presented for public consultation, which the FAA believed would improve passenger knowledge and avoid confusion:[13]

- Each passenger over 12 years of age must be given one copy of the printed briefing card upon entering the airplane.
- The cards must be pertinent to the type and model of an airplane being used on the flight.

FIGURE 20.6 Nine covers of ditching decade safety leaflets (left to right, top to bottom): Air India (c. 1960), Pacific Northern Airlines (c. 1961), Philippine Airlines (c. 1957), Air France (1947), Alitalia (c. 1952), Swissair (c.1952), Qantas (c.1955), TWA (1949), Colonial Airlines (c.1948).

The first proposal raised quite some comments by the airlines. By distributing the pamphlets, the idea was that passengers were promoted to keep them. This would not only raise costs for the airlines but also multiply the amount of printed material highlighting an airplane emergency, which would not be good for an airline's reputation. An additional fear, which possibly was not more than an excuse, was that the negative promotion pamphlets would litter around at airports.[14] In the final rule, the FAA deleted the requirement for distributing the safety cards. The airlines, keen to retain the cards on board and their numbers in check, happily and voluntarily added a 'do not remove from aircraft' text.

The second proposal was well received and took effect in the U.S. on October 24, 1967.[15] Passengers no longer needed to find out which aircraft type they were in. This removed a likely area of confusion. Some U.S. airlines already issued type-specific cards; others had what was called fleet cards. These now had to be replaced.

Other countries followed with requiring briefings and safety cards. IATA, the international organization representing airlines, in 1968 did a survey of 'safety briefing literature', as they called it, as in use among its members, and used it to draft guidelines so as to achieve some consistency.[16] They advised against photographs and were in favor of simple line drawings as they better convey the essence of the message, without distracting backgrounds. As to color, while acknowledging that this was valuable, IATA warned against overuse. The maximum number of languages should be three. Aviation jargon should be avoided, as should be phrases not familiar to a foreign public, such as 'topping up a life vest'. The IATA guidelines did not delve into testing safety cards for comprehension.

The Society of Automotive Engineers' cabin safety panel published in 1976 an Aerospace Recommended Practice (ARP 1384) for passenger information cards. The next year, the FAA issued an Advisory Circular on the subject, which partly relied on the ARP.[17] It also gave hints for the oral briefing, and later also for videotaped briefings. The guidance material of the SAE and the FAA has been regularly updated and still forms the leading guidance material for safety cards and briefings. In Germany, since October 2004, the *Luftfahrt-Bundesamt* (LBA) regularly updates guidance to EASA regulations. It is issued outside the EASA system and followed by some German airlines.[18]

ICAO issued in 2018 *a Manual on Information and Instructions for Passenger Safety.*[19]

20.6 DESIGNING AND TESTING SAFETY CARDS

In 1973, two behavioral psychologists who worked for Douglas, Beau Altman, and Dan Johnson, started a company dedicated to making safety cards. They called it Interaction Research Corporation (IRC). One of their development activities was the testing by naive persons of their products. They used the feedback to improve the artwork until a 90% level of understanding was achieved.[20] Dan Johnson sat on the SAE panel and initiated the ARP mentioned earlier. Both testified in 1977 in a House of Representatives hearing on passenger education.[21]

In 1981, Carl Reese, a collector of safety cards and former flight attendant, started a one-man company for making safety cards, called 'Cabin Safety, Inc.'. He also had the illustrations, which he made himself, tested for comprehensibility. From the latter 1980s, more such companies emerged, most of which were located in the state of Washington, in the vicinity of Boeing. Reese however operated from the U.S. east coast before moving to Canada.

Florian Jentsch, in his 1992 thesis described hereunder, discerned two kinds of tests for verifying the adequacy of safety cards, or, for that matter, briefings:[22]

- Conceptual tests: Various designs and certain features of safety cards are shown by trained interviewers to test participants who then attempt to interpret and verbally describe the depicted information. This method is the most often used.
- Behavioral tests: participants are asked to perform a specific task after receiving safety information, for example, donning oxygen masks after reading the respective part on a passenger safety briefing card.

20.7 VIDEO

Motion pictures have been shown on board airplanes for decades, using cinema-type movie projectors. They were unlikely used for presenting safety instructions. When video equipment replaced the projectors, the option of using the new medium for that purpose emerged, providing an alternative for life briefings. This was in the 1970s and limited to long-haul aircraft. Initially, the footage consisted of video recordings of flight attendants performing their oral briefing. In 1990, Aer Lingus introduced the first computer-animated safety briefing.[23] The reason for such animation was to improve the level of attention by passengers. Aer Lingus, together with an Irish film-producing company, had established the psychological principle that passengers identify with the character who provides the demonstration. They explained:

> Given the heterogeneity of passengers it can be very difficult to select a human-role model that the large majority of passengers perceive positively. By using an abstract animated character these barriers are removed, with passenger less likely to be as subjectively critical of an animated character as they would a human-role model.

In an effectiveness study in 1995, Aer Lingus found that the video presentation, which was used on long-haul routes (i.e. transatlantic), scored much better than the traditional demonstration by cabin crew, as employed on its short-haul (i.e. continental) routes.

Since then, animated video presentations have become the international norm for long-haul routes. Many airlines added a national element to their presentations. This met two goals: attracting the attention of passengers, and national promotion. Air New Zealand is a good example. It uses such themes as the indigenous people or the hobbit as the main thread. (The Hobbit movies were largely shot in New Zealand.) Air France shows elements of French culture, KLM Delft blue tiles, popular with tourists. Korean Airlines uses a virtual influencer who is popular on social media. While these artistically created videos show all the requisite subjects, they tend to do those outside a cabin environment. In domestic U.S. operations, live demonstrations remained the norm.

20.8 STUDIES AND RESEARCH

In 1985 Nora Marshall of the NTSB did an in-depth study on passenger safety education.[24] She reviewed the passenger safety cards, oral briefings (including demonstrations of e.g. life vest donning), and videotaped briefings. She found that safety cards in many instances did not meet the FAA guidelines, which actually were also found to contain errors. She observed that there were no standards for testing safety cards, and that, in general, no testing was performed, with the exception of IRC. (She was apparently unaware of Reese.)

Cranfield University in 1989 performed both conceptual and behavioral research on the safety cards and safety briefings. For the cards, their effectiveness in conveying safety information was measured by having subjects don a life vest, fasten seat belts, or assume the brace position. Knowledge of other subjects (oxygen mask use, exit location, and operation) was assessed by means of questionnaires. Four safety card types were tested, varying in the use of diagrams or photographs, the amount of text, and symbols.[25]

As to briefings, Cranfield investigated the effect of varying its content on passenger attention and ability to carry out safety procedures. The same topics as for the cards were tested, in the same form (activity or knowledge retention). Variations were in the briefing contents (standard, without any demonstration of equipment, or modification), who did it (cabin crew or captain), and the duration between the briefing and the emergency activity. Uniquely, this research was done in an aircraft. No other safety education research is known that took place in the actual setting of an aircraft. In the Cranfield case, it was their Trident which they had earlier used for competitive evacuation trials. In general, the participants performed well for simple tasks, but less for the more complicated tasks such as life vest donning and exit operation. One recommendation was that card designers should consult non-aviation personnel to ensure that naive passengers can comprehend the information. Cranfield found that in providing safety information to passengers, a balance must be struck between giving a sufficient level of detail and not frightening passengers.

Among aviation students, evaluating the comprehension of safety briefings and safety cards is a popular means for honing their academic skills. In 1992, Florian Jentsch, a Master's Degree candidate at the Embry Riddle University in Florida, organized conceptual tests of contemporary safety cards in conjunction with universities in three European countries: France, Germany, and the UK. He exposed differences in interpretation based on culture and language group.[26] A very common difference was that Europeans associated exits with the color green and Americans with the color red. This was because these colors were so used in buildings and ships. The study's range was quite limited as the four countries share many cultural elements. One of the recommendations therefore was for a broader study, involving various Asian, African, and other continent's cultures. No such study was found and likely not done but would certainly have exposed more differences.

In his thesis, Jentsch cited conceptual testing by Finnair when they introduced the MD-11. In a novel approach, Finnair posed school children aged 11 and 12 open-ended questions about what they thought was meant by each presented part of its safety card. 'Many children mistook the drawing of a uniformed flight attendant opening one exit, while a non-uniformed person opened a different exit, for a separation of doors available to passengers and crewmembers'. In the final version, the woman figure was no longer in uniform.

In 2001 Cranfield again researched passenger education.[27] This time the topic was the method of opening a Type III exit and how this could be improved by a personal briefing and placarded diagrams. The test article was an indoor Boeing 737-200 fuselage, with a hatch-type exit weighing 21.5 kg. It was found, as expected, that more detailed briefings resulted in better opening times. Quite interestingly, the main outcome of the briefing was that it reduced the hesitation time taken by participants to start to operate the exit. Placarded opening diagrams were an additional positive element. Both the briefing and the diagrams instilled a sense of responsibility and better prepared the participants for the task. The time taken for the actual opening did not differ significantly.

In Canada, in 2002 the Transportation Development Centre studied how to improve the effectiveness of briefings for passengers with sensory and cognitive disabilities. A test video was scripted and exposed to 32 participants, who were deaf, blind, or had other communication-limiting impairments and compared to a regular video. It was shown that indeed significant improvements could be made for the impaired.

More research has been done on both the safety briefings and the safety cards, for example, by the Australian Transport Safety Bureau in 2004 and by FAA's CAMI in 2008.[28] They identified issues with the level of attention that passengers pay to the briefing (live or video) and cards and their comprehensibility, particularly of the printed cards. Luca Chittaro of the University of Udine, Italy, proposes to use an interactive safety video which he found would increase both the level of attention and the comprehensibility.[29]

20.9 EFFECTIVITY IN ACCIDENTS

When the FAA introduced the requirements for oral briefings in 1956 and printed safety leaflets in 1965, it had no evidence other than common sense that they would work. It was of course known that at least some passengers listened to briefings and read the cards. But have accidents indeed proven that they were effective?

The NTSB in their 1985 study reversed the question and listed accidents with passenger education problems. For the period 1962 to 1985, it cataloged 21 such cases of which one occurred outside the U.S. not involving a U.S. air carrier. Briefings were reported as too short, inadequate, or hard to hear. Cards were reported as difficult to follow or incorrect. In two cases, mismatches were found between the briefing and the equipment on board, and in one case between the briefing and the information on the leaflet.

There are very few accident investigation reports that mention the efficacy of safety information on survival. The report of a 1967 Convair 880 crash in Cincinnati mentioned a passenger who had followed the instructions on the safety card for tightening the seat belt and the brace position.[30] He was one of the few survivors of this crash which was impact non-survivable to the majority of occupants. In a 1971 Convair 580 accident a passenger who had thoroughly familiarized himself with exit locations survived, together with a person that followed him. The accident was survivable, but other occupants died of asphyxiation due to problems with opening the main door.[31] This person tried several of the emergency exits, a scenario that is reminiscent of the 1943 Trammel accident.

And then, there is a case where opinions conflict as to whether passenger education was indeed a survival factor. In the Pago Pago accident, cited earlier, of 96 occupants only five passengers survived. The accident report says:[32]

> All the survivors reported that they listened to the pretakeoff briefing and read the passenger information pamphlet. These actions prepared them for the evacuation by stressing the location of the nearest exit and the procedures to be followed in an emergency. The movement of most of the passengers, including many of the passengers in the overwing area of the aircraft, to the front and rear exits indicates that they either did not comprehend the pretakeoff briefing or they reacted to the emergency without thinking.

Critics said that the NTSB's conclusion in the second sentence is quite bold and not supported by facts. As those passengers had died, they could not be interviewed. It is therefore not known whether or not they had listened to the briefing and studied the leaflet and what motivated them to move away from the overwing exit area. In his book *Clipper 806*, John Godson mentioned that the rescuers discovered more than 20 bodies neatly stacked one on top of the other behind the forward boarding door. He speculated that while the aircraft was still sliding on the ground, passengers already moved forward and aft to the doors (through which they had boarded), with the flight attendants still in their seats, as trained.[33] He continued:

> As the ground run continued—and quite possibly because it seemed so gentle—others joined those rushing for the exits. This caused a human jam-up around them. Some of the first persons must have studied the Emergency Instruction folders; they managed to get at least one door unlocked.

But none of the doors had opened. Godson had studied Pan Am's emergency instructions for the 707 and found the following instructions for the main entrance and galley doors:

> To open—simply lift and rotate the handle fully [. . .]. Push door out.

He surmised that the passengers did not get them open in time as this instruction conflicted with what needed to be done: He explained:

> All that has to be done, once the locking handle has been turned, is to PULL THE DOOR INSIDE—the exact opposite of what the printed emergency instructions say is to be done.

Figure 20.7 shows the airplane, post-crash with the forward door inside, its initial position after release of the handle.

Godson reckoned that the passengers indeed had carefully studied the safety booklet and acted accordingly, but that these instructions tragically were false. A version of events quite at odds with that of the NTSB. But whose version is right? We shall never know. Godson, at least, admitted he speculated.

FIGURE 20.7 Boeing 707 Pago Pago crash, January 30, 1974.

A case in which several education methods were cited as having contributed to survival is that of the hijacked Ethiopian Airlines 767 that crashed in the water off the beach of Grande Comore in November 1996. The accident was partially survivable. An informal report mentioned that:[34]

> The 767 was now gliding with just the standby instruments and ram air turbine. The first officer went to the rear of the cabin to find passengers wearing their life jackets and inflating them. He and the cabin crew then helped the passengers deflate the life jackets, showed them how to reinflate them, and how to assume the brace position. The cabin crew kept repeating the instructions. They stored any loose items in the cabin and checked that all passengers wore life jackets; and
> Some passengers died because they inflated their life jackets inside the cabin. They had got caught in the water and pushed upwards to the ceiling with the rising water. They were trapped and drowned in the fuselage. Many survived the initial impact but, maybe in a sense of panic, did not hear the captain's instructions not to inflate life jackets.

Trisha Ferguson, the CEO of Interaction Group, remembered from a TV interview of a surviving passenger who credited her survival to the safety card (made by Interaction) that instructed not to inflate the life vest inside the aircraft.[35]

Quite possibly, all methods (briefing by captain, check by first officer, safety card) added up.

NOTES

1. Press Summary of Report of the Investigation of the Accident to the Imperial Airways Aircraft G-ADUU (Cavalier) on January 21, 1939, Office of the Air Attaché British Embassy, Washington D.C., March 25, 1939.
2. CAR 41.507, 1945.
3. DR 52-26.
4. Pan American World Airways, Inc., off the Coast of Oregon in the Pacific Ocean, March 26, 1955, CAB Accident Investigation Board, SA-304, Released November 15, 1955.
5. Air Safety Board, Hearings Before a Subcommittee of the Committee on Interstate and Foreign Commerce, House of Representatives, 81st Congress, Second Session, February 22, 1950, p. 129.
6. Press Summary Cavalier.
7. Human Factors in Air Transportation—Occupational Health and Safety, Ross A. McFarland, 1953, p. 581.
8. Air France—Preston City, Connecticut August 3, 1954, CAB Accident Investigation Report, F101-54, Released April 18, 1955.

9. DR 50-8, 40.31.
10. DR 52-26.
11. Amdt 40-20, 41-6, 42-6 (Effectivity Date Postponed by Amdt 40-4, 41-10, 42-9).
12. Amdt 121-1.
13. NPRM 66-26.
14. De Wolkenridder (KLM Employee Magazine), 14 October 1967.
15. Amdt 121-30.
16. Guidance Material for Passenger Emergency Evacuation Briefing Cards, Letter IATA to Member Airlines, April 5, 1968.
17. Passenger Safety Information Briefing and Briefing Cards, Advisory Circular 121-24, Department of Transportation, Federal Aviation Administration, June 23, 1977.
18. Passenger Safety Briefing Cards (SBC) and Safety Briefing Videos (SBV), LBA-B2-Circular 12/2020, Luftfahrt-Bundesamt, Revision 4, February 2021.
19. Manual on Information and Instructions for Passenger Safety, Doc 10086, International Civil Aviation Organization, First Edition, 2018.
20. The Influence of Cross-Cultural Differences on the Interpretation and Understanding of Aircraft Passenger Safety Briefing Cards, Florian G. Jentsch, Embry Riddle Aeronautical University—Daytona Beach, March 1992.
21. Aviation Safety (Aircraft Passenger Education-The Missing Link in Air Safety), Hearings Before the Subcommittee on Investigations and Review of the Committee on Public Works and Transportation, U.S. House of Representatives, 95th Congress, First Session, July 12, 1977.
22. The Influence of Cross-Cultural Differences.
23. Computer Inflight Safety Videos, in Cabin Safety, Published by the Journal for Cabin Safety Training, Vol. 3, No. 2, 1997.
24. Safety Study—Airline Passenger Safety Education: A Review of Methods Used to Present Safety Information, NTSB, October 25, 1985.
25. Passenger Attitudes Towards Airline Safety Information and Comprehension of Safety Briefings and Cards, P.J. Fennell, H.C. Muir, CAA Paper 92015, December 1992.
26. The Influence of Cross-Cultural Differences.
27. An Investigation into Methods of Briefing Passengers at Type III Exits, Ann M. Cobbett, Paul Liston, Helen Muir, Cranfield University, CAA Paper 2001/6, May 2001.
28. Public Attitudes, Perceptions and Behaviours towards Cabin Safety Communications, Australian Transport Safety Bureau Report B2004/0238, by Andrew Parker, Synovate Pty Ltd, June 2006; Effective Presentation Media for Passenger Safety I: Comprehension of Briefing Card Pictorials and Pictograms Cynthia L. Corbett, Garnet A. McLean, DOT/FAA/AM-08/20, September 2008.
29. A Comparative Study of Aviation Safety Briefing Media: Card, Video, and Video with Interactive Controls, Luca Chittaro, Transportation Research Part C: Emerging Technologies, 85, December 2017, p. 415.
30. Aircraft Accident Report, Trans World Airlines, Inc., Convair 880, N821TW, Constance, Kentucky, November 20, 1967, NTSB-69-05, Adopted August 27, 1969.
31. Aircraft Accident Report, Allegheny Airlines, Inc., Allison Prop Jet Convair 340/440, N5832, New Haven, Connecticut, June 7, 1971, NTSB-AAR-72/20, Adopted June 1, 1972.
32. Aircraft Accident Report, Pan American World Airways, Inc., Boeing 707-321B, N454A, Pago Pago, American Samoa, January 30, 1974, NTSB-AAR-77-7, Report Date October 6, 1977.
33. Clipper 806, The Anatomy of an Air Disaster, John Godson, Contemporary Books, Inc., 1978.
34. Simpleflying.com/ethiopian-airlines-flight-961-cabin-crew-perspective/, Visited 7 March 2024.
35. Simpleflying.com/trisha-ferguston-journey-female-ceo-aviation-industry/, Visited 7 March 2024.

21 Epilogue

21.1 HISTORY SUMMARIZED

The previous chapters reviewed the century-old history of cabin safety. They showed the development in sentiments toward the subject by both industry and society. Before World War Two, cabin safety simply was not an issue. Indeed, airplane cabins had seats and seat belts, fire extinguishers, first-aid kits, and exits, but these had not come about from a well-planned cabin safety scheme.

During the war, the historical meeting of aviation experts in Chicago promoted the formulation of safety regulations, including those for cabin occupants, starting the first wave of attention on cabin safety. This took place in the U.S., which had become the leading aviation nation. Other countries, with some exceptions, followed the examples set by the U.S.

In 1947 a horrific accident, in which people were seen dying while attempting in vain to escape an airplane on fire, pointed to the need for action. Post-crash survivability became topical. American Airlines invented the escape chute as a means for rapid egress, which was quickly adopted across the industry. Structural crash loads were improved.

Dr. Barry King of the medical division of the U.S. CAA staged tests involving humans to determine the parameters for an optimum evacuation. A new regulatory system for specifying the number and sizes of exits was devised, which would last to this day. Separately, NASA's Gerard Pesman studied the mechanisms of crashing and subsequent fires by catapulting airplanes against walls so that he could estimate the time available for egress. If King and Pesman had compared notes, they would have concluded that 90 seconds was a good evacuation time target.

While the aircraft manufacturers generally embraced the new rules, the airlines were more reluctant. Their trade organization argued that resources and funds could better be spent on preventing accidents rather than mitigating the consequences. They successfully quashed a proposal for an array of axes on board but eventually had to accept other cabin safety measures. Meanwhile, air transport airplanes increasingly crossed seas and oceans, and in the process occasionally struck water. In the mid-1950s, cabin safety attention shifted to ditchings and life rafts.

Yet, accidents on land which should be survivable but in which people died continued to happen. It needed people like Howard Hasbrook who worked for a non-profit, non-government organization to investigate these and pinpoint areas for cabin improvement. His advice was heeded by the larger airlines, and there was even a move to install seats with energy-absorbing features, tested dynamically. His advocacy work, however, did not put to work the rulemakers in Washington, D.C.

The advent of the jets around 1960 stirred a renewed interest in cabin safety. The union for stewardesses stated that the service girls on board, incidentally all young, white, and pretty by selection, had an important safety role, yet lacked proper training and a license. The airlines were not yet convinced.

The new jets were not immune to crashing and the first that suffered an accident, in July 1961, which should have been survivable to all on board, but was not, raised renewed attention to survivability. It led to new rules for the ability of airplanes to be evacuated by setting standards for such subjects as lighting, marking, evacuation tests, and safety cards. A second accident, in November 1965, underlined their importance and led to more measures. The manufacturers, again, were co-operative and came up with further suggestions to improve the rules. Training standards for flight attendants, as they were now called, were set and imposed on the air carriers. Thus, in 1972 the second wave of cabin safety improvements ended, leaving a sentiment that cabin safety was complete.

But accidents continued to happen and increasingly brought to light a phenomenon that so far had been underestimated: the flammability of interior materials. Yes, there had been rules for that since Chicago, but they were largely based on the scenario of a cigarette-initiated fire. Plastics had gradually become the main material for interiors, but their perilous flammability characteristics had been ignored during the gradual process.

It took a series of accidents in the 1970s with post-crash fires involving cabin materials to change the mood. Accidents in Anchorage (1970), Chicago (1972), and Pago Pago (1974) had many fatalities directly attributable to the cabin fire. Smoke and toxicity rules were proposed but rejected again in favor of an approach in which all fire characteristics would be balanced for an optimum outcome. Much research and development was needed, carried out by FAA's Technical Center. Its pace was too slow in the eyes of congressmen and became the subject of several House of Representatives hearings. Eventually, new rules for both seat cushion blocking layers and heat release of other cabin materials were introduced in 1986 and 1988, effective both to new airplane types and new samples of existing types.

A new scenario that manifested itself in 1973 (Paris) and again in 1983 (Cincinnati) was that of a fire that started in-flight and went out of control. The same measures as taken for the post-crash scenario helped to mitigate those but additionally led to on-board fire prevention measures.

Concurrently, an extensive crash dynamics research program was conducted to find an optimum between occupant protection and undue engineering or economic burdens. The program consisted of the assessment of human impact injury criteria, analytical modeling techniques, full-scale component testing, and the deliberate crash of a remotely controlled Boeing 720. New rules for the dynamic testing of seats, in two directions (forward and downward) were introduced in 1988. Unlike the flammability rules, they only applied to new airplane types. Newly assembled airplanes of existing types would only be affected from 2009.

While these third-wave measures were put in place, two more significant cabin safety events occurred. An accident in the United Kingdom dramatically exposed the drawbacks of the so-called self-help exits, or Type III exits. Typically located over the wing in single-aisle airplanes, they are meant to be opened in an emergency by passengers. The other event was not an accident, but the low-profile approval of a modification by the FAA that led to an outcry by unions and others. The overwing exits of the twin-aisle Boeing 747 (which are not dependent on operation by passengers), were allowed to be sealed off. This was seen as a serious degradation of safety. Both events led to a major re-assessment of the exit and evacuation rules and provisions, thus extending the third wave several years. Following that, however, the sentiment re-emerged that cabin safety was complete.

Of course, it was not. If only, because society is not static and neither is technology. They require constant adaptation of practices to such events and new features as unlawful actions (9/11), pandemics, battery-powered laptops and tablets, and passenger's physical and behavioral changes.

21.2 REACTIVE, NOT PROACTIVE

This historical review highlights a common thread in cabin safety development: its reactive nature. With one exception, cabin safety improvements resulted from an accident or, more often, a series of similar accidents. In some cases, these were not enough to change things, and more pressure was needed from unions, politicians, or both. Pro-activity in cabin safety was rare. The term tombstone engineering has been coined in this respect.

The exception was the provisions for oxygen. Ross McFarland's research work that had started with his 1935 expedition to Chile formed a basis for a set of regulations that was finished in 1950 and only needed one substantial update, in 1958, to account for the higher operating altitude of the jets. As accident history has since proven, it was first time right.

21.3 STAMINA

The creation and introduction of the exit table in 1951 took a mere 16 weeks from research publication to rule. That included publication of the rule proposal, processing comments, and five weeks between rule publication and effectivity.

That record has never been matched again in cabin safety. On the contrary, there are quite a few candidates for the opposite record: the longest duration from first concept to implementation. Of course, such a record is not actively sought. Here is a shortlist:

- On the simple subject of allowing symbols in lieu of text for marking exits, it took Europe 23 years from initiation to the regulatory change (1994–2007), with the U.S. still allowing it by means of exemptions, only.
- In the U.S., a law for licensing cabin crew was first proposed in 1961 but rejected. Only 42 years later, another such bill was adopted and cabin crew started to receive licenses.
- Dynamic testing of passenger seats was first suggested in 1956 by Howard Hasbrook. A forward-fit requirement for such seats became effective in 2009 in the U.S. and in 2021 in Europe, so after 53 and 65 years, respectively. Admittedly, industry had not waited for that and had introduced it earlier.

While some people may have witnessed the first example from start to finish, few will have had the stamina to witness the other two.

21.4 REJECTION RULE

Quite a few cabin safety rules were rejected, as the 1949 saga of the axes showed plus the many subjects discussed in Chapter 10—Regulation Proposals that were Rejected. In all cases, this was done before they became final. Once final, it appeared very difficult to withdraw a rule. Occasionally, airlines wondered why they carried equipment that weighs a lot but seems to be never used. How often have life vests and oxygen equipment saved lives? Is a second axe on board really needed, or even the first? Accident experience has shown that tail exits, which were amply credited when they were introduced in the 1960s, have rarely been used in life-threatening evacuations. And when so, it led to people becoming trapped. But such an experience has not resulted in a withdrawal of the tail exit rules.

In a bold move, Henk Wolleswinkel, Deputy Director General of Civil Aviation, the Netherlands, suggested reconsidering some cabin safety rules. This was when he addressed the Very Large Transport Aeroplane Conference in October 1998 on behalf of the Minister of Transport.[1] He opined that oxygen generators had killed many more people in the Valujet case than they had ever saved. In a crash of a very large airplane, he said, loads would not reach 16 g and thus such seats would not be needed. Life rafts were archaic and not helpful for polar flights. And the 90-second criterion could be relaxed in the light of airplane structures with better burn-through characteristics. His plea for reconsideration was not followed up. History has taught that the only effective rule for rejection is to reject a rule before it becomes a rule.

21.5 U.S. DOMINANCE CHALLENGED

There is no doubt which country dominated the history and development of cabin safety. That was the U.S. Its institutions for aviation research and its resources and procedures for rulemaking, including its consultation and transparency properties, are second to none. Its output, in the form of reports, firm requirements, and rule gestation documentation, all funded by the U.S. taxpayer, was gladly and *gratis* accepted by other countries in the world. In return, the U.S. aviation industry benefited from this international recognition.

But from about 1995 a second aviation rulemaking force emerged in Europe. Airbus had become a world player of proportions equal to Boeing and stimulated a strong European aviation authority. Boeing learned that European authorities (then in the form of the Joint Aviation Authorities—JAA) would no longer automatically accept findings by the FAA and had to change its strategy and take Europe more seriously. In the wake of the Manchester and Kegworth accidents, the UK, and Europe at large, became more concerned with cabin safety and made funds available for research.

The JAA was succeeded by EASA, which had its own research budget, in around 2003. But as cabin safety by then had matured, its influence on cabin safety development remained relatively limited. Yet, EASA introduced concepts and rules that diverge from, and go beyond, those originated in the U.S. Harmonization efforts for airworthiness aspects are well under way, but on the operational side, there is still room for consolidation.

In 2028 it will be 100 years after Guggenheim funded a study for Americans to learn from the Europeans. Since then, cabin safety has seen a huge evolution and some diversity. In the interest of crew and passengers, would it be appropriate to perform a study aimed at cabin safety harmonization at a global scale?

NOTE

1 Opening Remarks by Mr. H. Wolleswinkel, The Deputy Director General of Civil Aviation on Behalf of the Minister of Transport of The Netherlands, Very Large Transport Aeroplane Conference, 13–16 October 1998.

Appendices

APPENDIX 1—ACCIDENTS REFERRED TO

Date (yyyymmdd)	Type	Operator	Location	Fatal	Survivors	Reference
19230914	DH34	Daimler Airway	Ivinghoe beacon	5	0	8.1.1
19240424	F3	KLM	North Sea	3	0	20.2
19290617	W.10	Imperial Airways	Near Dungeness	7	6	3.1.1;20.3
19310331	F-10	TWA	Bazaar, KS	8	0	3.1.4;10.2
19340727	Condor	Swissair	Tuttlingen	12	0	8.1.2
19341220	DC-2	KLM	Rutbah Wells	7	0	5.5.2.1
19350506	DC-2	TWA	Atlanta, MO	5	6	4.2;10.2
19350720	DC-2	KLM	Pian San Giacomo	13	0	8.1.2
19360407	DC-2	TWA	Mt Chestnut Ridge, PA	12	2	8.1.2
19370506	LZ 129	DZR	Lakehurst, NJ	35	62	3.1.4;8.1.1
19370728	DC-2	KLM	Near Brussels	15	0	5.5.2.1
19390121	S23	Imperial Airways	Atlantic Ocean	3	13	3.2.1;20.4
19390326	DC2	Braniff	Oklahoma City, OK	8	4	3.2.2
19401108	Ju.90	Lufthansa	Brauna	29	0	8.1.2
19410226	DC-3	Eastern Air Lines	Near Atlanta, GA	8	8	3.2
19411003	S-42	Pan American	San Juan, PR	2	25	13.5.1.3
19430802	C-46	USAAF	Lahe	1	24	10.2
19430728	DC-3	American Airlines	Trammel, KY	20	2	3.2.3;3.3.4.1;5.5.3.1;5.5.3.2;7.2.3;20.3;20.9
19460118	DC-3	Eastern Air Lines	Cheshire, CT	17	0	5.5.2.2
19460711	L-049	TWA	Reading, PA	5	1	12.2.1
19470529	DC-4	United Air Lines	NY La Guardia	43	5	2.1;5.4.2;7.2;8.2;9.3.5;10.2;12.3.1;21.1
19470530	DC-4	Eastern Air Lines	Bainbridge, MD	53	0	10.2
19470613	DC-4	Pennsylvania Central	Near Charles Town, WV	50	0	10.2
19480121	L-649	Eastern Air Lines	Boston, MA	0	25	5.4.2

19480617	DC-6	United Air Lines	Mount Carmel, PA	43	0	13.5.2.4
19490815	DC-4	Transocean	Off Lunga Point	8	50	7.3.1
19491129	DC-6	American Airlines	Dallas, TX	28	27	5.4.2
19500614	DC-4	Air France	Bahrain	13	38	7.3.1
19501031	Viking	BEA	London Heathrow	28	2	5.5.1.2.2
19510114	DC-4	National Airlines	Philadelphia, PA	7	21	8.2
19520119	DC-4	Northwest Airlines	Sandspit, AK	36	7	7.3.1
19520211	DC-6	National Airlines	Newark, NJ	29	34	7.4
19520411	DC-4	Pan American	San Juan, PR	52	17	7.3.1
19520825	Tudor	Air Work	Trapani	7	50	7.3.1
19521207	L-1049	TWA	Fallon NAS, NV	0	40	8.2
19521209	Dove	Pacific Airmotive	Staten Island, NY	2	2	7.4
19530803	L-749	Air France	Kastellorizo	4	38	7.3.1
19540615	DC-4	Great Lakes	Gage, OK	0	82	8.2
19540619	DC-4	Swissair	Off Folkestone	3	6	7.3.1
19540803	L-1049	Air France	Preston City, CT	0	37	20.4
19540905	L-1049	KLM	Shannon	28	28	7.3.1
19550326	377	Pan American	off Oregon	4	19	7.3.4; 8.2;20.4
19560402	377	Northwest Airlines	Seattle, WA	5	33	7.3.4;14.4.1
19560630	L-1049/DC-7	TWA/United	Grand Canyon, AZ	128	0	4.4
19561016	377	Pan American	Mid-Pacific Ocean	0	31	7.3.4
19600714	DC7	Northwest Airlines	Off Polillo Is	1	57	7.3.4
19600914	L-188	American Airlines	New York La Guardia, NY	0	76	7.2.3
19610711	DC-8	United Airlines	Denver, CO	17	105	7.4;9.1;9.2.1;9.3.1;9.3.5;12.3.2;12.7;20.5;21.1
19611108	L-049	Imperial Airlines	Richmond, VA	77	2	9.1;9.2.1
19611221	Comet	BEA	Ankara	27	7	13.5.2.4
19620923	L-1049	Flying Tiger Line	Atlantic Ocean	28	48	7.3.4
19621022	DC-7	Northeast Airlines	Off Biorka Is., AK	0	102	7.3.4
19651111	727	United Airlines	Salt Lake City, UT	43	54	8.3.6.1;9.1;9.3;9.3.3.1;9.3.5;10.4;10.7
19670305	DC-8	Varig	Monrovia	51	39	10.4
19671120	880	TWA	Cincinnati, OH	70	12	20.9

(*Continued*)

(Continued)

Date (yyyymmdd)	Type	Operator	Location	Fatal	Survivors	Reference
19700419	DC-8	SAS	Rome	0	65	11.2
19701127	DC-8	Capitol International	Anchorage, AK	47	182	11.2;21.1
19710607	580	Allegheny Airlines	New Haven, CT	30	3	20.9
19711113	DC-8	Air Canada	Over Canada	0	123	14.6.2
19721208	737-200	United Airlines	Chicago Midway, IL	43	18	8.3.6;21.1
19721229	L-1011	Eastern Airlines	Everglades, FL	101	75	11.2
19730401	L-1011	not reported	En route	0	235	6.6
19730711	707	Varig	Paris Orly	123	11	10.4;11.2;11.5.2.1;11.5.4;13.5.2.2
19731102	DC-10	National Airlines	Near Albuquerque, AZ	1	126	6.6
19740130	707	Pan American	Pago Pago	97	4	10.4;11.2;11.3;11.5.2.2;20.9;21.1
19741003	DC-10	not reported	Near Brownsville, TX	0	65	6.6
19750501	DC-10	not reported	en route	0	194	6.6
19750507	707	Pan American	Near St Johns	1	183	6.6
19750608	737-200	Frontier	Near Eagle, CO	0	7	6.6
19750807	727	Continental Air Lines	Denver, CO	0	134	8.3.6
19751112	DC-10	Overseas National	New York JFK, NY	0	139	15.3; 17.3.6
19760102	DC-10	Overseas National	Istanbul	0	376	17.3.6
19760623	DC-9	Allegheny Airlines	Philadelphia, PA	0	106	17.3.2
19770327	747	Pan American	Tenerife	335	77	11.2;13.3
19771103	747	El Al	Near Belgrade	1	Unknown	6.6
19780301	DC-10	Continental	Los Angeles, CA	4	196	5.5.3.3;13.4.1
19800819	L-1011	Saudia	Riyadh	301	0	10.4;19.4.2
19820113	737-200	Air Florida	Washington airport, VA	74	5	13.2;13.3;17.3.5
19820123	DC-10	World Airways	Boston, MA	2	210	13.2
19820209	DC-8	Japan Airlines	Tokyo Haneda	24	150	13.2
19820913	DC-10	Spantax	Malaga	51	342	10.4
19821111	707	Arrow Air	Near Miami, FL	1	2	6.6
19830602	DC-9	Air Canada	Cincinnati, OH	23	23	10.4;13.2;13.3;13.5.2.2;13.5.2.4;13.5.3;13.5.3.1;19.1
19840322	737-200	Pacific Western	Calgary	0	119	13.2
19840830	737-200	Cameroon Airlines	Douala	2	114	13.2

Appendices

19850511	737–200	Saudi Arabian	Doha	0	104	13.2
19850812	747	Japan Airlines	Near Ueno village	520	4	11.2
19850822	737–200	British Airtours	Manchester	55	83	8.3.6.3;10.3;10.4;10.9;10.10;13.1;13.2;13.3;13.5.2.5;13.5.3; 13.5.3.2;14.3.2.1;14.3.2.3;14.3.2.4; 14.3.2.10;18.5.4;21.1
19871115	DC-9	Continental	Denver, CO	28	54	14.2.1
19880428	737–200	Aloha Airlines	Near Maui, HI	1	94	6.6
19880626	A320	Air France	Habsheim	3	133	17.3.3
19880831	727–200	Delta Airlines	Dallas Ft Worth, TX	13	95	17.3.3;17.3.4
19890209	DC-9	Evergreen International	En route	1	1	6.6
19890108	737–400	British Midland	Kegworth	47	78	10.3;13.3;15.5;17.3.2
19890309	737–200	USAir	Near Dayton, OH	1	76	6.6
19890224	747	United Airlines	Near Hawaii	9	346	6.7.2
19890719	DC-10	United Airlines	Sioux City, IA	111	185	13.3;13.5.1.3
19900125	707	Avianca	Near New York JFK, NY	73	85	13.5.1.3
19900214	A320	Indian Airlines	Bangalore	92	54	10.4
19910201	737–300	USAir	Los Angeles, CA	21	68	6.6;13.5.3;14.3.2.4
19920730	L-1011	TWA	New York JFK, NY	0	292	14.7.2.1;15.3
19930426	737–200	Indian Airlines	Aurangabad	55	63	10.4
19930914	A320	Lufthansa	Warsaw	2	68	10.4
19931104	747	China Airlines	Hong Kong	0	296	19.4.2
19940810	A300	Korean Air	Jeju	0	160	10.4
19950821	EMB-120	Atlantic Southeast Airlines	Carrollton, GA	8	21	14.6.2
19960511	DC-9	Valujet	The Everglades, FL	110	0	6.6;21.4
19960613	DC-10	Garuda	Fukuoka	3	272	10.4
19961123	767	Ethiopian Airlines	Off Grande Comore	125	50	14.6.2;20.9
19990824	MD-90	Uni Air	Hualien	0	96	10.4
19990831	737–200	LAPA	Buenos Aires	63	27	10.4
20020415	767	Air China	Busan	129	37	10.4
20020207	777	United Airlines	En route	0	154	14.6.2
20040929	Dornier 228	Kato Air	Bodø	0	8	14.6.2
20050802	A340	Air France	Toronto	0	309	10.4;10.7;13.5.2.4;14.7.2.1;15.5;17.3.2;17.3.3;17.3.6;19.4.2

(Continued)

(Continued)

Date (yyyymmdd)	Type	Operator	Location	Fatal	Survivors	Reference
20050814	737–300	Helios Airways	Near Grammatiko	121	0	6.6
20070916	MD-80	One Two Go Airlines	Phuket	90	40	10.4
20060709	A310	Sibir Airlines	Irkutsk	125	78	10.4
20080117	777	British Airways	London Heathrow	0	152	10.7
20080610	A310	Sudan Airways	Khartoum	30	184	10.4
20090225	737–800	Turkish Airlines	Amsterdam	9	126	17.3.2
20100824	ERJ-190	Henan Airlines	Yichun	44	52	10.4;17.3.3
20121225	Fokker 100	Air Bagan	Heho	1	70	10.4
20130706	777	Asiana Airlines	San Francisco, CA	3	304	17.3.2;17.3.3;19.4.2
20150908	777	British Airways	Las Vegas, NV	0	170	15.3
20161028	767	American Airlines	Chicago O'Hare, IL	0	170	15.3
20160803	777	Emirates	Dubai	0	290	10.4;17.3.3
20180731	190	Aeromexico Connect	Mexico City	0	103	10.4;17.3.3
20190509	Sukhoi 100–95	Aeroflot	Moscow Sheremetyevo	41	37	19.4.1
20240102	A350	Japan Airlines	Tokyo	0	379	17.3.3;19.4.1;19.4.2

APPENDIX 2A—U.S. REGULATIONS 1926–1936 (PRE-FEDERAL REGISTER)

Regulations 1926–1936 (Pre-Federal Register)

Name	Effectivity Date	Subject	location
Air Commerce Regulations	Midnight, December 31, 1926	Air Commerce Regulations	https://babel.hathitrust.org/cgi/pt?id=mdp.39015019911851&seq=381, p. 359
Information Bulletin No. 7	June 1, 1928	Air Commerce Regulations	https://archive.org/details/AirCommerceRegulations/page/n7/mode/2up
Aeronautics Bulletin No. 7	September 1, 1929	Air Commerce Regulations	Mentioned in Air Commerce Bulletin, November 15, 1929, but not available online
Aeronautics Bulletin No. 7-A	September 1, 1929	Airworthiness Requirements of Air Commerce Regulations	Mentioned in Air Commerce Bulletin, November 15, 1929, but not available online
Aeronautics Bulletin No. 7-E	Midnight, May 15, 1930	Air Commerce Regulations Governing Scheduled Operation of Interstate Passenger Air Transport Services	https://books.google.nl/books?id=o1D8Xsx-n2UC&printsec=frontcover&hl=nl&source=gbs_ge_summary_r&cad=0#v=onepage&q&f=false
7-E interpretation	July 15, 1930	Interpretation of Regulations Governing Scheduled Operation of Interstate Passenger Air Transport Services	https://books.google.nl/books?id=o1D8Xsx-n2UC&printsec=frontcover&hl=nl&source=gbs_ge_summary_r&cad=0#v=onepage&q&f=false
Aeronautics Bulletin No. 7-A	January 1, 1931	Airworthiness Requirements of Air Commerce Regulations for Aircraft	https://books.google.nl/books?id=o1D8Xsx-n2UC&printsec=frontcover&hl=nl&source=gbs_ge_summary_r&cad=0#v=onepage&q&f=false
Aeronautics Bulletin No. 7-E	October 1, 1931	Air Commerce regulations governing scheduled operation of interstate passenger air transport services effective as amended October 1, 1931	In Air Commerce Bulletin, September 15, 1931
7-E interpretations	October 1, 1931	Interpretations of regulations governing scheduled operation of interstate passenger air transport services effective as amended October 1, 1931	In Air Commerce Bulletin, September 15, 1931
Aeronautics Bulletin No. 7-F	March 1, 1933	Airworthiness Requirements for Aircraft Components and Accessories	https://babel.hathitrust.org/cgi/pt?id=uc1.b2860853&seq=19
Aeronautics Bulletin No. 7-A	October 1, 1934	Airworthiness Requirements for Aircraft	https://babel.hathitrust.org/cgi/pt?id=uc1.c2551299&seq=5
Aeronautics Bulletin No. 7-E	October 1, 1934	Air Commerce Regulations Governing Scheduled Operation of Interstate Passenger Air Transport Services	https://babel.hathitrust.org/cgi/pt?id=uc1.c2551299&seq=12
Aeronautics Bulletin No. 7-E, amdt 2	January 2, 1936	Cabin attendants for operations between 15,000 and 18,000 ft.; operations above 18,000 ft.	Published in Air Commerce Bulletin, January 15, 1936

APPENDIX 2B—U.S. REGULATIONS 1937–1964

Regulations 1937–1964

Amdt #	CAR	FR Page	FR Date	Effectivity Date	Subject	DR, NPRM	DR Date	Comments
	CAR 04	2 FR 1899	24-Sep-37	1-Nov-37	Airplane Airworthiness			Redesignated in 1946 into CAR 04a (11 FR 14134) and in 1948 into CAR 4a (13 FR 5486)
	CAR 15	2 FR 1931	24-Sep-37	1-Nov-37	Aircraft Equipment Airworthiness			Replaced from 1947 by the TSO system; CAR 15 rescinded in 1952
	CAR 40	2 FR 2032	30-Sep-37	1-Nov-37	Scheduled Airline Certification (Interstate)			
	CAR 61	2 FR 2044	30-Sep-37	1-Nov-37	Scheduled Airline Rules (Interstate)			
Amdt 41-0	CAR 41	10 FR 8528	10-Jul-45	1-Sep-45	Certification and Operation Rules for Scheduled Air Carrier Operations Outside the Continental Limits of the United States			
Amdt 04-0	CAR 04	11 FR 71	3-Jan-46	9-Nov-45	Airplane Airworthiness; Transport Categories			Redesignated in 1946 into CAR 04b (11 FR 14134) and in 1948 into CAR 4b (13 FR 5486)
Amdt 03-0	CAR 03	11 FR 409	9-Jan-46	13-Nov-45	Airplane Airworthiness; Normal, Utility, Acrobatic, and Restricted Purpose Categories			Redesignated in 1948 into CAR 3 (13 FR 5486)
	CAR 06			1-Aug-46	Rotorcraft Airworthiness			Adopted May 3, 1946, retitled in 1956 into Rotorcraft Airworthiness; Normal Category
Amdt 42-0	CAR 42	11 FR 5213	14-May-46	1-Aug-46	Nonscheduled Air Carrier Certification and Operation Rules			
	CAR 42	14 FR 1427	31-Mar-49	1-Jun-49	Irregular Air Carrier and Off-Route Rules			Complete revision of CAR 42
	CAR 40	18 FR 2267	21-Apr-53	1-Apr-54	Scheduled Interstate Air Carrier Certification and Operation Rules	52–33	6-Dec-52	Merge of 40 and 61, effectivity date postponed several times (18 FR 8867)
	CAR 07	21 FR 3743	2-Jun-56	1-Aug-56	Rotorcraft Airworthiness; Transport Categories	55–11	7-May-55	
Amdt 46-0	CAR 46	23 FR 2264	8-Apr-58	1-Oct-58	Scheduled Air Carrier Helicopter Certification and Operation Rules	56–2	28-Jan-56	
Amdt 41-0	CAR 41	27 FR 1977	1-Mar-62	1-Mar-63	Certification and Operation Rules for Certificated Route Air Carriers Engaging in Overseas and Foreign Air Transportation and Air Transportation within Hawaii and Alaska	60–19	1-Dec-60	Complete revision of CAR 41

Appendices

Amdt 91–0	FAR 91	28 FR 6704	29-Jun-63	30-Sep-63	General Operating and Flight Rules	63–3	1-Feb-63	
Amdt 42–0	CAR 42	28 FR 7124	12-Jul-63	11-Nov-63	Aircraft Certification and Operation Rules for Supplemental Air Carriers, Large Commercial Operators, and Certificated Route Air Carriers Engaging in Charter Flights or Other Special Services	62–39	22-Aug-62	Complete revision of CAR 42
Amdt 135–0	FAR 135	29 FR 2988	5-Mar-64	7-Sep-64	Air Taxi Operators and Commercial Operators of Small Aircraft	62–48	8-Nov-62	
Amdt 27–0	FAR 27	29 FR 15694	24-Nov-64	1-Feb-65	Airworthiness Standards; Normal Category Rotorcraft	64–29	23-May-64	
Amdt 29–0	FAR 29	29 FR 16149	3-Dec-64	1-Feb-65	Airworthiness Standards; Transport Category Rotorcraft	64–30	28-May-64	
Amdt 23–0	FAR 23	29 FR 17955	18-Dec-64	1-Feb-65	Airworthiness Standards; Normal, Utility, and Acrobatic Category Airplanes	64–17	14-Apr-64	
Amdt 25–0	FAR 25	29 FR 18289	24-Dec-64	1-Feb-65	Airworthiness Standards; Transport Category Airplanes	64–28	2-Jun-64	
Amdt 121–0	FAR 121	29 FR 19186	31-Dec-64	1-Apr-65	Domestic, Flag, and Supplemental Air Carriers and Commercial Operators of Large Aircraft; Certification and Operation	64–40	26-Aug-64	

APPENDIX 2C—U.S. FINAL RULES AND PRECEDING PROPOSALS SINCE 1941

Final Rules and Preceding Proposals Since 1941

Amdt	FR Page	FR Date	Effectivity/ Compliance Date	Airwo.	Operation	IP	FP	EP	LS	II	FA	Subject	DR,NPRM #	Date of DR,NPRM
94	6 FR 784	6-Feb-41	1-May-41		61				√			Oxygen	Unknown	
120	6 FR 3099	26-Jun-41	1-Jul-41		61				√		√	Oxygen, cabin attendant	Unknown	
122	6 FR 3826	1-Aug-41	1-Oct-41		61				√			First-aid	Unknown	
129	6 FR 4691	13-Sep-41	1-Oct-41	04	61						√	Seat belt sign	Unknown	
130	6 FR 4753	17-Sep-41	Immediate		61						√	Seat belt sign	Unknown	
61-13	8 FR 14602	28-Oct-43	1-Feb-44		61			√				Exit marking	43	08-Nov-43 (not in FR)
04-1,04-4,41-3, 42-2,61-2	11 FR 11351	4-Oct-46	1-Nov-46	04	41,42,61		√					Fire prevention	Unknown	
04b-5	12 FR 3933	18-Jun-47	10-Jun-47	04		√						Crash loads	Unknown	
4b-13, 41-5, 42-2, 61-6	14 FR 5307	26 Aug 1949	21-Oct-49,1-Mar-50	4b	41, 42, 61			√				Oxygen, flight crew PBE	(46-1,47-8) (14 FR 1333)	
CAR 42, supplement 3	14 FR 7031	22 Nov 1949	Immediate		42			√	√	√	√	Seat belts, fire extinguisher, exits, evacuation equipment, survival equipment, first-aid kits	None	
4b-2,15-3,41-1, 42-3,61-1	15 FR 29	6 Jan 1950	6-Feb-50	4b	41, 42, 61	√						Seat belts	(46-8;47-9)	26-Nov-46, 21-May-47
4b-4	16 FR 11759	21-Nov-51	20-Dec-51	4b				√				Evacuation provisions	(51-8)	4-Oct-51
4b-6	17 FR 1087	5-Feb-52	5-Mar-52	4b			√	√				Crash loads, fire extinguisher	Unknown	
Supp. 14,11,20	17 FR 2748	29-Mar-52	upon publication		41,42,61						√	First-aid kits	None	
40-18	20 FR 6515	3-Sep-55	1-Jan-56		40						√	Crash axe	50-8,51-6, 54-25,55-8	Multiple, 23/03/1955
40-20,41-6,42-6; 40-4	20 FR 8848	2-Dec-55	31-May-56, 31-Aug-57		40,41,42				√			Exit lighting, flotation equipment	52-26,53-15,55-5	29-Aug-52, 11-Aug-53, 17-Feb-55
4b-5 (1957)	22 FR 1546	9-Mar-57	9-Apr-57	4b				√				Evacuation provisions	56-25	6-Oct-56
Supp. 43 to CAM 42	22 FR 3841	1-Jun-57	15-Jun-57		42						√	First-aid kits	None	
4b-6 (1957)	22 FR 5562	16-Jul-57	12-Aug-57	4b					√		√	Life line, cabin pressure altitude maximum	56-28	27-Nov-56

4b-8,40-11,41-17,42-14	23 FR 2590	19-Apr-58	17-May-58	4b	40,41,42	√	Flight attendant seat location	(22 FR 9116)	15-Nov-57
Supp. 37 to CAR 4b	23 FR 2789	26-Apr-58	5-May-58	4b		√	Credit for inflatable slides, aisle width	None	
4b-9,40-12,41-18,42-15	23 FR 6743	30-Aug-58	1-Sep-58	4b	40,41,42	√	Supplemental oxygen	58-7	4-Apr-58
4b-11	24 FR 7067	1-Sep-59	1-Oct-59	4b		√	Exit table, flotation means	(24 FR 128)	7-Jan-59
40-21,41-28,42-23	24 FR 9765	5-Dec-59	1-Jan-61		40,41,42	√	Training program approval	59-3	27-Jun-59
40-36,41-44,42-39	27 FR 1453	16-Feb-62	20-Mar-62		40,41,42	√	Exit lighting	61-20	30-Sep-61
4b-12	27 FR 2986	30-Mar-62	3-May-62	4b		√	Aisle width	61-12	8-Jun-61
40-43	29 FR 5627	28-Apr-64	26-Oct-64		40	√	Seat belt wearing, sign adherence	63-20	14-Jun-63
40-44,41-9, 42-8	29 FR 5941	6-May-64	2-Nov-64		40,41,42	√	Light in life vest and life raft	63-32	5-Aug-63
25-1,121-2	30 FR 3200	9-Mar-65	7-Jun-65	25	91,121	√	Evacuation provisions and procedures, briefing, flight attendants	63-42	29-Oct-63
121-7	30 FR 6725	18-May-65	16-Aug-65		121	√	Flight attendant training	62-9	10-Mar-62
121-17	31 FR 1146	28-Jan-66	1-Sep-66		121	√	Flotation equipment	65-12	19-Jun-65
25-9,121-20	31 FR 8911	28-Jun-66	30-Jun-66	25	121	√	Exit signs, marking, lighting, megaphones	66-13	7-Apr-66
25-15,121-30	32 FR 13255	20-Sep-67	24-Oct-67, 1-Oct-69	25	121	√ √ √	Head injury protection, underseat stowage, fire testing, isolation of fuel lines, exit table, type A exit, tail exits, overwing escape route slip resistance, evacuation demonstration, emergency lighting, flight attendant uniform distribution	66-26	29-Jul-66
25-20,121-46	34 FR 5543	22-Mar-69	23-Apr-69	25	121	√	Head injury protection, evacuation demonstration, flight attendant numbers	68-28	31-Oct-68
121-54,135-12	34 FR 19130	3-Dec-69	1-Apr-70		121,135	√	Flight attendant briefing methods	69-4	30-Jan-69
121-55	35 FR 84	2-Jan-70	2-Feb-70		121	√	Flight attendant training	69-14	4-Apr-69
135-18	35 FR 10098	19-Jun-70	19-Jul-70		135	√	Evacuation demonstration, evacuation provisions, markings, signs	68-37	7-Jan-69
25-32,121-84	37 FR 3964	24-Feb-72	1-May-72	25	121	√	Storage compartments, underseat storage, fire testing, passenger compliance with instructions, exit opening times, wing escape route width, emergency lighting	69-33	12-Aug-69

(*Continued*)

(Continued)

Final Rules and Preceding Proposals Since 1941

Amdt	FR Page	FR Date	Effectivity/ Compliance Date	Airwo.	Operation	IP	FP	EP	LS	II	FA	Subject	DR,NPRM #	Date of DR,NPRM
121-88	37 FR 5605	17-Mar-72	15-Jun-72		121						√	Flight attendant number	70-35	11-Sep-70
25-34,121-99	37 FR 25354	30-Nov-72	31-Dec-72	25	121			√				Rear exit security	72-15	24-Jun-72
	38 FR 12207	10-May-73	10-Jul-73		252							Smoking restrictions		
121-105	38 FR 21493	9-Aug-73	8-Sep-73		121						√	Public address and interphone systems	72-6	2-Mar-72
121-113	39 FR 42675	6-Dec-74	9-Dec-74		121,135				√			Oxygen for medical use	73-19	18-Jun-73
25-38	41 FR 55454	20-Dec-76	1-Feb-77	25			√					PBE in isolated compartments	75-10	
25-39	42 FR 2052	10-Jan-77	10-Feb-77	25				√				Type A exits	A74-19,75-40	10-May-74, 23-Dec-75
121-133,135-44	42 FR 18392	7-Apr-77	16-May-77		121,135						√	Passengers who may need evacuation assistance	74-25	5-Jul-74
121-143	43 FR 22643	25-May-78	26-Jun-78		121	√					√	Flight attendant training, briefing, retention of items of mass	77-12	21-Jul-77
25-44,91-154,121-148	43 FR 46230	5-Oct-78	29-Sep-78, 04-Dec-78	25	91,121	√					√	Seat belts, flight attendant training, briefing	77-20	1-Sep-77
25-46,121-149	43 FR 50578	30-Oct-78	1-Dec-78	25	121				√	√	√	Evacuation demonstration, exits, markings, lighting, raft capacity, passenger address, and interphone systems	75-26	10-Jun-75
25-51,121-155, etc.	45 FR 7750	4-Feb-80	6-Mar-80	25	121		√	√			√	Flight attendant seats, storage compartments, floor surfaces, signs, ashtrays	75-10,75-31	07-Mar-75, 11-Jul-75
25-53,121-159	45 FR 41586	19-Jun-80	31-Aug-80	25	121		√				√	Flight attendant seating, lower-deck service compartments, signs, passenger address system	78-7,78-7A,75-31	Multiple, 11-May-78
25-54	45 FR 60154	11-Sep-80	14-Oct-80	25				√				Hand fire extinguishers	75-31	11-Jul-75
121-176	46 FR 61450	17-Dec-81	18-Jan-82		121			√			√	Evacuation demonstration	81-1 (11–3)	19-Jan-81
25-58,121-183	49 FR 43182	26-Oct-84	26-Nov-84	25	121			√				Floor lighting	83-15	11-Oct-83
25-59,121-184	49 FR 43188	26-Oct-84	26-Nov-84	25	121		√					Seat cushion flammability	83-14	11-Oct-83
121-185	50 FR 12726	29-Mar-85	29-Apr-85, 16-Jun-86		121		√					Fire extinguishers	84-5	17-May-84

121–188	51 FR 1218	9-Jan-86		121		Emergency medical equipment	85–9	14-Mar-85
25–61,121–189	51 FR 26206	21-Jul-86	20-Aug-86	25	121	√	Improved flammability standards	85–10	16-Apr-85
121–193	52 FR 20950	3-Jun-87	6-Jul-87		121	√	Protective breathing equipment	85–17	10-Oct-85
121–194	52 FR 21472	5-Jun-87	6-Jul-87		121		Carry-on baggage program	86–6	27-May-86
25–64	53 FR 17640	17-May-88	16-Jun-88	25		√	Improved seat safety standards	86–11	17-Jul-86
25–66,121–198	53 FR 32564	25-Aug-88	26-Sep-88	25	121	√	Improved flammability standards	85–10,85–10A	16-Apr-85, 11-Jun-85
121–204	54 FR 22270	22-May-89	31-Jan-90		121	√	Protective breathing equipment		
25–67,121–205	54 FR 26688	23-Jun-89	24-Jul-89	25	121	√	Location of exits (60 ft rule)	87–10	20-Oct-87
25–70,121–209,135–34	54 FR 43922	27-Oct-89	27-Nov-89	25	121,135	√	Passenger address system independent source	86–5	27-May-86
121–214,135–36	55 FR 8054	6-Mar-90	5-Apr-90		121,135	√	Exit row seating	89–8	13-Mar-89
25–72	55 FR 29756	20-Jul-90	20-Aug-90	25		√	Exit uniform distribution, over-sized exits, alternate exits	84–21	3-Dec-84
121–220	55 FR 51078	11-Dec-90	11-Dec-90		121	√	Protective breathing equipment		
25–74	56 FR 15450	16-Apr-91	16-May-91	25		√	Fire extinguishers	89–1	12-Jan-89
25–76,121–228,135–43	57 FR 19220	4-May-92	3-Jun-92	25	121,135	√	Improved access to Type III exits	91–11	9-Apr-91
121–230,135–44	57 FR 42662	15-Sep-92	15-Oct-92		121	√	Child restraint systems, fire extinguishers, evacuation capability, passenger briefing	90–6	1-Mar-90
25–79,121–233	58 FR 45224	26-Aug-93	27-Sep-93	25	121	√	Evacuation demonstration, exit lighting, passenger address system	89–23	8-Sep-89
121–236,135–47	59 FR 1780	12-Jan-94	12-Jan-94		121,135	√	First-aid kits	ATA petition	
121–241,135–52	59 FR 42974	19-Aug-94	1-Mar-96		121,135		Flight attendant duty and rest	93–3	31-Mar-93
121–250,135–57	60 FR 65940	20-Dec-95	19-Mar-99		121,135		Flight attendant CRM training		
121–251,135–58	60 FR 65832	20-Dec-95	19-Jan-96		121,135	√	Commuter operations major revision, lavatory for protection	95–5	29-Mar-95
121–255,135–62	61 FR 28416	4-Jun-96	3-Sep-96		121,135	√	Child restraint systems	95–7	9-Jun-95
25–87	61 FR 28684	5-Jun-96	5-Jul-96	25			High-altitude operations	89–31	22-Nov-89
25–88	61 FR 57946	8-Nov-96	9-Dec-96	25		√	Number and location of exits	90–4	22-Feb-90
25–91	62 FR 40702	29-Jul-97	28-Aug-97	25		√	Crash loads	95–14	29-Aug-95
None	64 FR 1076	7-Jan-99	7-Jan-99		121,135		Crewmember interference, portable electronic devices	None	

(*Continued*)

(Continued)

Final Rules and Preceding Proposals Since 1941

Amdt	FR Page	FR Date	Effectivity/Compliance Date	Airwo.	Operation	IP	FP	EP	LS	II	FA	Subject	DR,NPRM #	Date of DR,NPRM
121–281,135–78	66 FR 19028	12-Apr-01	12-Apr-04		121,135					√		Emergency medical equipment (AED, EMK)	00–03	24-May-00
None	69 FR 39292	29-Jun-04	12-Jun-05		121,135						√	Country of assembly information	None	
25–116,121–306	69 FR 62778	27-Oct-04	28-Nov-05, 28-Nov-07	25	121			√		√		Flight attendant assist space, assist handle, outside viewing means, interior doors, portable oxygen equipment	96–9	24-Jul-96
25–117,121–307	69 FR 67492	17-Nov-04	17-Dec-04	25	121			√				Evacuation demonstration	95–9	18-Jul-95
121–314,135–100	70 FR 50902	26-Aug-05	26-Sep-05		121,135	√						Child restraint systems	none	
121–315	70 FR 56542	27-Sep-05	27-Oct-09		121	√						Improved seat safety standards	88–8,S02–17	17-May-88
121–326	71 FR 40003	14-Jul-06	14-Aug-06		121,135	√						Child restraint systems	121–314,135–100	26-Aug-05
121–334	72 FR 45629	15-Aug-07	15-Oct-07		121							Flightdeck door monitoring	05–07	21-Sep-05
121–366	78 FR 67800	12-Nov-13	12-Nov-14		121						√	Identification of flight attendants, approval of training devices	08–07	12-Jan-09
25–138	79 FR 13515	11-Mar-14	12-May-14	25					√			Security of lavatory oxygen provision	13–01	9-Jan-13
121–373	80 FR 58575	30-Sep-15	30-Oct-15		121	√						Child restraint seats: disclosure of seat dimensions	14–03	1-Apr-14
121–374,135–133	81 FR 33098	24-May-16	23-Jun-16, 22-Aug-16		121,135				√			Portable oxygen concentrators	14–08	19-Sep-14
121–386	87 FR 61452	12-Oct-22	10-Jan-23		121						√	Flight attendant duty and rest	A19–10,22–01	25-Sep-19, 2-Nov-21
25–148,25–151	88 FR 39152	15-Jun-23	11-Jul-23	25						√		High-altitude operations	19–3	5-Apr-19
25–150,121–389	88 FR 41295	26-Jun-23	25-Aug-23	25	121							Installed physical secondary barrier	22–5	01-Aug-22
25–153,121–393	89 FR 68094	23-Aug-24	22-Oct-24	25	121,135		√					Flammability testing performance standards	19–09	3-Jul-19
				25	121,135		√					Flammability testing performance standards	S23–12	17-Aug-23

Domains: 'IP: Impact Protection, FP: Fire Protection, EP: Escape Potential, LS: Life Support, II: Information and Instructions, FA: Flight Attendants'

APPENDIX 2D—WITHDRAWN U.S. PROPOSALS

Withdrawn proposals

DR,(A)NPRM	Issued	Withdrawn	Subject
51-6	1-Sep-51	30-Jul-52	Emergency lighting
51-6	1-Sep-51	30-Jul-52	Passenger briefing
55-8	23-Mar-55	3-Sep-55	Second axe and chop marks
56-26	17-Oct-56	14-Dec-62	Flotation equipment
69-2	11-Jan-69	18-Aug-70	Smoke hoods
A69-30	30-Jul-69	superseded 12Feb75	Compartment interior materials (smoke emission)
A70-14	25-Mar-70	17-Jul-73	Smoking on board aircraft
A74-38	30-Dec-74	24-Aug-78	Toxic gas emission
75-3	12-Feb-75	24-Aug-78	Smoke emission
A75-13	13-Mar-75	22-Jun-81	Crewmember clothing: flammability standards
75-26 proposal 7-25	10-Jun-75	30-Oct-78	Crash loads: addition of 1.5 g rearward
75-26 proposal 7-25	10-Jun-75	30-Oct-78	Lower-deck crashworthiness provisions
75-26 proposal 7-39,7-79	10-Jun-75	30-Oct-78	Evacuation alarm system
75-26 proposal 7-41	10-Jun-75	30-Oct-78	Multi-deck exit requirements
75-26 proposal 7-44	10-Jun-75	30-Oct-78	High-intensity lights at each flight attendant station
75-26 proposal 7-45	10-Jun-75	30-Oct-78	Passageways between decks
75-31 proposal 8-38	11-Jul-75	11-Sep-80	Lavatory-occupied sign
75-31 proposal 8-54/8-120	11-Jul-75	11-Sep-80	PBE at each flight attendant seat
75-31 proposal 8-59	11-Jul-75	11-Sep-80	Placard on flight attendant seat: flight attendant only
75-31 proposal 8-118	11-Jul-75	24-Aug-78	Compartment interior materials: retrofit application of 60 s vertical burn test
81-1 proposal 11-6	19-Jan-81	2-Aug-82	Third megaphone
81-1 proposal 11-7	19-Jan-81	2-Aug-82	Independent power source for PA system
81-1 proposal 11-14	19-Jan-81	17-Dec-81	Reduction of flight attendant number with passenger seats blocked
88-11	30-Jun-88	Unknown	Improved Survival Equipment for Inadvertent Water Landings
89-9	14-Apr-89	6-Jun-96	Flight attendant requirements: reduced minimum number during stops
95-1	30-Jan-95	3-May-02	Revised access to Type III exits (20 to 13 inch)
A98-2	18-Feb-98	26-Aug-05	Child restraint systems

APPENDIX 3—EXIT TYPES AND DIMENSIONS

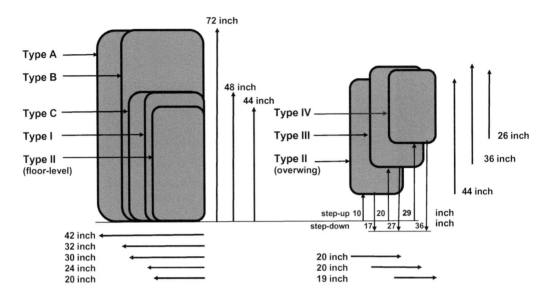

As applicable:

   From 1951 for exit Types I, II (floor-level), and IV
   From 1951 for exit Type III, except for step-up and step-down heights
   From 1957 for exit Types II (overwing) and Type III
   From 1967 for exit Type A
   From 1996 for exit Types B and C

Index

Acts, conferences, conventions, hearings, legislation

A

Aeronautics Bulletin, 15–17, 19, 26, 27, 71, 106
Agency Task Force, 131
Air Carrier Access Act of 1986, 212
Air Commerce Act, 25–27
Air Commerce Regulations, 25, 26, 27
Air Navigation Act (UK), 286
Air Navigation Order (UK), 225
Airworthiness Directive, xvii, 77, 114, 157, 192
Aviation and Transportation Security Act, 226
Aviation Medical Assistance Act, 251

C

CAA-CAB Working Group Subcommittee Emergency Evacuation, 39, 41, 55
Chicago Convention, 31, 33, 43, 46, 48, 50, 52–53, 55, 105, 162, 240, 300
Civil Air Regulations (CAR), 14–15, 17, 20, 26–27, 29, 47, 69, 106
    Chapter or Part 03 or 3, 27–28, 47
    Chapter or Part 04, 17–18, 20, 28, 34, 44, 46, 50–52, 60, 164
    Part 04a or 4a, 27–28
    Part 04b or 4b, 27–30, 45, 47, 49, 82, 91–92, 111, 255
    Chapter 15, 17, 26
    Chapter or Part 40, 20, 26–28, 44, 51, 61, 72, 92–93, 106–**108**, 115, 119, 225
    Part 41, 27–28, 44, 60–61, 69–72, 81, 92–93, 107–110, 115–116, 119
    Part 42, 27–28, 46, 60–61, 69, 71–72, 81, 92–93, 107–108, 115, 119, 292
    Part 46, 109
    Chapter or Part 61, 26–28, 60, 69, 71, 81, 106–107
Civil Rights Act, 99
congressional hearings, 38–39, 110, 145, 153–156, 183, 301

E

EASA Certification Specifications, 31
    CS-25, 31,217, 218, 220, 222, 240, 248
    CS-MMEL, 208
EASA Part Cabin Crew, 31, 101
Equal Opportunity Act, 99

F

FAA Reauthorization Act of 2003, 225
    of 2018, 71, 121, 176, 241
    of 2024, 239, 243, 281
Federal Aviation Act, 27, 29
Federal Aviation Regulations (FAR), 29, 76, 101, 157–158, 183, 193
FAR 23, 27, 188
FAR 25, 27, 29–30, 91–92, 112, 132, 134, 158–159, 172, 174–175, 187, 191, 194, 201, 207–208, 213, 218, 222, 241–242, 249, 251, 256–257, 266
FAR 91.607, 59
FAR 121, 27, 72, 108–109, 115–116, 172–174, 178, 188, 190, 192–193, 213, 218–219, 223, 230
FAR 127, 109
FAR 135, 27, 72, 109, 116, 218

I

ICAO
    Annex, 31, 34, 105, 121, 240
    Document, 31, 240
Information Bulletin, 25, 27

J

Joint Aviation Requirements (JAR) JAR-25, 30, 150, 207, 243, 266
JAR-26, 150, 215
JAR-OPS, 31, 215, 224, 228, 233, 234

P

Paris Convention, 29, 31

S

Seattle Conference, 181, 195–197, 200–202, 213, 270
Special Aviation Fire and Explosion Reduction (SAFER), 153, 155, 158, 184, 192, 195
Special Board of Inquiry on Air Safety, 80, 142
Special Conditions, 241, 265, 282

U

UK parliament select committee inquiry, 144, 146, 184

V

Very Large Transport Aeroplane Conference, 241, 302
Vision 100-Century of Aviation Reauthorization Act, 120

W

White House Commission on Aviation Safety and Security, 249

Cabin Safety Subjects
Generic

A

air contamination, 121–122, 159, 183, 238, 240, 247–248, 281

320   Index

C

cabin air quality, *see* air contamination
Cabin Safety Subject Index (CSSI), 240, 248

D

Derivative, xvii,112, 133, 139–140, 175, 216, 218, 256–258

E

equivalent (level of) safety finding, 222, 256–257

F

forward fit, xvii, 202, 238, 249, 302

G

grandfather right *or* grandfathering xvii, 208, 216, 220, 254, 257–258

I

infant, 17, 41, 46, 126, 142, 169, 171, 186, 189–191, 206, 238, 244, 249–250
installed physical secondary barrier, 228–*229*

R

retrofit, xvii, 77, 130, 132, 150, 158, 189, 194, 217, 238, 248–249

S

seat *or* seating, 1, 2, 5–6, 9–10, 12, 16–18, 33–35, 42, 44–47, 51, 56–59, 62, 69–70, 72–74, 79, 83, 86–91, 96, 100, 102, 107–110, 112–117, 126, 129, 131–136, 138, 140, 144, 147, 150, 155–156, 159, 162, 167–172, 174, 176, 181, 184, 186–192, 194–200, 203, 206–218, 220, 225, 228, 230–233, 242–244, 247–250, 254, 256–258, 261, 264–265, 280, 282–283, 292, 300
    seat dimensions, 242, 250

T

type certificate *or* type certificated *or* type certification, xvii, xviii, 22, 28, 44, 56, 77, 80, 92, 112, 114, 117, 134, 138–140, 155, 172, 188, 197, 208, 218, 234, 249–250, 254, 282

U

union, 8, 99, 113, 116, 120, 145, 153, 155, 176, 184, 197, 202, 208, 213, 215, 217, 222, 227, 234, 242, 255, 300–301

Impact protection

C

child restraint, 184, 189–191, 240, 244, 249
crash load, 46–48, 88, 132, 137, 181, 191, 206–207, 238, 300

D

dynamic test *or* dynamic testing, 43, 89, 131, 155–156, 187–189, 238, 248–249, 264–265, 301–302

G

g load (forward direction)
    6 g, 45–47, 264
    9 g, 45, 47, 62, 155, 181, 185, 187, 264
    16 g, 187–189, 238–239, 248–249, 264, 285, 302
    20 g, 47, 155, 249
    40 g, 47, 131

H

head injury *or* head injury criterion (HIC), 131, 188, 244

S

safety belt *or* seat belt, 1–3, 9–10, 12–13, 16–18, 22, 33, 35–37, 44–47, 61–62, 100, 110, 113–114, 129, 156, 160, 170, 188–189, 207, 209, 225, 243–244, 249, 264–265, 267, 291–292, 295, 297, 300
    supplemental loop belt, 206, 250
seat
    aft *or* rearward facing, 9, 45, 87, 142–144, 184, 245
    flight attendant *or* cabin attendant *or* jump, 111–114, 116, 130, 154, 156–157, 186, 192, 297
    side facing, 139
    track, 35
stowage compartment, overhead, 138, 186
    underseat, 138–139

T

turbulence, 7, 16, 110, 118, 160, 191, 238, 243–244, 261, 286

Fire protection

A

anti-misting kerosene (AMK), 155, 186
ash container *or* ashtray, 18, 48–49, 157, 192

E

escape slide radiant heat resistance, 184, 186

F

fire
    in-flight, 7, 42, 146, 149, 154, 183, 192–193, 271
    post-crash, 33, 42, 146, 153–155, 158, 186, 250, 301
fire extinguisher, 1–3, 9–10, 15, 18, 33, 37, 48–**50**, 118–119, *191*–193, 230, 283, 300
    with Halon, 191, 250
fire-proof, 49
fire resistant, 49, 192
flame resistant, 48, 49, 132
flammability, 6, 49, 62, 126, 132, 139–140, 147, 154–155, 158, 181, 183–184, 193–194, 239, 250, 265, 300–301
flash resistant, 49

Index

H

heat release, 184, 191, 193–195, 250, 264–266, 280, 285, 301

P

Portable Electronic Device (PED) fire risk, 284–285
protective breathing equipment (PBE), *see* smoke hood

S

seat cushion fire blocking layer, 158–159, 183–184, 186, 191–192, 194, 265–266
smoke emission, 153, 158, 193–194, 250
smoke hood, 129, 131, 141, 144–149, 154, 184, 192–*193*
smoking, 10–11, 17–18, 22, 37, 48–49, 60–61, 100, 106–107, 122, 129, 159–160, 183, 238, 292

T

toxic gases *or* toxicity, 43, 132–133, 145–147, 153–154, 156–159, 183, 191, 193–195, 209, 301

Escape potential

0–9

60-foot rule, 175, 181, 183, 197

A

Airworthiness Notice 79, 150, 209, *210*–211, 213
aisle width, 1, 58, 91, 127, 167, 184
axe, 5, 79–81, 130, 228, 300, 302

B

baggage, 1, 12, 42, 48, 83, 85, 100, 110, 118, 121, 132, 135, 139, 149, 172, 176, 189, 225, 238–239, 241, 243, 267, 281, 283–285

C

chop marks, 79–81
chute, *see* slide
crowd *or* crowded *or* crowding, 14, 34, 52, 55, 59, 130, 158, 179

D

descent assist means, 38, 50, 53–54, 57, 59, 62, 241, 256, 266, 280, *see also* ladder, rope, slide, stair
door, entrance, 2, 10, 20–21, 38, 56, 109–110, 118, 126–127, 134–135, 297
door, internal, 129, 251

E

emergency *or* escape slide, *see* slide
emergency lighting, 7, 15, 19, 21, 39, 58, 62, 79–82, 84, 121, 126, 128–129, 134–137, 139–140, 145, 173, 195, 282, 300
  floor lighting *or* floor proximity emergency escape path marking (FPEEPM), 183, 195, 266, 281
  luminous paint, 14, 20, 50, 52–53, 58, 80–82

evacuation demonstration *or* test, 6, 34, 39–40, 59, 109, 115, 117, 126, 128–129, 133–134, 137, 145, 155, 159, 162–179, 184, 196–197, 201–202, 208, 230–231, 233–234, 239–242, 254, 278–279, 281, 300
  injuries from, 162, 167, 174–176, 241
  simulated handicapped, or injured persons, 39, 169–170, 177, 212
exit *or* emergency exit
  access to, 58, 126, 135, 184, 197, 209–211, 213–215, 220, 258
  actual use *or* usage, 5, 14, 38–39, 55, 83, 126–127, 130, 157, 158, 164, 170, 184, 201, 209, 212–213, 267–268, 269–280, 297
  automatically disposed hatch (ADH), 217–218, **219**, 220
  ease of operation or opening, 18, 53, 62, 139, 209–210, 212–213, 215–216, 218, 296
  excess, 135, 140
  hatch, 10, 14, 19, 21, 35, 48, 53, 56, 58, 74, 112, 167, 178, 206, 209–218, 220, 233, 258, 296
  marking *or* sign (inside), 15, 20, 58, 79, 81–82, 126, 128, 134–135, 139–140, 196, 222, 241
  marking (outside), 53, 80–81, 129
  opening instructions *or* diagrams, 58, 80–81, 87, 129, 214, 220, 296
  table, 51, 56–57, 89–90, 133–134, 138, 140, 197–201, 254, 258, 301
  uniform distribution, 112, 134, 197, 201
exit types
  tail, 111–112, 130, 135, 137, 140, 143, 172, 199, **256**–257, 270, 272–280, 285, 302
  Type A, 112, 134, 139–140, 159, 170, 173, 175–176, 192, 196, 198–**201**, 202, 232–233, 258–259, 318
  Type A+, 258
  Type B, 200–**201**, 257, 259, 318
  Type C, 200–**201**, 216, 219, 318
  Type I, 41, **56**–58, 90, 116, 129, 133–135, 137–138, 170, 172, 192, 198, **199**–**201**, 202, 208, 216, 233, 254–259, 318
  Type II, **56**–58, 89–90, 133–134, 138, *199*–**201**, 318
  Type III, **56**–58, 89–90, 133–135, 138–139, 150, 170, 172, 178, 181, 183, 197, **199**–**201**, 202, 206, 208–220, 233, 240–241, 243, 255–259, 270, 296, 301, 318
  Type IV, **56**–59, 89–90, 133, 138, 172, **199**, **201**, 255, 269, 318

L

ladder or rope ladder or telescoping ladder, 38–40, 53
Latin Square, 145, 212, **255**, 258
luggage, *see* baggage

P

passageway 51–52, 58, 150, 209–210, 213–215, 217–218, **219**, 220, 258
Persons with Reduced Mobility, *see* special categories of passengers

R

rope, 38–40, 50, 53–54, 62, 256

S

slide *or* escape slide *or* evacuation slide *or* chute, 33, 39, 54–55, 59, 62, 79–80, 82, 91–92, 119–120, 134, 139–140, 162, 167, 169–177, 184, 186, 191–192, 197, 199–201, 207–208, 216, 230, 241, 250–251, 256–259, 266–268, 277, 279, 300
special categories of passengers (SCP), 177, 218, 240, 249
stair *or* stairs, 39, 50–51, 53–54, 130, 135, 172, 241, 256
step-down distance or height, 41, **56**–57, 89, 164, 170, 172, 214, 254–256, 318
step-up distance or height, 41, **56**–57, 89, 214, 255–256, 318
strobe lights *or* flashing lights, 135, 147–148, 211

Life support

A

Automatic External Defibrillator (AED), 120, 238, 251

D

dinghy, *see* life raft
ditching, 34–35, 37, 51, 58, 62, 79–80, 82–87, 92, 103–104, 109–110, 118, 129, 139, 171, 174, 222, 241, 288–293, 300

F

first-aid *or* first-aid equipment *or* first-aid kit *or* medical box, 2, 9–10, 15, 21, 29, 33, 37, 39, 59–60, 92, 103, 117–119, 202, 223, 230, 251, 281, 300
flashlight, 21, 87, 118
flotation cushion, 92, 131, 205, 222

L

life belt *or* life jacket *or* life preserver *or* life vest, 3–4, 9–11, 13, 15, 21, 37, 59, 83–84, 86–87, 91–92, 118, 222, 230, 244, 255, 266, 286, 289–292, 294–295, 298, 302
life raft, 11, 13, 21, 37, 60, 83–87, 92–93, 117–118, 171, 174, 230, 266, 290–292, 300, 302

M

medical box, *see* first-aid kit
medical kit, 120, 183, 202, 238, 251, 281

O

oxygen *or* oxygen masks (excluding PBE related), 5–7, 15, 21, 33, 42–43, 60–62, 65–77, 79, 100, 106–107, 109, 121, 129, 145–146, 157, 206, 224–225, 230, 238, 248, 264, 291, 294–295, 301–302

P

portable oxygen concentrator, 75

R

rescue, 5, 7, 11, 13, 83–84, 86–87, 92, 96, 130, 148, 157, 189–190, 222, 291, 297

S

survival equipment (other than for water survival), 60, 146
arctic *or* frigid areas *or* polar survival, 7, 60, 62, 118, 223
desert, 7, 118
tropical, 60, 62

Information and instructions

B

brace-for-impact position, 2, 87, 189, 238, 244–247, 295, 297–298
briefing card, *see* safety card

F

fasten seat belt instruction *or* sign, 1, 13, 23, 37, 46, 60–61, 93, 129, 160, 225, 243–244, 291, 295

M

megaphone, 129, 284

N

no smoking instruction *or* placard *or* sign, 18, 22, 37, 48, 60–61, 93, 106, 129, 157, 192, 225, 292

P

Public Address system (PA), 61, 129, 160, 238, 285

S

safety briefing, 7, 61, 83, 154, 203, 225, 244, 285, 295–296
safety card *or* safety leaflet *or* safety pamphlet, 9–10, 35–37, 46, 60–62, 67, 72, 83–84, 126, 130, 154, 168, 198, 212, 218, 222, 225–226, 244, 264, 282, 285, 287–298, 300

U

use oxygen sign, 60–**61**, 69

Cabin professional

C

cabin attendant *or* cabin crew *or* cabin personnel *or* cabin staff, *see* flight attendant

F

flight attendant, 6–7, 12, 14, 18, 20, 39, 48, 60–61, 67–74, 76, 83–87, 93, 95–122, 126–130, 134, 139, 145–147, 150, 154–158, 164, 167, 169, 170, 173, 174, 176–179, 183–184, 186, 192–193, 196–197, 206–208, 211–213, 215, 218, 222, 225, 227–228, 230–235, 238–244, 247–248, 251, 255, 257–258, 266–268, 271, 278, 280, 282, 284, 290–292, 294–298, 300, 302
attestation *or* certificate or licence, 105, 108, 120, 230, 234, 300, 302
duty and rest times, 95, 105, 121, 184, 234–235

Index

number of *or* ratio, 6, 95, 102, 107–110, 115–117, 129, 155, 174, 206, 230–234
training *or* drills, 95–96, 105, 108, 117–120, 129, 154–155, 167, 169, 171–172, 174, 178, 193, 230, 234, 240–241, 248, 251, 266–268, 280, 300

P

purser *or* steward *or* stewardess, *see* flight attendant

ORGANISATIONS

Airlines

A

Aer Lingus, 295
Air California, 173
Air Despatch, 96, 100
Air Florida, 181, 183
Air France, 83–84, 97–99, 101, *119*, 244–*245*, 292–*293*, 295
Air India, *293*
Air New Zealand, 295
Air Union, 95
Airwork, 35–*36*, 83
Alitalia, *293*
Allegiant Air, 242
Allegheny, 173
Aloha Airlines, 74, 76
American Airways *or* Airlines, 11, 13, 39–40, 42, 54, 82, 89, 96, 98–99, 103, 105, 117, 222, *259*, 300
American Export Airlines *or* American Overseas Airlines, 28, 107, 290
American Trans Air, 208
Ansett Airlines of Australia, 96
Avelo Air, 242

B

BOAC, *46*, 79, 99, 118, *246*, 291
Boeing Air Transport, 96
Braathens, 173, 233
Braniff, 13, 99, 145, 173
Breeze Airways, 242
British Airways, 196, *198*, 211, 240
British European Airways, *144*
British South American Airways, 101

C

Cebu Pacific, 99
Channel Airways, *136*
Chicago and Southern Air Lines, 14
Colonial Airlines, *293*
Comair, 188
Compagnie Aérienne Française, 95
Continental Airlines, 97–98, 118, 207

D

Daimler Airway, 95, 99
Dan Air, 144
DELAG, 95
Delta Airlines, 98, 169
DLT, *72*

E

Eastern Air Transport *or* Eastern Airlines, 11, 13, 38, 96–97, 100, 197
Emirates, 102
Ethiopian Airlines, 298

F

Finnair, 296
Flying Tiger Line, 87, 92
Frontier Airlines, 242

G

Germania, 216
Great Lakes, 103

H

Hapag-Lloyd, 216
Hawaiian, 173
Hughes Air West, 155

I

Imperial Airlines, 127–128
Imperial Airways, 9–*10*, 13, 95, 287

J

Japan Airlines (JAL), 99, 154

K

KLM (Royal Dutch Airlines), 48, 67, 84–*85*, 88, 96, 98–99, 101, 103–104, 118, 121, 164, 287–*288*, 295
Korean Airlines, 295

L

Lufthansa, 95–96, 175, *246*

M

Martinair, 228
Mexicana, 95

N

National Airlines, *88*, 207
North Central, 173
Northwest Airlines *or* Northwest Orient Airlines, 28, 68–69, 84, 86–87, 97, *246*, 290

O

Overseas National Airways (ONA), 160, *267*

P

Pacific Northern Airlines, *293*
Pacific Southwest Airlines (PSA), 173
Panagra, 67
Pan Am *or* Pan American Airways *or* Pan American
 World Airways, 11–12, 21, 28, 35, 39–*40*,
 60, 67, 69, 83–84, 86, 88, 96–101, 103,
 107, 116–118, 168–170, 173, 189–190, 197,
 290–292, 297, *298*
Philippine Airlines, *293*

Q

Qantas, *293*

R

Republic, 173

S

Sabena, 99
SAS, 35, 85, 173, *222–223*
Scoot, 99
Spirit Airlines, 242
Sterling, 173, 233
Stout Air Services, 96
Sun Country Airlines, 242
Swissair, 84, 96, *291*, *293*

T

Tasmanian Aerial Services, 96
Transcontinental Air Transport, 96
Transocean Airlines, 83
TWA, 11–12, 14, 26, 28, 39, 54, 67, 69, 96, *97*, 98, 103, 107, 118, 177, 183, 289–290, *293*
Tyrolean Airways, 177

U

United Air Lines *or* United Airlines, 5, 11, 14–*15*, *19*, 22,
 28, *37*–38, 80, 87, 96, 98, 105, 120, 126, 128,
 130, 136–137, 148, 160, 164, 167, *168*–171, 176,
 188, 259, 289–290, 292

V

Valujet, 75

W

Western Air Express, 96

Aircraft manufacturers and types

A

Aero Commander, 137
Aerospatiale, 211
Airbus, 148, 175–176, 194, 197, 200, 211, 212, 215, 222,
 226, 228, 254, 258, 302
 A220, 218

A300, 61, 173, 176, 208, *276*
A310, 147, 176, 201, 258, *276*, **277**
A320, 30, 91, 113, 175–176, 197, 200, 208, 211, 215,
 216, 218, **219**, 220, 258, 266, *276*
A321, 218, **219**, 220, *259*
A330, 114, 175
A340, 114, 148, 175, 188, 197, 244, 265–266, 268, *276*
A350, 175, 222, 258, 266, *276*, 284
A380, 102, 175–176, 232, 241
Airspeed Ambassador, 34
Antonov 24, *114*
ATR *or* ATR 42/72, *129*, 211, 220, 222, 225
Avro 642, 96
 Tudor, 34, 101
 York, 289

B

BAC One Eleven, 112, 133, 135, 199, 224, 256, *277*
Beechcraft 99,109
 D-18, **163**, 164
Boeing, 12, 89, 134, 137, 140, 144–145, 149, 156, 159, 170,
 172–173, 175–177, 183–184, 196, 216–217, 220,
 222, 228, 254, 256–258, 265, 282, 294, 302
 Boeing 80 *or* 80A, 96, 106
 Boeing 247, 11, *19*, 66
 Boeing 307, *12*, 21, **53**, 65, 69, 71, *97*, 110, **163**
 Boeing 314, 12, 51
 Boeing 377, 21, 34, 39, *40*–41, 49, 50, **53**, 86, 103
 Boeing 707, 73–74, 79, 89, 91, 116, 149, 153–154, 157,
  168–169, 257, *276*, 297–298
 Boeing 717, *148*, 256–257, 285, *298*
 Boeing 720, 145, 169, 186, 213, 301
 Boeing 727, 73, *111*–112, 128, 130, *131*, 133, 135, 137,
  143–145, 172, 199, 256–257, 259, 265–266,
  277, **277**
 Boeing 737, xvii, 73–75, 91, 134, 139–140, 181, *182*,
  197–198, 200, 208, *210*–212, 215, 218, 257,
  259, *276*
 Boeing 737 Original (-100, -200), xvii, xviii, 181–183,
  209, 211, 215–216, 296
 Boeing 737 Classic (-300, -400, -500), xvii, 208, 215,
  240, 244, 264
 Boeing 737 Next Generation (-600, -700, -800, -900),
  xvii, *112*, 175, 200, *216*–217, *219*, **219**, 258, 265
 Boeing 737 Max 7, 8, 9, 10, xvii, xviii, 175, **219**, 258
 Boeing 747, 73–74, 76, 117, 134, 139, 154, 159,
  173–174, 177, 181, 183–184, 193, 196–*198*, 207,
  232, 248, 259, *276*, 282, 284, 301
 Boeing 757, 193, 208, *214*
 Boeing 767, 175, 193, 201, 208, 215, 228, 232, *276*, 298
 Boeing 777, 114, 148, 174–175, 188, 265–266, *276*, 282
 Boeing 787, 73, 175, *221*–222, 238, 248, 265
 Boeing 2707, *170*
 Boeing B-29, 69
 Boeing C-97, **53**
 Boeing C-135, 143
Bombardier CS, 218
Bristol Brabazon, 34
British Aerospace (BAe), 194, 197, 257
 146, 30, *113*, 232, 247, 257, *276*–**77**
 Jetstream, 41 188
Burnell CBY-3, 282

Index

C

Canadair Regional Jet (CRJ), 188, *277*, **277**
COMAC ARJ-21, 256
Concorde, 21, *76*, 170, 173
Consolidated Liberator, 289
Convair, 39, 135, 137, 264
    Convair 37, 34, **53**–54, 162–*163*
    Convair 104, **53**–54
    Convair 240, 34, 39, 41, 50, **53**, 84–*85*
    Convair 580, 297
    Convair 880, 89, 91, 169, *276*, 297
Curtiss C-46 *or* CW-20 Commando, 28, 42, *44*, **53**, 142, **163**
    Condor, 96, 106

D

De Havilland, 2, 46
    Comet, 34, *46*, 79, 89, *114*, 192, *276*
    D.H. 34, 95
    D.H. 86, 96
    Dove, 87
    Trident, *see* Hawker Siddeley
De Havilland Canada Dash, 8 174, 177
    Twin Otter, 109
Dornier, 2
    228, 228–*229*
    328, 174
    Komet, *3*
Douglas, 35, 41, 76, 79, 137, 194, 254–256, 294
    C-9A, 177
    C-124, 214
    C-133, 155, 159
    DC-2, 11, 13, 26, 48, 66, 96, 106, 110, 142
    DC-3 *or* DST *or* C-47*or* Dakota, 12–15, 20, 22, 28, 34, 42, 48, 50, **53**, 59, 67, 96, 110, 143, 231, 289
    DC-4 *or* C-54, 5, 34–35, 38–*40*, 42, 50, **53**, 83, 91, 102–103, 120, 142, 144, **163**–164, 167–*168*
    DC-6, 34, *37*, 39, 41, 50, **53**, 87–*58*, 192
    DC-6B, 35, 88, 222
    DC-7 (1946), **53**–54
    DC-7 *or* DC-7C, 56, 79, 86–88, 149, 169
    DC-8 (1946), **53**–54
    DC-8, 73, 79, 87, 89, 91, 126–*127*, 130, 153–154, 169, 173, 255, 259, *276*–**277**
    DC-8-60, 137, *276*
    DC-9, 73–75, 112, 133, 135, 176, 198–199, 206, 255–257, 264, *277*, 289
    DC-9-30, 172–173, 177, 256
    DC-9-41, 173
    DC-9-50, 173, 257
    DC-10, 54, 73–74, 149, 173–174, 181, 184, 189, 192, 197, 200, 207, 256, *267*, *276*

E

Embraer 190, 218, 266, *276*
    195, 266

F

Fairchild, 255
    C-82 Packet, 42
    C-119, 42
    F-27, 89
Fairchild-Hiller, 137
Farman, 2
Fokker, 2, 11, 74, 88–89, 112, 133, 143, 176, 178–179, 194, 196, 197, 208, 211–212, 254–255, 258
    Fokker 50, 30, *72*, 224–225, 232, 258, 277
    Fokker 70, 112, 258
    Fokker 100, 30, 112, *178*, 198, 208, 212, 215, *277*
    Fokker F-VII *or* F-7, *17*, 96
    Fokker F-10, 11, 96, 106, 142
    Fokker F-27 *or* Friendship, 88–89, 134, 143, 173, 231, 233, 255
    Fokker F-28, 112, 133, 173, 176, 199, 212, 233, *277*
Ford Trimotor, 11, 96, 106

G

Grumman, 137
    C-2 Greyhound, 143
    Gulfstream, 1 145

H

Handley Page, 2
    Hastings, 143
    Hermes, 83
    W.10, 9
Hawker Siddeley Trident *or* Trident Two *or* Trident Three, *136*, *144*, *149*, 211, 224, *277*, **277**, 295

I

Ilyushin, 35
    Il-12 *or* Il-14, 35
    Il-62, 224

J

Jet Commander, 133
Junkers, 2
    G.38, 282
    Ju 90, 96

L

Lear Jet, 133, 137, 208
Lisunov Li-2, 96
Lockheed, 137, 156, 170
    10 *or* 12, 106
    49 *or* L-749 *or* Constellation, 34, 38–39, 41–42, 50, **53**–54, 57, 69, 79–80, 81, 84, 87–88, 102–103, 121, 127, 145, **163**–164, 270
    C-5, 143
    C-141, 143
    Electra, 82, 89, 134
    Jetstar, 133, 145
    L-89 Constitution, 34, **53**–54
    L-1011, 73–74, 153, 173, 177, 192, 207
    L-1649 Starliner, 79, 88, 169
    L-2000, 170
    Lodestar, 118

LZ 10 *Schwaben,* 95
LZ-129 *Hindenburg,* 12, 95

M

Martin, 34, 135, 264
    2–0–2, 34, 50–51, **53**, **163**
    4–0–4, 85
McDonnell Aircraft, 137
McDonnell Douglas (MDD), 137, 145, 156, 173, 256
    MD-80, 173, 257, *277*, **277**, 285
    MD-11, 174–175, 233, *276*, 296

N

North American Aviation, 137
Northrop Gamma, 67

R

Republic RC-2, **53**–54

S

Saab, 211
    340, 30, 174
Saunders-Roe Princess, 34
Sikorsky S-38, 11, 19
    S-40, 96
    S-42, 189
Sud-Est Armagnac, 35
    Caravelle, 79, 89, 112, 133, 135, 224, 256, *277*
    Languedoc, 34
Sud-Ouest Bretagne, 34

T

Trislander, 232
Tupolev, 104 79
    114, 136

V

Vickers Varsity *or* Viking, 34, 143
    VC-10, 149
    Viscount, 34, 79, 89

Other Organisations
A

Association of European Airlines (AEA), 228, 243
Aerospace Industries Association (AIA), 128, 137
Aircraft Accident Investigation Board (AAIB) (UK), 146, 150, 182, 209, 264
Air Cruisers, 85, 91
Airline Pilots Association (ALPA), 38
Airline Stewards and Stewardesses Association (ALSSA), 105, 110
Air Transport Association (ATA), 6, 39, 55, 75, 80, 105, 207
Airworthiness Authorities Steering Committee, 30
American Association of Airport Executives, 148
Association of Flight Attendants (AFA), 143, 155, 173, 184

Association of Professional Flight Attendants (APFA), 228
Australian Transport Safety Bureau, 296
Aviation Consumer Action Project (ACAP), 202
Aviation Crash Injury Research (AvCIR), 37–38, 88
Aviation Rulemaking Advisory Committee (ARAC) *or* Aviation Rulemaking Committee (ARC), 75, 77, 113, 175, 198, 218, 222, 238–239, 241–243, 250, 254, 281
Aviation Safety Engineering Research (AvSER), 88, 169

C

Cabin Safety, Inc., 294
Civil Aeronautics Authority (CAA) *or* Civil Aeronautics Administration (CAA), 26–27, 39, 47, 48, 60, 80, 100, 118, 134, 164, 250, 254–255, 257
    Air Safety Bureau, 27
    Office of Aviation Safety, 164
    Medical Division, 33, 39, 62, 85, 300
Civil Aeronautics Board (CAB), 15, 26–27, 29, 34, 38, 44, 47–50, 52–54, 59, 69–70, 78, 80–84, 91–92, 103, 105, 109–110, 114–116, 118, 126–127, 132, 143, 159–160, 162, 164, 167–168, 228, 243, 255, 289, 292
    Bureau of Aviation Safety *or* Bureau of Safety Investigations *or* Safety Bureau, 27, 29, 38–39, 48–49, 132
Civil Aviation Authority, UK (CAA), 30, 146–147, 149–150, 176, 209–214, 217, 220, 239, 243, 257, 259
Civil Aviation Safety Authority, Australia (CASA), 231
Columbia University, 69
Cornell University, 37, 45, 87–88, 167
Cranfield Institute *of* Technology *or* Cranfield University, 149–150, 153, 183, 191, 211, 214–215, 217, 221, 240, 282, 287, 295–296

D

Daniel Guggenheim Fund for the Promotion of Aeronautics, The, 2–3, 9–11, 142, 303
Department of Civil Aviation (Australia), 144
Department of Commerce, 27
    Aeronautics Branch, 25, 27, 106
    Aircraft Accident Board, 27, 30
    Aviation Business Bureau, 11
    Bureau of Air Commerce, 25–27, 29, 66, 69
Department of Health and Human Services, 122
Department of Labor Occupational Safety and Health Administration, 122
Department for Transport (DfT) (UK), 227
Department of Transportation, 27, 29, 176, 243
    Office of the Inspector General, 176
Du Pont, 132, 137
Dutch Civil Aviation Authority *or Rijksluchtvaartdienst,* 112, 133, 208, 255, 258

E

Embry Riddle University, 40, 296
Environmental Protection Agency, 122
European Association of Aerospace Industries (AECMA), 228, 243

Index

European Civil Aviation Conference (ECAC), 30, 232–**233**
European Commission *or* European Union, 31, 218, 234, 248, 250
European (Union) Aviation Safety Agency (EASA), 25, 31, 77, 102, 147, 150, 208, 217–220, 222–225, 228, **233**, 240–242, 248–250, 258, 285, 294, 303

F

Federal Aviation Agency *or* Federal Aviation Administration (FAA), 25, 27, 29, 31, 47, 71, 74–77, 82, 88, 92, 109–117, 119–122, 127–128, 131–135, 137–140, 145–149, 153–160, 165, 168–178, 181–184, 186, 189–195, 197–202, 206–208, 212–220, 222–228, 230, 233–234, 238–244, 247–251, 254–255, 257–258, 265, 281–282, 292, 294, 296, 301–302
    Civil Aeromedical Institute (CAMI), 41, 87–88, 126–127, 144–146, 155–156, 169–170, 177, 197, 213–215, 217, 239, 242, 244, 259, 264, 269–270, 281, 296
    Exit Seat Working Group, 218
    National Aviation Facilities Experimental Center (NAFEC) or Technical Centre (TC) or William J. Hughes Technical Center, 132, 149, 155–156, 159, 184–*185*, 191, 194–195, 214–215, 217, 239, 301
    Long Beach ACO, 199
    Northwest Mountain Region, 270
    Seattle ACO, 196
Flight Safety Foundation (FSF), 41, 54, 81, 88–89, 103, 105, 145, 158, 240
Food and Drug Administration, 122
Fraunhofer ITEM, 248

G

General Accounting Office *or* Government Accountability Office, 195, 239
George Washington University (GWU), 39, 41, 56–57, 171

H

House of Commons (UK), 176

I

IIT Research Institute, 149
Interaction Group *or* Interaction Research Corporation, 294, 298
International Air Transport Association (IATA), 240, 287, 294
International Board for Research into Aircraft Crash Events (IBRACE), 244, 247
International Civil Aviation Organization (ICAO), 25, 30–31, 33–34, 52, 81, 84, 101, 105, 121, 143–144, 224–227, 230, 234, 239–241, 244, 248, 250, 284–285, 291–292, 294 Bulletin, 159
International Commission for Aerial Navigation (ICAN), 29, 31
International Society for Air Safety Investigators (ISASI), 6

J

Joint Aviation Authorities (JAA), 25, *30*–31, 150, 188, 200–201, 207, 214–218, 220, 222–224, 227–228, 233–234, 238, 241, 243, 248, 302–303
    Cabin Safety Study Group, 150, 208, 215, 217, 220, 243, 248

L

Luftfahrt-Bundesamt (German CAA), 225, 294

M

Messerschmitt-Bölkow-Blohm (MBB), 200–202
Ministry of Aviation *or* Air Ministry (UK), 13, 130, 291

N

National Advisory Committee for Aeronautics (NACA), 15, 21, 33, 42–43, 62, 81
National Aeronautics and Space Administration (NASA), 42, 156, 186–*187*, 300
    Ames Research Center, 184, 192
    Langley Research Center, 156
    Lewis Research Center, 89
National Air Carrier Association (NACA), 242
National Bureau of Standards (NBS), 132, 194
    Fire Protection Section, 132
National Fire Protection Association, 81
National Institute for Occupational Safety and Health, 159
National Research Council, 247–248
National Transportation Safety Board (NTSB), 25, 27, 29, 74, 76, 87–88, 113, 119–120, 148, 155–158, 190, 193, 197, 202, 215, 228, 239, 244, 249, 265, 287, 295–297
NLDB study group, 244, *247*

O

Ohio State University (OSU), 158, 184, 194

R

Regional Airlines Association (RAA), 228
RGW Cherry & Associates, 239
Royal Aeronautical Society (RAeS), 239, 283
Royal Air Force (RAF), 47, 143, *289*

S

San Diego Air & Space Museum, 39
SCI-SAFE, 146
Society of Automotive Engineers (SAE), 54, 89, 294
Southern California Safety Institute, 240
Stewardesses for Women's Rights, 147

T

Transportation Development Centre, 296
Transportation Security Administration, 226
Transport Canada, 222
TÜV Rheinland, 177, 250

U

United States Air Force (USAF), 91, 144
    Military Airlift Command (MAC) *or* Military Air Transport Service (MATS), 39, *40*, 143
University of Greenwich, 240, 269–270, 282
University of Southampton, Sound and Vibration Research, 149
University of Udine, 296
U.S. Navy, 47, 85, 143
U.S. Office of Education, 100, 118

Periodicals

A

Aviation *or* Aviation Week *or* Aviation Week and Space Technology, 22, 88, 103, 120
Aviation Herald, The, 75, 242–243
Aviation Safety Journal (FAA), 181–*182*

B

British Medical Journal, 45
Business Week, 99

C

Chicago Tribune, 101

F

Federal Register, xvi, xvii, 8, 26, 29, 70
Flight International, 101
Flying, 143

Persons

A

Altman, Beau, 294
Armstrong, Harry G., 73
Ashford, Ron, 176

B

Bakker, Geeri, 101
Balleyguier, Henri, 95
Barry, Kathleen, 101
Biden, president, 281
Bongertman, Hilda, 67, 96
Boyle, James, 91
Broderick, Tony, 190
Buck, Robert, 54
Butcher, Nick, 239, 283
Byron, William D., 13

C

Carroll, John, 87
Chandler, Richard, 155
Cherry, Ray, 149, 239
Chittaro, Luca, 296
Church, Ellen, 95–96
Clinton, president, 249

Cooper, D. B., 143
Cutting, Bronson M., 26, 142

D

De Haven, Hugh, 37, 45
Diener, Nelly, 96
DuBois, Eugene F., 37, 45

E

Enders, John, 158

F

Farrier, Thomas, 6
Ferguson, Trisha, 298
Finucane, Matthew, 184
Fontaine, Jeanne, 95

G

Galea, Ed, 269–271, 280, 282
Gardlin, Jeffrey, 242
Gaume, James, 76, 225
Godson, John, 297
Goglia, John, 113
Gorodetskaya, Elsa A., 96
Granger, Nellie, 96

H

Haldeman, George, 164
Hasbrook, A. Howard, 6, 33, 38, 79–80, 87–89, 126, 128, 138, 143, 249, 264, 300, 302
Hill, Richard (Dick), 159
Housley, Mary Francis, 103
Hubert, Ronan, 261

I

Inouye, senator, 247

J

Jentsch, Florian, 294, 296
Johnson, Dan, 294
Johnson, Lyndon B. president, 99

K

Kennedy, president, 29
King, Barry G., 6, 33, 39, 41, 51, 55, 62, 85, 103, 105, 163, 167, 269, 300
King, James, 88
Kirchner, Otto, 54, 89
Koplin, Klaus, 200
Kubis, Heinrich, 95

L

Lauterbach, Edith, 167
Lederer, Jerome, 54, 89, 105

Index

Lightfoot, Jim Ross, 190
Littlewood, William G., 42, 89, 105, 255
Lovelace, Dr., 68

M

Marshall, Nora, 295
McFadden, Ernest, 144, 146
McFarland, Ross A., 6, 14, 47, 50, 54, 65, 67–69, 73, 103, 144, 121, 301
McLaughlin, Helen, 100
McLucas, John, 207
McSweeney, Thomas, 199–200
Messel, George van, 88
Mica, John, 226
Mineta, Norman, 154–156, 183
Ming, Connie, 101
Monroe, Marilyn, 103
Muir, Helen, 150, 211, 240
Muller, miss, 103

N

Nader, Ralph, 159–160

O

Oto, Yukio, 220

P

Paltridge, Shane, 144
Parker, Natalie, 103
Patterson, William (Pat), 5, 167–169
Pesman, Gerard J., 43, 300
Pinkel, Irving, 42, 89
Povey, Nick, 149

Q

Quinn, Rowland, 105, 118, 120–121

R

Rampin, Jean-Marc, 220
Ranter, Harro, 261
Reese, Carl, 294–295
Roads, Barbara, 117
Robson, R. C., 120
Rickenbacker, Eddie, 13
Rockne, Knute, 11, 142
Roebuck, John A., 148, 255

S

Sanderson, Jack, 95
Sarkos, Constantine (Gus), 159, 184
Six, Robert, 207
Snow, Clyde, 87
Snyder, Richard, 47
Spence, steward, 13
Stapp, John Paul, 37

T

Taylor, Frank, 153–154
Teare, Donald, 45
Truman, president, 141, 143

U

Uzzell, Sarah, 267

V

Veryioglou, George, 177
Vicente, Núñez, 283
Virr, Lionel, 243

W

Watson, Edna, 13
Wecklein, Donald, 240
Wells, Mary, 99